Warriors
in
Mr.
Lincoln's
Army

Warriors in Mr. Lincoln's Army

Native American Soldiers Who Fought in the Civil War

Quita V. Shier

TRUE DIRECTIONS
AN AFFILIATE OF TARCHER PERIGEE

iUniverse®

WARRIORS IN MR. LINCOLN'S ARMY
NATIVE AMERICAN SOLDIERS WHO FOUGHT IN THE CIVIL WAR

iUniverse books may be ordered through booksellers or by contacting:

iUniverse
1663 Liberty Drive
Bloomington, IN 47403
www.iuniverse.com
1-800-Authors (1-800-288-4677)

Because of the dynamic nature of the Internet, any web addresses or links contained in this book may have changed since publication and may no longer be valid. The views expressed in this work are solely those of the author and do not necessarily reflect the views of the publisher, and the publisher hereby disclaims any responsibility for them.

Any people depicted in stock imagery provided by Thinkstock are models, and such images are being used for illustrative purposes only.
Certain stock imagery © Thinkstock.

ISBN: 978-1-5320-2716-1 (sc)
ISBN: 978-1-5320-4042-9 (hc)
ISBN: 978-1-5320-2717-8 (e)

Library of Congress Control Number: 2017910446

Print information available on the last page.

iUniverse rev. date: 02/23/2018

Contents

Preface ix

Acknowledgments xi

Introduction 1

The Oath Taken at Enlistment...17

Enlistment Papers...18

Officers of Company K...20

Enlisted Men—Letter A...33

Enlisted Men—Letters B and C...70

Enlisted Men—Letters D and E... 111

Enlisted Men—Letters G, H, I, and J 122

Enlisted Men—Letters K, L, and M 181

Enlisted Men—Letters N, O, P, Q, and R...261

Enlisted Men—Letters S, T, V, and W 316

Discharge Papers 474

Photographs 476

Selected Names for Handwriting Analysis 485

Bibliography 493

Index...543

To the Anishinabek elders who were friends of mine and who also supported my book project. The elders are listed as follows:

Winifred (Winnie) Wabakek and her brother-in-law, Bob Wabakek, were master basket makers and supplied me with wonderful keepsakes. I held public sales of their baskets in my home and at my church.

Don and Ida Stevens (the Red Arrow family) were known for their basket making. Don was a descendant of Company K soldier Thomas Nelson, who was the son of Chief David Nelson, also known as Chief Shoppenagonce or "Little Needles." Don and his friend Maria Myers conducted a sacred blessing of Mother Earth the day before breaking ground for the construction of our new home.

Ceremonial Chief Eli Thomas (Little Elk), whose wit and wisdom were always enjoyed. Eli was a black ash basket maker, storyteller, powwow dancer, and revered elder of the Saginaw Chippewa Indian tribe. I treasure the chief's craftwork that I collected over the years.

James (Jim) and Lena Strong shared their personal histories with me over many cups of coffee enjoyed in the welcome atmosphere of their home. Lena was a direct descendant of Michigan's "Marathon Runner" Anishinabe Pottawatomi Chief White Pigeon and was very proud of her heritage. Jim was chief of the Saginaw Chippewa Tribal Council from 1941 to 1943 and from 1949 to 1950. The couple's black ash baskets give a touch of beauty and grace to our home.

Hazel (*Sah-gas-no-quah*) Lavoie was the daughter of an Anishinabe Methodist minister and a crafts person in her own right. She made three dolls for me and used beautiful stitching and beadwork. Hazel was a wonderful storyteller of Anishinabe history and oral traditions. It was she who bestowed upon me the honorary Anishinabequa name of *Wob-be-nung-go-quah*, which means Morning Star.

Chief Louis (Louie) Pontiac was an artist with glass beads and a pleasant conversationalist. He made exquisite beaded necklaces, and I have several of these treasures in my collection.

Gerry (*Nom-bi-zhe-qua*) Jackson made beautiful hand-painted ceramic pottery bowls, several of which she gave to me. The most prized piece in my collection of her work is her signature "feather bowl." As an accomplished pianist, Gerry would entertain her guests with various styles of music from the compositions of J. S. Bach to jazz.

Lahy Bailey made some wonderful porcupine quill boxes that I have on display. I always enjoyed talking to Lahy when he discussed his handicrafts at powwow gatherings.

Although these wonderful people have walked on, I will always remember them because I was honored to be in their presence, and I miss the pleasure of their company.

Preface

Many years ago, as I was enjoying breakfast with my paternal Croatian grandparents on a sunny summer morning, Grandpa asked me to fulfill a special request. He encouraged me to do something for the American Indians—those folks who had been given a raw deal from the US government and were all but forgotten in their needs.

Grandpa worked in a local coal mine and owned a grocery store. He could speak five languages and was schooled as far as his little village of Svte Rok could take him. As an avid reader, especially of history, he had a great respect for learning.

Archeological digs were in progress around our little town in central Illinois and had been for quite some time. Several ancient Indian campsites had been uncovered, and articles about the excavations were printed in the local newspaper for several weeks. I became fascinated with the discoveries and wanted to learn more about these ancient people.

With this awakening of interest, I promised my grandpa that I would pursue his request. My search for knowledge and understanding about American Indians began. I was just ten years old.

My parents were more than happy to take me to the city library on Saturdays so that I could check out books about American Indian tribes and their histories.

When I was a premed student at Illinois Wesleyan University, I happened to see a book titled *Michigan in the Civil War* on a study break in the university library. There was a section in the book about the Anishinabek (American Indians) in Company K of the First Michigan Sharpshooters who fought in that war. It was then that I decided that someday I would research the men in this company and write a book about them and their families.

After earning a master's degree in environmental science from the University of Illinois and a move to Michigan with my husband and six-month-old son, I began my research about the Anishinabek of the Wolverine State. In this process, I met and made some very dear friends who introduced me to the elders on a nearby Anishinabek reservation. The elders in turn taught me about their history and culture. Tutored by these wise people, I soon became an educational resource person for information about the three main tribes of Michigan and developed programs for schoolchildren from kindergarten through high school. I lectured many times at my children's schools and in various cities in the state.

In the mid-1970s, I conducted a one-year class at Delta College, University Center, about the Anishinabek. The class was given especially for teachers in the tri-county area but was also open to anyone. The tribal elders delighted in coming to these classes and enjoyed the experience of teaching their culture and life ways to the students.

Often I would host the elders who would demonstrate their art of black ash basket weaving and sell their crafts in my home and at my church. As a thank-you for their opportunity to sell their crafts at church, one of the elders made four beautiful black ash offering baskets and gave them to me to present to our minister. Today those baskets are as beautiful as ever and are still being used.

It is the author's hope that *Warriors in Mr. Lincoln's Army* will engender not only appreciation for the service of the men of Company K, First Michigan Sharpshooters, but also the recognition that they deserve for their loyalty and sacrifice for the Union cause in a war that ultimately defined our nation.

With the completion of this book, I have fulfilled the promise that I made to my grandpa to do something for the American Indians.

To fully understand the profiles in this book, it is strongly suggested that the introduction be read first.

Acknowledgments

After my twenty-six years of research and writing about Company K of the First Michigan Sharpshooters, I have many people to thank for their kind help and support of my project. I am indebted to the following people for their contributions that helped me to finish my book. *Miigwetch* to all of you.

My husband, George, who has been a constant and faithful supporter of my decision to adopt this project and has helped me with critique, proofreading, and computer savvy. Also, special recognition to my family – my late parents, my sister, Chiqeeta Jameson, who is also an author, and our children, who supported my goal of informing the public about this special group of men.

The "Bones Ladies" friends with whom I enjoyed traveling on many genealogy trips—Marcia Brandle, Wilma Diesen, Barb Fox, Gale Hock, and Nancy Lackie—and who encouraged me, contributed information, and kept tabs on my progress through the years. A special thank-you to Barb Fox for some independent research that she did for me in Oceana County.

Dr. Helen Hornbeck Tanner, an internationally known ethnohistorian of American Indian history and literature, a research associate at the Newberry Library in Chicago, Illinois, secretary of the Michigan Commission on Indian Affairs, and an expert witness in legal matters involving Indian treaty rights. Helen was my mentor and friend who gave me inspiration, knowledge, and support for my book project.

Yvonne Surateaux Hoag, a mentor and friend. I enjoyed Von's companionship when we traveled many Indian trails together in the pursuit of knowledge and understanding of the Anishinabek people.

David and Beverly O'Keefe, our friends who took time out from a scheduled trip to Washington, DC, to snap some photos, as a favor to me, of Charles Agahgo's military stone in the Alexandria National Cemetery in Alexandria, Virginia.

Malcolm and Patricia Chase, our friends who graciously provided room, board, and transportation on several of my trips to the National Archives in Washington,

DC. Their hospitality and generosity enabled me to have the time to procure copies of all the Company K files that I needed for my research.

Debbie Diesen, who is a friend and an author in her own right, for information about pension laws and their application to the Company K soldiers, their wives, and their children.

Bud and Avis Wolfe, our friends who so generously shared conversations, photos, and information about the Payson Wolf and George Nelson Smith families. My appreciation also to the couple for the loan of Rev. Smith's diaries, for pictures of Payson and Mary Jane, and for a copy of a letter sent by Payson to Mary Jane.

Suzette Psyhogeos, for the time spent and the effort involved in her in-depth research of William Neveau and the Neveau family. Suzette is an excellent genealogist.

Alice Cadotte and Sherrie Peterson, for additional help and photos in the Neveau family research.

Ellie Schroeder, a friend and also an author who suggested iUniverse as a publisher for my book.

Patrick Mayotte, for hosting our visits with him and the time that he spent in conversation and showing us the grave of Henry Waasegiizhig (Henry Condecon). Also, Patrick's additional information about the Waasegiizhig family was most appreciated and beneficial for Henry's file.

Chris Calkins, a historian at the Petersburg, Virginia, National Battlefield, for his information about the protocol of burying deceased Civil War soldiers in military cemeteries.

Dr. Margaret Ann Noodin, for the time and effort that she took in her translations of Charles Allen's Anishinabemowin letters.

Dr. Helen Peltier Roy, for her additional input in the translations of the Charles Allen letters.

Simon Otto, for permission to use the photograph of his grandfather, Marcus Otto, and appreciation for copies of his publications about the Anishinabek that he autographed and sent to me.

Nichole Garret of the Albion College Archives, for the research and material that she sent to me about Joseph Wakazoo.

Mrs. Gretchen Emory, for hosting a visit with her and for the fascinating information that she shared with me about Amos Crane and the Madosh family history.

Susan J. Lafernier, for the information that she sent to me about John Bird and Amos Crane.

George Wunderlich and Terri Reimer of the National Museum of Civil War

Medicine, for their insightful knowledge about various medical treatments used during the Civil War.

Susan Schank, for conversations about Joseph Kakakee and for information that she sent to me about Joseph, his wife, and her relatives and Joseph's sojourn in Canada.

Alberta Wells, for correspondence, historical information about her grandfather, Thomas Wezoo, and for the photograph of Thomas, his wife, and daughter. Alberta was most helpful with her generous contributions to my project.

Curtis Chambers, the tribal chairman of the Burt Lake Band of Ottawa and Chippewa Indians, Inc., and Harbor Master of Cheboygan, Cheboygan County, and Loretta Parkey, tribal enrollment and historian of the Burt Lake Band. Curtis and Loretta hosted me on a visit and shared information on the Burt Lake Village, Cheboygan County, burnout of 1900 and of Chief Kejigowi and his son, Simon.

F. Lawrence McFall Jr., author, historian, and outstanding researcher. Upon my request, Lawrence found the cause of Amable Kitchibatise's death and solved the mystery of the location of his grave. Mr. McFall sent an autographed copy (with a personal message) of his book *Danville in the Civil War* to me as a gift.

Nancy Bonifield, for the in-depth research that she did for me on the Cornelius Hall family and the Hall relatives.

Bruce Johnson, Jane Toombes, and Eric for information about the history of Ontonagon County. Additional thanks to Jane for a copy of her book *Chippewa Daughter*, which is centered around the Lake Superior country.

Chad Avery, a dedicated Anishinabe genealogist and historian, for his translations of the meanings of several Anishinabek names and historical information regarding those names.

Mark Keller, author and researcher, for copies of his publications about the Anishinabek people. Over the years, Mark and I shared lunches, coffee times, and phone conversations when he would advise me as to the areas of research that I should investigate.

William E. (Bill) Lind, a very knowledgeable researcher in the Military History Department of the National Archives in Washington, DC. Bill mentored me in the process of researching military, pension, and hospital records for the men of Company K. He also gave me a private tour of the military history storage areas of the archives, which are closed to nonemployees. I owe Bill a great deal of appreciation. He was a kind and thoughtful man.

Harold Moll, a prolific researcher and author who recorded the genealogies and history of the Anishinabek people in Gratiot, Isabella, and Midland counties. He was especially helpful with information about the Gruet, Peshekee, and Chief Bemassikeh families and their relationship to Rev. Miessler and his Lutheran mission called Bethany. What remains of Bethany and its cemetery are located on Pine River Road outside of St. Louis in Gratiot County.

Beth Seator, who is very knowledgeable about Thomas and Mary Kechittigo. My husband and I spent a lot of time with Beth and learned quite a bit of information about the Kechittigo family that is not common knowledge. Beth showed us some of Mary's beautiful baskets, which are in Beth's possession and are her treasures.

Nancy Stone of the Crawford County Historical Society, for her information about the Kechittigo family.

Ruth Ann Fradenburg-Kelley of the Oceana County Historical Society, for her information on the Anishinabek of Oceana and Mason Counties.

Kay Lynn Lund and her staff at the Midland, Michigan, Church of Jesus Christ of Latter-Day Saints Family History Center, for her kind and supportive help of my research, and for assistance in the use of the center's collections of vital records.

Father Albert Langheim, OFM, a fellow Illini, for his kind assistance in aiding me in my research of the records in Cross Village, Emmet County. My appreciation also to Father Al for a signed copy (with a personal message) of his booklet *The Catholic Mission at Cross Village—The First 200 Years*.

Father Andy Buvala of Kateri Tekakwitha Catholic Church in Peshawbestown, Leelanau County, for aiding me in my research of Louis Shomin and for guiding me to Louis's grave in the church cemetery.

Alonzo Sherman, for a copy of his book of Michigan GAR (Grand Army of the Republic) Civil War veterans' posts.

Amy Becker and Jane B. John of the Peter White Public Library of Marquette, Marquette County, for information on the Graveraet family.

Rosemary Michelin of the Marquette County Historical Society, Inc., for her information about Garret Graveraet and the Graveraet family.

Diane Hawkins of Hastings Public Library, Hastings, Barry County, for assistance in the research of Rev. James Selkirk of the Episcopal church in Barry County and John Kesis of the Bradley Indian Mission in Allegan County.

George Levy, for the gift of an autographed copy of his book about Camp Douglas titled *To Die in Chicago*.

Margaret Cook at the College of William and Mary in Williamsburg, Virginia, for a copy of the entry in the *Charles Campbell Diary* that mentions Louis Marks and his demeanor in captivity.

Boston Public Library, Boston, Massachusetts, for a copy of the *Boston Evening Transcript* of June 30, 1864, page 4, that mentions the names of the *Indians Captured Among the Yankee Prisoners* at Petersburg, Virginia.

William R. Erwin Jr., senior reference librarian of the Special Collections Library of Duke University, Durham, North Carolina, for copies of pages mentioning Company K and the Sharpshooter Regiment from the George Harry Weston, Jeremiah Stuart, and Constant C. Hanks collections.

Rebecca Zeiss, for her beautiful graphic design for the cover of my book.

Kyle Crampton, for a copy of an archival research report for the Niipissing Cemetery in Isabella County.

Geraldine Moore Schram, for her outstanding graphoanalysis of the signatures of seventeen selected men of Company K.

Frank Boles, the director of the Clarke Historical Library, Central Michigan University, and Clarke Library archivists Evelyn Leasher and Marian J. Matyn, for their kind assistance during my years of research.

Dorothy Reuter, for the gift of a signed copy of her book *Methodist Indian Ministries in Michigan 1830–1890*.

Dawn Eurich, archivist of Special Collections of the Detroit Public Library, for permission to use pictures of Company K officers and men from the library's photographic collections.

Carol Ardis, for copies of pictures of Cornelius Hall and his wife in Carol's private collection.

Pamela Welliver, president of the Wexford County Historical Society, for a copy of a picture of the Cornelius Hall family held at the county museum.

Vicki Catozza, reference assistant in the Research Center Reference Division of the Western Reserve Historical Society, for permission to use a copy of a letter from Joseph Wakazoo to Rev. Samuel Bissell.

Alex Forist, collections curator of the Grand Rapids Public Museum, Grand Rapids, for permission to use a copy of the photograph of Aaron Pequongay (Aaron Sargonaquatto) and his family.

Carolee R. Gillman of the Grand Rapids History and Special Collections, Archives, Grand Rapids Public Library, Grand Rapids, for permission to use a copy of the photograph of Joseph Tazhedewin (Joseph Poneshing) and family.

Shelley Williams, director of the White Lake Community Library, White Hall, Muskegon, for the location of a newspaper article about the death of George Stoneman.

Karen Jania, reference archivist of the Bentley Historical Library, University of Michigan, for permission to use photographs and newspaper articles of the Graveraet family from the Emerson R. Smith Papers held in the collections of the Bentley Library.

David Koch, reference archivist, Presbyterian Historical Society, Philadelphia, Pennsylvania, for the citation information for Rev. Peter Dougherty's original diaries describing his Indian Mission Church (Grand Traverse Bay) and the session minutes (1843–1871) of the church.

Stuart Frohm, retired photographer and reporter for the *Midland Daily News*, for his articles and pictures highlighting my lectures about the book project. Many thanks, Stu.

Linda I. Flook-Birnbaum, program support assistant for the Department of Veterans Affairs, Beverly National Cemetery in New Jersey, for her photos of Samuel Kaquatch's military headstone in the Philadelphia National Cemetery, Philadelphia, Pennsylvania.

Laura Wickstead, Virginia Room librarian, Roanoke Public Libraries, Roanoke, Virginia, for her research of Benjamin Kewacondo.

Margaret Briggs, for her information about the men of Company K.

Reference Department of the Alice and Jack Wirt Public Library, Bay City, Bay County, for copies of two obituaries of Company K soldier William Collins.

Barbara (Manley) Herndon, professional genealogist, for her research on Thompson Nauquam.

A special thank-you to my late mother for the use of her personal medical resource, *Blakiston's Illustrated Pocket Medical Dictionary,* that she used in her career as a surgical nurse.

Company K, First Michigan Sharpshooters

Introduction

The American Civil War ended 152 years ago. There has been a renewed interest in all aspects of this war as witness to the many books, articles, movies, and television presentations. It seems that people need to reflect upon the meaning and the tragedy of a conflict so uniquely American in order to understand the greatness of this country.

New information has been discovered from heretofore unknown diaries and personal accounts. Battles have been scrutinized, analyzed, and described in the most sanguine manner, impressing upon our people that this war was tragic because it was so personal. Friendships were destroyed, and many families were forever separated due to divided loyalties. But in the end, the Union was preserved, and time itself brought healing to this nation.

The Anishinabek

Of the military men who served in this drama of untold suffering, little has been written about the experiences of the American Indian (indigenous) participants. Indigenous soldiers and sailors from various states served bravely for both the Union and the Confederacy. One such brave fighting unit for the north was Company K of the First Michigan Sharpshooters called the all-Indian Company.

Company K was unique because it was the only company in the entire sharpshooter regiment, and in all other military units in Michigan, that had only indigenous enlisted men on its roster. There were Anishinabek men of the state who did serve in other Michigan units of artillery, cavalry, and infantry, but they were in companies with nonindigenous men.

Company K of the First Michigan Sharpshooters consisted of 137 enlisted indigenous men, one Anishinabe officer and two non-Anishinabe officers, which gives the total count of 140 men in that company. The first line officers of Company K were in command by July 1863. There were changes in the line officers as the war progressed due to illness, resignation and death.

With the exception of three American Indian men who were members of other tribes in other states and those Anishinabek from Canada, the rest of the warriors who enlisted in Company K were all members of the three main tribes of Michigan: the Ojibwa or Ojibwe (also referred to as Chippewa), the Odaawaa (or Odawa/Ottawa), and the Bodawatomi (or Potawatomi). Together these main tribes are known as the People of the Three Fires and refer to themselves as the Anishinabe (singular) or Anishinabek in the plural form. The feminine singular form is Anishinabekwe. Anishinabe means man (human being) and denotes a man, woman or child.

Forty one enlisted men and one Anishinabe officer in Company K were killed in battle or died of wounds or disease while in the military.

Anishinabek Attempt to Join the Military

At the beginning of the Civil War in 1861, many young Michigan Anishinabek men who, by law, were not subject to wartime draft flocked to the induction centers to try to enlist in the Union army. A well-known American Indian of his day, Dr. George Copway, who was an educated Methodist missionary, visited Michigan in May 1861 to enlist a company of chosen Anishinabek men to serve as scouts for the Union army. It was reported that over two hundred Anishinabek offered their services at the Straits of Mackinac to answer his call but were refused by the Michigan authorities who succumbed to their prejudicial feelings. Even the state Indian agent, D. C. Leach, strongly disagreed with any Indian involvement in the war. But also in 1861, many Michigan newspapers and numerous neighbors of the Anishinabek reported that these people were known to be loyal and trustworthy and would be good soldiers if allowed to enlist in the army.

Organization of the First Michigan Sharpshooters

The First Michigan Sharpshooters began its organization in the winter of 1862/63. The regiment was headed by Captain Charles V. DeLand of Michigan's Ninth

Infantry, who was commissioned as colonel of this new regiment. By this time, the enlistments had changed from three months to three years, as it became apparent that the war would not end soon.

Bounties were offered to volunteers to encourage enlistments. The federal government offered a hundred-dollar bounty in which twenty-five dollars was given upon enlistment, and the balance was to be paid when mustered in. In some local areas such as Detroit, there were additional monetary inducements ranging from ten to thirty dollars.

In January 1863, the sharpshooter regiment was ordered to its headquarters at Camp Chandler in Kalamazoo, and recruitment was pursued with vigor.

By March 1863, the state offered a fifty-dollar bounty to enlistees. Also, according to the Enrollment Act of March 3, 1863, those non-Anishinabek men who were drafted (ages twenty-one to forty-five) could hire substitutes and pay them $300 or be exempted from military duty by paying the government $300. When a substitute accepted the draftee's money and enlisted, he was not entitled to a bounty at enlistment because of the lump sum he had received from the draftee.

With local area money, state and federal bounties, in addition to a private's pay of thirteen dollars a month, a recruit would have sufficient funds to support his family in his absence. As a comparison, a laborer's pay in the nineteenth century was about fifty cents a day when he could find work.

The regiment left Kalamazoo in April 1863 and moved its camp to Dearborn near Detroit, Wayne County, to guard the US Arsenal.

Memories of the 1862 Santee Sioux Uprising

As the numbers of Union wounded and dead mounted daily, there was another call for additional troops from Michigan. This time the army reconsidered the enlistment of Anishinabek men into the Union ranks. However, memories of the 1862 Santee Sioux uprising in Minnesota were still vivid in the minds of many non-Anishinabek in Michigan. The uprising and subsequent killing of many settlers by Santee braves was due mostly to the callous indifference and bungling government bureaucracy in the distribution of food and supplies that were to be given to the Sioux families in the treaty agreements for ceding the Santee lands to the US government. The lack of concern and the display of apathy were not only despicable and inhumane but also deprived the desperate, starving Santee of the basic necessities they so badly needed. Feeling helpless in finding supplies and the food that they needed to feed their families, the Santee warriors rebelled and went to war with the recent settlers and the US Army. Sadly, many Santee and members of their families also died in this brutal and unnecessary conflict.

In the minds of many of Michigan's non-Anishinabek, the thought of arming the Anishinabek men was unthinkable. Michigan newspapers were full of accounts of "Shall the Indians Be Armed?" and the debate raged throughout the state. Fear and prejudice against the Anishinabek was very evident at this time. However, the need for more men prevailed over fears of armed Indians, and it was decided that Anishinabek men would be encouraged to enlist in Michigan military units, especially Company K.

Enlistment of the Anishinabek

By the end of April 1863, there was an effort to get the word out that Anishinabek men were wanted to form an all-Indian company, Company K, for the First Michigan Sharpshooters. Also, there was a special need for bilingual leaders for this company, as there would be enlisted men who did not speak English or who were not comfortable speaking a language that they did not know very well.

As the word spread, the Anishinabek men began to arrive at various state enlistment centers in May to join Company K. As the number of enlistments increased throughout May, June, and July, some Native American men from other US tribes and from Canada would also join their brethren in this company.

Before they left for training and guard duty at the US arsenal in Dearborn, the enlisted men were feted to "drum feasts" hosted by their families in their respective settlements. The drum kept the rhythm during the dances and was always considered the heartbeat of the people.

At these war dances and feasts, the enlistees' families gave the men gifts of specially decorated, beaded leather pouches that contained sacred items, including tobacco. These gatherings, which were celebrated for centuries, honored the warriors as they prepared for war. Speeches were given, and special prayers were said, not only for the men but for their families who would be left behind. The men of the Christian faith also received small testaments printed in the Anishinabe language. Farewells were said as the enlistees embarked for Dearborn. Aching hearts feared that this departure would be the last time that some of the soldiers and their families would see each other. In separation, the families would suffer desolation and hardship. These situations were compounded by the knowledge that some of their soldier boys would lie under strange soil in battlefields and prison cemeteries far from home and not in family ancestral burial grounds.

As the Anishinabek men arrived at Dearborn, they were taken in small groups to Detroit for their muster-in and were to be given the remainder of their enlistment bounty (seventy-five dollars) due at that time.

The soldiers of Company K were promised the same pay and benefits as their non-Anishinabek comrades, and the US government honored that promise. The men received their uniforms, accoutrements, and .58-caliber Springfield Rifle Muskets from the regimental quartermaster. They wasted no time in personalizing their gun stocks with carvings of birds, animals, and floral designs. These decorated rifles would become highly prized trophies for the Confederates who captured Anishinabek soldiers. The rifles would not be relinquished by the rebels until General Robert E. Lee surrendered the Confederate army at Appomattox Court House, Virginia, on April 9, 1865.

Enlistments for Company K increased after July 4, 1863. Patriotic speeches were given by recruiting officers at various Anishinabek settlements and reservations around the state. These officers were accompanied by some of the Anishinabek men who had already enlisted into Company K and were resplendent in their uniforms. The presence of these soldiers in Union blue added a touch of excitement to the gatherings.

The recruitment for the First Michigan Sharpshooters was only partially completed by July 7, 1863, when the regiment was mustered into United States service. Companies that had been mustered were A, B (which did have the only other Anishinabek members, William Duverney and John Kedgnal, who were half brothers), C, D, E, and F. Companies G, H, I, and K would subsequently be mustered when most of the recruitment was completed.

Reasons Why the Anishinabek Enlisted

What would induce the young Anishinabek men of Michigan to want to join the military of a country that didn't recognize them as citizens of the United States? Several reasons can be stated.

First, Michigan was their home even though they were uprooted from their original places of habitation and relocated to other parts of the state due to treaties and subterfuge. They would fight for their homeland.

Second, many Anishinabek were finding it harder to make a living for their families. Many of the families were desperately poor. They were becoming marginalized both socially and economically. Money offered as an incentive for enlistment was hard to refuse, and the Anishinabek were promised (as previously mentioned) that they would be paid on the same scale as non-Anishinabek soldiers of their regiment.

Third, the Anishinabek genuinely feared that they would become slaves like the African Americans in the south if the Confederates won the war.

Then there was a young man's dream of going on an adventure. Good friends and relatives from the same home areas would enlist together as they felt a sense of pride and camaraderie in representing their people in the war. But this adventure would turn to sheer hell with untold agony, disease, death, and disillusionment for many of the soldiers.

Lastly, there was the time-honored warrior tradition. Young Anishinabek men considered themselves to be warriors (*Ogitchedaw*) and knew that it was their duty and sense of honor to protect their homes and families from any and all harm.

Occupations and Life Ways

The occupations of the Anishinabek men who enlisted in Company K were varied in scope and included hunters, farmers, fishermen, lumberjacks, boatmen who sailed the Great Lakes and also ferried passengers from the mainland to nearby islands, teamsters, mechanics, skilled carpenters, ministers, and laborers. Among this group was an Anishinabe second lieutenant who, being well educated, was a school teacher and gifted in the fields of art and music.

The name given to an individual Anishinabe or Anishinabequa in a ceremony after a child's birth was very important, and its meaning was sacred to Anishinabek culture and traditions. A name was the very essence of a person's being and an indicator of the values a boy or girl would embody in life.

In addition to the names given to them at birth, many of the Company K men would also take several different names in their lifetimes for various cultural, traditional, and religious reasons as well as for military service. Sometimes this practice of taking several names would cause difficulties for the widows when they submitted pension applications for their deceased husbands' military service.

The men of Company K also came from a variety of religious backgrounds. A number of the men were educated in missionary schools associated with Baptist, Congregational, Lutheran, Methodist, Presbyterian, and Roman Catholic churches. In addition to their Anishinabek names, many of the men adopted English names upon Christian baptism. There were also those men who retained the practice of their Anishinabek traditional religious and cultural beliefs.

Marksmanship Required for Enlistment

The requirements for enlisting as a sharpshooter were stringent, extremely difficult, and centered on a man's ability to be an outstanding marksman. In practice sessions, the men were required to make a "string," or a line of five shots, a hundred yards offhand or two hundred yards at rest within an eleven-inch bull's-eye. The best marksman could hit the bull's-eye at three hundred yards. Since ammunition was expensive, most of the Anishinabek were crack shots who learned to make every bullet count when hunting to supply food for their families.

The sharpshooters were trained to be skirmishers who harassed the enemy with sniper fire. When needed, they would defend and lend their support to artillery and other regiments. But their main duty was to kill the officers of the opposing forces and thereby cause confusion and disunity in the enemy's ranks.

Chief Naugechegumme Addresses the Men of Company K

When the regiment was stationed at the Dearborn Arsenal, the well-respected Anishinabe leader, Ojibwe Chief Naugechegumme (also spelled Naugjekomeh), spoke to the men of Company K. The following extract is from the chief's speech on July 11, 1863, and is found on page 13 of the *Detroit Advertiser and Tribune*. The microfilm copy of the chief's speech is held in the Clarke Library on the campus of Central Michigan University in Mt. Pleasant, Isabella County. An extraction from the chief's speech is as follows:

The company was called together and sat under the shade trees on the arsenal grounds. The chief arose and addressed the men by calling them "My Children" and told them that he had traveled quite far to see them and to counsel them. He told them that he had observed them in camp and on the parade grounds to see if they had behaved like true sons and noble braves.

The chief admonished the men to listen to his words and he would advise them. He emphasized the importance of obeying their officers, to discharge every duty to their country and to be loyal to the great father—the President of the United States—who was paying them for their service.

The men were told to abandon evil of all kinds and to throw away any liquor as it would disgrace them, their fathers, their families and their chiefs.

The chief also told them to rise early in the morning, work, train and leave nothing undone in the evening.

They were told to save their money because their fathers, who took care of them and gave them instructions, were growing old and, being left behind, they would need assistance.

Challenged to face the enemy, to drive them away and not to turn their backs, the chief reinforced their bravery as men and not boys. He reminded them that they were descendants of great chiefs and brave warriors who fought and died with honor.

When faced with death the chief told the men to have confidence in the Great Spirit and, if they died, their forefathers would welcome them into the spirit world as brave sons. The chief concluded his speech by instructing the men to bring honor, and not disgrace, to their families, to the President and to their homeland.

The Regiment Is Deployed

When the last companies were mustered and the regiment was complete, the sharpshooters left the Dearborn Arsenal on August 16, 1863, and traveled to Camp Douglas in Illinois. Camp Douglas was located four miles southeast of downtown

Chicago, Cook County, and was a confine for Confederate prisoners. The men of the regiment would serve as prison guards for seven months.

On St. Patrick's Day, March 17, 1864, the First Michigan Sharpshooters left Camp Douglas for the war at the front. They would arrive in Annapolis, Maryland, on March 21 and be attached to General Ambrose E. Burnside's Ninth Corps.

The engagements in which the First Michigan Sharpshooters participated can be found in many books detailing the military battles of the Civil War. Especially noted is Raymond J. Herek's excellent account in his book *These Men Have Seen Hard Service.*

Wartime experiences affected not only the men but also their families. Regular monthly payments issued by the army were delayed when the troops were on fast marches or engaged in fierce battles. These delays resulted in limited funds received at home.

Poor and inadequate food, wounds incurred by the men and the infirmities that resulted from these injuries, illnesses, and mental stress, known today as post-traumatic stress disorder, would hinder many of the men from making a living to support their families when they returned home from the war.

Medical Treatment in the Civil War and Postwar Issues

In 1861, the United States was not prepared for the medical challenges to come and had very few general hospitals. Many of the medical procedures and medicines given to the soldiers were primitive and dangerous (especially the use of mercury compounds) compared to today's medical practices. But sadly, it's often through wars that we advance our medical knowledge and improve treatments and procedures.

Among the many medical advancements that were instituted during the middle and latter years of the Civil War were the following: (1) improved ambulance corps and the triage method (those most likely to survive were given preference in emergency treatment) were implemented and executed by Dr. Jonathan Letterman; (2) different types of orthopedic surgeries were performed, and improved designs for prosthetics were used to give a better fit to the stumps left after the amputations of arms and legs; (3) antiseptics such as bromine and iodine used toward the latter years of the war were applied to wounds to hinder infections; (4) pain relief through the use of morphine and opium; (5) ether and chloroform used as anesthetics during surgery;

and (6) quinine given for the treatment of malaria. Even plastic surgery made its debut during the Civil War.

At the end of the Civil War in 1865, many large American hospitals and the medical procedures in use were close to the state-of-the-art for that time in history.

Dr. Thomas Holmes of Washington, DC, improved the embalming process for deceased soldiers during the Civil War, but this service was expensive and not affordable for most families of men who were not officers.

The problems that occurred from the men's wartime experiences also caused stress, mainly post-traumatic stress disorder, between couples, which took its toll on their marriages and relationships. Among the symptoms of this disorder are irritability, explosive temper, and difficulty forming close relationships. It was impossible for the families to relate to their soldiers' war experiences or to understand the terror of their nightmares caused by this terrible condition. In many cases, alcohol and opiates were sought as solace from both mental and physical pain. For some soldiers, alcohol and drug addiction would plague them during their remaining years.

Postwar Pensions

To compound these situations, government red tape was a tremendous obstacle in acquiring postwar pensions for many of the veterans and their survivors. If the men were married by their traditional accepted custom and practice, there were no marriage certificates, just the verbal agreement between the couples and their parents. Not having a legally recognized certificate of marriage meant that the wife, in the case of the pensioner's death, needed family or friends to testify for her in a court of law that she and her husband were married according to tribal practice. These witnesses would also swear to the validity of the marriage and list the children under the age of sixteen who would be beneficiaries of pensions. Some pensions were not granted due to insufficient or conflicting information and the lack of communication.

Postwar pensions covered in the soldiers' profiles are explained with regard to what act of Congress, and the date, the pension was issued. The process of obtaining a pension began with an *application* to which a number was assigned. If the application was approved, then a *certificate* number was assigned and the recipient would receive a pension. If no certificate number is listed, then the pension was either denied or possibly given at a later date upon further information and proof. For additional information about the different Civil War pension acts (from 1862 to 1921), the reader should refer to *The Bureau of Pensions: Its History, Activities and Organization* by Gustavus A. Weber (Baltimore, Maryland: Johns Hopkins Press, 1923).

Postwar Activities

After their service, many of the men of Company K joined various posts of the Grand Army of the Republic (or GAR). This organization and its first post were formed as a patriotic Civil War Union Veterans' society by Dr. B. F. Stephenson in Decatur, Illinois, in 1866. The objects of the GAR were: (1) to preserve the bonds that the men had formed fighting in battles together; (2) to exhibit kindness and give assistance to those men in need; (3) to help and support their comrades' widows and orphans and aid in the education of these orphans; (4) to protect and assist the disabled soldiers regardless of their misfortune; and (5) to remember and perpetuate the memory of their deceased comrades.

Membership in the GAR was a valuable asset to the veterans. It allowed them to come together with other men who had gone through similar experiences and who would understand and share their inner feelings. Many times, as the years passed, the men of various posts provided military protocol for the funerals of deceased veterans. The post meetings also provided enjoyment and opportunities for the men to express their patriotism by marching in parades and in Memorial Day observances.

By an act of the War Department issued during the Civil War, all soldiers discharged from service by reason of wounds received in battle were entitled to a bounty of a hundred dollars no matter how short their terms of service.

Introduction to Profiles

The biographical profiles of the officers and enlisted men of Company K of the First Michigan Sharpshooters are taken from compiled military service records, pension records, and medical records found in the National Archives in Washington, DC, military papers in the State of Michigan Archives and Library, county records of births, marriages, and deaths, state and church vital records, newspaper accounts and source material granted by permission from various county archives, libraries, museums, and historical societies both in and out of the state of Michigan.

The names used for the profiles were taken from the original enlistment roll called the *Descriptive Roll of Company K, First Regiment Michigan Sharpshooters, Volunteers, 1861–1866* found in the State of Michigan Archives. With the help of Anishinabek friends, many of the names were corrected where necessary, considering the many mistakes made in phonetic translations at the time of enlistment and in the papers of various government agencies. But there are Anishinabek names of which the spellings are questionable.

The reader will note that, according to the amount of information available, some profiles are more extensive than others. Each profile is a complete independent document able to stand alone and still be an inclusive part of the whole book. Therefore, there is some repetition of information.

Each man's profile has its own bibliography in the back of the book. Instead of a numbered footnote system, sources are italicized and are located at the ends of appropriate sentences in the profiles.

The author wishes to inform the reader that the profiles are not about the generals, military maneuvers, or the battles of the Civil War. They are about the infantrymen known as grunts who bore the burden of fighting and dying in this terrible conflict and the officers who led them into battle. Who were these fighting men of Company K? Who loved them and what happened to them?

For the readers' interest, the following names are just a few examples of the total number of profiles found in this salute to the *Warriors in Mr. Lincoln's Army*:

Charles Allen, a very bright student from a well-known family who was educated in a mission school. Charles took advanced education at Twinsburg Institute (the Ottawa School) in Twinsburg, Ohio. He wrote several letters home in the Anishinabe language to his beloved family. These letters have been translated for the author by linguists who specialize in the Anishinabe language and are included in the soldier's profile.

Louis Genereau Jr., who, when dying of tuberculosis, entreated those who attended him in death to please take care of his wife and little family. They meant the world to him, and he was very worried about their futures.

Joseph Gibson, whose mother and sister revered education and made sure that Joseph attended Rev. Peter Dougherty' Presbyterian Mission School after he broke both legs when he was collecting maple syrup with his family. Their devotion was so strong that the mother and sister took turns carrying Joseph on their shoulders on the two-mile journey to and from school. Joseph died of starvation in a prison camp.

Garret A. Graveraet, the well-educated, trilingual son of Henry Garret and Sophie

(Bailly) Graveraet Jr. His health was never strong, but he rose to the responsibilities of what he was asked to do. Second Lieutenant Graveraet was known to be an excellent teacher and an accomplished musician and landscape painter. He wrote several letters in English to his family, and the copies are included in his profile. Garret was loved and admired by all who knew him.

Henry Garret Graveraet Jr., whose mother was an Anishinabequa of well-connected lines. He was descended from a Netherlands Dutch family whose ancestors fought in the Revolutionary War and in the War of 1812. Henry was Garret Graveraet's father.

Jacob Greensky, the son of the well-known and respected Methodist minister Rev. Peter Greensky. Jacob, his brother, Benjamin, and Rev. Greensky built a log frame church on a rise called Greensky Hill in what is now Charlevoix County. The church is still active with services in the original building. Today this house of worship is called Greensky Hill Mission Church.

Joseph Hannin and *David Lidger,* who were members of the Oneida tribe of the Iroquois Confederation. Both men journeyed from New York state to Michigan and enlisted in Company K at Detroit. Their tribe has a long association with the American government as allies in war and in peace. The Oneida, who fought with the Patriots and not the British in the Revolutionary War, are still known today as "America's First Allies."

Joseph Kakakee, who disappeared after the war. In reality, he went to Canada, married, had a family, and then returned to Michigan without his wife and children. The author solved a problem for one of his descendants by offering information about Kakakee's life in Michigan. The descendant in turn provided information to the author about Kakakee's life in Canada.

Thomas Kechittigo, a well-known, log-driving lumberjack (a river hog) who navigated Michigan rivers in the spring run and worked for various lumber companies. He taught a sharpshooter from another unit how to disguise himself with vegetation and told him to roll in the dirt to cover the blue color of his uniform. Tom was well liked by the officers and men of Company K and in his postwar life was a guest at many dinners given by the well-known lumber barons of Crawford County. Mary, Tom's wife, was the true love of his life. Tom and Mary eloped because Mary's father wanted her to marry a Frenchman.

Amable Kitchibatise, who dictated a letter home to his wife reassuring her that he was okay, not to worry, and expressed concern for her and their children. The letter was sent from a Danville, Virginia, prison. Of course, he wasn't all right. He later died of bronchitis and was buried under a stone with another man's name inscribed on the stone. Amable's cause of death, the place of his death, and the location of his grave have finally been found thanks to an outstanding researcher who gave this information to the author.

Josiah Light, a man who buried his wife and two children the summer before he was killed in a hunting accident. During the fall, after Josiah's death, Josiah's son was also killed in a hunting accident. The tragedies that Josiah and his family experienced would seem to rival those of Job in the book of Job found in the Holy Bible's Old Testament.

Louis Marks, who was brought out of a Petersburg tobacco warehouse prison to show the people gathered in front of the prison what an Indian looked like. Amid insults and laughter, Louis was asked to remove his kepi to show the children his thick black hair. Who had the last laugh at the end of the war?

James and *John Mashkaw,* the sons of Chief John Mashkaw. Both brothers died in battle on the same day, which resulted in a double tragedy for their family. There were no descendants of either soldier.

Daniel Mwakewenah, the greatly admired chief of his Ottawa people. He was keen on sending the Anishinabek children to mission schools for education. Daniel was shot in the hand and died a short time later from an infection in that hand. Because he was so well liked and admired, Daniel's body was embalmed, placed in a handsome coffin, and sent on its way to Emmet County. The casket arrived in Saginaw of Saginaw County on its way north and was buried in Saginaw's Brady Hill Cemetery until it could be transported to the chief's home. For some reason, the order did not come to send the remains north, so Daniel still lies beneath a military stone in said cemetery.

Thomas Nelson, the son of David Nelson, who was also known as Chief David Nelson Shopnagon or Shoppenagans (Little Needles). When on a furlough home to Saginaw City to recover from a battle injury, Thomas was badly injured defending an elderly man who had been attacked by another man for no cause. The elderly gentleman died a short time later. The attacker was fined a small sum of money but served no jail time. Thomas Kechittigo and Chief Shoppnegons were friends and are buried near each other in the Grayling, Crawford County Cemetery.

Antoine Scott, who was recommended twice for the Medal of Honor for his bravery in the Battle of the Crater. He died in 1878. At the time of the Civil War, the Medal of Honor was not awarded posthumously. Five non-Anishinabek members of

14

the First Michigan Sharpshooters, who were recommended for the medal, lived long enough to receive their honors in 1896. It is sad that the only Anishinabe soldier from Michigan who was recommended twice for the Medal of Honor did not live to receive this prestigious award for his outstanding service for the Union cause.

Joseph Wakazoo, who was a descendant in a long line of distinguished Ottawa chiefs. Joseph was well educated, having attended Albion Seminary (now Albion College in Albion, Michigan) and Twinsburg Institute in Twinsburg, Ohio. He and Charles Allen were classmates at the institute. Joseph became a missionary and spent some time in Canada. After he returned from Canada, Joseph went to Minnesota where he studied for the ministry. He was ordained into the Episcopal Church and served the Anishinabek of Minnesota until his death. Joseph was a cousin to Payson Wolf.

Henry Waasegiizhig, who was also known as Henry Condecon. He was descended from a long line of Anishinabek chiefs and lived in both the Upper Peninsula of Michigan and in Wisconsin. Henry worked as a land looker (estimator of timber) for various lumber companies and was admired for his business savvy. He traveled to Washington, DC, as a representative of his tribe for negotiations with the US government. Because he was fluent in English, Henry had no need of an interpreter.

Thomas Wezoo was very active in his Methodist Mission Church and attended many church camp meetings on the Pottawatomi reservation at Athens, Calhoun County. Thomas considered it the honor of his life to have shaken the hand of his president, Abraham Lincoln, when Lincoln visited the wounded soldiers at City Point, Virginia. Just a few days after this momentous event for Thomas, Mr. Lincoln was assassinated.

Payson Wolf, who was a descendant of highly respected Ottawa chiefs of the Maingun (or Wolf) and Wakazoo families and a cousin and Company K comrade of Joseph Wakazoo. Payson was associated with Rev. George Nelson Smith's Congregational Church Mission in Northport of Leelanau County. He fell in love with the minister's daughter, Mary Jane, and she with him. They were classmates together in Smith's mission school. The young couple wanted to marry, but the contemplation of such a marriage was not well received by either the Anishinabek or the non-Anishinabek of Smith's church. Rev. Smith believed and taught that the Anishinabek were equal to the non-Anishinabek in every way, and if he did not honor the couple's wishes, everything he had taught about cultural relations would be for naught. Rev. Smith agreed to officiate at the couple's wedding, and a short time later, Payson built a nice home for his young bride. Even though he loved his wife and bicultural family and had friends and family in both cultures, Payson felt conflicted. He didn't know just where he really belonged. To add to this struggle, his war experiences and the terrible confinement in a prison camp would change him in a dark and troubling way. Mary Jane and the couple's thirteen children watched Payson's downward spiral but were powerless to help him.

The Oath Taken at Enlistment

I _____ DO SOLEMNLY SWEAR, THAT I WILL BEAR TRUE FAITH AND ALLEGIANCE TO THE **UNITED STATES OF AMERICA,** AND THAT I WILL SERVE THEM HONESTLY AND FAITHFULLY AGAINST ALL THEIR ENEMIES OR OPPOSERS WHOMSOEVER; AND THAT I WILL OBSERVE AND OBEY THE ORDER OF THE PRESIDENT OF THE UNITED STATES, AND THE ORDERS OF THE OFFICERS APPOINTED OVER ME, ACCORDING TO THE RULES AND ARTICLES OF WAR.

Enlistment Papers

VOLUNTEER ENLISTMENT.

STATE OF MICHIGAN,

Town of *Pent Water* County of *Oceana*

I, *Cornelius Hall* born in *Ionia County*
in the State of *Michigan* aged *Twenty* years,
and by occupation a *Farmer*, Do HEREBY ACKNOWLEDGE to have
volunteered this *Third* day of *September* 186*4*
to serve as a **SOLDIER IN THE ARMY OF THE UNITED STATES OF AMERICA**,
for the period of *One Year* unless sooner discharged by proper authority. Do
also agree to accept such bounty, pay, rations and clothing, as are, or may be, established
by law for volunteers. And I, *Cornelius Hall* do solemnly swear,
that I will bear true faith and allegiance to the **UNITED STATES OF AMERICA**, and that
I will serve them honestly and faithfully against all their enemies or opposers whomsoever; and that I will observe and obey the orders of the President of the United
States, and the orders of the officers appointed over me, according to the Rules and
Articles of War.

Sworn and subscribed to, at *Grand Rapids*
this *3d* day of *September* 186*4*,   *Cornelius Hall*

BEFORE *me*

I CERTIFY ON HONOR, That I have carefully examined the above named volunteer agreeably to the General Regulations of the Army, and that in my opinion he is
free from all bodily defects and mental infirmity, which would, in any way, disqualify
him from performing the duties of a soldier.

Alonzo Hall
                Examining Surgeon.

I CERTIFY, ON HONOR, That I have minutely inspected the volunteer *Cornelius
Hall* previously to his enlistment, and that he was entirely sober
when enlisted; that, to the best of my judgment and belief, he is of lawful age; and
that, in accepting him as duly qualified to perform the duties of an able-bodied soldier, I
have strictly observed the Regulations which govern the recruiting service. This soldier
has *Black* eyes, *Dark* hair, *Dark* complexion, is *5*
feet *8* inches high.

Capt N. Wisley   *Sharp Shooters*
First Regiment of Michigan Volunteers, (Infantry,)
            RECRUITING OFFICER.

Volunteer enlistment paper of Private Cornelius Hall, Company K, First
Michigan Sharpshooters. National Archives, Washington, DC.

SUBSTITUTE
VOLUNTEER ENLISTMENT.

STATE OF _Mich_   *City* TOWN OF _Lansing_

I, _Robert Valentine_ _____ born in the State of _Mich_ , aged _23_ years, and by occupation a _Hunter_ Do HEREBY ACKNOWLEDGE to have agreed with _Joseph Mills_ , Esq., of _4" Ward city of Lansing Lingham Co Mich_ to become his **SUBSTITUTE** in the Military Service, for a sufficient consideration paid and delivered to me, on the _24_ day of _August_ , 186_4_; and having thus agreed with said _Joseph Mills_ , I DO HEREBY ACKNOWLEDGE to have enlisted this _24"_ day of _august_ 186_4_, to serve as a **Soldier** in the **Army of the United States of America**, for the period of _9_ year , unless sooner discharged by proper authority : I do also agree to accept such bounty, pay, rations, and clothing, as are, or may be, established by law for soldiers. And I do solemnly swear that I will bear true and faithful allegiance to the **United States of America;** that I will serve them honestly and faithfully against all their enemies or opposers whomsoever; and that I will observe and obey the orders of the President of the United States, and the orders of the Officers appointed over me, according to the Rules and Articles of War.

Sworn and subscribed to at _Jackson_ this _24"_ day of _aug_ 186_4_

BEFORE me _R S Berry_

       His
Robert X _Valentine_
       mark

capt & Pro mar
2d Dist Mich

We certify, on honor, That we have carefully examined the above-named Volunteer Substitute agreeably to the Regulations, and that, in our opinion, he is free from all bodily defects and mental infirmity which would in any way disqualify him from performing the duties of a soldier; that he was entirely sober when enlisted; that he is of lawful age, (not under 18 years;) and that, in accepting him as duly qualified to perform the duties of an able-bodied soldier, and as a Substitute in lieu of _Joseph Mills_ _Enrolled in_ , ~~drafted in~~ _4" Ward city of Lansing Michigan_ , 186_, we have strictly observed the Regulations which govern in such cases. This soldier has _black_ eyes, _black_ hair, _dark_ complexion; is _5_ feet _6½ in_ inches high.

R S Berry
Provost Marshal.

Volunteer substitute enlistment paper of Private Robert Valentine, Company K, First Michigan Sharpshooters. National Archives, Washington, DC.

Officers of Company K

Andress, Edwin V., Captain

Enlistment: Entered into the service of Company K of the First Michigan Sharpshooters as captain on June 23, 1863, at the Detroit Arsenal in Dearborn, Wayne County, for three years. Commissioned by Governor Austin Blair on July 22, 1863.

Age: Twenty-five, born July 29, 1838, in Leeds County, Ontario, Canada.

Occupation: Not stated

Residence: Chesaning, Saginaw County

Physical Description: Not stated. Officers were not asked personal information unless they entered the military at a lower rank.

Mustered: July 22, 1863, in Detroit, Wayne County

Military Service: Captain Edwin V. Andress, as a recruiting officer looking for sharpshooters, went to Oceana County just shortly before July 4, 1863. It was suggested that he go to the Anishinabek Reservation near Elbridge, as several men there had expressed an interest in entering the service but had not been accepted.

Andress arranged to be one of the speakers at the July Fourth celebration and was given an honored place on the program. He delivered a stirring, patriotic speech, which was translated into the Anishinabe language by Louis Genereau Sr. Following Andress was Chief Paybawme, who addressed the crowd with patriotic fervor.

As a result of the intense speechmaking, about twenty-five young Anishinabek men from the area, led by Louis Genereau Jr., stepped forward to enlist in the sharpshooter regiment. The enlistees were assigned to Company K and then taken on the boat, *Charles Mears,* to the Detroit Arsenal at Dearborn for induction and training (*Hartwick and Tuller*).

It is assumed that Captain Andress was popular with his Anishinabek men, who knew that he respected them and their culture. One writer mentioned that Andress was a fluent "speaker" of the Anishinabe language, but the author doubts this statement without further proof. If Captain Andress were a fluent speaker of the Anishinabe language, then he would not need interpreter Louis Genereau Sr. to translate his speech into the Odawa (or Ottawa) dialect at the July Fourth celebration. Genereau was present to be an interpreter for Andress.

During the Battle of Spotsylvania, Virginia (the Ni River), on May 9, 1864, Andress sustained a gunshot (missile) wound to the right foot, near the metatarsal bone of the second toe, and flesh wounds on three fingers of his right hand. Stretcher bearers took him to the division aid station where his wounds were washed and hastily bandaged. He was given whiskey for shock and an opium pill for pain.

Andress was then sent by ambulance wagon to a depot hospital at Fredericksburg, Virginia. The hospital was located at or near attorney John Marye's house, on Marye's Heights. At the hospital, the wound on his foot was treated with simple cold water dressings. The dressings consisted of folded lint rinsed in cold water, placed on the wounds and held in place with a cloth wrap or adhesive plaster (*Schaadt).* His fingers were also washed in cold water and wrapped with simple water dressings. Treatment with cold water was thought to suppress wound inflammation. Opium pills were again offered to the soldier.

From the depot hospital, Andress was sent by ambulance wagon through Fredericksburg to the wharf at Belle Plain Landing, nine miles northeast of Fredericksburg on Potomac Creek. At the landing, he was taken by hospital steamer to Seminary USA General Hospital in Georgetown, DC, and admitted on May 12. Similar medical treatment was administered to him at this hospital, and he was given a hearty diet of fresh fruits and vegetables and breads and grains of various types.

Andress was given a furlough on May 16. On July 4, 1864, the captain requested an extension to his leave of absence due to his wounds.

On July 7, Andress was admitted to Division No. 1, USA General Hospital at the Navy Yard in Annapolis, Maryland, for surgery. He was anesthetized with ether and underwent surgical treatment for the wound in his foot. During the surgery, the doctors discovered that his right leg had become ulcerated. According to the Adjutant General's Office, and also according to a medical opinion at that time, the possible cause of the ulcers was secondary syphilis. If so, compounds of mercury were applied to the ulcers as treatment (*Bollet*). But the ulcers could also have been caused from vascular damage resulting in varicose veins. In this case, Andress would have been anesthetized with ether, as previously mentioned, and the sores and dead tissue would have been removed with a scalpel. This process of tissue removal was called debridement. Iodine was then applied around the wound, and a weak solution of bromine was put into the cavity of the sore (*Evans*). After the procedure, a cloth bandage was applied to the wound and secured with adhesive plaster. A definitive diagnosis as to the cause of the ulcers in Andress's right leg was not recorded.

Discharged: Due to the nature of his wounds, Captain Andress was mustered out and honorably discharged for disability on July 26, 1864. He was paid money owed to him for his service at his discharge and returned to Michigan.

Biography: Edwin Von Shultz Andress was the son of Socrates and Mary (Ladd) Andress. His siblings were Abbot "Abb," James T., Mary Ann, Charles A., and Wilson Rufus.

Edwin married Mrs. Ellen (or Nelly) Louise Hooppell, the widow of Robert (or William) Hooppell, on August 1, 1874, in Detroit, Wayne County. Robert (or William) Hooppell, a petty officer in the United Kingdom Royal Navy, died at age thirty-one of pulmonary tuberculosis on July 2, 1872, in the County of Devon, England. According to one record, Ellen was born November 29, 1852, in Tregony, Cornwall, England. Another record states that she was born on November 29, 1856, in London, England (*Hooppell Family Genealogy*). Rev. Supply Chase, minister of the Gospel, presided at the marriage of Edwin and Ellen.

In 1878, the Andress family moved to Weldon near Onyx, Kern County, California, and then later to Onyx where the family settled on a ranch.

The Andress couple were the parents of four children: Earnest Albert Socrates, born May 28, 1876; Jessie Mary, born April 3, 1878; Charlotte (or Lottie) Ethel, born October 28, 1880; and Charles Von Edwin, born November 25, 1883.

Application #311,699 for an invalid pension was filed for Andress on September 25, 1879. He received Invalid Pension Certificate #201,283, which paid thirty dollars a month until his death.

Edwin died of consumption (or tuberculosis) at age forty-six on October 10, 1884, at Onyx. His funeral was held on October 12, and he was buried in Little Cottage Grove Cemetery of said city.

With the help of Edwin's brother, Charlie, Ellen and her children remained on the family ranch and raised beef cattle.

On October 21, 1889, Ellen Andress married for the third time to John Wood (of Illinois) in Kern, California. The marriage was short-lived, and she was subsequently divorced from Wood in 1891. After the divorce, Ellen resumed her former husband's name of Andress.

Application #547,567 for a widow's pension was filed for Ellen on April 20, 1892.

She received a Widow's Pension Certificate #882,283, which paid thirty dollars a month until her death.

On July 5, 1892, Application #554,030 for a minor children's pension was filed for Ellen. She received a Minor Children's Pension Certificate #379,908 for ten dollars a month for her youngest child, Charles, until November 24, 1899, when he attained the age of sixteen.

Ellen Andress died on October 7, 1924, in Kernville of Kern County and was buried at Wofford Heights of said county.

Driggs, William J., First Lieutenant

Enlistment: Commissioned a first lieutenant in Company K of the First Michigan Sharpshooters by Governor Austin Blair on July 22, 1863.

Age: Twenty-four, born February 14,1839, in New York County, New York.

Occupation: Soldier, having previously enlisted as a corporal in Company L of the Michigan Sixth Cavalry on August 29, 1862. Transferred to Company C of the Seventh Cavalry on November 12, 1862.

Residence: East Saginaw, Saginaw County

Physical Description: Five feet eleven and a half inches tall, with hazel eyes, light brown hair, fair complexion.

Mustered: December 20, 1863, in Detroit, Wayne County

Military Service: On June 26, 1864, when his regiment was before Petersburg, Driggs sent a letter to his father, John Driggs, a United States Republican congressman who represented Michigan's Sixth Congressional District. In the letter, Driggs lamented the fact that his deafness had become progressively worse due to the explosions of artillery shells. He related that he could hear neither field commands from his superiors nor challenges from sentinels unless given in a very loud tone of voice. Therefore, he considered himself unfit for the discharge of picket duty and felt it necessary to tender his resignation. In conclusion, Driggs related that he had, to the best of his ability while suffering from his infirmity, led his company of Anishinabek men since the first fight at the Battle of the Wilderness. He was proud of this accomplishment.

Congressman Driggs consented to his son's wish to resign from his command and wrote a letter on his son's behalf to General Orlando B. Wilcox. Included in this correspondence were the letters he received from William, in addition to a letter from William to Secretary of War Edwin M. Stanton, in which Lt. Driggs expressed his reluctance as to his need to resign from the army.

Lieutenant Driggs was very proud of his "Indian Company," as he called his men, and stated in his letter how bravely and desperately they had fought. He believed that since he had no Anishinabe officer left to interpret, that the company should be relieved from further duty at the immediate front. He preferred that the company should have some time to recuperate, seek new recruits, and have new officers assigned to the unit.

Discharged: First Lieutenant William J. Driggs was mustered out and honorably discharged for the disability of severe deafness on July 6, 1864. He reentered the service as a second lieutenant in the Eleventh United States Infantry on February 23, 1866. After he was promoted to first lieutenant on July 28, 1866, he was transferred to the Twentieth Infantry on September 21, 1866. First Lieutenant Driggs mustered out of the army permanently on January 1, 1871, and returned to his home in Saginaw.

Biography: William Jefferson Driggs was the eldest child of John Fletcher and Anna Marie (Hawley) Driggs. As stated previously, John F. Driggs was a well-known US Republican congressman from Saginaw. William's siblings were Emma Frances, Truman Erastus, Irene Hawley, and Florence Nightingale. As a child, William contracted scarlet fever, which left him partially deaf. He would suffer from poor health for the rest of his life. When William told his father that he wanted to join the army, John expressed a concern that his son's deafness would increase due to his exposure to artillery discharges in the service. Against his father's wishes and the concern of the family physician, but due to his anxiety to serve his country, Driggs enlisted in the army.

After his military service, Driggs worked in the Railway Mail Service for thirty-two years in Saginaw. In the latter years of his postal service, he was a superintendent and had the responsibility of receipt and dispatch of mails. William Driggs did not marry.

On November 12, 1890, Application #959,557 for an invalid pension was filed for Driggs. Invalid Pension Certificate #811,039 was granted to him in which he received eight dollars a month. His monthly payments were increased to twenty-four dollars and remained the same until his death. Driggs was an active member of the GAR Gordon Granger Post #33 in Saginaw. In 1910, he moved to Evart, Osceola County, and resided with his sister Mrs. N. W. Ely.

On December 12, 1914, at the age of seventy-five, William J. Driggs died of acute nephritis (or inflammation of the kidneys) in Evart. His body was taken to Saginaw accompanied by comrades of Evart's GAR Sedgwick Post #16.

Funeral services for Driggs were conducted by Rev. Nelson F. Bradley from the First Congregational Church of Saginaw on Tuesday, December 15, 1914. He was laid to rest in his family's plot in Saginaw's Forest Lawn Cemetery and accorded military honors from his GAR post.

Graveraet, Garrett A., Second Lieutenant

Enlistment: Entered into the service of Company K of the First Michigan Sharpshooters as a second lieutenant on June 9, 1863, at Little Traverse (renamed Harbor Springs in 1881), Emmet County, for three years. Commissioned by Governor Austin Blair on July 22, 1863.

Age: Twenty-three, born January 10, 1840, on Mackinac Island, Mackinac County.

Occupation: Artist, musician, and teacher

Residence: Little Traverse

Physical Description: No description given. Officers were not asked personal questions unless they entered the service at a lower rank.

Mustered: July 22, 1863, in Detroit, Wayne County

Military Service: Second Lieutenant Garret A. Graveraet, upon receiving his commission, was detailed on July 31, 1863, on an order from Regimental Colonel Charles V. DeLand to recruiting service. He was to seek additional enlistments for Company K among the Anishinabek men in their settlements near Lake Michigan. Sergeant Francis Tabasasch of the same company was ordered to go with Graveraet and to assist him in his duties.

After their recruiting requirements were completed, Second Lt. Graveraet and Sgt. Tabasasch rejoined their regiment at the Detroit Arsenal in Dearborn.

On August 17, 1863, Second Lieutenant Graveraet traveled with the sharpshooters to Camp Douglas, a confine for rebel prisoners, in Chicago, Cook County, Illinois, for their first assignment outside of Michigan. The men of the regiment would guard the prison.

One year later, on St. Patrick's Day, March 17, the sharpshooters were ordered to Annapolis, Maryland, to prepare for battlefield assignments. While in camp in

Maryland, Second Lt. Graveraet, who did not enjoy the best of health, was seen to be very active on the repair detail. He was cheerful and never refused his duty to lead his men in various camp duties.

After the sharpshooters were ordered to the front in Virginia, Second Lt. Graveraet continued to be an example to his men with his bravery and leadership. He distinguished himself in three severe battles before he died of wounds in a Washington, DC, hospital in June 1864.

During the Battle of Spotsylvania on May 12, 1864, Garret received word from one of the men of his company that his father, Sergeant Henry Garret Graveraet Jr., had suffered a gunshot wound to his head. Garrett hurried to the spot where Henry had fallen, but upon his arrival, he saw that his father was dead. That evening, with permission from First Lieutenant and Adjutant Edward J. Buckbee, Garrett, with Buckbee and some other men from Company K, retrieved Henry's body and buried it. Garret marked the grave in hopes that the body could be recovered and that he would be able to arrange to take his father home to Michigan where Henry would be reburied (*Herek from Buckbee).* But that hope of taking his father home would not be realized.

After sundown on June 17, 1864, during the Battle at Petersburg, Second Lt. Graveraet was seriously wounded. He was leading his company on an assault against rebel artillerymen when he sustained a gunshot wound in the upper left arm (humerus bone) from either a missile ball or a piece of shrapnel from the explosion of an artillery shell (Garrett remembered it to be a missile ball). The missile fractured the shaft of the humerus bone near his shoulder (*Smith).*

Garrett was taken by stretcher bearers or ambulance wagon to his division aid station where bleeding was stopped by tourniquet or compression and bandages were applied to stabilize his wound.

From the aid station, Garret was taken by ambulance wagon to his division hospital farther to the rear of the action. That evening, the surgeons administered chloroform to the lieutenant and amputated his left arm near the shoulder. It's not certain whether a circular or a flap method of amputation was used. In either case, the end of the bone was smoothed with bone-biting forceps or rasps. The skin, if the circular method were used, or the flaps of the muscle and skin of the flap procedure were brought together and were sewn loosely with silk or wire sutures (*Kuz and Bengtston).* Whiskey was administered for shock, and an opium pill was given for pain.

After surgery, the raw wound area was dressed with a pad of folded flannel, or whatever cloth was available, that was coated with a soothing ointment called cerate. Cerate was made of beeswax mixed with oils, fatty substances, or resins (*Bollet*). A muslin bandage roll was wrapped over this pad and around the stump and the shoulder area. The stump area would be supported in starch or plaster splints to limit motion. An opium pill or whiskey was given to the patient for pain.

On June 19, Garrett was taken by ambulance wagon to the military railroad, put on a mattress in a boxcar, the floor of which was cushioned with straw or hay, and sent to City Point, Virginia. He was taken from the train by ambulance wagon and transported to a wharf at City Point. Garrett was taken from the wharf, put on the hospital steamer, *George Leary*, and transported to Armory Square USA General Hospital in Washington, DC.

He arrived at Armory Square Hospital on June 20 and was lodged in Ward Q. His wound was treated with a tincture of iodine and fresh dressings, and his pain was again eased with opium pills. A diet that consisted of fresh fruits and vegetables and breads and grains of various types was ordered for him.

While in the hospital, Garrett wrote a letter (found in his pension papers) to his mother, Sophia, and to his sister, Josine, on June 22, 1864. The letter is as follows:

Washington, D.C. June 22, 1864

Dear Mother & Sister,

On Friday last evening the first charge on the enemy's outworks near Petersburg, Va., I was wounded in the left arm by a Minnie ball and the arm had to be amputated below the shoulder, which was done that evening. I think I shall be discharged before long and come home if my arm does well. The Dr. thinks it will do well.

I've had no opportunity to write about father's death. Don't be discouraged about me.

Mother's kind teachings and prayers is all that has kept me up. I have thought of them a great deal and I feel determined to become a Christian if possible. This fighting for my country is all right, it has brought me to my senses.

I expressed from Warrenton Junction early in May four hundred dollars to Hon. D.C. Leach, to be given to him to mother. That is I enclosed that amount in a letter to Mr. Leach and gave the letter unto the hands of our paymaster who promised to have it expressed from

Washington. Now I want to know if you have received it? Please write to me immediately. Address the letter to me at

Armory Square Hospital
Ward Q Bed 45
Washington City, DC

A letter from you will do me good. Don't be uneasy.

Affectionately.
Garrett A. Graveraet

Shortly after he had written his letter, Garrett's condition deteriorated, and his pain grew more intense. After lingering for ten days, he died at 4:00 p.m. on June 30, 1864. Garrett's death was detailed in a letter to Sophia Graveraet by Joseph Finch, ward master of Armory Square Hospital.

The official record of Garret's passing in the hospital was noted in *The Medical and Surgical History of the War of the Rebellion*. Graveraet, G. A., Lieut., K, First Michigan Sharpshooters, age twenty-four, June 17, 1864. Left arm, died June 30, 1864 (*Medical*).

Garrett's body was turned over to friends on the day of his death. Among those friends was Congressman John F. Driggs who sought out Dr. Thomas Holmes, who was a noted embalmer and lived in Washington, DC. As Dr. Holmes prepared Garrett's body for burial, Congressman Driggs expedited the process to have Garrett's body temporarily buried in the Historic Congressional Cemetery in Washington. Second Lt. Garrett A. Graveraet was laid to rest, with full military honors, on July 8, 1864. His burial site was designated as Site R77/184 (*Cemetery*).

Dr. D. M. Bliss, surgeon in charge of Armory Square Hospital, wrote to Mrs. Sophia Graveraet and informed her of her son's death. He also mentioned that he would arrange to have the body returned home on October 1, 1864.

A letter from Little Traverse on behalf of Sophia Graveraet was written by US government interpreter for Indian affairs, Richard Cooper, on July 25 in response to Dr. Bliss's letter. Mr. Cooper requested that the $130 left in Lt. Graveraet's account be used to pay the expenses for shipping Graveraet's body home sooner than October 1. Cooper further stated that if that plan were possible, he would make arrangements to ship the body to Detroit in care of Bissel and Gillets Warehouse. From Detroit, the body would then be sent on to Little Traverse by way of the propeller boat *Hunter*. If this plan were not feasible, then Dr. Bliss was advised to send money, left after shipping expenses, to Mrs. Graveraet in care of Mackinac Indian Agent DeWitt C. Leach.

On July 26, 1864, assistant ward master of Ward Q at Armory Square Hospital, Joseph Finch, wrote a letter to Sophia Graveraet in which he described Garrett's last days. In the letter, Finch mentioned that Garrett knew that he was dying and had requested that his body be sent home. Finch further related that Garrett suffered quite a lot and that his case was terminal due to an infection called septicemia (or blood poisoning due to pathogenic bacteria) that had spread to his heart. Finch also mentioned that US Congressional Representative John F. Driggs, father of Lt. William J. Driggs, had visited Garrett several times, along with other friends and comrades. A Catholic priest had also been in to see Garrett several times to talk to him and to give him comfort. Representative Driggs personally asked Dr. Holmes to prepare Garrett's body for burial upon Garrett's death.

Mr. Finch further related to Sophia that the medical personnel did all they could to help Garrett. He reassured her that Garrett was a good soldier, a true officer, and a gentleman and liked by all the men of his regiment. Finch concluded that he regretted the loss of her only son and hoped that God would hold her in His care.

Second Lt. Garrett A. Graveraet's body was disinterred from the Congressional Cemetery on November 5, 1864, and shipped to Detroit by way of the instructions previously noted from Richard Cooper's letter. It's assumed that Congressman John F. Driggs was instrumental in expediting the transfer.

It was Sophia's decision to have Garrett's body taken from Little Traverse to Mackinac Island and buried in the family plot in Ste. Anne Cemetery. His reburial on Mackinac Island took place sometime after November 5, 1864. Garrett's military stone stands beside his father's memorial stone in that cemetery.

In a fitting tribute to this young man, Lt. William J. Driggs said of him, "He never shrank from danger. At the battle of the Wilderness and at Spotsylvania he remained constantly with the men, sharing their dangers and encouraging them to stand their ground. He had often complained of his health, which was usually very feeble, and I had frequently urged him to remain at the hospital or in camp. But this he would not do. He was determined to be with his men. He was the most popular officer in the regiment and his loss was deeply felt" (*Detroit Advertiser and Tribune*).

Mackinac Indian Agent DeWitt C. Leach was reported to have greatly admired Graveraet and considered him a hero.

Discharged: No discharge given. Died from wounds while in the hospital.

Biography: Lieutenant Garrett A. Graveraet was born on Mackinac Island,

Mackinac County, on January 10, 1840. He was the second child and first son of Henry Garrett and Sophia (or Sophie) Hortense (Bailly) (pronounced Bay-e) Graveraet Jr.

Through his mother, who was a daughter of Joseph and Angelique (McGulpin) Bailly, Garrett was descended from French, Scots-Irish, and Anishinabek lineages *(Bailly)*. From his father, who was the son of Henry Garrett and Charlotte (Livingston) Graveraet Sr., Garrett was descended from English, Anishinabek, and Netherlands Dutch ancestors *(Graveraet)*.

Garrett's siblings were: Sophia Alice, born in 1836 or 1837; Marie Rosine, born February 16, 1842; and Joseph, born in 1848.

Being an excellent student, Garrett acquired a very good education for his time. He was fortunate to have his mother (who was well educated) as his first teacher in 1845 at the Catholic Mission School at Point St. Ignace (or St. Ignace), Mackinac County. The school was under the directorship of Bishop Peter Paul Lefevre of Detroit, Wayne County. The Graveraet family lived near the school when Sophie was a teacher there from 1840 to 1855 *(Lefevere 1)*. During that time, Henry found what work he could do to augment the wages that Sophie would contribute to the family income.

Henry had complained that Sophia's wages as a teacher were just not enough in combined family income and that it was increasingly difficult for him to find work in St. Ignace. He wanted to move back to the island to find a job, but he was indecisive as to when he wanted to move from St. Ignace.

On September 20, 1847, Sophia wrote to Bishop Lefevere and requested a raise in salary in order to pay for family expenses and also to keep the school open *(Lefevere 2)*.

On May 12, 1848, Sophie received a certificate of deposit for thirty-six dollars from Bishop Lefevre *(Lefevere 3)*.

As Garrett grew to manhood, he helped his father with fishing, hunting, and farming. He enjoyed woodland experiences with Anishinabek friends, while he learned refined ways from his mother. Under Sophia's supervision, Garrett became an apt pupil and scholar. In addition to English and Anishinabe languages, he soon became proficient as a French speaker. He loved literature, music, and art and became an accomplished violinist as well as a portrait and landscape painter.

The 1860 federal census of Michigan listed the Graveraet family living on Mackinac Island, but Joseph was not included in the family tally. During his residence on the island, Garrett worked as a clerk in a mercantile store to help with family expenses.

Shortly before the Civil War, Garrett's family returned to Little Traverse. While living in Little Traverse, Garrett received a government appointment to teach in an Anishinabek school. No doubt this experience sharpened his interpersonal skills. But it seemed that prolonged confinement in the closed space of a classroom was injurious to his health. So after a few years at the school, he resigned from his teaching position. Garrett was not strong physiologically and often complained of his feeble health.

Soon after he submitted his resignation (in early 1863), he received a request from the military authorities in Michigan to raise a company of Anishinabek volunteers for the First Michigan Sharpshooters. Being linguistically proficient and adept at cultural mediation, Garrett was the perfect choice as a recruiter. He knew many of the Anishinabek men personally and was well liked by them. Garrett joined the army, was awarded his commission of second lieutenant on July 22, 1863, by Governor Austin Blair, and zealously entered the recruiting service.

Knowing that his mother and sister were wholly dependent upon him and that Henry was not able to provide stable support (he may have had an issue with alcohol), Garrett provided for his family's future needs. Just before he left for the service, he bought a house and a one-fourth lot in Little Traverse for his mother. He had the house fully furnished.

While in the service, Garrett sent his wages home and kept only the money needed for his own expenses.

When he died at age twenty-four, Garrett, who did not marry, left not only his immediate family but also many friends and comrades who mourned his loss. He was an admirable young man who was known not to drink alcohol or use foul language. Garrett bridged the Anishinabek and non-Anishinabek cultures by his ease of living in both worlds and was loved by all who knew him.

Application #78,414 for a widow's pension was filed for Sophie on January 9, 1865. She received Widow's Pension Certificate #61,689, which paid eight dollars a month.

In 1877, Sophie decided that instead of a widow's pension, she wanted to submit an application for a dependent mother's pension from her son's service. Garrett had always seen to her needs, and Henry's pension was not enough support for her elderly years.

In lieu of Henry's pension, Application #230,334 for a dependent mother's pension was submitted for her on March 12, 1877, and her widow's pension payments were discontinued.

Sophie Graveraet was granted a Dependent Mother's Pension Certificate #177,583 in which she was paid fifteen dollars a month commencing on April 20, 1877. She received these payments until her death. The devout grand lady of the Henry G. Graveraet Jr. family died in Petoskey, Emmet County, on January 7, 1892, at about the age of eighty-five. Her final resting place is an unmarked grave in the Holy Childhood of Jesus Cemetery in Harbor Springs of Emmet County.

Enlisted Men—Letter A

Agahgo, Charles, Private

Enlistment: Enlisted as a private on July 4, 1863, at Elbridge, Oceana County, by Captain Edwin V. Andress, First Michigan Sharpshooters, for three years.

   Age: Twenty-four, born about 1839 in Ada, Kent County.

   Occupation: Farmer

   Residence: Pentwater, Oceana County

   Physical Description: Five feet nine, black eyes, black hair, and a dark complexion. Examining physician was Dr. Jacob B. McNett, assistant surgeon, First Michigan Sharpshooters.

   Mustered: July 11, 1863, in Detroit, Wayne County, by Lieutenant Colonel John R. Smith, US Army

   Military Service: In March 1864, Private Agahgo became ill while on guard duty at the confine for Confederate prisoners, Camp Douglas, Chicago, Cook County, Illinois. At the post hospital, Agahgo complained of a persistent cough that became worse and so weakened him that he was kept in his bed for an unspecified period of time. He recovered and caught up with his regiment after the men had left for Annapolis, Maryland, on March 17, 1864, St. Patrick's Day.

   On May 13, 1864, the day after the initial Battle of Spotsylvania in Virginia, Agahgo was so weak that he was taken by ambulance wagon to a depot hospital, possibly at or near attorney John Marye's house close to Marye's Heights in Fredericksburg, Virginia. He was kept for observation until May 15.

   From Fredericksburg, Private Agahgo was sent by ambulance wagon on May 15 to a wharf at Belle Plain Landing, Virginia, nine miles northeast of Fredericksburg on Potomac Creek. After he arrived at the wharf, Agahgo was transferred to a hospital steamer and sent to Alexandria, Virginia.

   On May 16, Agahgo was admitted to L'Ouverture General Hospital in Alexandria with a diagnosis of inflammation of the lungs. Later, the diagnosis was changed to erysipelas. Erysipelas is also known as "St. Anthony's Fire" and "The Rose" and is an acute, infectious disease caused by bacteria called *Streptococcus pyogenes* (*Rutkow*). This illness is characterized by a spreading inflammation (of redness and tenderness) of the skin and subcutaneous tissues. The inflammation is accompanied by the formation of blisters. If the disease spreads into the lymph nodes, it can pass into the bloodstream and cause "pyemia" or "blood poisoning" (*Bollet*). In this case, heart valves and lungs can be damaged. Pyemia in the nervous system can cause meningitis or inflammation of the membranes of the brain and spinal cord.

Since it was not recorded in a medical report that Agahgo incurred a gunshot wound that became infected, it is assumed that he may have suffered from spontaneous erysipelas. This condition could have occurred due to an infection at the site of a small break or cut in the skin. Because of the contagious nature of this disease, Agahgo was isolated in a separate area away from other patients.

Various treatments for Agahgo's illness could have included the following: a laxative of castor oil; a diaphoretic of Dover's powder, which is a powder of ipecac and opium that produces sweating; a cathartic of "blue mass," which is calomel (or mercurous chloride) to purge his system; a tonic of ferric chloride and quinine for fever; an external poultice of yeast or a compound of lead applied to his chest; or his body was painted with a tincture of iodine or bromine (*Ibid.*). Also, his body could be smeared with oil, fresh lard, or glycerin to exclude air from the blisters and give him some comfort (*Evans*). Nutrients of milk, chicken broth, and beef tea were ordered for his diet. Alcohol was added as a stimulant, and opium pills were given for pain.

After a seven-month stay in the hospital, Private Charles Agahgo became delirious on January 17, 1865, and died while in a coma at 3:00 p.m. on January 19. The doctors conducted a postmortem examination of Agahgo and found a severe infection and swelling of the vessels of the meninges (or membranes) that cover the brain. This discovery was evidence that the disease had spread to his nervous system.

The official notation of Agahgo's death can be found in the *Medical and Surgical History of the War of the Rebellion, 1861–1865, Volume VI*, and is as follows:

> Case 29. – Private Charles Agugo, Co. K, lst Mich. Sharpshooters, was admitted May 16, 1864, with rheumatism. There is no record of his case until Jan. 7; 1865, when he was attacked with erysipelas, ushered in by a decided chill. The fauces and right side of the face first became affected; the inflammation then crossed the nose and involved

the entire left side of the face; there was much swelling and both eyes were closed. He was treated with tincture of iron, quinine, stimulants and a nutritious diet. Delirium set in on the 17th. He died comatose on the 19th. Post mortem examination: The membranes of the brain were highly congested. Other organs normal.— Act. Ass't Surgeon Lewis Heard, L'Ouverture Hospital, Alexandria, Va. *(Medical)*

On January 21, 1865, Private Agahgo's body was placed into a coffin and taken to Alexandria National Cemetery in Alexandria, Virginia. Formal services and military protocol were afforded the deceased, which included a chaplain, military escort from the hospital to the cemetery, the firing of arms, and a placement of an individual temporary headboard with information about the deceased (*Encyclopedia*). Today, Private Agahgo lies at rest in Section B under military headstone #3391. The name on his stone reads "Charles Agorgo."

An inventory of Agahgo's personal effects included one forage cap, one great coat, one uniform coat, one blouse, two pairs of trousers, three flannel shirts, one pair of cotton drawers, one pair of boots, two pairs of shoes, one pair of socks, one vest, one tin cup, one canteen, and one haversack.

Discharged: No discharge given. Died of disease while in the hospital.

Biography: Charles Agahgo, whose family name was derived from the Anishinabe word *kag,* which means "porcupine," was the son of Agahgo and his wife (*Baraga)*. He may have received some education at a Protestant or Catholic Church-related school. Charles is thought to have had at least two brothers, named Peinsoah and Shoega.

Charles married Pahgutchquay (or Pawgawchequay) Kaguageme on May 15, 1857. The marriage was conducted according to accepted Anishinabe custom and practice (an agreement between the couple and their parents) at Lowell, Kent County. Sometime later, Charles and Pahgutchquay moved to Elbridge, Oceana County.

The couple were the parents of two sons: Pahbamashay, born on December 5, 1862, and Wawbegonese, born on November 25, 1864. Wawbegonese (or Wabekanis) died of an illness on July 3 or 6, 1867, at the age of three.

Pahgutchquay's Application #115,521 for a widow's pension was filed for her on November 18, 1865.

On June 1, 1865, Pahgutchquay (who was also known by her English name of

Lucy), as widow, received Certificate #456,213, which paid one hundred dollars. The certificate was issued as additional bounty due to the soldier for his service.

Application #184,346 was filed for Pahgutchquay on February 4, 1870, for a minor's pension for Pahbamashay. Joseph Taunchy was appointed guardian by the court and was worthy of his responsibility.

Pahgutchquay's widow's pension was approved on March 13, 1872. She received Widow's Pension Certificate #156,567, which paid eight dollars a month plus two dollars a month for Pahbamashay until he reached the age of sixteen. The monthly payments were retroactive to April 11, 1870. The minor's pension was not approved since Pahbamashay was already covered under his mother's widow's pension.

Lucy (Pahgutchquay or Pawgawchequay) Agahgo died in Elbridge on October 9, 1914, and was buried in said county.

Allen, Charles, Sergeant

Enlistment: Enlisted as a sergeant on June 12, 1863, at Northport, Leelanau County, by First Lieutenant William J. Driggs, First Michigan Sharpshooters, for three years.

Age: Nineteen, born about 1844 in Grand Traverse (now Old Mission), Old Mission Peninsula, on Grand Traverse Bay, Grand Traverse County.

Occupation: Farmer

Residence: Northport

Physical Description: Five feet eight and a half inches tall, black eyes, black hair, and a dark complexion. Examining physician was Dr. Arvin F. Whelan, surgeon, First Michigan Sharpshooters.

Mustered: June 22, 1863, in Detroit, Wayne County, by Lieutenant Colonel John R. Smith, US Army

Military Service: When with his regiment as they guarded the munitions at Dearborn Arsenal in Wayne County, Sergeant Charles Allen was granted a twenty-day furlough on July 12, 1863. The furlough was for the purpose of recruiting duty among the Anishinabek in northern Michigan.

He was granted a second furlough for recruiting duty in Northport of northern Michigan in early August of the same year. During this second furlough, he enlisted his friend Private Payson Wolfe, who accompanied him back to the Detroit Arsenal in Dearborn. Both men were eager to defend their country and to prove themselves worthy warriors for their people.

Families and friends gathered at Union Dock in Northport to see the two men off to their military adventures. No one could possibly have known the horror and bloodshed that was awaiting these soldiers as their wooden steamer, *Tonawanda*, departed from the dock at 1:00 p.m. One soldier would come home with post-traumatic stress disorder and broken health caused by his experience in battle and as a prisoner of war in Andersonville, Georgia. The other soldier would be wounded so badly that he died an agonizing death in a Fredericksburg, Virginia, depot hospital.

Sometime between September and October 1863, when the regiment was guarding Confederate prisoners at Camp Douglas in Chicago, Cook County, Illinois, Allen was selected for promotion. Company K Captain Edwin V. Andress chose Allen and promoted him to the rank of first sergeant (or orderly sergeant). He would be the first soldier of Company K to be promoted to that rank. Andress believed that because Allen was well educated in the Presbyterian Mission schools and at Twinsburg Institute at Twinsburg, Ohio, possessed fluency in his bilingual ability, and was of the highest character in his interpersonal skills and leadership, he would be an excellent choice for that position.

The rank of first sergeant entailed a close working relationship with Captain Andress in which Allen was responsible for the completion of all daily paperwork for his company and the execution of all orders given by Captain Andress (*Kautz*). First Sergeant Allen was paid twenty dollars a month for his service (*Ibid.*).

When he was stationed at Camp Douglas, Allen wrote several letters home to his family (in pension papers). At least three letters written in October and December 1863 and February 1864 were written in Anishinabemowin (Anishinabe [Indian] language) and translated into English for the author by Dr. Helen Roy and Dr. Margaret Noodin (*Roy* and *Noodin*). The letters describe the loneliness of distance and the yearning for family that every soldier experiences.

The translation of letter #1 is as follows:

Chicago
Camp Douglas October 27, 1863

I love you all, Loved ones,

Again today I am thinking of you all. We are still well, here where we are. I often think of you in my loneliness but I have a little paper

37

that is called a "pass" that allows me to leave the fort, yet I don't go out at night because it is not a good time to be out. Remember there are soldiers who sometimes flee in loneliness. Also, two days ago, I meant to tell them that here, while some went out and others were resting, one was begging to pass the time. I think of you often here in Chicago. I go to Chicago sometimes and there at least I am not lonely. But I am doing well and at least am not sick. Sometimes young Iroquois women visit us and we try to look out for them and pray their boss will give them more work. This gives me some comfort as a soldier. Yesterday morning I met Stephen Shawasung and Apangishimo who greeted us and visited for a while. They heard from cousin Dan Rodd that you are well and people look good back home but we miss them. (?) Sometimes after I eat and fall asleep to rest, I think of the ones who are with me always staying with me forever sitting with me in my home as I see them in my prayers. If only it could happen on this earth. One day I will be with my loved ones in heaven. This is what I write for today and I pray all of you there will quickly write back. I wonder if you will use the $15. I would love it if you send a picture of my relatives.

Yours
Greetings, greetings.
Your Son or Brother or Friend
Sgt. Charles Allen

On November 29, 1863, Allen, suffering from a simple case of measles, was admitted to the USA Post Hospital at Camp Douglas. Treatment consisted of isolation and close observation until the symptoms began to subside and his rash disappeared. Charles returned to duty on December 7.

The translation of letter #2 is as follows:

Headquarters Co. K 1st. Michigan S.S.
Camp Douglas Chicago Ill, December 21 1864

My Loved Ones,

Once again I am writing to tell you that I am still doing well, while knowing all of you are also doing well. It would make you cry how much I laugh at them I tell you. As I am writing to you all it is Sunday today. We rode out from Detroit so we dreaded returning there yesterday we arrived at last. That's the third time we've been sitting here riding around so once more as always we must go there. Last summer I was gone for so long from camp here where we live. This was when the Indian soldiers got really drunk over at Detroit. This was made possible because of that American who poured the alcohol. So then he was put on trial and the Anishinaabeg who were his companions thought about it and were witnesses while I translated for them and then we rode out from there. At last we went before staying too long and allowing the bootlegger to again be among the Anishinaabe soldiers who had done bootlegging with him. It's as if he was always causing trouble even before he was a soldier. So this is my correspondence and greeting to you.

Greetings to you then,
Charles Allen

The translation of letter #3 is as follows:

Camp Douglas Chicago Feb 28 1864

I love you
My loved ones,

I received your letter a while ago and was happy to know you all are doing well. I should also let you all know that I am doing fine.

Then our mother will come here in spring. Then we will definitely be paid on the 10th of March. So we always got the soldier's pay in the fall, now I had to sell some things I think then they paid us and later when the steam boat came around is when I sent you all the money. I think I can get things by boat if put them in letters. I always think to send you all money since you've taken on more burden to get by and I should also say that I will try to see you all in Spring and I'll arrive soon if given permission.

So that's all.

Greetings.
Charles Allen

During the Battle of the Wilderness in Virginia on May 6, 1864, Allen suffered a gunshot wound in his left side while attacking the rebel lines. The missile ball entered the lower point of the left scapula (or shoulder blade), just grazed the point of the scapula, and exited near the coracoid process (the upper part) of the blade. In its trajectory, the ball penetrated the chest wall and lodged in the left lung.

Sergeant Allen was taken by ambulance wagon from the battlefield to his division aid station where bleeding from the wound was stopped with compression. He was then transported by ambulance wagon to a depot hospital farther behind the lines at Fredericksburg, Virginia. This hospital was at or near attorney John Marye's house close to Marye's Heights.

At the hospital, Allen's wound was cleaned with water, and he was administered chloroform for surgery. The doctors used their fingers to probe the wound in order to find the missile. The ball was found, removed with a forceps and the wound was bandaged with cold water dressings. Cold water dressings consisted of lint dipped into water, applied to the wound, and held in place with a cloth bandage or adhesive plaster (*Schaadt*).

After the soldier awakened from surgery, he was given whiskey or an opium pill for pain. Since Charles was judged to be a terminal case, he was not sent on to a general hospital. Instead, he was made as comfortable as possible, given an opium pill for pain, and set off to the side to die. Other men less seriously wounded and with better chances of survival would benefit from what care could be given to them by the overworked and stressed hospital staff.

One of the Ninth Corps surgeons working at the depot hospital that bloody May was Dr. William Howell Reed. He was reported to have described the suffering and stated, "In one corner, upon a stretcher, lay a soldier. He was wounded through the lungs, and breathed only with sharp stitches of pain" (*Reed*). Could that soldier have possibly been Sgt. Charles Allen? Dr. Reed further described the horrid conditions of filth, blood, and vermin that infested the depot hospital. He also noted that sometimes the wounded would be taken outside and placed on the lawn so that they could have some relief from the sweltering heat inside of the crowded hospital (*Ibid.*).

After suffering in extreme pain for two weeks, First Sergeant Charles Allen died at the Fredericksburg Depot Hospital on or about May 20, 1864. He was the first soldier from Company K to die of wounds received in battle.

Allen's body was placed on a stretcher, covered with a blanket or a tarp, and taken to a cemetery near to the hospital. At the cemetery, the covering was removed, and Charles's remains would have been laid next to other dead soldiers in a trench and covered with dirt (*Ibid.*). His name, rank, and unit were written on a wooden board that was placed at the head of his burial site. A chaplain's prayers may have been said at his burial (*Ibid.*).

After the war, the soldiers' remains were removed from the trenches, placed into coffins, and reburied a few hundred yards from the depot hospital in the newly designated Fredericksburg National Cemetery (*Guide*). Since there is no mention of Charles Allen's name in the national cemetery records, it's assumed that his headboard was lost to the elements or used for firewood before his body was moved. With no way to identify Allen's remains, he was reburied under a stone labeled "Unknown"—just one of the 12,000 unknowns in that vast cemetery (*Ibid.*).

Discharged: No discharge given. Died of wounds while in the hospital.

Biography: Charles Allen, who did not marry, was the sixth of fifteen children born to Naishkaze (or Naskasa) and Ahchijekwa (or Onjeequa). He was a cousin to Company K comrade Thomas Miller, who was also known as Thomas Kahgee. The Naishkaze family included: Penasequa, born 1834, lived two years; Wasequanaby, born 1836, lived eleven months; Anekotoqua, born 1838, lived one and a half years; a boy child born 1840, died young; Shagonaby, born 1842, lived twelve years; Charles, born 1844, died at age nineteen of wounds received in the Civil War; Mary Ann, born 1846; Nancy, born 1848, died young; Margaret, born 1849, died young; Jacob, born 1851, who married Kenisteen Bababwa in 1870 and drowned at the age of thirty-two in 1884 in Grand Traverse; Otashahnah, born 1852, died young; Susan, born at her father's spring sugar bush camp in 1853–1856 and married Aaron Sahgahnahquato (also known as Aaron Pequongay) in 1870; George, born 1858 and married Eliza Manitowash; William, born 1860 and died in 1890; and another child named Nancy, born 1862.

On Sunday, June 4, 1843, Naishkaze (or Naskasa) and Ahchijekwa (or Onjeequa) were baptized into the Christian faith by Presbyterian missionary Rev. Peter Dougherty (*Craker*). The baptisms took place at Dougherty's Grand Traverse Mission Church, "Old Mission," on Old Mission Peninsula in Grand Traverse County. At their baptisms, the couple chose the English names of Moses and Anna and the family surname of Allen. When at Old Mission at Grand Traverse, Charles, Mary Ann, Nancy, and Margaret were also baptized into the Presbyterian Church. The Allen family was known to be very active in the mission church and school activities, and they were seen as regular attendees at the summer church camp meetings (*Dougherty*).

The Allen children who lived through early childhood attended Dougherty's mission school. It was in this school that they learned to read, write, and speak in English and were encouraged to expand their knowledge of the Anishinabe language. In addition to said studies of languages, other courses offered included reading, writing, arithmetic, geography, history, astronomy, and philosophy. The girls learned sewing, cooking, and laundry work. The boys were taught mechanics and how to farm. Charles was considered an excellent student in all of his classes.

School classes were held year-round, but many students were needed by their parents to help during the seasonal cycle of work and could not attend school on a regular basis. The best attendance was during the very cold months of winter when the students' fathers hunted fur-bearing animals for their pelts.

After the revised State Constitution became law in 1850, Anishinabek who were not members of any organized tribe could become citizens of the state and be able to vote. Consequently, they could then buy government lands and settle upon them (*Clifton*).

Due to the pressure of white settlers in the Grand Traverse area, the Anishinabek selected land for themselves on the Leelanau Peninsula. Since the government had set aside the counties of Grand Traverse, Charlevoix, and Emmett for settlement, the Anishinabek began to leave Old Mission and resettle on the west side of the bay on the peninsula.

Rev. Dougherty decided to follow the migration of his Anishinabek church members and relocated his mission near the little settlement of Omena in Leelanau County in 1852 (*Tanner*). Omena is derived from the Anishinabe word *Omanah,* which means "It is so?" as a response to any statement made by the Anishinabek (*Romig*). Rev. Dougherty named his church the Grove Hill New Mission Church.

In addition to the church, Dougherty again established a school where the Allen children, and others, continued their education. It was at New Mission where Margaret, Jacob, William, and Nancy were baptized, and where Charles was received as a member in the church on Sunday, May 22, 1859. Susan Allen joined the New Mission Church on January 3, 1869.

Being an excellent student, Charles was urged to continue his higher education at Twinsburg Institute of higher learning in Twinsburg, Summit County, Ohio. This private select school was instituted by Congregational minister Rev. Samuel Bissell (1797–1895). Allen attended the school with his friend and future Company K comrade, Joseph Wakazoo, for the session commencing April 9, 1860, to March 9, 1861 (Catalogue). Allen and Wakazoo probably stayed in rooms in the school dormitory or boarded out with families in town. The school curriculum was difficult, and Rev. Bissell emphasized a classical education. Classes included courses in mathematics, languages, writing, penmanship, and music and art. The school year was divided into three sessions over a forty-two-week period.

The Allen family was of modest means and depended for support upon the money that Charles earned before his enlistment and money that he sent home before his death in the service. Moses, who had a crippled arm and no team of horses with which to work his farm (assessed at $150), tried to provide for his family by selling fish. He sold off some of the eighty acres he received in a government patent, which netted some income, but the money was hardly enough to pay taxes. Anna earned some money from selling her baskets. The older boys contributed what they could to the family by also fishing and selling their catch. In total, the family's income was less than fifteen dollars a month.

Annie Allen's Application #280,616 for a mother's pension was filed for her on March 11, 1881. A Mother's Pension Certificate #251,466 was granted to her on January 31, 1889. Her payments were eight dollars a month retroactive to March 11, 1881, and were increased to twelve dollars a month retroactive to March 19, 1886. She received this amount until her death at age eighty-five on April 23, 1899, at her home in Omena. Old age was listed on her death certificate as the reason for her demise.

Amderling, Peter, Private

Enlistment: Enlisted as a private on September 26, 1864, at Ontonagan, Township of Rockland, Ontonagon County, by A.E.B. Mann, First Michigan Sharpshooters, for three years.

Age: Twenty-one, born about 1843 in La Point, Madeline Island, Ashland County, Wisconsin.

Occupation: Laborer

Residence: Rockland, Ontonagon County, in Michigan's Upper Peninsula

Physical Description: Five feet eleven, dark eyes, dark hair, and a dark complexion. Examining physician was Dr. George M. Landon, surgeon, Company D, Fourth Michigan Cavalry.

Mustered: October 20, 1864, in Detroit, Wayne County, by Captain and Provost Marshal Mark Flanigan, Twenty-Fourth Michigan Infantry. Peter joined his company on November 4, 1864, at the brigade headquarters at Peebles Farm in Virginia.

Military Service: When Peter was mustered in Detroit, the officer in charge mistakenly spelled his surname as Anderson, and Amderling. The true spelling of his family surname was Anotagan.

Peter's cousin, John Bensus or Benesis, also known as John Beneshia Bird or John Bird, was mustered into Company K at the same time as Peter, and they traveled together to join their unit. The money that Peter sent home to his parents was their main support.

In February 1865, Peter became ill with a cold during the battles before Petersburg, Virginia, when the troops were in their trenches and suffering from inclement weather. His cold became worse with the inhalation of powder from the smoke of exploding shells. To compound his troubles, he developed diarrhea from the poor quality of available food.

As his health began to deteriorate, Peter developed a constant cough with bloody sputum. He was confined to his tent and unable to perform any military duties. Company K comrades Henry Waasegiizhig (also known as Henry Condecon) and Leon Otashquabono tried to care for Peter in his discomfort. Henry and Peter had grown up together. Henry's mother was a relative of Peter's mother, and Henry and Leon were Peter's closest friends and tent mates in the company.

In addition to his friends' help, Peter received some treatment from the regimental surgeon while confined to his tent. A purgative such as calomel or "blue mass," which contained mercurous chloride, may have been given to him to clear his intestinal tract (*Bollet*). Because his symptoms became worse, Peter was sent by ambulance wagon to the military railroad, put on a mattress in a boxcar, the floor of which was cushioned with straw or hay, and sent to the depot hospital at City Point, Virginia, around March 1865 (*Pfanz*).

Private Anotagan remained at this hospital until the middle of May when the hospital and its patients were relocated to Alexandria, Virginia, in order to follow the Ninth Corps. Peter was taken by ambulance wagon to the wharf at City Point, transferred to a hospital steamer, and taken to Alexandria. He remained at the hospital until July 8 when he was sent to Washington, DC.

On July 9, Peter was admitted to Lincoln General Hospital in Washington with the diagnosis of hemoptysis (the spitting of blood from the larynx, trachea, bronchi, or lungs). His condition was also thought to be from subacute gastritis (or inflammation of the stomach).

At Lincoln General Hospital, Anotagan was given a liquid diet of broth until his stomach could recover and he was able to handle a healthy diet of fresh fruits and vegetables. He was also given a medication for diarrhea called "laudanum," which is a mixture of a tincture of opium in alcohol (*Blakiston*). Peter was ordered to strict bed rest. He returned to duty on July 21 still plagued with a persistent cough.

Discharged: Private Peter Anotagan was mustered out and honorably discharged at Delaney House in Tenallytown, DC, on July 28, 1865. He returned to Detroit on the steamer *Morning Star*. On August 7, 1865, Anotagan was paid money owed to him for his service at Jackson, Jackson County.

Biography: Peter was one of five children born to John Baptiste and Oshabens (Ozhobinse or QuisNoQua) Anotagon. The couple was married by Catholic Bishop Frederic Baraga in 1842 at LaPoint, Wisconsin. Peter's siblings were Mary, Angelic, William, and John. Mary and Peter were born at LaPoint. The other children were born after their parents moved to Ontonagon County, Michigan. Mary married Antoine Bebamise, and Angelic married Edward Matchigabo.

Before he entered the service, Peter hunted to supply meat for his family and worked at other jobs to add to the family's support. His father owned no property for farming and was barely able to hunt and trap.

After his discharge, Peter worked on the boats on the Great Lakes with his cousin and Company K comrade, John Benisus (Beneshia or Bird), to earn extra money to support his family. While working on the boats, Peter's health continued to deteriorate to the point that he could no longer perform his duties. When Peter was too ill to work, his brother John continued to hunt and work odd jobs to maintain family subsistence.

In 1870, the Anotagon family moved to Hancock, Houghton County. According to John, Peter died sometime during the month of February 1872 at Portage Lake in Keweenaw County of Michigan's Upper Peninsula. But Peter's father, John B. Anotagan, stated that Peter died in Hancock. John Benisus (or Bird), on the other hand, recollected that Peter died in Houghton. In any case, the cause of death was consumption (or tuberculosis) of the lungs. He probably had this disease from the onset of his chronic cough in February 1865. Peter was buried in an Anishinabek cemetery in Houghton County. His brother William died the same spring.

Since Peter never married, he left his parents, sisters Angelic and Mary and their spouses, and brother John as his sole survivors.

About 1884, John Baptiste and Ozhobinse Anotagan, son John, and Angelic and Edward Matchigabo moved to Odanah, Ashland County, Wisconsin. Mary Bebamise died before the family moved back to Wisconsin.

Peter had been bilingual, but his parents and siblings were not. This fact necessitated an interpreter for depositions given by family members for the pension application made first by Ozhobinse. Application #493,206 for a dependent mother's pension, for her son's service, was filed for Ozhobinse on December 30, 1890.

Ozhobinse Anotagan died February 4, 1892, in Odanah. She was preceded in death by her son John, who died on February 5, 1891. Her pension application was rejected on the grounds that she, the claimant, had died before the application could be processed. Therefore, no one was entitled to the soldier's accrued pension under her application.

A dependent father's pension Application #591,887 was filed for John B. Anotagan on March 16, 1894. At the time the application was filed, John was living with his daughter Angelic and her husband. He was granted Dependent Father's Pension Certificate #402,007 on September 28, 1894. The pension was retroactive to March 16, 1894, and paid twelve dollars a month. Due to the notification of John Baptiste Anotagan's death at Odanah, his pension was dropped on November 3, 1900.

Andrew, John, Private

Enlistment: Enlisted as a private on May 18, 1863, at Isabella City (now Mt. Pleasant), Isabella County, by First Lieutenant William J. Driggs, First Michigan Sharpshooters, for three years.

    Age: Eighteen, born about 1844 or 1845 in Lapeer County.

    Occupation: Farmer

    Residence: Isabella City

    Physical Description: Five feet five, black eyes, black hair, and a dark complexion. Examining physician was Dr. George L. Cornell, assistant surgeon, First Michigan Sharpshooters.

    Mustered: May 26, 1863, in Detroit, Wayne County, by Lieutenant Colonel John R. Smith, US Army

    Military Service: While eating his dinner in the entrenchments before Petersburg, Virginia, on June 25, 1864, Private John Andrew suffered a gunshot wound in his right thigh from a Rebel sharpshooter. The missile entered the anterior aspect of the thigh near the groin and exited in the fold of the thigh and buttock.

John was carried by stretcher to his division aid station behind the entrenchments where his wound was washed and hastily bandaged. From the aid station, John was taken by ambulance wagon to his division hospital farther behind the front lines. In this hospital, the wound was again cleaned with water and treated with a simple water dressing. Simple water dressings consisted of folded lint rinsed in cold water, put on the wounds, and held in place by cloth wraps or adhesive plaster (*Schaadt*). An opium pill was offered to the patient for pain.

On June 30, John was taken by ambulance wagon to the military railroad, put on a mattress in a boxcar, the floor of which was cushioned with straw or hay, and taken to the depot hospital at City Point, Virginia. Similar medical treatment was continued.

A few days later on July 3, 1864, the soldier was taken to the wharf at City Point, transferred to a hospital steamer and sent to L'Ouverture USA General Hospital at Alexandria, Virginia. At L'Ouverture, Andrew's wound was treated much the same—simple water dressings. A tincture of iodine was also used to periodically cleanse the wound, and opium was offered for pain (*Evans*). During his time in the hospital in Alexandria, John enjoyed a hearty diet of all that he could eat of meats, fresh fruits and vegetables, and various breads and grains.

Private Andrew was given a furlough from the hospital on August 12 for thirty days.

On September 19, he was back in L'Ouverture and remained through October and November. On December 6, Andrew was transferred from L'Ouverture to USA General Hospital of Grace Church Branch in Alexandria, Virginia. Similar treatment was continued.

On February 14, 1865, Private Andrew returned to duty but still suffered from the effects of his wound, which had a constant drainage. Much improved by May 1865, he was assigned from his unit to be a policeman in the provost guard (a detail of military police under the command of an officer, the provost marshal) at the Brigade Headquarters in Washington, DC. Also, in June 1865, he was detailed for an unspecified task in the Quartermaster Department in same city.

Discharged: Private John Andrew was mustered out and honorably discharged at Detroit, Wayne County, on August 14, 1865. He was paid money due to him at his discharge and returned home.

Biography: John Andrew was the son of Andrew and Keywaytinse (or Mary)

Nayshekaywawsung. His siblings were: Andrew, born in 1842; Melissa, born in 1844; and Esther, born in 1846. John and his siblings were second cousins to Company K soldier William Collins.

On July 5, 1868, John, age twenty-three, married Eliza (or Mawjeseyeanoqua) Neyome, age eighteen, in Isabella, Isabella County. Eliza was the daughter of Mark and Ogabah Neyome. Mark was an Anishinabe doctor who treated patients with herbs, roots, and poultices in the manner according to the traditional ways of the Anishinabek. Rev. Robert Palmer Sheldon, Methodist minister and teacher of the Sheldon School for Anishinabek children north of Mt. Pleasant, officiated at the marriage of the couple (*Reuter*). Witnesses to the marriage were Rev. John P. Williams and Susan Sheldon. Both John and Eliza resided in Isabella at the time of their marriage. They were members of the Anishinabe Methodist Episcopal Church.

Five children were born to John and Eliza (Neyome) Andrew after they moved to Oregon Township in Lapeer County. The children were: Allen, born in 1872, died in 1873; Daniel, born May 24 (or November 15), 1875; Emma, born May 5 (or June 16), 1879; Mary, born May 1 (or April 7), 1881; and an unknown child, born in October 1883 and died several months later.

During the years after his service, John's health steadily declined. He suffered from diarrhea, and his wound oozed constantly (due to infection) and gave him continual discomfort. His father-in-law, Mark Neyome, and his cousin and Company K comrade, William Collins, treated John's illnesses in the traditional Anishinabek manner with herbs and poultices.

When he was able, he worked for his neighbor and friend, Joseph D. Slater, and for others who had jobs for him. He also made baskets to sell.

On September 26, 1882, John's Application #460,944 for an invalid pension was filed for him. He was granted Invalid Pension Certificate #252,595 in 1883, which paid eight dollars a month.

A few months before his death, John moved in with his friend Barney Whittemore (also known as Whitman or Pamawedunk) and his wife, Mary, in Taymouth Township of Saginaw County. This move was needed so that Eliza could have assistance from Barney's family to help care for John.

John Andrew died on January 19, 1884. His death was caused from blood poisoning (or septicemia) from his gunshot (missile) wound and the systemic complications that resulted from the septicemia (*Rutkow*). He was buried in the Wheaton (or Whedon) Chippewa Indian Cemetery, also known as Taymouth

Cemetery, in Taymouth Township. John Andrew's military stone incorrectly reads "John Anderson" instead of John Andrew.

After John's death, a dependent widow's Application #324,169 was filed for Eliza on March 3, 1885. Sadly, her death on June 15, 1886, in Oregon Township left her three children as orphans and canceled her application for a widow's pension.

Because he was respected and trusted by the Andrew family, Joseph D. Slater was appointed as legal guardian for the Andrew children shortly after Eliza died. Application #359,322 for a pension for dependent children was filed for Slater on August 16, 1887.

On October 21, 1890, Daniel, Emma, and Mary Andrew were granted a Pension for Minor Children Certificate #276,735 under the supervision of their guardian. The pension paid eight dollars a month retroactive from January 20, 1884. Later, the payments were increased to twelve dollars a month retroactive to 1886. An extra two dollars a month was added for each child until April 12, 1897, when the youngest child, Mary, attained the age of sixteen.

Aptargeshick, Oliver, Private

Enlistment: Enlisted as a private on June 17, 1863, at the Dearborn Arsenal, Wayne County, by Sergeant Joseph O. Bellair, First Michigan Sharpshooters, for three years.

Age: Nineteen, born about 1844 on Walpole Island, Lambton County, Ontario, Canada.

Occupation: Farmer and hunter

Residence: Walpole Island First Nation Indian Reserve on Walpole Island, Ontario, Canada

Physical Description: Five feet and a half inch tall, dark eyes, dark hair, and a red complexion. Examining physician was Dr. George L. Cornell, assistant surgeon, First Michigan Sharpshooters.

Mustered: June 17 or 19, 1863, in Detroit, Wayne County, by Lieutenant Colonel John R. Smith, US Army

Military Service: Private Oliver Aptargeshick was admitted to his regimental hospital, the US General Hospital at the United States Naval Academy in Annapolis, Maryland, on April 8, 1864. He was suffering from diarrhea and stayed in the hospital for about a week. Treatment for his diarrhea consisted of a diet of barley water, rice water, broth from meat extracts, soups, coffee, and tea. Citrus juices and fresh vegetables were added to his diet when his system could tolerate the change. Dover's powder, composed of a mixture of ipecac and opium, was administrated to induce perspiration (*Evans*). Also, castor oil as an emetic was ordered to induce vomiting, astringent enemas of silver nitrate were given, and oral turpentine and calomel (mercurous chloride) were added to his medications *(Bollet)*. A tincture of opium, or opium in alcohol called "laudanum," was also given to Oliver. He returned to his regiment about the middle of April.

Some military records state that Oliver was reported missing in action in a battle before Petersburg, Virginia, on June 17, 1864, and that he died in the hospital of wounds received in action. The nature of the wounds was not specified. A few other military records reported that Oliver died of disease while in the hospital.

In reality, Oliver was admitted to Pavilion #3 of Lincoln USA General Hospital in Washington, DC, on June 21. The doctors diagnosed his ailments as joint inflammation or rheumatism of the large joints brought on by some form of dysentery/diarrhea (*Ibid.*). His treatment for the rheumatism would have included opiates for severe joint pain and quinine or potassium iodide for their mild anti-inflammatory effect (*Ibid.*). He was treated with cool baths and compresses to reduce inflammation (*Ibid.*). The diarrhea was treated as mentioned previously.

To set the record straight, Oliver died at Lincoln USA General Hospital on July 9, 1864, not of wounds but of pulmonary congestion, which is the abnormal collection of blood in the lungs *(Blakiston)*. This report is in his pension papers and is recorded in his *Hospital Record Subject to the Order of the Surgeon General United States Army* and in his *Record of Death and Interment*. An inventory of his clothing included one uniform coat, one pair of trousers, one haversack, one canteen, one pair of shoes, and one forage cap.

On July 10, Private Oliver Aptargeshick's body was placed in a coffin and taken to Arlington National Cemetery in Arlington, Virginia. Formal funeral services were accorded the deceased, which included a chaplain, a military escort from the hospital to the cemetery, and the firing of arms. An individual temporary headboard with name and military unit of the deceased was placed at the head of the soldier's grave site *(Encyclopedia)*. Today, Private Aptargeshick lies at rest under military stone #5732 in section 13 of said cemetery. The stone reads "Oliver Aptargeshick."

Discharged: No discharge given. Died of pulmonary congestion while in the hospital.

Biography: Other spellings of Pvt. Oliver Aptargeshick's name were Ahreotergeshig and Avpetargezhik, to name a few of the many different spellings.

He left a family on Walpole Island to mourn his death. Today, there are descendants with the family name of Aptakezhick who live on the island and relate that they believe that the meaning of their name is "half day" or "day." Presently, some of the family members are known by the name of Day.

A few years ago, a granite stone was erected by the Walpole Island Veterans' Society to honor the memory of one of their fellow First Nation members, Oliver Aptargeshick. The stone was added to previous memorials honoring Walpole Island warriors who died in action in past wars. The name on the stone reads "Oliver Ar-Pe-Targe-Zhik," which, roughly translated as it is spelled, could mean "Talking Cedar." There is no pension file for Oliver Aptargeshick.

Arwonogezice, James, Private

Enlistment: Enlisted as a private on September 1, 1863, at Little Traverse (renamed Harbor Springs in 1881), Emmet County, by Second Lieutenant Garrett A. Graveraet, First Michigan Sharpshooters, for three years.

Age: Twenty-five, born April 10, 1838, at Old Mission, Old Mission peninsula on Grand Traverse Bay, Michilimackinac County. Today, Old Mission is in Grand Traverse County.

Occupation: Farmer

Residence: Pentwater, Oceana County

Physical Description: Five feet ten, black eyes, black hair, and a dark complexion. Examining physician was Dr. George L. Cornell, assistant surgeon, First Michigan Sharpshooters.

Mustered: On October 21, 1863, at Camp Douglas, Chicago, Cook County, Illinois, by an officer named Capt. Lowe. During their deployment in Chicago, the Michigan Sharpshooters guarded Confederate prisoners at the Camp Douglas confine.

Military Service: On April 16, 1864, while in his camp near Annapolis, Maryland, James caught a severe cold and was sent to his regimental hospital, the US General Hospital at the United States Naval Academy, in Annapolis. It had rained for two weeks after the regiment arrived in Maryland, and many of the men were suffering from the effects of the inclement weather. One of the regimental surgeons ordered warm fluids for James's catarrh (the inflammation of the mucous membranes of the nose and throat) and bed rest.

In the weeks previous to the battle at Petersburg, Virginia, on June 17, 1864, James was frequently exposed to severe weather conditions. Not having sufficient protection from the elements, he suffered a second bout with a bad cold. This time, on June 17, the cold settled in his lungs. He was not sent to his division hospital but was treated in his tent by Dr. Thomas Eagleson, assistant surgeon for the Michigan Sharpshooters. His treatment was the same as previously mentioned. James was sick for about two months and was excused from military activities for that time. He returned to duty in August.

In May 1865, James was detailed as a company cook.

In June, he was assigned to an undisclosed duty in the Quartermaster Department in Washington, DC.

Discharged: Private James Arwanogezhik was mustered out and honorably discharged on August 11, 1865, at Detroit, Wayne County. He was paid money owed to him at his discharge and returned home.

Biography: When James signed his own name on legal papers, he wrote it as "James Arwonogezice." If he signed his last name as Wassagejig, which was another spelling that he used, the translation meant "dawn daylight" or, to be more specific, "lightsky" derived from the words *wasseia* and *gijig* (*Baraga*). James was the son of Aronogezhic and Waysay (or Mary) Obasha.

The first marriage for James was to Sophia Grooseneck in about 1859–1860. The couple had twelve children, all of whom died in childhood or early adolescence.

After his discharge, James continued to complain of a constant cough and trouble with his lungs, which kept him from maintaining a steady job. He sought help from a local Anishinabequa medicine woman known as Mrs. Nawgesic. She treated him with herbs in the traditional Anishinabek manner. When he was able, James did work in the lumber camps to help support his family.

An invalid pension Application #669,457 was filed for James on April 17, 1889. In the application, he cited disease of the lungs (contracted while in the service), which led to a general decline in his health after his discharge from the army.

During the years after his service, James was an active member of the GAR Woolsey Post #399 at Northport, Leelanau County. On September 30, 1889, he was listed on the membership roll as quartermaster sergeant of his post. He was also a member of GAR Baxter Post #119 of Charlevoix, Charlevoix County.

After the war, James was very active as a local Anishinabe lay preacher in one of the Methodist churches in Charlevoix County. He also served for a short time as pastor for the Honor Indian Mission near Crystal Lake in Benzie County (*Reuter*). In May 1889, James was one of the trustees of the Anishinabe Methodist Episcopal Church of Susan Lake (or Greensky Hill Indian Mission) in Hayes Township of Charlevoix County. He was said to have donated four or five acres of land that was used for this church's mission (*Ibid.*).

James received his Invalid Pension Certificate #527,059 on January 28, 1891. It was not issued for any disability incurred while in the service but for postwar disease of heart, lung, liver, and rheumatism. It's not clear why James would have received an invalid pension when William Caybaicoung (or Cabecoung) claimed the same postwar infirmities but did not receive a pension. James's monthly pension payments were twelve dollars retroactive to July 12, 1890. His monthly pension payments were increased to fifteen dollars in 1908, and by 1913 he received twenty-seven dollars a month in support.

After Sophia died on March 7, 1896, in Charlevoix, James married for the second time to Louisa Naongaby (or Naubakaka) on December 12, 1896, in the same city. Rev. J. W. Wallenbeck, a Methodist minister, officiated at the ceremony. James and Louisa were the parents of one daughter, Anna, born July 22, 1897. Anna died of acute gastritis (acute or chronic inflammation of the stomach) on December 4, 1908.

James was a resident at the Soldiers' North Home in Grand Rapids, Kent County, from December 7, 1901, to May 1, 1907. He left the home at his request. In January 1908, James moved to Duane, Mahnomen County, Minnesota, where he notified the pension office of his new location. He remained in Minnesota for a short time and then moved back to Michigan before June 13, 1911, to settle in Kewadin, Antrim County.

Sometime before or after he moved to Minnesota, James divorced Louisa. On November 6, 1912, he married for the third time to Margaret Tapakea, widow of John Tapakea. A Rev. Johnson officiated at the marriage in Kewadin.

On May 17, 1917, at age eighty-five, James Arwonogezice died of senile pneumonia, caused by a weak heart. His death occurred at his home at Bay Shore, Hayes Township, Charlevoix County.

James's funeral was conducted from the Methodist church of Charlevoix, and he was buried in the Brookside Cemetery in said city. His Charlevoix GAR post provided military honors at his burial. The newspaper obituary stated that James was buried in the Old Indian Cemetery at Bay Shore.

Margaret Arwonogezice submitted Application #IC527,059 for a widow's pension on September 19, 1928. The application was refused. The reasons cited were: (1)

That Margaret would have had to have been married prior to June 27, 1905, in order to apply for a pension under the act of May 1, 1920. Since she married James in 1912, she was not entitled to a pension under that act. (2) As the soldier was not pensioned for any disability incurred in his service, under the general law, the widow would not be entitled to a pension under that law.

But since there was an accrued pension amounting to twelve dollars due to her husband from the date to which he was last paid, Margaret was eligible to claim the accrued monies. She could receive these monies provided that she could prove that she was James's legal widow. It's not known if Margaret supplied the required proof.

Ashkanok, Joseph, Private

Enlistment: Enlisted as a private on July 14, 1863, at Little Traverse (renamed Harbor Springs in 1881), Emmet County, by Second Lieutenant Garrett A. Graveraet, First Michigan Sharpshooters, for three years.

Age: Eighteen, born January 13, 1845 or 1847, in Canada.

Occupation: Farmer

Residence: LaCroix (renamed Cross Village in 1875), Emmett County

Physical Description: Five feet ten, black eyes, black hair, and a dark complexion. Examining physician was Dr. Arvin F. Whelan, surgeon, First Michigan Sharpshooters.

Mustered: July 20, 1863, in Detroit, Wayne County, by Lieutenant Colonel John R. Smith, US Army

Military Service: While in action at the Battle of Spotsylvania on May 12, 1864, Joseph suffered a gunshot wound to the upper portion of his left arm (or humerus). The injury resulted in damage to the deltoid and triceps muscles and the radial nerve. Fortunately, the missile did not strike the bone. He also suffered from hearing loss due to concussions caused by the bursts of cannon shells.

The soldier walked or was taken by ambulance wagon to his division aid station. At the aid station, hand compression or a tourniquet was applied to his arm to stop the bleeding, and his wound was cleaned with water and bandaged with simple cold water dressings. Cold water dressings consist of lint dipped into cold water, applied to the wound, and held in place with a cloth bandage or adhesive wrap (*Schaadt*). He was given whiskey for shock and an opium pill for pain.

Joseph was then taken by ambulance wagon to his division hospital farther behind the lines where iodine was applied to the entrance and exit wounds to impede infection, and simple dressings were continued as treatment.

From the division hospital, Joseph was then taken by ambulance wagon to a depot hospital in Fredericksburg, Virginia, at or near attorney John Marye's house near Marye's Heights. At this hospital, simple cold water dressings were continued for treatment of his wound. Joseph was again offered whiskey and an opium pill for pain.

On May 15, Joseph was sent by ambulance wagon from the depot hospital to a wharf at Belle Plain Landing, Virginia, nine miles northeast of Fredericksburg, on Potomac Creek. Upon arrival at the wharf, he was transferred to a hospital steamer and taken to Mount Pleasant USA General Hospital in Washington, DC. He was admitted under the name of "Eskinaw" to Mount Pleasant Hospital on May 16. The same treatment of simple dressings was continued, and his wound was periodically cleansed with a tincture of iodine or iodine in alcohol (*Evans*). A hearty diet of fresh fruits, vegetables, and an assortment of breads and grains was ordered for him.

Joseph was given a three-week furlough from the hospital on May 31, 1864. He was readmitted to Mt. Pleasant Hospital on June 21 and returned to duty with his regiment on July 9, 1864.

In May 1865, Ashkanok was detailed from his unit to be a policeman for the provost guard at the Brigade Headquarters in Washington, DC. The provost guard is a detail of military police under the command of an officer—the provost marshal. While in DC, he was also assigned to a detail at the Quartermaster Department.

Discharged: Private Joseph Ashkanok was mustered out and honorably discharged at Detroit on August 11, 1865. He was paid money due to him at his discharge and returned home to LaCroix.

Biography: On November 23, 1869, Joseph (also called Wawshawwawnawshe) married Elizabeth Gissiswabe in Cross Village. She was born in that village on March 6, 1852, the daughter of Mary Ann and Frank Gissiswabe (or Kenwaba). Rev. John Bernard Weikamp, Catholic priest of Holy Cross Church of said village, officiated at the marriage *(Langheim)*. The ceremony was witnessed by Michael Kinis and Augustin Kimiwanaam/August Shomm.

According to Elizabeth, when Joseph entered the service, he used the name Ashkanok although he was always known to his family and friends as Joseph Jawenashi.

Elizabeth and Joseph Jawenashi-Ashkanok were the parents of seven children: John, born August 14, 1870, died May 3, 1871; William, born April 10, 1872; Bruno, born November 7, 1874; Rosa, born May 21, 1877, died November 27,

1885; Theresa, born December 21, 1879; Gregory (or George 1.), born September 9, 1883, died August 4, 1885; and Gregory (or George 2.), born March 24, 1886, died September 4, 1888. All the children were baptized in the rite of the Holy Cross Catholic Church during the same year in which each child was born (*Holy Cross*).

Throughout his civilian life, Joseph would suffer greatly from the wound that he received in battle. The damage to the arm would eventually result in atrophy and weakness of the muscles of the forearm and hand—a very painful condition. The injury would also severely restrict his ability to earn a living for his family.

Even though he suffered physically, Joseph would try to attend his GAR meetings and functions when he was able. He was a member of the GAR George Washington Post #106 of Cross Village, and served for a term as the post's sergeant major.

On January 6, 1877, Joseph's Application #229,500 for an invalid pension was filed for him.

Invalid Pension Certificate #147,960 was granted to Joseph on January 3, 1878. He received his pension due to his inability to perform manual labor, which was directly related to the wound that he received in the line of duty. Payments were retroactive to December 1877. At first his monthly checks totaled only two dollars. Over the years, he received several increases in payments until his monthly disability check totaled six dollars. From August 27, 1912, to May 31, 1914, Joseph received monthly checks of seventeen dollars.

Joseph Jawanashi-Ashkanok died of paralysis of the heart. In this occurrence, the heart is in a condition of "asystole," which is faulty or imperfect contraction of the cardiac ventricles, especially of the right ventricle, as seen in the last stages of mitral disease when the heart stops beating or contracting (*Blakiston*). Joseph's death, at age sixty-nine, occurred in Cross Village on May 31, 1914. He was buried in Holy Cross Cemetery on June 2. A military stone with the name "Joseph Ach Aw Nach" marks his burial site.

On June 16, 1914, Application #1,029,588 for a widow's pension was filed for Elizabeth Jawanashi-Ashkanok.

She received her Widow's Pension Certificate #778,421 in 1915. The pension paid eight dollars a month until her death at age sixty-five. Elizabeth succumbed to severe asthma on March 17, 1917, in Cross Village. She was buried near her husband in said cemetery.

Ashkebug, George, Private

Enlistment: Enlisted as a private on July 9, 1863, at Northport, Leelanau County, by Second Lieutenant Garrett A. Graveraet, First Michigan Sharpshooters, for three years.

Age: Twenty-eight, born about 1835 in Northport.

Occupation: Teamster (or wagoner)

Residence: Northport

Physical Description: Five feet seven and a half inches tall, black eyes, black hair, and a dark complexion. Examining physician was Dr. Arvin F. Whelan, surgeon, First Michigan Sharpshooters.

Mustered: July 20, 1863, in Detroit, Wayne County, by Lieutenant Colonel John R. Smith, US Army

Military Service: Private George Ashkebug's name may be derived from the Anishinabe word *Ashkibagad,* which translates to "leaves of trees and bushes are budding" (*Baraga*).

George received a contused (or bruise) wound to the forehead and left eye from a piece of shrapnel caused by the burst of a cannon shell at the Battle of Spotsylvania, Virginia, on May 12, 1864. He walked or was taken by ambulance wagon to the division aid station where his wounds were cleaned with water and hastily bandaged. He was given whiskey for shock and an opium pill for pain.

From the aid station, George was taken by ambulance wagon to his division hospital farther behind the lines. At this hospital, his eyes were irrigated with saline and borax solutions, and cold compresses were put on his forehead and left eye to relieve the swelling. On May 14, George was taken by ambulance wagon through Fredericksburg to a wharf at Belle Plain. At the wharf, he was transferred to a hospital steamer and sent to L'Ouverture USA General Hospital in Alexandria, Virginia, where he was admitted on May 16.

The doctors at the L'Ouverture Hospital irrigated his eyes with saline and borax solutions. Simple water dressings that consisted of folded lint rinsed in cold water, to suppress inflammation and control bleeding, were applied to his forehead and left eye. The dressings were held in place by cloth wraps or adhesive plaster (*Schaadt*). He was offered whiskey and an opium pill for pain. George returned to duty the latter part of May.

On August 4, Ashkebug was sent from his regiment to the Sickel Barracks USA General Hospital in Alexandria and admitted on August 5. The soldier was suffering from debility or weakness. Alcohol and tonics were given as treatment for his debility. A diet of meats, fresh fruits and vegetables, and whole grains was ordered for him.

During his stay at the hospital, George complained of lung troubles. He told the doctors that he thought that he had developed these troubles due to exposure to inclement weather while in the trenches and on picket duty before Petersburg.

On December 6, Ashkebug was transferred from Sickel Barracks to L'Ouverture Hospital—the Grace Church Branch of L'Ouverture—in Alexandria. Due to his weakened condition, he remained in the hospital until February 14, 1865, when he returned to duty.

Discharged: Private George Ashkebug was mustered out and honorably discharged at Delaney House, Tenallytown, DC, on July 28, 1865, and returned to Detroit on the steamer *Morning Star*. He received money owed to him for his service on August 7 at Jackson, Jackson County.

Biography: George Ashkebug was also known as Andrew George Ashkebug, George Estabrook, and by his Anishinabe name of Acheahuahakwa. He had at least two sisters, named Margaret and Nancy.

Before and right after the Civil War, George worked odd jobs in the Charlevoix area for his friend Mr. John S. Dixon, a local justice of the peace. He also worked as a seaman on the Great Lakes.

On March 13, 1870, George, age thirty-seven, married Mary Micksawba (or Michisaba), age thirty-six. Mary's father was Louis Michisaba of Charlevoix, Charlevoix County. The marriage was officiated by Mr. Dixson in Dixson's home. Joseph R. Dixson, Dixson's son, and Louis Michisaba witnessed the ceremony. Mary's siblings were: Theresa, born 1834; Joseph, born 1837; Margaret, born 1842; William, born 1844; Alexander, born 1846; and Issac, born 1848.

George and Mary were the parents of two children: John, born about 1873; and Jonah (also called Junius or Junie), born July 18, 1878. Junius (Junie) was named after Joseph Dixon's younger brother, Junius.

After his service and during the rest of his life, George complained of a rupture (or hernia) that oozed a constant discharge. His hernia was probably caused by strenuous activity or from an injury during his service. Sometimes he experienced a great deal of pain and was not able to keep a job for any length of time. His father-in-law bought a truss for George to wear to give him more support.

George provided for his family by fishing, cutting wood, or hauling supplies when he was physically able. His coughing was constant, and the pain in his chest became worse. As the months passed, he became weaker and appeared more emaciated. At times he would vomit blood, a sign of consumption (or tuberculosis).

Sometime during 1880, George separated (but did not divorce) from his wife and family in Charlevoix. He moved to Northport where he lived with his sister, Margaret (or Negonnebequay), and her husband, John Agatchie. Mary and the boys went to live with Mary's father in Charlevoix Township. She supported herself and her family by doing washing and housecleaning for the people of Charlevoix.

Application #508,907 for an invalid pension was filed for Ashkebug on March 22, 1884. He cited injuries to his groin and to his left eye, which resulted in impaired vision during his service.

When living with his sister and family, George may have attended some of the meetings of the GAR Woolsey Post #399 in Northport.

In May 1886, when Ashkebug was cutting some wood for his sister, he reinjured his hernia and was confined to bed. His last few days of life were spent in agony as he sat bent over in a forward position in a chair. His pain was constant until death came as a relief on July 23. Cause of death was determined to be a strangulated hernia. A strangulated hernia occurs when the circulation of the blood and the fecal material are blocked. If unrelieved, this condition leads to ileus (an intestinal obstruction) and necrosis (tissue death) of the intestine (*Blakiston*). The pain experienced by this condition is excruciating.

As a gesture of love and devotion to their brother, Margaret and John Agatchie mortgaged their team of horses to a Northport general store merchant, Mr. Thomas Copp, for a suit of clothes in which to bury Ashkebug. The Rev. John Jacob, Anishinabe Methodist minister in Northport, officiated at Ashkebug's funeral. George was buried in the Anishinabe Onumenese Cemetery, which is directly across the Leelanau Peninsula from Northport. A military stone marks his grave site.

In addition to his estranged wife and children, Ashkebug also left a sister, Nancy, and his wife's sister, Teresa Micksawba, as surviving relatives.

Application #392,567 for a widow's pension was filed for Mary on April 8, 1889. Finally, on February 12, 1895, an Invalid Pension Certificate #883,425 was granted to Ashkebug for the injury to his left eye. The pension paid four dollars a month retroactive to March 22, 1884. Mary, as legal widow, received these payments that were due to her husband (even though he had died) but only up to the time of his death on July 23, 1886.

Mary received a Widow's Pension Certificate #395,613 on May 5, 1899. It was granted under the General Act of June 1890. This act was more liberal and granted payments to widows of men who served for ninety days regardless of the causes of the deaths of their husbands. The pension payments were retroactive to August 12, 1890, and paid eight dollars a month. Also, an extra two dollars a month was included in the certificate for Junius until he reached the age of sixteen on July 9, 1893. Pension payments for Mary were dropped on June 30, 1903, due to notification of her death sometime before that date.

Ashkebugnekay, Amos, Private

Enlistment: Enlisted as a private on July 4, 1863, at Pentwater, Oceana County, by Captain Edwin V. Andress, First Michigan Sharpshooters, for three years.

   Age: Thirty-two, born about 1831 in Kent County, Michigan.

   Occupation: Laborer

   Residence: Pentwater

   Physical Description: Five feet ten, black eyes, black hair, and a dark complexion. Examining physician was Dr. Jacob B. McNett, assistant surgeon, First Michigan Sharpshooters.

   Mustered: July 11, 1863, in Detroit, Wayne County, by Lieutenant Colonel John R. Smith, US Army

   Military Service: Amos was given a twenty-day furlough in December 1863 while on guard duty with his regiment at the camp for Confederate prisoners, Camp Douglas, Chicago, Cook County, Illinois. In January 1864, he was detailed on recruiting service at Pentwater.

   In a battle at Petersburg, Virginia, on June 17, 1864, Ashkeybugnekay, fourteen other men of Company K and many of Amos's regiment were captured by the rebels and held in a tobacco warehouse. A few days later, they were sent south in cattle railcars to a confine for Union prisoners, Camp Sumter (also called Andersonville Prison), in Andersonville, Georgia.

   While in the stockade at Andersonville, Amos was exposed to the cruelty and inhumanity of prison life. It was in these conditions, after three months' confinement, that Amos's legs began to swell and he was in so much pain he couldn't walk. His Company K comrade, William Newton, and a friend, Edger Baker of the Seventh Illinois Infantry, carried him to a small stream that ran through the camp in order to bathe his legs in the cold water. The water seemed to ease his pain and the inflammation. This stream was the main source of water for the camp and was so badly polluted that its existence was a vector for disease and death.

Amos was admitted to the prison hospital as #15312 on October 20, 1864, with the diagnosis of scorbutus or scurvy, which is a nutritional disorder caused by the lack of vitamin C, chronic diarrhea, and rheumatism. He received what little help was available in medical attention. Another prisoner, George P. Miller, fed Amos and cared for him as best he could. On many nights, Amos and his friends would plot as to just how they would try to escape, swim the rivers, and make their way back to the Union lines.

After ten miserable months at Andersonville, Amos and other prisoners were sent by cattle railcar to Camp Lawton at Millen, Georgia. He was exchanged by the rebels at Camp Fisk, near Vicksburg, Mississippi, about April 21, 1865.

Upon his release at Camp Fisk, Amos started to look for a way to travel to Memphis, Tennessee. He wanted to board a steamer that would take him to the Union Camp, Camp Chase, in Ohio.

As fate would have it, Amos found room on the packet steamer *Sultana,* as did his paroled Company K mate Louis Miskoguon.

The *Sultana* was a side-wheel vessel, 260 feet long, and designed to carry only 376 passengers. But as the steamer left the dock at Memphis, Tennessee, it was grossly overloaded with 2,400 people. Most of the passengers were Union soldiers recently freed from prison camps. The steamer had started its ill-fated journey north on the Mississippi River from New Orleans on April 21. Amos considered it his good luck to find passage on the *Sultana* as his way to get to Camp Chase. He had a three-day wait before departure.

On April 27, 1865, after two brief stops on its way north, the *Sultana's* massive boilers exploded at 2:00 a.m., seven miles above Memphis, Tennessee (*Potter*). Amos, who was a good swimmer, and his Company K comrade, Louis Miskoguon, were among the five hundred survivors who jumped from the boat into the cold, muddy water of the Mississippi River. The lucky survivors were taken to several Memphis area hospitals. More than 1,800 people died when they were scalded, burned, or drowned (*Ibid.*). Truly, the demise of the *Sultana* was America's greatest maritime disaster.

Amos was admitted to Adams USA General Hospital where he was treated for chills and exhaustion. He was released on April 30 and booked passage on another steamer.

On May 3, Amos arrived at Camp Chase to rest, recuperate, and to have a medical exam. He was granted a furlough of thirty days on May 17 and returned to duty on June 17. Since he was last paid April 30, 1864, he was given three months' extra pay due to his former prisoner-of-war status.

Discharged: Private Ashkebugnekay was mustered out and honorably discharged on August 1, 1865, at Detroit. He was given money owed to him for his service at the time of his discharge

Biography: Amos's name "Ashkebugnekay" can be translated as an interpretation of the word "green" in the Anishinabe language. He was known to his family and all of his Anishinabek friends by the name of Ashkebugnekay. To non-Anishinabek folks, he was known as Amos Green and used this name after his discharge.

Amos was the son of Puctah (or Amomawshing) and Julia (Nawance) Green. All the people who knew Amos considered him to be an excellent hunter, swimmer, and runner.

In 1880, an Amos Green is listed in Custer Township of Mason County. This family included a wife Nancy, age thirty, a son Daniel, age eight, and a son Louis, age three.

In one of his pension papers, Amos related that his first wife died before he entered the service in 1863.

Amos was well thought of by his friends and neighbors, both Anishinabek and non-Anishinabek, and they considered him to be an honest man worthy of credit and confidence.

He was one of the first landowners of Mason County and received a patent for a homestead of 160 acres on which he grew crops and raised livestock. The land description was southeast quarter of section 23 in township 18 north of range 16 west of Michigan Meridian in Custer Township. He was issued his certificate #4920 on December 5, 1884 (*Land Records*).

During the years after his discharge, Amos was an active member of the GAR Sam Haight Post #348 in Scottville of Mason County and enjoyed getting together and visiting with old buddies from his army days.

Ashkebugnekay-Green's Application #474,654 for an invalid pension was filed for him on March 6, 1883. He cited disability from rheumatism, the effects of scurvy during his imprisonment, and disease of the heart.

In his later years, the swelling in his legs, due to the effects of scurvy while in the southern prison camp, grew worse. It became increasingly difficult for him to work his old team of horses on his land and to support his family by manual labor.

Amos received an Invalid Pension Certificate #344,840 on December 24, 1886.

The pension paid two dollars a month retroactive to March 6, 1883, and four dollars a month retroactive to February 3, 1886.

On July 4, 1891, Amos, age sixty-eight, married Ohawwauben (or Shawwauben), age fifty-eight. She was the daughter of Aeway and Miskeonkodoqua. The marriage was officiated by William Neilan, justice of the peace, in Weldon Creek of Mason County. Witnesses to the ceremony were R. H. Hawley and Joseph Elliot, who was an Anishinabe Methodist minister and interpreter and was active in the Anishinabek missions.

On two separate papers, Amos testified that he had no living children by 1898.

In the 1900 federal census, Amos was listed with Mary (or Shawwauben), his wife, a granddaughter Katie, a granddaughter Lilly, and a grandson Eddie.

Amos's monthly payments were increased to twenty-four dollars a month on August 7, 1905, retroactive to May 17, 1903. From September 1905 to June 1906, Amos received another increase that amounted to thirty dollars a month.

Amos Ashkeybugnekay-Green died on June 19, 1906, at his home in Weldon Creek. The immediate cause of his death was heart failure aggravated by organic heart trouble.

He was buried in an unmarked grave in the Mason County Riverside Cemetery. Military honors from his GAR post were accorded him at his burial site.

Ashman, Daniel, Corporal

Enlistment: Enlisted as a corporal on May 18, 1863, at Isabella City (now Mt. Pleasant), Isabella County, by First Lieutenant William J. Driggs, First Michigan Sharpshooters, for three years.

Age: Seventeen, born about 1846 in Isabella County.

Occupation: Farmer

Residence: Isabella City

Physical Description: Five feet six, black eyes, black hair, and a dark complexion. Examining physician was Dr. George L. Cornell, assistant surgeon, First Michigan Sharpshooters.

Mustered: May 26, 1863, in Detroit, Wayne County, by Lieutenant Colonel John R. Smith, US Army

Military Service: Corporal Daniel Ashman was reported to have been a drummer for his company (*Fancher*). By 1862, President Lincoln forbade allowing boys under the age of eighteen to enlist into the army under any circumstances. But if the boy had the permission of his parents, his enlistment was accepted. This may have been the case with Ashman since he was only seventeen when he entered the army. His superiors must have thought that he showed some maturity by enlisting him at the rank of corporal. During the duration of the war, 100,000 boys under the age of eighteen enlisted in the Union army.

As a drummer, Ashman learned fifteen different drum calls for the men in the ranks and twenty additional calls for skirmishes. On the field of battle, the drum was indispensable since it could be heard over the din of cannons, musket fire, and the frantic shouts of the officers. A drum was the link between life and death for the soldiers. Many times, the drummer boy was the prime target for sharpshooters (*Life of a Drummer*).

Ashman's workday began at 5:00 a.m. when he would summon the men for their different duties. In addition to roll call, there were calls for breakfast, dinner, drills, and lights out (*Ibid.*).

When his drumming skills were not needed, Ashman was busy with other camp duties, such as relaying messages and scouting out food from the surrounding farms. After a battle, Daniel donned a white armband and, as a stretcher bearer, helped remove the wounded from the field (*Ibid.*).

Corporal Ashman was admitted to US General Hospital at the United States Naval Academy at Annapolis, Maryland, on April 15, 1864, with the diagnosis of opthalmia or conjunctivitis. This affliction causes inflammation of the conjunctiva or mucous membrane of the eye. At the hospital, Ashman's eyes were washed with cold water and solutions of saline and borax. Nitrate of silver in water was applied to the inside of his eyelids, and chloride of sodium was also used to wash his eyes (*Dorwart*). Quinine, iron, and cod-liver oil were given orally to ease pain and clean out the digestive tract.

Ashman improved his diet by taking advantage of the plentiful food available at the hospital. He returned to his company on April 22.

Daniel, along with others of his regiment, was taken prisoner as his company charged the enemy's defenses during a battle at Petersburg, Virginia, on June 17, 1864. He was held for a few days in a former tobacco warehouse and then sent by cattle railcar to an open stockade confine for Union prisoners, Camp Sumter (also called Andersonville Prison) in Andersonville, Georgia. It wasn't long before Ashman's health began to deteriorate.

On October 25, 1864, Ashman was admitted to the prison hospital with scorbutus or scurvy, which is a nutritional disorder caused by the deficiency of vitamin C. He received what limited medical attention was available and then returned to the prison grounds on November 2. Another prisoner, Company K buddy Joseph Williams, also known as Joseph Nesogot, took care of Ashman during his illness.

Because of the approach of Sherman's Union army on his "March to the Sea," prisoners were sent to confines farther inland. According to official government records of November 11, 1864, Ashman, Williams, and the other prisoners were transferred by train from Andersonville Prison to Camp Lawton in Millen, Georgia. Lawton was another open stockade prison that subjected the prisoners to the mercy of the elements and was known, at that time, to be the largest prison in the world.

At Camp Lawton, Joseph Williams continued to care for Daniel as best he could but to no avail. By that time, Daniel was so weak from his illness that he died on or about November 15, 1864. His body was taken by his comrades or guards from the hospital to a "dead house" where all usable clothing was removed from the body. A numbered tag may have been attached to the body for later reference. Then, as quickly as possible, Daniel's remains and those of other prisoners were taken by wagon to the cemetery some distance from the prison grounds (*Encyclopedia*).

At the cemetery, Ashman's body was laid without a covering and shoulder to shoulder with other bodies in a trench about four feet deep. The remains were then covered with dirt. A small wooden board with some identification about Ashman may have been placed at the head of his grave (*Ibid.*).

Daniel's death at Camp Lawton was verified in a deposition given by Joseph Williams (Joseph Nesogot) on July 19, 1869. Joseph was with Daniel when Daniel died. After his death, Daniel Ashman's rank was reduced from corporal to private on July 1, 1865, with no reason given for his demotion.

At the end of hostilities, the remains of Union prisoners who died at Camp Lawton were disinterred and sent to the Beaufort National Cemetery in South Carolina for reburial. Inquiries made to this cemetery revealed that there is no burial record, by name, of Daniel Ashman's remains having been reinterred in South Carolina. But many of the remains transferred from Camp Lawton to Beaufort were listed as "unknown." Private Ashman, unfortunately, may have been one of those unknowns.

Discharged: No discharge given. Died of disease while a prisoner of war.

Biography: With the name Ashman, it's possible, but only a guess, that Daniel may have been a member of that well-known Michigan family. There is no pension file for Daniel Ashman.

Awanakwad, Petros, Private

Enlistment: Enlisted as a private on June 8, 1863, at Little Traverse (renamed Harbor Springs in 1881), Emmet County, by First Lieutenant William J. Driggs, First Michigan Sharpshooters, for three years.

Age: Twenty-five, born about 1838 in Cheboygan, Cheboygan County.

Occupation: Farmer

Residence: Little Traverse

Physical Description: Five feet six, with black eyes, black hair, and a dark complexion. Examining physician was Dr. Arvin F. Whelan, surgeon, First Michigan Sharpshooters.

Mustered: June 20, 1863, in Detroit, Wayne County, by First Lieutenant William J. Driggs, First Michigan Sharpshooters

Military Service: Sometime during the months of September and October 1863, while his regiment was guarding Confederate prisoners at Camp Douglas south of Chicago, Cook County, Illinois, Private Boetius (Petros or Peter) Awanakwad became sick of an undisclosed illness. He was sent home on sick furlough for thirty days and reported back to his regiment in November. A soldier named "Peter Nawaquot" on the enlistment roll, with just a notation of being sick in October 1863, may have been another entry for Peter (Petros) Awanakwad.

Petros fell ill with intermittent (or malarial) fever on September 26, 1864. He was sent to his division field hospital where he was given quinine for his fever. Quinine was dispensed either in the form of powdered cinchona tree bark in water or whiskey, or in the form of pills containing pure quinine sulfate (*Bollet*). Whiskey worked better because it masked the bitter taste of the quinine.

On September 28, Petros was taken by ambulance wagon from his division field hospital to the military railroad. He was put on a mattress in a boxcar, the floor of which was cushioned with straw or hay, and sent to the depot hospital at City Point, Virginia. At City Point, the doctors continued his quinine treatment and administered a diaphoretic called Dover's powder (a combination of ipecac and opium) for his diarrhea and for the maintenance of his bowels *(Ibid.)*. Cold wet cloths were put on his head, and he was fed a bland diet.

Complicating his malarial condition and diarrhea, Petros came down with a bout of chronic bronchitis. On September 28, Petros was taken to a wharf at City Point, transferred to a hospital steamer, and taken to L'Ouverture USA General Hospital in Alexandria, Virginia. He was admitted to L'Ouverture on October 1.

The doctors again administered Dover's powder and added spirit of niter, also called potassium nitrate or saltpeter, to treat his bronchial condition (*Evans*). Petros was confined to strict bed rest and given a bland diet followed by citrus juices and fresh vegetables when tolerated. He returned to duty with his regiment on October 25.

On February 20, 1865, during the siege of Petersburg, Virginia, Awanakwad was severely wounded by the burst of a rebel cannon shell that penetrated his bombproof shelter just behind the breastworks. A piece of shrapnel from the shell burst fractured his right femur (or thigh bone) and severed the femoral artery, which resulted in a great loss of blood. Sgt. Francis Tabasasch and Pvt. Louis Shomin, who shared the bombproof with Petros, witnessed the incident and summoned help immediately. Francis and Louis must have felt devastated because they knew that the large amount of blood loss would result in their buddy's death.

Petros was immediately taken by stretcher bearers to the aid station, a short distance from the breastworks, where a tourniquet was applied to his thigh and bandages were hastily applied to his leg. He was given whiskey for shock and an opium pill for pain.

After his initial treatment, Petros was then taken by ambulance wagon to the First Division USA Field Hospital of the Ninth Army Corps farther behind the lines at a place called Meade Station. At this hospital, chloroform was administered to him, and his leg was amputated near the hip. The surgical procedure used was probably the flap method because of the speed in which it could be performed and the larger amount of soft tissue that would remain after amputation to cover the end of the stump (*Schaadt*). The stump was washed and dressed with adhesive plaster bandages (*Ibid.*). Opium was given for pain.

Due to shock and a great loss of blood, Petros died later that same day. He was the last soldier from Company K to die in wartime hostility.

The next day, Private Petros Awanakwad's body was placed into a four-foot-deep trench, covered with a blanket (if available) and then with soil at the Ninth Corps Hospital Cemetery at Mead Station (*Encyclopedia*).

Later, Petros's body was removed from the cemetery at Mead Station and interred at Popular Grove National Cemetery four miles south of Petersburg. He was placed into a coffin, if one were available, and buried with a religious service and military protocol (firing of arms) in grave #0561 (*Ibid.*).

Grave #0561 corresponds with the name Pe-to-zo-ourquitte on the cemetery list, but the stone reads in error as "Jaco Penaswonquot."

There was a Jaco Penaswonquot who died at Andersonville Prison in Andersonville,

Georgia, and was buried on the prison grounds of that confine. His stone in the prison cemetery reads "S. Ricott."

The author believes that Petros Awanakwad and Petozoourquitte are the same man. There is a similarity in the spellings of Petros, Pe-to-zo, Betos Awanakwad, and Wonquot. The date of death (March 29, 1865) for a man called Petozoourquitte listed on the descriptive roll of Company K could actually be the date of Petros Awanakwad's reburial (under the name of Petozoourquitte) in Poplar Grove Cemetery. It's known that the remains of the men buried at Meade Station were removed to Popular Grove National Cemetery when the cemetery was established in 1866. Petros's body could have been one of the first to be reburied in Popular Grove before it became a national cemetery.

Discharged: No discharge given. Died of injuries while in the hospital.

Biography: Petros (or Peter) Awanakwad's parents may have been a couple named David and Jane Owanoquet, but that's only an assumption. Other spellings of Petros (or Peter) Awanakwad's name included Boetius Awanakwad (the name on his marriage certificate as recorded by the priest), Pierre Banquot, Pease Banquot, Petres Almonoquot, Peter Awwawnawquot, Petozoourquitte and Patrick Owanoquot.

On June 3, 1859, Boetius (Petros) Awanakwad, age twenty, married Teresa Maiangowi (Waganachasee) Atawish, age sixteen, at Wawgawnawkezee (or Middle Village) in Emmet County. Theresa was born on July 2, 1843. Her father's name was William Atawish, her mother's name is unknown. The marriage was officiated by Father Seraphim Zorn, who was a Roman Catholic missionary living at La Croix (renamed Cross Village in 1875) in said county. Witnesses were Michael Medweashe and Mary Kinisikwe, both of Middle Village. In 1860, Petros (possibly listed as Patrick Owanoquet in the census of that year) and his family were living in La Croix.

Petros and Teresa Awanakwad were the parents of three sons: Baziel, born April 16, 1857, at Middle Village and baptized on May 6; Antoine, born 1860 and died as an infant; and Benjamin, born October 1, 1861, at Middle Village and baptized on October 13. Although Baziel was born before his parents were married, Petros acknowledged him as his son and provided for him.

Application #113,206 for widow's pension was filed for Teresa on October 19, 1865, under the first Pension Act of Congress approved July 14, 1862. Under the 1862 Act, a pension was granted to those who were left without provision for their maintenance and support by the death of the soldier.

Teresa received a Widow's Pension Certificate #128,324 on April 28, 1869, which paid eight dollars a month retroactive to February 21, 1865. She also received an additional two dollars a month for each son, retroactive to July 25, 1866, until each boy attained the age of sixteen. Teresa did not allow her children to be adopted and provided for them as best she could. She was known in the community to be a very good mother.

In April 1900, a woman by the name of Mary Ann Ahpetahgshegoquay, a resident of the township of Suttons Bay in Leelanau County, claimed to be the mother of Private Petozoourquitte. Application #718,265 for a dependent mother's pension, under the Act of 1862, was filed for Mary Ann on April 26, 1900.

The name Petozoourquitte actually does appear on the Descriptive Roll of Company K, as mentioned previously, but does not appear on any military records in the War Department. The actual records, of course, are under the name of Petros Awanaquad. Therefore, Mary Ann's application was rejected on April 9, 1903, for the reason that the records of the War Department failed to show that the soldier, Petozoourquitte, was in the service as alleged.

Teresa Awanakwad died at the age of sixty-seven on October 19, 1910, at Good Hart. The cause of death was not recorded. She was buried in grave #F21 in the Anishinabek cemetery next to St. Ignatius Catholic Church in Good Hart, Emmet County.

Enlisted Men—Letters B and C

Battice, John, Private

Enlistment: Enlisted as a private on August 24, 1864, in Jackson, Jackson County, by Captain R. J. Barry, captain and provost marshal for the Michigan Third District, for three years.

Private Battice was a substitute for Daniel W. Van Auken, who was enrolled in the Fourth Ward, city of Lansing, Ingham County. This substitution was credited to the Third Congressional District, Thirty-Fifth Subdistrict, Fourth Ward, Lansing, and satisfied the requirement for a man needed from the Third District. As the principal or enrolled draftee, Van Auken would have paid Battice about $300 to be his substitute. As a volunteer substitute, Battice was not entitled to an enlistment bounty because of the generous lump sum he received as a substitute. But as an enlisted substitute soldier, he was eligible (as were regular enlisted men) for a hundred-dollar bounty if he was discharged from the service by reason of wounds received in battle.

There were non-Anishinabek men who avoided the service by finding substitutes. Many of these men visited the Michigan reservations and areas with Anishinabek populations. They sought out the men and offered lump sums of money to them if they agreed to serve as substitutes. The Civil War era was a time in which most Anishinabek people were in need of monetary support to provide for their families. The offers of money were hard to refuse.

Age: Nineteen, born about 1845 in the state of Michigan.

Occupation: Hunter

Residence: Possibly in Michigan's Upper Peninsula. Town not listed.

Physical Description: Five feet eleven and a half inches tall, black eyes, black hair, and a dark complexion. Examining physician was Dr. H. B. Shank, surgeon of the Board of Enrollment of the Third District of Michigan.

Mustered: August 24, 1864, in Jackson, Jackson County, by Captain R. J. Barry, captain and provost marshal for the Michigan Third District

Military Service: John may have come through his war experience unscathed since no medical records were found that mentioned disease or wounds incurred while he was in the service.

Discharged: Private John Battice was mustered out and honorably discharged at Delaney House in Tenallytown, DC, on July 28, 1865. He returned to Detroit on the steamer *Morning Star*. On August 7, he was paid money due to him for his service at Jackson, Jackson County.

Biography: Other spellings of Battice were Battin, Battise, and Baptiste. The true identity of the John Battice who enlisted into the Michigan Sharpshooter regiment might be found in one of the following five entries, or maybe not found. There are federal land records for Battice no. 1, 2, and 3 found in the land records of the US Department of the Interior, Bureau of Land Management.

(1.) John Battice, a laborer living in Nottawa Township of Isabella County, found in the 1880 federal census with his wife, Mary (or Wawwawsemoquay). John and Mary were members of the Anishinabek First Indian Methodist Episcopal Church of Mt. Pleasant, the Isabella Indian Mission Church. In 1880, the couple was listed as the parents of Peter, born about 1876, and Joseph, born about 1879. By 1886, two daughters had joined the family. They were Mary, baptized in the church on February 2, 1885, and Anna, baptized in the church in 1886; Ira joined the family in 1890, and Lizzie was born about 1892. Only Mary, Ira, and Lizzie are listed in the 1900 federal census for Isabella County, Wise Township. John is not listed with the family in 1900. An oversight or death? Mary is thought to have died between 1906 and 1913.

This John Battice, spelled Battise, was allotted forty acres in Nottawa Township of Isabella County by reason of the first article of the treaty of August 2, 1855, and the second article of the treaty of October 18, 1864, with the Chippewas of Saginaw, Swan Creek, and Black River. The land description was the southwest quarter of the northwest quarter of section 11 in township 15 north of range 5 west in the state of Michigan containing forty acres. He received his certificate on August 20, 1872.

(2.) John Battice or John Baptiste, who was one of the first landowners of Mason County, received a patent for sixty acres in section 21 township 17 north range west in Eden Township. This John (who also went by the name of Flamcowawbenew and Wawbawsway) received his patent on August 16, 1872, with proof on June 30, 1875.

John Battice-Baptiste was enumerated in the 1870 census as living in Custer, Mason County, and listed with his known living descendants on the Durant Roll of March 4, 1907. His children included Joseph, age thirty, married with one child and living in Signer, Wisconsin; Ira, age nineteen, living in Fergus, Saginaw County; and Lizzie, age eleven, living in Fergus. Mary is not listed and is presumed dead or not living with John by that date. The similarity between the names of the children of John (1) and Mary and John (2) is quite noticeable. Could John (1) and John (2) be the same man?

(3.) John Battise who held a patent for sixty-five and eight-tenths acres in Chippewa County in the Upper Peninsula due to the treaty concluded July 31, 1855, between the Ottawa and Chippewa Indians of Michigan. The land description is lot numbered 6 of section 11 and the northwest quarter of the northwest quarter of section 23 in township 47 north of range 3 west, in the district of lands subject to sale at Marquette, Michigan. He received Certificate #1410 issued on May 21, 1873. This man may have been the John Battice who was recruited in the Upper Peninsula.

(4.) John Battice, a resident of Hartford, Van Buren County, who was also known as Shobtise and John Blackman, and whose children were Lewis, Benedict, Joseph, Moses, and a daughter, Shaneya.

(5.) John Battice, age thirty-eight (listed a little older than would be expected according to his age on his enlistment paper), a farmer and a resident of Elbridge Township in Oceana County in the 1870 federal census. John is enumerated with his wife, Angeline, age twenty-eight, and their children: Leroy, age eighteen; Michael, age sixteen; and Joseph, age six. It is assumed that Angeline is a second wife, considering her age, and the mother of Joseph. This John was also a first land-owner in Elbridge Township of Oceana County. There is no pension file for a "John Battise, Baptiste, or Battice."

Benasis, John, Private

Enlistment: Enlisted as a private on September 10, 1864, at Algonquin in Ontonagan County of Michigan's Upper Peninsula by A.E.B. Mann, First Michigan Sharpshooters, for three years.

Age: Twenty-two, born about 1842 in Ontonagan County.

Occupation: Laborer and boatman

Residence: Algonquin in Ontonagan

Physical Description: Five feet eleven, dark eyes, dark hair, and a dark complexion. Examining physician was Dr. George Landon, First Michigan Sharpshooters.

Mustered: October 20, 1864, in Detroit, Wayne County, by Captain Mark Flanigan, captain and provost marshal of the Twenty-Fourth Michigan Infantry

Military Service: John enlisted on the same date as that of his cousin and Company K comrade, Peter Anotagon. See file on Peter Amderling (or Anotagon). John, with Peter, joined the regiment at Peebles farm in Virginia on November 4, 1864. No records of disease or wounds received while in the service have been found for John.

In May and June 1865, Private Benasis is reported to have been assigned as a brigade pioneer, as was his comrade, Amos Chamberlain, in April 1864. To be a brigade pioneer was, to say the least, not high on any soldier's list of enjoyable endeavors. Pioneers were soldiers selected (detached from their units to form a mobile workforce) from regiments who repaired the roads and bridges, removed obstacles, worked on entrenchments and fortifications, constructed mines and approaches, and prepared burial sites. Private Benasis may have been assigned to a battalion that repaired or built a military prison (or brig) in the vicinity of Georgetown, DC, where the sharpshooters were stationed during those months.

To denote the pioneer rank, John would have worn an armband on the left sleeve of his uniform jacket, which showed two yellow-colored crossed hatchets (or axes). The same design may have been on the top of his kepi (or cap). This badge also served as a pass and allowed the wearer less hassle from camp guards. As an incentive, pioneers received an extra four cents a day in pay.

Discharged: Private John Benasis was mustered out and honorably discharged at Delaney House in Tenallytown, DC, on July 28, 1865. He returned to Detroit on the steamer *Morning Star.* On August 7, Benasis was paid money due to him for his service at Jackson, Jackson County.

Biography: John was known to his family and friends as John Benashins (his proper surname), John Beneshia Bird, and John Bird. The names Benashins and Beneshia are derived from the Anishinabe word *bineshi,* which means "small bird" (*Baraga*). After the war, John would sign his name as "John Bird" on depositions for his fellow army buddies.

Both before and after the war, John worked as a laborer and boatman on the Great Lakes with his cousin Peter Anotagon.

At age thirty-eight John married Josephine Josephs, age thirty, on November 6, 1881, in Arvon, Baraga County. Walfred Been, justice of the peace, officiated at the ceremony. Witnesses were Olof Zellard and Mary Beck.

By reason of the Treaty with the Chippewa of September 30, 1854, John was entitled to an allotment of eighty acres of land, which he selected, on the L'Anse Reservation in Baraga County. The land description was north one half of the northwest one-quarter section 12 township 51 north, range 32 west. His allotment was approved in 1894, but John deeded the acreage to a James B. Smith in 1896 (*Lafernier*).

In later years, John and his family lived at the Kewawenon Anishinabe Methodist Episcopal Mission north of the Village of L'Anse. Living on the mission property encouraged John to become involved in church ministry as a lay preacher. When serving his church, John was called "Little Bird." True to his Anishinabek Christian culture, he and his wife were known to have attended the church summer camps and sing fests. The mission church is known today as the Zeba United Methodist Indian Church (*Reuter*).

Suffering from the effects of old age, John Bird died on May 9, 1907, at his residence in L'Anse Township of Baraga County. He is buried in the Anishinabek Pinery Cemetery (or Methodist Episcopal Mission Cemetery) located between L'Anse and Zeba of Baraga County. John's Company K army buddy and good friend Amos Crane is also buried in the same cemetery. There is no pension file for John Benasis.

Bennett, Louis, Private

Enlistment: Enlisted as a private on June 7, 1863, at Little Traverse, Emmet County, by First Lieutenant William J. Driggs, First Michigan Sharpshooters, for three years.

Age: Thirty-one, born August 19, 1832, on Mackinac Island, Mackinac County.

Occupation: Farmer and fisherman

Residence: Little Traverse (renamed Harbor Springs in 1881)

Physical Description: Five feet nine, black eyes, black hair, and a dark complexion. Examining physician was Dr. George L. Cornell, assistant surgeon, First Michigan Sharpshooters.

Mustered: June 22, 1863, in Detroit, Wayne County, by Lieutenant Colonel John R. Smith, US Army

Military Service: Before his service, Louis Bennett was known as Louis Bennett Beaubien Jr. He dropped the surname of Beaubien when he enlisted.

Private Bennett, who was more than ready to fight for his country and may have been disappointed in his lack of progress to be at the front, was reported to have deserted his guard post at Camp Douglas on the evening of November 15, 1863. Camp Douglas was located in Chicago, Cook County, Illinois, and was a confine for Confederate prisoners who were guarded by the Michigan Sharpshooters.

Although the November date was mentioned in the court-martial record, other military records stated that Bennett deserted his post on either September 4 or 24, 1863. The military record further stated that he was arrested in Buffalo, New York, on October 21, 1863.

From Buffalo Bennett was sent to the depot headquarters for drafted men in Elmira, New York, and received there on October 27. He spent the rest of his time under arrest in a military prison until he was returned under guard to his regiment, which was entrenched before Petersburg, Virginia, on December 27, 1864. He remained under arrest and in confinement until his trial by court-martial.

On February 25, 1865, by Special Order 39, a trial by a general court-martial was ordered to convene on March 6 to hear the case of desertion against Private Louis Bennett and to pronounce judgment. The following case and judgment are found in Bennett's military file.

After a delay, the court-martial was finally held on April 20, 1865, at the headquarters of the First Division of the Ninth Army Corps before Judge Advocate Joseph O. Bellair. Sgt. Francis Tabasasch testified that Private Louis Bennett was a good soldier and had a good reputation among his peers. Pvt. Bennett testified in his own behalf that he did not fully understand the rules and regulations of the army when he joined, nor the trouble that his unauthorized leave of absence would cause. He also related that he was a good and loyal soldier for the United States and fully intended to rejoin his regiment.

The court found Private Bennett guilty of desertion as charged. The sentence was as follows: "the Court does therefore sentence the said Private Louis Bennett, K Company, First Michigan Sharpshooters, to make good all time absent from his regiment and forfeit all pay for the same period of time. The Court is thus lenient for the reason that the prisoner is a member of the Ojibway tribe of Indians and at the time of desertion was unacquainted with the rules and customs of the US service." Private Bennett was lucky. The war was at an end, and the necessary paperwork would have been an added hassle. Therefore, the court did not pursue its judgment against Bennett, and he was returned to duty on April 20, 1865 (*Records*).

Discharged: Private Louis Bennett was mustered out and honorably discharged at Delaney House in Tenallytown, DC, on July 28, 1865. He returned to Detroit on the steamer *Morning Star*. On August 7, he was paid the money owed to him for his service at Jackson, Jackson County.

Biography: Louis Bennett Beaubien Jr. was the son of Louis Bennett and Christine Outapitakawnay (or Chippewa) Beaubien Sr. (*Beaubien Family*). His siblings were: Therese, born 1827; Margaret, born 1828; Christine, born 1822; Mary, born 1834; Charles, born 1836, and Joseph, born 1842. Louis was baptized on August 19, 1832, the day of his birth, in Ste. Anne Church on Mackinac Island (*Ibid.*).

Louis married Rachel St. Andre Jr., daughter of Charles Bodequin and Rachel Pond St. Andre Sr., in October 1865 on Mackinac Island. The sacrament of marriage was officiated at Ste. Anne Church. Charles was born in France, and Rachel Pond St. Andre is listed in the census as a native of Canada.

Rachel St. Andre Jr.'s siblings were: Charles Bernard, born 1841; Clement, born 1843; Adolph, born 1855; Mary Louisa, born 1847; Victorie, born 1849 (died before 1860); James Isadore, born 1852; Eli, born 1854; Jeremiah, born 1857; and brother and sister twins, Maxime and Catherine, born 1859. As their father did, the St. Andre boys would earn their living by fishing.

Louis and Rachel were the parents of one child, Mary J., born July 16, 1866.

Louis Bennett, who worked long hours as a fisherman in all kinds of inclement weather, died November 19, 1869. He succumbed from inflammation of the pleura (or inflammation of the serous membrane that envelops the lungs) (*Blakiston*). At the time of his death, Bennett and his family were living in Holmes Township (on Mackinac Island) of Mackinac County. He was buried in Ste. Anne Cemetery on said island.

After Louis's death, Rachel Bennett gave Louis's discharge paper to an attorney, Mr. Josiah F. Wendell, of Milwaukee, Wisconsin, for safekeeping. She also gave instructions to Wendell to submit an application for a widow's pension for her and to give the discharge paper to Mary when the pension was received.

Rachel St. Andre Bennett died of tuberculosis on June 10, 1880, on Mackinac Island. It seems that Mr. Wendell, according to his story, tried to make contact with Mary in 1888 when he visited Mackinac Island to locate her but was told that Mary had died.

At age twenty-four, Mary Bennett was living in St. Ignace in Mackinac County and was employed as a cook in a hotel there. It was at the hotel that Mary met Joseph Coles, age twenty, a hotel porter who immigrated to the United States from England in 1885.

Mary Bennett and Joseph Coles were married on June 26, 1889, in St. Ignace by Cornelius Bennett, justice of the peace. Witnesses to the ceremony were Jessie Bennett and Joseph Juelenette.

On April 16, 1890, Mary, sometimes listed as Marie (Bennett) Coles, and her husband were living in Mancelona, Antrim County. Joseph was a day laborer, and Mary worked as a general stock storekeeper.

While living in Mancelona, Mary wrote a letter to Mr. Wendell requesting that her father's discharge paper be sent to her. This letter dispelled any doubts that she was deceased. Wendell wrote back to Mary explaining to her that her mother had given her father's discharge paper to him for a security fee of twenty dollars. He also related that he had tried to find her to give the discharge paper to her. Wendell told Mary that he would be glad to send the paper to her on the condition that she pay the security fee. It seems that Mary was not able to pay the fee.

On September 14, 1891, Application #529,495 was filed for Mary (age twenty-five) in order to obtain a minor's pension. She was informed that she would need to send in her father's discharge paper. Mary again wrote to Wendell and asked that he send her father's discharge paper to her. Since she was unable to pay the twenty-dollar fee, Wendell again denied Mary's request.

To aid Mary's case, Special Examiner E. C. Parkinson was sent to Mr. Wendell's home in Wisconsin to procure the discharge paper. Parkinson related, in no uncertain terms, that according to the act of Congress of May 21, 1872, it was unlawful to withhold a discharge paper from the relatives of a military person for any reason. He also told Wendell that, as an attorney, Wendell could be disbarred if he did not hand over the paper to him. Parkinson returned to Michigan with the discharge paper, and it was received by Mary on January 16, 1892. Mary's application for a minor's pension was refiled for her.

Since Mary (Bennett) Coles was over the age of sixteen when she applied for a minor's pension, her application was denied.

On August 15, 1914, while living with her husband in Kingsley, Grand Traverse County, Mary died of cancer of the bowel. She was buried in Mancelona of Antrim County.

Joseph and Mary Coles did not have children.

Burns, Peter, Private

Enlistment: Enlisted as a private on June 10, 1863, at East Saginaw, Saginaw County, by First Lieutenant William J. Driggs, First Michigan Sharpshooters, for three years.

Age: Twenty-one, born about 1842 in Kent County.

Occupation: Farmer and hunter

Residence: Isabella City (now Mt. Pleasant), Isabella County

Physical Description: Five feet five, dark eyes, dark hair, and a ruddy complexion. Listed as a "half blood Indian." Examining physician was Dr. George L. Cornell, assistant surgeon, First Michigan Sharpshooters.

Mustered: June 16, 1863, in Detroit, Wayne County, by Lieutenant Colonel John R. Smith, US Army

Military Service: On November 18, 1863, while on guard duty with his regiment at the confine for Confederate prisoners, Camp Douglas, Chicago, Cook County, Illinois, Private Burns was promoted to fourth corporal in place of William Collins, who was reported as deserted.

On April 1, 1864, Burns was promoted to fourth sergeant to fill the vacancy of Charles Wabesis, who was reduced in rank. Wabesis's reduction in rank was due to him being charged with a felony while he was stationed in Chicago (see file on Charles Wabesis).

On April 18 and 19, 1864, while in camp near Annapolis, Maryland, Burns was reported sick. He was sent to his regimental hospital, the US General Hospital at the United States Naval Academy in Annapolis, and returned to duty on April 20.

Burns was diagnosed with diarrhea on June 24, 1864, and either walked or was transferred by ambulance wagon to his division hospital farther behind the lines. The doctors at the hospital prescribed tartar emetic and castor oil to induce vomiting (*Bollet*). Dover's powder, a mixture of ipecac and opium, was administered to induce perspiration, and an opium pill was given for pain (*Ibid.*). Boiled water, diluted coffee and tea, barley water, rice water, and broth of meat extract were ordered for his diet. He remained in the division hospital from June to late August. During that time, he was promoted to the rank of sergeant.

On August 27, 1864, Sergeant Burns was transported by ambulance wagon from the division hospital to the military railroad where he was put on a mattress in a boxcar, the floor of which was cushioned with straw. He was then taken to the Depot Hospital at City Point, Virginia. At this hospital, his status was downgraded to severe diarrhea and debility or weakness. Alcohol and tonics for his debility were added to his medications, and his diet was continued.

As his health became worse, Sergeant Burns was conveyed by ambulance wagon to the wharf at City Point on September 8. He was transferred from the wharf to a hospital steamer for his trip to Douglas USA General Hospital in Washington, DC.

Peter was admitted to Douglas General on September 9. Similar orders were given for his medication and diet. Now suffering from chronic dysentery (inflammation of the colon with intense diarrhea and blood in the stools), the doctors added acetate of lead or nitrate of silver combined with opium for Burns's treatment (*Evans*). When considered beneficial and tolerable, citrus juices and fresh vegetables were included in his diet. His condition continued to weaken.

On September 14, 1864, Sergeant Peter Burns died at age twenty. He was attended in his last hours by Dr. F. W. Norris, assistant surgeon.

The next day, Burns's body was placed into a coffin, and he was given a military escort from the hospital to Arlington National Cemetery in Washington, DC. A religious service was held at the cemetery, and he was honored with military protocol (the firing of arms). A temporary headboard with information of the deceased was placed at the head of his grave site. Today, Sergeant Peter Burns lies at rest in section 13 of said cemetery under military stone #8141.

Discharged: No discharge given. Died of disease while in the hospital.

Biography: Peter Burns, who did not marry, was the son of Mack Burns and an Anishinabequa mother who lived in Isabella City at the time of Peter's death. There is no pension file for Peter Burns.

Bushaw, Augustus, Private

Enlistment: Enlisted as a private on June 18, 1863, at Little Traverse, Emmet County, by Second Lieutenant Garrett A. Graveraet, First Michigan Sharpshooters, for three years.

Age: Twenty, born about 1843 in Little Traverse.

Occupation: Farmer

Residence: Little Traverse (renamed Harbor Springs in 1881)

Physical Description: Five feet eight, black eyes, black hair, and a dark complexion. Examining physician was Dr. Arvin T. Whelan, surgeon, First Michigan Sharpshooters.

Mustered: July 22, 1863, in Detroit, Wayne County, by Lieutenant Colonel John R. Smith, US Army

Military Service: When in camp near Annapolis, Maryland, Private Bushaw became ill with diarrhea. He was admitted to his regimental hospital on April 22, 1864. His illness was caused from the lack of vitamin C found in fresh fruits and vegetables. This condition was often called scorbutic taint or scurvy. The appalling lack of sanitation practices in camp also contributed to the incidences of diarrhea.

The doctors at the hospital prescribed an emetic to induce vomiting (*Bollet*). A mixture of ipecac and opium, called Dover's powder, and potassium nitrate were administered to induce perspiration and also to reduce fever (*Ibid.*). A tincture of opium in an alcoholic solution, called laudanum, was given for pain as well as for the diarrhea (*Ibid.*).

Boiled water, diluted coffee and tea, barley water, rice water, and broth made of meat extract was the diet prescribed for Bushaw. As his health improved and his digestive tract became more tolerant, the doctors added citrus juices, fresh fruits, and vegetables to his diet. He rejoined his regiment in late April.

Bushaw became ill again on June 10, 1864. He was taken by ambulance wagon to the military railroad, put on a bed of straw in a box car and taken to the wharf at City Point, Virginia. At the wharf, he was transferred to a hospital steamer and sent to Mt. Pleasant USA General Hospital in Washington, DC. His diagnosis was, again, chronic diarrhea. He was given opiates for joint pain and quinine and potassium iodide for their mild and anti-inflammatory effects (*Ibid.*). At Mt. Pleasant Hospital, Bushaw was given alcohol and acetate of lead, or nitrate of silver combined with opium, for pain in addition to the treatments previously mentioned (*Evans*). A bland diet was continued until citrus juices and fresh vegetables could be added as tolerated.

On June 18, Bushaw was sent by hospital steamer from Washington, DC, to Haddington USA General Hospital in West Philadelphia, Pennsylvania, for further treatment. He returned to duty on July 10.

On July 18, Bushaw was again transferred by steamer and admitted to Lincoln USA General Hospital in Washington, DC. He was given a furlough for thirty days on September 5, 1864.

While he was at home, Bushaw was able to obtain fresh fruits and vegetables, and his health improved. In October, he returned to his regiment.

In late June 1865, Bushaw again became ill with chronic diarrhea. He was sent from his regiment's base at Tenallytown, DC, to Chestnut Hill Hospital in Philadelphia.

From Philadelphia, Private Bushaw was sent to Harper USA General Hospital in Detroit, Michigan, on July 5, 1865. It was at Harper that the doctors discovered that Bushaw also suffered from chronic rheumatism. Chronic rheumatism was thought to be the painful inflammation of the large joints. This condition often accompanied chronic diarrhea and scurvy. For the rheumatism, Bushaw was given laudanum (a tincture of opium in alcohol) and nighttime Dover's powder for pain. Oral colchicum, called meadow saffron, and iodide of potassium were also prescribed for the rheumatism (*Ibid.*).

A bland diet was ordered for Bushaw. When he could tolerate them, fresh fruits and vegetables were added to his meals.

For the remainder of the month of July and until August 11, 1865, Augustus remained at Harper Hospital quite sick from his infirmities. Sometime during his tenure in the hospitals, he was mistakenly reported to have deserted. The charge of desertion was removed in July 1865.

Discharged: Private Augustus Bushaw was mustered out and honorably discharged on August 11, 1865, at Detroit. At the time of his discharge, he received payment due to him for his service and returned to Michigan.

Biography: Augustus Bushaw was the son of Charles, a Canadian trader of merchandise, and Angelic Beauchamp. Beauchamp (pron. Bow-shaw) is the correct French spelling of the family surname. He was also known by the name of Augustin Bemassawe (name on his marriage certificate) and Augustus Boushaw. Augustus's siblings listed in the census of 1870 were: Lucy, born 1828; Angelique, born 1845; William, born 1866; and Catherine, born 1870.

At age twenty, Augustus married Lucene (Lucy), age seventeen, the daughter of Paul and Martina (or Martha) Wasson. Rev. Father Louis Sifferath, a Roman

Catholic priest, officiated at the marriage of the couple on February 5, 1862, at Little Traverse. Witnesses to the marriage were Dennis Downing and William Sagina. Lucy's siblings in the 1860 federal census included Andrew, born 1851; Victoria, born 1853; Agnes, born 1856; and Mary, born 1859.

Augustus and Lucy were known to have had the following twelve children all born in Little Traverse: Angelica, born 1864; William, born 1866; Charles, born April 10, 1867, and died October 8, 1868; Mary Martina, born April 6, 1868, and died of cerebrospinal meningitis (inflammation of the membranes of the brain and spinal cord) in 1869; Catherine, born November 2, 1869, and died on August 30, 1870, of chronic diarrhea; Rosa, born 1870; a second Mary, born in May 1871 and died June 2, 1871, of spinal meningitis; a third Mary, who died at one month of age on June 2, 1874, of cerebrospinal meningitis; Louis, born June 1875 and died of chills and fever three months later on September 4, 1875; Anna, born in 1876; Martin, born June 26, 1878; and Mary Wasson, born in February 1881 and died on February 22, 1882, of inflammation of the lungs called pneumonitis.

Charles Beauchamp died of chronic diarrhea on September 1, 1871, at the age of sixty-five. His widow, Angelic (or Angelica), died of tuberculosis at age seventy-five on January 30, 1876, at Little Traverse.

In addition to farming on his acreage in Friendship Township of Emmet County, Augustus enjoyed being a member of the GAR J. B. Richardson Post #013 in Harbor Springs. At these meetings, he enjoyed visiting with his former Company K buddies.

Lucy Bushaw died at the young age of thirty-nine at Harbor Springs on September 15, 1884.

Augustus Bushaw, weakened by his wartime illnesses and the hard work of farming, died March 23, 1887, in Harbor Springs. He was given military honors from his GAR post and buried in Lakeview Cemetery of said city. Augustus lies at rest beneath a military stone (last name spelled "Boushaw") and, most probably, his wife's burial is not far from his grave site. There is no pension file for Augustus Bushaw.

Cabecoung, William, Private

Enlistment: Enlisted as a private on May 18, 1863, at Isabella City (now Mt. Pleasant), Isabella County, by Lieutenant William J. Driggs, First Michigan Sharpshooters, for three years.

Age: Nineteen, born about 1844 in Tuscola County.

Occupation: Farmer

Residence: Isabella City

Physical Description: Six feet tall, with black eyes, black hair, and a dark complexion. Examining physician was Dr. George L. Cornell, assistant surgeon, First Michigan Sharpshooters.

Mustered: May 26, 1863, in Detroit, Wayne County, by Lieutenant Colonel John R. Smith, US Army

Military Service: At the end of April 1864, while on duty with his regiment, Corporal Cabecoung became ill with severe pain in his chest, frequent coughing, and difficulty breathing.

On May 3, 1864, he was sent by ambulance wagon from his company quarters through Fredericksburg to the wharf at Belle Plain Landing, Virginia. At the landing, he was put on a hospital steamer and sent to USA General Hospital in Fairfax Seminary near Alexandria, Virginia. The doctors diagnosed his illness as pneumonia or inflammation of the lungs called pneumonitis. They ordered blisters to promote absorption through the skin (*Evans*). Topical applications of mustard plasters and turpentine wraps were used as counter irritants (*Bollet*). Oil of turpentine and camphor were given orally for the treatment of diarrhea (*Schaadt*). Opium was also administered for pain. After a short stay, Cabecoung returned to his regiment.

William was reported to have been sick in June. He was taken by ambulance wagon to the military railroad, put on a mattress in a boxcar, the floor of which was cushioned with straw or hay, and sent to the Depot Hospital at City Point, Virginia. The doctors diagnosed his problem as severe bronchitis. Painful cupping and blistering were ordered for treatment. He returned to duty with his regiment on July 14.

Cabecoung was listed as sick with bronchitis again in August and was returned to the hospital in City Point for a short stay. He rejoined to his regiment in September 1864.

On May 1, 1865, Cabecoung was promoted to the rank of full corporal.

Discharged: Corporal William Cabecoung was mustered out and honorably discharged at Delaney House in Tenallytown, DC, on July 28, 1865. He returned to Detroit on the steamer *Morning Star*. On August 7, he was paid money due to him for his service at Jackson, Jackson County.

Biography: William's surname is derived from either the Ojibwa (or Chippewa) word Kakabika, which means "a cascade or cataract" or from the Ojibwa (or

Chippewa) word Kakabikang, which translates "in a place where there is a waterfall" (*Baraga*). Another spelling for Cabecoung was Kabaicoung. He was also known as Chippen or William Chebbin.

Prior to 1854, William lived with his grandmother in Lapeer County. It's known that William had at least one brother, named Seogun.

After the war, William returned to Isabella City to live for a short time. He then moved to East Saginaw, Saginaw County, where he married, according to the traditional Anishinabek custom and practice (consent of the couple and their parents), to Gezhonquotoqua in May 1877. Gezhonquotoqua was the daughter of Sahgoncotoqua (or Nancy Jacob) and sister to Julia David, who was married to Company K soldier Albert Church.

William and Gezhonquotoqua were the parents of two children: James (or Kahbazahchewon), born November 1, 1879, and Charlotte (or Nahwahchewonoqua), born April 1, 1882. Both children were baptized by an Anishinabe Methodist minister named William Turner.

Gezhonquotoqua died in 1884 or 1885. Shortly after his wife's death, William took his children and moved to Quanicassee in Tuscola County.

Application #930,155 for an invalid pension was filed for William on August 28, 1890. He cited rheumatism, heart disease, and lung problems. The application was rejected on the grounds that his infirmities were not caused by his war service.

William died of a heart attack (another record states death due to inflammation of the bowels) in Quanicassee, Wisner Township, on August 7, 1891. His death occurred while he was cutting hay with a mowing scythe.

It is reported that William Cabecoung (Chebbin or Chippen) was buried in an Anishinabek cemetery in the Quanicassee area. He was accorded military honors by members of a GAR post in said county.

After her father's death, Charlotte lived with her grandmother, Nancy Jacob, in Fergus, Saginaw County.

An attorney from Pinconning, Samuel S. Carson, was appointed guardian to the Cabecoung children on December 3, 1892. Application #576,105 for a pension for minor children was filed for Carson on February 28, 1893.

The application was rejected on May 22, 1897, on the grounds that the claimants were unable to submit evidence that the soldier's death was due to the effects of his military service. Even if the application were approved, both children had already attained the age of sixteen, and their benefits would have been discontinued.

Carter, Charles, Private

Enlistment: Enlisted as a private on June 22, 1864, in the field near Petersburg, Virginia, by Lieutenant Henry V. Hinckley, First Michigan Sharpshooters, for three years.

> **Age:** Twenty-one, born about 1843 near Hagerstown, Maryland.
>
> **Occupation:** Farmer
>
> **Residence:** Hagerstown
>
> **Physical Description:** Five feet ten, with black eyes, black hair, and a dark complexion. Examining physician was Dr. Arvin F. Whelan, surgeon, First Regiment, Michigan Sharpshooters.
>
> **Mustered:** July 7, 1864, in the field near Petersburg, Virginia, by Lieutenant Otis Fisher of the Eighth US Infantry
>
> **Military Service:** Private Charles Carter was killed in action as he charged the enemy's defenses on July 30, 1864, in the Battle of the Crater before Petersburg, Virginia.

As with so many men who died that terribly hot day, Carter's final resting place is unknown. The battle was a fiasco for the Union army, so his body was probably found by the Confederates, who, with indifference and disrespect, put it into a trench and covered it with dirt (*Encyclopedia*). Charles may have left a family who would mourn his death and his burial in a strange land so far from his ancestors' resting place.

> **Discharged:** No discharge given. Killed in action.
>
> **Biography:** Charles Carter may have heard of the bravery of Company K and of the sharpshooter regiment during the war. Since the company was an all American Indian unit fighting for the Union and Carter was a Union sympathizer, he probably felt that he could serve with his Native American brothers and contribute to the cause of saving the Union. Also, his service would earn some much-needed cash. Hagerstown is near the border with Virginia, so he could have easily made his way to join up with the sharpshooters in the field.

To what tribe could Charles Carter have been a member? Considering that his home was Hagerstown, Maryland, he may have been from the Lenni Lenape (or Delaware) tribe of northern Maryland (*American Indians in Maryland*). Also, he may have come from the southern offshoot of the Lenni Lenape called Nanticoke or the "tidewater people" of southern Maryland (*Nanticoke/Southern Delaware*).

After the British conquest of the eastern coast, some Nanticoke people moved westward, but most of the southern group stayed behind in its traditional territories. This part of the Nanticoke tribe was known for aiding, protecting, and providing for escaped slaves during the eighteenth century. In fact, some of the Nanticoke language was known to have been infused with West African Mandika language.

Charles probably sympathized with the southern slaves and felt strongly about fighting to help them gain their freedom. In addition to Native American heritage, one can speculate that Carter may have also had some Mandika roots in his ancestry. There is no pension file for Charles Carter.

Chamberlain, Amos, Private

Enlistment: Enlisted as a private on June 13, 1863, at East Saginaw, Saginaw County, by First Lieutenant William J. Driggs, First Michigan Sharpshooters, for three years.

Age: Twenty-two, born about 1841 in Lapeer County.

Occupation: Farmer and hunter

Residence: Isabella City (now Mt. Pleasant, Isabella County)

Physical Description: Five feet nine and a half inches tall, black eyes, dark hair, and a ruddy complexion. Examining physician was Dr. Arvin F. Whelan, surgeon, First Michigan Sharpshooters.

Mustered: June 16, 1863, at Detroit, Wayne County, by Lieutenant Colonel John R. Smith, US Army

Military Service: During the months of January and February 1864, while on guard duty with his regiment at Camp Douglas, Private Amos Chamberlain was detailed as a company cook. Camp Douglas was located in Chicago, Cook County, Illinois, and was a confinement for Confederate prisoners.

In April 1864, Amos served as a brigade pioneer as did his comrade, John Benasis (or John Bird), in May and June 1865. To be a brigade pioneer was, to say the least, not high on any soldier's list of enjoyable endeavors. Pioneers were soldiers selected (or detached from their units to form a mobile workforce) from regiments who repaired roads and bridges, removed obstacles, worked on entrenchments and fortifications, constructed mines and approaches, and prepared burial sites (*Kautz*).

To denote the pioneer rank, Chamberlain would have worn an armband on the left sleeve of his uniform jacket, which showed two yellow-colored crossed hatchets (or axes). The same design may have been on the top of his kepi (or cap). This badge also served as a pass and allowed the wearer less hassle from camp guards. Brigade pioneers received an extra four cents a day in pay.

Also, during the month of April, Amos was admitted to his regimental hospital. He was diagnosed as having ulcers. At the hospital, the doctors prescribed a bland diet of rice water, barley water, milk, and broth made of meat extract. Later in April, Amos returned to his regiment.

While the regiment was before Petersburg in June 1864, Chamberlain contracted chronic diarrhea, which would result, in later life, in the weakening of his kidneys, heart, and lungs. Treatment for his diarrhea at the division hospital, farther behind the lines, consisted of a bland diet (as mentioned above), medications including Dover's powder that contained a combination of ipecac and opium to induce sweating, and doses of turpentine and castor oil to induce vomiting (*Bollet*). A tincture of opium in an alcoholic solution called laudanum was given for pain as well as for diarrhea (*Ibid.*).

On August 26, 1864, Chamberlain was again sent to his division hospital, this time with the complaint of remittent fever (or malaria). While at the hospital, Chamberlain was given quinine in the form of powdered cinchona tree bark mixed into water or whiskey, or pills of purified quinine sulfate for the fever. Whiskey worked better because it masked the bitterness of the quinine *(Ibid.*).

The next day, he was sent by ambulance wagon to the military railroad, put on a mattress in a boxcar, the floor of which was cushioned with straw or hay, and sent to the Depot Hospital at City Point, Virginia. At the hospital, Chamberlain's fever was again treated with quinine, and he was given acetate of ammonia as a diuretic. Turpentine was administered to maintain his bowels during bouts of diarrhea. Opium pills were given for pain.

Still suffering from a fever and chronic diarrhea, Chamberlain was taken by ambulance wagon to a wharf at City Point on September 8 and transferred to a hospital steamer. The steamer took him to Grant USA General Hospital at Willets Point, New York Harbor. Similar treatment, as mentioned previously, was given to Amos at Grant Hospital. Fresh fruits and vegetables, which were more easily obtained, were added to his diet.

On September 22, he was sent from Grant General Hospital to USA Convalescent Barracks, Fort Wood, Bedlow's Island, New York Harbor. Similar medical treatment and diet were continued.

Deemed to have sufficiently recovered from the fever and diarrhea, Chamberlain returned to his regiment on September 27, 1864. On May 1, 1865, Private Amos Chamberlain was promoted to the rank of corporal.

Discharged: Corporal Amos Chamberlain was mustered out and honorably discharged at Delaney House, Tenallytown, DC, on July 28, 1865. He returned to Detroit on the steamer *Morning Star*. On August 7, he was paid money due to him for his service at Jackson, Jackson County.

Biography: Amos (or Pahnosewawnequat) Chamberlain, whose name was also spelled Chamberlin, was the son of Harry (or Meshezhegog), which translates "Big Skunk," and Jane Bradley Chamberlain (*Avery*). His siblings were: Mary Ann, born 1845, died in 1866; Margaret, born 1846 and married Charles Fisher; Lucy, born in 1858; Eliza, born 1861; and Amanda, born 1865 (*Gruett*).

Amos, at age twenty-five, married Sarah Nawoquayasenoquay (or Kewequahnaby), age fifteen/sixteen, on September 16, 1866. She was the daughter of chief Kawgaykezhick and his third wife, Wawtwaybogee, and was the granddaughter of Chief Bemassikeh. See profile on Daniel Pemassegay. The marriage was officiated by Rev. John Irons, an Anishinabe Methodist minister, at Isabella City. Witnesses were John Collins, a Company K buddy, and Meshezhegog. Sarah died before 1874. There were no children of this union.

There is a legal marriage recorded in Isabella County on August 30, 1874, between Amos and a Nancy Jackson. The couple had a son named William (or Mochoghezhick) who was baptized in 1875. The baptism took place in the First Methodist Episcopal Church—Isabella Indian Mission.

Amos and Nancy separated, but the legal marriage between the couple was never terminated.

Amos married for the third time to Jane George in 1879. The marriage was according to traditional Anishinabek custom and practice (an agreement of the couple and their parents). Jane (George) Chamberlain was held in high esteem by her people as a practitioner of traditional Anishinabek medicine.

On August 2, 1882, Amos joined the Isabella Indian Mission. He was also a member of the GAR Wa-bu-no Post #250 in Mt. Pleasant where he enjoyed getting together with his veteran buddies.

Amos and Jane Chamberlain were the parents of: Harvey (or Meshezhegog), born 1883; Charley (or Ah Nyaack), born 1894; and Esther (or Terbepekequah), born 1898. The couple remained together until Amos's death.

Amos was allotted forty acres in Wise Township of Isabella County by reason of the first article of the treaty of August 2, 1855, and the second article of the treaty of October 18, 1864, with the Chippewas of Saginaw, Swan Creek, and Black River. The land description was southeast one-quarter of the southeast one-quarter, section

33, township 16 north, range 3 west. The certificate was issued on May 27, 1871 (*Land Records*).

An invalid pension Application #460,960 was filed for Amos on September 26, 1882. He received his Invalid Pension Certificate #379,643 on December 23, 1887, for chronic diarrhea and general disability. His monthly checks amounted to two dollars a month retroactive to December 26, 1882, and were increased to four dollars a month retroactive to December 23, 1885.

Amos Chamberlain died of pneumonia on August 18, 1909, in Denver Township of Isabella County. He was buried on the Chamberlain family's rural property. A memorial stone marked "Chamberlain" denotes the family burial plot.

On October 26, 1909, Application #929,391 was filed for Jane Chamberlain for a widow's pension. Jane's application was denied on April 23, 1910, since Nancy (Jackson) Chamberlain was never legally divorced from Amos and was still living. Also, because of the previous legal marriage, Jane was not entitled to the accrued pension due to the soldier at the time of his death.

Jane (George) Chamberlain suffered from epilepsy and died at the age of eighty on July 24, 1911. She may be buried near Amos.

Chatfield, Charles, Private

Enlistment: Enlisted as a private on May 18, 1863, in Isabella City (now Mt. Pleasant), Isabella County, by First Lieutenant William J. Driggs, First Michigan Sharpshooters, for three years.

Age: Nineteen, born about 1844 in Lapeer County.

Occupation: Farmer

Residence: Isabella County

Physical Description: Six feet one, with black eyes, black hair, and a dark complexion. Examining surgeon was Dr. George L. Cornell, assistant surgeon, First Michigan Sharpshooters.

Mustered: May 26, 1863, at Detroit, Wayne County, by Lieutenant Colonel John R. Smith, US Army

Military Service: Private Chatfield was reported to have deserted from his regiment on July 19, 1863, while the sharpshooters guarded the Detroit Arsenal in Dearborn.

He was arrested in Isabella County on November 26 and delivered by Benjamin K. Land to Captain Strickland at Dearborn on December 3.

Chatfield was then sent to Camp Douglas in Chicago, Cook County, Illinois, to rejoin his regiment that had been sent there to guard Confederate prisoners. He was restored to duty by Colonel Charles V. DeLand on December 7, 1863.

On February 28, 1864, Chatfield was admitted to the USA Post Hospital at Camp Douglas where the doctors diagnosed his ailment as pneumonia. A blister plaster to promote absorption of poison away from the lungs was applied to his chest *(Bollet)*. He was given "blue mass," composed of calomel (or mercurous chloride) for a purgative and opium for pain. Also, he may have been given Dover's powder that contained ipecac and opium to induce sweating and decrease body temperature *(Ibid.)*. He returned to duty on March 9.

On April 16, Chatfield was admitted to his division hospital with the complaint of diarrhea. The doctors treated his diarrhea with castor oil (an emetic) to induce vomiting, oral turpentine to manage the bowels, and Dover's powder to induce perspiration *(Ibid.)*. Additional opium was given for pain, and a bland diet of barley water, rice water, and broth made from meat extract was ordered.

On April 22, Charles was sent to Division 1, USA General Hospital at the United States Naval Academy (Navy Yard) in Annapolis, Maryland, with a case of scrofula (or tuberculosis) of the lymph nodes of the neck. Treatment consisted of the application of a tincture of iodine as a paint to the swollen neck glands *(Evans)*. Complete bed rest and a healthy diet were ordered for the soldier. Private Chatfield returned to duty on May 2.

During a battle near Petersburg, Virginia, on June 17, 1864, Chatfield incurred a wound described as a "slight contusion (or bruise) on his back" from a missile ball. The skin was not broken. He was taken to a division aid station behind the lines where the wound was washed and hastily bandaged with a simple dressing that consisted of folded lint rinsed in cold water, to decrease inflammation, and held in place by a cloth wrap or adhesive plaster *(Schaadt)*. He was given whiskey for shock and an opium pill for pain and was sent back to his company.

On June 24, Charles was sent to his division hospital with the diagnosis of intermittent fever (or malaria). He was given quinine in the form of powdered cinchona tree bark mixed with whiskey or water or pills containing pure quinine sulfate for his fever *(Dorwart)*. Whiskey worked better because it masked the bitter taste of quinine. A bland diet was again ordered for Charles.

After he returned to duty on July 4, Chatfield was again afflicted with diarrhea. He was taken by ambulance wagon to the military railroad, put on a mattress in a boxcar, the floor of which was cushioned with straw or hay, and taken to the Depot Hospital near City Point, Virginia. He remained at this hospital until July 6. For his diarrhea, the doctors administered much the same treatment as previously mentioned.

On July 6, Chatfield, now suffering from a more severe case of diarrhea, was sent to the wharf at City Point and transferred by a hospital steamer to DeCamp USA General Hospital at David's Island, New York. He was admitted as a patient on July 10. After his treatment, Charles was given a furlough for thirty days on August 16, 1864.

When Chatfield returned from his furlough in September, records show that he was again in the hospital sick of disease (probably diarrhea). He returned to the hospital with the same complaint in January 1865 and remained there until sometime in late May.

Discharged: No record of discharge has been found for Private Charles Chatfield. He may have been released on furlough from the hospital, given a discharge for disability, or deserted and went home while still suffering from his illness. He is last reported as "absent from his regiment, sick of disease" as of May 1865. If he did not desert his regiment, a discharge paper could have been given to Chatfield at a later date. From the following record, it appears that Charles Chatfield survived his service after 1865.

Biography: Charles Chatfield was the son of Thomas (also known as Thomas Shaygonaybe) and Margaret (Wawsawchewawnequay) Chatfield. His known siblings were Julia, Mary Ann, Shawwawnekezhick, Franklin, Mary, Anos, Thomas, John A., Kaybaycheoquay, Susan, and Naywawdaygezhegoquay (*Gruett*). He may have been a relative of Samuel C. Chatfield, a Company K comrade. Both Charles and Sam were born in Lapeer County, Michigan.

According to the 1868 Gruett Saginaw Chippewa Index, a Charles Chatfield is known to have married Kawwawnawnoquay (also known as Sophia), the daughter of James and Wawsaychewawnoquay Fisher (*Ibid.*). Their children were a daughter, Pemaysewawnaquodequay, and a son, Penaysewawmawquot (or Jonas). Jonas died at age six of colic on November 24, 1873. Kawwawnawnoquay was a sister to Wawwawsawmoquay, who married Thomas Nelson, a Company K comrade of Charles (*Ibid.*).

Eighty acres were allotted to Charles by reason of the first article of the treaty of August 2, 1855, and the second article of the treaty of October 18, 1864, with the Chippewas of Saginaw, Swan Creek, and Black River. Forty acres were located in Denver Township of Isabella County with a land description of southwest quarter of the northwest quarter, section 21, township 15 north, of range 3 west. The certificate was signed on May 27, 1871 (*Land Records*).

The second forty acres, by reason of the same treaties, were located in Chippewa Township of Isabella County with a land description of southeast quarter of the northwest quarter, section 12, township 14 north, range 4 west. The certificate was signed on August 20, 1872 (*Ibid.*).

Charles Chatfield died on August 18, 1909, in Mt. Pleasant and is buried in an Anishinabek cemetery in Isabella County. There is no pension file for Charles Chatfield.

Chatfield, Samuel C., Private

Enlistment: Enlisted as a private on May 18, 1863, in Isabella City (now Mt. Pleasant), Isabella County, by First Lieutenant William J. Driggs, First Michigan Sharpshooters, for three years.

Age: Twenty-six, born about 1837 in Lapeer County.

Occupation: Farmer

Residence: Isabella County

Physical Description: Five feet nine, with black eyes, black hair, and a dark complexion. Examining physician was Dr. George L. Cornell, assistant surgeon, First Michigan Sharpshooters.

Mustered: May 26, 1863, at Detroit, Wayne County, by Lieutenant Colonel John R. Smith, US Army

Military Service: In January and February 1864, while on guard duty with his regiment at Camp Douglas in Chicago, Cook County, Illinois, Chatfield was detailed as a company cook. Camp Douglas was a confine for Confederate prisoners.

During the war in June 1864, Sam, who suffered from an undisclosed illness, was taken by ambulance wagon from his regiment to the military railroad. He was put on a mattress in a boxcar, the floor of which with straw or hay, and sent to the depot hospital at City Point, Virginia. He remained at the hospital until he was released in August.

On Friday, August 19, 1864, a day that was marked with dry, oppressive heat, Private Samuel C. Chatfield made the ultimate sacrifice. He was killed in action while on a charge against the enemy's defenses at Weldon Railroad near Yellow House (also called Globe Tavern) outside of Petersburg, Virginia.

If his body was recovered by Union soldiers, he was buried in his uniform, or wrapped in a blanket and placed in a hastily dug individual grave or in a trench with other deceased Union soldiers somewhere in the vicinity of the battlefield. His burial was without ceremony, and a board with his name and unit (if known) was placed at the head of his grave site. That marker has long disappeared, and his grave site is unknown. If Samuel was found by the rebels, he was put (with indifference and disrespect—a casualty of war) into a hastily dug trench with other dead Union men and covered with dirt (*Encyclopedia*). Sam left a family who not only grieved at his death but mourned that he was not buried in the land of his ancestors.

Discharged: No discharge given. Killed in action.

Biography: Samuel C. Chatfield (sometimes written Samuel W. Chatfield and W. Samuel Chatfield) was the son of William (Shawwaw nawnawquot, which means "southern cloud") and Kinnequay (which means "golden eagle") Chatfield (*Avery*). His siblings were: Warren, who married Otawzhewaw; Mary, who married James Paaheninne; Penayse (or Edmund/Edwin); Nancy and Lyman (*Gruett*). It is noted that Samuel C. Chatfield and Charles Chatfield were both born in Lapeer County and enlisted on the same day from the same place. They may have been relatives.

Sam married Charlotte (or Nawzewawbawnoquay) Natahbenego (*Ibid.*). The ceremony took place on December 20, 1855, in the home of Anishinabe Methodist Episcopal missionary Rev. John Irons and his wife, Margaret, in Midland, Midland County. The marriage rite was officiated by Rev. Peter O. Johnson, Anishinabe Methodist missionary, and witnessed by Showshowonebise, Emilia Nawgawnequam, Cornelius Bennett, and Charles H. Rodd. Missionary Irons was the schoolteacher for Rev. Johnson's Kecheassining mission on the Tittabawassee River near present-day Midland (*Reuter*).

The couple were the parents of Joshua (or Keywaykezhick), born June 12, 1856 or 1860; Andrew, born in 1861, and died of tuberculosis at age eleven in 1872; and Martha, born October 7, 1861. Martha died in 1866.

Samuel C. Chatfield was allotted forty acres in Union Township of Isabella County by reason of the first article of the treaty of August 2, 1855, and the second article of the treaty of October 18, 1864, with the Chippewas of Saginaw, Swan Creek, and Black River. The land description was southwest quarter of the northwest quarter, section 1, in township 14 north, of range 4 west. The certificate was issued on May 27, 1871 (*Land Records*).

A dependent widow's pension Application #74,004 was filed for Charlotte Chatfield on November 29, 1864. From all indications, it seems that this claim was abandoned sometime after March 1872 due to the lack of further communication and follow-up by the widow and her lawyer.

Charlotte's second marriage was to James Nicholson sometime before 1868. After their marriage, the couple moved to the northern part of the state. In any case, Charlotte's second marriage would have nullified her claim for a dependent widow's pension since her second husband was expected to support her and her children.

Church, Albert, Private

Enlistment: Enlisted as a private on June 10, 1863, at East Saginaw, Saginaw County, by Lieutenant William J. Driggs, First Michigan Sharpshooters, for three years.

Age: Twenty, born about 1843 in Genessee County.

Occupation: Farmer and hunter

Residence: St. Charles, Saginaw County

Physical Description: Five feet eleven, dark eyes, dark hair, and a dark (ruddy) complexion. Examining physician was Dr. George L. Cornell, assistant surgeon, First Michigan Sharpshooters.

Mustered: June 16, 1863, at Detroit, Wayne County, by Lieutenant Colonel John R. Smith, US Army

Military Service: Previous to his enlistment in the sharpshooter regiment, Albert Church joined Company M of the Eighth Michigan Cavalry Regiment on April 28, 1863, at Venice, Michigan, under the name "James Moses." He is reported to have deserted the cavalry on May 22, 1863, at Mt. Clemens, Macomb County. Church stated that the reasons for his desertion from the cavalry were that he was young and not happy to be separated from his people. He also stated that the Anishinabek men, who told him that they would enlist with him, decided that they would not join the cavalry. He felt alone, so he left his troop.

After he heard that a sharpshooter unit had been raised for service and that one company had all Anishinabek men, Church decided to cast his lot with them. So, his second enlistment, under the name of "Albert Church," is as reported above in the First Michigan Sharpshooter regiment. But after his enlistment in this regiment, Church deserted again, this time on July 19, 1863.

He was returned to his regiment on November 12, 1863, after being restored to duty by Col. Charles V. DeLand on October 23. By the time Church was restored to duty, the sharpshooter regiment had been guarding Confederate prisoners since the middle of August 1863 at a confine called Camp Douglas in Chicago, Cook County, Illinois.

In the process of his desertion, Church lost his .58-caliber Springfield Rifle Musket and all accoutrements. As a consequence for his lack of responsibility, his pay was docked for the cost of the lost equipment. It's most likely that Private Church was not aware that he had violated the twenty-second (which became the fiftieth) article of war that defined desertion.

On June 1, 1864, Pvt. Church was listed as "sick" (no specifics) and sent by ambulance wagon from his division hospital behind the lines to a Depot Hospital at Fredericksburg, Virginia, for treatment. This hospital may have been at or near attorney John Marye's house on Marye's Heights.

This date was the beginning of Church's long list of ailments and his frequent stays in various hospitals.

On June 10, Albert was sent from the Depot Hospital by wagon to a wharf at Belle Plain, Virginia. From Belle Plain, Church was taken by hospital steamer to Mount Pleasant USA General Hospital in Washington, DC, with the diagnosis of "phthisis pulmonalis" (old term for pulmonary tuberculosis and for any disease characterized by emaciation and loss of strength due to diseases of the lungs). He was admitted on June 11. At this hospital, Church was fed a hearty diet, ordered to strict bed rest, and exposed to as much fresh air as possible. There wasn't any effective treatment for tuberculosis until the use of antibiotics in the 1950s.

Private Church was transferred from Mt. Pleasant Hospital on June 17 to Haddington USA General Hospital in West Philadelphia, Pennsylvania, and arrived on June 18. His diagnosis was "organic disease of the heart." From Haddington he was transferred to USA General Hospital, Turner's Lane, in Philadelphia on June 22, 1864, and admitted on June 24. His case was labeled "debility and anemia." His anemia was treated with a hearty diet, and he was returned to duty on July 11.

On July 17, 1864, Pvt. Church was again reported ill and was taken by ambulance wagon to the military railroad. At the railroad, Church was put on a mattress in a boxcar, the floor of which was cushioned with straw or hay, and sent to City Point, Virginia. Albert was then taken by a hospital steamer from a wharf at City Point and transported to Lincoln USA General Hospital in Washington, DC. He was admitted to this hospital on July 18. Church's diagnosis was again that of "consumption" (old term used for progressive tuberculosis). As mentioned previously, there was no effective treatment for tuberculosis until the middle of the twentieth century.

The soldier was transferred to USA General Hospital in York, Pennsylvania, on July 28, diagnosed with typhoid fever. He was admitted to the general hospital on July 29. Treatment for the symptoms of typhoid consisted of Dover's powder (ipecac and opium) for diarrhea, cooling the body with water, or water and alcohol for fever reduction, and small doses of turpentine for intestinal ulcers (*Schaadt*). Pvt. Church was isolated, confined to bed, and fed liquid or bland diets.

Albert was returned to duty on October 27, 1864. At the time of his discharge, he apparently suffered from chronic diarrhea.

Discharged: Private Albert Church was mustered out and honorably discharged at Delaney House, Tenallytown, DC, on July 28, 1865. He returned to Detroit on the steamer *Morning Star*. On August 7, Church was paid money due to him for his service at Jackson, Jackson County. There is no pension file for Albert Church.

Biography: Albert Church (also known as James Moses) married Julia David according to Anishinabek custom and practice (with the consent of the couple and their parents) in the spring of 1863 at St. Charles (also called Indian Town), Saginaw County. Julia was the daughter of Nancy Jacob and a sister to Gezhonquotoqua, who was the wife of Company K soldier William Cabecoung. Albert and Julia were the parents of two daughters, Nancy, born in June 1870, and Susan, born in September 1874.

After Albert returned home from the service in 1865; an Anishinabe doctor, Henry Crevis (or Quewis), treated him in the traditional way with herbs for chronic diarrhea.

Church's health continued to decline until his death in February 1875 due to complications of diarrhea and tuberculosis.

He is buried in section B, row 1, of the St. Charles Riverside Cemetery in St. Charles. His headstone mistakenly reads "James Church."

Application #243,472 for a widow's pension was filed for Julia (husband's name is spelled "Chirch" instead of "Church") on April 4, 1879. The application was denied on the grounds that according to the War Department, Albert Church was deemed a deserter. He left Company M of the Eighth Michigan Cavalry Regiment without discharge, joined Company K of the First Michigan Sharpshooters, and deserted again.

Church was accused of signing up in both arms of the service under different names solely to obtain the fifty-dollar state bounty, given upon each enlistment, which was a violation of the fiftieth article of war.

Because Church deserted his cavalry unit and then joined the sharpshooters, he was considered in a constant state of desertion during the whole period of his enlistment in the sharpshooter regiment.

Julia's pension claim was rejected, reopened, and then abandoned for lack of further evidence from her and her attorney. Such a sad situation for a widow who needed a pension for monetary support for her and her children.

Julia Church died sometime after 1893.

Collins, Jacob, Private

Enlistment: Enlisted as a private on June 10, 1863, at East Saginaw, Saginaw County, by Lieutenant William J. Driggs, First Michigan Sharpshooters, for three years.

    Age: Thirty, born about 1833 in Saginaw County.

    Occupation: Farmer and hunter

    Residence: Isabella City (now Mt. Pleasant) Isabella County

    Physical Description: Five feet eight, dark eyes, dark hair, and a dark (or ruddy) complexion. Examining physician was Dr. George L. Cornell, assistant surgeon, First Michigan Sharpshooters.

    Mustered: June 16, 1863, at Detroit, Wayne County, by Lieutenant Colonel John R. Smith, US Army

    Military Service: On April 15, 1864, Collins was admitted to his regimental hospital with an undisclosed illness.

    During the Battle of the Crater before Petersburg, Virginia, on July 30, 1864, Private Collins sustained a severe gunshot (missile) wound in his upper left arm. The missile splintered the humerus (the bone in the upper arm above the elbow) and rendered the arm useless. He was taken immediately behind the lines to a division aid station where a tourniquet was used to stop the bleeding. The wound was washed and bandaged, and splints (to immobilize the arm) were applied (*Bollet*). A swallow of whiskey or an opium pill for pain was offered to Collins. He was then taken from the aid station by ambulance wagon and transported to his division hospital farther behind the lines.

    At the division hospital, powdered morphine may have been sprinkled into the wound (*Ibid.*). A fresh simple water dressing of lint rinsed in cold water, to help control bleeding and keep inflammation in check, was applied to the wound and held in place by a cloth wrap or adhesive plaster (*Schaadt*). A new splint was applied to his arm. He was given whiskey or an opium pill for pain.

    After treatment at the division hospital, Collins was then taken by ambulance wagon to the railroad where he was put on a mattress in a boxcar, the floor of which was cushioned with straw or hay, and transported to the USA Depot Field Hospital at City Point, Virginia.

At the depot hospital, fresh bandages and a replacement splint were applied to Jacob's arm, and he was given an opium pill or whiskey for pain. The doctors at City Point decided not to amputate Collins's arm but to continue the conservative treatment in the use of a splint (*Kuz and Bengston*).

On August 3, Collins was taken to a wharf at City Point, transferred to a hospital steamer, and taken to Campbell USA General Hospital in Washington, DC. At Campbell, the wound was again dressed with simple bandages, and another splint was applied, which allowed for drainage from the injury. The same treatment for pain was continued.

While he was a patient at Campbell Hospital, Collins was deemed unfit for transfer to the Veteran Reserve Corps. His wound was so severe that it left his arm useless. He was given a furlough on November 21, 1864, and readmitted to Campbell Hospital on January 21, 1865. He remained at Campbell until April 13, 1865.

Discharged: Private Jacob Collins was mustered out at Campbell Hospital and given a certificate of disability for an honorable discharge on April 13, 1865. He was paid the money owed to him for his service at his discharge and returned to Michigan.

Biography: Scant information is available about Jacob Collins except that he married a woman named Eliza. It is not known if the couple had a family. Collins was unable to find work because of total disability. Application #76,663 for an invalid pension was filed for Collins on July 10, 1865.

Jacob Collins died due to complications of his wound in the winter of 1867 or 1868 in Isabella County and was buried in an Anishinabek cemetery in said county. He may have been related to John and William Collins.

On May 30, 1870, Jacob's wife, Eliza, applied for a widow's pension under the same application number of her husband's claim. But before she could be notified of the status of her claim, Eliza died on June 30, 1875, in said county.

Collins, John, Private

Enlistment: Enlisted as a private on May 18, 1863, at Isabella City (now Mt. Pleasant), Isabella County, by Lieutenant William J. Driggs, First Michigan Sharpshooters, for three years.

Age: Twenty-one, born about 1842 in Saginaw, Saginaw County.

Occupation: Farmer

Residence: Isabella City

Physical Description: Five feet seven, black eyes, black hair, and a dark complexion. Examining physician was Dr. George L. Cornell, assistant surgeon, First Michigan Sharpshooters.

Mustered: May 26, 1863, at Detroit, Wayne County, by Lieutenant Colonel John R. Smith, US Army

Military Service: While the Michigan Sharpshooters were assigned to guard Confederate prisoners at Camp Douglas, Chicago, Cook County, Illinois, Private John Collins was granted a furlough from duty on July 12, 1863.

Sometime between September and October 1863, Collins lost his .58-caliber Springfield Rifle Musket and had his pay docked for replacement.

John was admitted to the USA Post Hospital at Camp Douglas on February 18, 1864, with the diagnosis of pneumonia. His treatment for pneumonia may have included blue pills of tartar emetic and calomel (or mercurous chloride that contains mercury) as purgatives to induce vomiting, and opiates to suppress coughing (*Bollet*). A sinapism (or mustard plaster) was placed on his chest and was thought to draw fluid away from the lungs and ease whatever caused the pain in the chest (*Internet*). Cupping and blistering were also used to promote the removal of fluid away from the lungs and into the skin. This method of treatment was called absorption (*Evans*). Private Collins was returned to duty on March 6.

On April 14, 1864, Collins was admitted to the Regimental Hospital of the First Michigan Sharpshooters in the field with intermittent fever (malaria) and diarrhea. He was given quinine made from powdered cinchona tree bark dissolved in whiskey or water, or pills of purified quinine sulfate for his fever. Whiskey worked better since it masked the bitter taste of quinine (*Ibid.-Bollet*).

For diarrhea, John was given an emetic (to induce vomiting) such as castor oil, astringent enemas of silver nitrate, oil of turpentine to control his bowels, and Dover's powder (a mixture of ipecac and opium) to induce perspiration (*Schaadt*). He was also given opium pills for pain.

His diet included boiled water, diluted coffee and tea, barley water, rice water, and broth made of meat extract. He returned to his regiment in June.

In June and July 1864, John was detailed as an attendant and took care of the sick and wounded in Armory Square Hospital in Washington, DC. During the months of September to November 1864, he was on detached service and assigned as an ambulance driver. From April to June 1865, Collins was again assigned as an ambulance driver, this time with the First Division Ambulance Corps.

Discharged: Private John Collins was mustered out and honorably discharged at Delaney House, Tenallytown, DC, on July 28, 1865. He returned to Detroit on the steamer *Morning Star*. On August 7, Collins was paid money owed to him for his service at Jackson, Jackson County.

Biography: There is no pension file for John Collins, who may have been the John Collins also known as Mawchechewon. His parents were Sawgawcheway and Theresa *(Avery)*. John married Tapesebequay, and the couple had one daughter, Mary Ann *(Ibid.)*. According to the Gruett Chippewa Index of 1868, John's siblings included a sister and two brothers, Henry and George *(Gruett)*. John may have been related to Jacob and William Collins, also of Company K.

A John Collins was known to have at least three allotments of land in Isabella County. These allotments were by reason of the first article of the treaty of August 2, 1855, and the second article of the treaty of October 18, 1864, with the Chippewas of Saginaw, Swan Creek, and Black River. Their descriptions are: (1) Southwest quarter of the northwest quarter of section 14 in township 14 north, of range 4 west, containing forty acres. The certificate was issued May 27, 1871 *(Land Records)*. (2) Southeast quarter of the southeast quarter of section 12 in township 15 north, of range 3 west containing forty acres. The certificate was issued on May 27, 1871 *(Ibid.)*. (3) East one half of the northeast quarter of section 23 in township 15 north, of range 4 west, containing eighty acres. The certificate was issued on May 27, 1871 *(Ibid.)*.

Collins, William, Corporal

Enlistment: Enlisted as a corporal on May 18, 1863, at Isabella City (now Mt. Pleasant), Isabella County, by Lieutenant William J. Driggs, First Michigan Sharpshooters, for three years.

Age: Thirty-three, born about 1830 in Lapeer County.

Occupation: Farmer

Residence: Isabella County

Physical Description: Five feet seven, dark eyes, black hair, and a dark complexion. Examining physician was Dr. George L. Cornell, assistant surgeon, First Michigan Sharpshooters.

Mustered: May 26, 1863, at Detroit Arsenal, Dearborn, Wayne County, by Lieutenant Colonel John R. Smith, US Army

Military Service: Corporal William Collins was detailed as a company cook during the month of September 1863. He was assigned to this task while on guard duty with his regiment at the confine for Confederate prisoners, Camp Douglas, in Chicago, Cook County. Illinois. He was also an interpreter for his superior officers during recruiting duties for Company K. William was reported to have deserted from his post at Camp Douglas while on furlough on October 22, 1863. Nothing more is known about this man's military service.

Discharged: No discharge given due to desertion in the line of duty.

Biography: William Collins was known to have been a cousin of John Andrew, a fellow soldier in Company K.

According to the Gruett Manuscript of 1868, William Collins's mother was Nepawnewawnoquay who died in 1865. His known siblings were Rebecca (Penaysewabanoquay) and Sawgawkeway, both of whom had died by 1868 (*Gruett*).

William and his first wife, whose name may have been Ternace, had a daughter, Eliza (or Natenegobequay?), who was born about 1858. After William's first wife died, he married for the second time to Theresa Sawgawchenay (*Ibid.*).

When William deserted to Canada (while on military furlough from Camp Douglas in October 1863), he took his daughter, Eliza, with him, leaving Sawgawchenay behind. Eliza was listed as living in Canada with her father in 1868. William may have been related to Jacob and John Collins of Company K.

William Collins is known to have had eighty acres of allotted land in Isabella County by reason of the first article of the treaty of August 2, 1855, and the second article of the treaty of October 18, 1864, with the Chippewas of Saginaw, Swan Creek, and Black River. The land description is the west half of the southwest quarter of section 23 in township 15, north, of range 4 west. The certificate was issued on May 27, 1871 (*Land Records*).

In January 1899, William Collins (who deserted in 1863) signed a deposition for his comrade, William Cabecoung, when Cabecoung applied for a pension. In the deposition, Collins listed his age as seventy-five and his post office address as Kawkawlin in Bay County. This court record attests to the fact that William Collins did return to Michigan from Canada after the end of the war.

There is a death certificate for a William Collins, who died of pneumonia caused by "la grippe" (or influenza), with the complication of old age, in Bangor Township of Bay County. His date of death is February 7, 1899. This William was described as an Indian basket maker, a widower, and aged seventy-five at the time of his death. According to the death certificate, the deceased was buried in the Indian Corner of Oak Ridge Cemetery of Bay City, Bay County. The death record is consistent with the information that is known about the Company K soldier.

There are two obituaries for this William Collins. One obit, from the *Bay City Tribune* of February 9, 1899, stated that Collins died at the home of friends in Monitor Township of said county (*Newspaper (1.)*).

The second obit, from the *Bay City Times Press* of February 9, 1899, stated that William Collins, who lived about a mile and a half north of Indiantown Church, died under the most distressing circumstances (*Newspaper (2.)*). It seems that he had been sick for about a week with influenza and no one had taken care of him before his death. An undertaker took charge of Collins's body and saw to his burial in said cemetery (*Ibid.*). There is a high probability that both obituaries are for the same William Collins of discussion. There is no pension file for William Collins.

Corbin, George, Corporal

Enlistment: Enlisted as a corporal May 18, 1863 (on his twenty-third birthday), at Isabella City (now Mt. Pleasant), Isabella County, by Lieutenant William J. Driggs, First Michigan Sharpshooters, for three years.

Age: Twenty-three, born May 18, 1840, in Saginaw County. His enlistment paper states twenty-seven as his age for a birth year of 1836.

Occupation: Farmer

Residence: Isabella County

Physical Description: Five feet seven, black eyes, black hair, and a dark complexion. Examining physician was Dr. George L. Cornell, assistant surgeon, First Michigan Sharpshooters.

Mustered: May 26, 1863, at Detroit, Wayne County, by Lieutenant Colonel John R. Smith, US Army

Military Service: In the fall of 1863, when his regiment was guarding Confederate prisoners at Camp Douglas at Chicago, Cook County, Illinois, Corporal Corbin suffered the loss of the sight of his left eye. He had contracted a severe cold, and due to complications, a corneal ulcer developed in that eye. In February 1864, Corbin was detailed as a company cook at the camp.

On April 15, Corbin was in the Regimental Hospital of the First Michigan Sharpshooters in the field with the complaint of intermittent (or malarial) fever. While in the hospital, quinine made from the powdered bark of the cinchona tree and mixed with water or whiskey (whiskey masked the bitterness of quinine), acetate of ammonia and spirit of niter (or potassium nitrate called saltpeter) were administered for his fever (*Evans*).

During the Battle of Spotsylvania on May 12, 1864, Corbin received a superficial gunshot (missile) wound to the right side of the chest, which resulted in severe contusions (or bruises). He was sent to his division first aid station and then to the division field hospital by ambulance wagon. At the field hospital, simple water dressings that consisted of folded lint dipped into water, placed on the wound area and held in place with a cloth wrap or adhesive bandage, were applied to his bruises (*Schaadt*). After his treatment, he returned to duty.

On June 11, 1864, while with his company at the James River, Virginia, Corbin was diagnosed with pneumonia and severe diarrhea at the regimental field hospital. During his stay at the hospital, Corbin's pneumonia was treated with "blue pills" that contained mercury, calomel (or mercurous chloride called blue mass), Dover's powder (ipecac and opium), a diaphoretic (to elicit perspiration), and a sedative (*Ibid.-Evans*). For his diarrhea, Corbin was given oil of turpentine, camphor (a diaphoretic), castor oil (a purgative), and opium pills for pain (*Ibid.-Evans*).

On June 27, George was taken by ambulance wagon to a military railroad where he was put on a mattress in a boxcar, the floor of which was cushioned with straw or hay, and sent to City Point wharf at City Point, Virginia. At the wharf, Corbin was transferred to a hospital steamer and taken to Mount Pleasant USA General Hospital in Washington, DC. At this hospital, the doctors applied liniment to Corbin's contusions. George's pneumonia was treated much the same as previously noted with the addition of a sinapism (mustard plaster) that was placed on his chest. The plaster was thought to draw fluid away from the lungs and eased whatever caused his pain (*Ibid.-Evans*).

For his severe diarrhea, Corbin was given an emetic (castor oil) to induce vomiting. His diet included boiled water, diluted coffee and tea, barley water, rice water, and broth made of meat extract. The aftereffects of the diarrhea and its medical treatments would plague him for the rest of his service and long after his discharge.

Corbin was sent from the General Hospital in DC to USA General Hospital at Broad and Cherry Streets in Philadelphia, Pennsylvania, still suffering with complications from the bruises received at the Battle of the Spotsylvania. The treatment given to him consisted of simple water dressings and liniment.

From the general hospital at Broad and Cherry Streets in Philadelphia, Corbin was put on a hospital steamer and taken to Summit House USA General Hospital in West Philadelphia, Pennsylvania. He was admitted to the hospital on July 2 where his bruises were again treated with applications of liniment and simple water dressings. Treatment was continued for the patient's diarrhea.

From Summit House, Corbin was sent to Satterlee USA General Hospital in West Philadelphia on August 24, suffering from continued complications of old bruise wounds and chronic diarrhea. He returned to duty on October 24, 1864.

On December 10, 1864, Corbin was admitted to Finley USA General Hospital in Washington, DC, complaining of chronic rheumatism, which caused severe swelling in his joints. The doctors administered opiates for pain and quinine and potassium iodide for their mild anti-inflammatory effect (*Bollet*). Warm baths and compresses were also used for their analgesic effect.

Corporal Corbin was given a furlough from the hospital for thirty days on January 3, 1865. He returned to the hospital on February 2 and received further treatment for his infirmities until he was returned to his regiment on April 30.

George returned to active duty on May 1, 1865, and was promptly promoted to sergeant on that date.

Discharged: Sergeant George Corbin was mustered out and honorably discharged at Delaney House, Tenallytown, DC, on July 28, 1865. He returned to Detroit on the steamer *Morning Star*. On August 7, George was paid money due to him for his service at Jackson, Jackson County.

Biography: George Corbin, also known as Puhquas and Wabmaygo, was the son of George (non-Anishinabe) and Betsey Petewanquot (which means "half cloud") Corbin Sr. (*Avery*).

George Jr. married his first wife, Sarah (who was also known as Kebayajewonoquay, Ogawbayquogewawnoquay, or Kanoushans) Williams, in Pinconning, Bay County, about 1855 or 1857. According to George, this marriage was by ceremony officiated by an Anishinabe minister. Another source (pension papers) stated that the marriage was by accepted Anishinabek custom and practice (the agreement of the couple and their parents). Sarah was the daughter of Ainnewawbe and Paysheminnequay.

Sarah and George were the parents of: Joseph, born 1857 and died of tuberculosis in 1903; John; Martha, born in 1862; and Thomas, who died of a kidney abscess in 1917. William, age six, and Mary, age four, are also listed as the couple's children in the 1868 Gruett Saginaw Chippewa Index (*Gruett*).

Eighty acres were allotted to Corbin in Isabella County by reason of the first article of the treaty of August 2, 1855, and the second article of the treaty of October 18, 1864, with the Chippewas of Saginaw, Swan Creek, and Black River. The acreage was located in the east half of the southeast quarter of section 30 in township 15 north, of range 4 west. A certificate was granted to him on May 27, 1871 (*Land Records*). An additional forty acres were allotted to Corbin in Isabella County by reason of said treaties and are described as the northeast quarter of the northeast quarter of section 14 in township 15 north, of range 5 west. A certificate was granted to Corbin on August 20, 1872 (*Ibid.*).

George was a very sick man when he returned home from the war and was treated with native medicinal herbs by the well-respected Jane (George) Chamberlain, who was an Anishinabequa medicine woman. She was the wife of Amos Chamberlain, who was George's Company K comrade.

It is reported that Sarah left George. She died about 1892.

George married for the second time to Margaret (Ogawbaygezhegoquay) Chamberlain in 1866 in Isabella County by Anishinabek custom and practice. Margaret's parents were Harvey and Jane (Bradley) Chamberlain. Margaret Corbin joined the First Methodist Episcopal Church, the Isabella Indian Mission, in 1877. George and Margaret had no children. After a period of time, Margaret left George. She is reported to have died around February 1, 1920.

George's health must have improved because he was working as a lumberjack (or shanty boy) in Sheridan of Clare County in 1880.

Corbin married for the third time to Mary Price about 1888 in the accepted Anishinabek custom and practice. The couple were the parents of a son, Louis. George and Mary stayed together until Mary died in 1895.

On March 8, 1888, Application #643,724 for an invalid pension was filed for George. He received an Invalid Pension Certificate #455,467 in November 1889. The pension paid fourteen dollars a month, retroactive from March 1888, for chronic diarrhea, rheumatism, and the loss of the sight in the left eye due to service-related causes. Corbin received his monthly payments until his death.

George, who sometimes attended Anishinabek Methodist churches, was aided in applying for his pension by Rev. Charles W. Campbell (also known as "Colonel"). Rev. Campbell was a Methodist minister of missions to the Anishinabe Bradley Chapel (at Delwin in Isabella County) and the North Branch Anishinabe Church.

The minister also helped other Anishinabek men of Company K with their applications for pensions.

The fourth marriage for George was to Eliza (Price) Paysheminnee (or Peshminee), a widow and sister to Mary Price, in 1897 by accepted Anishinabek custom and practice. Her father was James Payshenause. Eliza died of heart failure at age thirty-eight on October 14, 1899.

George married for the fifth and final time to Nancy Pashnee Shaw (daughter of William and Eliza Pashkeesweskum Pashnee), who had divorced John Shaw. George and Nancy first lived together, according to Anishinabek custom and practice, in 1900. On March 11, 1921, the couple was married in a Christian ceremony by Rev. L. L. Hanthorne of the First Methodist Episcopal Church. Witnesses to the ceremony were William Dempsey and Minnie Walker.

During his postwar years, George was an active member of the GAR Wa-bu-no Post #250 of Mt. Pleasant, and enjoyed visiting with his army buddies.

George Corbin died at the age of ninety-one on Sunday, May 20, 1928, at 2:00 p.m. at his home in Delwin in Denver Township, Isabella County. His burial place is uncertain, but he is known to have owned a plot in River Lawn Cemetery of Denver Township. During his last illness, Corbin was frequently visited by Rev. Campbell. The minister was also present to help the family after Corbin died.

Application #1,619,363 for a widow's pension was filed for Nancy Pashnee Corbin on July 19, 1928. She was considered by law to be George's legal wife and widow. But she was awarded only the accrued payment (in 1932) from George's pension up to the time of his death. Nancy was denied her widow's pension because George's death was attributed to arterial sclerosis and not to the ailments for which he was pensioned. She died November 14, 1938, in Isabella County.

Crane, Amos, Private

Enlistment: Enlisted as a private on August 24, 1864, at Jackson, Jackson County, by Captain R. J. Barry, provost marshal, for three years.

Private Crane was a substitute for Mackinaw Indian Agent DeWitt C. Leach, which satisfied the requirement for a man from the Third Congressional District, Thirty-Fifth Subdistrict, Fourth Ward of the city of Lansing, Ingham County. As the principal or enrolled draftee, Leach would have paid Crane about $300 to be his substitute. As a volunteer substitute, Crane was not entitled to an enlistment bounty because of the generous lump sum he received as a substitute. But as an enlisted substitute soldier, he was eligible (as were regular enlisted men) for a hundred-dollar bounty if he was discharged from the service by reason of wounds received in battle.

There were non-Anishinabek men who avoided the service by finding substitutes. Many of these men visited the Michigan reservations and areas with Anishinabek populations. They sought out the men and offered lump sums of money to them if they agreed to serve as substitutes. The Civil War era was a time in which most Anishinabek people were in need of monetary support to provide for their families. The offers of money were hard to refuse.

Age: Twenty-eight, born about 1836 in Baraga County.

Occupation: Hunter

Residence: L'Anse, Baraga County

Physical Description: Five feet nine, black eyes, black hair, and a dark complexion. Examining physician was Dr. H. B. Shank, surgeon of the Board of Enrollment of the Third District of Michigan.

Mustered: August 24, 1864, at Jackson by Captain R. J. Barry, provost marshal

Military Service: While deployed on the skirmish line during the siege of Petersburg, Virginia, in 1864, Amos was exposed to inclement weather conditions. He contracted a cold that settled in his lungs and caused a debilitating cough and pain in his chest. As his condition became worse, complications developed that compromised his immunity, and he contracted early pulmonary tuberculosis.

Instead of being admitted to a field hospital for his illness, Dr. Thomas Eagleson of the Sharpshooter Regiment treated Amos in camp. Crane was confined to his bed for complete rest and was given opiates for pain. There was no real treatment for tuberculosis until the 1950s when antibiotics were first used to treat the disease.

Due to his weakened condition, Amos was detailed in the Quartermaster Department in Washington, DC, during the later part of 1864.

In May 1865, Crane was assigned as a policeman from his unit to the provost guard in same city.

Discharged: Private Amos Crane was mustered out and honorably discharged near Delaney House, Tenallytown, DC, on July 28, 1865. He returned to Detroit on the steamer *Morning Star*. On August 7, Amos was paid money due to him for his service at Jackson, Jackson County.

Biography: Amos Crane's first marriage at the age of twenty-three was to a twenty-year-old woman named Heighday (or possibly Emeline) about the year

1857 or 1858 in L'Anse, Baraga County. Amos listed his birthplace as Wisconsin. The couple had a daughter named Caroline born in 1859. Nothing more is known of this marriage or of what happened to the mother and daughter.

Amos's second marriage was to Charlotte Madash (or Mawdosh) in 1867 in L'Anse. Rev. George Blaker, an Anishinabe Methodist minister, officiated at the ceremony. Rev. Blaker was a Methodist Church missionary pastor to the Kewawenon Anishinabek Mission. The mission was known later as Zeba United Methodist Indian Church Mission, located north of the village of L'Anse (*Reuter*).

In conversations with a researcher, and with material received from this person, the author learned the following information about the Noquet tribe and Charlotte Madash's ancestors (*Emory*).

It seems that Father Jacques Marquette (1637–1675) mentioned a small tribe of Algonquin Indians (about 150 people) who lived along the shore of Lake Superior, which today is the location of Marquette County in Michigan's Upper Peninsula. This tribe was known as the Noquet (*No'ke* or "bear foot") who migrated four times a year according to the seasons.

Two men of this Noquet tribe (Marje Gesick and Mudwayosh or Ma Dosh) were brothers, and both men were chiefs of their tribe at different times. Marje Gesick led miners to iron deposits, and Mudwayosh signed the Millard Fillmore treaty, which provided for reservations east of the Mississippi in 1853.

The Noquets freely mixed with the Chippewas at Keweenaw Bay in Houghton County, and Bay Mills and Sault St. Marie in Chippewa County, also located in the Upper Peninsula. Eventually, these bands absorbed most of the Noquets.

The Madash (Madosh) family is the only family who can easily be traced to the original Noquet tribe, who traditionally lived in the area as previously mentioned. Many descendants of these people are still living in Marquette County and are known as the last of the Noquets.

Today the word Noquet has been shortened to Noc and appears in the names of Big Bay de Noc and Little Bay de Noc in the Upper Peninsula.

Amos and Charlotte (Madash) Crane were the parents of ten children. Six of these children died before their father's death in 1891, including a known child, Mary, born in 1869 and died in 1870. The four remaining children were: Julia, born October 19, 1873, who married Dougal (also known as William) Shaw, the son of Louis and Marie Cameron Shaw, on March 13, 1893; Isaac Amos, born November 20, 1875, and died in February 1898; Hannah (or Anna), born January 27 or 29, 1877, and died of tuberculosis on November 25, 1896; and Lucy, born

March 23, 1889, and died of tuberculosis in January 1898. The actual death record states that Lucy died on December 13, 1906. Except for Julia, the three remaining Crane children died unmarried and without issue. Hannah (or Anna) and Isaac were known to have attended the Mt. Pleasant Indian School in Isabella County.

Dougal (or William) and Julia (Crane) Shaw were the parents of: Louis, born ca. 1894; Frances, born ca. 1901; and Sarah, born ca. 1903.

Amos Crane was allotted eighty acres of land under the September 30, 1854, treaty with the Chippewa Indians of Lake Superior (the L'Anse area) and the Mississippi. The land description is the south half of the southeast quarter of section 13 in township 51 north of range 32 west. Certificate #163 was issued to Amos on July 19, 1875 (*Land Records*).

On June 21, 1886, Application #613,733 for an invalid pension was filed for Amos. He reapplied for his pension under the liberal Act of 1890 and received an Invalid Pension Certificate #879,592.

Shortly after he received his pension certificate, Amos died of tuberculosis on April 13, 1891. He did not leave a will at his death.

Amos Crane is buried in the Anishinabek Pinery Cemetery (the Methodist Episcopal Mission Cemetery) located between L'Anse and Zeba in Baraga County. Amos's son, Isaac Amos, and Amos's army buddy and good friend, John Benashins (Beneshia) Bird, are also buried in the Pinery Cemetery.

Charlotte's Application #521,987 for a widow's pension was filed for her on August 5, 1891. She received Widow's Pension Certificate #357,756 on November 21, 1892, retroactive to August 5, 1891, for support for her children, in which she was to receive fourteen dollars a month.

Before she received her widow's pension certificate in 1892, Charlotte Crane married for the second time to Joseph Halfaday in L'Anse on November 19 of said year. The ceremony was officiated by Rev. Fergus O. Jones, a Methodist Episcopal minister.

Since Charlotte had remarried and had a husband to support her and her children, her widow's pension was nullified from the date of her remarriage to Halfaday. She had only received one payment of twelve dollars to the time of her remarriage.

On February 27, 1893, a William Owen was granted guardianship of Hannah and Lucy in order to obtain benefits due them as minor children (under the age of sixteen) from a pension for minor children. Application #571,551 was filed for Owen on March 7, 1894.

A Pension for Minor Children's Certificate #399,158 was issued, and payments of twelve dollars a month for each girl commenced in 1895.

Since Julia Crane married Dougal Shaw, and Hannah (Crane) Halfaday died of tuberculosis on November 25, 1896, Lucy was the only child to receive continued benefits since she was still under the age of sixteen at her father's death. Payments were received by William Owen for Lucy's support until March 22, 1905, when she attained the age of sixteen. Lucy died of tuberculosis on December 13, 1906.

Court records relate how Amos's heirship estate was distributed to his wife, Charlotte, and to his surviving heirs from the date of the hearing on February 17, 1915 (*Lafernier*).

Charlotte (Crane) Halfaday died at age seventy-nine of bronchial pneumonia on April 23, 1930, in Baraga County and is buried in said county. Her daughter, Julia, predeceased her on January 17, 1928, at the age of fifty-five in L'Anse Village.

Enlisted Men—Letters D and E

Dabasequam, Jonah, Private

Enlistment: Enlisted as a private on June 24, 1863, at Little Traverse (now Harbor Springs), Emmett County, by Second Lieutenant Garrett A. Graveraet, First Michigan Sharpshooters, for three years.

Age: Twenty, born about 1843 in Charlevoix (at that time in Emmet County).

Occupation: Farmer

Residence: Little Traverse

Physical Description: Five feet ten, black eyes, black hair, and a dark complexion. Examining physician was Dr. Arvin F. Whelan, surgeon, First Michigan Sharpshooters.

Mustered: July 20, 1863, at Detroit, Wayne County, by Lieutenant Colonel John R. Smith, US Army

Military Service: Private Jonah Dabasquam was killed in action during the Battle of Spotsylvania, Virginia, on May 12, 1864. If his body were found and identified on the field held by Union troops, it would have been buried near the battle site. Jonah's body would have been left in its uniform or wrapped in a blanket, buried without ceremony in a pine box (if available), and put into a single grave or in a trench with other dead soldiers (*Encyclopedia*). Soil would have been placed over Jonah's body, and a board with information as to his name and unit placed at the head of his grave site. Headboards were easily lost due to weathering and theft and would result in the remains being "unknown" when disinterred (*Ibid.*).

Since there is no information as to Jonah's final resting place, it can be assumed that he may have been buried with indifference in rebel-held ground or later reburied as an unknown Union soldier in Fredericksburg, Virginia, National Cemetery (*Guide*). His family mourned his death and his burial so far away from the soil in which his ancestors were laid.

Discharged: No discharge given. Killed in action.

Biography: Jonah Dabasequam (also known as Kemwanashkam), who did not marry, was the son of John Dabasequam (also known as John Kemwanashkam) and his wife, Nockenoqua? There is confusion and disagreement as to the true spelling of the family's surname.

John married Jonah's mother, who died in the summer of 1856 or 1857, at Old Mission according to Anishinabek custom and practice (with the consent of the couple and their parents). Old Mission was established by Presbyterian minister Rev. Peter Dougherty in the spring of 1839 (*Craker*).

Jonah, while in the service, was the sole support for his family and sent most of his pay home.

After Jonah's death, John Dabasequam was employed for ten years by John Denahy, who was a friend and neighbor of the family. Denahy considered John a good worker who earned an honest day's wages. As he became weak and feeble with age, he could no longer work. Due to his situation, John was given money from the poor funds of the county for his support.

While he was living in Kewadin in Antrim County, Application #341,004 for a dependent father's pension was filed for John on June 18, 1886. He was referred to as John Labasquam on his application papers. Since he could no longer work to support himself and had no property to farm, John needed all the help that he could get. His one surviving son was unable to help him.

Having received no further evidence needed from John, nor from his lawyer, to process the claim for John's pension between 1892 and 1895, the application was abandoned by the US Pension Office.

David, John, Private

Enlistment: Enlisted as a private on May 19, 1863, at East Saginaw, Saginaw County, by Lieutenant William J. Driggs, First Michigan Sharpshooters, for three years.

Age: Twenty-one, born about 1842 in Saginaw County.

Occupation: Hunter and laborer

Residence: Isabella City (now Mt. Pleasant), Isabella County

Physical Description: Five feet seven, black eyes, black hair, and a dark complexion. Examining physician was Dr. George L. Cornell, assistant surgeon, First Michigan Sharpshooters.

Mustered: May 26, 1863, at Detroit, Wayne County, by Lieutenant Colonel John R. Smith, US Army

Military Service: In August 1863, when he was on guard duty for Confederate prisoners with his regiment at Camp Douglas in Chicago, Cook County, Illinois, Private David was reported to have deserted his post.

He was arrested, returned to duty by Colonel Charles V. DeLand, and fined $16.88 from his pay for his arrest. Sometime after he deserted his post, he lost his .58-caliber Springfield Rifle Musket. Upon his return to his regiment, his wages were docked for its replacement.

Private David was admitted from his regiment to Division No. 1, USA General Hospital at the United States Naval Academy (Navy Yard) in Annapolis, Maryland, on April 22, 1864 with the diagnosis of typhoid fever. Typhoid is an intestinal infection spread by ingesting water or food contaminated with the bacteria *Salmonella typhosa (Blakiston).* Symptoms of typhoid fever include a continuous rising fever, fatigue, headache, a rose-colored rash on the chest and abdomen, mental depression, and occasional bloody stools.

David's treatment of typhoid fever included most of the following medicines and procedures: tartar emetic to evacuate the stomach and rid the body of irritating substances (*Evans*); castor oil to provoke bowel movements and cleanse the colon (*Ibid.*); Dover's powder, a diaphoretic (to induce perspiration) and sedative powder that contained ipecac and opium (*Ibid.*); calomel (mercurous chloride), a purgative that contained mercury (*Schaadt*); oil of turpentine given orally or by enema (*Ibid.*); quinine and opium given to reduce fever (*Ibid.*); applications of cloths dipped into cold water, and sponge baths with cold water or water and alcohol were also used to reduce fever (*Ibid.*).

Bed rest, isolation, avoidance of extreme environmental temperatures, and liquid or bland diets were ordered for the patient.

Private John David died on May 4, 1864. The items that he left at his death were one pair of trousers and one pair of shoes.

Since he had died in a general hospital, John was given a more proper burial, which included a coffin, religious services, a military escort from the hospital to the cemetery, military protocol that included the firing of arms, and an individual headboard with information about him and his unit. He was buried in grave #618 in Ash Grove US Cemetery near the hospital (*Encyclopedia*).

On May 6, 1864, Private David's remains were removed from Ash Grove and reburied in the Annapolis National Cemetery at Annapolis, Maryland. His military stone is #1078 in section K and reads "Jno. Davis." He may or may not have had the same burial protocol as was previously accorded him.

Discharged: No discharge given due to death by disease while in the hospital.

Biography: John David, also known as Taybawsegay (or Tabaseka), was the son of Shawnekesshig (the correct spelling of the father's name), also known as Aishdawnawquot (which means "cloud crossing"), and his first wife, Mary Howdedo (*Avery*). The couple was married in 1832. When John's mother died, about 1861, his father remarried and had children with his second wife.

John, who never married, was his father's and step family's sole support, and they were totally dependent upon him.

After his son's death, Shawnekesshig was destitute, with no other monetary means of support for him and his second family. He supplied food for his family by hunting and fishing. Only three acres of land (half-cleared and half-wooded) were in Shawnekesshig's possession.

Application #381,855 for a dependent father's pension was filed for Shawnekesshig on October 4, 1888. He died in July 1893 in Quanicassee, Tuscola County.

Shortly after Shawnekesshig's death, his second wife remarried. John's father's pension application was denied on July 10, 1894, due to the occurrence of his father's death before his claim was referred for special examination.

John's stepmother was not entitled to receive the claim (dependent mother's pension) upon her first husband's death because she was not John's birth mother.

Dutton, Luther, Private

Enlistment: Enlisted as a private on June 2, 1863, at East Saginaw, Saginaw County, by Lieutenant William J. Driggs, First Michigan Sharpshooters, for three years.

Age: Nineteen, born about 1844 in Saginaw County.

Occupation: Farmer and hunter

Residence: Taymouth Township, Saginaw County

Physical Description: Five feet nine, black eyes, black hair, and a ruddy complexion. Examining physician was Dr. George L. Cornell, assistant surgeon, First Michigan Sharpshooters.

Mustered: June 16, 1863, at Detroit, Wayne County, by Lieutenant Colonel John R. Smith, US Army

Military Service: Private Dutton is reported to have deserted his regiment at the Dearborn Arsenal, Wayne County, on July 19, 1863. He was arrested in Genessee, Genessee County, on September 8, 1863, and was returned to Camp Douglas, Chicago, Cook County, Illinois, where his regiment was guarding Confederate prisoners.

Dutton was restored to duty by Colonel Charles V. DeLand on September 14, 1863, and his pay was docked seventeen dollars for the expense of his arrest.

During a battle before Petersburg, Virginia, on June 17, 1864, Private Dutton sustained a gunshot wound (flesh wound) in the anterior portion of his right thigh. The missile entered three inches above his right knee, and in its transit it badly damaged the muscles of the thigh. Fortunately, the missile missed striking the femur (or thigh bone).

Dutton was taken by stretcher to an aid station where his wound was washed and any bleeding was stopped. A cold water dressing was applied to his wound. Cold water dressings were composed of lint rinsed in cold water, placed on the wound, and held in place by a cloth wrap or adhesive plaster (*Schaadt*). He was given whiskey or an opium pill for pain.

The soldier was then taken by ambulance wagon to his division hospital farther behind the lines where similar treatment was given to him, including the application of bromine to the wound to impede infection.

On June 18, Dutton was taken by ambulance wagon to the military railroad. He was laid on a mattress in a boxcar, the floor of which was cushioned with straw or hay, and sent to the Depot Hospital at City Point, Virginia. At the hospital, applications of bromine to the wound and cold water dressings were continued as treatment. Dutton was also offered opium pills for pain.

On June 19, Dutton was taken to a wharf at City Point, transferred to the hospital steamship *Connecticut*, and taken to Annapolis, Maryland.

He was admitted to Division 1, USA General Hospital at the United States Naval Academy (Navy Yard) in Annapolis, Maryland, on June 20 where bromine and cold water dressings were again applied to his wound. In addition to his injury, Dutton suffered from a severe cold contracted from exposure while in the trenches before Petersburg.

Private Dutton was given a twenty-five-day furlough from the hospital on August 2.

On September 1, 1864, he was ordered to report to Major L. J. Barry, who was in command of the Detroit Barracks in Michigan. After further examination,

Dutton was authorized to be sent back to Annapolis, to rejoin his regiment, but the order was canceled.

Instead of returning to Annapolis, Dutton, who still suffered from his wound, was admitted to USA Post Hospital, Detroit Barracks, on September 2, 1864. He remained in the Post Hospital until February 25, 1865, when he was transferred to St. Mary's USA General Hospital in said city.

Dutton remained at St. Mary's Hospital until his discharge. The doctors determined that he was permanently disabled from his wound and was suffering from the early stages of tuberculosis.

Discharged: Private Luther Dutton was mustered out and honorably discharged from St. Mary's General Hospital in Detroit on May 11, 1865, on special order (discharge for disability) of the War Department of May 2, 1865. He was paid the money owed to him for his service at his discharge and returned home.

Biography: Luther Dutton, also known as Luke Dutton, Isidor Abendunk, and Chittimon, was the son of Rev. Thomas (or Sawgawchewayosay) and Lucy (or Mawdewaygewawnoquay) Dutton. Rev. Dutton was a local Methodist minister associated with the Taymouth Indian Methodist Mission in Saginaw County (*Reuter*).

Rev. Dutton was also an Ojibwa (or Chippewa) chief of the Swan Creek and Black River Bands.

The minister was allotted eighty-five and twelve-hundredths acres in Isabella County by reason of the treaty with the Chippewa of Saginaw, Swan Creek, and Black River in the provision of the first article of the treaty of August 2, 1855, and the second article of the treaty of October 18, 1864. Rev. Dutton was one of the signers of that treaty before his death in 1864. The land description is the east half of the northwest quarter of section 2, in township 15 north, of range 3 west. The certificate was signed on May 27, 1871. Since Rev. Dutton was deceased by then, his heirs inherited his property.

The minister was also one of the chiefs who signed the 1864 Treaty that concerned the Chippewa of Saginaw, Swan Creek, and Black River in regards to several townships of land on Saginaw Bay that were released to the state.

Luke's siblings were: Sarah (who married William Moses); a brother Naywawdaykezhick (or Thomas), who died in 1864 at age nineteen; Susan; Edwin; Mawnedogezhick (or Franklin), who died at age fifteen on June 30, 1872; and Nawwawgewawnoquay, a half sister, who married Kawtegaykoonse. Nawwawgewawnoquay was the daughter of Rev. Dutton and a previous wife known as Ogawdwaydawgewawnoquay (*Gruett*).

Luke married Charlotte (or Oshawgaw) Wabegemos (which means "little white chief") in the spring of 1862 in Taymouth Township of Saginaw County by traditional Anishinabek custom and practice (with consent of the couple and their parents) (*Avery*). Charlotte was the daughter of Moses Wawbegemos and Wawwawbawnoquay (*Ibid.*). The couple had two children: Lucy, born in 1865, and Thomas, born in 1867.

On May 22, 1865, Luke Dutton submitted a declaration for the purpose of obtaining the seventy-five dollars due in bounty money, arrears of pay, and other sums of money due to him for his service. It's not certain whether he was paid the money owed to him.

Luke Dutton had forty acres of allotted land in Isabella County by reason of the first article of the treaty of August 2, 1855, and the second article of the treaty of October 18, 1864, with the Chippewas of Saginaw, Swan Creek, and Black River. The land description is the southwest quarter of the southwest quarter of section 4 in township 15 north, of range 5 west. The certificate was issued on August 20, 1872 (*Land Records*).

Application #154,054 for an invalid pension was filed for Luke on March 22, 1870. He did not see its approval due to his death in June 1870 while living on his father's farm in Taymouth Township. After he died, Luke's certificate for his allotted land was passed on to his heirs.

Luke Dutton's demise at the young age of twenty-five/twenty-six was due to tuberculosis and complications of his war wound. After his funeral, Luke was buried in the Wheaton Chippewa Indian Cemetery in Taymouth Township. His father is also buried in the same cemetery. Charlotte (as a widow) was listed by the name of Elizabeth on the 1870 federal census.

Application #193,145 for a widow's pension was filed for Charlotte on January 19, 1871. She received pension #952,031 for eight dollars a month, and two dollars a month for each of her two children before her second marriage.

Charlotte's second marriage was to Stephen Kawgayawshe (or Stephen James) in 1884 in Mt. Pleasant, Isabella County. The marriage was officiated by Stephen Hart, justice of the peace. The couple had one child, Bessie, who married Charlie Chamberlain. Stephen James died on May 12, 1912, when the couple was living in Ogemaw County.

When Charlotte remarried, she was considered by the government as not eligible to receive widow's benefits from her first husband's service. Her second husband was expected to support her.

After Stephen's death, Charlotte was again eligible to reapply as the lawful widow of Luther Dutton and receive her widow's pension. Application #193,145 for a remarried widow's pension was refiled for Charlotte (age eighty) on March 22, 1923, when she was living in Isabella County.

A Remarried Widow's Pension Certificate #952,031 was granted to Charlotte sometime in 1924, in which she was awarded about twelve dollars a month until her death.

Etarwegeshig, John, Private

Enlistment: Enlisted as a private on July 5, 1863, at Pentwater, Oceana County, by Lieutenant Edwin V. Andress, First Michigan Sharpshooters, for three years.

Age: Twenty-six, born about 1837 in Kent County.

Occupation: Laborer

Residence: Pentwater

Physical Description: Five feet nine, black eyes, black hair, and a dark complexion. Examining physician was Dr. Jacob B. McNett, assistant surgeon, First Michigan Sharpshooters.

Mustered: July 11, 1863, at Detroit, Wayne County, by Lieutenant Colonel John R. Smith, US Army

Military Service: In late September 1863, Private John Etarwegeshig was reported to have deserted from his guard post at the confine for Confederate prisoners, Camp Douglas, in Chicago, Cook County, Illinois. He was arrested on October 4 and returned to his regiment. An undisclosed amount of money was withheld from his pay to cover the expenses for his arrest.

John wrote several letters to his mother while he was a guard at Camp Douglas and sent money to her. Two of those letters (found in the pension papers) were in English as follows:

Letter #1

Camp Douglas
Chicago, Illinois
October 2, 1863

Dear Mother,

I write you a few lines this time. Dear Mother enclose please find money $45.00 I desire you to use $5.00 only and spend it as you may think best and keep forty dollars until such time as I may return so that I may use it as I may think but what I have been paid I have spent it all. I advised my brother to send his money along with mine and he gave me no answer. If he had we would have been able to send you sixty dollars. This is all I have to say at present. I have not been very well for a long time. My desire has been this for a long time to go and see you all. This is all I have to say. Answer soon.

I am John Wa me gwon

Letter #2

February 24, 1864
Camp Douglas Chicago, Illinois

Paw co te go quay

I write you this present time. Some time ago I presumed to send you a little money. I am sorry to say I have not got the money at present. I thought to borrow a little money for you and did get a little for you. This I can return as soon as I get paid for my services here. I think in a little while we shall get paid and then I can return it. I did not intend at this time to write to you fully what I might have done and in my next I will be able to say particularly about my circumstances. The money I am now sending you it may probably not be good money. If so return it to me at once. I am glad to inform you that my health is about half good. My comrade has been sick. This is all. In regard to Uncle's likeness, send it to me, without fail. This I think will cost about one dollar and in return I will send mine.

Nin Wa me gon

On May 12, 1864, Private Etarwegeshig was killed in action during the Battle of Spotsylvania, Virginia. His death was due to wounds to his shoulder and body caused by missile balls.

There is no record of where John is buried. Since the Battle of Spotsylvania was a tactical draw between the Union and the Confederate forces, John's body could have been found and buried by the rebels in what territory those forces held at the end of the battle. If that were the case, John was probably buried, without much care or respect, with other dead Union soldiers in a trench or a shallow grave and considered unknown (*Encyclopedia*).

If John fell in Union-held territory by the end of the battle, he would have been buried without ceremony. His body was either left in his uniform or wrapped in a blanket, possibly put into a coffin, if one was available, and laid in an individual grave or in a common grave with other deceased Union soldiers. If he were known, a board with John's name and unit would have been placed at the head of his burial site (*Ibid.*).

Identification boards placed at burial sites were often stolen for firewood or weathered so badly that any markings would disappear before the bodies could be transferred to national cemeteries. It's possible that John's body was disinterred from the battlefield, moved to Fredericksburg National Cemetery, and reburied along with other unknown Union soldiers (*Guide*). In any case, John's family mourned his death and knew that he would have preferred to have been buried in the land of his ancestors and not in strange soil.

Discharged: No discharge given. Killed in action.

Biography: John Etarwegeshig, also known as John Wamegwon, was one of six children born to Reechee (?) and Pawcotegoquay (also spelled Pohketogoquay, Pahtegoquah, and Pahtegoquay) Etarwegeshig. "Etarwegeshig" translates to English as "light at both ends of the day" or a "dawn to dusk day" as mentioned in his pension papers.

Reechee deserted his wife in 1849 and remarried in the traditional Anishinabek custom and practice (with consent of the couple and their parents) to another woman. Desertion and separation were considered as a divorce in traditional Anishinabek social mores. He died in the spring of 1862 and was buried on the Anishinabek reservation near Little Traverse (now Harbor Springs) in Emmet County.

John's mother married for the second time, by Anishinabek custom and practice, to James Tahyawquawgon (Taquahgwon means "Black Partridge") in April 1849. The marriage took place in Ada Township of Montcalm County.

James had eighty acres of wild unimproved land when he married Pawcotegoquay. But when he died of tuberculosis in August 1864, that land passed to his heirs from his first marriage and not to Pawcotegoquah and her children.

Before his enlistment, John worked by the month as a laborer in Pentwater and hunted and fished to provide for his family. He had provisions and groceries delivered to his mother by shopkeeper/grocer Harvey Sayles and promised to pay for the provisions when he returned home from Pentwater for visits. He honored his promise.

Being the dutiful and attentive son that he was, John bought a pair of buckskin shoes for his mother and made arrangements with Harvey Sayles to continue to supply provisions and groceries to his family after his enlistment. He seemed to be very close to his mother as noted in the content of his letters that he sent to her from the army.

John did not marry. His surviving half siblings, one brother and two sisters, who were under sixteen at the time of his death were: Notenisquom, age fourteen, born about 1850; Nahtahwegeshig, age twelve, born about 1852; and Wahwatchchenodin, age ten, born about 1854.

According to the time scale of the first and second marriages, and the birthdates given by Pawcotegoquah of the three youngest siblings, the father of these children was most likely her second husband, Jim Taquahgwon (or Tahyawquawquon).

Because she had personal property that only amounted to about $300 and no means of support, Application #173,481 for a dependent mother's pension was filed for Pawcotegoquah Etarwegeshig on March 29, 1869. The application was filed under the Act of July 14, 1862.

After much red tape and complaints from Indian Agent George Lee about the lack of care or attention given to the widow's request for a pension, Pahtegoquah finally received her Dependent Mother's Pension Certificate #178,297 on July 30, 1877 *(Lee)*. The pension was retroactive to March 18, 1875 (date that the claim was completed) and paid eight dollars a month until her death. To make ends meet, Pahtegoquah made and sold baskets to earn additional money.

She applied for an arrears of a mother's pension—the money due to her from the date of her son's death on May 12, 1864. By right she was to receive eight dollars a month in arrears retroactive from 1864 up until March 17, 1875, when the payments would be terminated. It's not certain whether she received these payments before her death.

Pawcotegoquah died at her residence near Hart, Oceana County, sometime between the end of 1877 and March 15, 1880. She was buried in said county.

Enlisted Men—Letters G, H, I, and J

Genereau Jr., Louis, Sergeant

Enlistment: Enlisted as a sergeant on July 4, 1863, at Elbridge, Oceana County, by Captain Edwin V. Andress, First Michigan Sharpshooters, for three years.

Age: Eighteen, born about 1845 in Hastings, Barry County.

Occupation: Farmer

Residence: Pentwater, Oceana County

Physical Description: Five feet six, black eyes, black hair, and a dark complexion. Examining physician was Dr. Jacob B. McNett, assistant surgeon, First Michigan Sharpshooters.

Mustered: July 11, 1863, at Detroit, Wayne County, by Lieutenant Colonel John R. Smith, US Army

Military Service: From August to October 1863, Sergeant Genereau was on sick furlough from his guard duty at the confine for Confederate prisoners, Camp Douglas, Chicago, Cook County, Illinois.

Genereau was admitted to Division No. 1, USA General Hospital at the United States Naval Academy (Navy Yard) in Annapolis, Maryland, on April 2, 1864 with the diagnosis of a light case of erysipelas of the face. Erysipelas is a severe skin infection due to the bacterium *Streptococcus pyogenes*, which causes a bright red rash on the body (*Blakiston*). His face was treated with an application of yeast poultices made from flaxseed or bread that applied heat and moisture to the affected area (*Bollet*). Castor oil was administered to him as a cathartic (or purgative), and opium pills were given for pain (*Evans*). Louis's condition greatly improved, and he was returned to duty on April 14.

On May 12, 1864, while engaged in the Battle of Spotsylvania, Virginia, Genereau sustained a gunshot wound to his lower left leg. The missile struck his leg just above the ankle and fractured the lower third of the fibula and the tibia called the "shin bone."

Louis was taken by ambulance wagon to the first aid station to have any bleeding stopped. A simple cold water dressing (lint soaked in cold water) was applied to his wounds and held in place with a cloth wrap or adhesive plaster (*Schaadt*). He was then taken to his division hospital farther behind the lines. The doctors anesthetized Louis with chloroform and removed two pieces of bone from the wound. They also eased Genereau's pain by placing powdered morphine into his wound and giving him opium pills. Bromine may have been applied to the wound to impede infection, and cold water dressings were used to cover the wound. Whiskey was administered as a tonic. Genereau's injured limb was then placed into a fracture box to keep it immobile (*Kuz and Bengtson*).

Louis's injury caused partial ankylosis (the stiffness or fixation of a joint) due to postoperative adhesions that occur when the injured portions of the bones fuse together. For the rest of his short life, Louis was somewhat lame in the left leg and needed the use of a cane for walking.

On May 25, Sgt. Genereau was transported by ambulance wagon from the division hospital to a wharf at Belle Plain Landing (situated on the Potomac Creek), Virginia. From the landing he was sent by hospital steamer to Washington, DC.

On May 26, he was admitted to Lincoln USA General Hospital in Washington. Water dressings and the use of a fracture box were continued as treatment for the soldier. Genereau was given a furlough of three months on June 22.

While on a furlough home to rest from his injuries, and having recently acquired a constant cough, Louis Genereau Jr., age twenty, married Louisa (or Lucy) Maria Duvernay/Duverney, age sixteen/seventeen. The couple were married on August 14, 1864, at Pere Marquette, Mason County, in a ceremony officiated by Rev. V. G. Boynton, a Methodist minister. A. A. Darling and Rev. Isaac Greensky (transcript of marriage named Rev. Peter Greensky) were witnesses to the ceremony.

Louisa, who was born September 1, 1847, in Grand Haven of Ottawa County, was the daughter of Charles, a native of Wisconsin and a sailor on the Great Lakes, and Eliza Lawrence Duvernay.

By his marriage to Louisa, Louis Jr. became a brother-in-law to William Duvernay and William's half brother, John Kedgnal.

After the war, John Kedgenal changed his name to John Henry Duvernay. These two men, members of Company B of the Michigan Sharpshooters, were the only other Anishinabek men in the sharpshooter regiment.

Louis Jr. returned from his furlough and was readmitted to Lincoln General Hospital on September 21, 1864. On September 28, Genereau left Lincoln General and was sent by hospital steamer to Satterlee General Hospital in West Philadelphia, Pennsylvania, where he was admitted on September 29.

While wrestling around with his comrades, Louis Jr. sustained an injury to his chest and right side in October 1864. He was treated with poultices that were applied to his chest and side.

Louis Jr. was again granted a furlough on November 4 and was readmitted to Satterlee Hospital on November 24 for further treatment. He was reported "absent without leave" on November 28 but returned to Satterlee on December 15. Genereau was released from the hospital and returned to his regiment at Petersburg on December 17.

On March 1 or 7, 1865, Sergeant Louis Genereau Jr. was reduced in rank from sergeant to private for an unspecified reason. Private Thomas Smith of Company K was promoted to sergeant in place of Genereau.

There is an oral story passed down through the Anishinabek generations living in Elbridge about the capture of Louis Genereau Jr. during the Civil War. The original printed version of this story appeared in the 1978 publication *The Tree That Never Dies,* edited by Pamela Dobson (*Oral History*). The story appears on page 29 and relates that Louis was captured and held by the rebels for a short time and then escaped to return to his regiment and tell of his ordeal. Since this account of capture and escape is about the Union attack on the salient at the battle at Petersburg on June 17, 1864, then the author has a problem with its authenticity. Louis's medical and military records list him as being a patient (due to his severe injury at the battle of Spotsylvania) in Lincoln General Hospital in Washington, DC, from May 26, 1864, to his furlough given at the hospital on June 22, 1864. Even though there is no mention of Louis's capture and escape, either by Louis, his comrades, or in Louis's pension papers, the rendition in Dobson's book is still a good story.

Discharged: Private Louis Genereau Jr. was mustered out and received an honorable discharge at Delaney House, Georgetown, DC, on July 28, 1865. He returned to Detroit on the steamer *Morning Star.* Louis was paid money owed to him for his service on August 7 at Jackson, Jackson County.

Biography: Louis Genereau Jr. (whose French surname means "generous or giving") was a son of Louis and Mary Ann (sometimes called Lucy) Genereau Sr. The family name was also spelled Genereaux and Genro. Louis Sr. was a noted Anishinabe of his band. Mary Ann's father was Black Cloud.

Louis Jr. was baptized on January 1, 1856, in the Methodist Episcopal

Church at the Oceana Indian Mission (near Hart and Pentwater), Oceana County. His siblings were William and Charles.

Louis Genereau Sr. was half Anishinabe and was a powerfully built man for his height of five feet seven and a half inches. He was known for his athletic wrestling ability. For many years, he was a United States interpreter for Indian Affairs and was well respected for his work between the Anishinabek and the US government. He had a trading post on the Grand River not far from Ionia in Ionia County. Louis Sr. was not a bad man, but he had a fondness for liquor and struck fear in others when he was in an inebriated condition.

In the spring of 1840, while in a drunken rage, Louis Sr. held H. B. Brownell, the father-in-law of Deacon Edwin Mason of Richland, in a fire until he died. On May 25 of that year, Louis Sr. was convicted of second-degree murder in the death of Brownell and sentenced to a term of ten years in the Jackson, Michigan, state prison (*Jackson*). While in prison, he learned the shoemaker trade (*Michigan Pioneer*).

After his pardon from the state prison on August 15, 1841, Louis Sr. went to Gull Prairie (now Richland) in Kalamazoo County. It was there that Rev. Leonard Slater, a Baptist missionary, wanted to help Genereau and personally built a fully outfitted cobbler shop for him (*Ibid.*). But Louis Sr. only worked at his trade in fits and starts, and in a short time he left his shop and rejoined his band (*Ibid.*).

By 1863, Genereau Sr. owned a farm in Elbridge, Oceana County, in the Elliott neighborhood and was instrumental in recruiting Anishinabek men for Company K of the Sharpshooter Regiment in July of that year.

In his early years, Louis Sr. was a staunch Methodist Episcopalian. In his later years, he embraced Catholicism (*Genereau Family*). Louis Genereau Sr. died of heart disease on January 17, 1881 (*Ibid.*).

After his discharge from the service, Louis Jr. returned to Michigan, his health taking a turn for the worse. He complained of pain in his kidneys and stomach, was partially disabled due to the wound in his left leg, and often bled from the lungs (a symptom of tuberculosis). He also complained of pain in his chest due to his injury in October 1864.

Being a dutiful son, Louis did what work he could, which was mostly helping his father raise corn and potatoes on the Genereau Sr. farm. But his ability to work grew less and less in the years after his service due to his declining health. He moved around with the aid of both a cane and crutches.

Louis Jr. sought medical help from his father-in-law, Charles Duvernay, an Anishinabe doctor who treated him in the Anishinabek traditional way with poultices and medicinal herbs. He was also treated in the nontraditional manner by a Dr. Shedrick of Hart.

Louisa and Louis Jr. were the parents of three children, who were baptized in the rite of the Methodist Episcopal Church at Elbridge. They were: Alice, born May 15, 1866, and died August 1868; Valena (or Evelina), born April 28, 1867, and died at nine months of age; and Levi, born July 10, 1868. Levi lived to adulthood and married Sarah Wawsaykezhick, the daughter of James and (?) Wawsaykezhick on April 2, 1889.

Application #103,131 for an invalid pension was filed for Louis Jr. on February 20, 1866. He received an Invalid Pension Certificate #72,070 for the gunshot (missile) wound to his left leg on September 26, 1866.

After being confined to his bed (in his father's home) for three months, Louis Genereau Jr., age twenty-six, surrounded by his loving wife and family and attended by Dr. B. McPherson, died of tuberculosis (caused by the tubercle bacillus *Mycobacterium tuberculosis*) at Elbridge on June 25, 1871. The payments of eight dollars a month for the injury to his ankle were terminated when Louis died.

It is reported in his pension papers that just before he died Louis said to his friends, "I am going to die very soon. I hope some of you would be kind enough to look after my bereaved wife and my poor little boy, and I hope that my pension may be transferred to them. I am dying of a disease that I brought home from the army."

Louis Jr. was buried in the Methodist Episcopal Indian Cemetery in Elbridge, which is now known as the *Genereau Family Burying Ground—An Early Methodist Cemetery*.

Sometime after Louis's death, Louisa and Levi moved to Petoskey in Emmet County to live with Louisa's brother John Henry Duvernay.

Louisa Genereau applied for accrued payments from Louis's pension. Application #208,852 for a widow's pension was filed for Louisa on March 29, 1873.

On November 17, 1884, Louisa Genereau was remarried to Benjamin Keway (who had been a cripple all of his life) at St. Francis Catholic Church in Petoskey. Father Pius Niermann, pastor at Harbor Springs, officiated at the marriage. Louis Keway and Magdalena Blackbird witnessed the ceremony. Ben Keway deserted Louisa a short time after their marriage.

Several appeals were made to the Pension Office about Louisa's need for support after her last application for pension was filed March 1, 1899. This last application was rejected because it was determined by the government that her first husband, Louis Genereau Jr., died of tuberculosis and not of a war-related injury. Also, Louisa had remarried and was then abandoned by her second husband. Since she could not furnish information as to what happened to her second husband, and she had not obtained a divorce (a long and lengthy procedure, especially for a woman), the government rejected her application.

After Keway abandoned Louisa, Louisa's son, Levi, took responsibility for the care of his mother.

On October 9, 1899, Application #706,520 for a pension for a minor child was filed for Levi. The application was denied because Levi was past the age of sixteen.

Suffering from cancer of the uterus, bladder, and rectum, Louisa (Duvernay) Genereau Keway died at her son's home in Petoskey on April 29, 1918. She had lived with Levi during the last year of her life. Louisa was buried on May 1, 1918, in an unmarked grave in the Duvernay family plot in Greenwood Cemetery in Petoskey, Emmet County.

George, David, Private

Enlistment: Enlisted as a private on May 18, 1863, at Isabella City (now Mt. Pleasant), Isabella County, by Lieutenant William J. Driggs, First Michigan Sharpshooters, for three years.

Age: Twenty-two, born about 1841 in Saginaw County.

Occupation: Farmer

Residence: Isabella City

Physical Description: Five feet eleven, black eyes, black hair, and a dark complexion. Examining physician was Dr. George L. Cornell, assistant surgeon, First Michigan Sharpshooters.

Mustered: May 26, 1863, at Detroit, Wayne County, by Lieutenant Colonel John R. Smith, US Army

Military Service: Private George was reported to have deserted on July 19, 1863, while his regiment guarded the state arsenal in Dearborn, Wayne County. He was arrested and returned to his regiment, which was then on guard duty at the confine for Confederate prisoners at Camp Douglas, Chicago, Cook County, Illinois. Colonel Charles DeLand restored him to duty on August 20. His pay was docked $41.60 for expenses incurred in his arrest, which left less money to send home to his family.

During the month of February 1864, while at Camp Douglas, George was detailed as a company cook.

On a charge against the rebels' works at the Battle of Spotsylvania, Virginia, on May 12, 1864, Private George sustained a gunshot wound to his head. The missile ball passed anteriorly-posteriorly through the scalp over the top of the right parietal bone of the skull and caused a contusion (or bruise) of the bone. David was taken to the aid station where cold water dressings were applied to his scalp. Cold water dressings were composed of lint dipped into cold water, placed on the wound, and secured with a cloth wrap or adhesive plaster (*Schaadt*). Private George was then taken by ambulance wagon to his division hospital where the doctors examined him and applied fresh cold water dressings to his head.

From his division hospital in the field, Private George was taken by ambulance wagon to the depot hospital at Fredericksburg, Virginia, and admitted on May 17. This hospital was at or near attorney John Marye's house close to Marye's Heights. Pvt. George remained at the depot hospital receiving similar treatment until May 24 when he was taken by ambulance wagon through Fredericksburg to a wharf at Belle Plain Landing (on the Potomac Creek).

At the wharf, he was put onto a hospital steamer and sent to Emory USA General Hospital in Washington, DC. The soldier was admitted to Emory on May 25. Cold water dressings were continued as treatment for the patient.

Private David George died comatose at Emory Hospital on May 26, 1864. His case was reported by Surgeon N.R. Mosely as follows:

The official report from the *Medical and Surgical History of the War of the Rebellion:*

> George, D. Private, Co. K, 1st. Michigan Shaarpshooters, aged 26 years, received, at the battle of Spotsylvania Courthouse, Virginia, May 12, 1864, a wound of the head, with contusion of the bone, in the right parietal region, by a conoidal musket ball. He was admitted into the field hospital of the 3rd. division, Ninth Corps, and transferred thence to Washington, and admitted, on May 25, into the Emery Hospital. He died comatose on the following day. The case is reported by Surgeon N.R. Mosely, U. S. V. (*Medical and Surgical*).

In his effects, Private George left one dress coat and one vest.

On May 27, Private David George's body was placed into a pine coffin and taken to Arlington National Cemetery in Washington, DC. Formal services were accorded to the deceased, which included a military escort from the hospital to the cemetery, a chaplain, and military protocol, which included the firing of arms and an individual temporary headboard for his grave site with information about the deceased *(Encyclopedia)*. The soldier was interred at 3:00 p.m.

Today Private David George lies at rest under stone #325 in section 27 of said cemetery.

Discharged: No discharge given. Died from wounds while in the hospital.

Biography: David George, also known as David Nayyawtoe (sometimes spelled Naygatoe), was the son of George and Nancy Nayyawtoe. David's half siblings, with his mother's first husband, were Maishkeawshe, I Yolk, and Ogeshegwawmquay *(Gruett)*.

David, who did not marry, hunted and trapped to support his family before he enlisted, and sent money home to his parents while he was in the service. Also, while on furlough, he supplied food and clothes to his dependent family. His father was crippled and advanced in age and could not provide any assistance in helping to support the family.

George and Nancy Nayyawtoe received eighty acres of treaty land in Isabella County by reason of the first article of the treaty of August 2, 1855, and the second article of the treaty of October 18, 1864, of the Chippewa of Saginaw, Swan Creek, and Black River. The land description is the east half of the southeast quarter of section 19 in township 15, north of range 3 west *(Land Records)*. Four acres were cleared and chopped by son David before he entered the service. Mr. Nayyawtoe's infirmities kept him from gaining subsistence from his land.

David George's death in the service rendered his parents quite destitute for support. Application #67,714 for a mother's pension was filed for Nancy Nayyawtoe on October 6, 1864.

She received a Mother's Pension Certificate #59,838 that was sent on November 20, 1865. The certificate paid eight dollars a month, retroactive from May 18, 1864, until her death.

Gibson, Joseph L., Private

Enlistment: Enlisted as a private on September 28, 1863, at Little Traverse (now Harbor Springs), Emmet County, by Second Lieutenant Garrett A. Graveraet, First Michigan Sharpshooters, for three years.

Age: Twenty-three, born about 1840 in Bear Creek Township, Emmet County.

Occupation: Farmer

Residence: Bear Creek Township

Physical Description: Five feet six, black eyes, black hair, and a dark complexion. Examining physician was Dr. George L. Cornell, assistant surgeon, First Michigan Sharpshooters.

Mustered: October 21, 1863, at Camp Douglas, Chicago, Cook County, Illinois, by Captain Lowe.

Military Service: While on guard duty with his regiment at the confine for Confederate prisoners at Camp Douglas, Joseph faithfully sent money home (when he was paid) for his family's support. He also sent letters and additional money to recruiting agent and businessman Richard Cooper in Little Traverse to buy groceries for his family. In his letters to Cooper, Joseph signed his name as Louis J. Gibson (in Pension papers). The content of one of his letters to Cooper is as follows:

> Headquarters Co. "K" 1 MI.S.S.
> Camp Douglas, Chicago, Ill.
> Feb. 22, 1864
>
> Mr. Richard Cooper,
>
> Please let my folks have 1 Bbl of flour and ½ Bbl pork and I will pay you as soon as we are paid which will now be soon about the 18th. of next month and oblige with respect.
>
> Yours
> Louis J. Gibson
> To R Cooper Esqr.
> Little Traverse, Emmet Co. Michigan

Private Gibson was captured by the rebels on June 17, 1864, while charging the enemy's defenses before Petersburg, Virginia. After he was held for a few days in an abandoned tobacco warehouse, Joseph was sent by cattle railcar to a Confederate camp for Union prisoners, Camp Sumter (also known as Andersonville Prison), in Andersonville, Georgia. The confine was an open stockade where the prisoners were exposed to the elements and inhumane treatment by their captors.

Due to the lack of proper food, Gibson succumbed to scurvy (the lack of vitamin C, due to the scarcity of fresh fruits and vegetables) and starved to death. His death, which was compounded by exposure, occurred on September 3, 1864. Company K comrade Louis Muskaguon testified that he saw Joseph die in the prison.

Gibson's body was taken by his comrades or prison guards to the brush arbor "dead house" outside of the stockade. At the dead house, the body was divested of any useful clothing and was added to the pile of corpses that awaited burial as soon as possible (*Encyclopedia*). Information about the man's unit, state, and date of death was collected by a record keeper known as Dorance Atwater (also a prisoner), who kept the "Atwater List" of those prisoners who died at Andersonville Prison. Atwater attached a numbered tag to the body for later reference.

As soon as possible, Gibson's body, in addition to the bodies of other dead prisoners, was taken by wagon to the cemetery grounds. His body was placed without a covering and shoulder to shoulder with other deceased soldiers into a trench. The remains were then covered with soil (*Ibid.*). A small post was placed at the head of Gibson's grave, and a number was carved into it. The number matched the number on the body tag and was also noted in the records known about the deceased.

Today, Private Joseph L. Gibson lies at rest under military stone #7741 in the Andersonville National Cemetery. Joseph was the first Company K prisoner to die in captivity at this prison.

Discharged. No discharge given. Died of disease while a prisoner of war.

Biography: Joseph L. Gibson (also known as Joseph Nabawnayasang and Louis J. Gibson) was the son of Louis and Lilla Nabawnayasang of Bear Creek Township. His known siblings in 1860 were: Paul, born ca. 1843; and Therressa, born ca. 1850.

Joseph attended Presbyterian Missionary Rev. Peter Dougherty's Anishinabek mission school at "Old Mission" (*Craker*). The mission was located on Old Mission Peninsula on Grand Traverse Bay and opened with twenty-five students on May 10, 1841 (*Ibid.*).

In addition to the regular studies of reading, writing (in English and Anishinabe), mathematics, and geography, the girl students were taught sewing, cooking, and housekeeping. The boys were taught to use tools and to farm (*Ibid.*).

It was known that Joseph was a very good student and took his studies and life skills seriously. He was equally at ease in both English and Anishinabe languages. Highly regarded, he had many friends.

The revised State Constitution was adopted in 1850 and made citizens of all those persons of American Indian descent who did not belong to any tribe. Now the Indians could buy government land, settle on it, and become citizens (*Ibid.*). White settlers were coming in rapidly and crowding the Anishinabek (*Ibid.*).

By 1852, the Anishinabek moved their homes from Old Mission to lands that they had selected and purchased on the west side of the bay on the Leelanau Peninsula. Their lands were located in the counties of Grand Traverse, Charlevoix, and Emmet (*Ibid.*). Rev. Dougherty decided to move his mission and relocate on land that was bought on the Mission Point on the bluff east of Omena in Leelanau County (*Ibid.*). He named his new mission "The Grove Hill New Mission Church" (*Ibid.*).

At New Mission, Joseph and the other students continued their studies under the tutelage of Rev. Dougherty and head teacher Rev. Andrew Porter.

While he studied at New Mission, Joseph adopted the surname of one of the teachers whom he greatly admired, a woman teacher (in charge of the female students) named Catherine Gibson (*Ibid.*). Joseph would use the name *Gibson* when he enlisted in the army.

Joseph's brother, Paul, and sister, Therressa, who admired teacher Gibson, also adopted her surname and attended the same school (*Report*).

Years later, Rev. Porter would relate the following story about Joseph Gibson from Porter's reminiscences of his days as a teacher at Old Mission school: "When school was suspended for sugar making in the spring of 1850, Joseph, about ten years of age, suffered a broken leg. The accident occurred as he helped his mother and sister collect maple sugar sap at their annual 'sugar bush.'" Author's note: Mr. Porter knew that Joseph's mother and sister were devoted to education, so when the school reopened, they took turns carrying Joseph for three-quarters of a mile to his school until his leg healed. But this young man, so well liked, died of cruel starvation in Andersonville prison camp (*Traverse*).

Joseph, who did not marry, was a devoted son. His father, Louis, was reported to have deserted his family and gone to Canada, according to depositions given in support for a mother's pension for Lilla. Joseph supported his mother and siblings by fishing and farming a plot of land.

Before he entered the service in 1863, Joseph sold his horse and some property for money to support his siblings and his aging mother in his absence. He expressed much anxiety about his mother and the family as he prepared to leave for the service.

Even though Joseph's family was in possession of a small log cabin and some homemade furniture worth about six dollars, Joseph's death at Andersonville Prison would leave his loved ones in hardship.

One unconfirmed source stated that Lilla was entitled to forty acres of wild land from the United States government by reason of the Chippewa and Ottawa Treaty of July 31, 1855.

Application #87,413 for a dependent mother's pension was filed for Lilla

Nabawnayasang on March 25, 1865. She was granted a Dependent Mother's Pension Certificate #84,868 on October 1, 1866, and received eight dollars a month. The payments were retroactive from September 3, 1864, until her death.

By 1870, Joseph's brother, Paul, was farming to support the family. It seems that the father, Louis, returned to the family from Canada since he was listed as a member of the household in the 1870 federal census. Daughters Ellen, age ten, and Lucy, age eight, born after Joseph died, were also included in the household for said year.

Going, Samuel, Private

Enlistment: Enlisted as a private on July 4, 1863, at Elbridge, Oceana County, by Lieutenant Edwin V. Andress, First Michigan Sharpshooters, for three years.

Age: Twenty, born about 1843 in Barry County.

Occupation: Laborer

Residence: Pentwater, Oceana County

Physical Description: Five feet eight and a half inches tall, black eyes, black hair, and a dark complexion. Examining physician was Dr. Jacob B. McNett, assistant surgeon, First Michigan Sharpshooters.

Mustered: July 11, 1863, at Detroit, Wayne County, by Lieutenant Colonel John R. Smith, US Army

Military Service: In September 1863, Private Going's wages were docked for a lost waist belt plate and bayonet while he was a guard at the confine for Confederate prisoners at Camp Douglas, Chicago, Cook County, Illinois.

On May 10, 1864, Going was promoted to the rank of corporal.

During the Battle of Spotsylvania, Virginia, on May 12, 1864, Going was shot in the head and died instantly while in action against the enemy. But according to different army records, Samuel's date of death varies from May 9 to 12. The War Department record lists Corporal Going as being killed in action on May 9, 1864, while engaged in the Battle of Spotsylvania near the Ni River. There is also a military record that states Samuel died of his head wound in the hospital at Fredericksburg, located at or near attorney John Marye's house at Marye's Heights, sometime after May 9. So, there would seem to be confusion as to which date of death is correct and just where the soldier's death occurred.

If Corporal Samuel Going was killed in action on the Union-held field of battle and identified as the Union soldier Samuel Going, he was left in his uniform, wrapped in a blanket before interment, and buried in a temporary grave until his reburial in a military cemetery. He may or may not have been buried in a pine coffin, depending upon its availability. A temporary wooden board with his name, unit, and date of death would have been placed at the head of Samuel's grave site as reference for future reburial (*Encyclopedia*).

After the war, Sam's body would have been removed from his burial on the battlefield. He would than have been reburied in the Fredericksburg National Cemetery (possibly with military honors) and again identified with a temporary wooden board. As soon as possible, a permanent stone would have been placed at the head of his grave site.

The reader should note that according to a letter written on January 27, 1871, from the Office of the Adjutant General, all the records of death for Samuel Going were reviewed by that office and a decision was made as to the accepted date of death for the soldier. The letter specifically states that "Final statement reports him killed in battle of Spotsylvania, Va. May 10, 1864, which is accepted as the correct date of death." The letter was signed by "J. P. Martin, Assistant Adjutant General."

Today, Samuel Going lies at rest under stone #2186 in the Fredericksburg National Cemetery, which states his name as "Samuel Gora."

Discharged: No discharge given. Killed in action.

Biography: Samuel was the son of Jonathan (John) and Martha Tondoqua and was also known as Sam Tondoqua. Tondoqua means "going" in English. The couple was married about March 15, 1836, at Gull Prairie in Barry County by Rev. Leonard Slater, who was a well-known Baptist missionary (*History 1.*). Rev. Slater established an Ottawa Indian Baptist mission and school at Prairieville in Barry County during the winter of 1836 or 1837 (*History 2.*).

After Sam's father died on December 25, 1853, Martha married secondly to Addison Shaw. Their marriage took place in 1856 in Allegan County.

In 1860, the members in the Shaw household included Addison, Martha, Samuel, Samson, and sisters Tochemahbum and Sebequa. Addison made baskets, hunted, trapped, and fished to support the family.

Previous to his enlistment, Samuel, who did not marry, worked for twenty dollars a month as a lumberjack for Mr. Allen Flagg of Pentwater. In addition to a portion of his wages that he earned from his work and gave to his mother, Sam also hunted, trapped, and fished with his stepfather to support his family. While in the service, Samuel sent most of his pay home.

After Samuel was reported killed in action, Martha Going Shaw was awarded

Treasury Department Certificates #142,713 and #481,376, which were issued on February 20, 1865, and July 23, 1868, for arrears of her son's pay. She also received two one hundred-dollar bounties due to Sam.

In 1871, Addison suffered a severe injury (an inguinal hernia) to his groin area due to an accident. The injury rendered him an invalid and unable to provide much support for his family. The only activity that he was able to do to support his family was to make and sell baskets for a meager income.

Martha's Application #192,965 for a mother's pension was filed for her on January 12, 1871. At that time, the family was living in Riverton of Mason County. She cited her son's death, her first husband's death, and the invalid condition of her second husband. She had sold her team of oxen, which was worth twenty dollars, for cash to buy food and made and sold baskets to supplement the family's income.

In 1888, Addison Shaw left Martha and went to the Mackinaw (Cheboygan County) area to live. Several more appeals were made, including a letter dictated by Martha, inquiring as to the status of her application for a mother's pension. After January 30, 1892, Martha's application was abandoned due to the lack of additional information needed to process her papers.

Graveraet Jr., Henry Garrett, First Sergeant

Enlistment: Enlisted as a first sergeant on July 7, 1863, at the Dearborn Arsenal, Wayne County, by Colonel Charles V. DeLand, First Michigan Sharpshooters, for three years.

Age: About forty-five to forty-seven, born on Mackinac Island, Mackinac County. Another record states that Henry was actually fifty-five, ten years over the age limit of enlistment. The author accepts Henry's birth (in 1816) as stated as such by his mother in a letter to Mackinac Indian Agent Henry R. Schoolcraft in 1836.

Occupation: Merchant

Residence: Little Traverse (now Harbor Springs), Emmet County

Physical Description: Five feet ten, blue eyes, dark hair, and a dark complexion (another source lists a white complexion). Examining physician was Dr. Arvin F. Whelan, surgeon, First Michigan Sharpshooters.

Mustered: July 20, 1863, in Detroit, Wayne County, by Lieutenant Colonel John R. Smith, US Army

Military Service: Henry was present when sixteen young Anishinabek were recruited by his son, Second Lieutenant Garrett A. Graveraet, for Company K from Little Traverse in Emmet County. He accompanied his son and the new recruits on the boat *Mears*, from Little Traverse to Dearborn where he also decided to join the company. At the time of his enlistment, Henry was judge of probate in Emmet County.

On a direct order from Colonel Charles V. DeLand, Sergeant Henry G. Graveraet Jr. accompanied Indian Agent Richard Cooper on August 3, 1863, for a recruiting mission (on detached service) for Company K among the Anishinabek. Mr. Cooper assisted with translation duties.

In September 1863, Henry was again listed on detached service.

On March 18, 1864, Henry, while still on detached service, was listed as sick in USA General Hospital in Cleveland, Ohio. His only medical record for that date lists his illness as syphilis caused by the microbe *Treponema pallidum* (*Blakiston*). If the diagnosis was correct, the ulcer or chancre on the primary site was treated by cauterization under anesthetic of ether or chloroform (*Schaadt*). Medicinals, such as tartar emetic to evacuate the stomach, castor oil to evacuate the bowels, and "blue mass" (or mercurous chloride) to prevent constipation, were administered to him (*Bollet*). Opium was given for pain (*Ibid.*). Also, drinks of sassafras and sarsaparilla were probably given to him. It's known that none of the therapies mentioned cured syphilis during that era.

While fighting in the same unit as his son at the Battle of Spotsylvania on May 12, 1864, it was reported that Henry was killed instantly by a gunshot wound to the head. Garrett, who was distraught at the loss of his father, carried Henry's body to safety behind the lines and buried him using a metal mess plate for a shovel (*Herek*). The grave was in an area called Beverly's Farm, and Garrett left a wooden marker for identification and reburial. Later, Company K comrades Leon Otashquabono and Joseph Wakazoo testified in a deposition that a bomb shell (or artillery cannon shell) burst had actually killed Henry.

Shortly after the battle, Henry's body was recovered and reinterred by a burial detail in the then newly designated Fredericksburg National Battlefield Cemetery in Fredericksburg, Virginia. The body may or may not have been wrapped in a blanket, then put into a pine coffin if one was available (*Encyclopedia*). Henry lies beneath stone #4366 inscribed "Sgt. H.G. Graveraets 1 Mich S.S." in division B of section C. A memorial stone for Henry was placed beside the gravestone of his son, Garrett, in St. Anne (Ste. Anne) Cemetery on Mackinac Island.

Henry was one of many who gave the supreme sacrifice during that bloody month of May. He would be sorely missed for his leadership among the Anishinabek soldiers and for his bilingual expertise.

Discharged: No discharge given. Killed in action.

Biography: Henry Garrett Graveraet Jr. was born on Mackinac Island in 1816 and was the oldest son of Henry Garrett and Charlotte Livingston/Livingstone Graveraet Sr. Charlotte, who was also known as Adaubetahgeezehgoquay or Midday Woman, was the daughter of Major Livingston/Livingstone and an Anishinabequa woman known as Amudwagewumaquaid. She gave Henry Jr. his Anishinabe name of Waygeemuhwee (which means Grand Chief). Henry was also known as Adjidjak or Crane *(Native Americans in Michigan 1., Graveraet Family Page)*.

In February 1836, Charlotte wrote a letter to the Mackinac Indian Agent Henry R. Schoolcraft to register the Anishinabek names of her children *(Schoolcraft)*. The meeting for the 1836 Treaty was to be held shortly after February with the Anishinabek of the vicinity, and Charlotte wanted the Graveraet family to be considered among the numerous claims that would be presented. The following Anishinabek names and ages of her family (she and Henry G. Sr. had fifteen children) and that of her mother were submitted to Indian Agent Schoolcraft. The children's names (including Charlotte's mother and herself) that were included in the letter are as follows:

Amudwagewumaquaid (Charlotte's Mother)
Adaubetahgeezehgoquay (Charlotte), born 1785 or 1796—Midday Woman
Adjidjak (or Crane) and Waygeemuhwee (or Grand Chief) (Henry G. Jr., born 1816)
Nenasequaid (or Sarah Ann, born 1818)—Partridge Woman
Wageenahnanoquaid (or Caroline Ann, born 1819)—North Wind Lady
Niahwasanogin (or Robert J., born 1820)—Eight Summers
Oshgoskittawaquaid (or Marie Louisa, born 1822)—Rising River Woman
Magegeanoquaid (or Alice, born 1824)—Grand Noise of Rapid Woman
Pakenaga (or Albert, born 1826)
Quakegeanoquaid (or Lucy Ann, born 1828)
Ashquequenabe (or John H., born 1830)
Kitchchnagan (or Anthony Wayne, born 1832)
Kanedenaquaid (or Mary Jane, born 1834)
Madeleine O., born 1836
Charlotte R., born 1838

George E., born 1839

Harriet, born 1843

Henry Jr.'s father (and Garrett's grandfather), Henry Garrett Graveraet Sr., served as a private in the Seventeenth United States Infantry during the War of 1812 and sustained a wound to his right hip during the Battle of Brownstown, Michigan Territory, on August 5, 1812. He helped to defend Fort Stephenson on Sandusky Bay, Ohio, on August 1, 1813, with Major George Croghan (*Native Americans in Michigan 2., Graveraet Family Page*).

On September 1, 1814, Henry G. Sr. (who learned to speak the Anishinabe language fluently) was appointed Indian interpreter by Territorial Governor Lewis Cass (*Ibid.*).

Henry G. Sr. was the son of Geritt (also spelled Gerret) Graverat, who was a silversmith and Indian trader of Dutch descent, who came from Albany, New York, to Detroit about 1772. His ancestors had come from the Netherlands and settled in New York about the middle of the seventeenth century. On May 1, 1767, Gerrit Graverat was listed as a private in Captain Abraham C. Cuyler's Company of the Granadier Company of First Battalion, Albany, New York, Militia (*New York Colonial Muster Rolls 1664–1775*).

In later years, Henry G. Sr. and Charlotte Graveraet lived in Marquette, Marquette County. Henry G. Sr. died December 31, 1860, and Charlotte died January 17, 1861. They lie at rest next to each other in Park Cemetery in Marquette, Marquette County, of Michigan's Upper Peninsula.

Henry G. and Sophia Hortense (Bailly) Graveraet Jr. were married on January 11, 1836, in Ste. Anne Catholic Church on Mackinac Island. The ceremony was officiated by Rev. Father F. J. Bonduel. Sophie was the daughter of Joseph (an early fur trader) and Angelique McGulpin (BeadWayWay or Mecopemequa) Bailly (pron. Bay-e). Joseph was born Honore Gratien Joseph Bailly de Messein on April 7, 1774, in Vercheres, Quebec. Angelique McGulpin's father was Makatoquet, or Black Cloud, chief of the Grand River Band of Ottawa (*Bailly*).

Henry G. and Sophie Graveraet Jr. were the parents of four children. They were: Sophia Alice, born 1836 or 1837; Garrett A., born 1840; Marie Rosine, born 1842; and Joseph, born 1848.

In the 1860 federal census, the Graveraet family was listed as living in Holmes Township on Makinac Island. Joseph was not listed.

Alice Graveraet married John Couchois on March 5, 1859, and died shortly after her marriage.

Rosine married first to Robert F. Wright on July 22, 1866. One child, Robert Henry Wright, was born in 1868. Rosine, her husband, Robert, and their son, Robert Jr., were living with Sophie in the 1870 Emmet County federal census.

The second marriage for Rosine was to John B. Couchois on July 1, 1873. They had one son, John Couchois. When John B. Couchois died, Rosine resumed her former surname of Wright. Her second son, John Couchois, who became a noted writer, adopted the name John C. Wright as his pen name.

While living on Mackinac Island, Henry was engaged in fishing and farming. In the winters, he would stay in the Lake Superior area while the family stayed behind. Henry was neither a constant nor stable support for his family due to his issue with alcohol.

Sophia helped support the family by earning a meager living as a teacher. She taught (including the years of 1844 to 1852) at a French Catholic school for Anishinabek at St. Ignace, Mackinac County. The school was under the superintendence of Bishop Peter Paul Lefevere of Detroit with whom she often corresponded. See Garrett A. Graveraet file. Sophia was one of Garrett's first teachers.

In her early teen years, Sophia was adopted and tutored by Madam Magdelaine Laframboise, "The First Lady of Mackinac Island." Under Madam Laframboise's guidance, Sophia was given an excellent education and was taught to be a refined lady and an exceptional hostess. As a noted storyteller, Sophia entertained many notables and government officials in the Graveraet home. One such notable was General Zachary Taylor, who became the twelfth president of the United States.

After the deaths of her husband and son, Sophia lived out her life in Harbor Springs.

Application #78,414 for a widow's pension (as previously mentioned in Garrett A. Graveraet's file) was filed for Sophia on January 9, 1865. She was granted a Widow's Pension Certificate #61,869, which paid eight dollars a month.

In 1877, Sophie decided that, instead of her widow's pension, she wanted to submit an application for a dependent mother's pension. Garrett had always seen to her needs, and Henry's pension was not enough support for her elder years. In lieu of Henry's pension, Application #230,334 for a dependent mother's pension was submitted for her, and her widow's pension payments were discontinued. The application was filed on March 12, 1877.

She was granted Dependent Mother's Pension Certificate #177,583 in which she was paid fifteen dollars a month commencing April 20, 1877. These payments from her son's service were received until her death.

Sophia sought solace from her grief in her Catholic Church and was seen attending Mass daily. She died in Petoskey, Emmet County, on January 7, 1892, at about the age of eighty-five. Her final resting place is an unmarked grave in the Holy Childhood of Jesus Cemetery in Harbor Springs of said county.

Greensky, Benjamin C., Private

Enlistment: Enlisted as a private on September 10, 1863, at Little Traverse, Emmet County, by Second Lieutenant Garrett A. Graveraet, First Michigan Sharpshooters, for three years.

Age: Twenty-four, born about 1839 in L'Anse, Baraga County.

Occupation: Farmer

Residence: Pine River Indian Methodist Mission (now Greensky Hill Mission) in Charlevoix, Emmet County (now Charlevoix County), where his father, Rev. Peter Greensky, was the minister.

Physical Description: Five feet four, black eyes, black hair, and a dark complexion. Examining physician was Dr. George L. Cornell, assistant surgeon, First Michigan Sharpshooters.

Mustered: October 21, 1863, at Camp Douglas Chicago, Cook County, Illinois, by Captain Lowe. Camp Douglas was a confine for Confederate prisoners and was guarded by the men of the First Michigan Sharpshooters for seven months.

Military Service: Private Benjamin C. Greensky was killed while charging the enemy's defenses during an early-morning frontal assault at the Battle of Spotsylvania, Virginia, on May 12, 1864 *(Frassanito)*. He had been promoted to corporal shortly before the battle.

Corporal Greensky's place of burial is not known but is most likely on or near the battle site. If Union forces recovered his body, they would have left him in his uniform or wrapped him in a blanket and buried him without ceremony. Burial would have been in an individual grave or in a trench with other deceased Union soldiers. A pine coffin (if available) might have been used to contain Greensky's body. Some sort of marker for identification would have been left at the head of the grave site *(Encyclopedia)*. But due to inclement weather conditions or theft, the marker may not have survived, leaving Greensky unidentified. He may have been disinterred and moved to Fredericksburg National Cemetery where he was reburied with other Union men who were also unknown.

If Greensky's body was retrieved by the Confederates after the battle, it would have been buried without much care or respect in a trench or mass grave with other unknown Union corpses *(Ibid.)*.

Discharged: No discharge given. Killed in action.

Biography: Benjamin C. Greensky is listed in the 1860 federal census for Grand Island of Alger County. The island is in Lake Superior opposite the shore of Munising in Alger County. Benjamin is listed as age eighteen and living in a house with other Anishinabek men. His occupation is that of hunter and fisherman, the same as the others of his household.

Ben was the son of Reverend Peter and Susan Greensky and the older brother to Jacob (see Jacob Greensky file for the story of Rev. Peter Greensky) and Henry.

On July 13, 1863, Benjamin C. Greensky married Emma Redbird in Northport, Leelanau County. The couple was married by Rev. Salmon Steele of the Methodist Episcopal Church. Witnesses to the ceremony were Miss Etta Tuttle and Mrs. Marsella M. Steele. There were no children of this marriage.

After Benjamin's death in the service, Application #68,228 for a widow's pension was filed for Emma Greensky on October 8, 1864. She received a Widow's Pension Certificate #40,449 on February 8, 1865, which paid eight dollars a month until her death at Northport.

Greensky, Jacob, Private

Enlistment: Enlisted as a private for one year on September 3, 1864, at Grand Rapids, Kent County, by Captain Norman Bailey of the First Michigan Sharpshooters and provost marshal for the Fourth District of Michigan. This enlistment was credited to the Fourth District, Pentwater, Oceana County, and satisfied the requirement for a man from that district.

Age: Eighteen, born about 1846 or 1847 at St. Mary's (Sault Ste. Marie—the Soo), Chippewa County.

Occupation: Farmer

Residence: Pine River Indian Methodist Mission (now Greensky Hill Mission) in Charlevoix, Emmet County (now Charlevoix County), where his father, Rev. Peter Greensky, was minister.

Physical Description: Five feet eight and a half inches tall, black eyes, dark hair, and a dark complexion. Examining physician was Dr. Alonzo Mate, First Michigan Sharpshooters.

Mustered: September 3, 1864, at Grand Rapids by Captain Norman Bailey, First Michigan Sharpshooters and provost marshal for the Fourth District of Michigan

Military Service: Private Jacob Greensky sustained a gunshot (missile) wound to his neck while charging the rebels' defenses during a battle before Petersburg on April 2, 1865. The missile entered the back of his neck and passed downward in a diagonal path to the small of his back where it exited the body. There were no fractures of the bones. He was taken by ambulance wagon to an aid station where any bleeding was stopped. Jacob was then taken to his division hospital in the field where the doctors applied bromine (to impede infection) and cold water dressings to the soldier's wounds. The water dressings were composed of lint dipped into cold water, applied to the wounds, and held in place with a cloth wrap or adhesive plaster (*Schaadt*). Opium pills were given for pain.

On April 3, Private Greensky was taken to the military railroad, put on a mattress in a boxcar, the floor of which was cushioned with straw or hay, and sent to the depot hospital at City Point. Treatment with bromine, the application of simple water dressings, and pain relief was continued (*Ibid.*).

On April 26, Greensky was taken from the hospital to a wharf at City Point, transferred to a hospital steamer, and taken to Slough Barracks, a General Hospital branch of the Third Division, USA General Hospital in Alexandria, Virginia. Similar treatment was given to Greensky at Slough Barracks.

Private Greensky was transferred to another area of Slough Barracks and admitted on April 27. Bromine and cold water dressings were continued. Medicines given by mouth to the patient included Dover's powder (powder of ipecac and opium) and antimony that induced diaphoresis, which caused an increase of perspiration (*Ibid.*). Potassium carbonate and colchicum (derived from meadow saffron) were also given to Greensky to induce diuresis or increase the output of urine (*Ibid.*). In addition to these treatments, he was given whiskey as a tonic and opium pills or morphine (by injection or administered topically into the wound) for pain, and placed on a milk diet (*Ibid.*).

While he was recuperating in the hospital, Greensky contracted measles on May 22. He was isolated from other patients and remained in the hospital until his discharge.

Discharged: Private Jacob Greensky was mustered out and honorably discharged from Slough Hospital on June 22, 1865. He was paid money owed to him for his service at the time of his discharge.

Biography: Jacob Greensky was the son of Rev. Peter and Susan Greensky.

His siblings were Benjamin (see profile on Benjamin Greensky) and Henry, who was born about 1850.

Rev. Peter Greensky was also known by his Anishinabe name of Shagasokicki or Showskawageshik. His father was Wesawin, and his brothers were Isaac and William (*Avery*). He was a well-known Ojibwa (or Chippewa) Methodist Episcopal minister born about 1807 at Sault Ste. Marie (or the Soo), Chippewa County, in Michigan's Upper Peninsula (*Reuter*). Peter was well educated in the Boys' School at the Soo.

As a young traditional medicine man, Peter was converted to the Christian belief under the firebrand preaching of the Canadian Mississauga Ojibwa Indian chief and Methodist evangelist minister, the Rev. John Sunday (also known as Shawundais) in 1831 *(Ibid.)*. He was one of Rev. Sunday's first Anishinabe converts in the Lake Superior country. Peter received missionary training at the Methodist Church School at Bay Mills in Chippewa County and received his local preaching license on September 1, 1844 *(Ibid.)*.

After his conversion, Peter burned his medicine bag and marveled at the beautiful and unusual colors that arose from the bag as it was consumed by the fire *(Conversation 1)*. This occurrence was a sign to Peter that he had chosen the correct path for his journey through life and that he was to share his religious beliefs with other Anishinabek *(Ibid.)*.

In addition to being well educated, the young minister had an excellent command of the English language. As he preached, he made quite a visual impression with his long black hair, long bone earrings that dangled from his earlobes, and a blanket wrapped around his body (*Walker*).

Rev. Greensky established the first Protestant mission near Charlevoix in the mid-1840s—the Pine River Methodist Indian Mission. The place chosen was near a meeting place where chiefs used to hold their councils—"the sacred circle of trees." Today the mission is located in Charlevoix County, but before the Civil War. it was in Emmet County.

In the 1850s, Rev. Greensky went to a sacred place to harvest logs to build a more permanent church at the site of the mission. The logs were floated between canoes on Lake Charlevoix on the way to the building grounds *(Conversation 2)*.

After the church was built, several chiefs gathered at the sacred "circle of trees" to bend the tops so they would not be used for lumber by the white men (*Ibid.*).

After 1846 and until 1859, Rev. Greensky was instrumental as an interpreter for Rev. Peter Dougherty as Dougherty established his Presbyterian missions in the Grand Traverse Bay area. In addition to being an interpreter, Rev. Greensky assisted Rev. Dougherty in the translations of church hymns and lessons from English to the Anishinabe language that were used in Dougherty's mission schools.

Jacob Greensky and his brother, Benjamin, attended Dougherty's mission school in their formative years of education. During their school years, the brothers sampled many of Rev. Dougherty's prized apples as they ran through the minister's orchard.

After forty-two days of illness, Susan Greensky, Peter's beloved wife, died of consumption (or pulmonary tuberculosis) in May 1860. Tuberculosis is caused by *Mycobacterium tuberculosis,* commonly known as the tubercle bacillus *(Blakiston)*. She was buried in the Pine River Cemetery behind the mission church. An unmarked white wooden cross marks her grave site.

After his discharge in 1865, Jacob returned to Pine River Mission to assist his father with mission church duties and to serve as a Methodist lay minister.

At the age of twenty, Jacob married Esther Wausemegayquay (or Wazhemegaw, Shabetise) Duvernay, age sixteen, on March 29, 1866. Esther was the daughter of John and Mary Ann (or Mawshemogoqua) Duvernay. Another source states that Esther's mother was Elizabeth Otaypagawamekay. John A. Horton, justice of the peace, officiated at the couple's wedding. Joseph Mixsauba and Amanda Horton, sister of the officiate, were witnesses.

Rev. Peter Greensky served the Pine River Methodist Indian Mission from 1859 to 1861 and from 1863 until his death on April 8, 1866. His demise was due to a rapidly progressing (or "galloping") fatal form of pulmonary tuberculosis called *florid pithisis (Ibid.)*.

After a great crowd of attendees witnessed Rev. Peter's funeral, the much-loved minister was buried next to his wife in the cemetery now known as the Greensky Hill Old Cemetery. His grave site is marked by a plain white wooden cross.

Following Rev. Greensky's death, Peter's brother, Rev. Isaac Greensky, went to the Pine River Mission to assist his nephew and to continue Rev. Peter's vision for his mission.

Jacob and Esther Greensky were the parents of Peter, born December 28, 1869; Alice, born September 15 or 29, 1872; Joseph; George, born January 23,

1878, and died in 1885; Adam, born December 25, 1881; Jane, born August 3, 1884; and a second George, born August 23 or 28, 1886.

Joseph, George (1), Adam, and Jennie (or Jane) all died before their father's death in 1887. George (2) married Susan Fisher on July 15, 1905, in Charlevoix. Justice of the Peace William Collins officiated at the ceremony.

In 1875, the Pine River Mission was renamed Greensky Hill Mission Church in honor of the beloved minister. Today the church is known as the Greensky Hill United Methodist Church.

Jacob continued to experience a steady decline in his health after he was discharged from the service. The scar wound (or cicatrix) in his neck, that was one inch in width and two and a half inches in length, caused extreme pain to the point that he could not support any weight on his shoulders. The cicatrix extended diagonally across the spinal column, covering the spinose processes of the seventh cervical and the two upper dorsal vertebrae.

There was a sinus (or cavity) leading to the wound from the lower scar. The sinus would break open every summer and ooze its watery matter. This wound limited Jacob's ability to do any heavy work. It left him partially disabled and resulted in his lack of holding a steady job, except lay preaching, in which to support his family.

In accordance with the treaty with the Ottawa and Chippewa of Michigan on July 31, 1855, party to the treaty of March 28, 1836, Jacob received a certificate for eighty acres of land approved on August 19, 1875. The land was located in Emmet County and was described as the north half of the northeast quarter of section 22 in township 35 north of range 5 west (*Land Records*).

On July 2, 1880, Jacob's Application #407,565 for an invalid pension was submitted for him. He received Invalid Pension Certificate #236,586 in April 1883, which paid four dollars a month.

About two years before his death, Greensky contracted a chronic cough. He also experienced such pain in his neck and shoulders that he could not lie down with any comfort. His cough developed into tuberculosis, which caused him to spit up blood and made it difficult for him to breathe. Susan Black, an Anishinabequa doctor, used traditional herbal treatments and attended Jacob during the last years of his life.

Jacob Greensky died at the age of forty-one at his home in Hayes Township, Charlevoix County, on August 31, 1887. His death was due to a combination of the effects of his war wounds and of tuberculosis. Rev. James Awanagezhik, who was Jacob's neighbor, friend, comrade in Company K, and a local Methodist lay preacher, was present at Jacob's death and officiated at his funeral.

The young Methodist lay minister was buried near his parents in the Greensky Hill Indian Methodist Cemetery behind the church. His grave site is marked by a plain white wooden cross.

Esther Greensky was known to be a fine basket maker and sold her baskets to earn much-needed money. Application #374,134 for a widow's pension was filed for Esther on June 7, 1888. She received a Widow's Pension Certificate #268,988 in 1890, which paid twelve dollars a month with two dollars a month for each of the two minor children (Alice and George (2)) retroactive from August 31, 1887 (their father's death) to September 4, 1890. By 1890, both children would have attained the age of sixteen and would no longer be eligible for dependent children's payments.

Esther's second marriage was to Reuben Willis on October 5, 1890.

In 1899, Antoine Block was appointed by the court to be guardian for the surviving Greensky children. A minor's pension Application #708,513 (for the second George Greensky) was filed for Block on November 14, 1899. The application was denied due to lack of further information needed to process the claim. When Esther remarried to Ruben Willis, he was expected by the government to support Esther and the minor children. Due to Esther's remarriage, her widow's pension was nullified.

Ruben Willis died February 2, 1901, in an accident in which he was run over by railroad cars.

Esther married for the third time to Thomas Anweshky on August 1, 1904. Thomas died April 17, 1913.

On January 3, 1917, Esther Anweshky, a widow for the third time, applied for a remarried widow's pension from her first husband's (Jacob's) service. It was rejected because she had no title to a pension as a former widow of the soldier due to the reason that she had contracted more than one marriage since his death in 1887.

Esther's son, George Greensky, reapplied for Application #708,513 on October 11, 1917, for a minor's pension. He wanted to check to see if he were eligible to draw any of his father's pension money since he was only one year old at the time of his father's death. The application was denied because his mother had received money for his support through her original widow's pension and because his father's death was not due to his army service but to tuberculosis. Jacob's wound in the service and his tuberculosis were reasons cited for Esther having received her original widow's pension in the first place!

Esther (Duvernay) Greensky Willis Anweshky died at her home in Bay Shore, Charlevoix County, sometime after 1917.

Gruet Jr., Peter, Private

Enlistment: Enlisted as a private on July 6, 1863, at the Dearborn Arsenal, Wayne County, by Lieutenant Edwin V. Andress, First Michigan Sharpshooters, for three years.

Age: Twenty-one, born in January between the years of 1846 and 1849 in St. Charles, Saginaw County.

Occupation: Hunter

Residence: Marquette, Marquette County

Physical Description: Five feet five, black eyes, black hair, and a dark complexion. Examining physician was Dr. Arvin F. Whelan, surgeon, First Michigan Sharpshooters.

Mustered: July 11, 1863, at Detroit, Wayne County, by Lieutenant Colonel John R. Smith, US Army.

Military Service: It is reported that Private Peter Gruet deserted on July 19, 1863, at Dearborn, Wayne County. There is no further record of his service in Company K except that his name appears on a list of deserters. This Peter Gruet is the same Peter Gruet who joined Company K, Ninth Michigan Cavalry Regiment on April 24, 1864, after he deserted from the First Michigan Sharpshooter Regiment.

Discharged: There is a record of a discharge for a Peter Gruett from Company K, Ninth Michigan Cavalry on July 21, 1865, at Lexington, North Carolina.

Biography: Peter Gruet Jr. was the son of Peter Gruet Sr. (also known as Kawkawchees Second) a trader, interpreter, guide, and farmer, and his wife, Abigail Tromble, who was of French descent. Peter Sr. and Abigail's marriage was officiated by George Raby, justice of the peace, on September 21, 1846, in Saginaw of Saginaw County. Peter Jr. had a full brother, Edward, born in 1842.

Peter Jr. and Edward were half brothers to Philip (who compiled the 1868 Saginaw-Chippewa Indian Family Index) and Madeline (or Keshegewahnoquay) Gruet through Peter Sr.'s first marriage to Peendugay (or Magdelina). Magdelina remarried to Sawgaw.

Peendugay was the daughter of Chief Bemassikeh of the Little Pines Band. The band lived near the Bethany Lutheran Indian Mission in Gratiot County. Peter Jr. was also a cousin of Company K comrade Daniel Pemassegay (*Moll*).

Peter Sr.'s brother, James, served as the interpreter for the mission, which was founded by Rev. E. R. Baierlein in May 1848 (see the profile of Daniel Pemassegay for the Bethany Mission). Peter Sr. purchased the mission property on October 17, 1866. James, Peter Sr., William, and a sister, Sophie, were the children of James Gruet Sr., a French trader, and an Anishinabequa wife. James Sr. was associated with the Mackinac Island fur trade firm of Gruet and LaFramboise *(Ibid.)*.

After he returned to civilian life, Peter Gruet Jr. married Julia (or Ogawbayawbwa) in 1865 by traditional Anishinabek custom and practice (with consent of the couple and their parents). Peter Jr. and Julia were the parents of a girl, Sally, born in 1865, and a boy born in 1868.

On May 20, 1878, Peter Gruet Jr. was appointed guardian for the four children of his Company K comrade Thomas Nelson. Nelson's wife had died, and Thomas was very ill. This appointment was requested by Nelson, and a good decision, since Peter was an uncle to the children and well liked by them.

Shortly after Thomas Nelson died, Peter Gruet and his family took the four Nelson children, Lucy, Frank, Daniel, and Jane, into their home to care for them.

There is no record of an application for a pension for Peter Gruet Jr.'s service in Company K, First Michigan Sharpshooters. Because of his desertion from the sharpshooter infantry to the cavalry troop, and no explanation given for his desertion, Gruet would not have been eligible for a pension.

Peter Gruett Jr. died sometime after 1881. There is no pension file for Peter Gruet.

Hall, Cornelius, Private

Enlistment: Enlisted as a private on September 3, 1864, at Grand Rapids, Kent County, by Captain Norman Bailey, First Michigan Sharpshooters and provost marshal for the Fourth District of Michigan, for one year. Enlistment credited to the Fourth Congressional District, Pentwater, Oceana County, to satisfy the requirement of a man from that district.

Age: Twenty, born April 8, 1844, near Ionia City in Ionia County.
Occupation: Farmer
Residence: Pentwater, Oceana County

Physical Description: Five feet eight, black eyes, dark hair, and a dark complexion. Examining physician was Dr. Alonzo Mate, First Michigan Sharpshooters.

Mustered: September 3, 1864, at Grand Rapids by Captain Norman Bailey, First Michigan Sharpshooters and provost marshal for the Fourth District of Michigan.

Military Service: On December 26, 1864, Private Cornelius Hall was admitted to a first division USA hospital in the field near Petersburg, Virginia, diagnosed with diarrhea.

Castor oil, a mild cathartic, was administered to the patient to empty the colon *(Evans)*. Also, podophyllin, a grayish powder made from the dried rhizome and roots of *Podophyllum peltatum*, a purgative, may have also been used *(Ibid.)*.

If Private Hall experienced cramping or abdominal pain for more than two days, then a half grain each of capsicum (dried fruit of *Capsicus frutenscens*—the bush red pepper or chili pepper) and camphor with a sixth grain of opium were given every two hours *(Ibid.)*.

During his treatment, the patient was confined to bed rest and given such foods as boiled rice, cracker-panada (a dish of bread or crackers boiled to a pulp and flavored), and toast and water or barley water until progress was seen in his condition.

On July 11, 1865, Pvt. Hall was considered well enough to be released from the hospital and returned to duty.

While in the line of battle before Petersburg on the morning of April 2, 1865, the soldier was wounded in the right hand. The little finger was broken, and the hand was badly cut and torn by a missile from a gunshot. He was taken to his first aid station where bleeding was stopped and his hand was hastily bandaged. From the aid station, Cornelius was taken by ambulance wagon to a first division hospital in the field farther behind the lines where the doctors applied a simple water dressing to the wounds. Simple water dressings were composed of folded lint rinsed in cold water and held in place by a cloth wrap or adhesive plaster *(Schaadt)*.

On April 3, he was taken to the military railroad put on a mattress in a boxcar, the floor of which was cushioned with straw or hay, and taken to the depot hospital at City Point where his wounds received the same treatment.

Private Hall remained in the City Point hospital for about fifteen days until he was discharged and returned to duty on April 18. He suffered quite a bit from the soreness and weakness of his hand and from rheumatism, which caused pain in his joints.

Discharged: Private Cornelius Hall was mustered out and honorably discharged by reason of Special Order #22 at Headquarters, District of Alexandria, Ninth Army Corps, dated May 20, 1865. He was paid money owed to him for his service at the time of his discharge and returned to Michigan.

Biography: Cornelius Ward Hall, known also as Negawnesay or Kawgaygawbowe, was the son of Frederick, known as Kawgaygawbowe, a Grand River Band Ottawa chief, and Brickerd (or Ann) (Mahwazoo) Hall. Today that Grand River Band is known as the Little River Band of Ottawa Indians.

Cornelius was baptized at the age of fourteen on November 21, 1858, by Rev. A. M. Fitch, minister of the Pentwater Methodist Episcopal Church in Oceana County. His baptism took place on the occasion of his brother Joseph's wedding to Mary (or Katherine?) in said city.

In addition to Cornelius, age eighteen, the 1860 federal census for Mason County included said parents; a brother, John, age nineteen; a sister, Masahaungeek, age five; and a sister, Taahquahne, age nine.

During the summer years of 1850–1860, Cornelius resided on the family farm with his parents and siblings. The Hall family, who were considered to be very good farmers, had 125 acres of woodland, fifty dollars' worth of implement machinery, $200 worth of livestock, and fifteen acres of tilled land under cultivation with grains and Irish potatoes. The farm was valued at $1,000 by the mid-1880s.

On September 20, 1865, Cornelius Hall married Miss Florence Nibnesey (or Nibnessey) Hill, who was known to be a premier basket maker. Rev. Isaac Greensky (brother to Rev. Peter Greensky), a Methodist Episcopal minister, officiated at the ceremony.

Cornelius (under the name "Cornelius Kawgaygawbaw") had 160 acres of land in Mason County under the Homestead Act of 1862. Its description is the southeast quarter of section 14 in township 18 north of range 16-west in the township of Pere Marquette (or Indian Town), which became Riverton Township in Mason County. His Homestead Certificate #3060 would be issued to him on June 13, 1878 (*Land Records*). Sadly, Cornelius would lose this property due to default of his mortgage on June 3, 1884.

By 1870, the federal census for Mason County listed the following Anishinabek Hall brothers (all farmers) and their families.

1. Peter, age forty-four, and Shazah, age twenty-eight, with their child, Clarissa, age five months.

2. Joseph, age forty-five, and Mary (or Katherine?), age thirty, with their children: Nancy, age fifteen; Sarah, age five; Battice, age three; and Celia, age four months.

3. John H., age thirty, and Mary, age twenty, with their children: Mary, age six; Ben, age four; and Chwnty, age two.

4. Cornelius, age twenty-eight, and Frances, age thirty, with their child, Isaac, age one.

5. George (Towokone), age ca. eighteen. He would marry Angeline Cobmoosa or Coubmosay.

6. Isaac, age ca. thirty. Wife, Mary? Daughter, Mary, age two.

Cornelius and Frances were the parents of several children, of whom only Isaac would outlive his parents. The offspring born to the couple were: Lucinda, or Lucy, who died of lung fever (or pneumonia) in July 1868 at the age of one year; Isaac, born July 5, 1870; a second daughter named Lucinda, or Lucy, born about 1871; Frederick, born in February 1880 and died of brain fever (or cerebrospinal meningitis) at the age of two years on April 19, 1882; Wilbor, born October 5, 1882, and baptized on the same date at the Riverton Indian Methodist Church in Mason County; and Alice, born June 30, 1885. Alice died of grippe (or influenza) at age seven on March 29, 1893.

Lucinda Hall married Henry Shawnosky, son of James Shenosky, on May 1, 1890. The couple's marriage was officiated by Lucy's father, Cornelius, justice of the peace. Isaac Hall would marry Maggie (or Kewondeway) Rapp, the daughter of David James and Mary Waugan Rapp, on December 23, 1894. Cornelius also officiated at this marriage. Maggie died of tuberculosis on January 19, 1908.

During his lifetime, Cornelius and his family resided on his farm at Pere Marquette, Mason County, from 1865 to 1884; St. Helens in Roscommon County from 1884 to 1885; and in Star City, West Branch Township, in Missaukee County from 1885 until his death.

When he lived in Mason County, Cornelius was an inspector of lands in Eden Township. He moved to Eden Township to take the place of a former inspector (who was familiar to him) and completed the remaining time for this gentleman's term of office.

On March 6, 1883, Application #474,772 for a pension was filed for Cornelius for his military service. He was granted an Invalid Pension Certificate #428,262 on September 26, 1890, for the sum of eight dollars a month for wounds to his right hand.

Due to default of the indenture of mortgage on his farm, Cornelius's property and tenements were seized by Sheriff John Bethune of Mason County and offered for sale on June 3, 1884. The property was bought by J. Davidson Burns of Kalamazoo County for the sum of $525.45.

After Cornelius moved to Missaukee County and took up residency on Star City Road, he became an active member of the GAR Caldwell Post #365 in Lake City. He proudly served as officer of the guard for his post in 1894.

Having experienced the death of several children at early ages, Cornelius would again know the pain of loss when three more of his loved ones died in 1897 during a four-month period. His wife, Florence, succumbed to paralysis (type not stated) at age fifty-four on April 13, and his granddaughter, Eunice Shawnosky, died of bilious fever (arising from the excess of bile in the intestine) on May 14 at one month of age (*Blakiston*). Cornelius's daughter, Lucinda Hall Shawnosky (Eunice's mother), died of milk leg or postpartum thrombophlebitis (the inflammation of a vein associated with a clot) on August 23 *(Ibid.)*.

Cornelius was elected twice to the position of justice of the peace for Missaukee County. His first term was from April 5, 1897, to April 4, 1901. His second term was from April 6, 1903, to its expiration date of July 4, 1907. When he was in office, Cornelius ruled on three land grants and purchases and arbitrated various land disputes. He also officiated at the weddings of twelve Anishinabek couples, including two of his children as mentioned previously.

Through further request applications, Cornelius's monthly allowance from his original pension was increased to twelve dollars on May 25, 1912, and to nineteen dollars a month on April 8, 1914.

Cornelius, who did not remarry, died at age seventy-three of Bright's disease (nephritis or chronic inflammatory disease of the kidney(s)) on August 5, 1917 *(Ibid.)*. His death occurred at his home in Missaukee County.

He was buried in Star City Cemetery on August 6 with religious and military honors from his Caldwell GAR Post. The cemetery is a short distance from the old Methodist Episcopal Church (no longer standing) in West Branch Township in said county. His grave site is shaded by a black cherry tree.

Known to have been a soft-spoken person, Cornelius was a caring, honest family man and a competent farmer. He possessed a good name for himself and his family and was well respected by all who knew him.

On September 6, 1917, Isaac Hall, as the only surviving son and heir-in-law, petitioned the Missaukee County Probate Court for his father's property in said county. Isaac was deemed to be the legal heir of his father by the court on October 12, 1917.

Isaac died a widower at age fifty-two on January 13, 1924, in Leelanau Township of Leelanau County. The cause of his demise was not listed on his death record.

Hamlin, James H., Private

Enlistment: Enlisted as a private on March 28, 1864, on Mackinac Island, Mackinac County by Dominic Murray, First Michigan Sharpshooters, for three years.

Age: Forty-three, born about 1821 in the Mackinac area.

Occupation: Fisherman

Residence: St. Ignace (or Point St. Ignace), Mackinac County

Physical Description: Five feet six, black eyes, black hair, and a dark complexion. Examining physician was Dr. George Landon, surgeon, First Michigan Sharpshooters.

Mustered: April 29, 1864, at Detroit, Wayne County, by Captain Warner Backlin, First Michigan Sharpshooters

Military Service: Private James H. Hamlin joined his regiment at North Anna River, Virginia, on May 26, 1864. He was captured while charging the enemy's defenses in a battle before Petersburg, Virginia, on June 17, 1864. He and other Union captives were taken by the rebels to a holding area (a tobacco warehouse in Petersburg) and kept for a few days. The captives were then put on cattle rail-cars and sent to the Confederate camp for Union prisoners, Camp Sumter (or Andersonville Prison), in Andersonville, Georgia.

On October 11, 1864, Pvt. Hamlin was admitted to the prison hospital with the diagnosis of scurvy (lack of vitamin C found in fresh fruits and vegetables).

Due to the inhumane conditions and the lack of proper food and water, Pvt. Hamlin died from scurvy on October 20, 1864. Pvt. Payson Wolfe, a Company K comrade, testified that he saw Pvt. Hamlin die from scurvy. He also related that he saw the rebel guards take him to the brush arbor "dead house" outside of the stockade.

When Private Hamlin was taken to the dead house by the guards, all usable clothing was removed from his body. Information about Hamlin was collected by a record keeper known as Dorance Atwater (also a prisoner), who kept the "Atwater

List" of those prisoners who died at Andersonville. Atwater attached a numbered tag to the body for later reference (*Encyclopedia*).

A short time later, Hamlin's body, along with other deceased soldiers, was taken by wagon to the burial ground about a mile from the prison.

At the cemetery, Hamlin's remains were placed, without a wrap and shoulder to shoulder with other deceased prisoners, into a four-foot-deep trench and covered with dirt. A small post with a number carved into it was placed at the head of his grave (*Ibid.*). This number matched the number on the body tag and was also noted in the records known about the deceased.

Today Private James H. Hamlin lies at rest under military stone #11,260 in Andersonville National Cemetery.

Discharged: No discharge given. Death from disease while a prisoner of war.

Biography: James (or Jacobert/Jackoba) H. Hamlin was born February 12, 1821. He was the son of Augustin and Angelique (or Kiminitchawgan) Hamlin Jr. and was baptized in Ste. Anne Catholic Church on Mackinac Island, Mackinac County. His siblings were: Angelique, born 1820; John B., born 1827; Moses, born 1829; Paul, born 1835; and Hyacinth (a boy), born 1838. The "H" in Hamlin's name could have stood for "Hatch," which was the middle name for James mentioned in Rosalie's application for a widow's pension on May 16, 1865.

At age thirty-three, James married Rosalie Jeandron (or Jeandreau/Gendron), age nineteen, on October 2, 1855, at Point St. Ignace (or St. Ignace Township), Mackinac County. Isaac Blanchard, justice of the peace, officiated at the wedding ceremony. Witnesses to the marriage were Widow Larcher and Mrs. Blanchard.

Rosalie was the granddaughter of Michael Sr. and Anabid Jeandron (or Gendron), early settlers of St. Ignace; the daughter of Michael Jr. and Mary Ann? Jeandron; and the sister of Michael Jeandron III, a member of Company K. Through marriage to Rosalie, James H. Hamlin became a brother-in-law to Michael Jeandron III (*RootsWeb*).

James and Rosalie (Jeandron) Hamlin were the parents of five children, all of whom were born at Point St. Ignace: Helen (or Ellen), born July 8, 1856 (who may have married a Lozon and died May 15, 1878); Michael, born April 25, 1858; James (Jacobent) H. Jr., born April 8, 1860; Augustin, born December 30, 1861; and Moses F., born February 27, 1864.

With the exception of Helen (or Ellen), the Hamlin children were baptized by the Rev. Father A.D.J. Piret at the St. Ignatius Loyola Catholic Church in St. Ignace on the following dates: (1) Helen was baptized by Father Jahan on August 14, 1856;

godparents were Moses Hamlin and Helene Messway. (2) Michael was baptized on April 16, 1858; godparents were Pierre Pont vulgo Robesco and Josette Perault. (3) Jacobert (or James Jr.) was baptized on May 6, 1860; godparents were Antoine (or Anthony) Martin and Helene Messway. (4) Augustine (or Augustus) was baptized on January 29, 1862; godfather was Aimable Ance (or Hens), and godmother was Marie Ann Evajibanoie. Augustine would marry Mary Beaudoin, born in 1871. (5) Moses was baptized March 6, 1864; godfather was Joseph Messway, and godmother was Angelique Hamlin. Moses would marry Elizabeth Belanger, born in 1874 at Carp River, Mackinac County.

Application #98,298 for a widow's pension was submitted for Rosalie on June 17, 1865. She received a Widow's Pension Certificate #76,732 on June 23, 1866, which paid eight dollars a month. Sometime later, Rosalie applied for an increase of her widow's pension. On July 25, 1866, she received a two dollars' increase for each of her five children, in addition to the eight dollars she was already allowed per month, making a total of eighteen dollars a month.

On August 4, 1870, Rosalie married for the second time to Moses F. Hamlin, a shoemaker, at Mackinac, (probably St. Ignace). He was a brother to her first husband, James H. Hamlin. Rev. J. A. Van Fleet officiated at the couple's wedding. Witnesses to the ceremony were Dr. J. H. Holister of Chicago and Miss Delia Gulett (or Gillett) of Marshal, Calhoun County.

When Rosalie remarried to Moses Hamlin, she was no longer eligible to receive a widow's pension for James's service. The US government expected her new husband to support her. Pension money for the children's support would continue to be paid through a court-appointed guardian for the children.

After the widow's remarriage in 1870, Bela Chapman, judge of probate of Mackinac County, appointed a Mr. Thomas Chambers on September 2, 1870, as guardian to the five Hamlin children.

The appointment for guardian was made on September 20, 1870. Application #193,717 for a pension for minor children was filed for Chambers on February 6, 1871. Chambers did receive (as guardian) a Pension for Minor Children Certificate #155,204 dated January 2, 1872. The same payments, as in the widow's pension, were continued and paid to Chambers for the children's support from the date of Rosalie's remarriage. The two-dollar extra monthly payments for each child ceased as he, or she, attained the age of sixteen. Total payments were stopped when the youngest child, Moses, turned sixteen on February 26, 1880.

On January 13, 1872, a Patent Certificate #498 was granted to James H. Hamlin for eighty acres by reason of the first article of the treaty concluded July 31, 1855, between the US Commissioners and the Ottawa and Chippewa Indians of Michigan. The land description is the west half of the southwest quarter, of section 12 in township 34 north, of range 6 west, in the District of Lands subject to sale at Traverse City, Michigan, in Emmet County. James's children inherited his patent.

Hannin, Joseph, Private

Enlistment: Enlisted as a private on February 3, 1865, at Mendon, St. Joseph County, by J. F. Lobdell, First Michigan Sharpshooters, and a notary public for Wayne County, for three years. Enlistment credited to Mendon in the Second Congressional District to satisfy the requirement for a man from that area.

Age: Thirty-five, born about February 3, 1830, in Oneida County, New York.

Occupation: Farmer and laborer

Residence: Mendon

Physical Description: Five feet nine and a half inches tall, black eyes, black hair, and a dark complexion. Examining physician was Dr. George Landon, surgeon, First Michigan Sharpshooters.

Mustered: February 4, 1865, at Detroit, Wayne County, by Major E. Detrhy, First Michigan Sharpshooters

Military Service: It was reported by Hannin (and verified by his Company K comrades, Thomas Kechittigo and Moses Thomas) that he suffered from sore eyes (due to exposure, dust, and a cold) and rheumatism (with extreme pain in his legs). These maladies were the result of severe cold weather and of standing in cold water in the trenches before Petersburg, Virginia.

Sgt. Kechittigo also stated that sometime during his service before Petersburg, Pvt. Hannin was reported to have been knocked breathless by the explosion of a shell near him. He was carried from the trenches to his division hospital behind the lines and remained in the hospital until he recovered.

Both Thomas and Kechittigo further related that a short time after the regiment had gone into camp outside of Washington, DC, Pvt. Hannin had become ill with yellow fever and diarrhea. He was admitted to a First Division, Ninth Army Corps field hospital on June 12, 1865, and spent about three weeks there.

The soreness in his eyes (severe conjunctivitis) was diagnosed as not of "vicious habits" (or venereal disease) and became worse accompanied by increased loss of sight.

Treatment for Hannin's yellow fever began with complete isolation. He was given calomel (a lump of mercurous chloride that contained mercury and called "blue mass"), quinine, opiates, and castor oil for fever and pain. Pvt. Hannin was also immersed in hot baths that contained four to eight ounces of mustard to produce perspiration (*Bollet*).

Among the medicines used to treat his diarrhea would have been calomel and ingested turpentine along with opiates for pain (*Ibid.*).

Hannin's eyes were treated with repeated washings of a dram of alum in a pint of tepid water and applications of silver nitrate in water to the inner surface of his eyelids (*Dorwart*).

Joseph returned to duty on July 6.

Discharged: Pvt. Joseph Hannin was mustered out and honorably discharged at Delaney House, Georgetown, Washington, DC, on July 28, 1865. He returned to Michigan on the steamer *Morning Star.* On August 7, Hannin was paid money due to him for his service at Jackson, Jackson County.

After he was paid, Hannin returned to the Oneida Indian Reserve, Delaware Township, County of Middlesex, Ontario Province, Canada.

Biography: Joseph Hannin stated in his pension papers that he was born February 1, 1830, in Oneida County, New York, and always considered himself a citizen of the United States. He was a member of the Oneida Indian Nation.

The Oneida Indian Nation—the *Ona yote ka o no*—the "Granite People" or "People of the Rock," was one of six tribes that were members of the Iroquois Confederation (*Richards*). The confederation included the Mohawk, Oneida, Onondaga, Cayuga, Seneca, and (after 1723) the Tuscarora tribes.

The Oneida cast their lot, along with a few members of the Tuscarora tribe, with the American Patriots and not with Great Britain in the Revolutionary War—the only tribe of the confederation to do so. Oneida tribesmen were of great help to the American Patriots and were faithful allies. The Patriots called the Oneida Nation their "First Allies." These allies provided information, warriors, scouts, and food to the Patriots (*Oneida*).

As a young child, Hannin and his family moved with many of the members of the Oneida Indian Nation from New York to Ontario, Canada sometime during the years of 1840/1841.

In 1858, Joseph Hannin married Laglete Sickles at the Oneida Indian Mission in

Muncy, Province of Ontario, Canada. Rev. Abraham Sickles, an ordained Oneida Indian Methodist Minister, officiated at the ceremony. Laglete may have been the daughter of the minister. Joseph and Laglete were the parents of two children: Jemima Sickles, born in June 1860, and Elijah Hannin, born in May 1877.

Joseph returned to the United States to join the First Michigan Sharpshooters and listed Mendon of St. Joseph County as his residence when he enlisted into Company K. There were Potawatomi Anishinabek who lived at or near Mendon, St. Joseph County. Company K comrade David Lidger also listed his residence as Mendon of said county before he enlisted into the sharpshooter unit. He too was a member of the Oneida Nation. Was there a reason that both Oneida men lived, for a short time, near the Potawatomi? Since both men were of the Oneida Nation and lived near Mendon, they more than likely knew each other.

After his military service, Hannin returned to his family in Canada.

On September 2, 1890, Application #928,331 for an invalid pension was submitted for Hannin from Melbourne PO, Middlesex County, Province of Ontario, Canada. It was rejected.

Hannin reapplied for an invalid pension in 1891.

In 1896, he received an Invalid Pension Certificate #905,849 for the reasons of rheumatism, partial blindness in his right eye, and weakness of sight in his left eye. The pension was granted under the generous Act of June 27, 1890, which allowed payments of six to twelve dollars to veterans who served for three months, were honorably discharged, and who suffered from physical or mental disabilities that kept them from earning a living. Pension payments to Hannin were six dollars a month. There was a discrepancy as to whether he received his first payment of $17.20. He claimed that he did not receive his payment but was given only a suit of clothes in lieu of his money by the attorney who handled his pension case.

Hannin's debilities left him unable to perform any meaningful manual labor. He seemed to be dependent upon neighbors and friends for charity, as well as his pension, to help support his family.

In 1904, Hannin received a four-dollar increase in his pension payments to total ten dollars a month.

By 1907, Hannin's pension payments were increased by two dollars, which resulted in a total payment of twelve dollars a month.

Joseph Hannin died January 7, 1916, at his home in Melbourne, Middlesex County, Ontario, Canada, and was buried in said county.

Hubert, Charles, Private

Enlistment: Enlisted as a private on August 9, 1863, at Detroit, Wayne County, by Lieutenant Garrett A. Graveraet, First Michigan Sharpshooters, for three years.

Age: Twenty-eight, born about 1835 in St. Ignace, Mackinac County.

Occupation: Sailor

Residence: Sault St. Marie (the Soo), Chippewa County, in Michigan's Upper Peninsula

Physical Description: Five feet seven, gray eyes, black/brown hair, and a brown complexion. Examining physician was Dr. Arvin F. Whelan, surgeon, First Michigan Sharpshooters.

Mustered: September 29, 1863, at Camp Douglas in Chicago, Cook County, Illinois, by Captain Duryea, First Michigan Sharpshooters. Another source stated that Charles was mustered at the Detroit Arsenal in Dearborn, Wayne County. Camp Douglas was the confine for Confederate prisoners where the sharpshooters were guards for seven months.

Military Service: On October 6, 1863, while Private Hubert was on guard duty at Camp Douglas, he was arrested. No reason was given for his arrest, but money was retained from his pay for his arrest.

Hubert was admitted from his regiment to Division No.1, USA General Hospital at the United States Naval Academy (Navy Yard) in Annapolis, Maryland, on March 23, 1864. He was suffering from severe otitis media – the inflammation of the middle ear (*Blakiston*). It was common during that time to treat an earache by putting sweet oil (such as olive oil) in the ear canal and applying a hot brick bound in cloth to the ear to help draw out the infection (*Denney*). Hubert was discharged from the hospital and rejoined his regiment on April 1.

On June 24, 1864, Pvt. Hubert sustained a back injury in the battlefield before Petersburg, Virginia. He was taken by ambulance wagon to the military railroad. At the railroad, Hubert was put on a mattress in a boxcar, the floor of which was cushioned with straw or hay, and sent to the depot hospital at City Point. At the hospital, Hubert was treated with poultices and mustard plasters that consisted of a mixture of ground mustard seed, flour, and water wrapped in a flannel cloth and secured to the patient's body with a cloth wrap or adhesive plaster (*Internet*). He was also given opium pills for pain,

After a few days, Hubert was taken to a wharf at City Point, transferred to a hospital steamer, and sent to Armory Square Hospital in Washington, DC. He was given similar treatment at Armory Square and released to rejoin his regiment on July 1.

When he was in the trenches before Petersburg on July 23, 1864, Pvt. Hubert sustained a gunshot (missile) wound to his left hand. His wound was assessed at a first aid station behind the lines and the bleeding was stopped. His hand was hastily bandaged and he was put on a boxcar at the military railroad (as previously described) and sent to the depot hospital at City Point.

It seems that Hubert's injury was a very painful flesh wound. The doctors at City Point treated his wound with the application of a simple cold water dressing. The dressing was composed of folded lint rinsed in cold water, placed on the wound, and held in place by a cloth wrap or adhesive plaster (*Schaadt*).

Pvt. Hubert was again taken to a wharf at City Point, transferred to the hospital steamer *DeMoley*, and sent to Mower USA General Hospital at Chestnut Hill near Philadelphia, Pennsylvania, on July 26. His wound was again treated with simple dressings.

Hubert remained at Mower Hospital until he was given a furlough of twenty days on September 5, 1864. He was to return to the hospital after his furlough.

Pvt. Charles Hubert was listed as deserted on January 6, 1865, from Mower Hospital. There is no record of his return to the hospital after his furlough.

Discharged: No muster out or discharge was found for Private Hubert.

Biography: Charles Hubert's father was Jack Hubert, who was the nephew of the chief of Grand Traverse. In the 1836 Census of Ottawa and Chippewa (or Ojibwa) Mixed Breed, a Hubert family, who lived in St. Ignace, included Jack (father), born in 1797 (no mother listed—she may have been deceased by 1836) and children: Margaret, born 1824; Louis, born 1827; Xavier, born 1831; Nancy, born 1833; and Charles, born 1835 (*Census*).

Charles was recorded as married on his military hospital papers and his wife, listed as Mrs. Charles Hubert, was thought to have lived in South Ste. Mary's or Sault Ste. Marie, Chippewa County. If he did desert his unit from Mower Hospital with no explanation, and if there was no discharge recorded due to his desertion, he would not have been eligible for a pension. There is no pension file for Charles Hubert.

Isaacs, John, Private

Enlistment: Enlisted as a private on May 16, 1863, at Port Huron, St. Clair County, by Frederick Dunn, First Michigan Sharpshooters, for three years.

Age: Twenty-one, born about 1842 in Sarnia, Ontario, Canada. Another record states that his birth was on Walpole Island, First Nation, Ontario, Canada.

Occupation: Farmer

Residence: Isabella City (now Mt. Pleasant), Isabella County

Physical Description: Five feet eight, black eyes, black hair, and a dark complexion. Examining physician was Dr. Jacob B. McNett, assistant surgeon, First Michigan Sharpshooters.

Mustered: May 26, 1863, at Detroit, Wayne County, by Lieutenant Colonel John R. Smith, US Army

Military Service: Private Isaacs was reported to have deserted his regiment on June 12, 1863, at Detroit. He was arrested at Detroit by C. Gebhard, provost marshal of the First District of Michigan on July 18, 1864. Isaacs had been seen on the towboat *Dispatch* by three men and identified as being a soldier who was wearing soldier's clothes. At his arrest, it was discovered that he had used the alias "Joseph Walker."

In addition to the thirty dollars deducted from his pay for the expense of his arrest, Isaacs was charged ten dollars per month from July 4, 1863, to July 4, 1864. Although he was not formally under a court-martial, since he had no record of further stoppages against him, John was sentenced to make good his absence of one year and twenty-three days by judgment and order of a general court-martial.

Pvt. Isaacs rejoined his regiment on November 4, 1864, at Peebles House, Virginia. He served faithfully with his unit and took his turn as a brigade guard until he was discharged. There is no record of illness or injury for John Isaacs during his military service.

Discharged: Private John Isaacs was mustered out and honorably discharged at Detroit under Circular 31 of the Adjutant General's Office on August 11, 1865. He received money due to him for his service at that time.

Biography: John may have been a brother or cousin to William Isaacs, who was also in Company K. There is no pension file for John Isaacs.

Isaacs, William, Private

Enlistment: Enlisted as a private on May 18, 1863, at Isabella City (now Mt. Pleasant), Isabella County, by Lieutenant William J. Driggs, First Michigan

Sharpshooters, for three years. He also filled out some enlistment papers in which he used the name "Wahnasega" and "Isaac Wahnasega" in addition to William Isaacs.

Age: Nineteen, born about 1844 in Saginaw County.

Occupation: Farmer and laborer

Residence: Isabella City

Physical Description: Five feet ten and a half inches tall, black eyes, dark hair, and a dark complexion. Examining physician was Dr. George L. Cornell, assistant surgeon, First Michigan Sharpshooters.

Mustered: May 26, 1863, at the Dearborn Arsenal, Wayne County, by Lieutenant Colonel John R. Smith, US Army

Military Service: Private William Isaacs, who, like John Isaacs, also used the alias "Joseph Walker." On December 3, Private Isaacs became quite ill while on guard duty at the confine for Confederate prisoners at Camp Douglas, Chicago, Cook County, Illinois. He was admitted to the USA Post Hospital where he was diagnosed with pneumonia.

The doctors prescribed opiates to relieve his pain and to suppress his cough. Cathartics (or purgatives) such as castor oil and turpentine were administered to cleanse his system *(Evans)*.

Cupping was an option in which blisters were formed and then drained—a very painful procedure *(Ibid.)*. A mustard plaster was probably used, as it was thought to draw out any poison in his lungs. The plaster was a poultice or a mixture of ground black mustard seed, water, and flour spread onto the inside of a cloth of cotton or flannel and applied to the chest *(Internet)*.

William returned to duty on December 19.

Sometime around June 1, 1864, while in the line of duty, an unexploded artillery cannon shell landed near Isaacs's feet, and the impact caused bacterial laden dirt to be thrown into his eyes. A short time later, Isaacs suffered ocular inflammation of his eyes called conjunctivitis (or opthalmia). This incident would result in severe damage to his eyesight.

William was taken by ambulance wagon to a division field hospital near White House Landing on the Pamunkey River where doctors repeatedly washed his eyes with a solution of a dram of alum in tepid water *(Dorwart)*. Also, nitrate of silver in water was applied to the inner portion of his eyelids *(Ibid)*.

On June 10 Isaacs suffered a gunshot wound (missile) to his right thigh. The missile entered a few inches above his right knee and exited just below the knee. He was taken from his division field hospital near White House Landing where he was put on a hospital steamer and transferred to Mount Pleasant USA General Hospital in Washington, DC, where he was admitted on June 11.

Treatment for his missile wounds consisted of the application of bromine to the wound sites to impede infection, and simple water dressings. Simple dressings consisted of folded lint rinsed in cold water, applied to the wounds, and secured in place with a cloth wrap or adhesive plaster (*Schaadt*). Treatment for the inflammatory condition of Isaac's eyes was continued.

On June 17, William was sent from Mt. Pleasant Hospital to Haddington USA General Hospital in West Philadelphia, Pennsylvania, and admitted on June 18. Similar treatments were continued, and a hearty diet was ordered for him. He remained at Haddington until he returned to his regiment on February 13, 1865. Due to the severity of his injuries, Isaacs performed only light duty until his discharge.

Discharged: Private William Isaacs was mustered out and honorably discharged on July 28, 1865, at Delaney House, Georgetown, Washington, DC. He returned to Detroit on the steamer *Morning Star*. Isaacs was paid money owed to him for his service on August 7 at Jackson, Jackson County.

Biography: William Isaacs may have been a brother or a cousin to John Isaacs, who was also a soldier in Company K.

After his discharge from the army, William Isaacs married Waingekeyzhegoquay (or Sarah), the daughter of William and Waindawbawnoquay Fisher. Sarah's siblings were: Mayyawsenoquay, Kaybayawsequay, Maydwayshemaw, and Penaysewekezhegoquay (*Gruett*). William and Sarah were the parents of a daughter, Emma, born sometime during the latter part of 1866.

In a letter written by William's granddaughter, Mrs. Blanche (Chatfield) West, Blanche mentioned that William deserted his wife and child a few years after Emma was born (*West*). There is no record of William having returned to his family.

After he left Sarah and Emma, Isaacs lived in the counties of Mecosta, Cheboygan, Crawford, Otsego, Emmett, and Charlevoix where he worked as a laborer and a lumberjack.

When he lived in Cheboygan County, he joined GAR Post #264 in Wolverine and enjoyed visiting with other veterans.

During his later years, Isaacs grew so increasingly feeble, due to pain and lameness in his right leg, that he was barely able to hold a laborer's job. Also, his eyesight continued to deteriorate. It's possible that Isaac's opthalmia could have been what was called keratoconjunctivitis, or chronic granulated sore eyes, caused by virulent bacteria. The dirt thrown into his eyes may have contained this bacterial agent. The ocular condition of inflammation of the cornea and conjunctiva can be of short duration, or it can last for months or years. Also, the affliction could have caused a continued severe visual debilitation and was known to be resistant to treatment used during the Civil War (*Altic*).

William Isaacs had thirty-eight and eighteen/one-hundredths acres of land in Isabella County by right of the first article of the treaty of August 2, 1855, and the second article of the treaty of October 18, 1864, between the United States and Chippewas of Saginaw, Swan Creek, and Black River of Michigan. Its location is described as the northwest quarter of the northwest quarter of section 2 in township 14 north of range 3 west. The patent certificate was issued to Isaacs on May 27, 1871 (*Land Records*).

On April 11, 1881, Application #419,031 for an invalid pension was filed for William. He received an Invalid Pension Certificate #348,099 in February 1887, which paid two dollars a month. In 1890, Isaacs received an increase to four dollars, which netted him a total payment of six dollars a month.

On March 13, 1895, while trapping in Cheboygan County twelve miles east of Wolverine, Isaacs's right foot was so badly frostbitten that he had to have all the toes amputated. The accident further decreased his ability to do any manual labor except to make a few baskets for additional income. Due to his increased disability from the trapping accident, Isaacs received an additional two dollars a month in 1899 to total eight dollars in monthly payments. By February 1905, he received twelve dollars a month in pension payments.

William Isaacs died on March 16, 1907, at his home in Boyne City, Charlevoix County. He was listed as buried in plot #89 in a section called "Potters Field" of Maple Lawn Cemetery in said city. His grave has been identified and is now marked with a military stone.

There is a questionable story about William's death and burial place. According to Louis (or Chelsea) Leaureux, who lived in Mt. Pleasant in 1958, William Isaacs (whom Leaureux thought had returned to Mt. Pleasant) died in Isabella County and was buried in the old Mount Pleasant Indian School Cemetery. This information was told to Mrs. Blanche West but was not verified by her since she was not able to visit the school cemetery to check out Louis's information (*Ibid.-West*).

Jacko, John, Private

Enlistment: Enlisted as a private on February 14, 1865, at Grand Rapids, Kent County, by Captain Norman Bailey, First Michigan Sharpshooters and provost marshal for the Fourth District of Michigan. The enlistment was for one year and was credited to the Fourth Congressional District, Leelanau, Leelanau County.

Age: Twenty, born about 1843 in Northport, Leelanau County.

Occupation: Laborer

Residence: Northport

Physical Description: Five feet eight, black eyes, black hair, and a dark complexion. Examining physician was Dr. Alonzo Mate, surgeon, First Michigan Sharpshooters.

Mustered: February 14, 1865, at Grand Rapids, Kent County, by Captain Norman Bailey, First Michigan Sharpshooters and provost marshal for the Fourth District of Michigan.

Military Service: While John was on picket duty in the breastworks before Petersburg, Virginia, on the evening of March 23, 1865, his clothing became soaked in the continuous cold rain of a severe storm that lasted all night. It wasn't long before he contracted a cold in his lungs. His tent mate, Albert Pesherbay (Peshawbey), commented that Jacko became so sick with chills that his whole body shook. He complained of severe headaches, fever, and pain in his joints and lungs. So intense was his illness that he was immediately admitted to a division hospital in the field near Petersburg on March 24. In the hospital, Jacko was diagnosed with remittent fever, severe bronchitis, and acute diarrhea.

Remittent fever is paroxysmal fever of sudden occurrence with exacerbations and remissions but without intermissions (*Blakiston*). Jacko's remittent fever was most probably a case of malaria. Malaria is an infectious disease caused by one of the genus *Plasmodium* and transmitted by infected mosquitoes of the genus *Anopheles (Ibid.).* The doctors treated the malaria with powdered quinine bark mixed with whiskey or water, or with pills of purified quinine sulfate. Whiskey worked better, as it masked the bitter taste of quinine. Quinine also provided pain relief (*Bollet*).

For his bronchitis, doctors treated Jacko with a mustard plaster, which was a poultice or a mixture of ground black mustard seed, water, and flour spread onto a cloth of cotton or flannel and applied to his chest (*Internet*). It was a belief that the plaster would draw out the poison that caused the bronchitis. Opiates were also administered.

Jacko was treated for his acute diarrhea with opiates in an alcoholic solution called laudanum (*Ibid.-Bollet*). Dover's powder that contained ipecac and opium was also used in the treatment of his diarrhea (*Evans*).

On March 26, Jacko was sent by hospital train to the depot hospital at City Point, Virginia, for further treatment. A bland diet of boiled water, diluted coffee and tea, barley water, rice water, and broth made from meat extract was ordered for Jacko. As his digestive tolerance improved, citrus juices and fresh fruits and vegetables were added to his diet.

He remained at this hospital until April 6 when he was moved to the Convalescent Camp Branch area of the same hospital.

Similar treatment and diet were continued at the Convalescent Camp Branch. Jacko remained at the Camp Branch area hospital until he returned to limited duty with his regiment about the middle of April. He suffered constantly with lung problems throughout the rest of his service.

Discharged: Private John Jacko was mustered out and honorably discharged on July 28, 1865, at Delaney House, Georgetown, Washington, DC. He returned to Detroit on the steamer *Morning Star*. Jacko was paid the money owed to him for his service at Jackson, Jackson County, on August 7.

Biography: John Jacko, who also signed his name as John Jocko, was born about 1843 or 1845, the son of Jacko (or Jake) and Mary Ann (or Ogawbayosaqua) Penaiswonquot. He was also known by the name Kahkebonoka, which translates as "window maker." The family's surname was also known as Shako. He was a nephew of Noah Wadasahmosay, who was Jake's brother and a third cousin to James Awanagezhik, a comrade in Company K. Jacko Penaiswonquot was also a member of Company K and died a prisoner of war at Fort Sumter (Andersonville Prison) at Andersonville, Georgia, on October 30, 1864.

One of John Jacko's brothers was Louis, known by the names of Louis Nahtahwinodin, which means "first wind," Louis Penaiswanquot, and Nahtahwinodin Jacko. Louis was a member of Company K but was not listed on the roster. The other Jacko siblings were Catherine, Susan, Simon, William, Andrew, and Mary Ann.

Sometime after his service, John Jacko married Angeline Wadash. The couple were the parents of Thomas, Joshua, Fred, Noah, and Abram. Angeline died at Good Hart, Emmet County, in July 1885.

On August 11, 1885, John Jacko married secondly to Susan Songa/Songo/Sonyo Andrews, who was the widow of Silas Andrews. Silas died in August 1884 at Horton Bay, Charlevoix County. Susan was born in Isabella City (now Mt. Pleasant),

Isabella County, in May 1849. She stated her address as East Saginaw, Saginaw County. The couple was married by Edwin R. Boynton, justice of the peace. The ceremony was witnessed by Peter Wells, Jacko's army buddy in Company K, and J. B. Sull.

John and Susan Jacko were the parents of Mary, born January 12, 1892; William, born in 1894 and died of convulsions on July 18, 1895; Martha, born September 15, 1896; Alice, born January 1, 1900; and Anthony, born in January 1902 and died of strangulation on June 16 of said year.

After his discharge from the army, John Jacko and his family lived in several Anishinabek settlements. They resided in Northport, Leelanau County, from 1865 to 1877 and Good Hart, Emmet County, from 1877 to 1887. After 1887, the Jacko family moved to Horton Bay, where they remained. Jacko was known to have worked in various lumber camps to help support his family.

John Jacko's health continued to deteriorate over the years after he left the military service. His coughing became much worse, and he began to spit up blood, which indicated the possibility of tuberculosis. He complained of stiffness in his joints and general overall pain in his body.

When he was able, he supported his family by loading wood onto sailing vessels on Pine Lake in Charlevoix County and by farming and fishing. But the work in the wood yard and on the farm became increasingly difficult for him. In the winter months, he would become bedridden for weeks at a time.

John was a member of the GAR Miles Norton Post #401 located in Horton Bay. He attended the post meetings, when he was physically able, and enjoyed the companionship of fellow veterans.

On September 29, 1888, Application #673,904 for an invalid pension was submitted for John Jacko. He received an Invalid Pension Certificate #896,246 on October 9, 1895, which paid ten dollars a month.

In September 1898, Jacko reported that he thought that his pension certificate was stolen from his house while he and his family were away. In lieu of the missing certificate, another certificate was sent to him in October 1899.

On June 6, 1906, Jacko's pension payments were increased by two dollars to a total of twelve dollars per month.

John Jacko died at the age of sixty-four on April 21, 1907, in Evangeline Township of Charlevoix County from complications brought on by pneumonia.

An obituary printed in the *Charlevoix Sentinel* on Thursday, April 25, 1907, mentioned that John Jacko had complained of being sick, with evidence of pneumonia, a week before he died. The obituary also stated that Jacko's death occurred in the lumber camp shack that he shared with fellow logger David Paul.

Cemetery records show that John was buried in an unmarked grave on April 22, 1907. His grave is in the GAR section of Maple Lawn Cemetery in Boyne City, Charlevoix County. Today a military stone marks his burial site.

Application #872,707 for a widow's pension was filed for Susan Jacko on July 5, 1907. Her husband's death left her and her children destitute. She did earn some money by selling the baskets that she made to people who frequented resort areas. Also, she received some monetary help from Charlevoix County.

Susan received her Widow's Pension Certificate #739,295 on March 27, 1912. The pension payments were eight dollars a month from July 5, 1907, and were increased to twelve dollars per month from April 19, 1908. In addition to Susan's monthly payments, there was a two dollar per month additional payment for each of her three minor children until each child attained the age of sixteen years. Therefore, her monthly pension payments totaled eighteen dollars a month with a decrease of two dollars a month as each of the three children reached the age of sixteen.

The last known place of residence for Susan Jacko was Mt. Pleasant, Isabella County, as of February 6, 1917.

Jacko, Natahwinodin, Private

Enlistment: Enlisted as a private on November 18, 1864, at Traverse City, Leelanau County, by Captain Norman Bailey, First Michigan Sharpshooters and provost marshal for the Fourth District of Michigan. The enlistment was for one year and was credited to the Fourth Congressional District, Bingham Township, Leelanau County. Even though this man enlisted, his name does not appear on the Sharpshooter roster as a member of Company K.

Age: Twenty-four, born about 1840 near Mapleton on Old Mission Peninsula in Leelanau County.

Occupation: Farmer

Residence: Leelanau County

Physical Description: Five feet nine and a half inches tall dark eyes, dark hair, and a dark (copper) complexion. Examining physician was Dr. Alonzo Mate, First Michigan Sharpshooters.

Mustered: November 18, 1864, at Grand Rapids, Kent County, by Captain

Norman Bailey, First Michigan Sharpshooters and provost marshal for the Fourth District of Michigan.

Military Service: It is the author's belief that Natahwinodin Jacko (also known as Louis Penaiswanquot or Pasanaquot) and Jacob Prestawin (or Pestawin) are possibly one and the same man. See file on Jacob Prestawin.

The physical descriptions, places of residence, and enlistment information for both men are identical. The differences were: Natahwinodin Jacko did not have an enlistment paper as Prestawin did but did have a certificate of disability for a discharge paper. The discharge paper listed the identical information ascribed to Prestawin, but Prestawin did not have a discharge paper.

On May 11, 1865, Natahwinodin Jacko, who was suffering from a high fever, was admitted to a division depot hospital near Alexandria, Virginia.

On May 22, he was transferred by hospital steamer to Mount Pleasant USA General Hospital in Washington, DC, diagnosed with typhoid fever and diarrhea. Typhoid fever is spread by eating food or drinking water contaminated with *Salmonella typhosa (Blakiston)*. Patients with typhoid fever exhibit generalized malaise, fever, and red skin lesions called "rose spots" (*Bollet*). Jacko was isolated from other patients.

The doctors reduced his fever with emetics, such as tartar emetic (composed of antimony and potassium), to induce vomiting and cathartics (or purgatives), such as castor oil, to cleanse his system (*Evans*). Cloths dipped into cold water and sponge baths with cold water, or water and alcohol, were also used. Other treatments for the fever could have included giving quinine, mercurials such as calomel (or mercurous chloride), and oil of turpentine by mouth (*Ibid.-Bollet*). Abdominal cupping and blistering agents were also used to increase blood flow (*Ibid.-Bollet*). Opium in alcohol called "laudanum" was administered for pain (*Ibid.-Bollet*).

Jacko's diarrhea was treated with castor oil and Dover's powder that contained ipecac (dried rhizome and roots of a member of the *Cephaelis* species) and opium (*Ibid.-Evans*). A bland diet of boiled water, diluted coffee and tea, barley water, rice water, and broth made from meat extract was ordered for Jacko. As his digestive tolerance improved, citrus juices and fresh fruits and vegetables were added to his diet.

Discharged: With two-thirds disability due to an imperfect recovery from an attack of typhoid fever and chronic diarrhea of seven weeks' standing, Private Natahwinodin Jacko was discharged from the service. He was given a certificate of disability for discharge from Mt. Pleasant Hospital on July 3, 1865. Dr. H. Allen, assistance surgeon in charge of the hospital, signed Jacko's discharge. The soldier was paid the money owed to him for his service at the time of his discharge.

Biography: Natahwinodin Jacko was also known as Louis Penaiswanquot. Natahwinodin means "first wind" and was this man's Anishinabe name. He was the son of Jacko (or Jacob) and Marianne (Ogabeosokwe) Penaiswanquot (Pasanoquot). See file on Jacko Penaiswanquot. His siblings were John (Kakebonoka or "window maker"), born about 1848 (see file on John Jacko); Catherine (or Nascan), born about 1850, who married Louis Manitowash; Susan (or Shawnosaqua), born about 1852; Simon, born about 1854; William (or Kahbenahe), born about 1856; Andrew, born about 1858; and Mary Ann, born about 1861. The first four children were born on Old Mission Peninsula near Mapleton, Grand Traverse County. The last four were born at Northport, Leelanau County. Natahwinodin Jacko (or Louis P.) did not marry.

After his father Jacob's death in Andersonville Prison, Natahwinodin Jacko enlisted in his father's company, Company K. His brother, John Jacko, also enlisted into Company K on a different date.

Natahwinodin Jacko (or Louis P.) returned home very ill. On July 25, 1870, Application #158,777 for an invalid pension was submitted for him at Traverse City, Grand Traverse County. The application was submitted under the Act of July 14, 1862 (disability incurred in the line of duty). He sited that the onset of his disability of weakness in his legs, after his discharge, was the result of the rigors of constructing breastworks while standing guard in the rain and from hard work and marching in the hot weather. He also felt that the crowded camp conditions and inclement weather contributed to his ongoing bout with typhoid fever and chronic diarrhea while he was on duty in Washington, DC.

On August 27, 1870, the Adjutant General's Office reported that the name Nahtahwinodin Jacko could not be found on the rolls of Company K. Not receiving any further communication from this man, the Pension Office subsequently abandoned his application for an invalid pension.

Even though quite ill, Natahwinodin Jacko tried to support his mother and siblings in whatever labor he could find. To compound his illnesses, he contracted tuberculosis.

He was taken to Harper General Hospital in Detroit on October 1, 1870, by the Indian agent and died in that hospital on November 29.

Natahwinodin Jacko was buried in section S, lot 14, row 3, of the Civil War

Section of Elmwood Cemetery in Detroit, Michigan. His headstone reads "Jacko Nat-Bah-Me-No-Ling, 1st. Michigan Infantry" (should be 1st. Michigan S.S.).

On December 23, 1896, Application #645,502 for a dependent mother's pension was filed for Marianne Penaiswanquot (Pasanoquot). This application was submitted under the more liberal Act of June 27, 1890, on Natahwinodin's (or Louis's) military service (soldier served ninety days and was honorably discharged). Many depositions were given by people who knew that the soldier Natahwinodin Jacko (or Louis P.) actually did serve in Company K.

Marianne's application for a dependent mother's pension was rejected on the grounds that she was already a pensioner under the service of her husband, Jacob Penaiswanquot (or Pasanoquot), and held a Widow's Pension Certificate #263,983, which paid twelve dollars a month. She was unaware that she could not receive two pensions at the same time.

Marianne Penaiswanquot died on July 15, 1905, near Suttons Bay in Leelanau County, while living with her son William.

Jackson, Edward Andrew, Private

Enlistment: Enlisted as a private on October 1, 1864, at Detroit, Wayne County, by J. F. Lobdell, notary public at Wayne County, for three years. The enlistment was credited to the First Congressional District, Hamtramck, Subdistrict Twelve, Wayne County.

Age: Twenty-seven, born July 4, 1837, in Hyde Park, New York.

Occupation: Laborer

Residence: Harwich, Kent County, Ontario, Canada

Physical Description: Five feet nine, black eyes, black hair, and a dark complexion. Examining physician was Dr. George Landon, surgeon, First Michigan Sharpshooters.

Mustered: October 1, 1864, at Detroit, Wayne County, by Captain Mark Flanigan, Twenty-Fourth Michigan Infantry

Military Service: At the time of his enlistment, Jackson, who resided in Harwich, Kent County, Ontario, Canada, traveled to Detroit, Michigan, to enlist into the sharpshooter regiment.

In late April 1864, while he was on duty with his regiment at Lynchburg, Virginia, Private Jackson was detailed from his unit to be a policeman for the provost guard at the Brigade Headquarters in Washington, DC. The provost guard was a detail of police under the command of an officer. Lynchburg was an island of Union sympathizers in a sea of Confederates.

Although no charges were given, Jackson was reported to have been confined to a Central Guard House in Washington, DC, sometime in early May 1865.

On May 12, 1865, he was transferred from the guard house to Stone USA General Hospital in DC, having been diagnosed with typhoid fever. He may have been in the guard house to isolate him from other personnel until he could be sent to the hospital. Typhoid fever is an acute infectious disease caused and spread by eating food or drinking water contaminated with bacteria called *Salmonella typhosa (Blakiston)*. The illness is characterized by fever, severe generalized malaise of restlessness and discomfort, possible diarrhea or constipation, and the presence of transient red skin lesions called "rose spots" on his skin (*Bollet*).

Edward was isolated from other patients at Stone General Hospital. His treatment for typhoid consisted of doses of calomel, or mercurous chloride called "blue mass," analgesics, quinine, and ingested turpentine (*Ibid.*). Painful cupping and blistering to increase blood flow was added to his treatment, and he was given opium in alcohol called "laudanum" for pain (*Ibid.*).

If Edward had diarrhea, he would have been given emetics such as tartar emetic to evacuate his stomach and cathartics such as castor oil to stimulate bowel movements (*Evans*). A bland diet of boiled water, diluted coffee and tea, barley water, rice water, and broth made from meat extract was ordered for Edward. As his digestive tolerance improved, citrus juices and fresh fruits and vegetables were added to his diet. He remained at Stone General Hospital until June 15.

Discharged: Private Edward Andrew Jackson was mustered out and honorably discharged on June 15, 1865, from Stone USA General Hospital, Washington, DC. He was paid the money due to him for his service at his discharge and returned to Ontario, Canada.

Biography: Edward Andrew Jackson was born July 4, 1834 or 1837, in Hyde Park, Dutchess County, New York. He was the son of bicultural parents, Peter and Hannah Jackson. Hannah was an Anishinabequa (*Jackson*).

After Jackson returned to Ontario, he gained employment at a saw mill in Blenheim, Kent County. He also worked as a mechanic. It was at the saw mill that he lost the first and second fingers of his right hand due to an accident sometime early in 1866. The injury caused inflammation and contraction of the tendons of the other fingers.

Due to his work in the saw mill, Jackson joined a Canadian fraternal benefit society called the IOF or the Independent Order of Foresters (*Foresters*). He was also known to be a member of the Royal Templars of Temperance (*Temperance*).

Jackson married Anna (or Annie) Sophia Nichols, who was described as a "white woman," on August 30, 1866, at the Chatham Arms Hotel in Chatham, Ontario. Annie was the daughter of Thomas and Sarah E. Nichols. The couple's marriage was performed by Presbyterian minister Rev. William Walker. Witness to the marriage was Martha Merrill, whose father owned the hotel where the wedding ceremony was held.

Andrew and Annie Jackson were the parents of twelve children: Laura Ada, born January 26, 1867; Howard Bartkett, born January 29, 1869; Edith Ann, born August 16, 1872; Orilla Mae, born June 30, 1873; Alice Louise, born August 6, 1874; Edward Andrew Jr., born September 5, 1876; Harriet Sophia, born November 12, 1878; George Henry, born February 27, 1880; Mary Ellen, born March 21, 1881; Lillian Isabelle, born April 14, 1883; and twins whose date of birth is unknown.

An invalid pension Application #1047,134 was filed for Jackson on August 11, 1891, for typhoid fever and the impaired use of his right hand.

The Jackson family moved to Michigan and made their home in Detroit sometime during 1891 after Edward's pension application was filed.

Edward received Invalid Pension Certificate #787,903 in June 1892, which paid twelve dollars a month for loss of index and middle finger and for impaired use of his hand. The payments were retroactive from August 11, 1891. The claim for typhoid fever was rejected in September 1892 since it was not construed as a valid claim for disability.

Edward Andrew Jackson died December 23, 1893, of inflammation of the lungs, also called pneumonia or pneumonitis, at the family residence in Detroit. His body was sent to Canada and buried in Evergreen Cemetery in Blenheim, Kent County, Ontario, on December 25. Jackson's gravestone is a cement reproduction of an ornate tree stump. As with the Fraternal Order of Woodmen of America, Jackson's Independent Order of Foresters made sure that the grave site of a fellow woodman would be marked and identified.

Jackson's pension #787,903 was reissued as an accrued pension to Annie on August 13, 1894, under "accrued pension" and "general law." This action was taken so that she could collect the money allotted her husband (for his accident) since his death.

After the accrued pension money had been paid, a widow's pension Application

#589,010 was filed for Annie Jackson on January 8, 1894. She had no means of support for herself, or for her children, save from her labor or the contributions of her children. Also, she had no property of any value except her clothes.

On August 13, 1894, Annie Jackson received a Widow's Pension Certificate #400,429. The monthly rate paid eight dollars a month (retroactive from January 8, 1894), plus two dollars for each of her three youngest children (George H., Mary E., and Lillian I.), which totaled fourteen dollars a month. Her monthly payments would be decreased by two dollars when each child reached the age of sixteen.

Annie Jackson died at the home of her daughter, Edith Trotter, in Ypsilanti, Washtenaw County, on July 16, 1913. Her body was sent to Canada and buried near her husband in said cemetery in Ontario.

Jackson, William, Private

Enlistment: Enlisted as a private on August 29, 1864, at Flint, Genessee County, by Captain R. Strickland, First Michigan Sharpshooters and provost marshal, for three years.

Private Jackson was a substitute for Newell Barnard, which satisfied the requirement for a man from the Sixth Congressional District, Ninety-Third Subdistrict, First Ward, city of Saginaw, Saginaw County. As the principal or enrolled draftee, Barnard would have paid Jackson about $300 to be his substitute. As a volunteer substitute, Jackson was not entitled to an enlistment bounty because of the generous lump sum that he received as a substitute. But as an enlisted substitute soldier, he was eligible for a hundred-dollar bounty (as were regular enlisted men) if he was discharged from the service by reason of wounds received in battle.

There were non-Anishinabe men who avoided the service by finding substitutes. Many of these men visited the Michigan reservations and areas with Anishinabek populations. They sought out the Anishnabek men and offered lump sums of money to them if they agreed to serve as substitutes. The Civil War era was a time in which most Anishinabek people were in need of monetary support to provide for their families. The offers of money were hard to refuse.

Age: Twenty-six, born about 1838 in Michigan.
Occupation: Hunter, living in the Saginaw area
Residence: Saginaw, Saginaw County

Physical Description: Five feet seven and a half inches tall, black eyes, black hair, and a copper complexion. Examining physician was Dr. E. G. Gale, surgeon of the Board of Enrollment of the Sixth District of Michigan.

Mustered: August 29, 1864, at Flint, Genesee County, by Captain R. Strickland, First Michigan Sharpshooters and provost marshal

Military Service: Jackson joined his regiment on September 15, 1864. Regimental hospital records show that William was reported to have been sick (illness not stated) during the months of September and October. He returned to duty sometime between November and December.

Discharged: Private William Jackson was mustered out and honorably discharged near Delaney House, Georgetown, Washington, DC, on July 28, 1865. He returned to Detroit on the steamer *Morning Star*. On August 7, he was paid money due to him for his service at Jackson, Jackson County.

Biography: There is no pension file for William Jackson.

Jeandron (Jondreau), Michael, Private

Enlistment: Enlisted as a private on March 14, 1864, at Mackinac Island, Mackinac County, by Dominic Murray, First Michigan Sharpshooters, for three years. The enlistment was credited to the Fourth Congressional District, St. Ignace, Mackinac County.

Age: Twenty-one, born about 1842 or 1843 in either St. Ignace, Mackinac County, or on Mackinac Island of said county.

Occupation: Fisherman

Residence: Saint Ignace, Mackinac County

Physical Description: Five feet five, gray eyes, black hair, and a dark complexion. Examining physician was Dr. George Landon, surgeon, First Michigan Sharpshooters.

Mustered: April 29, 1864, at the Detroit Arsenal, Dearborn (or Detroit), Wayne County, by Captain Warner Backlin (Werner Boecklin), US mustering officer

Military Service: Private Michael Jeandron joined his regiment at North Anna River, Virginia, on May 26, 1864. He was captured while charging the enemy's works in a battle before Petersburg, Virginia, on June 17, 1864. He and other Union captives were taken by the rebels to a tobacco warehouse in Petersburg. After a few days, the captives were put on cattle railcars and sent to the Confederate prison camp called Camp Sumter (or Andersonville Prison) in Andersonville, Georgia.

On December 26, 1864, Pvt. Jeandron, who was exposed to inhumane conditions and the lack of proper food and water, was admitted to the prison hospital with the diagnosis of acute diarrhea. His body had become emaciated, and debility and depression set in due to this painful, exhausting, and protracted disease.

Finally, on January 5, 1865, Jeandron died in the prison hospital. His body was taken by his comrades or guards from the hospital to a brush arbor "dead house" where all usable clothing was removed from the body. Information about Jeandron was collected by a record keeper known as Dorance Atwater (also a prisoner) who kept the "Atwater List" of those prisoners who died at Andersonville. Atwater attached a numbered tag to the body for later reference. Then, as quickly as possible, Jeandron's body was put into a wagon with other corpses and transported to the cemetery about a mile from the prison stockade (*Encyclopedia*).

At the cemetery, Jeandron's remains were placed, without a wrap and shoulder to shoulder with other dead prisoners, into a four-foot-deep trench and covered with dirt. A small wooden post with a number carved into it was placed at the head of his grave, which identified the soldier and his unit (*Ibid.*). This number matched the number on the body tag and was also noted in the records known about the deceased.

Today Private Michael Jeandron lies at rest under military stone #12,396 in the burial ground that is now known as Andersonville National Cemetery.

Discharged: No discharge given due to death by disease while a prisoner of war.

Biography: The Company K soldier Michael Jeandron, whose name was also spelled Jondreau, Jondrau, Jaudron, and several other different ways, was a grandson of Michael and Anabid Jaudron Sr., who were early settlers of St. Ignace, Michigan. Michael and Anabid arrived about 1807.

Michael Sr. was awarded a private land claim, Claim #1, for 480 acres, which was the first claim at St. Ignace Point, now known as Graham's Point. He had lived on the land since 1807, was in possession of a home and some outbuildings, and was engaged in farming on July 1, 1812. This claim was verified by the officers of the court on July 25, 1823, and confirmed by the commissioners on October 28, 1823 (*Claims*).

Approved as the true owner of Claim #1, Michael Sr. entered this claim with the registrar of the land office at Detroit in 1828 (*Ibid.*).

Jaudron Sr. was an active member of his community and was listed as a member of the Mission Church that was built in that area in 1837.

Michael Sr. and Anabid were the parents of Michael Jr., who married a Mary Ann?

Michael and Mary Ann Jeandron Jr. were the parents of Rosalie, born 1835; Antoine, born 1838; Mary Ann, born 1841; Michael III (the Company K soldier), born 1842 or 1843; and John Baptist, born 1844. Michael III did not marry.

After Michael Jeandron Jr. died (before 1850), his widow, Mary Ann, married Jean Baptiste Perrault and brought a stepfather to her children. Jean Baptiste Perrault, Mary Ann Jeandron Perrault, and the Jeandron children (mentioned above) are listed in the 1850 federal census of St. Ignace in Michilimackinac County.

In 1860, Michael III worked as a laborer and resided in the household of Joseph Rabelard, a fisherman, and his wife, Elizabeth, in the township of St. Ignace in Mackinac County.

The Jeandron children, Michael III, John Baptist, Anthony (Antoine), and Mary Ann, had eighty acres of land in the Emmet County area by reason of a treaty of July 31, 1855, between the US commissioners and the Ottawa and Chippewa Indians of Michigan, parties to the treaty of March 28, 1836. The land description was the south half of the southeast quarter of section 34 in township 35 north of range 5 west. Certificate #555 was granted to the Jeandron children and their heirs on January 13, 1872 (*Land Records*).

Michael Jeandron III's sister, Rosalie, married James Hatch Hamlin (see file on James H. Hamlin) a comrade of Michael's in Company K. Hamlin also died in Andersonville Prison.

John, David, Private

Enlistment: Enlisted as a private on January 27, 1865, at Detroit, Wayne County, by Johnston Mower, First Michigan Sharpshooters, for three years. Credited to the Second Congressional District, La Grange, Cass County.

Age: Nineteen, born about 1846 in Bay City, Bay County.

Occupation: Laborer

Residence: La Grange Township

Physical Description: Five feet four and a half inches tall, black eyes, black hair, and a dark complexion. Examining physician was Dr. George Landon, surgeon, First Michigan Sharpshooters.

Mustered: January 28, 1865, at Detroit, Wayne County, by Captain Mark Flanigan, provost marshal

Military Service: Shortly before February 23, Private David John (along with William John) was apprehended on a charge of desertion from his regiment. He was returned to his regiment on February 24 by military guards. It was reported (and substantiated by Company K comrades John Wesley and Freeman Sutton) that when the regiment was before Petersburg, Virginia, on April 3, 1865, Private David John was injured. Supposedly, David sustained an injury to his right ear and a flesh wound to the right side of his head caused by a missile ball. John reported that no surgeon or assistant surgeon treated him for his wounds. No medical record of said injuries has been found.

Discharged: Private David John was mustered out and honorably discharged near Delaney House, Georgetown, Washington, DC, on July 28, 1865. He returned to Detroit on the steamer *Morning Star*. On August 7, he received money due to him for his service at Jackson, Jackson County.

Biography: David John married Mary Quewis according to traditional Anishnabek custom and practice (agreement of the couple and their parents) on September 2, 1878, at Custer, Mason County. Other records state that the last name of Mary was Geiawis and the marriage date was May 1873.

David and Mary John were the parents of two children: Joseph, born September 1, 1879, and Nancy, born March 5, 1881.

On September 8, 1888, Application #671,594 for an invalid pension was filed for David John. He also requested a replacement certificate in lieu of his lost discharge. He reported that he carried his discharge paper with him in a pocket and when he walked in a severe storm, it became saturated and spoiled. A replacement discharge paper was sent to John's attorney on September 22, 1888.

According to his pension papers, David John was struck by a train on March 2, 1889, as he walked along the track of the Pere Marquette railroad near his home in Fountain, Mason County. David sustained contusions about his head and face, his nose was completely torn off, and a fraction of the base of his skull was missing. David was carried home in an unconscious state, and Dr. John Hincks, who practiced medicine in Manistee, was summoned. These injuries, in addition to his extensive internal injuries, were sufficient to cause David's death on March 4. He was buried somewhere near his home in said county.

Mary tried to complete her husband's claim for a pension, but it was denied.

She then decided to apply for a widow's pension. A widow's pension Application #605,687 was submitted for her on December 7, 1894.

Due to insufficient additional evidence needed, Mary John's application was abandoned, and she did not receive a widow's pension.

David John may have been a relative of Company K soldier William John. Considering the family surname "John" is known among the Potawatomi people in the area in which he lived, David John was probably a member of the Potawatomi tribe.

John, William, Private

Enlistment: Enlisted as a private on January 27, 1865, at Detroit, Wayne County, by Johnston Mower, First Michigan Sharpshooters, for three years. Credited to the Second Congressional District, White Pigeon, St. Joseph County.

Age: Twenty, born about 1845 in Bay City, Bay County.

Occupation: Laborer

Residence: White Pigeon

Physical Description: Five feet seven, black eyes, dark hair, and a dark complexion. Examining physician was Dr. George Landon, surgeon, First Michigan Sharpshooters.

Mustered: January 28, 1865, at Detroit, Wayne County, by Captain Mark Flannigan, provost marshal

Military Service: Shortly before February 23, Private William John (along with David John) was apprehended on a charge of desertion from his regiment. He was returned to his regiment on February 24 by military guards.

On February 25, 1865, Private William John was admitted to his division hospital in the field near Petersburg, Virginia. He was diagnosed with an indolent, or slow-healing, ulcer on the inner side of the right arm near the axilla (or armpit). Indolent ulcers have little tendency to heal and are inclined to grow an excess of connective tissue (*Blakiston*).

At the division hospital, John was anesthetized with chloroform, and the dead tissue and other foreign material around the sore was debrided (or removed) with a scalpel (*Bollet*). After the tissue was removed, iodine was applied to the skin around the wound to impede infection, and a weak solution of bromine was put into the cavity of the sore (*Evans*). At the conclusion of the surgery, a cloth bandage was applied to the wound and secured with adhesive plaster.

On March 1, Private William John was transferred by ambulance wagon to the military railroad and put on a mattress in a boxcar, the floor of which was cushioned with straw or hay, and sent to the depot hospital at City Point. Similar treatment was given to John at this hospital.

William was taken to a wharf at City Point on March 16 and transferred to the hospital steamer *State of Maine* on March 18. He was then transported to Washington, DC, and admitted to Colombian College USA Hospital on March 19. His ulcer was treated in a similar manner, and he was released from the hospital on June 16 to rejoin his regiment.

Discharged: Private William John was mustered out and honorably discharged near Delaney House, Georgetown, Washington, DC, on July 28, 1865. He returned to Detroit on the steamer *Morning Star*. On August 7, John was paid the money due to him for his service at Jackson, Jackson County.

Biography: It is thought that William John may have been a brother or a cousin of Company K soldier David John. Considering that the family surname "John" is known among the Potawatomi people in the area in which he lived, William John was probably a member of the Potawatomi tribe. There is no pension file for William John.

Enlisted Men—Letters K, L, and M

Kabaosa, Louis, Private

Enlistment: Enlisted as a private on July 4, 1863, at Elbridge, Oceana County, by Captain Edwin V. Andress, First Michigan Sharpshooters, for three years.

Age: Twenty-seven, born about 1836 in Kalamazoo, St. Joseph County.

Occupation: Laborer

Residence: Pentwater, Oceana County

Physical Description: Five feet seven and a half inches tall, black eyes, black hair, and a dark complexion. Examining physician was Dr. Jacob B. McNett, assistant surgeon, First Michigan Sharpshooters.

Mustered: July 11, 1863, at Detroit Arsenal, Dearborn, Wayne County, by Captain Edwin V. Andress, First Michigan Sharpshooters

Military Service: On the way to the front with his regiment in April 1864, Private Kabaosa was taken ill. On April 17, he was sent to his regimental hospital near his encampment outside of Annapolis, Maryland, where his illness was diagnosed as scrofula or tuberculosis of the cervical (neck) lymph nodes. Kabaosa was sent from his regimental hospital by ambulance wagon to Division No.1, USA General Hospital at the United States Naval Academy (Navy Yard) in Annapolis and remained there until April 26. He was still a patient when his regiment proceeded to the front.

The doctors at the hospital treated his scrofula with applications of tincture of iodine applied as a paint to the swollen nodes of his neck (*Evans*). He was given opiates for pain, ordered to strict bed rest, and given a hearty diet.

On April 27, Kabaosa was transferred by hospital steamer from the Annapolis hospital to Mower USA General Hospital at Chestnut Hill, near Philadelphia, Pennsylvania, where similar treatment was continued. He returned to duty with his regiment on July 11.

Private Kabaosa was admitted to Lincoln USA General Hospital in Washington,

DC, on July 18, 1864, with a diagnosis of valvular disease of the heart. He was granted a furlough on August 5 and readmitted to Lincoln General Hospital on September 21.

Louis was transferred from Lincoln General Hospital to Satterlee USA General Hospital in West Philadelphia on September 29. At that time, he was diagnosed with chronic bronchitis. His treatment included applications of mustard plasters to his chest and doses of quinine and opium for pain. A mustard plaster is a poultice that includes powdered black mustard seed and flour combined with water or egg white. This mixture was spread on the inside of a flannel or cotton cloth dressing and applied to the back or chest of the patient. It was thought that the plaster stimulated the immune system and drew out the "poison" that caused the bronchial illness (*Internet*). Louis was deemed sufficiently well enough to return to duty on December 17, 1864.

Discharged: Private Louis Kabaosa was mustered out and honorably discharged at Delaney House, Georgetown, Washington, DC, on July 28, 1865. He returned to Detroit on the steamer *Morning Star*. On August 7, he was paid the money due to him for his service at Jackson, Jackson County.

Biography: Louis Kabaosa is known to have married a woman whose first name was Susan. The couple lived in Elbridge Township of Oceana County and were the parents of two sons: Paul, born in 1860, and James, born in 1869 or 1870.

Louis died of consumption (tuberculosis) of the lungs at age thirty-four on July 9, 1870, and was buried in said Township. There is no pension file for Louis Kabaosa.

Kabayacega, George, Private

Enlistment: Enlisted as a private on August 29, 1864, at Flint, Genesee County, by Captain R. Strickland, provost marshal for the Sixth District of Michigan, for three years.

Private Kabayacega was a substitute for John L. Barnard, which satisfied the requirement for a man from the Sixth Congressional District, Saginaw County, First Ward of Saginaw City. As the principal or enrolled draftee, Barnard would have paid Kabayacega about $300 to be his substitute. As a volunteer substitute, Kabayacega was not entitled to an enlistment bounty because of the generous lump sum that he received as a substitute. But as an enlisted substitute soldier, he was eligible for a hundred-dollar bounty (as were the regular enlisted men) if he was discharged from the service by reason of wounds received in battle.

There were non-Anishnabek men who avoided the service by finding substitutes. Many of these draftees visited the Michigan reservations and areas with Anishinabek populations to specifically seek out these men. They offered lump sums of money to them if they agreed to serve as substitutes. The Civil War era was a time in which most Anishinabek people were in need of monetary support to provide for their families. The offers of money were hard to refuse.

Age: Thirty, born about 1834 in Michigan.

Occupation: Hunter

Residence: St. Charles Township, Saginaw County

Physical Description: Five feet three, black eyes, black hair, and a copper complexion. Examining physician was Dr. E. G. Gale, surgeon of the Board of Enrollment of the Sixth District of Michigan.

Mustered: August 29, 1864, at Flint, Genesee County, by Captain R. Strickland, provost marshal of the Sixth District of Michigan

Military Service: On or about March 11, 1865, while in the trenches before Petersburg, Private Kabayacega incurred injuries to both of his eyes. The explosions of artillery shells created large amounts of dust and particulate in the air, including whatever bacteria resided in the dirt. This bacteria-infused dust caused severe inflammation of the corneas and conjunctivas of George's eyes and seriously impaired his vision (*Altic*). Dr. Thomas Eagleson, assistant surgeon for the regiment, washed George's eyes with water, applied nitrate of silver in water to the inside areas of his eyelids, and sent him back to his company (*Dorwart*). Ultimately, the inflammation, which is called keratoconjunctivitis, would result in permanent injury to the soldier's eyes and contribute to his partial blindness.

George had also developed a severe cough (which affected his lungs) from exposure to inclement weather. The regimental doctors diagnosed his cough as acute bronchitis and ordered Dover's powder (a diaphoretic and sedative powder that contained a mixture of ipecac and opium) and spirit of nitre (or saltpeter) as treatments (*Evans*).

Discharged: Private George Kabayacega, who was known by his superiors to have been a good soldier, was mustered out and honorably discharged at Delaney House, Georgetown, Washington, DC, on July 28, 1865. He returned to Detroit on the steamer *Morning Star*. On August 7, he was paid the money due to him for his service at Jackson, Jackson County.

Biography: George Kabayacega was also known as George Sockatup, a hunter known for his excellent eyesight before the war. He had at least one brother by the name of John Babawash.

George's first wife and children died when the family lived in St. Charles Township of Saginaw County and before George enlisted in the army in 1864. At that time, he owned some land in Isabella County and did establish a residence there, but his main residence was in St. Charles Township.

George married secondly to Mary Smith (a childless widow of a William Smith) on June 24, 1875, at the home of Peter David in St. Charles Township. The couple was married by Rev. A. S. Fair, who was the minister of the Methodist Episcopal Church in St. Charles. St. Charles was also called "Indian Town." The marriage was witnessed by William Turner, who was an Anishinabe Methodist Episcopal minister, Chief James Fisher, Peter David, and George's brother, John Babawash.

During his postwar years, Kabayacega earned a meager living by making ax handles and chopping wood as long as his failing eyesight would permit. What a burden it must have been for George to remember his perfect prewar eyesight and to realize that the shadow of blindness was descending upon him. When engaged in his chores, George wore goggles to protect his eyes. Mary earned some money for the couple by making and selling baskets.

Anishinabe doctor, Henry Quewis, treated Kabayacega's eyes with native medicinal herbs and poultices. George's health continued to become worse due to the weakened condition of his lungs.

On May 10, 1879, Application #285,396 for an invalid pension was filed for George Kabayacega. He was issued a new discharge certificate because he had reported that the original certificate had fallen from his pocket and was lost. He was granted Invalid Pension Certificate #437,815 for disease of the eyes, which paid four dollars a month retroactive from July 29, 1865. George received payments from his pension until his death.

On March 30, 1882, George Kabayacega walked from his home to the town of St. Charles to purchase twenty-five pounds of flour and some oil to fill his oil can. That day was very cold and bitter. Also, the water was quite high along the banks of streams and ditches and was several inches over the road on which Kabayacega walked to return home. He probably chilled as he walked and stopped to rest at a high place on the road near the house of Norman Ballard. The next morning, Ballard found George's mud-covered body in the middle of the road with his head lying on the bag of flour that was tied up in a shawl. The oil can was found beside the body.

It was inferred from the report of his death that he had been drinking (as evidence of an empty whiskey bottle beside his body). Also, it was thought that he had become wet when he walked in the water and had apparently frozen to death during the previous evening.

George Kabayacega was buried in section C of the St. Charles Township Cemetery known as Riverside.

On December 21, 1887, Application #411,141 for a widow's pension was filed for Mary Kabayacega, who was also known as Mary Sockatup. At first the application was denied because the soldier's death was not chargeable to his military service but due to exposure.

Mary applied again for her pension on July 18, 1890, and this time she was granted a Widow's Pension Certificate #285,353, which paid eight dollars a month from said date. She received the pension due to the same reason that her husband had received his pension—the inflammation of his eyes that resulted in near blindness due to his military service.

Mary Kabayacega died of endocarditis or inflammation of the lining membrane of the heart and its valves (*Blakiston*). Her death occurred at her home in St. Charles Township on January 15, 1909. She may be buried in Riverside Cemetery near her husband. George and Mary did not have children.

Kadah, Joseph, Private

Enlistment: Enlisted as a private on September 9, 1863, at Elbridge, Oceana County, by Captain Edwin V. Andress, First Michigan Sharpshooters, for three years.

Age: Twenty-one, born about 1842 in Lowell, Kent County.

Occupation: Farmer

Residence: Elbridge Township, Oceana County

Physical Description: Five feet six, black eyes, black hair, and a ruddy complexion. Examining physician was Dr. George L. Cornell, assistant surgeon, First Michigan Sharpshooters.

Mustered: September 29, 1863, at Camp Douglas in Chicago, Cook County, Illinois, by Captain Duryea. The camp was a confine for Confederate prisoners and was guarded by the soldiers of the First Michigan Sharpshooters for seven months.

Military Service: On July 3, 1864, Private Joseph Kadah was sent from the field to his division hospital with the complaint of diarrhea and high fever. He was taken by ambulance wagon to the military railroad, put on a mattress in a boxcar, the floor of which was cushioned with straw or hay, and sent to the depot hospital at City Point, Virginia. He was admitted to the hospital on July 4, where his illness was confirmed.

The doctors at City Point treated Kadah's fever with quinine and cold water baths (*Evans*). Quinine was made from powdered cinchona tree bark dissolved in water or whiskey. Whiskey worked better because it masked the bitter taste of the quinine. Quinine was also dispensed as pills of purified quinine sulfate.

To treat his diarrhea, Joseph was given an emetic (to induce vomiting) such as castor oil and astringent enemas of silver nitrate and turpentine (*Ibid.*). Dover's powder (a mixture of ipecac and opium) was given to the patient to induce perspiration, and opium pills were administered for pain (*Ibid.*).

Private Kadah was taken to a wharf at City Point on July 6, transferred to a hospital steamer, and sent to DeCamp USA General Hospital at David's Island, New York. He was admitted to DeCamp on July 10 where he was given similar treatment for fever and diarrhea.

Kadah's diet consisted of boiled water, diluted coffee and tea, barley water, rice water. and broth of meat extract. Fresh fruit, fruit juices, and fresh vegetables were added to this regimen when his digestive system could tolerate the change.

The soldier remained at DeCamp until October 3 when he was sent to St. Mary's USA General Hospital in Detroit, Michigan, and admitted on October 5.

Similar treatment was given to Kadah at St. Mary's. In addition to his fever and diarrhea, he was also diagnosed with chronic rheumatism. The only treatment for rheumatic pain during the Civil War was to administer opiates, and quinine or potassium iodide for their anti-inflammatory effect. Cool baths and cold compresses were also ordered for the patient to reduce inflammation (*Bollet*). Private Joseph Kadah died in the hospital on October 23, 1864.

On October 24, Joseph's body (which may or may not have been embalmed) was placed into a coffin and given a military escort from St. Mary's Hospital to Detroit's Elmwood Cemetery in Wayne County. At the cemetery, a short religious service would have been provided, and military protocol with the firing of arms was presented (*Encyclopedia*). The name on his present military stone reads "Joseph Hagler (should be Kadah) Pvt. Co. K, 1st. Mich Sharp Shooters, Civil War, 1864."

Discharged: No discharge given due to death from disease while in the hospital.

Biography: Joseph's last name was also spelled Kadat on his enlistment paper. During the conversation at his enlistment, the officers may have misunderstood Joseph as he said his family surname. The name Kadah could have been spelled Cadeau (Ca-doh), or Cadotte/Cadot with a silent *t* that showed evidence of Joseph's Metis (French-Indian) ancestry. There is no pension file for Joseph Kadah.

Kakakee, Joseph, Private

Enlistment: Enlisted as a private on August 31, 1864, at Grand Rapids, Kent County, by captain and provost marshal for the Fourth District of Michigan, Norman Bailey, First Michigan Sharpshooters, for three years. Credited to the Fourth Congressional District, Chester, Ottawa County.

   Age: Thirty-five, born about 1823 or 1829 in Pere Marquette, Mason County.

   Occupation: Laborer

   Residence: Chester Township, Ottawa County

   Physical Description: Five feet seven and a half inches tall, black eyes, black hair, and a dark complexion. Examining physician was Dr. Alonzo Mate, surgeon, First Michigan Sharpshooters.

   Mustered: September 1, 1864, at Grand Rapids, Kent County, by Captain Norman Bailey, First Michigan Sharpshooters

   Military Service: No military medical record of illness or injury for Private Kakakee has been found. However, by his own statement and those of some others in his company, Joseph related that he received a back injury while the regiment was before Petersburg, Virginia. It seems that Kakakee and three others of his company were ordered to break down some rebel breastworks with axes near Petersburg before sunrise in late March or early April 1865. Kakakee stated that he fell and slid down on some timber while engaged in this chore and injured his lower back. He did not seek medical help from the regimental doctors. He also complained of rheumatism, both during and after his war years, that exacerbated his back pain.

   Discharged: Private Joseph Kakakee was given an honorable discharge for disability on May 20, 1865, at Alexandria, Virginia. Joseph was mustered out at Delaney House, Georgetown, Washington, DC, on June 3, 1865. He was paid the money owed to him for his service at that time and returned to Michigan.

   Biography: Joseph Kakakee's name is derived from the Anishinabe word *kekek,* which means "Sparrow Hawk" (*Baraga*). He stated in his later pension papers that the correct way to write his name was Joseph Meshekakak (which is derived from *mishikekek* and is translated as "Kite" or a bird of prey (*Ibid.*). He had at least one sister, Labadah (or Sarah King), who was an Anishinabequa medicine woman.

Sometime before 1848, Joseph went to Ontario, Canada. He met and married a widow named Mary Polly (Crane) Sunego, who was born in Saltfleet Township, Hamilton, Ontario, about 1806.

Mary (or Mayaawigiizhigokwe, which means Right in the Sky Woman) Polly (Crane) Sunego was the daughter of Otesoo, the war chief of the Otter Clan, and the widow of Bunch Sunego (or Tyetiquob). Bunch was the son of Osunego (or Asanagoo, which means "Black Squirrel"), a Mississauga tribal chief from the Eagle clan (*Nahnebahwequa—Wikipedia*).

Mary and Bunch Sunego were married around 1823 and were both baptized into the Credit Mission of the Wesleyan Methodist Church in 1825. The couple had nine children. Only the oldest, Catherine or Nahneebahwequa (which translates as "Standing Upright Woman"), and the youngest, Mary, survived to adulthood (*Ibid.*).

Catherine married William Sutton from England. As an adult, Catherine (Sunego) Sutton became an Ojibwa spokeswoman and a well-known Methodist missionary among her people (*Ibid.*).

After Bunch Sunego died (about 1842), Mary Polly (Crane) Sunego married Joseph Kakakee. Following their marriage, the couple took possession of lots 32 and 33 in Sarawak Township, Grey County, on the shores of Georgian Bay in Ontario. In order to hold the title to their lots, the Kakakee couple was to improve twenty-five acres of land for farming (*Grey County*).

Joseph and Mary (Sunego) Kakakee had two children born in Owen Sound of Grey County: Martha, born in 1848, and Moses, born in 1851 (*Ibid.*). Mary married John Snake. Moses married a white widow and was on the Chippewas of Nawash Band Council for many years. He died in 1903 in Cape Croker and was buried there (*Ibid.*).

Joseph, Mary, their two children, and Mary's youngest daughter, Mary Sunego, were found in the Sarawak Census of 1851. Another child, Joseph Finger, was listed in the same census as living with the Kakakee family. It was not uncommon for Indian families to adopt children. The Kakakee family was listed in the records of the Credit Mission Wesleyan Methodist Church (*Ibid.*).

Mary (Sunego) Kakakee was not only very active in the Methodist mission, she also participated in the church's *Dorcas Society*. The society was named after Dorcas (or Tabitha), a seamstress who was described in the Holy Bible's Acts of the Apostles for her charitable giving. The society's members provided clothing to the poor (*Ibid.*).

Mary was considered a pious, intelligent Indian woman who went through some sorrowful times in losing Bunch and all but two of her Sunego children at early ages. Her Christian fortitude gave her strength and peace (*Ibid.*). On the other hand, Joseph Kakakee was sometimes given to intemperance and more than once embarrassed Mary while he was in an inebriated state.

Joseph improved his acreage, planted some crops, and trapped and fished to earn a living for his family. Around 1857, the Department of Indian Affairs of Canada decided to offer the lots for sale to new immigrants who came into the area looking for farmland. This was quite a blow to the resident Indian families. Joseph may have become frustrated because he had made many improvements to his lot and would not get his money back (*Ibid.*). He had also heard a rumor that the Indians would be moved to Manitoulin Island.

For whatever reason, Joseph left Mary and their two children between 1851 and 1857 and disappeared (*Ibid.*). No one knew why he had left his family or where he had gone. In reality, Joseph went back to Ottawa County, Michigan, and lived there until he enlisted into the Union army in 1864.

Although Joseph and Mary remained married until Mary's death, there is no evidence that Joseph visited his family in Ontario or had any correspondence with them (*Ibid.*). Why did Mary not take her Kakakee children and go with Joseph to Michigan? Anishinabek family relationships are very strong, especially those with ties to ancestral homes and family burial grounds. Mary's home was in Sarawak, and her surviving children with Bunch Sunego were established there too. She probably didn't want to leave Canada, or her children she had with Bunch, for an area with no ancestral ties.

It seems that neither Joseph nor Mary was interested in dissolving their marriage. Somehow, Joseph knew of Mary's death in 1897 in Cape Croker, Ontario. He had always referred to Mary as his wife before she died.

Joseph was an uncle to Aaron Sargonquatto (also known as Aaron Pequongay or Puhquonga) and worked with him in a sawmill in Manistee of Manistee County before 1861. He was also Aaron's Company K comrade.

After he returned from his service in 1865, Joseph settled in the Custer Township area of Mason County. He sought treatment for his ailing back from his sister,

Sarah King. She treated Joseph in the traditional Anishinabek manner with herbs and poultices.

On May 20, 1872, Joseph petitioned the Circuit Court of Mason County and the US Pension Office to inform them that he had lost his discharge paper. He knew that without a discharge paper he would not receive consideration for a pension when he applied for one. Joseph reported that he had lost the paper somewhere between Ludington and Indiantown (or East Riverton) in Mason County sometime between January 15 and January 20, 1872. Also, he mentioned that a diligent search was made for the paper, but it was not found.

Recognized as one of the first landowners of Mason County, Joseph was issued a Homestead Certificate No. 0100 for 160 acres in Branch Township on November 20, 1877. His land description was the southeast quarter of section 32 in township 18 north, of range 15 west (*Land Records*).

Joseph was noted to be very good with an ax and could square timber when his back or his rheumatism wasn't bothering him. But as the years passed, Kakakee's physical ailments became worse, and he was unable to support himself by manual labor.

Dr. A. D. Kibbee was Joseph's personal doctor and detected Joseph's heart disease as well as his trouble with rheumatism. Dr. Kibbee treated Joseph's ailments but was known to have made the comment to him that a "fondness for whiskey" did not improve his infirmities.

On November 5, 1889, Application #737,101 for an invalid pension was submitted for Joseph. At that time, he was still a resident of Custer Township in Mason County and had received a replacement certificate of discharge. Joseph referred to Mary as his wife in his pension application.

Sarah King and a Joseph Smith (who said that he was Joseph Kakakee's grandson) were living with Joseph in said township. This Joseph Smith could have been the Joseph Finger who was listed as living with the Kakakee family in the 1851 census of Grey County, Ontario. According to Mary (Sunego) Kakakee's descendants, there is no known blood connection between Joseph Finger and the Kakakee family, which leads to the speculation that Joseph Finger-Smith may have been adopted by the Kakakee family. If this speculation is true, then Joseph, as a young adult, may have made trips back and forth between Michigan and Canada to visit his extended family.

An Invalid Pension Certificate #619,312 was granted to Joseph under the liberal Act of June 27, 1890, which stipulated that: the recipient have served three months;

was given an honorable discharge; the widow was married to the soldier prior to said date, and she was without other means of support. The pension was retroactive to November 5, 1889, and paid six dollars a month for the ailments of rheumatism and disease of the heart. The monthly payments were increased to eight dollars in 1892. Joseph's claim for additional payments for a back injury was denied.

There is no record that Mary Crane (Sunego) Kakakee received pension payments from Joseph's service after 1896. So, it's assumed that Mary died sometime after said date. It's possible that Joseph Finger-Smith was told of Mary's passing when he was on a visit to Canada and then related this information to Kakakee.

Joseph Meshekakak (Meshekakack) Kakakee died of pneumonia on May 12, 1901. He was buried in the Old Riverside Indian Burial Ground next to the Custer City Cemetery (or Riverside Cemetery) in Custer, Mason County. A military stone marks his burial site.

Kaquatch, Samuel, Private

Enlistment: Enlisted as a private on June 15, 1863, at Little Traverse (now Harbor Springs), Emmet County, by Second Lieutenant Garrett A. Graveraet, First Michigan Sharpshooters, for three years.

Age: Eighteen, born May 15, 1845, in Little Traverse.

Occupation: Farmer and hunter

Residence: Little Traverse

Physical Description: Five feet ten and a half inches tall, dark eyes, dark hair, and a ruddy complexion. No examining surgeon was listed.

Mustered: July 20, 1863, at Detroit, Wayne County, by Lieutenant Colonel John R. Smith, US Army

Military Service: On January 15, 1864, Private Samuel Kaquatch became ill while on guard duty with his regiment at Camp Douglas. The camp was a confine for Confederate prisoners at Chicago, Cook County, Illinois, that the sharpshooters guarded for seven months.

He was immediately admitted to the USA Post Hospital where the doctors diagnosed his illness as pneumonia and treated him with mustard plasters. Mustard plasters consisted of a poultice or a mixture of ground black mustard seed, water, and flour spread on a layer of cotton or flannel cloth and applied to the chest or back. The moist heat that was generated by the mixture was thought to be beneficial in drawing out the "poison" that caused the pneumonia (*Internet*). Samuel was given pills that contained a compound cathartic or purgative of dried bitter apple, jalap, gum-resin, and mercurous chloride known as calomel (*Dorwart*). His cough was suppressed, and his pain was eased with doses of opiates.

Samuel was left in the post hospital to recover his strength when his regiment left Chicago on March 17 for the front in Virginia. He returned to duty with his regiment on April 23.

During a charge against the enemy's breastworks in a battle at Petersburg, Virginia, on June 17, 1864, Kaquatch suffered a flesh wound in the lower right forearm from a missile ball. He was sent immediately to a first aid station where any bleeding was stopped and the wound was hastily bandaged. From the aid station Kaquatch was taken by ambulance wagon to the division hospital in the field behind the lines near Petersburg. At this hospital, a tincture of iodine was applied to and around the wound to impede infection (*Evans*). A simple water dressing of lint dipped into cold water was applied to the wound and secured by a cloth wrap or adhesive plaster (*Schaadt*). Opium pills were given to the soldier for pain.

On June 20, 1864, Private Kaquatch was taken by ambulance wagon to a military railroad. He was put on a mattress in a boxcar, the floor of which was cushioned with straw or hay, and sent to the wharf at City Point. From City Point, he was transferred by hospital steamer to Lincoln USA General Hospital in Washington, DC, and admitted to the hospital on June 21.

He remained at Lincoln General until June 27 when he was sent to USA General Hospital at Broad and Cherry Streets in Philadelphia, Pennsylvania, and admitted on June 28. His wound was again treated with applications of iodine and simple water dressings.

From USA General in Philadelphia, Kaquatch was transferred and admitted to Summit House, USA General Hospital (at Kingsessing St.) in West Philadelphia on July 2.

While a convalescent at Summit House on August 3, the doctor in charge of Samuel's ward gave Kaquatch a pass to the city and told him to get some exercise to help him regain his strength.

During that evening, Kaquatch had imbibed a little too much. When he returned to the Summit House Hospital, the guard would not admit him in his inebriated condition. Angry and upset at having been turned away by the guard upon his return to the hospital, Kaquatch decided to walk along the Philadelphia and Baltimore Railroad tracks for lack of anything else to do, and maybe just to cool his anger. What happened next resulted in Samuel's unnecessary death that could have been prevented if the guard would have readmitted him to the hospital.

There are conflicting stories of just where Kaquatch's death occurred after he was denied reentry to the hospital and where he was buried. One story stands out as the most credible. With further research needed to find the truth in the conflicting stories, the Pension Department requested that the records of the War Department and of the Surgeon General's Office be reexamined. In addition to the records, research was requested for any articles related to Kaquatch's death as reported in the *Philadelphia Ledger*.

The final accepted version of Private Kaquatch's demise is detailed in the following two depositions (found in pension papers) given on October 3, 1891, and October 5, 1891, respectively, as it pertained to Sophia Kaquatch's dependent mother's pension case. Please notice the different names of the same hospital that are mentioned. The name Summit House Hospital was later changed to Citizen's Hospital, and the building was abandoned after the war ended in 1865.

Deposition number one is as follows as given by Mr. David R. Birch, Clerk, in the *Ledger* office in Philadelphia:

> I am a clerk in the Editorial Department of the "Philadelphia Ledger" and have charge of the old files of that paper. I find the following published item under the heading of "Local Affairs" in the issue of Thursday, August 4, 1864.

> Soldier killed:------Samuel Gaywick, a soldier 20 years old, who was run over on the Baltimore railroad on Tuesday night, died at the Citizens Hospital. The coroner held an investigation on the body, and it was testified that the deceased was intoxicated when he was run over. A verdict in accordance with the facts was rendered.
>
> The forgoing is a correct transcript of the article as published.
>
> David R. Birch

Deposition number two given by T. King Walker, chief clerk of the accounts of the Philadelphia and Baltimore Railroad Company located at Broad Street Station in Philadelphia, is as follows:

> I find the following entry recorded therein:

Samuel Gewehick, Co. K, 1ˢᵗ. Michigan S.S. was run over and killed on August 2ⁿᵈ. (1864) by an engine and train of cars which were coming from the wharf. The accident happened on Washington Avenue below Broad Street. The man was drunk and lying on the track. He had applied for admission to the Citizens Vol. Hospital, but the guard refused him on account of his condition. The following was the verdict of the Coroner's Jury. Samuel Geweshick, Indian, age twenty years, killed by a train of cars of the Philadelphia and Baltimore Railroad Company on 2ⁿᵈ. Inst. on Gray's Ferry Road.

I certify the forgoing to be a correct transcript of the Record of Accidents, contemporaneous with the period named, and is in my own handwriting.

T. King Walker

Author's note: the date of death on Samuel's hospital record was recorded as August 3 and mentioned that he was run over by railroad cars near Broad and Prince Streets in Philadelphia.

It seems that Samuel, who probably felt tired and weak, in addition to being inebriated, lay down on the tracks of the Philadelphia and Baltimore Railroad to sleep. Since he did not hear the train that was coming from the wharf, the engine and cars passed over him. One of Samuel's legs was crushed from where it was attached to the body to the lower part of the leg, and he sustained massive injuries. He was taken immediately to Summit Hospital where he died an hour later from a great loss of blood.

Samuel's death in the hospital on August 3 was witnessed by his Company K comrade and friend George Stoneman. Stoneman was a patient at Summit House at the same time as Kaquatch and was also given a pass that same evening. He witnessed Samuel's death on the railroad tracks and saw him die in the hospital. Stoneman's account is taken from the surgeon general's report of March 29, 1869, when Samuel's father, Michael, applied for a dependent father's pension on Samuel's service.

The notation that Samuel Kaquatch died at Harrisburg is found on Kaquatch's pension card. The notation is a mistake since Samuel was killed in Philadelphia.

It was reported that Samuel was buried, soon after his death, in Glenwood Cemetery in Philadelphia. Since undertaker Mr. John C. Rulon (or Ruton) was in charge of Samuel's burial, he may have provided embalming services and also a casket. Sam's body probably had a military escort to the cemetery complete with a religious service and the firing of arms (*Encyclopedia*). A temporary wooden marker that included Samuel's name and unit was placed at the head of his grave.

On October 1, 1864, Private Samuel Kaquatch's body was disinterred from Glenwood Cemetery and reburied in Philadelphia National Cemetery. A temporary wooden marker was placed at the head of his grave site until a permanent stone marker was supplied. Today Private Kaquatch lies at rest under military stone #614 in section B of said cemetery. His surname on the stone is spelled Kagwaitch.

No information has been found as to what, if any, discipline was meted out to the guard who refused Samuel's reentry to the hospital. As a patient, Samuel should have been readmitted regardless of his inebriated condition. He was recuperating from a wound received in the line of duty.

Discharged: No discharge given due to accidental death while in the service.

Biography: Samuel was the son of Michael, a fisherman, and Sophia (Achkwegijigokwe) Kaquatch. Samuel's surname was also spelled Kagwaitch and Kegwetch, as reported in his pension file. Michael and Sophia were married by Rev. Father Francois Pierz at the Holy Childhood of Jesus Catholic Church of Little Traverse (now Harbor Springs) on February 13, 1843.

In the 1860 federal census of Emmet County, Samuel, age fifteen, was listed with his parents and his siblings, who were: Angela (Angilique), age eight; Eli, age four; and Peter, age two. Ambrose, whose name was sometimes written as "Abram," would join the family on February 8, 1864.

Samuel was baptized in the Holy Childhood of Jesus Catholic Church on May 17, 1845. Even though he remained unmarried, he was known to be a hard worker who supported his family from the time that he could hold a job. Before the war, he earned his living as a fisherman.

Samuel's parents were uneasy about their son's enlistment into the service and fearful for his safety but were supportive of his decision to fight for his homeland. Being the dutiful son that he was, he promised them that he would send his pay home for their support as often as he could.

Sophia Graveraet testified that she and her family were close friends of the Kaquatch family and that she was often their interpreter for family business. Sophie's son, Second Lieutenant Garrett A. Graveraet, also of Company K, kept an eye on the young man and sent Sam's money home for him. Once, while on a recruiting furlough home, Graveraet personally delivered an unspecified amount of Samuel's money to his parents.

At the time of Samuel's death, one brother, Ambrose, was the only child under sixteen of Samuel's siblings who was still living.

After his son's death, Michael sold off four acres of land to pay taxes and to support the family.

Application #171,075 was submitted for Michael Kaquatch on January 29, 1869, in order to obtain a dependent father's pension. His health had failed, and he had become quite infirm.

Michael's pension application was rejected in 1870 due to the decision that Samuel was not in the line of duty when he received his fatal injuries.

A last will and testament was made by Michael Kaquatch on January 21, 1875. In the will, Michael bequeathed all of his lands to his wife, Sophia. The properties were situated in the town of Little Traverse in Emmet County and in the town of Burt, known as Indian Village, in Cheboygan County (*Will*). Upon Sophia's death, these holdings were to be transferred to their son Ambrose.

Michael Kaquatch died at his home in Little Traverse on June 16, 1876.

Due to age, infirmities, and needs, Sophia sold off most of the landholdings to provide for much-needed subsistence and to pay the mortgage and taxes. The only landholding not sold was the forty-acre lot on which Sophia continued to live after Michael's death.

By 1879, Ambrose had died and left Sophia with no living children to help support her. Since most of the Kaquatch land was sold off to pay for necessities and taxes, Sophia became dependent upon the charity of others. Dr. Carlos D. Hampton, superintendent of the poor for the Emmet County Poor Fund, was especially attentive to her situation.

On November 8, 1879, Application #254,020 was submitted for Sophia in order to obtain a dependent mother's pension. Applications were resubmitted over the years of 1884, 1886, 1888, 1889, 1890, and 1891. Each application was rejected on the grounds that the soldier was not in the line of duty when he was killed by a train.

Finally, on March 3, 1893, by a special act of Congress, the Committee on Invalid Pensions referred the bill H.R. 8498 that granted a Dependent Mother's Pension Certificate #369,429 to Sophia Kaquatch (*H.R. 8498*). The bill was granted because Samuel Kaquatch, even though he was killed in an accident while not in the actual line of duty, was, at that time, a patient at the hospital and recovering from wounds incurred while he was on active duty.

Sophia's pension paid twelve dollars a month from March 3, 1893, until her death at Harbor Springs in April 1903.

Kahgayahsung, Solomon, Private

Enlistment: Enlisted as a private on May 18, 1863, at Isabella City (now Mt. Pleasant), Isabella County, by Lieutenant William J. Driggs, First Michigan Sharpshooters, for three years.
   Age: Twenty-four, born about 1839 in Midland, Midland County.
   Occupation: Farmer
   Residence: Isabella, Isabella County
   Physical Description: Five feet nine, black eyes, black hair, and a dark complexion. Examining physician was Dr. George S. Cornell, assistant surgeon, First Michigan Sharpshooters.
   Mustered: May 26, 1863, at Detroit, Wayne County, by Lieutenant Colonel John R. Smith, US Army
   Military Service: After August 31, 1863, there is no record of discharge or any other information about Solomon Kahgayahsung on the company rolls.
   Discharged: No record for a discharge has been located.
   Biography: Solomon Kahgayahsung, also known as Solomon Foster, was listed as the son of Wawbegawneskum and Omaywawwegezhegoquay in the 1868 Gruett Saginaw Chippewa Index. He was also reported as having died at the age of twenty-five, before 1868 (*Gruett*). His siblings were Marcus and a sister named Shawwawnawsenoquay (*Ibid.*).

Solomon is said to have married a woman named Mary (?). The couple had one son, John, born in 1861 or 1862. Another record states that Solomon married a woman named Margaret and was the father of Eliza Kahzheawsung. This information has not be substantiated. No further information about Solomon Kahgayahsung has been found.

There is a question as to the possibility of Solomon Kawgayahsung and Solomon Otto possibly being the same man.

Kahgayahsung enlisted on May 18, 1863, but there is no further military record for a man by that name.

Solomon Otto has a complete record and was known to have been a brother of Marcus Otto also of Company K. He enlisted on May 18, 1863, the same day that Marcus Otto and Solomon Kahgayahsung enlisted. Could Solomon Kahgayahsung and Solomon Otto be the same man? Some of the Otto descendants think that the two men are one in the same. There is no pension file for Solomon Kahgayahsung.

Kechittigo, Thomas, Sergeant

Enlistment: Enlisted as a sergeant on May 3, 1863, in Buena Vista, East Saginaw, Saginaw County, by First Lieutenant William J. Driggs, First Michigan Sharpshooters, for three years.

Age: Twenty-seven, born about May 15, 1835 or 1836, (or May 3, 1836) in what is now known as Zilwaukee, Saginaw County. Another record states that his birth occurred in Saganing, Arenac County.

Occupation: Laborer

Residence: Saginaw County

Physical Description: Six feet tall, with black eyes, black hair, and a dark complexion. Examining physician was Dr. George L. Cornell, assistant surgeon, First Michigan Sharpshooters.

Mustered: May 26, 1863, at Detroit, Wayne County, by Lieutenant Colonel John R. Smith, US Army

Military Service: Although his name is spelled Thomas K. Chetego in the enlistment record, it appears as Thomas Kechego and Kechetogo on his enlistment paper. Most often his name was spelled Kechittigo, Ke Chittigo, or shortened to Chittigo or Chettigo.

Thomas was well thought of and respected by his superior officers. He was considered to be very dependable and a go-to guy when matters needed attention. He was admired and loved by his company comrades. During his military years, newspaper writers and fellow soldiers referred to him as "Big Tom," because of his muscular build and height, and "Old Choctaw," which was a corruption of the name Chittigo (*Campbell*).

Tom was a crack shot, so he was one of the best sharpshooters in the regiment. He carried a stick about a foot long and an inch thick on which he made a notch for every rebel that he killed. He could never understand why the soldiers, when in battle, wouldn't roll in the dust to camouflage their blue uniforms so as not to show a contrast with their surroundings. So, he always encouraged his comrades to cover their heads and chests with leaves, twigs, or cornstalks to blend in with nature. "Make self like corn," he was reported to have said. Tom was known to give the same advice to men of other state units, especially when he and his company joined them on advanced picket or sharpshooter duty.

One of those sharpshooters from another state unit was First Sergeant Wyman S. White of Company F, Second United States Sharpshooter Regiment from New Hampshire. In his diary, he mentioned one occasion when he was sent to the Ninth Corps as a sharpshooter during the Wilderness Campaign of 1864. When he joined the corps, Wyman met a Michigan sharpshooter who was an American Indian. The Indian instructed Wyman to use the cornstalks from the field they were in to camouflage their uniforms and themselves as they worked their way to the bushes in front of the rebel lines. The Indian told Wyman to "make self like corn." The two soldiers reached their destination without drawing fire (*White*).

Wyman and the Indian kept the rebels from using their guns for the remainder of the day. After dark, both men returned to their respective units. They would never meet again. Wyman reported in his diary that the Indian was pleasant company even though he said very little in conversation (*Ibid.*). The author believes that this Indian soldier was Sgt. Thomas Kechittigo.

On the forenoon of May 12, 1864, during the Battle of Spotsylvania, Sgt. Kechittigo suffered a gunshot wound (missile) in his left forearm. The missile struck the upper third of his forearm on the radius side, below the elbow, cutting away the muscles and weakening the arm. In its transit through the muscles, the missile narrowly missed both the ulna and the radius bones. He was helped to the rear by Company K comrade Private John Waubenoo and then taken to an aid station where his wound was assessed. At this station, any bleeding was stopped, and his wound was cleaned with cold water and hastily bandaged. He was given whiskey as a tonic and an opium pill for pain.

Thomas was then sent by ambulance wagon to his division hospital in the field and farther behind the lines. At this hospital, his wound was treated with a tincture of iodine (to impede infection) and simple cold water dressings, which consisted of folded lint rinsed in cold water, placed on the wound, and held in place with a cloth wrap or adhesive plaster (*Schaadt*). It was in this battle that Tom was mistakenly reported as having died of his wound on May 14, 1864.

On May 13, Kechittigo was transferred by ambulance wagon to a depot hospital in Fredericksburg, Virginia, where he received the same treatment when the staff could attend to him. From pictorial evidence of American Indian men photographed after the battle, this hospital was at or near attorney John Marye's house on Marye's Heights. Many private residences and public buildings were pressed into service as depot hospitals in said city. Due to the staggering numbers of wounded men and overworked staffs in these hospitals, the men received less than adequate care before they were sent to the general hospitals in the north. It was known that the care the men received in the general hospitals was the best available at that time.

Tom remained at the depot hospital for one day and two nights and was then transferred by ambulance wagon to a wharf at Belle Plain, Virginia.

From Belle Plain, Thomas was transported to a hospital steamer and sent to L'Ouverture USA General Hospital in Alexandria, Virginia, where he was admitted on May 16. His wound was treated with a tincture of iodine, to ward off infection, and fresh simple cold water dressings (*Bollet*). Ice wraps were also used to reduce wound inflammation. Pain management was as previously mentioned.

Kechittigo remained at L'Ouverture Hospital for about four weeks and was then granted a furlough of thirty days on June 14. He returned to L'Ouverture on July 15 for further treatment. On July 28, 1864, Tom returned to duty with his regiment.

On April 3, 1865, while in the trenches before Petersburg, Virginia, Sgt. Kechittigo was wounded for the second time. A rebel artillery shell burst near him, and a piece of shrapnel struck his left shoulder with such force that it threw him hard to the ground. The fall caused several bruises to his shoulder and chest. Company K comrades Sgt. Francis Tabasasch and Pvt. Albert Pesherbay helped Thomas to a safe area. He then walked, or was assisted, to the aid station behind the lines where his injuries were assessed. After whiskey was offered as a tonic and an opium pill for pain, Thomas was then sent by ambulance wagon to his division hospital farther behind the lines.

At the division hospital, his bruises were treated with salves, and he was again offered an opium pill for pain. A short time later, he was released and rejoined his regiment in the field.

Discharged: Sergeant Thomas Kechittigo was mustered out and honorably discharged at Delaney House, Tenallytown, DC, on July 28, 1865. He returned to Detroit on the steamer *Morning Star.* On August 7, Thomas was paid money due to him for his service at Jackson, Jackson County.

Biography: Thomas Kechittigo, also known by his personal Anishinabe name of Neodegezhik, was the son of Abram (or Abraham) and Elizabeth (or Chinggwaychewaynoquay) Keychetego. The name "Keychetego" was the family surname as spelled in the Gruett Saginaw Chippewa Index of 1868 (*Gruett*). He was also a nephew of Chippewa Chief Naugechegumme (or Naugjekomeh). Elizabeth was of one-quarter French heritage. Thomas's father, Abram, was allotted eighty acres in Isabella County by reason of the August 2, 1855, treaty with the Chippewas of Saginaw, parties to the treaty of January 14, 1837, and that portion of the band of Chippewa Indians of Swan Creek and Black River parties to the treaty of May 9, 1836. Its location is described as the north one half of the northwest quarter section 28 township 17 range 4 east (*Land Records 1*). Thomas's mother died before 1855, and his father died in 1857. One brother died at an early age. There were no sisters. He provided for himself as best he could by trapping and hunting with his trusty gun and faithful pet dog. Tom's meals were few and far between, but he survived. As he approached manhood, he made his living by farming, as did many of his people.

In 1861, Thomas and six friends tried unsuccessfully to enlist in the army at Saginaw to fight in the Civil War. They were told that the non-Anishinabek were afraid that "the Injuns would get crazy and murder and scalp all the women and children"—a fear arising from past wars between the two cultures. Also, some non-Anishinabek believed that the Anishinabek were not civilized.

On June 2, 1862, Rev. A. W. Curtis, minister of the Gospel, officiated at the marriage of Thomas and Artoa (or Alva) Kawgaybequay or Kagebiqua in Arenac County. Another record states that their marriage was 1860 or 1861. Tom and Artoa were the parents of several children, of which two are identified. A daughter named Frances was born about 1863, and a son named Ogawbayawgemo was born about 1864 or 1865.

Artoa was notified (mistakenly) on May 14 that Tom had been killed on May 12, 1864, at the Battle of Spotsylvania. Application #54,783 for a widow's pension was filed for her on June 20, 1864. After the application was sent in, Tom returned home on a thirty-day furlough given to him on June 14 to rest from his battle injuries. To her great surprise and happiness, Tom's arrival home dispelled the inaccurate information that he had died of his wounds. The government was notified of the mistake, and Artoa's pension application was canceled.

On January 30, 1866, Application #101,234 for an invalid pension was filed for Thomas. He received an Invalid Pension Certificate #264,702 on July 29, 1866, which paid two dollars a month for the injury he incurred to his left arm while in the line of duty. During his postwar years, Tomas experienced periodic pain in his shoulders and chest due to the previously mentioned fall caused by the force of shrapnel from a shell burst.

After he returned from the war, Thomas, according to his recollections, lived in Saginaw County for two years, Pinconning in Bay County for ten years, Oscoda in Iosco County for fifteen years, Mackinac Island in Mackinac County for one year, and the rest of his life in Grayling in Crawford County.

Before and after the war, Tom was employed as a "shanty boy" (or lumberjack) in the forests and as a "river hog" on the AuSable River, where he was known for his dexterity, agility, and expertise in driving logs through the turbulent waters of the spring run. He had excellent balance that was aided by his spiked boots and a peavey pole, which saved his life many times. To keep up his strength as a lumberjack, Tom consumed about 8,000 calories every day, especially during the winter season.

Being an industrious man, he was also engaged as a farmer, hunter, trapper, river guide, fisherman, and railroad worker to provide for his family. He also found employment in the area lumber mills.

Artoa and the children died in a smallpox epidemic about 1872 in Au Sable.

Thomas received a Homestead Certificate #483 for eighty acres (under the name of "Thomas Chittego") on the AuSable River in Iosco County. His patent was granted on April 15, 1873. It's description was the north half of the northwest quarter of section 15 in township 24 north of range 7 east (Land Records 2).

Tom's second marriage was to Mary Ann (Campau/Campeau) Elke, the widow of William (or Bill) Elke, on October 23, 1875, in East Saginaw of Saginaw County. Rev. H. H. Wilson, a presiding elder of the African Methodist Episcopal Church, officiated at the ceremony. John Hall and John M. Lowery were witnesses to the marriage.

Mary was the daughter of a Frenchman known as Andrew Campau/Campeau and his Anishinabequa wife, Manya (or Mary). She was born in Lapeer County on August 15, about 1845. Her known siblings were a brother, Andrew Jr., who was an Isabella County merchant, and two sisters, Elizabeth and Eliza. Before his death in 1873, Bill and Mary Elke had one son, John, who predeceased his mother.

It seems that Mary's father did not want her to marry Thomas since he had another man (of French ancestry) in mind for her to marry. But love prevailed, and Tom and Mary eloped. They were a happy couple and were reported to have been the parents of Mary, born around 1875 or 1876; a son born in 1877; Minnie, born about May 3, 1884, in Pinconning of Bay County and died the same year; twins Angeline and Adeline, born January 3, 1887; and Elzia (a son), born about 1893 and died in 1896. Daughter Mary married Lewis Williams, a laborer, in Pinconning, Bay County, on May 17, 1890.

About 1895, Tom and Mary moved with their younger children to Grayling of Crawford County where Tom built the family home overlooking the Au Sable River. The couple became active members in the Grayling Methodist Episcopal Church.

Attending the same church as the Kechittigo family was the only other Anishinabek couple who lived in Grayling—Chief David Shoppenagonce (or Shawbwawnegoonse—"Little Needles") and his wife. The Kechittigos and the Shoppenagonce families were good friends. The chief was also known as David Nelson, and he and his first wife, Mary Awnemequoung (or Amnemequon), were the parents of Thomas Nelson, who was a Company K comrade of Tom Kechittego (*Avery*). See the file on Thomas Nelson.

In his retirement years, Tom was invited many times to the homes of lumber barons Nells Michelson and Rasmus Hanson in whose lumber camps he had worked. In their presence, and other guests, he would enjoy dinner with questions and conversations about his life as a lumberjack. Tom was well respected by these men and a favorite guest (*The Avalanche*). Many times Mary would attend with Tom on these outings accompanied by the Shoppenagonce family. On these occasions, the couples were allowed to decorate the parlor to their liking in which they would demonstrate Anishinabek life ways with songs, dances, storytelling, and craft sales (*Ibid.*).

For thirty years, Thomas Kechittigo was active in the GAR Sculley Post #265 at Omer, Arenac County. He served as its guard and color bearer, in which he carried and presented the flag for ceremonies for fifteen years.

When he and his family moved to Grayling in the mid-1890s, he became a member of the GAR Marvin Post #240.

Thomas was active as a marshal at GAR camp meetings, seeing to their protection and order. He received a badge of honor for exemplary work in carrying out his duties.

Over the years, the muscles in his left arm atrophied so much that Thomas sought an increase in his monthly pension payments to help him to support his family. His payments were increased from two to eight dollars. By 1912, he received thirty dollars a month. In the act approved on May 11, 1912, any veteran who received an honorable discharge and suffered a disease or a debilitating injury while in the service was to be paid a maximum of thirty dollars a month regardless of his length of service.

Considering that he was left an orphan in his early life and was exposed to rough circumstances, Thomas, as an Anishinabe, learned to walk with ease in the white man's world. He became an honored and respected citizen whose friendship was treasured by all who knew him. Thoroughly independent, Tom maintained a comfortable dwelling for his family and saw to their support. The Kechittigo home hosted many visits from neighbors and friends alike.

Thomas dictated two letters to former Major Julian E. Buckbee of the First Regiment, Michigan Sharpshooters. The first one, dated November 13, 1886, was written on GAR Scully Post (located in Omer of Algonac County) stationery, and told of Thomas's interest in seeing his former regimental officer and army comrade again at the annual GAR meeting in Lansing. The second letter, written in 1892, told of his interest in his old army friend's postwar years and of the disappointment of not seeing him at that year's GAR meeting. Thomas also related to Buckbee that he was still a "Big Indian," that he could still kick six feet high, didn't feel old, and that he was as good a man as he was in his war years. He also said that he was glad to see so many of his comrades at the annual meeting but was surprised that he did not know many of them because they looked so old and gray.

In his later years, Kechittigo's health steadily declined due to his age, tuberculosis (as affirmed by his doctor), and to his injuries incurred in the military. He was also plagued with rheumatism.

Thomas died from a severe attack of rheumatism on April 24, 1916, at about the age of eighty-one. His death occurred at Grayling Mercy Hospital. Thomas's funeral service was held from his M.E. Church in Grayling. On April 26, he was given a burial by military protocol in Elmwood Cemetery presented by his GAR Marvin Post in said city. Thomas lies beside two of his children in lot 3, block 36, grave A.

Thomas Kechittigo's obituary appeared in the April 27, 1916, Grayling newspaper, *The Crawford Avalanche.* In the obituary, it was stated that Mr. Kechittigo had always been recognized as an honorable and respected citizen and that by his own labor he was independent and maintained a comfortable home for his wife and family. Thomas and his wife were loyal and consistent members of the M.E. Church for many years. The article further stated that Mary, his wife, survives but that the state of her health and her age makes it almost sure that she will join him very soon. Rev. Mitchell conducted the funeral service, which was attended by nearly every soldier in the area whose health would permit. The article concluded that the ladies of the GAR also attended in a body to pay their last respects. It must have been a comfort to Mary to have her lady friends join her in her mourning.

Informed of Thomas's passing, the *Fraternal Order of Woodmen of America* furnished a tombstone for Thomas's grave. The stone is unusual because it is in the shape of a tree stump and stands about five feet tall. The monument echoes the sentiment that no woodman shall rest in an unmarked grave—a testimonial to true brotherhood.

After Thomas's death, Application #1,118,084 for a widow's pension was filed for Mary on April 2, 1918. She mentioned in her pension deposition that Thomas was always known as *Thomas Chittigo,* and she didn't know just where the prefix "Ke" came from. This sentiment was echoed by the author's Anishinabequa friend Mrs. Hazel Lavoie, who lived in Oscoda of Iosco County and knew Thomas Chittigo's history.

Mary, who still had a keen mind and whose opinions were valued by all of her friends, continued to live in the Grayling home she had shared with Thomas. She supported herself by taking in washing and making beautiful baskets, which were prized by all who purchased them. Known as a very neat housekeeper, she was loved by her neighbors and had a wide circle of friends. Mary's vegetable garden was the envy of many who observed her hard work and saw the fruits of her labor.

In her younger days, Mary was active in the affairs of the Women's Relief Corps, the sister organization to the GAR, and was considered one of its esteemed members.

Now a widow, the Soldiers' Relief Society helped Mary in her time of need.

Beth Seator of Grayling reminisced with the author about her very early childhood memories of Mrs. Chittigo and the Chittigo home. Beth would accompany her grandmother when the two would visit with Mary and buy some of Mary's beautiful baskets. She recalled how pleasant and clean the house smelled and how it was filled with the wood that Mary would use to make baskets. Mary was always glad to see Beth and her grandmother and enjoyed her visits with them.

Many appeals were made by Mary's friends to the US Pension Agency on Mary's behalf and stressed that she was a worthy recipient of a widow's pension. A picture of Mary and Tom (taken around 1915) was found in Tom's pension papers. In the picture, Tom is proudly wearing his Ninth (IX) Army Corps pin and his GAR badge. Finally, sometime after 1920, Mary Chittigo received a Widow's Pension Certificate #889,115, which paid about eight dollars month until her death.

Having become feeble with age, Mary Chittigo's nephew, Lyman Williams, and his wife of Rosebush in Isabella County lived for a short time with Mary to care for her before her death. Mary was not ill, but her life was fading away.

Mary Ann Campau Elke Chittigo died at about the age of eighty-eight at her home on Friday, February 24, 1933, at 3:30 a.m. Her funeral service was held the following Monday from the Michelson Memorial Methodist Church in Grayling with Rev. H. J. Salmon officiating. Her obituary was full of praise and admiration for the grand old lady. Mary's burial was in Elmwood Cemetery near her husband. Listed in the Grayling *Avalanche* newspaper as surviving the deceased was one daughter, Mary Elke Bigjoe, of Omena, Leelanau County, and two nephews, Mr. Williams of Rosebush, Isabella County, and Jack Williams of Beaverton, Gladwin County.

Kejikowe, Simon, Private

Enlistment: Enlisted as a private on July 6, 1863, at Little Traverse (now Harbor Springs), Emmet County, by Second Lieutenant Garrett A. Graveraet, First Michigan Sharpshooters, for three years.

Age: Twenty-three, born about 1840 in Cheboygan County.

Occupation: Farmer

Residence: Burt (Burt Lake), at Colonial Point in Cheboygan County

Physical Description: Five feet eight, black eyes, black hair, and a dark complexion. Examining physician was Dr. Arvin F. Whelan, surgeon, First Michigan Sharpshooters.

Mustered: July 20, 1863, at the Detroit Arsenal, Dearborn, by Lieutenant Colonel John R. Smith, US Army

Military Service: On May 12, 1864, at the Battle of Spotsylvania, Virginia, Private Simon Kejikowe sustained a severe gunshot (missile) wound to the left side of his body. He was taken to a field aid station behind the lines where his wound was assessed, washed, and hastily bandaged. Simon was then taken by ambulance wagon to his division hospital in the field for further treatment which consisted of a simple water dressing. This dressing consisted of lint soaked in cold water, placed on the wound (which may or may not have been treated with a tincture of iodine), and secured with a cloth wrap or adhesive plaster (*Schaadt*). He was given whiskey or opium pills for pain.

Due to the severity of his wound, Simon was then taken by ambulance wagon to a depot hospital in Fredericksburg, Virginia. This hospital was at or near the home of attorney John Marye on Marye's Heights. Iodine, water dressings, and pain management were continued for Private Kejikowe.

Dr. William Howard Reed was one of the Ninth Corps surgeons who worked at this depot hospital and described the suffering of the soldiers and the terrible conditions of filth, blood, and vermin that infested the place.

Sometimes, according to Dr. Reed, the wounded would be taken outside and placed on the lawn so that they could have some fresh air and relief from the terrible heat inside the hospital (*Reed*).

Although there was no official confirmation, Private Kejikowe was reported as dead on the muster rolls for September and October 1864. He probably died of his wound in the Fredericksburg hospital, as his name is not borne on subsequent rolls for his company.

Assuming that Kejikowe died in the depot hospital, his body would have been put on a stretcher, covered with a blanket or a tarp, and taken to a cemetery close to the hospital. At the cemetery, the blanket was removed, and Simon's body would have been laid next to other dead soldiers in a trench and covered with dirt (*Ibid.*). A wooden board with name and unit (if known) was placed at the head of his grave site. Prayers may or may not have been said at his burial (*Ibid.*).

Soon after the war, the soldiers' remains were removed from the hospital burial trenches and reburied individually (possibly in caskets, if available) in the newly designated Fredericksburg National Cemetery (*Guide*). No religious service would have been provided.

Since there is no record of Simon Kejikowe having been reburied (by name) in said cemetery, it's assumed that Simon's headboard suffered a demise through inclement weather or was removed for firewood. Without identification, Simon's remains are probably now under a stone labeled "Unknown" in the Fredericksburg National Cemetery (*Ibid.*).

Discharged: No discharge given due to assumed death in a military hospital, as his name does not appear on subsequent company rolls.

Biography: Simon Kejikowe, who did not marry, was the son of Chief Joseph and Julia Gijigowi. Kejikowe was also spelled Kieshegoway, Kechegowe, Keeshagoway, and Kigegoway. Chief Joseph was the headman of the Cheboygan Band of Odawa (or Ottawa) who lived near Burt Lake at Colonial Point.

Simon's siblings were a brother, Enos, who was also known as Elias or Ignatius, and a sister named Catherine.

As the nearest of kin, Simon's brother and sister were known to have applied for Simon's remaining arrears of pay from his service. They noted that Simon died from wounds received in the line of duty. But since each sibling had attained the age of sixteen at the time of their application, they were not entitled to any pension payment.

On July 22, 1890, at the age of fifty, Enos Kejikowe died of blood poisoning (septicemia) from a leg wound.

In October 1890, a disastrous fire was deliberately set and implicated Cheyboygan County's Sheriff Ming, his deputies, and a timber speculator, John McGinn, in a land grab (*Traverse*). The fire burned out the Burt Lake settlement at Colonial Point (*Conversations*). The main causes of the tragedy involved the misrepresentation and total disregard for the differences between "annuity payments (from treaties) versus taxes" by the town's local officials and the state's lack of responsibility in dealing with the Anishinabek's trust land (*Friday*). This terrible event left the people of the settlement homeless and destitute. There is no pension file for Simon Kejikowe.

Kenewahaneby, John, Private

Enlistment: Enlisted as a private on February 14, 1865, at Grand Rapids, Kent County, by Captain and provost marshal for the Fourth District, Norman Bailey, First Michigan Sharpshooters for one year. Credited to the Fourth Congressional District, Leelanau, Leelanau County.

Age: Seventeen, born about May 16, 1848, in Ahgostatown, Leelanau Township, in Leelanau County (his mother's testimony). John's age is listed as twenty years, eleven months on his official enlistment sheet.

Occupation: Laborer

Residence: Leelanau Township

Physical Description: Five feet five and a half inches tall, black eyes, black hair. and a dark complexion. Examining physician was Dr. Alonzo Mate, surgeon, First Michigan Sharpshooters.

Mustered: February 14, 1865, at Grand Rapids by captain and provost marshal for the Fourth District, Norman Bailey, First Michigan Sharpshooters.

Military Service: Private John Kenewahaneby's service to his country was short-lived. On March 2, 1865, he was taken by ambulance wagon from his regiment to a division hospital, near Petersburg, Virginia, with the diagnosis of double pneumonia.

The doctors treated John's pneumonia with the application of mustard plasters and poultices to his chest or back. The plasters consisted of a mixture of ground black mustard seed, flour, and water wrapped in a flannel cloth (*Internet search*). The moist heat was thought to be beneficial in ridding the body of so-called poisons. Opium pills were administered for pain. The young soldier died the next day.

After his death on March 3, John's body was put on a stretcher, covered with a blanket, and taken to the cemetery at nearby Meade Station. The blanket was removed, and the body was put into a trench with other dead bodies and covered with dirt. His name and unit were written on a wooden board that was placed at the head of his grave. Prayers may or may not have been said at his grave site (*Reed*).

On April 17, 1866, the farm of Rev. Thomas B. Flower, located on Vaughn Road four miles south of Petersburg, was chosen as the site for the new Poplar Grove National Cemetery for Union soldiers.

During the summer of 1866, John Kenewahaneby's remains were moved from Meade Station and reburied (possibly in a casket) in Poplar Grove Cemetery. No religious service was conducted (*Conversation*). Today John lies at rest under a military stone in grave #189. The name on his stone reads "John Kenewancic."

Discharged: No discharge given due to death from disease while in the hospital.

Biography: John was also known as John Kenewahnaneppi/Keniwahnaneppi or, as explained by an interpreter, correctly spelled as *Kenewahaneby,* which means "everlasting (or evergreen) tree"; John Kenewnuhneba (which means "eagle summer"); and John Penaiquon (his baptismal name), which was also spelled Banagua/Banagwa. He was the son of Joseph Banagua (or Penaiquon) and Margaret/ Margarette Negonbequay Banagua/Penaiquon.

Margaret testified (and substantiated by her cousin George Allen, a brother to Charles Allen, who was a member of Company K) that she and Joseph were married on July 14, 1847, at Omena (Mission Point near Northport) in Leelanau County. Witnesses were Joseph Asagon and Gabina. Joseph was the son of Banagua Kewegabawe and Margaret (Maria on the wedding license) Nodiniquom, who was the daughter of Klotchi. Margaret related that the marriage was performed by Father Francois Pierz, a Catholic missionary to the Anishinabek.

There is some discrepancy as to the exact date of John's birth. It's reported that Joseph Banagua died in a drowning accident sometime in the late 1850s at St. Joseph, Berrien County. There is also a discrepancy as to the exact date of when Joseph drowned.

As soon as he was old enough, John Kenewahaneby (or Banagua) worked in a sawmill in Traverse City in Grand Traverse County and was employed at loading vessels and chopping cordwood to make enough money to buy clothes and food for himself and for his mother and sister. He was a dutiful son, a hard worker, and Margaret's sole support.

After her son's death in the service, Margaret's log house burned in September 1865, and all of its contents were destroyed. She did receive the remainder of the bounty money due to her son and a small government annuity of about four dollars a year, which ceased in 1873.

Even though she raised potatoes, corn, and beans in a small rented garden plot and made baskets to sell, times were tough for a widow who was in failing health. She was destitute. In those days, a woman could not make a living as a man could, so Margaret depended upon friends and neighbors for help. Among those friends were the Allen family (John's Company K comrade Charles Allen's family) and Aaron Sargonquatto (also known as Aaron Pequongay or Puhquonga), who was a Company K comrade of John's and who was a second cousin to John's mother, Margaret.

In 1866, Margaret and a man named John Akahche (Kahche or Ogotchee), a cousin to Margaret's first husband, John Banagwa, began cohabiting without marriage as husband and wife. It seems that Margaret's son, John, had asked Akahche to help Margaret survive if he, John, were killed in the service. Akahche offered Margaret a place to live so that he could help take care of her and support her. She accepted the offer. After she agreed to Akahche's offer, Margaret was then known as Margaret Akahche.

The combined work efforts of Margaret and John, who worked his forty acres of land with two ponies, helped the couple to support each other. The land was worth about five dollars an acre, but only five of the forty acres were cleared for farming.

Application #281,385 for a dependent sister's pension was filed for an Eliza Penegwah Keway on March 19, 1881. Eliza is not mentioned as a daughter of Joseph and Margaret Banagwa, or as a sister to John, in any of Margaret's (or other's) depositions.

On her application, Eliza claimed that her parents were Joseph and Mary (or Bashenenabe) Penegwah (as the name was spelled on the application), that she was born about 1855, and that she was a sister to John Penegwah, the Company K soldier. Eliza's application was rejected on account of claimant's failure, after a reasonable time, to furnish the necessary proof to establish the validity of her claim as a sister to the soldier.

On June 16, 1890, Application #426,267 was filed for Margaret Penaiquon Banagua Akahche for a mother's pension. It was rejected on the basis that she was living as a "mistress" (in the US government's opinion) with a man who was not her husband or the father of her son but who was supporting her in the eyes of the law. Therefore, she was not a dependent who deserved a pension.

Application #695,639 for a dependent mother's pension was submitted for Margaret under the name of Margarette Banagua on April 6, 1899. This effort was a resubmission since the first attempt was rejected.

The second submission was successful under Sec. 4707 as amended by the Act of June 27, 1890, concerning pensions for dependent mothers and fathers. The amendment (in the widow's case) was a more liberal interpretation under said act since it considered a widow "who was without other means of support than her daily labor." By 1899, John Akahche was at an advanced age and had some ailments that prevented him from fully supporting Margaret.

Margaret finally received Dependent Mother's Pension Certificate #498,877 issued on August 30, 1900. The pension payments were twelve dollars a month and were retroactive to April 6, 1899.

Margaret Penaiquon (Banagua) Akahche, who suffered from rheumatism and failing health, died on April 3, 1906, at Northport.

Application #959,919 was submitted for John Akahche for a dependent father's pension on March 1, 1911. The application was rejected on the grounds that the claimant was not the father of the soldier. Therefore, Akahche had no title to a pension under the law.

Kesas, John, Private

Enlistment: Enlisted as a private on August 23, 1864, at Kalamazoo, Kalamazoo County, by Rollin C. Kenison, provost marshal for the Second District of Michigan, for two years. He signed his name "Ke sas" on his enlistment paper.

Private Kesas was a substitute for Edgar W. Gilkey of Richland, Kalamazoo County, which satisfied the requirement for a man from the Second Congressional District, Kalamazoo County, town of Richland. As the principal or enrolled draftee, Gilkey would have paid Kesas about $300 to be his substitute. As a volunteer substitute, Kesas was not entitled to an enlistment bounty because of the generous lump sum that he received as a substitute. But as an enlisted substitute soldier, he was eligible for a hundred-dollar bounty (as were regular enlisted men) if he was discharged from the service by reason of wounds that he received in battle.

There were non-Anishinabek men who avoided the service by finding substitutes. Many of these men visited the Michigan reservations and areas with Anishinabek populations. They sought out the men and offered lump sums of money to them if they agreed to serve as substitutes. The Civil War era was a time in which most Anishinabek people were in need of monetary support to provide for their families. The offers of money were hard to refuse.

Age: Thirty, born about 1834 in Michigan.

Occupation: Farmer

Residence: Richland, Kalamazoo County

Physical Description: Five feet six, black eyes, black hair, and a dark complexion. Examining physician was Dr. N. V. Nitekurk, (?) surgeon of the Board of Enrollment of the Second District of Michigan.

Mustered: August 23, 1864, at Kalamazoo by First Sergeant E. M. Clift, Thirteenth US Infantry mustering officer for Provost Marshal R. C. Dennison

Military Service: Private John Kesas joined his company and regiment on September 15, 1864, and apparently served the duration of his service without being wounded. He did suffer from a persistent cough during his term of service, which could have been an early symptom of consumption (or tuberculosis).

Discharged: Private John Kesas was mustered out and honorably discharged at Delaney House, Georgetown, Washington, DC, on July 28, 1865. He returned to Detroit on the steamer *Morning Star.* On August 7, John received payment due to him at Jackson, Jackson County for his service.

Biography: The name Kesas is derived from the word *giizis* or *gisiss* and means "sun." Gisiss could also mean moon or month, depending on how the word is used (*Baraga*). John's name was also spelled Keeses, Kesis, and Kesses.

John Kesas (who also used the name John Kahawawe) of Wayland, Allegan County, married Betsey Quaquawata (who was listed as Betsey Wildcat on the couple's wedding license) also from Wayland on March 15, 1858. Another record stated that Betsey was also known as Mary Nottaway. Rev. James Selkirk, the pastor of the Episcopal Mission Church, officiated at the marriage of the couple in his home (or parsonage) in said town. The ceremony was witnessed by Sarah Baikus and John Johnson. Sarah Isaacs and Eliza Burch of Athens, Calhoun County, were also present at the ceremony. Today the mission church is known as the Bradley Indian Church on the Anishinabek (both Ottawa and Potawatomi) settlement at Bradley, Allegan County.

John and Betsey were the parents of Eliza, their only child, born October 20, 1861.

On May 10, 1864, Betsey Kesas died. She was attended in her illness by Sarah Isaacs and Eliza Burch. Betsey is buried in the Bradley Indian Mission Cemetery in Wayland Township, Allegan County.

As a widower, John saw to the care of his daughter with relatives and friends and then enlisted in the army on August 23, 1864.

Toward the end of his service and after his discharge in 1865, Kesas was constantly sick and suffered greatly from a severe cough and a disease of the lungs. These symptoms were probably from consumption (or tuberculosis). It was reported that he also had inflammatory rheumatism. John doctored with patent medicines and was treated by an Anishinabequa doctor, Granny David, who gave him traditional herbs and poultices for his ailments.

John Kesas experienced a continuous physical decline at the Bradley settlement and died on October 20, 1867, as was recorded in the last papers of his file.

Henry Pashmahme, Eliza Burch, and Sarah Isaac cared for Kesas during his last days and were present at his death. He was buried near his wife in said cemetery and lies at rest beneath a military stone.

John and Betsey's daughter, Eliza, married a man named Adam Shipman. Missionary and Minister of the Gospel N. Weston officiated at the ceremony on February 28, 1883, on Walpole Island, Canada. Sometime after their marriage, the couple moved back to Michigan and resided in Athens.

Eliza's Application #391,344 for a minor's pension was filed for her on March 21, 1889. Her application was based upon the claim that she was under the age of sixteen at her father's death and therefore would be entitled to a pension as a surviving minor.

On January 18, 1894, Eliza's application was rejected on the grounds that she had no title to a pension because she had already attained the age of sixteen prior to the date of filing her claim. She resubmitted her application on June 8, 1911, and it was again rejected for the same reason on March 25, 1913.

Kewacondo, Benjamin, Private

Enlistment: Enlisted as private on February 15, 1864, in Holmes Township, outside of the Village of Mackinac Island of Mackinac County, for three years. The enlistment was credited to St. Ignace of Mackinac County by Joseph Jenae, First Michigan Sharpshooters.

Age: Twenty-one, born about 1843 in Canada.

Occupation: Boatman. On July 22, 1863, Benjamin listed his occupation as a house servant in the US Civil War Draft Registration Records, 1863–1865 on page 286.

Residence: St. Ignace, Mackinac County

Physical Description: Five feet ten, black eyes, black hair, and a dark complexion. Examining physician was Dr. George Landon, surgeon, First Michigan Sharpshooters.

Mustered: April 29, 1864, at Detroit, Wayne County, by Captain Werner Boecklin (or Warner Backlin)

Military Service: Benjamin, being a boatman, may have worked as: a fisherman on the Great Lakes; on the ferry boats that crossed Lake Huron to Mackinac Island from St. Ignace and Mackinaw City; and at loading and unloading boats when they arrived at port. In these possible occupations, Benjamin was exposed to a lot of pressure on his legs and back, aggravated by prolonged standing and strenuous work.

Sometime after his enlistment, Private Kewacondo complained of pain and soreness in his right leg. When he was with his regiment in Virginia, he was admitted to his division hospital for treatment. Benjamin was diagnosed with a painful indolent ulcer (a break in the skin that refuses to heal) on his right leg (*Blakiston*). The ulcer was probably caused by poor circulation due to vascular disease or varicose veins.

The doctors at the division hospital applied simple cold water dressings to the ulcer. These dressings were composed of folded lint dipped into cold water, applied to the sore, and held in place by a cloth wrap or adhesive plaster (*Schaadt*). Whiskey or an opium pill was given to the patient for pain.

On May 13, Kewacondo was taken by ambulance wagon to a depot hospital in Fredericksburg, Virginia. This hospital was at or near attorney John Marye's house at Marye's Heights. The doctors at the depot hospital continued the cold water dressings and pain management.

On May 15, Benjamin was taken by ambulance wagon from the depot hospital to the wharf at Belle Plain, Virginia, and put on to a hospital steamer bound for Washington, DC. He was admitted on May 16 to Douglas USA General Hospital in said city.

At Douglas General, the surgeons anesthetized Benjamin with ether and removed the dead tissue from the sore with a scalpel. This surgical procedure is called debridement (*Bollet*). Iodine was applied around the area of the wound, and a weak solution of bromine was put into the cavity of the sore (*Evans*). After the medicinal applications were applied, the leg was wrapped in a dry bandage and secured. Opiates for pain were again administered to the patient.

Private Kewacondo was transferred from Douglas Hospital to Satterlee USA General Hospital in West Philadelphia, Pennsylvania, and admitted on May 18. Similar treatment was continued, and Benjamin was confined to a resting position with his leg elevated. Now, for the first time since his enlistment, he was served nourishing food, as the doctors prescribed a healthful diet to speed his recovery. Private Kewacondo was released from Satterlee Hospital and returned to duty with his regiment on August 26, 1864.

Discharged: Private Benjamin Kewacondo was mustered out and honorably discharged on July 28, 1865, at Delaney House, Washington, DC. He returned to Detroit on the steamer *Morning Star* and received payment due to him for his service on August 7 at Jackson, Jackson County.

Biography: No pension record for Kewacondo (sometimes spelled "Kewaconda") has been found. Although it seems that he disappeared after his discharge in 1865, the author found a later military record for a *Benjamin Kewaconda* who was also from Canada. In this record, a Benjamin Kewaconda enlisted in Company E of the Tenth United States Cavalry (*Register*).

The record further states that this Benjamin Kewaconda joined the unit on May 4, 1867, at Detroit for a period of five years. The enlistee was twenty-two years of age, single, from Georgian Bay, Canada, and listed his profession as a sailor. His physical description was stated as dark eyes, dark hair, and a dark complexion. He measured six feet in height.

After the Civil War, the Ninth and Tenth United States Cavalry units consisted of all African American enlistees (with Caucasian officers) and were engaged in fighting the American Indians on the western frontier. It's known that Indians were also referred to as "colored" in the military and in some census records of the nineteenth century. Maybe Benjamin was looking for a different kind of war experience as a cavalryman and took the first opportunity to do so.

Benjamin must not have thought that the cavalry was challenging enough, or maybe he thought it was too demanding. He may not have liked fighting against fellow American Indians, or he may have even gotten himself into some kind of trouble. Anyway, after about two years of service, Kewaconda deserted the cavalry on August 21, 1869, and again vanished from records until 1886.

A final notation on an *American Civil War Soldiers Record* states that a Benjamin

Kewaconda, who served the Union as a sharpshooter from Michigan, died on December 17, 1886, in Roanoke, Virginia (*Record*).

After he deserted the cavalry, Benjamin could have found work on the railroads in southeastern Virginia. After all, he had spent time in that part of the country as an army sharpshooter. Railroad construction was at its boom following the Civil War, and workers could earn good wages. Benjamin may have died of some disease or in an accident while working on the railroad. In any case, if he died in Virginia, his burial site has not been located.

The two previous military service records of Benjamin Kewaconda and Benjamin Kewacondo show the author enough similarities in their records to possibly be the same man. There is no pension file for Benjamin Kewaconda/ Benjamin Kewacondo.

Kitchibatise, Amable, Private

Enlistment: Enlisted as a private on August 24, 1863, at Northport, Leelanau County, by Second Lieutenant Garrett A. Graveraet, First Michigan Sharpshooters, for three years.

Age: At his enlistment, Amable gave his age as twenty-two, born at La Croix (renamed Cross Village in 1875), Emmet County. According to another record, Amable was listed as being born in 1830, which would make him age thirty-three at enlistment.

Occupation: Farmer

Residence: La Croix

Physical Description: Five feet eleven, black eyes, black hair, and a dark complexion. Examining physician was Dr. George L. Cornell, assistant surgeon, First Michigan Sharpshooters.

Mustered: October 4, 1863, at Camp Douglas, Cook County, Illinois, by Capt. Lowe. Camp Douglas was a confine for Confederate prisoners and was guarded for seven months by the men of the First Michigan Sharpshooters.

Military Service: Private Amable Kitchibatise was assigned as a cook for his company during the months of December 1863 and March and April 1864.

Amable was captured at the Battle of the Crater on July 30, 1864, before the besieged city of Petersburg, Virginia. The rebels sent him to Danville by cattle railcar on the Richmond and Danville Railroad. The train trip extended from

Petersburg through Burkville Junction, Clover Station, and South Boston to a stop at Danville Prison in Danville, Virginia. In Danville, Amable was confined in a converted tobacco warehouse (*McFall Jr.*).

Shortly after he was locked in the prison and before his situation became deplorable, Amable dictated a letter (that was written by a fellow prisoner and sent to Amable's wife, Elizabeth). The letter is as follows:

> Danville
>
> August the 5th, '64
>
> Dear wife
>
>   I now inform you that I am a prisonor and I am well and hoping that these few lines will find you in good helth. I am in a good room and well fed and I hope that my 4 little Children are well. Dear wife I would like to be with you but I cant very well leave this good place. I was Captured on August the 30. Direct your letter to Danville no 3 building, no 1 flour.
>
> Charles
>
> Amable John

Instead of August 30, the date should read July 30. The soldier who wrote the letter for Amable signed his name "Charles" first as the writer for Amable's dictation. Amable may have signed his own name. This letter was the last communication that Elizabeth would receive from her husband. How Amable must have suffered from homesickness and worry as Elizabeth's heart ached with concern for Amable and how she would care for their children in his absence.

There were six former tobacco warehouses used as prisons in Danville. Prison #3, where Amable was confined, was located near the intersection of Union and Spring Streets in the city of Danville and was constructed of wood and measured forty by a hundred feet. The building was three stories tall located near the Dan River and was a holding area for both Union officers and men (*Ibid.*). Sentries placed outside of the building were stationed on the two most vulnerable sides of the prison, and two sentinels were placed on the ground floor inside the building. Iron bars secured the windows, and very large oak doors closed off escape attempts (*Ibid.*). According to his letter, Amable was confined on floor number one of said building. Confederate guards were usually placed between the officers and enlisted men, if they were confined together, to keep them separated and unable to communicate with each other.

During the months of August and September 1864, Amable's meals would have consisted of cornbread and sometimes a soup that included bits of rancid bacon. Fresh meat (a rarity) was sometimes included in the soup as well as some cabbage leaves and "cow peas" (or southern black-eyed peas), which, most of the time, contained worms. The gritty water used for the soup came from the muddy Dan River (*Ibid.*).

On May 10, 1865, while at camp in Georgetown, Washington, DC, Sergeant Francis Tabasasch and Private Louis Shomin of Company K happened to meet and talk with some Union soldiers who had been released from the Danville Prison and discharged from Alexandria, Virginia. The soldiers told Tabasasch and Shomin that they had seen Amable in that prison and knew that he had died there around March 1, 1865. One of the soldiers was Charles H. De Puy of Company H of the First Michigan Sharpshooters. It is known that Charles was confined for a short time in the same area as Amable and was most probably the "Charles" who wrote the letter, dictated by Amable, to Amable's wife.

While in captivity, Amable was admitted to the prison hospital as Amiab J. on November 22, 1864, suffering from bronchitis. According to the medical records of the prison hospital, Amable died of bronchitis on February 22, 1865, without leaving the hospital (*Ibid.*). The inhumane conditions of prison life, the lack of proper clothing to keep warm in the winter, and the epidemics of dysentery, smallpox, and other diseases brought on by starvation would certainly have contributed to prisoners' deaths.

After he died, Amable's body was moved to a dead house where his remains were tagged with his name and unit. But we have a bit of confusion here. It seems that Amable's Company K comrade, Amos Ashkebugnekay, who was also captured on June 17, 1864, at Petersburg, may have been held briefly in Prison #3 before he was shipped off to Andersonville Prison in Georgia. Amos survived the prison camp and the *Sultana* maritime disaster to return home. Somehow Ashkebugnekay's first name of "Amos," preceded by the initial J, was listed as the surname of the dead soldier instead of Amable's name. Both men were known by prison authorities to be in Company K of the First Michigan Sharpshooters.

When Amable was removed from the dead house and taken to the prison cemetery, he was laid, without a covering, into a trench with other dead prisoners. Dirt was placed over his body, and a wooden board with name and unit was placed at the head of his grave (*Encyclopedia*). So the name on the board (and later on his military stone) was mistakenly listed as *J. Amos Mich* instead of *Amable Kitchibatise Mich.*

When the Danville, Virginia, National Cemetery was established in December 1866, the remains of soldiers who died in the prison were disinterred from the mass graves and reburied in that cemetery. Wooden markers were used to identify the graves until military stones replaced the markers (*Danville*).

Today the body of Amable Kitchibatise is the one that actually lies in Plot E in said cemetery under stone #1167 that reads *J. Amos, Mich.* A 152-year-old mystery as to how and where Amable Kitchibatise died and what stone marks his burial place is finally solved. The solution to this mystery is credited to the fine detective work of author F. Lawrence McFall Jr.

Elizabeth Kitchibatise must have been devastated when she was told by a former prisoner of Amable's death. She then realized the reason why she did not receive more than one letter. Also, she knew that if he were alive, he would have returned to her and the family because he was a good husband and father who would not desert his family. In her broken heart, Elizabeth acknowledged that Amable was buried under prison soil and not, if he could have wished it differently, in the land of his ancestors.

Sergeant Charles H. De Puy would be awarded the Medal of Honor on July 30, 1896, for his gallantry in action at the Battle of the Crater fought at Petersburg, Virginia, on July 30, 1864 (Bozich).

Discharged: No discharge given due to death by disease while a prisoner of war.

Biography: Amable Kitchibatise, also known by the names Amabilis Egawanige, Kitche Batist, Amable Ketchebatist, and Amable John Baptist (his proper name), was born about 1830. The name Amable is derived from the Latin word *amabilis,* which means "amiable" and "lovable." He was baptized at Holy Cross Mission Church at La Croix (now Cross Village), Emmet County, in 1831. Kitchibatise is the name derived from the Anishinabe word *kitchi,* which means "big" and the word "baptist" (*Baraga*). The Anishinabek also pronounced John the Baptist as Shabatise. Due to his stature, Amable was often referred to as "big Amable John Baptist."

Amable married Elizabeth (Sobede in Anishinabek) Agawwawnegay (or Omyarwadoux/Mishquado), who was born about 1831 or 1832 at Burt Lake, Cheboygan County. She also was known as Josette and Lizette. The couple was married on Manitoulin Island, Canada, on January 4, 1849. A local Catholic priest performed the rite of marriage and a friend, Francis Wasegijig, witnessed the ceremony.

Amable and Elizabeth were the parents of five children: Margaret, born April 1851 or 1852; Francis, born December 10, 1853, baptized the same year, and died by 1865; Catherine, born December 7, 1856, and baptized the same year; Mary, born September 30, 1859, baptized the same year, and died October 26, 1867; and Joseph, born December 12, 1862, baptized the same year, and died September 11, 1878.

During the time of Amable's service and imprisonment, Elizabeth and the children were destitute for support, but she didn't abandon her children, nor did she permit them to be adopted.

Mr. Thomas Downing, clerk for the Circuit Court of Emmet County, approved funds to be given to Elizabeth from the county's Volunteers for Poor Families Relief Fund. This fund was supervised by the county treasurer. The allowance averaged five dollars, and this sum was granted to her on a monthly basis over the years of 1864 to 1867.

On October 5, 1865, Application #111,210 for a pension for a widow with dependent children was filed for Elizabeth. She was granted Widow's Pension Certificate #128,866 on May 10, 1869. The pension paid eight dollars per month retroactive from March 15, 1865, plus two dollars extra for each child (retroactive from July 25, 1866) until that child attained the age of sixteen. Margaret, who was over sixteen, Catherine, and Joseph were Elizabeth's only surviving children by the time she received her pension certificate in 1869.

In 1870, as a member of the Traverse Bay Bands of Odawa (or Ottawa) and Ojibwa Anishinabek, Elizabeth's name appeared on the census roll as having received her annuity payment from the government. The annuity payment was given due to past tribal treaty negotiations with the US government. Elizabeth's monthly pension payments were increased from eight dollars to twelve dollars on March 19, 1886.

On September 11, 1885, Application #330,708 for a pension for minor children was filed for the oldest daughter, Margaret, who was age thirty-three, and signed her maiden name as Margaret Chibidice. Her married name was Ononegos. She applied for a pension for children under sixteen years of age. Her thought was that even though her mother's pension certificate was received in 1869 and that the two dollars extra payments for the children were retroactive to 1865 when she was thirteen, then she would be eligible for the two dollars extra per month until she reached the age of sixteen in 1868. Note: The name "A. Chibadice" listed on the descriptive roll of Company K of the First Michigan Sharpshooters is the same man as Amable Kitchibatise.

Margaret's application was rejected on May 11, 1887, because her mother, Elizabeth, was still living and was receiving a mother's pension.

Sometime in her later years, Elizabeth Kitchibatise moved from Cross Village to Brutus in Emmet County. By the time that Elizabeth had moved to Brutus, her monthly pension payments were increased to twenty-five dollars a month. She died at her said home on September 8, 1918.

Lamourandere, Thaddeus, Private

Enlistment: Enlisted as a private on July 4, 1863, at Elbridge, Oceana County, by Lieutenant Edwin V. Andress, First Michigan Sharpshooters, for three years.

Age: Twenty-one, born about 1842 in Ionia County.

Occupation: Laborer and logger

Residence: Pentwater, Oceana County

Physical Description: Five feet ten, black eyes, black hair, and a dark complexion. Examining physician was Dr. Jacob B. McNett, assistant surgeon, First Michigan Sharpshooters.

Mustered: July 11, 1863, at Detroit, Wayne County, by Lieutenant Colonel John R. Smith, US Army

Military Service: Sometime during the months of September and October 1863, while he was guarding Confederate prisoners at Camp Douglas, Chicago, Cook County, Illinois, an assessment was made against Taddy's wages because he lost his waist belt and plate. Being a faithful son, it was quite evident to Taddy that not having been diligent about his equipment cost him some of his monthly pay that he could have sent home for his family's support.

Private Thaddeus "Taddy" Lamourandere was killed in action at the Battle of Spotsylvania, Virginia, on May 12, 1864. His burial site is not known.

If Taddy's body was found on the ground controlled by the Union forces, it would have been left in its uniform, wrapped in a blanket (if available), placed into a wooden coffin (if available), and buried in a trench with other dead Union soldiers. A wooden board on which his name and unit, if known, was recorded, was placed at the head of his burial site (*Encyclopedia*).

On the other hand, if Taddy died on rebel-held ground, he would have been unceremoniously buried with indifference and disrespect in a mass grave and unknown to anyone (*Ibid.*).

After the war, the remains of the Union dead (both known and unknown on Union-held ground from this battle) would have been disinterred and reburied in the Fredericksburg, Virginia, National Cemetery (*Guide*).

At the time of his death, Private Lamourandere was last paid by Paymaster Maj. Haskins to include April 30. He was owed $6.40 for his last twelve days (at sixteen dollars a month) by the paymaster.

Discharged: No discharge given. Killed in action.

Biography: Thaddeus "Taddy" Lamourandere (Lamorandiere) was the son of Etienne (also known as Steve or Akin) and Mary Ann (?) Lamourandere. Etienne may have been descended from Etienne Rocbert-de-la-Morandiere (b. 1668) and Elizabeth Duverger (b. 1673) de-la-Morandiere of Montreal, Quebec, Canada. Etienne and Mary Ann were married by a Catholic priest in Newaygo, Newaygo County, in May 1839. The marriage was witnessed by the couple's friends and neighbors, James and Sophia Lawrence.

In addition to Taddy, the other Lamourandere children were (by approximate dates): Stephen, born 1850; Mary, born 1852 (deceased by 1888); James, born 1854; Jane, born 1856; Charlotte, born 1859; Charley, born 1860 and killed by a train in 1883; Sarah, born 1862; Mitchell, born 1863; Margaret, born?; Terresa, born 1867; and Phillip, born 1869. They were members of the Grand River Band of Odawa (or Ottawa) Anishinabek.

Taddy, who did not marry, lived with his family in a log cabin on the Anishinabek reservation near Pentwater in Oceana County. He was known to be a good, steady worker and, along with his father and brothers, helped to support the family.

The Lamourandere men worked mostly in Newaygo County for a logging company and also for loggers Elihu Cooper and Henry J. Orton. In the winter, they also worked in the woods as lumberjacks, and in the spring, they ran log rafts on the rivers. Taddy earned about one dollar a day at these jobs and used his wages to help buy groceries and necessities. He also worked for businessman Samuel Rose and other settlers who would often donate flour and groceries to Taddy's family. The combined family yearly income averaged about $200.

By 1866, Etienne, Mary Ann, and the younger children moved from Oceana County to Garfield Township in Newaygo County and remained there. It was reported by businessman David Willard, who knew the parents, that Etienne may have owned a few acres (in Newaygo County) worth about two to three dollars an acre and had cleared it for a garden.

Etienne was known to be quite a robust man for his age and a steady, sober hard worker. He had mainly supported his family by making boats, fishing, hunting, making baskets, picking blueberries, and tanning deer and other wild animal hides in addition to his job as a logger.

By 1869, Etienne became severely crippled with rheumatism and was plagued with a continuous cough. He was not able to continue his logging work, and due to his advanced years, he could not contribute as much as he had previously to the family's support. But he and Mary Ann continued to sell their baskets and the wild fruit they collected for their meager subsistence. Etienne also continued to work at whatever he could physically manage. Mary Ann added to the family's income by selling corn and other vegetables from her garden.

On March 29, 1886, Application #352,584 for a dependent mother's pension was submitted for Mary Ann. She continued to apply even though one examiner had requested that her application be denied on the basis that Etienne made enough money to support her.

Mary Ann Lamourandere did not receive a pension. She died on July 26, 1890, at her home in Brooks Township, Newaygo County. Among those friends who were present at her death and attended her funeral were James and Sophia Lawrence, who had witnessed Etienne's and Mary Ann's wedding.

On October 16, 1890, Application #481,509 for a dependent father's pension was submitted for Etienne. At that time, he was without any other means of support except by the kindness of friends. Finally, he was granted a Dependent Father's Pension Certificate #339,577 on October 31, 1891. The pension payments were twelve dollars a month, retroactive to October 16, 1890, and were received until his death.

Lidger, Daniel, Private

Enlistment: Enlisted as a private on February 4, 1865, at Detroit, Wayne County, by J. F. Lobdell, notary public for Wayne County, for one year (Descriptive Roll states three years). Credited to the Third Congressional District, Mendon, Subdistrict Nineteen, St. Joseph County.

Age: Twenty-eight, born about 1837 in Oneida (or Oneida County), New York.
Occupation: Laborer

Residence: Mendon, St. Joseph County

Physical Description: Five feet eight, black eyes, black hair, and a dark complexion. Examining physician was Dr. George Landon, surgeon, First Michigan Sharpshooters.

Mustered: February 4, 1865, at Detroit, Wayne County, by Major E. Detshy

Military Service: Private Lidger served his short stint in the army without any record of illnesses or wounds.

Discharged: Private Daniel Lidger was mustered out and honorably discharged on July 28, 1865, at Delaney House, Georgetown, Washington, DC. He returned to Detroit on the steamer *Morning Star* and received payment due to him for his service on August 7 at Jackson, Jackson County.

Biography: No pension file has been located for Daniel Lidger, but there is other information known about his background. Daniel's last name was also spelled Lidyer, and in some records, his first name was referred to as David.

Daniel listed his birthplace as Oneida, New York, as did Company K comrade Joseph Hannin, which suggests, as with Hannin, that Daniel was a member of the Oneida tribe of the Iroquois Confederation.

The Oneida Indian Nation—the *Ona yote ka o no*—the "Granite People" or "People of the Rock," was one of six tribes who were members of the Iroquois Confederation (*Richards*). The confederation included the Mohawk, Oneida, Onondaga, Cayuga, Seneca, and (after 1720) the Tuscarora tribal nations.

The Oneidas cast their lot, along with some members of the Tuscarora Nation, with the American Patriots and not with Great Britain in the Revolutionary War—the only tribal nation of the confederation to do so. Oneida tribesmen were of great help to the American Patriots and were faithful allies. The Patriots called the Oneida Nation their "First Allies," and they are considered as such to this day. These allies provided information, warriors, scouts, and food to the Patriots (*Oneida*). Due to the brave sacrifices of the Oneidas and the Patriots in the bloody Battles of Oriskany and Saratoga, the alliance was able to turn the tide of the war in favor of the young nation. The French, who were impressed with the outcomes of these battles, decided to enter the fray and support the Patriot cause.

Daniel's residence, before he enlisted at Detroit, was Mendon of St. Joseph County. In that area of the state, Daniel, like his comrade Joseph Hannin, would have lived near Potawatomi Anishinabek. Daniel may have returned to Oneida, New York, after his service and then moved to Canada and died there, as did Joseph Hannin.

Since both men were of the Oneida Nation, they may have been acquainted with each other before they enlisted. Why did the two men live in Mendon, Michigan, before they enlisted?

Light, Josiah, Private

Enlistment: Enlisted as a private on July 4, 1863, at Elbridge, Oceana County, by Captain Edwin V. Andress, First Michigan Sharpshooters, for three years.

Age: Eighteen, born about 1845 in Kalamazoo, Kalamazoo County.

Occupation: Laborer

Residence: Near Pentwater, Oceana County

Physical Description: Five feet six, black eyes, black hair, and a dark complexion. Examining physician was Dr. Jacob B. McNett, assistant surgeon, First Michigan Sharpshooters.

Mustered: July 11, 1863, at the Detroit Arsenal, Dearborn, Wayne County, by Lieutenant Colonel John R. Smith, US Army

Military Service: Private Josiah Light was promoted from the ranks to corporal on May 1, 1865.

The only notation of an illness or injury was that of Light being treated for otitis media (earache) on April 17, 1864, while in the field. The doctors administered drops of sweet oil (olive oil) into Josiah's ear canal and applied heat to his ear with warm compresses or with hot bricks wrapped in heavy cloth. Opiates were given for pain (*Internet*).

Discharged: Corporal Josiah Light was mustered out and honorably discharged at Delaney House, Georgetown, Washington, DC, on July 28, 1865. He returned home to Michigan on the steamer *Morning Star*. On August 7, Light was paid money owed to him for his service at Jackson, Jackson County.

Biography: Josiah Light was the son of David, a farmer, and Sarah Missaugequay Light. Sarah was sometimes called Sophia. His known siblings were a brother, Paul, and sisters Aury and Jane (or Peshagacahkequay).

In the 1870 federal census of Crystal Township in Oceana County, Josiah was listed as a farmer with his wife, Marian (Mary) (or Shabbeshequay), and their children: Joseph, age two, and Juliette, age six months. Josiah and Marian lost a son at six days of age in 1872.

By the 1880 federal census, both David and Josiah's families were living in Eden Township of Mason County. David was listed with his wife (known as Sophia) and a daughter, Jane (or Peshagacahkequay), age thirty-two. Josiah was listed as a laborer living with Maryan (Marion) and their children: Joseph (or Wabegena), age twelve; Henry (or Wawsaygeezhink), age ten; Caroline, age five (born in 1875 and baptized on May 15 of that year in the Methodist Riverton Indian Mission of said county); and David, age two. Josiah and his family were probably members of the Riverton Indian Church (*Riverton*).

On July 3, 1884, Josiah's sister, Jane (or Peshagacahkequay—listed as married), died of tuberculosis at age thirty-six. During that same summer, Josiah's wife, Marian (Mary), also died.

An obituary notice for Josiah Light in the *Ludington Record* described his death that happened on October 23, 1884:

> It is reported that Josiah Light, an Indian was out hunting with another man and in going through the bushes the other man was behind, when his gun accidentally discharged, and the charge lodged in Light's body; one arm was blown to pieces. He was taken home but died soon after. He has buried his wife and two children this past summer. He was a very quiet and inoffensive man, and was respected by all he was also a cripple, having lost one leg at the knee. It was a very sad case. *(Obituary)*

For as much as is known about Josiah Light, it's certain that he did not lose a leg at the knee in the Civil War. If Josiah actually did lose a portion of his leg, it must have been by an accident after his discharge from the army.

Josiah was buried in the Eden Township Old Indian Cemetery near his wife and two of his children.

On November 3, 1884, Josiah and Mary's son, Joseph (or Wahbegena), age sixteen/seventeen, who worked as a laborer, was accidentally shot and died of his wound. Joseph was buried near his parents and siblings in said Indian cemetery. One can only imagine the tragedy and the pain of loss suffered by this family.

Josiah's father, David Light, died at the advanced age of ninety-six from hemorrhage of the bowels on September 4, 1896, at his home in Custer Township of Mason County.

There is no pension file for Josiah Light.

Marks, Louis, Private

Enlistment: Enlisted as a private on June 1, 1863, at Bear River (now Petoskey), Emmet County, by First Lieutenant William J. Driggs, First Michigan Sharpshooters, for three years.

> **Age:** Twenty-four, born about 1839 at St. Clair, St. Clair County.
>
> **Occupation:** Farmer
>
> **Residence:** Bear River
>
> **Physical Description:** Five feet eleven, dark eyes, dark hair, and a dark complexion. Examining physician was Dr. Arvin T. Whelan, surgeon, First Michigan Sharpshooters.
>
> **Mustered:** June 22, 1863, at Detroit, Wayne County, by Lieutenant Colonel John R. Smith, US Army
>
> **Military Service:** While on guard duty with his regiment at Camp Douglas, Private Louis Marks was taken ill. The sharpshooters were in charge of the confine for Confederate prisoners at the camp in Chicago, Cook County, Illinois. Louis was admitted to the USA Post Hospital on November 18, 1863, with the diagnosis of morbilli (or measles), an acute, infectious, and highly contagious disease caused by a virus (*Blakiston*). The only treatment given to the patient consisted of quarantine, small doses of whiskey as a sedative, rest, proper care, and a nourishing diet. He returned to guard duty on November 27.

When Private Marks was at the front during the months of March and April 1864, he was assigned as a cook for Company K.

In depositions given about Louis Marks for his father's application for a dependent father's pension, it was attested to by several credible sources (including comrades Sgt. Francis Tabasasch, Joseph Ashkanak, and Payson Wolf) that Louis was wounded in the lower back on his right side. He was reported to have received the wound either by gunshot (missile) or by a piece of timber that splintered when hit by shrapnel from the burst of a cannon shell. It was related by these deponents that Marks was carried immediately to the rear and transported to his division hospital (name not stated) for treatment. They reported that the wound was said to have occurred during action on May 9, 1864, at the Battle of the Ni, near the Ni River on the way to Spotsylvania, Virginia. There is no evidence to support this information about Louis's wound either from the War Department or from Louis's medical records.

In a battle before Petersburg, Virginia, on June 17, 1864, Louis was captured by the rebels while charging the enemy's defense works. He was one of a group of fifteen Anishinabek soldiers among three hundred Union prisoners taken to a tobacco warehouse in Petersburg and confined to the third floor of the building. The warehouse was located near the river on Short Market Street.

There is a story about Louis Marks in the *Charles Campbell Diary,* which is kept at the College of William and Mary in Williamsburg, Virginia (*Diary*). On June 17, 1864, Campbell recorded in his diary that he took his children and some other folks to the foot of Short Market Street to see the Indian prisoners among the Yankees held in the third-floor area of the tobacco warehouse. He related that a Confederate lieutenant, who was in command, brought two of the Indians to the outside for the children and others to see because they had never seen Indians. The two soldiers, dressed in Yankee uniforms, told Campbell that they were Ottawas from Michigan and belonged to a Michigan regiment. They said that their names were Louis Marks and Edward?—something that Campbell couldn't understand. They also told Campbell that they had been in the army for twelve months and had seen no fights until the battle on June 17. Campbell mentioned that one of the men did not speak English very well and did not have much to say. He did describe the prisoners as robust men with tawny skin color, straight black hair, dark eyes, taciturn disposition, and grave looking. One of the Ottawa men removed his cap, at Campbell's request, so that the children could see his hair. Campbell asked the men how they happened to be taken prisoner. They responded that they could not explain how it happened. The Confederate guard, who was standing by, laughed heartily at that response. Campbell remarked to the prisoners that he supposed that their capture was accidental and something they couldn't help.

It's the author's opinion that the men's robust appearance and proud demeanor were carefully studied by the locals and made an impression upon the children. As true warriors, they would not explain just how they were captured. After this encounter, the men were returned to the warehouse.

A short time later, Louis and the other captives were sent by cattle railcars to Camp Sumter (also known as Andersonville Prison) in Andersonville, Georgia.

On October 11, 1864, Louis was admitted to the prison hospital as #14,837 and was suffering from scorbutus (or scurvy). Scurvy is a condition brought on by the lack of vitamin C found in fresh fruits and vegetables. This condition caused Louis to have spongy, bleeding gums, loose teeth, a sallow appearance, and extreme weakness. These symptoms were exacerbated by insufficient food, severe diarrhea, and rheumatism (*Bollet*). Inhumane treatment and abominable living conditions also contributed to Louis's poor state of health.

Private Marks was released from Andersonville Prison and paroled at Savannah, Georgia, on November 20, 1864. He made his way to College Green Barracks General Hospital at Annapolis, Maryland, on November 27.

At the hospital, the doctors treated Louis's condition with hearty foods that would combat his scurvy. His meals contained plentiful amounts of onions, raw potatoes (potatoes lose much of their vitamin C during the cooking process), cabbage, tomatoes, squash, beets, cider, and fresh bread. Lemons and oranges were added to his diet when they could be obtained (*Ibid.*).

Marks was then sent to Camp Parole Hospital near Annapolis on December 1 for further treatment for his condition. Camp Parole was a camp for paroled prisoners in which both captured Confederates and former Union prisoners who had been paroled by the South were sent for exchange. The camp was also a holding area for Union soldiers who had deserted and whose units were in the area. Doctors on staff provided medical treatment for the sick and wounded. Private Marks was granted a furlough of twenty days on December 31. After his furlough, the soldier returned to active duty with his unit.

Discharged: Private Louis Marks was mustered out and honorably discharged at Annapolis, Maryland, on June 28, 1865. It is noted on his muster-out that Louis was due three months' extra pay per a telegram from the War Department dated May 30, 1865. Marks left for Detroit on July 28 on the steamer *Morning Star.* He was paid money owed to him for his service on August 7 at Jackson, Jackson County.

Biography: Louis Marks was the son of Pesa Teisji (or Tanashe) and Mary Nadnusokwe Teisji. According to Louis's father, the couple was married in the old L'Arbre Croche Roman Catholic Mission Church (now Holy Childhood of Jesus Catholic Church) at Harbor Springs by Father Francis X. Pierz. Pesa related that he thought that Father Pierz officiated at the marriage sometime around June 22, 1848.

Upon conversion to Christianity and baptism, Pesa took the name of Enos Marks. He also went by the name of Enos Mark Otanashe (or Odanashe).

Louis Marks was reported, by his father, Enos, to have married, but neither his wife's name nor the date of their marriage has been located. Enos also stated that Louis and his wife had no children.

After his return from the service, Louis was described as a man of broken health who suffered from the effects of scurvy and the wound he supposedly incurred in the service. His health was so severely damaged by his war experiences that he could not earn a living for himself or his family. Louis's father tried to care for his son and did rely upon local charity for help. For a short time after his discharge, Louis stayed with a Company K comrade Payson Wolfe at Northport and then returned to his father's home in Bear River.

Before the war, Louis supported his parents with hunting and fishing and whatever work he could find. His mother died before he joined the army.

Louis Marks had eighty acres of land in Emmet County by reason of the treaty of July 31, 1855, between the commissioners of the United States and the Ottawa and Chippewa Indians of Michigan, parties to the treaty of March 28, 1836. The description is the west half of the northeast quarter of section 17 in township 34 north of range 6 west. He was granted a certificate on August 19, 1875 (*Land Records*).

According to the Department of the Interior Pension Office, Louis Marks died from complications of the disease that he suffered in the prison camp and not from any injury. His death occurred on April 2, 1877. He was buried in Bear Creek Township.

Enos Marks relied upon local charity and help from a nephew, Hyacinth Succo, for his support. Application #277,355 for a dependent father's pension was filed for Enos on August 18, 1880.

The claim for pension was denied on April 29, 1892, on the grounds that at the time of Louis's death, Enos testified that Louis had a wife but no child who survived him. Enos also testified that Louis's wife died in 1878, just a year after Louis had succumbed to the illness that he had acquired in the army. Other depositions stated that Louis had neither wife nor child who survived him.

Under the law, the parents of a soldier have title to a pension only where it is shown that the soldier left neither wife nor minor child who survived him. But since Enos testified that Louis did leave a wife, the government refused his application.

The claim for Enos was also rejected because no evidence could be found that Louis suffered a wound that contributed to his death.

In the 1870 federal census, Louis Marks at age twenty-nine is listed as the head of the household of Enos Marks, but no wife nor child of his is named in the list. If there was a wife reported (by Enos) to have died in 1878 (a year after Louis died), why is she not listed in the 1870 census? Could Enos have misunderstood when asked if the soldier had any dependents? Since the federal census is taken every ten years, it's also possible that Louis could have married between late 1870 (after the census enumeration for that year) and 1877.

It seems probable (as witness to the 1870 federal census) that Louis never married, and if he didn't marry, Enos would have been eligible for a dependent father's pension.

Sometime before 1901, Enos Marks died. Hyacinth Succo then tried unsuccessfully to apply for a pension to compensate him for taking care of Enos in his final years. Hyacinth's claim was abandoned in 1902.

Marquette, Frank (Francis), Private

Enlistment: Enlisted as a private on October 24, 1864, at Grand Rapids, Kent County, by Captain Norman Bailey, First Michigan Sharpshooters and provost marshal for the Fourth Congressional District of Michigan, for one year. Enlistment credited to Assyria, Barry County, of the Fourth Congressional District.

Age: Thirty-five, born about 1829 in Canada.

Occupation: Hunter

Residence: Assyria

Physical Description: Five feet 5¾ inches tall, black eyes, black hair, and a ruddy complexion. Examining physician was Dr. Alonzo Mate, surgeon, First Michigan Sharpshooters.

Mustered: October 24, 1864, at Grand Rapids, Kent County, by Captain Norman Bailey, First Michigan Sharpshooters and provost marshal for the Fourth Congressional District of Michigan

Military Service: Private Frank Marquette joined his unit on November 11, 1864, at Peebles House, Virginia.

He was taken by ambulance wagon to his division hospital near Washington, DC, on May 25, 1865, suffering from diarrhea and a high fever. Treatment for Frank's illness may have included Epsom salt (magnesium sulfate) and quinine for fever, castor oil (a cathartic) in the morning to evacuate the bowels, opium for pain in the evening, and fresh fruit juices when tolerated by the patient (*Evans*). Ipecac (the rhizome and roots of a plant of the *Cephaelis* species), used as an emetic and nauseating expectorant, was also given in addition to said treatments (*Blakiston*).

On May 29, he was transferred to Carver General Hospital in Washington, DC, and admitted on May 30. Even though no specific disease was listed on his medical card, similar treatment for the previously mentioned disorders was continued.

Discharged: Due to his illness, Private Frank Marquette was mustered out and honorably discharged from Carver Hospital on June 27, 1865. He was paid money owed to him for his service at his discharge and returned to Michigan.

Biography: Frank Marquette may have returned to Barry County after his hospitalization and died there, or have gone back to Canada for the remainder of his years.

A possible answer as to why Frank Marquette, who was born in Canada, listed his residence as Assyria in Barry County before he enlisted into the army can be found in the Honorable W. W. Potter's *History of Barry County* (*Barry*). Mr. Potter relates that Barry County was ideal Indian ground that attracted the Anishinabek people from all three tribes—the Chippewa (or Ojibway), Ottawa (or Odawa), and Potawatomi who settled there and established their villages in the early 1700s. The ancient burial grounds and corn fields were witness to the early settlement of these people. Some of their descendants live there today.

Because the Anishinabek had occupied the Barry County area for such a long time, it's possible that some of them had moved there from Canada. Maybe Frank had relatives among these folks. It may also be that due to a possible familial connection and his desire to enlist in the Michigan Sharpshooter Regiment, Frank may have decided to journey from Canada to Barry County and take up residence with some of his relatives before he enlisted. There is no pension file for Frank Marquette.

Mashkaw, James, Private

Enlistment: Enlisted as a private on July 4, 1863, at Pentwater, Oceana County, by Captain Edwin V. Andress, First Michigan Sharpshooters, for three years.

 Age: Thirty-one, born about 1832 in Kent County.

 Occupation: Laborer

 Residence: Pentwater

 Physical Description: Five feet eight and a half inches tall, black eyes, black hair, and a dark complexion. Examining physician was Dr. Jacob B. McNett, assistant surgeon, First Michigan Sharpshooters.

 Mustered: July 11, 1863, at Detroit, Wayne County, by Lieutenant Colonel John R. Smith, US Army

 Military Service: Private James Mashkaw (older brother to John Mashkaw) was killed in action while advancing against the enemy's works during the Battle of Spotsylvania, Virginia, on May 12, 1864. Jim's brother, John, was also killed during the same battle. To lose two sons on the same day was tragic and a very sad day for the Mashkaw family. At the time of his death, Pvt. Mashkaw was last paid by Paymaster Major Haskins to include April 30, 1864.

If the Union forces controlled the field after a battle, James's body may have been identified or recognized as a Union soldier. If so, his body would have been left in its uniform, wrapped in a blanket, put into a coffin if one was available, and buried without ceremony either individually or in a trench with other Union dead. An effort would have been made to inscribe a wooden board with the deceased's name and unit (if known) and place the board at the head of the grave. Wooden markers were known to have been destroyed by inclement weather and also to have been taken by people who needed firewood (*Encyclopedia*). If the marker disappeared, then James's remains were unknown when he was disinterred and moved to the Fredericksburg National Cemetery. It's quite possible that he is buried in the national cemetery under a stone labeled "Unknown."

Since it's not known where James is buried, it's also possible that he was killed on rebel-held ground. If this was the case, his body was at the mercy of the victors who treated his remains with indifference and disrespect (*Ibid.*). If so, James's remains lie in a rebel-dug trench with other bodies that are unknown and forgotten. It's certain that he was not forgotten by his grieving family.

Discharged: No discharge given. Killed in action.

Biography: James (Jim) Mashkaw, also known as Kahkuhgewa, was the oldest son of John Maishkaw (or Mashkaw) Sr., a principal man (or chief) of one of the Grand River Odawa Bands and his wife, Wahonoquay. He was also a grandson of Chief Kewaytowaby (Kee-o-to-aw-be), who was a signer of the Treaty of the Ottawa, Chippewa, and Potawatomi concluded at Chicago, Illinois, on August 29, 1821 (*Letter*).

Old Chief Kewaytowaby held a government certificate for eighty acres of land situated eight or nine miles above the city of Grand Rapids in Kent County. Sometime after he received the certificate, it was stolen by an unscrupulous party, and the land was sold. The certificate was never found.

Chief John Maishkaw (or Mashkaw) Sr. and Wahonoquay embraced Christianity and were reported to have been married on February 12, 1837, although the date may have been February 12, 1831. The name Mashkaw may be derived from the Anishinabe word *Mashkawa*, which means "strong" (*Baraga*).

Prior to the Civil War, the Mashkaw family lived near Hart in Oceana County. James (also called Jim) Mashkaw (or Kahkuhgewa) married Chigahmequa (also known as Kehgumegua) on August 6, 1858, at Pentwater. Joseph Elliott, an Anishinabe interpreter and justice of the peace, officiated at the ceremony. Isaac and Martha Bennett were witnesses to the marriage. There were no children of this union.

In addition to James, his wife, Chigahmequa, and his parents, the following Mashkaw siblings were also listed in the 1860 federal census of Pentwater in Oceana County. They included: John, age eighteen; To bun done (or Peter), age sixteen; sister, Shawahnahung, age fourteen; brother, Mishkeahsega (or Isaac), age nine; and brother and a male child, Gosa, age two.

Before he joined the Union army, James hunted, fished, and worked at what jobs he could find to help support his wife and his parents. During his service, he sent money home for their living expenses.

On July 5, 1864, Application #56,218 for a widow's pension was filed for Chigahmequa Mashkaw. She was granted a Widow's Pension Certificate #32,329 shortly after filing her application. The exact amount of payments that she received per month was not stated, but it is presumed that her certificate paid from eight dollars to twelve dollars a month until her death.

Mashkaw, John, Private

Enlistment: Enlisted as a private on July 4, 1863, at Elbridge, Oceana County, by Captain Edwin V. Andress, First Michigan Sharpshooters, for three years.

Age: Twenty-two, born about 1841 at Prairieville, Barry County.

Occupation: Laborer

Residence: Pentwater, Oceana County

Physical Description: Five feet eight, black eyes, black hair, and a dark complexion. Examining physician was Dr. Jacob B. McNett, assistant surgeon, First Michigan Sharpshooters.

Mustered: July 11, 1863, at Detroit, Wayne County, by Lieutenant Colonel John R. Smith, US Army

Military Service: Private John Mashkaw (younger brother to James Mashkaw) was killed in action during the Battle of Spotsylvania, Virginia, on May 12, 1864. He died during the same battle as his brother, James, as the brothers were advancing against the enemy's works. His burial place is unknown. To lose two sons on the same day was tragic and a very sad day for the Mashkaw family. At the time of his death, Pvt. Mashkaw was last paid by Paymaster Major Haskins to include April 30, 1864.

If the Union forces controlled the field after a battle, John's body may have been identified or recognized as a Union soldier. If so, his body would have been left in its uniform, wrapped in a blanket, put into a coffin, if one was available, and buried without ceremony either individually or in a trench with other Union dead. An effort would have been made to inscribe a wooden board with the deceased's name and unit (if known) and place the board at the head of the grave. Wooden markers were known to have been destroyed by inclement weather and also to have been taken by people who needed firewood (*Encyclopedia*). If the marker disappeared, then John's remains were unknown when he was disinterred and moved to the Fredericksburg National Cemetery. It's quite possible that he is buried in the national cemetery under a stone labeled "Unknown."

Since it is not certain where John is buried, it's also probable that he was killed on rebel ground. If that was the case, his body was at the mercy of the victors, who treated his remains with indifference and disrespect (*Ibid.*). So, it's possible that John's remains may lie in a rebel-dug trench with other bodies that are unknown and forgotten. It's certain that he was not forgotten by his grieving family.

Discharge: No discharge given. Killed in action.

Biography: John Mashkaw was the son of Chief John Maishkaw (or Mashkaw) Sr., a principal man (or chief) of one of the Grand River Odawa (Ottawa) Bands, and his wife, Wahonoquay. He was also a grandson of Chief Kewaytowaby (Kee-o-to-aw-be), a signer of the Treaty of the Ottawa, Chippewa, and Potawatomi concluded at Chicago, Illinois, on August 29, 1821 (*Letter*).

Old Chief Kewaytowaby held a government certificate for eighty acres of land situated eight or nine miles above the city of Grand Rapids in Kent County. Sometime after he received the certificate, it was stolen by an unscrupulous party, and the land was sold. The certificate was never found.

Chief John Maishkaw (or Mashkaw) Sr. and Wahonoquay embraced Christianity and were reported to have married on February 12, 1837, although the date may have been February 12, 1831. The name Mashkaw may be derived from the word *Mashkawa,* which means "strong" in the Anishinabe language (*Baraga*).

Prior to the Civil War, the Mashkaw family lived near Hart in Oceana County.

In addition to John and his parents, the Mashkaw siblings who were also listed in the 1860 federal census of Pentwater included: James Mashkaw, age thirty; James's wife, Chigahmequa (also known as Kehaguhmegua), age thirty-five; To bun done (or Peter), age sixteen; sister, Shawahnahung, age fourteen; brother, Mishkeahsega (or Isaac), age nine; and a male child, Gosa, age two.

Before entering military service, John, who did not marry, hunted, fished, and worked at what jobs he could find to help support his parents. During his service, he sent home what money he had for their living expenses.

After notification of the deaths of both James and John, Maishkaw (or Mashkaw) Sr. and Wahonoquay were destitute for monetary help. Their daughter-in-law, James's wife, Chigahmequa, would receive pension money from her husband's service, as she was a direct beneficiary. At that time, the aged parents relied on what charity was given to them by the county as well as help from their neighbors.

On May 13, 1869, Application #175,170 was submitted for Maishkaw (or Mashkaw) Sr. for a father's pension (or dependent father's pension). It was rejected on September 28, 1869, because his wife was still living. A mother's pension is considered first unless she is deceased before the father. For reasons unknown, the brief for application was reopened, and Maishkaw (or Mashkaw) Sr. was granted a Father's Pension Certificate #196,008 on January 12, 1872, which paid about eight dollars a month until his death.

Application #201,624 was submitted for Wahonoquay for a mother's pension (or dependent mother's pension) on March 7, 1872. She received a Mother's Pension Certificate #163,762 on January 30, 1874. Her monthly payments were eight dollars a month, retroactive to May 13, 1869 (the date that her husband applied) until her death.

Due to their destitute circumstances, both parents received a pension based on their son John's service. Since John had no wife or child to benefit from his service, his parents were next in line to receive pension funds.

Miller, Thomas, Private

Enlistment: Enlisted as a private on June 13, 1863, at Northport, Leelanau County, by First Lieutenant William J. Driggs, First Michigan Sharpshooters, for three years.

Age: Nineteen, born about 1844 in Grand Traverse (also known as Old Mission) on Old Mission Peninsula located on the East Arm of Grand Traverse Bay.

Occupation: Farmer

Residence: Omena, Leelanau County

Physical Description: Five feet eight, black eyes, black hair, and a dark complexion. Examining physician was Dr. Arvin T. Whelan, surgeon, First Michigan Sharpshooters.

Mustered: June 22, 1863, at Detroit, Wayne County, by Lieutenant Colonel John R. Smith, US Army

Military Service: After his regiment was sent from Chicago to the front, Private Miller was taken by ambulance wagon to a Regimental Hospital of the First Michigan Sharpshooters on April 18, 1864. He complained of a slight cough but did not seem to be very sick.

He was transferred by ambulance wagon on April 22 to Division No. 1, USA General Hospital at the United States Naval Academy (Navy Yard) in Annapolis, Maryland diagnosed with "catarrh." Catarrh is an old term that meant the inflammation of the mucous membranes, particularly those of the air passages of the nose and throat, with an exudation containing mucus (*Blakiston*). The doctors ordered a healthy diet, warm fluids, and bed rest. Miller stayed at the hospital for treatment while his unit proceeded on to their next location. On May 2, he returned to his regiment.

On May 11, 1864, Private Miller was again taken by ambulance wagon to a hospital, this time to Augur USA General Hospital near Alexandria, Virginia, diagnosed with bronchitis. His treatment consisted of the application of mustard plasters to his chest, which was thought to draw what was considered poison away from the lungs. Mustard plasters consisted of a mixture of ground mustard seed, flour, and water wrapped in a flannel cloth and applied to his chest (*Internet search*). He was also given oral medication that included Dover's powder (combination of ipecac and opium) for diarrhea, spirit of nitre (or saltpeter) for his cough, and doses of quinine and opium to relieve pain (*Evans*).

Still quite ill, Miller was transferred by hospital steamer from Augur Hospital to Carver USA General Hospital in Washington, DC, on May 21, as his condition had become worse and he developed pneumonia. The doctors continued his previous treatment with the addition of painful cupping and blistering to his chest to promote more adsorption or the drawing out of fluid from the lungs (*Bollet*).

On June 1, Private Miller was transferred by hospital steamer from Carver General Hospital to Mower USA General Hospital at Chestnut Hill, near Philadelphia, Pennsylvania. It was at this hospital that Dr. J. Hopkinson diagnosed his condition as that of "phthisis," the old term for pulmonary (or lung) tuberculosis. There were no medications that were effective against TB during the Civil War, and treatments for this scourge would not appear until about the middle of the twentieth century.

While at Mower Hospital, Private Thomas Miller was mustered, but not paid, for the months of May, June, July, August, and September 1864. His last payment from Paymaster Major Larned was for December 1863. Dr. Hopkinson applied for a furlough for sick leave for Thomas, and it was approved by Dr. Jonathan Letterman, surgeon, Department of the Susquehanna.

On August 11, 1864, by command of Major General Couch, Thomas was granted a twenty-day furlough for sick leave from Mower Hospital so that he could return to Grand Traverse County for a period of rest. Miller was furnished transportation from Philadelphia to Pittsburgh, from Pittsburgh to Detroit, and then from Detroit to Traverse City. He then made his way to Omena.

While on sick leave, Private Thomas Miller died at the home of his mother's sister, Ann Shondasequa Miller, in Omena on October 15, 1864. Cause of death was not identified, but it was most likely that Miller died of tuberculosis. Thomas's aunt notified the government of his death that occurred while on a furlough for sick leave. A notation of the same was made on the soldier's casualty report.

Thomas Miller's funeral was held at Rev. Peter Dougherty's Omena Presbyterian Church called New Mission or Grove Hill. New Mission was established at Omena, Leelanau County, by Rev. Dougherty in 1852 after he and his congregation moved from Old Mission (or Grand Traverse), which was established in 1839 in Grand Traverse County (*Craker*). After the service, the young respected warrior was laid to rest in the cemetery behind the church.

Discharged: No discharge given due to death by disease while on sick leave.

Biography: Thomas Miller was also known as Thomas Kahgee. He was the son of Henry Kahgee, also known as Thomas K. Miller, and Sarah Nahwenahmikoqua Miller Kahgee. Thomas's parents were married by the Presbyterian missionary Rev. Peter Dougherty about September 25, 1843.

Sarah had joined the mission church previous to her marriage to Henry and was baptized on June 4, 1843. Thomas's aunt, his mother's sister Ann (or Shondasequa) Miller, was baptized into the Old Mission Presbyterian Church by Rev. Dougherty on June 4, 1843. Henry joined the church on January 7, 1844. Thomas's adopted sister, Isabella, was also baptized by Rev. Dougherty on May 18, 1845. The Kahgee family was well represented in the Old Mission Church.

Thomas's other connections to the Old Mission Church were through his relationship as a nephew of Daniel Rodd, who was an interpreter and teacher at Rev. Dougherty's Mission School. He was also a cousin to Charles Allen (of the Naishkaze family), who was a Company K comrade and whose family also belonged to the Mission Church.

Sometime before 1860, Henry and his family moved to Little Traverse (now Harbor Springs). Thomas's mother, Sarah, is reported by Henry to have died in the summer of 1860.

After his mother's death, Thomas went to live with his aunt Ann, with whom he was very close.

Henry stated that after his wife died, he remarried to a woman named Teressa but had no children with her. Henry and Teressa Kahgee were listed in the 1870 federal census of Charlevoix County. But did Henry actually marry Teressa after Sarah's death, or did he abandon Sarah and Thomas and then marry or just live with Teressa? According to Ann, Henry abandoned his family for Teressa.

After Thomas's death, his aunt Ann notified the government on February 25, 1865, that Henry Kahgee had actually abandoned his wife and child some years before and left no property whatsoever for their support. She stated that she had taken in the mother and child to live with her and saw to their needs. And, according to Ann, Sarah, before her death in 1860, had asked Ann to take care of her son and see to his support. It seems that Sarah had her questions then about Henry's faithfulness and dependability. There is no mention as to what happened to the adopted daughter, Isabella. Ann did as her sister requested and took in Thomas and his mother until Thomas entered the service.

Ann stated that Thomas had made a will and appointed her to be the administratrix during his sick leave home in 1864 and before his death on October 15 of that year. In the will, Thomas stated that his aunt was to receive all the money due to him from the army. Ann's deposition was attested to by David Awkowesay and Dominik Wedegowesh.

On January 29, 1866, Henry Kahgee, then a resident of Charlevoix, Charlevoix County, stated that his son never married or left a child who survived him. So Application #187,836 for a dependent father's pension was filed for Henry (under the name of H. Kahgel) on June 14, 1870, and again on June 22, 1880.

Henry stated that he owned about thirty-two acres at the Grand Traverse Bay area in Leelanau County before the war. Ann repudiated that statement. He also stated that his son, Thomas, helped to support the family by working with him on the property and by making maple sugar to sell. Now, without his son's help, Henry found himself to be destitute.

Henry said that while Thomas was home on sick leave in 1864, he was under the care of his aunt.

On January 2, 1885, Ann (or Shondasequa) Miller was awarded a government

Certificate #243,659 from the Treasury Department in which she (as administratrix) received $134.84 arrears of pay due to Thomas Miller from June 18, 1864. There is no pension file for Thomas Miller.

After all the statements made by Henry Kahgee and Ann Miller were studied by officials in the US Pension Office, it was decided that Henry Kahgee's application for a father's pension be rejected on July 7, 1885. The application was rejected on the grounds that Henry had indeed abandoned his wife and son.

Misisaius, Edward, Private

Enlistment: Enlisted as a private on September 10, 1863, at Little Traverse (now Harbor Springs), Emmet County, by Second Lieutenant Garrett A. Graveraet, First Michigan Sharpshooters, for three years. The regimental descriptive roll states that Edward Misisaius enlisted at Northport, Leelanau County, on June 14, 1863, by Second Lieutenant Garrett A. Graveraet.

   Age: Twenty-five, born about 1838 in Muskegon, Muskegon County.
   Occupation: Farmer
   Residence: LaCroix (renamed Cross Village in 1875), Emmet County
   Physical Description: Five feet nine, black eyes, black hair, and a dark complexion. Examining physician was Dr. George L. Cornell, assistant surgeon, First Michigan Sharpshooters.
   Mustered: October 4, 1863, at the confine for Confederate prisoners at Camp Douglas, Chicago, Cook County, Illinois, by Captain Lowe. Another record of muster states that the date was October 21, 1863. At that time, the confine was guarded by the soldiers of the First Michigan Sharpshooters for seven months.
   Military Service: Private Edward Misisaius was wounded during a battle near Spotsylvania, Virginia, on Wednesday, May 18, 1864. He incurred a flesh wound of the right hand (another medical record states a wound in the left hand) caused by a missile and was taken immediately to an aid station to assess his wound. Any bleeding was stopped, and the hand was washed and hastily bandaged. He was given whiskey or an opium pill for pain. Edward either walked from the aid station or was taken by ambulance wagon to his division hospital in the field farther behind the lines.

At the division hospital, Edward's hand was again washed with cold water and treated with simple water dressings. Simple water dressings were composed of lint soaked in cold water, applied to the wound, and secured with a cloth wrap or adhesive plaster. A tincture of iodine may or may not have been applied to his wound before the dressing was secured. He was given whiskey for shock and an opium pill for pain (*Schaadt*).

On May 19, Edward was transferred by ambulance wagon to a depot hospital in Fredericksburg, Virginia (possibly attorney John Marye's house on Marye's Heights). At this hospital, as time permitted from an overworked staff, Edward's flesh wound was cleaned with potassium iodide or liquid iodine, and simple water dressings were applied and changed as often as possible (*Bollet*). He was offered whiskey and opium pills for pain.

A Ninth Corps physician, Dr. William Howard Reed, described the horrid conditions of blood, filth, and vermin that infested the hospital at Fredericksburg. He noted that when the sweltering heat inside of the crowded hospital became unbearable, the wounded and dying would be moved to the outside and placed on the lawn to give them some relief (*Reed*).

Private Edward Misisaius was consistently reported as "absent—wounded" during the months following his injury and up to May and June 1865. He was last paid to April 30, 1864, and there is no record of his discharge. Two scenarios of Edward's demise are possible:

(1.) If Edward died at the Fredericksburg depot hospital, it could have been from septicemia (blood poisoning), which is a systemic disease produced by microorganisms and their poisonous products in the bloodstream, to name one possible cause (*Blakiston*). Assuming that he died at this hospital, his body would have been put on a stretcher and covered with a blanket. The remains were then taken with other dead bodies to a burial trench near the hospital, where the blanket was removed and the body was laid next to other dead soldiers and covered with dirt. Edward's body may have been put into a coffin, if available, before burial. His name and unit were written on a wooden board that was placed at the head of his burial site (*Encyclopedia*). Prayers may or may not have been said at his burial.

After the war, soldiers' remains were removed from the burial trenches, placed into coffins (if available), and reburied a few hundred yards from John Marye's property in the newly designated Fredericksburg National Cemetery (*Guide*). Since there is no record of Edward Misisaius's name in the national cemetery records, it's assumed that his headboard could have been lost to the elements or used for firewood before his body was disinterred. With no way to identify

Edward's remains, he was most likely reburied in the national cemetery under a stone labeled "Unknown," just one of the twelve thousand unknowns in that vast bivouac of the dead (*Ibid.*).

(2.) The second scenario for Edward's disappearance would be that he was sent home, possibly on a furlough for sick leave, and died. Or he may have just left the hospital and died along his route home. There is no record of his return to duty after his admission to the hospital in Fredericksburg. Hence, no discharge was given to Edward. Sadly, another soldier lost in the shuffle of war.

Discharged: There is no record of discharge for Private Edward Misisaius.

Biography: In addition to the surname spelling mentioned previously, Edward's last name was also spelled Misissinse, Misisains, Misissins, Minisiance, and Minissisance. There is no pension file for Edward Misisaius.

Miskoguon, Louis, Private

Enlistment: Enlisted as a private on September 10, 1863, at Little Traverse (now Harbor Springs), Emmet County, by Second Lieutenant Garrett A. Graveraet, First Michigan Sharpshooters, for three years.

Age: Thirty, born about 1833 in Kalamazoo, Kalamazoo County.

Occupation: Farmer

Residence: Charlevoix, Emmet County (now Charlevoix County)

Physical Description: Six feet tall, hazel eyes, black hair, and a dark complexion. Examining physician was Dr. George L. Cornell, assistant surgeon, First Michigan Sharpshooters.

Mustered: October 21, 1863, at Camp Douglas, Chicago, Cook County, Illinois, by Capt. Lowe. The regimental descriptive roll states that Private Miskoguon was mustered in Chicago on October 2, 1863. The First Michigan Sharpshooters spent seven months as guards for Confederate prisoners at the camp.

Military Service: On June 17, 1864, while attacking the enemy's works in a battle at Petersburg, Virginia, Private Miskoguon was captured by the rebels. He was held for a few days in a tobacco warehouse in Petersburg and then sent by cattle railcar to Camp Sumter, Andersonville Prison in Andersonville, Georgia.

In the prison, he and other members of his regiment, along with thousands of other men, endured starvation and inhumane treatment in one of the most infamous confines in American history. Even though a military record reported him "missing on 17 June 1864" and "captured on 30 July," he had actually been a prisoner since June 17 when he was captured at said battle.

Miskoguon was admitted to the prison hospital at least twice (sometime in August and again on December 2, 1864) with scorbutus or scurvy (lack of fresh food containing vitamin C) and chronic diarrhea. Records show that on April 1, 1865, Miskoguon was released from prison and possibly processed at Camp Fisk near Vicksburg, Mississippi. His plan was to board a steamer at Vicksburg and travel to Camp Chase, Columbus, Ohio. As a paroled prisoner at Camp Chase, he would receive medical treatment, a bath, a suit of clothes, and a short furlough home.

Louis was able to secure passage for his trip to Camp Chase on the ill-fated steamer *Sultana* and was listed on the transport's manifest as "S. Kogan." A Company K comrade, Amos Ashkebugnekay (or Amos Green), was also on the steamer (see file on Ashkebugnekay) as it made its way to Columbus.

The *Sultana* was a side-wheel vessel, 260 feet long, and designed to carry only 376 passengers. But as the steamer left the dock at Memphis, Tennessee, on April 27, 1865, it was grossly overloaded with 2,400 people. Most of the passengers were Union soldiers recently freed from prison camps. Around 2:00 a.m. on said date, the steamer's three boilers exploded about seven miles above Memphis (*Potter*). More than eighteen hundred people died when they were scalded, burned, or drowned (*Ibid.*). The tragedy of the *Sultana* was America's greatest maritime disaster.

Louis was a lucky man, as was Amos Ashkebugnekay-Green. The two men, who were good swimmers, were among the five hundred people who survived the tragedy.

Rescued from the murky, cold water of the Mississippi River, Louis was taken to Overton USA General Hospital in Memphis, suffering from contusions (or bruises). The doctors at the hospital probably treated Louis's bruises with cold compresses and salves and gave him opium pills for pain. On April 29, Louis was transferred to a Soldiers Home in Memphis to rest before his trip to Camp Chase.

He took another steamer out of Memphis and arrived at Camp Chase sometime in May 1865. The camp was a training camp for Union soldiers, a parole camp for the exchange of Union and Confederate prisoners, and a prison camp for Confederates. The Confederate cemetery held 2,260 remains. Doctors were on staff to treat injured and ill soldiers of both Union and Confederate allegiance. Louis's treatment at Camp Chase would have included a hearty diet, along with fresh fruits and vegetables for his scurvy, and Dover's powder (mixture of ipecac and opium), along with acetate of lead or nitrate of silver for his diarrhea (*Evans*). Louis could also rest, relax, and have refreshing baths.

After staying at Camp Chase for an unspecified time, Louis returned to Michigan. He was last paid to April 30, 1864.

Discharged: Private Louis Miskoguon's honorable discharge was issued by reason of Special Order No. 178 at Headquarters, Department of Washington, on July 19, 1865. He was mustered out and returned to Michigan on July 28 on the steamer *Morning Star*. On August 7, Louis received payment due to him at Jackson, Jackson County.

Biography: Louis Miskoguon, also known as Kewaquiskum and Awkebemosay, was the son of Michael and Sophia Miskoguon. In the 1860 federal census for the Township of Charlevoix, Emmet County, Louis's siblings included: Josephine, born ca. 1840; Joseph, born ca. 1851; Michael, born ca. 1854; and Moses, born ca. 1857.

In his young years, Louis attended Rev. George Nelson Smith's Congregational Church mission school in Northport, Leelanau County. In addition to the studies of both the Anishinabe and English languages, spelling, writing, geography, mathematics, and history, he learned how to be a farmer and to use tools.

Among his classmates was Payson Wolf, with whom he would become lifelong friends and a comrade in Company K. He would also become a good friend of Payson's future wife, Mary Jane Smith, also a classmate and the daughter of Rev. and Mrs. Smith.

Louis married Susan Miscowacowt (as spelled on the marriage certificate), also known as Susan Misconaquot, on May 1, 1853, at Northport. The couple's marriage was officiated by Rev. Smith. A friend of Presbyterian minister, Rev. Peter Dougherty, Rev. Smith established missions (as did Rev. Dougherty) among the Anishinabek—those of Old Wing Colony Mission of Allegan County in 1838 and in the Northport area in 1849.

Susan's father was Louis Misowalket. She was known to also use the names Josette or Josephina as her first name and Miscogeon and Kewaquiskum as her surnames.

Louis and Susan settled in Burgess, Hayes Township, Charlevoix County, and were the parents of eight children: Joseph, born 1855; Mitchell, born 1857; Moses, born 1859; Aiken, born 1861; Louis, born 1863; John, born 1866; and twins, Frank and Mary, born 1868. Mitchell died in 1872, Aiken died in 1888, and John died in 1907.

After his return from the service, Louis's health continued to deteriorate due to diarrhea that he had succumbed to while a prisoner of war. A local doctor treated him but with little success. Louis Miskoguon died on July 5, 1870, at Burgess and is buried in Charlevoix County.

Sometime after Louis's death, Susan married Simon Sanequaby (Louis's Company K comrade) in the traditional Anishinabek custom and practice (agreement of the couple and their parents). See file on Simon Sanequaby. Susan used the names Josette Giwegoshkam and Susan Miskogeon when she lived with Simon.

Susan and Simon were the parents of a son, James, born in 1873, and a daughter, Margaretta, born in August 1875. Margaretta died four months after her baptism on February 22, 1876, at Holy Childhood of Jesus Catholic Church at Harbor Springs, Emmet County. Since her parents were not married in the eyes of the church, Margaretta was listed as illegitimate on her baptismal certificate.

Sometime after Margaretta's baptism, Susan and Simon agreed that they would go their separate ways and discontinued their relationship—a divorce in Anishinabek custom and practice.

In 1884, Simon solemnized his third and last marriage to Maria Maksauge Madwes (or Madwens) in the Holy Childhood of Jesus Catholic Church. Susan remained unmarried.

Susan was now alone, destitute, in failing health, and depended greatly upon her oldest son, Joseph, for care. She decided to apply for a widow's pension on Louis's service. On January 15, 1889, Application #387,091 for a widow's pension was filed for Susan Miscogeon. She resubmitted her application on July 19, 1890.

Payson Wolf, Louis's army comrade and good friend, testified on Susan's behalf of his longtime friendship with Louis (and Susan) in an affidavit for Susan on January 22, 1894. He was also in Andersonville Prison with Louis, having been captured with him on June 17, 1864. Payson further testified that he had talked with Louis, who was also paroled from prison and on his way home to Michigan when they were both at Camp Chase in Ohio.

Susan finally received a Widow's Pension Certificate #391,056 on February 15, 1894, which paid eight dollars a month retroactive to July 19, 1890.

Sometime after 1894, Susan Miskoguon moved to Wolverine, Cheboygan County. On May 16, 1919, she was found dead in bed. Her place of death was listed as Mentor in Cheboygan County. Susan's demise was attributed to old age complicated by cardiac insufficiency. She was buried on May 18 in a cemetery in Wolverine.

Mixonauby, Thomas, Private

Enlistment: Enlisted as a private on September 3, 1864, at Grand Rapids, Kent County, by Captain and Provost Marshal Norman Bailey, First Michigan Sharpshooters for one year. This enlistment was credited to Pentwater, Oceana County, and satisfied the requirement for a man from that area in the Fourth Congressional District.

Age: Thirty-nine, born about 1825 in Kalamazoo, Kalamazoo County.

Occupation: Fur trader

Residence: Pentwater, Oceana County

Physical Description: Five feet ten, black eyes, dark hair, and a dark complexion. Examining physician was Dr. Alonzo Mate, surgeon, First Michigan Sharpshooters.

Mustered: September 3, 1864, at Grand Rapids by Captain and Provost Marshal Norman Bailey, First Michigan Sharpshooters

Military Service: Private Thomas Mixonauby was ill for most of his time in the service. He was taken by ambulance wagon to his division hospital behind the lines before Petersburg, Virginia, on September 29, 1864, experiencing severe bouts of vomiting. On the same day, Thomas was taken by ambulance wagon to the military railroad and put upon a mattress in a boxcar, the floor of which was cushioned with straw or hay, and sent to the depot hospital at City Point, Virginia. There was no explanation of the cause of his vomiting on his medical cards. On October 29, he was granted a twenty-day furlough home from the hospital at City Point.

Dr. E. H. Pratt of Pentwater examined Thomas on November 8 and concluded that he was unable to travel back to his unit due to his illness.

On November 15, Mr. D. L. Jones, a US teacher to the Chippewas and Ottawas who lived on the Indian reserve in Mason County, penned a letter to one of the surgeons at the depot hospital. He included Dr. Pratt's letter of Mixonauby's diagnoses with his letter. Jones's letter follows, as it was written and found in Thomas's pension file.

U. S. Teacher To the Chippewas and Ottawas

Reference

Hon. D. C. Leach

Indian Agent

Indian Reserve, Mason County Mich November 15, 1864

Surgeon of General Hospital, City Point, Virginia,

Dear Sir, In behalf of Thomas Mixonauby Private in Mich 1st. S.

S. Indian Company K who came home on sick furlough and his time being nearly expired wishes to inform you that he is so very sick that he is unable to get out or leave his bed but little is the same kind of sickness and vomiting that he had while in hospital and seems to linger eats but little and vomits up very soon.

Mixonauby is sick at my house we are 25 miles from one Doctor who has been to see him once and says his case is a bad one we are 75 miles from the RR in a new or wilderness trust of the county no way for him to go out at this season of the year except on foot or on horse Thomas is a good and well meaning soldier and his return has a good effect among his people he tells them much and it has a good and proper influence he desires you to assist and do what you can to get his furlough extended one month if then he is able to ride he says he will come life or death.

Yours truly

D. L. Jones

This is to certify that what I have with in regard to Mixonauby is true.
D. L. Jones, U. S. Teacher To the Chippewas and Ottawas.

On December 1, 1864, a second doctor, Dr. J. J. Kittredge of Pentwater, examined Thomas and reported that he was extremely sick and unable to travel. Also, it was the doctor's opinion that Thomas's condition was so bad that he would never be able to do duty as a soldier.

On December 27, 1864, Dr. Pratt wrote another letter to the depot hospital at City Point reconfirming Thomas's inability to travel. As his condition became increasingly worse, Thomas remained at Mr. Jones's house through most of the month of January 1865.

Finally, Thomas was sent to the General Post Hospital at the Detroit Barracks and was admitted on January 31, 1865, for treatment for pneumonia. The doctors at the barracks treated his pneumonia by giving Thomas Epsom salt (or magnesium sulfate) to purge his system, Dover's powder (a combination of ipecac and opium) as a diaphoretic, and painful cupping and blistering to promote absorption (or drawing away) of so-called poisons from the lungs and into the skin (*Evans*). Mustard plasters made with ground black mustard seed mixed with flour and water and spread on a cotton or flannel cloth were applied to the chest. This method was also thought to be beneficial in drawing poisons away from the lungs (*Internet search*).

Thomas was taken to St. Mary's USA General Hospital in Detroit on February 25, diagnosed with erysipelas—an acute, infectious disease due to the bacterium *Streptococcus pyogenes* and characterized by a spreading inflammation of the skin. The doctors treated Thomas's erysipelas by painting the inflamed area of the skin with applications of diluted bromine or chlorine in water. He was also given a cathartic (castor oil) as a laxative for purging his system and quinine for fever (*Schaadt*). But the inflammation can spread beneath the skin and infect the lymph nodes. From the lymph nodes, the infection can be passed into the bloodstream and cause pyemia or blood poisoning (*Bollet*). Pyemia can produce further systemic complications and death.

On March 12, 1865, Private Thomas Mixonauby died at St. Mary's Hospital. The doctors concluded that he died of erysipelas. Since Thomas died in a general hospital, he was given a more proper burial which included a coffin, religious services, a military escort from the hospital to the cemetery, military protocol (firing of arms) and an individual headboard with information about him and his unit. But, the location of Thomas's grave in a Detroit area cemetery is not known.

Discharged: No discharge given due to death from disease while in the hospital.

Biography: Thomas Mixonauby (also spelled Micksenawbay), age thirty-six, married Tishpah, age forty, on March 23, 1856, at the Anishinabek Colony near Leighton in Allegan County. The marriage was officiated by Rev. David Thomas, a Methodist missionary and interpreter who served the Methodist Nottawa Mission. Witnesses to the ceremony were Niwahskeskum and Pashshawbun. The Nottawa Mission encompassed four stations or "preaching places" in the three counties of Allegan, Barry, and Calhoun (*Reuter*).

At the time of their marriage, both Thomas and Tishpah listed their home as the "Indian Colony" near Leighton. Tishpah testified that there were no children under the age of sixteen at the time of Thomas's death in 1865. But two daughters, Me Nou Qua, age six, and Mary Ann, age five, were listed in the 1860 federal census of Pere Marquette, Mason County. The girls may have preceded their father in death.

Thomas had eighty acres of land in the Grand River bands area by reason of the treaty of July 31, 1855, between the commissioners of the United States and the Ottawa and Chippewa Indians of Michigan. The land description is the west half of the northeast quarter of section 30 in township 18 north of range 16 west. He was granted a certificate #374 on October 22, 1875, ten years after his death (*Land Records*). Thomas's children inherited his land.

Sometime after Thomas died in 1865, Tishpah Mixonauby moved to Riverton in Mason County. She was sent a receipt on March 17, 1866, for thirty dollars that was owed to Thomas for his service.

On May 9, 1871, Application #196,012 for a widow's pension was submitted for Tishpah. She was granted a Widow's Pension Certificate #158,183, which was dated June 1, 1872. Tishpah received pension payments of eight dollars a month retroactive to May 9, 1871, and her monthly rate was increased to twelve dollars commencing on March 19, 1886. Since she had reported that she had lost her pension certificate, a new certificate was sent to her, which included the increased amount of twelve dollars in monthly payments.

Tishpah Mixonauby died on March 10, 1904, near Custer, Mason County, and is buried in said county.

Mixunasaw, William, Private

Enlistment: Enlisted as a private on July 9, 1863, at Northport, Leelanau County, by Second Lieutenant Garrett A. Graveraet, First Michigan Sharpshooters, for three years.

   Age: Twenty-six, born about 1837 (birthplace not stated).
   Occupation: Farmer
   Residence: Northport
   Physical Description: Six feet tall, dark eyes, black hair, and a dark complexion. Examining physician was Dr. Arvin T. Whelan, surgeon, First Michigan Sharpshooters.
   Mustered: July 20, 1863, at Detroit, Wayne County, by Lieutenant Colonel John R. Smith, US Army
   Military Service: Private William Mixunasaw was captured by the rebels on June 17, 1864, while charging the enemy's works in a battle before Petersburg, Virginia. As with other captives taken during that battle, he was housed briefly in a tobacco warehouse in Petersburg and then sent by cattle railcar to Fort Sumter (Andersonville Prison) in Andersonville, Georgia. As a prisoner, he was subjected to starvation and inhumane treatment. Being denied fresh fruits and vegetables containing vitamin C, William's health soon deteriorated due to scorbutus (or scurvy).

On October 26, 1864, Private Mixunasaw died of scurvy. His body was taken by his comrades or prison guards to the brush arbor dead house outside of the stockade, where any useful clothing was removed from the body. Information about Mixunasaw was collected by a record keeper known as Dorance Atwater (also a prisoner), who kept the "Atwater List" of those prisoners who died at Andersonville. Atwater attached a numbered tag to the body for later reference. Then, as quickly as possible, William's remains, along with other bodies, were taken by wagon to the cemetery grounds about a mile away from the prison and which is now known as Andersonville National Cemetery (*Encyclopedia*).

At the cemetery, William's body was laid, without a covering and shoulder to shoulder with other dead prisoners, in a trench about four feet deep. The remains were then covered with dirt (*Ibid.*). A small post was placed at the head of his grave with a number carved into it. The number on the post matched the number on the body tag and was also noted into the records known about the deceased. Today, William lies at rest beneath military stone #11,511 that states his name as "W. Mackswaser."

Discharged: No discharge given due to death from disease while a prisoner of war.

Biography: William Mixunasaw, age twenty-one, married Mary Animekewasega, age fifteen, on August 15, 1856, at Northport, Leelanau County. The marriage was officiated by the couple's pastor, Rev. George Nelson Smith, who was a Congregational minister and missionary among the Anishinabek of Allegan and Leelanau County (Northport) areas. The couple did not have children. Other spellings of William's surname name include Misinawsa, Mesinasaw, Mixernasa, and Mesenawsa.

After William's death at Andersonville Prison, Application #87,267 for a widow's pension was filed (with the help of Rev. Smith) for Mary on March 25, 1865. She was granted a Widow's Pension Certificate #66,237 on March 7, 1866, and received eight dollars a month retroactive to October 27, 1864. In addition to Mary, Rev. Smith assisted many of the local Anishinabek veterans, and veterans' widows, to collect money owed to them and their dependents from the US government.

Sometime after 1866, Mary's health began to decline, and she became blind. As her world became increasingly dark, she asked Rev. Smith to baptize her.

On Sunday, February 23, 1868, Rev. Smith held a Sabbath meeting in the home of an elderly Anishinabequa widow who lived in the Anishinabek settlement of Onumunese. The village was about three miles southeast of Northport. Among those who attended the service was Mary Mixunasaw. Upon her profession of faith in Jesus Christ and his teachings, Rev. Smith anointed her with the sacrament of baptism (*Smith*).

Mary Mixunasaw died at the age of twenty-eight at noon on March 11 of said year. Her funeral was held at her home in said village and was attended by Rev. George and Mrs. Arvilla Smith and many serious solemn Anishinabek. Mary was said to have died very happy in her professed faith (*Ibid.*). The young widow was buried in the small cemetery adjacent to the village.

Mogwahgo, George W., Private

Enlistment: Enlisted as a private on February 23, 1864, at Schoolcraft, Kalamazoo County, by R. C. Dennison, captain and provost marshal, First Michigan Sharpshooters, for three years. This enlistment was credited to Constantine, St. Joseph County, and satisfied the requirement for a man from that area in the Second Congressional District.

Age: Twenty-three, born around March 15, 1840 or 1841, near Constantine, St. Joseph County. Another record lists his birthplace as Indiana.

Occupation: Farmer

Physical Description: Five feet four, dark eyes, dark hair, and a dark complexion. Examining physician is not known since Mogwahgo's volunteer enlistment paper is missing from his military file.

Mustered: February 24, 1864, at Kalamazoo, Kalamazoo County, by R. C. Denison, captain and provost marshal, First Michigan Sharpshooters

Military Service: During the Battle of Spotsylvania, Virginia, on May 12, 1864, Private George Mogwahgo received a gunshot (missile) wound to the ring finger of his left hand, which partially severed the digit. He was taken to an aid station behind the lines where any bleeding was stopped by compression and the wound was washed and hastily bandaged. He either walked or was taken by an ambulance wagon to his division hospital farther behind the lines.

At the division hospital, Dr. Arvin T. Whelan, surgeon, First Michigan Sharpshooters, anesthetized George with chloroform and probably used a surgical flap (muscle and skin coverage) procedure following the complete amputation at the joint of what was left of George's third finger (*Kuz and Bengtson*). After surgery, the skin and muscle flaps were brought together to form a stump and sewn together with silk or wire sutures. A porous mass of the separated threads of linen or cotton called "charpie" was used to dress the stump of the finger and absorb wound drainage. The dressing was secured with adhesive plaster (*Schaadt*). A palmar (toward the palm of the hand) splint was applied to the hand to stabilize it. George was given opium pills or administered powdered morphine though a small cut in the skin for postoperative pain.

On May 15, George was sent through Fredericksburg, Virginia, by ambulance wagon to Belle Plain Landing. From the landing, he was transferred to a hospital steamer and sent to Mount Pleasant USA General Hospital in Washington, DC.

George was admitted to Mt. Pleasant Hospital on May 16, where the doctors watched his wound closely and changed the dressings frequently. The patient was fed a nourishing diet, and pain control was continued.

On May 30, Private Mogwahgo was given a thirty-day furlough from the hospital.

During his furlough home to the Nottawaseppi Huron Band of Pottawatomi Anishinabek reservation in Athens Township near Athens, he was thrown from a horse that he was riding and broke his left leg. The only treatment he received was from an Anishinabe doctor known as Jim Duck. Due to his injury, he couldn't walk for many months. Consequently, George couldn't travel without help for the duration of the war. For the rest of his life, he suffered permanent lameness in his left leg.

Not able to read or write English but considering himself a good soldier, George thought that the military would understand that something must have happened to him that would have prevented his return on time and would know that he would return to duty when he was able. He didn't understand that the military didn't operate under those assumptions. Since notification of his injury at home was not received by his company at the termination of his furlough, he was branded a "deserter" on June 30, 1864.

Discharged: No discharge given at the end of the war due to the charge of desertion on his record.

Biography: George Mogwahgo (also spelled Moogargoe) was the son of Chief John Mogwahgo (also spelled Moguago) and his wife, Roxana. John was headman of the Nottawaseppi Huron Band of the Potawatomi who were living on a reservation near Athens, Calhoun County, just prior to the Civil War.

During the winter of 1839 or 1840, John and Roxana Mogwahgo, and others of their band, went on a journey to the Wabash in Indiana to hunt deer. In the early spring of 1840, the band returned to the St. Joseph River for the purpose of spring trapping on their way back home. It was during the full moon of March 1840 or 1841 (around the fifteenth) that George was born at a place near Constantine, St. Joseph County, Michigan. Other records state that George was born in Indiana. His boyhood home was the reservation, previously mentioned, near Athens.

George had a younger sister, Cynthia, born about 1844, and a younger brother, Cyrus, who died at the age of two before 1850. Cynthia would marry James Mingo of Albion, Calhoun County, on September 10, 1864.

George married, under the name of G. Moogwah at age eighteen, to Sarah Kukpashkummoquay, age sixteen of Barry County, on July 11, 1858, at Leighton in Allegan County. Another record states that the date of the marriage was August 1, 1858. Rev. Henry Jackson, an Anishinabe Methodist minister and interpreter, officiated at the ceremony. Witnesses to the wedding were S. P. Wellard and Rush Wellard.

George and Sarah were the parents of a daughter, Mary, born about 1888, who would later marry William Shagonaby (or Shagonabe).

About 1876, George contacted former Captain George H. Murdock of the First Michigan Sharpshooters to aid him in applying for an invalid pension. The papers that were prepared (but not yet sent) were lost when George's cabin caught fire and burned.

It was years later that someone explained to George that in order to obtain an invalid pension, he had to convince the government to remove the charge of desertion from his military record and grant a discharge to him. During the months of September and October 1915, several depositions were taken from friends (including Company K comrade Thomas Wezoo) and acquaintances who attested to the honorable character of Mogwahgo.

On October 15, 1915, by direction of the secretary of war and in accordance with the provisions of the act of Congress of March 2, 1889, the charge of desertion of June 1, 1864, against Mogwahgo was removed. Also, the implied charge of desertion of June 30, 1864, that arose from his failure to return from his furlough was removed. A belated discharge certificate for disability was issued to him and was amended to show the date June 30, 1864, when he left the service.

After he received his belated honorable discharge, Application #1,421,484 (under the act of May 11, 1912) for an invalid pension was submitted for George on October 23, 1915, and again on February 5, 1916. He received Pension Certificate #1,177,292 on February 25, 1916, which paid eighteen dollars a month retroactive to October 23, 1915. His rate was increased to twenty-one dollars a month from March 15, 1916.

On February 1, 1916, George Mogwahgo gave an interesting account to a notary public of his induction and military experience for his pension claim. The account was written down as follows and found in his pension papers:

> That he was enlisted at Schoolcraft, Kalamazoo County, Michigan, but his home was at Athens, Calhoun County, Michigan. He was examined and received his uniform at Kalamazoo, Michigan about Feb. 23-1864. From Kalamazoo he was sent to Rendesvous Camp at Grand Rapids, Michigan and stayed there about one week. From there he was sent to Camp Douglas near Chicago where he was kept about one month being drilled and then was sent to Annapolis Md. and was drilled there about one month. Then he went to Alexandria, Va. and was there about one week. He was then sent to the front and was soon after engaged in the Battle of the Wilderness and a few days later in the Battle of Spotsylvania Court House. Claimant was wounded – had the third finger of his left hand shot off and was sent to Mount Pleasant Hospital on the north side of Washington DC. After being there two or three weeks, he was given a sick furlough for 30 days and while on furlough he was thrown from a horse and his left leg badly broken. He was unable to get around on this leg for a long time and for that reason could not rejoin his company for duty.

It seems that George had "itchy feet" because he admitted on his pension declaration that he had lived in several places: in Athens of Calhoun County until 1866; in Jackson County from 1866 to 1873; in Hamilton of Allegan County from 1873 to 1912; and he changed places several times since 1912. By 1915, George was back in Athens.

On November 3, 1921, George filed a request for an increase in pay under the act of May 1, 1920. In May 1922, he resubmitted his request, and it was accepted. George was paid seventy-two dollars a month retroactive to November 3, 1921.

Sarah died and left George a widower. He applied and was admitted to the Michigan Soldiers' Home (Veterans' Home) in Grand Rapids, Kent County, on February 9, 1917. George was discharged from the home, at his own request, on September 4, 1917. He was readmitted on February 6, 1920, and discharged again on June 9, 1921. His final readmission was on February 9, 1923.

George Mogwahgo died of mitral valve disease of the heart in the hospital of the Soldiers' Home on May 16, 1923. His funeral was held 2:00 p.m. on May 18, and he was buried in the home cemetery now known as Grand Rapids Veterans Facility Cemetery. He lies at rest in grave #7132 of plot 7, row 19, grave 8. A Rev. Palmer officiated at his service, and military honors were conducted.

At his death, the nearest relatives listed were a daughter, Mary W. Shagonaby(e), wife of William Shagonaby(e), mentioned previously, of Heath Township, Allegan County, and Hamilton Douglas, who also lived in said county.

Mwakewenah, Daniel, Private

Enlistment: Enlisted as a private on August 15, 1863, at Bear River (now Petoskey), Emmet County, by Indian Agent Richard Cooper (an interpreter, storekeeper, and recruiter among the Anishinabek), First Michigan Sharpshooters, for three years.

Age: Forty-six, born about 1817 at Pentwater, Oceana County. Another record states that he was originally from the Grand Traverse Bay area.

Occupation: Farmer

Residence: Bear River

Physical Description: Five feet ten, black eyes, black hair, and a dark complexion. Examining physician was Dr. George L. Cornell, assistant surgeon, First Michigan Sharpshooters.

Mustered: October 21, 1863, at Camp Douglas, Chicago, Cook County, Illinois, by Captain Lowe. The camp was a confine for Confederate prisoners and was guarded for seven months by the sharpshooters.

Military Service: Private Daniel Mwakewenah, who was well liked by his comrades and superior officers, was very instrumental in recruiting many of the men who joined Company K. He was very skillful in the use of his rifle and was said to have killed about thirty-two rebels, many of them officers, during the Battle of the Wilderness, Virginia, on May 5 or 7, 1864 (*Newspaper*).

During the Battle of Spotsylvania, Virginia, on May 12, 1864, Daniel incurred flesh wounds in the face and right arm. In pain, and shortly after he received these wounds, a rebel sharpshooter took aim at Daniel and shot him in the left hand, which nearly severed the first, second, and third fingers (*Ibid.*). Being unable to reload his rifle, Daniel was taken with other wounded men to an aid station where the bleeding from his wounds was stopped. His wounds were washed, hastily bandaged, and whiskey and opium pills were offered for pain. Daniel was then transferred by ambulance wagon to his division hospital farther behind the lines. Considering the seriousness of his wounds, emergency surgery was performed at this hospital. The surgeon anesthetized Daniel with chloroform and probably used a surgical flap procedure following the complete amputation of what was left of his three fingers. The flaps of skin and muscle were brought together to form a stump and sewn together with silk or wire sutures (*Kuz and Bengtson*). After the surgery, the stumps of the fingers were dressed with a porous mass of separated threads of linen or cotton called "charpie," which absorbed wound drainage. The dressing was secured with adhesive plaster (*Schaadt*). A palmar (toward the palm of the hand) splint was applied to the hand to stabilize it. Daniel was given an opium pill, or powdered morphine was administered through a small cut in the skin for postoperative pain.

On May 17, Daniel was taken by ambulance wagon to the depot hospital at Fredericksburg, Virginia (*Ibid.-Newspaper a.*). This hospital was possibly at or near the home of attorney John Marye on Marye's Heights. Considering the crush of wounded soldiers, Daniel's bandages were changed when the staff had time to do so, and pain management was continued.

Daniel was transferred by ambulance wagon from Fredericksburg to a wharf at Belle Plain Landing, Virginia, on May 27.

From the landing, Daniel was transferred to a hospital steamer and taken to Armory Square USA General Hospital in Washington, DC. He was admitted to said hospital on May 28. At Armory Square, the doctors changed Daniel's surgical dressings frequently, watched the wounds closely, and continued pain control. Like the other wounded, Daniel was fed a nourishing diet, which was a patient advantage at the large general hospitals.

Shock from the injuries, the loss of blood from his wounds, and septicemia (which is a systematic disease produced by microorganisms and their poisonous products [infection] in the bloodstream) hastened his demise. The infection in the blood had progressed to Daniel's heart and resulted in his death at 10:00 p.m. on June 5, 1864.

Daniel's effects, left at his death, included one overcoat, one pair of trousers, one pair of shoes, and one blanket. He was last paid to April 30, 1864.

In writing a report after Daniel's death, First Lieutenant Lemuel R. Nichols stated that "Private Mwakewenah was a brave and good soldier."

Because Daniel was so well respected, Congressman John F. Driggs (father of First Lieutenant William J. Driggs) arranged to have the private's body embalmed by Dr. Thomas Holmes. Dr. Holmes was the well-known Washington, DC, physician who also embalmed Lt. Garrett A. Graveraet's body and had it sent back to Michigan.

Dr. Holmes had Daniel's remains placed into a handsome coffin. A metal plate with his name, the cause of his death, and the date and name of the battle in which the fatal wounds were received was attached to the box. The coffin was placed in charge of an officer who sent it on its way to Bear River, Michigan, by way of Saginaw City, Saginaw County, on June 7, 1864 *(Ibid.-Newspaper b.)*.

Several days later, Daniel's body arrived in Saginaw City. Since there was not sufficient time to notify Mwakewenah's relatives of plans to return the body to Bear River, Daniel was buried in lot 12, section 2-D of Brady Hill Cemetery in said city. He was probably accorded military honors, possibly including a chaplain or some form of military protocol, at his burial. The interment in the city cemetery was intended to be only temporary, as the plan was to send Daniel's body to Bear River when arrangements, and the cost of shipment, could be made with his relatives. As weeks became months and months turned into years, Daniel's body remained at rest at Brady Hill. Finally, a military stone was ordered for Daniel's grave from Sheldon and Sons in West Rutland, Vermont, on August 21, 1888. The stone marks his grave site today.

Discharged: No discharge given due to death from wounds while in the hospital.

Biography: Daniel's surname of Mwakewenah is translated as "Standing Bear." The preface Mwake is derived from the Anishinabe word *Makwa,* which means bear *(Baraga)*. Other spellings of his name include Mahkewenan, Mahkewenah, and Mahkewenaw.

On June 3, 1843, Daniel joined and received the rite of baptism at Rev. Peter Dougherty's Old Mission (at first called Grand Traverse) Presbyterian Church. On that date, Daniel also took the English surname of Wells *(Dougherty)*.

Old Mission (for Ottawas and Chippewas) was located on the east shore of Grand Traverse Bay, which was the first Protestant church in that region, having been established in 1839. Daniel was very active in the lay ministry of the church *(Ibid.)*.

At the time that he joined the Old Mission Church, Daniel was listed as having a wife, Quequejeahnoqua. She also joined the church, received the rite of baptism, and took the English name of Phoebe Wells on January 7, 1844. Rev. Dougherty mentioned this account in the June 1846 notes of his *Minutes of the Session of the Indian Mission at Grand Traverse Bay, Michigan (Ibid.)*.

Daniel was acknowledged as having presented his daughter, Harriet, age six months, for baptism during July 1844. It is assumed that Phoebe was her mother. But it's not clear just what happened to Phoebe and Harriet, as there is no further mention of them. According to later pension papers, Daniel was known not to have had a wife before his marriage to Catherine. It's possible that Daniel and Phoebe may have had a marriage of Anishinabek custom and practice (agreement of the couple and their parents) and not by ceremony conducted by clergy or justice of the peace.

In December 1847 or 1848, Rev. Peter Dougherty officiated at the wedding of Daniel and Catherine Ningasigekwe at the Presbyterian Old Mission Church. Catherine was born at Middle Village, also called Good Hart, in Emmet County.

By 1852, the pressure for land settlement by the non-Anishinabek increased. The Anishinabek began to leave their mission on Old Mission Peninsula (now Grand Traverse County). They selected parcels of land, which were set aside for them by the government, on the western shore of Grand Traverse Bay on Leelanau Peninsula.

Rev. Dougherty decided to follow his flock and build another mission and school. The minister sought permission from his superiors on the Presbyterian board to move from the Presbyterian Old Mission to the site of a New Mission, and his request was granted (*Craker*).

The land purchased for the New Mission was located at Mission Point in Leelanau County on the bluff a little east of, and including, Omena. Omena means "It is so?" in the Anishinabemowen language. The place acquired the name "Omena" from Rev. Dougherty's habitual response to statements made by the Anishinabek (*Romig*). He was the first postmaster of Omena in 1858. Rev. Andrew Porter (who was a teacher at Old Mission) was sent by Rev. Dougherty to oversee the building process at Mission Point.

Rev. Dougherty named his new settlement at Omena Grove Hill New Mission Church. The school house was also known as Grove Hill. Early settlers referred to the Dougherty Mission as the Grove Hill Seminary since each building rested upon a hill (*Ibid.-Craker*).

Also, in 1852, a request was made of Rev. Dougherty by Daniel Mwakewenah to establish a mission and school at Bear Creek (or Muhquh Sebing), Emmet County. Rev. Dougherty sponsored and supported the appointment of Rev. Porter to see to the completion of this task and to oversee its operation.

Rev. Porter arrived at Bear Creek on the boat *Eliza Caroline* to see to the details of establishing a mission and school. When the missionary arrived and left the vessel, he was greeted by Daniel Mwakewenah, who offered the use of the best room in his own home until the mission house could be built (*Traverse Region*).

Shortly after Porter's arrival, Daniel was elected chief of the Bear River Band of Odawas (or Ottawas).

About this time, Chief Daniel Mwakewena, who represented his people at Bear Creek (now called Petoskey, Emmet County), and Chief Andrew J. Blackbird, an Anishinabe, who represented his people from L'Arbre Croche (now called Cross Village, Emmet County), journeyed to Washington, DC. The two men traveled specifically to lobby for their Anishinabek (the Odawa [or Ottawa] people) and to appeal to the government for the return of their old lands in the said areas. The men were successful because a large tract of land in the Muhqua Sebing and L'Arbre Croche localities was eventually returned to that area's Anishinabek.

In the 1860 federal census of Bear Creek Township in Emmet County, Daniel Mwakewenah, age forty-six, was listed with a woman named Mary, age forty-five (probably Catherine); a boy named Joseph, age eighteen and listed as a field hand; and a girl named Mary, age fourteen. It is noted that Joseph (born around 1842) could be another child of Phoebe and Daniel before Daniel married Catherine. Daniel was listed on said census as owning the value of $250 of real estate and $300 of personal estate.

By 1863, two sons had joined the Mwakewenah family. John was born on January 15, 1861, and George arrived on April 30, 1863. Rev. Dougherty baptized the boys in the rite of the Presbyterian Church soon after their births.

Before he enlisted, Daniel did not have much time to enjoy parenting John and George. George would never know his father. Likewise, John would not have remembered his dad, either, as the little boy was just two years of age when Daniel left for the army.

After Daniel's death, Application #74,331 was submitted for Catherine Mwakewenah for a widow's pension on December 3, 1864. She received her Widow's Pension Certificate #47,176 on May 16, 1865. The certificate paid eight dollars a month retroactive to June 5, 1864.

Catherine Mwakewenah married for the second time to Edward Noaka, a farmer, from Bear Creek Township on March 13, 1866, in Charlevoix, Charlevoix County. The ceremony was officiated by John Horton, justice of the peace.

Due to her remarriage and having a husband to support her, Catherine's pension payments from Daniel's service were stopped. She died on December 18, 1866. After her death, the court declared her children to be orphans in need of a guardian.

On January 22, 1868, in a letter of guardianship, Dennis L. Downing, judge of probate for Emmet County at Little Traverse (now Harbor Springs), appointed Mrs. Ann Rodd as guardian for John Mwakewenah, age seven, and George Mwakewenah, age five. Mrs. Rodd (spelled Rood in the court papers) was the wife of Daniel Rodd, a teacher and interpreter at Rev. Dougherty's Old Mission School, and the couple was well known to the young brothers (*Probate*). By that time, the boys' sister, Mary Mwakewenah, had attained the age of twenty-two and was no longer a minor.

Mrs. Rodd filed Application #157,537 for pension for minor children on February 11, 1868. She received a Pension for Minor Children Certificate #125,489 on March 2, 1869, which paid eight dollars a month retroactive to March 14, 1866. She also filed for an additional two dollars a month for each child and received such amount on February 18, 1869, retroactive to July 25, 1866. The pension payments would cease when the youngest child, George, attained the age of sixteen on April 30, 1879.

Daniel and Catherine Mwakewenah's children, Mary, George, and John, may have attended Rev. Porter's school at Bear Creek during their early years. If they did attend this school, they would have been instructed to be proficient in English as well as their native language, learned the principles of Christianity, and acquired domestic, farming, and scholastic skills that would help them earn a living.

At age nineteen, George Mwakewenah of Charlevoix County married Catherine Kewakondo, age seventeen, of Bear Creek, Emmet County, on July 15, 1880. Justice of the Peace Hiram Parker officiated at the ceremony in Bear Creek.

Enlisted Men—Letters N, O, P, Q, and R

Narquaquot, Joseph, Private

Enlistment: Enlisted as a private on July 4, 1863, at Elbridge, Oceana County, by Captain Edwin V. Andress, First Michigan Sharpshooters, for three years.

Age: Twenty-five, born about 1838 in Grand Rapids, Kent County.

Occupation: Farmer and hunter

Residence: Pentwater, Oceana County

Physical Description: Five feet six, dark eyes, black hair, and a dark complexion. Examining physician was Dr. J. B. McNett, assistant surgeon, First Michigan Sharpshooters.

Mustered: July 11, 1863, at Detroit, Wayne County, by Lieutenant Colonel John R. Smith, First Michigan Sharpshooters

Military Service: Private Joseph Narquaquot became ill while he was on guard duty with his regiment for Confederate prisoners at Camp Douglas in Chicago, Cook County, Illinois. He was admitted to the Post Hospital on December 5, 1863, and diagnosed with pneumonia. The doctors treated Joseph's pain and suppressed his cough with opiates and "blue mass" (or calomel), which contained mercury (*Bollet*). Mustard blister plasters and moist heat were applied to his chest to help draw out (absorb) so-called poisons from his lungs and into his skin. A mustard plaster consisted of ground mustard seed mixed with flour and water, spread onto a cotton or flannel wrap, and applied to the chest (*Internet*). According to the office of the surgeon general, Joseph was reported to have died of pneumonia on either December 11 or 12

Joseph was buried in Chicago's old North Side City Cemetery, which is now Lincoln Park, six miles north of Camp Douglas. He was probably accorded burial protocol for a Union soldier. A headboard was placed at his burial site.

When City Cemetery was closed, Joseph's remains were to be transferred to Chicago's Rosehill Cemetery. He was supposed to be reinterred there along with other Union prison guards who served at Camp Douglas. But the grave site for Private Joseph Narquaquot has not been found at Rosehill Cemetery. Was it possible that his body was sent home to his family after expenses for embalming and travel were negotiated? Was his grave marker lost when his remains were transferred to Rosehill? Was he possibly reburied in Oak Woods Cemetery, instead of Rosehill, somewhere near the site of the twelve unknown Union guards?

The Confederate dead from City Cemetery were not transferred to Rosehill due to the outcry that rebels should not rest alongside Union dead. So, in 1867, the government purchased a section of Oak Woods Cemetery in Chicago's Hyde Park where the Confederate prisoners were reburied in two acres known as "Confederate Mound" (*Levy*).

Twelve Union guards, who died of smallpox in the Camp Douglas Post Hospital and were buried across from the camp, were also reburied in trenches in Oak Woods Cemetery (*Ibid.*). But in the removal and transport of these twelve coffins to the cemetery, the headboards were thrown aside, thus erasing the identities of the guards' remains (*Ibid.*).

Oak Woods Cemetery officials had the burial trenches covered with about six feet of earth to bring the sunken plot up to ground level, thus obscuring the trenches.

Today there are twelve government military stones located in front of the Confederate Monument. These twelve stones are only symbolic since the Union remains are lost to identity in the burial trenches (*Ibid.*).

Discharged: No discharge given due to death from pneumonia while in the post hospital.

Biography: Joseph Narquaquot married Eliza Wabbegema on May 7, 1858, at Grand Haven, Ottawa County, by traditional Anishinabek custom and practice (with mutual agreement of the couple and their parents). Joseph and Eliza were the parents of one child, Eliza, born February 7, 1864, just two months after her father's death.

Eleven years after Joseph's death, Eliza's Application #214,752 for a widow's pension (and child under sixteen years of age surviving) was filed for her on April 6, 1874. At the time of her application, she and Eliza were living in Riverton, Mason County.

Eliza Narquaquot received a Treasury Certificate #272,254 from the second auditor's office, which allowed her to receive Joseph's pay to include December 10, 1863. However, she did not receive a pension. In addition to pneumonia listed as the cause of Joseph's death, a second report was submitted that told a different story. That report stated that Joseph died of secondary syphilis. The US Pension Office requested follow-up reports to settle this discrepancy, but the reports were not received by that office. Therefore, Eliza's pension application was not accepted, and her claim was abandoned.

Narwegeshequabey, Jackson, Private

Enlistment: Enlisted as a private under the names of Jackson Narwegeshequabey and Noah Weashkidba on June 24, 1863, at Ionia, Ionia County, by Captain Edwin V. Andress, First Michigan Sharpshooters, for three years. The accepted name for this soldier is Jackson Narwegeshequabey.

Age: Twenty-two, born about 1841 in Lapeer, Lapeer County.
Occupation: Hunter
Residence: Isabella City (now Mt. Pleasant), Isabella County
Physical Description: Five feet eight, black eyes, black hair, and a dark complexion. Examining physician was Dr. J. B. McNett, assistant surgeon, First Michigan Sharpshooters.
Mustered: July 11, 1863, at Detroit, Wayne County, by Lieutenant Colonel John R. Smith, First Michigan Sharpshooters
Military Service: Federal department and regimental records report that Private Jackson Narwegeshequabey was captured by the rebels while attacking the enemy's works on July 30, 1864, at the Battle of the Crater before Petersburg, Virginia.

In depositions taken in March and June 1866, John Collins and Joseph Williams (also known as Joseph Nesogot), members of Company K, testified that they saw Narwegeshequabey captured. Although war department records and regimental records state that the date of capture was July 30, 1864, at the Battle of the Crater, both men testified to the date of capture as actually being June 17, 1864, before Petersburg, Virginia.

John stated that he never saw the prisoner again. Joseph stated that he was also taken prisoner at the same time as Jackson and that both men spent five months at Camp Sumter, also called Andersonville Prison, in Andersonville, Georgia. John further stated that when the rebels heard that Union General William T. Sherman was gaining Confederate ground, the prisoners were transferred to Camp Lawton in Millen, Georgia, on November 11.

On November 26, 1864, the prisoners at Camp Lawton were sent to a stockade prison area in Savannah, Georgia, to wait for parole. Williams was paroled, but Private Narwegeshequabey remained a prisoner. Joseph concluded that he had heard nothing further from Jackson, nor did Jackson return home. According to Williams, if Jackson didn't die, he would surely have returned to his people. Williams did comment that Jackson was quite ill when he left him in Savannah. It can be assumed, from Williams's testimony, that Jackson died of disease at Savannah while still a prisoner of war. Narwegeshequabey is most likely buried somewhere in the Savannah area.

Discharged: No discharge given due to death while a prisoner of war.

Biography: Jackson Narwegeshequabey, who was also known as Nowkeshe, was the son of Mawmawkechewing (or Beaver) and Kawgayyar Narwegeshequabey. Beaver and Kawgayyar were married according to Anishinabek custom and practice (the consent of the couple and their parents) in Chesaning, Saginaw County, in 1826. They were the parents of several children in addition to Jackson, who remained single during his short life.

On January 28, 1867, a Treasury Certificate #285,914 was issued to Beaver and Kawgayyar Narwegeshequabey (Act of July 22, 1861). The certificate paid arrears of pay due to include July 3, 1864, and a seventy-five-dollar bounty due Jackson at his enlistment, payable upon his muster-out. The couple was also issued Treasury Certificate #404,473, which allowed a hundred-dollar bounty, issued February 19, 1868 (Act of July 28, 1866).

Beaver died at Oscoda, Iosco County, in June 1874, and left Kawgayyar dependent upon her own labor and contributions from friends for support.

Having become feeble with age, Application #562,857 was filed for Kawgayyar (under the name of Narwegeshequabe) for a dependent mother's pension on October 28, 1892. She received a Dependent Mother's Pension Certificate #387,630 on December 18, 1893, which paid twelve dollars a month retroactive to October 28, 1892.

In August 1898, Kawgayyar Narwegeshequabey was deemed incompetent, and Mr. Frank Squanda of East Saginaw, Saginaw County, was appointed as her guardian on September 2, 1898. Squanda received the payments from Kawgayyar's pension and was entrusted to allocate them to her use.

Kawgayyar Narwegeshequabey died at her home in Buena Vista, Saginaw County, sometime shortly after Squanda received her pension payment on September 4, 1900. The Pension Office was notified of Kawgayyar's death, and the payments were stopped on November 20, 1900. Kawgayyar is buried in said county.

Nauquam, Thompson, Private

Enlistment: Enlisted as a private on June 24, 1863, at Little Traverse (now Harbor Springs), Emmet County, by Second Lieutenant Garrett A. Graveraet, First Michigan Sharpshooters, for three years.

Age: Twenty-three, born about 1840 in Little Traverse.

Occupation: Farmer

Residence: Charlevoix, Emmet County (now Charlevoix County)

Physical Description: Five feet eight and a half inches tall, black eyes, black hair, and a dark complexion. Examining physician was Dr. Arvin T. Whelan, surgeon, First Michigan Sharpshooters.

Mustered: July 20, 1863, at Detroit, Wayne County, by Lieutenant Colonel John R. Smith, First Michigan Sharpshooters

Military Service: Private Thompson Nauquam is reported to have deserted his guard post at the confinement for Confederate prisoners at Camp Douglas, Chicago, Cook County, Illinois, on or about September 21, 1863. There is no further military record for this man.

Discharged: No discharge given due to the claim of desertion.

Biography: Thompson Nauquam was the son of Tobias and Babeshe Nauquam. His known siblings were Philip, John, Isaac, Peter, and Louis. In addition to Tobias, Thompson and his older brothers, Philip and John, were engaged in successful farming in Hayes Township of Charlevoix County by 1870.

According to the federal census of 1870, Thompson and his first wife, Mary Ann, whom he married around 1863–1864, were the parents of Jacob, age six, and John, age two. Other children who joined the family in the following years were: Martha, born ca. 1873; James, born December 25, 1881; and Margaret, born December 20, 1884.

Thompson's second marriage was to Mariah (also known as Mary or Negahnegishia) Shepherd on February 6 or 13, 1892, in Hayes Township of Charlevoix County. Methodist minister Rev. John Kewaygeshik (also known as Kewayesig) officiated at the ceremony. Rev. Kewaygeshik was a supply pastor associated with the Methodist Indian Mission Circuit based in Petoskey, Charlevoix, and Elk Rapids (*Reuter*).

Thompson and Mary were the parents of a daughter named Nancy, who was born in 1894 and died of tuberculosis at age seven on November 11, 1901.

There is no pension file for Thompson Nauquam. Since he deserted his post at Camp Douglas in Chicago, Thompson probably thought that his short stint in the military was not to his liking. It could also be that since he, his father, and his brothers were successful farmers, a pension for service was not needed for income. Since he deserted and there is no record of an explanation for the circumstances of his desertion, Thompson would not have been eligible for a pension.

Nelson, Thomas, Corporal

Enlistment: Enlisted as a corporal on May 18, 1863, at Isabella City (now Mt. Pleasant), Isabella County, by First Lieutenant William J. Driggs, First Michigan Sharpshooters, for three years.

    Age: Twenty-seven, born about 1836 in Isabella County.

    Occupation: Farmer

    Residence: Taymouth Township, Saginaw County

    Physical Description: Six feet one, black eyes, black hair, and a dark complexion. Examining physician was Dr. George L. Cornell, assistant surgeon, First Michigan Sharpshooters.

    Mustered: May 26, 1863, at Detroit, Wayne County, by Lieutenant Colonel John R. Smith, First Michigan Sharpshooters

    Military Service: On February 7, 1864, Corporal Nelson became ill while on guard duty with his regiment at the confine for Confederate prisoners at Camp Douglas in Chicago, Cook County, Illinois. He was admitted to the USA Post Hospital diagnosed with "remittent fever" (fever with temporary cessation of symptoms) or malaria. Malaria is caused by a genus of protozoa called *Plasmodium* that is transmitted by infected mosquitoes of the genus *Anopheles* (*Blakiston*). Thomas was treated with doses of quinine made from powdered cinchona tree bark mixed with water or whiskey (whiskey masked the bitterness of quinine) or with pills of purified quinine sulfate (*Bollet*). He returned to duty on March 3.

    On May 12, 1864, at the Battle of Spotsylvania, Virginia, Corporal Nelson suffered a gunshot (missile) flesh wound in the upper third of his right thigh near the hip. Comrades Antoine Scott and William Isaac(s) testified that they carried Nelson to an aid station behind the lines where any bleeding was stopped by compression or tourniquet and his wound was washed and hastily bandaged.

    The soldier was then taken by ambulance wagon to his division hospital farther behind the lines. In this hospital, the doctors washed his wounds and applied iodine to both entrance and exit sites to impede infection. The conical missile had cut the thigh muscles so severely that Nelson's leg would be permanently weakened. Simple water dressings of lint, dipped into cold water, held in place with a cloth wrap and secured with an adhesive bandage were applied to his thigh (*Schaadt*). After his treatment for the leg injury, Nelson was given whiskey or opium pills and possibly powdered morphine, applied to a slit in the skin, for pain. He remained at the division hospital until May 17 when he was taken by ambulance wagon to the depot hospital in Fredericksburg, Virginia.

The depot hospital in Fredericksburg was at or near attorney John Marye's house on Marye's Heights. Corporal Nelson was given similar treatment for his wounds at that hospital.

Thomas was transferred by ambulance wagon from Fredericksburg to Belle Plain Landing, Virginia, on May 24. He was put on a hospital ship and sent to Harewood USA General Hospital in Washington, DC, where he was admitted on May 25 for further treatment since he had suffered partial loss of the use of his right leg. On June 6, he was granted a forty-five-day furlough from the hospital to his home in East Saginaw.

On June 23, while on furlough in East Saginaw, Nelson was involved in an unfortunate incident. It seems that during Nelson's conversation with an acquaintance, W. H. Beach, who was an old resident and highly respected citizen of that area, a man named McDonald approached Nelson and began to scuffle with him. As Nelson threw McDonald down upon the sidewalk, another man, named Wallace, approached Nelson and beat him severely in the face. When Beach reprimanded Wallace for his outrageous conduct, Wallace turned upon Beach and beat him so badly that the elderly man died two days later. The assailants were taken before a justice of the peace immediately after the altercation, and each was fined fifteen dollars (*Newspaper*).

Due to Nelson's wounds and the severe beating that he sustained in June, Dr. H. C. Farrand, a physician in East Saginaw, wrote a letter to Harewood Hospital on August 6. In the letter, Dr. Farrand requested an extension of Nelson's furlough since he was unable to return at the proscribed time due to the extent of his injuries. The extended furlough was granted by First Lieutenant William J. Driggs, and Nelson returned to Harewood on September 3.

Thomas was granted a second furlough of twenty days on October 25 from Harewood. He lost his furlough papers during his second trip home and was given replacement papers to return to the hospital on November 16.

Corporal Nelson was taken by hospital steamer from Harewood to Augur USA General Hospital near Alexandria, Virginia, on November 26.

While Nelson was at Harewood and Augur Hospitals, Lieutenant Driggs's father, Congressman John F. Driggs, visited him often and considered him a good soldier and a worthy man. Also, when he was a patient at the two hospitals, Nelson was diagnosed with phthisis, the old term for pulmonary tuberculosis (*Ibid.-Blakiston*).

On November 28, 1864, Corporal Nelson was examined for transfer to Company A of the Fourteenth Regiment Veterans Reserve Corps. It was quite obvious to the examining physicians that Nelson was not able to fulfill his duties in combat service since he had only partial use of his right leg. As mentioned previously, Nelson was considered a good soldier. He was also well liked and known for trying to do his duty. Therefore, he was granted the transfer to the VRC on January 15, 1865, by order of the War Department. In the Veteran Reserve, Corporal Nelson would do light duty, such as serve as a hospital nurse or clerk, and therefore be able to continue his military duty with pay. But it was soon evident that Nelson was too sick and disabled by his wounds to even fulfill his reserve corps duties.

Discharged: Corporal Thomas Nelson was mustered out and given a certificate of disability for discharge on July 10, 1865, at Washington, DC. He was paid the money due to him for his service upon discharge and returned home.

Nelson received a hundred-dollar bounty in January 1868, which was given to him pursuant to an act of compensation passed on July 28, 1866. As stated in the introduction, this act provided a hundred dollars to any soldier who was given a discharge due to serious, incapacitating wounds received in battle, no matter how short his term of service.

Biography: Thomas Nelson (or Ahpetahgezhick) was the son of David and David's first wife, Mary Awnemequoung Nelson. David was also known as Chief David Shoppenagonce ("Little Needles") or Shawbwawawnegoonse and was a well-known and respected chief of the Chippewa (*Avery*). He was a hunter, trapper, expert marksman, and nature guide for hunters and anglers. "Little Needles" was also a member of the highest order of the Midewiwin—the Grand Medicine Society.

Often Chief Shoppenagonce would join with his good friend Thomas Kechittigo, and sometimes Tom's wife, Mary, to participate in Indian social evenings hosted by Mr. Nels Michelson, a lumber baron of Grayling, Crawford County. These evenings were pleasant affairs in which the participants told Indian stories, sang native songs, and performed war dances. Bountiful suppers were served, and Indian crafts were sold to add to the treasury of the Ladies Aid Society of the Grayling Methodist Episcopal Church. Shoppenagonce and the Kechittigos were members of said church. As many as 175 people from town would attend these affairs (*Avalanche*).

Old Chief Shoppenagonce died on December 25, 1911, and left quite an historical legacy. He was buried in Elmwood Cemetery in Grayling (*Ibid.*).

At age twenty-three, Tom married Mary Wawwawsawmoquay Fisher, age eighteen, on January 6, 1859, at Taymouth, Saginaw County. She the daughter of James and Wawsaychewawnoquay Fisher. The marriage was officiated by Austin Smith, justice of the peace, and witnessed by Justus Ashman and Rev. Thomas Dutton. Rev. Dutton was chief (or head man) and an Anishinabe Methodist minister associated with the Taymouth Anishinabek Methodist Mission. He was also the father of Luther (or Luke) Dutton, who was a comrade of Tom's in Company K.

Mary Fisher Nelson's siblings were: Keshegewawnoquay, who married Rev. Daniel Whedon; Taybawgwawsegayquay, who married Rev. Nathan Whedon; Kawwawnawnoquay (also known as Charlotte), who married Samuel Chatfield, a Company K comrade and brother-in-law to Mary's husband, Thomas; OShaw-wawneghegoquay; Shawwawnepenayne; and Julia (also known as Ogawbayawbwa), who married Peter Gruett Jr. Peter was also a Company K comrade and brother-in-law to Thomas. Both Whedon men were associated with the Taymouth Indian Mission.

Thomas and Mary were the parents of five children: Elizabeth, born September 15, 1864; Lucy or Louise (also known as Wesawbawnoquay), born August 20, 1866; Frank, born September 15, 1868; Daniel, born October 10, 1870; and Jane, born August 3, 1872. All the children were baptized by Alex Chippeway, an Anishinabe lay minister of the Salem and Bradley Indian Missions near Allegan of Allegan County (*Reuter*).

Frank Nelson was a laborer in his adult years and remained unmarried. He died on May 10, 1890, at age twenty-four from consumption (tuberculosis) and complications from the amputation of one of his arms due to an abscess.

Thomas Nelson had forty acres of land in Isabella County under the first article of the treaty of August 2, 1855, and the second article of the treaty of October 19, 1864, with the Chippewa of Saginaw, Swan Creek, and Black River. The land description is the northeast quarter of the southeast quarter of section 5 in township 15 north of range 4 west. He was granted a certificate on May 27, 1871 (*Land Records*).

Before he entered the service, Thomas was described by friends and neighbors as a healthy, robust young man. Upon his return home, friends and relatives could see the steady decline in his health due to his wound and the early stage of pulmonary tuberculosis, which he may have contracted while in the service. The wound in his right thigh became a constant running sore and gave Thomas much difficulty and pain in walking. His leg was also very swollen from the site of the wound up to his right side. Thomas tried to hold a job in whatever he could find to support his wife and five children and worked briefly for lumberman G. W. Foster in Saginaw County.

Application #106,301 for an invalid pension was submitted for Thomas on April 10, 1866.

Mary died in 1875 and left Thomas as sole caretaker for their children. He struggled on as best he could. Finally, on February 2, 1876, Thomas received Invalid Pension Certificate #137,579, which paid four dollars a month retroactive to July 11, 1865.

Anishinabek doctors Eliza Grewett and Thomas's father-in-law, James Fisher, treated Thomas's wounds in the traditional manner with herbs and poultices. As his health continued to decline, a neighbor and friend, Barney Whitemore (Whitmore or Pamawedunk), and his wife, Lucy, helped care for Thomas and his children.

When he realized that death was near, Thomas asked his brother-in-law and Company K comrade, Peter Gruet Jr., if he would be guardian to his children (see Gruet file). Gruet agreed, knowing that the Nelson children were as fond of him as he was of them.

On August 26, 1877, Thomas Nelson died in Taymouth Township. His death certificate lists the cause of death as inflammation of the lungs, but his war injury and tuberculosis may also have contributed to his demise. He was buried (possibly with military honors) in the Chippewa Indian Cemetery (Wheaton/Wheadon Cemetery) on Seymour Road, Birch Run, in Taymouth Township.

After Nelson died, Peter Gruet Jr. took the youngest children, Lucy, Frank, Daniel, and Jane, to live with him and his family. The combined families are found under the name "Peter Gressett" on the 1880 federal census of the town of James in Saginaw County.

On May 20, 1878, Peter Grewett (or Gruet) Jr. was appointed guardian for the youngest children of his brother-in-law and army buddy by the probate court of Saginaw County.

Application #289,420, to obtain a dependent children's (a minor's—or children under sixteen) pension was filed for Grewett (or Gruet) Jr. on January 30, 1882. He applied in order to obtain money to help in providing for the three youngest Nelson children—Frank, Daniel, and Jane. The application for the minor Nelson children was not approved for Gruet because, sometime after 1882, Peter Grewett (or Gruet) Jr., as claimant, died. It's hoped that the older Nelson children, friends of the family, or another appointed guardian would have assumed some responsibility and care for the youngest siblings.

Nesogot, Joseph, Private (Also Known as Private Joseph Williams)—See the Joseph Williams File

Neveaux, William, Corporal

Enlistment: Enlisted as a corporal on July 8, 1863, at La Pointe, Madeline Island, Ashland County, Wisconsin, by Lieutenant William A. McClelland, First Michigan Sharpshooters, for three years.

Age: Sixteen, born February 9, 1847, in La Pointe.

Occupation: A sailor (or crewman) on Great Lakes freighters

Residence: La Pointe

Physical Description: Five feet four and a half inches tall, dark brown eyes, black hair, and a dark complexion. Examining physician was not listed.

Mustered: July 20, 1863, at Detroit, Wayne County, by Lieutenant Colonel John R. Smith, First Michigan Sharpshooters

Military Service: Corporal William Neveaux was reported to have joined his regiment as a drummer. Read about the duties of a drummer in Daniel Ashman's file. In March 1864, he was detailed to the Color Guard where he had the honor of escorting and guarding the regiment's colors and its color bearers.

From May 28 to July 11 of the said year, William was detailed by his captain to be an interpreter at Armory Square General Hospital in Washington, DC, by special order to the "Defenses of Washington." Most likely, he was employed by the hospital staff as an interpreter for the wounded and sick Anishinabek soldiers.

In August 1864, Neveaux was listed as ill or sick of disease. The diagnosis was not given. It is assumed that his illness was the result of conditions caused by inclement weather, poor camp hygiene, and substandard food.

A notation on his pension papers mentioned a wound near his spine caused by a piece of metal from a shell burst. The place of the battle was not noted. Treatment of such an injury would have included simple cold water dressings. These dressings were made of folded lint soaked in cold water, put on the wound, and held in place by a cloth wrap or adhesive plaster. The dressings were changed frequently (*Schaadt*).

In September 1864, William served again as a hospital attendant at Armory Square General Hospital. During his war years, William wrote frequently to his brother, Joseph, with whom he was close, about his experiences, and received many letters back from Joseph.

For reasons not given, Corporal Neveaux was reduced to the rank of private on May 1, 1865.

Discharged: Private William Neveaux was mustered out and honorably discharged on July 28, 1865, at Delaney House, Georgetown, Washington, DC. At that time, he requested that all correspondence be sent to his brother, Joseph Neveau, at La Pointe. William returned to Detroit on the steamer *Morning Star*. On August 7, he was given payment due to him for his service at Jackson, Jackson County, and returned home to La Pointe.

Biography: William Neveaux (also known as William Neveau) was the son of Alexis (or Alexander) and Maria (or Mary) Ojamajikwe/Ogemahquay (Bassinet) Neveaux. Alexis was born about 1797 in Quebec, Canada. Maria was an Anishinawbequa native born in Wisconsin about 1800. She was the daughter of Jean Baptiste and? Bassinet or Bazinet (pron. Bass-in-a).

Alexis worked as a voyager (or boatman) in the fur trade at Montreal, Ile de Montreal, Quebec, Canada, for about three years beginning in 1818. As a voyager, Alexis would travel far, work tirelessly, and live simply. The voyager men were of stocky build and paddled their canoes for long hours. They would subsist for months on pea soup, corn mush, bison pemmican, and pork fat (*Sivertson*). Voyagers earned low wages, and most of them were indentured French Canadians or Metis—those of mixed French Canadian and North American Indian heritage.

Sometime around the years of 1821 or 1822, Alexis emigrated from Canada to Sault Ste. Marie (the Soo), Chippewa County, Michigan, where he met and married Maria Bassinet.

After their marriage, Alexis and Maria went to Wisconsin, where they had the following children: Mary, born at Wisconsin River; Margarette, born in 1823 in Lac Du Flambeau; Michel, born in 1827 in St. Croix; and Louis, born about 1830 at Snake River (*Research*).

Following Louis's birth, the family moved to La Pointe, Madeline Island, Ashland County, Wisconsin. At La Pointe, the following children joined the family: Nancy, born about 1836; Jean Baptist, born December 17, 1837; Joseph, born April 4, 1842; and William, born February 9, 1847.

All the Neveaux children were baptized soon after their births in the rite of the Roman Catholic Church. William was baptized on February 14, 1847, by Catholic missionary Father Otto C. Skolla. Godparents for William were Amable and Sophie Dufort *(Ibid.)*.

By the 1850 federal census of La Pointe, Alexis Neveaux had accumulated real estate valued at $1,000. In the various census tallies, he was listed as a laborer and fisherman in addition to being a voyager. He would be elected supervisor of the town of La Pointe in 1871.

At age twenty-four, William married first to Sophie Lemieux, age sixteen, on March 28, 1869, in a ceremony officiated by Catholic missionary Father John Chebul. Witnesses to the marriage were Ignatius and Charlotte Robidoux. Sophie was the daughter of Jean Baptiste and Adelaide Gosslin Lemieux *(Ibid.)*.

William and Sophie had two daughters: Mary, born 1869; and Adalaide (or Adelia), born February 26, 1872. Adelia died April 21, 1912.

Sophie Neveaux died at the age of twenty-seven on February 9, 1874. Her funeral Mass was conducted by Rev. Father Francis H. Pfaller *(Ibid.)*.

William's second marriage was to Elizabeth Newago, the daughter of Louis and Charlotte Gosselin Newago. The couple was married in a Catholic rite on April 15, 1874, in Bayfield, Ashland County, Wisconsin. Father John Chebul officiated at the ceremony, which was witnessed by John Buffalo and Charlotte Belanger.

The Neveaux couple were the parents of the following children: Alexis, born February 17, 1876; Joseph, born October 20, 1877, who married Lucy Dufault; Charlotte, born September 26, 1879, who married Antoine Buffalo; John, born February 14, 1881, and drowned at age sixteen on December 18, 1898, when he fell through the lake ice while skating; Elizabeth, born March 13, 1885; Louis William, born June 4, 1888; and Narcissus Nelson (known as Nelson), born July 2, 1896. He served in World War I and did not marry.

Nelson was a caretaker for summer residents on Madeline Island *(On The Rock)*. He died in 1967 and is buried in the St. Joseph Catholic Mission Cemetery, which is also known as Middlefort and Old Indian Cemetery at La Pointe.

During his postwar years, William Neveaux earned what living he could for his family by fishing and working on the boats in the Great Lakes. He suffered quite a bit from rheumatism in his right arm and shoulder, which caused him much pain in the rigors of fishing.

On September 5, 1899, Application #1,234,919 for an invalid pension was filed for William Neveaux under the more liberal Act of June 27, 1890. This act covered those soldiers who served ninety days or more, had an honorable discharge, and was designated for the benefit of widows and children. William stated that his infirmities of rheumatism in the right arm and shoulder kept him from being able to work.

The first claim was abandoned due to a misunderstanding and the failure of Neveaux to appear for examination. So, on May 13, 1908, William reapplied for a pension under the Act of February 6, 1907, in which he cited the same reasons and used the same application number.

Neveaux received Invalid Pension Certificate #1,148,992 on August 17, 1908, which paid twelve dollars a month. On May 31, 1912, William again petitioned the US Pension Office to be placed on the pension roll of the United States under the provisions of the Act of May 11, 1912, a more liberal act than that of the Act of February 6, 1907, which preceded it. On June 3, 1912, William's pension payments increased to seventeen dollars a month.

Neveaux enjoyed getting together in camaraderie with his GAR friends of Bayfield's A. E. Burnside Post #249. In September 1913, the *Bayfield County Press* printed the following entry:

> Veterans Meet on Madeline Island
>
> In September, 1913, Col. Frederick Woods held a gathering of Civil War veterans at his summer home at Nebraska Row on Madeline Island. He arrived aboard his yacht at 11:45 am. in Bayfield, and took the party over to the island. They consisted of Bayfield's GAR "boys" and a few "camp followers." They were treated to a meal of "good old army pork and beans" and "pie just like mother used to make." After the meal, they enjoyed conversation and cigars on the Colonel's veranda (Bayfield).

Listed among the twenty-three old soldiers who attended the dinner was William Neveaux, age sixty-eight, of the First Michigan Sharpshooters.

According to the treaty concluded September 30, 1854, with the Chippewa Indians of Lake Superior and the Mississippi, and subsequent legislation that included the act of Congress approved on August 1, 1914, William Neveaux received some land in Wisconsin. He was allotted sixty acres located in the north half of the south half of the southwest quarter and the north half of the south half of the south half of the southwest quarter of section 13 in township 46 north of range 2 west. William was granted a certificate on September 5, 1919, which passed to his heirs. He was also allotted twenty acres located in the south half of the southwest quarter of the southeast quarter of section 4 in township 48 north of range 3 west. William was granted a certificate for this acreage on February 16, 1924, which passed to his heirs (*Land Records*).

William Neveaux died at the age of sixty-eight on October 16, 1914, at La Pointe. His death was attributed to angina pectoris, which is caused by paroxysmal pain characterized by severe constriction about the chest occurring suddenly due to emotional stress or physical exertion (*Blakiston*). Having complained of rheumatism during the war and after his discharge, William may have had rheumatic fever sometime during his early life that would have weakened his heart as he grew older.

William's burial was attended by members of his post and conducted with religious and military protocol. His burial site is marked with a military stone and is in the St. Joseph Catholic Mission Cemetery in La Pointe (*Cadotte*).

After William's death, Application #1,036,907 for a widow's pension was filed for Elizabeth on November 13, 1914. She received a Widow's Pension Certificate #788,633 on April 9, 1915, which paid twelve dollars a month retroactive to November 13, 1914. By 1930, having attained the age of seventy-five, Elizabeth received monthly pension payments of forty dollars. This amount was the maximum monthly payment allowed to the widow of a Civil War Union veteran.

Elizabeth Neveaux suffered a stroke in January or February 1939 and required constant care until her death at 11:00 p.m. on July 30 of said year. She may be buried near her husband in St. Joseph's Cemetery.

Newton, William, Private

Enlistment: Enlisted as a private on July 4, 1863, at Elbridge (another document states Pentwater), Oceana County, by Captain Edwin V. Andress, First Michigan Sharpshooters, for three years.

Age: Seventeen, born February 2, 1846, in "Grand River Land" (Grand Rapids area) Kent County.

Occupation: Laborer

Residence: Pentwater, Oceana County

Physical Description: Five feet five, black eyes, black hair, and a dark complexion. Examining physician was Dr. Jacob B. McNett, assistant surgeon, First Michigan Sharpshooters.

Mustered: July 11, 1863, at Detroit, Wayne County, by Lieutenant Colonel John R. Smith, First Michigan Sharpshooters

Military Service: Records show that William lost his .58-caliber Springfield Rifle Musket sometime between September and October 1863, and his pay was docked for its replacement. The loss took place when the sharpshooters guarded the Confederate confine at Camp Douglas in Chicago, Cook County, Illinois.

On June 17, 1864, during a battle at Petersburg, Newton was reported missing in action when, in reality, he was captured by the rebels while charging the enemy's breastworks. He was held for a few days in an old tobacco warehouse in Petersburg and then put on a train of cattle cars with other prisoners and taken to Camp Sumter. This camp, also called Andersonville Prison, was located in Andersonville, Georgia. At this prison camp, he was subjected to inhumane conditions and deprivation.

In November 1864, as General William T. Sherman closed in on southern strongholds, Pvt. Newton and other prisoners were sent by cattle railcar from Andersonville Prison to Camp Lawton Prison at Millen, Georgia. He remained there until November of said year when he was sent to another stockade prison camp in Savannah, Georgia, to await his release from confinement. Newton was finally paroled from Savannah on November 26, 1864, and found his way to Camp Parole, Maryland, on December 3, 1864.

Camp Parole was a camp for paroled prisoners in which both captured Confederates and former Union prisoners who had been paroled by the South were sent for exchange. The camp was also a holding area for Union soldiers who had deserted and whose units were in the area. At this camp, Newton was treated by physicians, had a bath, given a new suit of clothes, and partook of nourishing food. On December 9, William was granted a thirty-day furlough.

Newton returned from his furlough to Camp Parole and was then sent to Camp Chase, Ohio, on February 16, 1865, where he reported on February 20.

Camp Chase was a military training camp for Union troops, which included a section for use as a prison camp for Confederate prisoners. The Confederate cemetery contains 2,260 graves. Newton was again granted a second furlough for thirty days on February 24. He returned to Camp Chase and was sent to the provost marshal in Washington, DC, on April 2 to rejoin his regiment on April 15.

Discharged: Private William Newton was mustered out and honorably discharged on July 28, 1865, at Delaney House, Georgetown, Washington, DC. He returned to Detroit on the steamer *Morning Star.* On August 7, Newton was paid the money owed to him for his service at Jackson, Jackson County.

Biography: William Newton (also known as Wawachen, Wabwahchin, and Itwogezhick) was the son of Oliver and Bootagogua Newton. He was known to have at least two brothers, John and Joseph, and a sister named Elizabeth.

After William returned from the service, he settled in Pentwater. His first marriage was to Martha Kewaquam (or Kewaquon) on November 24, 1866. The ceremony was conducted by Harvey Sayles, justice of the peace, and took place at the Taboum school house in Elbridge Township of said county. The couple were reported to have owned 160 acres of government homestead land, which William farmed about twelve miles from Pentwater. William and Martha remained together for a year and then separated. There were no children of this marriage. Martha died about 1875 in Pentwater and was buried in the Catholic cemetery near Sayles Corners in Elbridge.

William married for the second time, according to accepted Anishinabek custom and practice (agreement between the couple and their parents) and before Martha died, to Alice Sahwatoqua (or Mashkeyashe) in 1868. The couple then moved to Scottsville, Mason County. William and Alice were the parents of three children: Benjamin, born about 1871; Martha, born about 1873; and John, born about 1876.

In his later years, William told his children that he could not marry their mother, Alice, since he was still legally married to his first wife, Martha, when he began living with Alice according to accepted Anishinabek custom and practice.

William and Alice's relationship was quite stormy, and the two finally separated sometime in 1877 or 1878 and sold all but four acres of their property. Alice moved to Free Soil, Mason County, and was still living there in August 1924.

After his separation from Alice, William moved to Leland, Leelanau County, in 1883, where he met and cohabited with Angeline Nebawnegezhik, the daughter of an Odawa (Ottawa) chief, Shanon Nebawnegezhick, and his wife, Nawbenaguay.

Application #762,351 for an invalid pension was filed for William on March 17, 1890. His health had steadily declined since he was released from Camp Lawton Prison in Georgia. Due to the privations of prisoner-of-war conditions and the exposure of prison life, William suffered from scurvy, chronic diarrhea, and weakness in his back and limbs due to rheumatism. These conditions constantly plagued him, interfered with his ability to make a living, and were the reasons that he sought an invalid pension.

William did seek medical help from the local Anishinabequa doctor, Bahqwahte-goqua, who treated him in the traditional manner with various medicinal herbs and poultices. She also did what she could for him when he was home on furlough and after his discharge from the service.

Newton reapplied for his pension on September 10, 1890. In early 1893, William and Angeline decided to make their relationship legal by Christian rite.

The couple chose Rev. John Jacobs as their officiant. Rev. Jacobs was a farmer and an Anishinabe Methodist Episcopal minister at the Northport, Leelanau County, Indian Mission Church (*Reuter*). William and Angeline were married at their home in Leland, Leelanau County, at 1:00 p.m. on March 19, 1893. Witnesses to the ceremony were Joseph Pamageshik of Traverse City and Aaron Pequongay (also known as Aaron Sargonquatto), a Company K comrade residing in Gills Pier. At the time of their marriage, William was forty-eight, and Angeline was thirty-six. Sometime after 1900, William and Angeline moved to Benzie County. The couple did not have children.

William's application was rejected in February 1902 because "a notable degree of disability was not shown under the Act of June 27, 1890." Finally, after several more attempts to obtain a pension, Invalid Pension Certificate #1,143,892 was granted to William under the Act of February 6, 1907, citing the same reasons outlined by William in his first application. His monthly pension payments totaled twelve dollars.

Under the Act of May 11, 1912, William's monthly pension payments were increased to seventeen dollars. These payments were again increased to twenty-three dollars and then to thirty dollars a month by February 1921.

Angeline and William attended Methodist Church camp meetings together, as was the custom of many of their people. During the singing of hymns, William was known to add his fine musical voice, which was appreciated by all who attended these meetings.

William joined the Woolsey GAR Post #399 based in Northport, Leelanau County, where he enjoyed the company of many of his service comrades.

After 1912, the couple moved their residence to Williamsburg, Grand Traverse County, where Angeline continued her devoted care of William. It's noted that William and Angeline took residence in both Yuba and Williamsburg.

On December 11, 1921, William left the following will found in his pension papers.

"Yuba, Michigan. I hereby leave or give my land of 4 acres and house to my Granddaughter Elizabeth Wasaquam. I am William

Newton." Witnesses: William Petoskey, Josephine Wistmon and Robert D. Agosa.

The amount of the estate was estimated at about $400. The little house was off the road and surrounded by heavy timber.

Elizabeth Wasaquam was the daughter of Julia, who was the daughter of a former marriage of Anishinabek custom and practice of Angeline with a man known as Louis John (or Shinknakahshie). William was very fond of Elizabeth and treated her as his own granddaughter. At the time that the will was probated, Elizabeth was living in Traverse City, Grand Traverse County.

William Newton died at the age of seventy-five at his residence at RR#2, Williamsburg, Acme Township, Grand Traverse County, on January 23, 1922. The cause of death was listed as mitral stenosis or a disease of the mitral valve of the heart causing obstruction to the flow of blood through the left atrioventricular opening (*Blakiston*). His place of burial is in the Yuba Cemetery near Acme in said county. A bronze plaque, which lies flush with the ground, is William's memorial marker.

On March 5, 1922, Application #1,184,599 was filed for Angeline Newton for the purpose of being placed on the pension roll of the United States under the provisions of the Act of April 19, 1908. She also sought the accrued pension due to her husband at the time of his death.

When her application was filed, she was living alone and trying to support herself by making baskets. Her reputation was that of a good person who took good care of her husband in his declining years.

Under the Act of May 1, 1920, Angeline was granted a Widow's Pension Certificate #956,009. She received thirty dollars a month, in which payments began on February 2, 1922.

On February 14, 1925, the First National Bank of Traverse City was appointed to be Angeline's guardian since she had been deemed incompetent. The reason for the guardian was to protect Angeline's pension income from being used by someone else. It was also considered that with this protection Angeline would not become a ward of the state. Her monthly payments were increased to forty dollars a month on July 4, 1931. During this time of being deemed incompetent, Angeline did visit her granddaughter, Elizabeth, and Elizabeth did see to some of her grandmother's needs when she returned the visits.

Angeline Newton died at her residence at RR#2, Williamsburg, on February 4, 1936. She was about the age of eighty-six, and the cause of death was listed as lobar pneumonia. Lobar pneumonia is an acute febrile (fever) disease involving one or more lobes of the lung due to infection by one of the pneumococci in the blood (*Ibid*). At her advanced age, Angeline did not have the strength to recover from her infection. Her place of burial was probably near her husband in Yuba Cemetery.

Mrs. Newton was one of the last two surviving widows of Company K men. She was followed in death by the last widow, Susan (Allen) Pequongay (Mrs. Aaron), on July 20, 1939, at her home in Traverse City. See file on Aaron Pequongay/Sargonquatto.

Ohbowakemo, James, Private

Enlistment: Enlisted as a private on February 1, 1864, at Kalamazoo, Kalamazoo County, by Captain J. A. Smith, First Michigan Sharpshooters, for three years. This enlistment was credited to the Second Congressional District, Kalamazoo County, Schoolcraft Township, and satisfied the requirement of a man from that district.

Age: Twenty-six, born about 1838 in Isabella County.

Occupation: Laborer

Residence: Schoolcraft, Kalamazoo County

Physical Description: Five feet nine, black eyes, black hair, and a copper complexion. Examining physician was Dr. N. O. Nitebeeck.

Mustered: February 2, 1864, by R. C. Dennison, provost marshal at Kalamazoo, Kalamazoo County

Military Service: During the Battle of Spotsylvania on May 12, 1864, Private James Ohbowakemo claimed that he was struck in the left side of the breast and shoulder by a large clod of dirt thrown by the explosion of an artillery shell. According to James's medical records, there is no evidence to support his claim of this occurrence.

Medical records do show that James was admitted to L'Ouverture USA General Hospital in Alexandria, Virginia, from his regiment on May 16, 1864, suffering from lobar pneumonia. Lobar pneumonia occurs when there is an acute febrile (or fever) disease involving one or more lobes of the lung due to infection by one of the pneumococci (*Blakiston*).

The doctors at L'Ouverture treated James's pneumonia with painful cupping and blistering (*Bollet*). This procedure was thought to be an anti-inflammatory measure that would help to draw out "poisons" away from his lungs and into his skin.

Opiates were given to the soldier for pain relief and cough suppression *(Ibid.)*. James remained at the hospital until he returned to duty with his regiment on October 25.

On June 28, 1865, Pvt. Ohbowakemo was admitted from his regiment to a division hospital near Washington, DC, suffering from diarrhea caused by poor food and contaminated water.

The doctors treated James's diarrhea with an emetic such as castor oil to induce vomiting and as a laxative to cleanse the system *(Ibid.)*. Dover's powder (a mixture of ipecac and opium) was administered to induce perspiration, and an opium pill was given for pain *(Ibid.)*. His diet consisted of boiled water, diluted coffee and tea, barley water, rice water, and broth of meat extract. James returned to his regiment on July 10, 1865.

Discharged: Private James Ohbowakemo was mustered out and honorably discharged on July 28, 1865, at Delaney House, Georgetown, Washington, DC. He returned to Michigan on the steamer *Morning Star*. On August 7, he was paid money owed to him for his service at Jackson, Jackson County.

Biography: James Ohbowakemo was also known as James R. Oshburn. As a young child, James lived around Grand Rapids in Kent County.

When he was a teenager, he moved with his family to Newaygo County, where he ran rafts on the Muskegon River for Mr. Henry Pego. About 1859, James moved to Isabella County.

James was married four times during his lifetime. Each marriage was conducted in accordance with traditional Anishinabek custom and practice (agreement of the couple and their parents). His first wife was Waindawbequay (whose father was Nayawpeting), whom he married in the fall of 1865 in Isabella County. She died at the age of twenty-three of consumption (or tuberculosis) in December 1871 in said county. There were accounts of children of this union, but they were reported to have died at very early ages.

Sometime in 1872, James married for the second time to Kapushkemoqua (or Peishkawmoquay). The couple were together for about six years and had two children who died in infancy. Kapushkemoqua died in 1878 and was buried in the Anishinabek burial ground in Nottawa Township of Isabella County.

In the spring of 1881, James married his third wife, Kewaytenoquay, in Nottawa Township. Before she married James, Kewaytenoquay had been previously married twice. She was first married to Quakegezhick, with whom she had a son, Wawsogon Jackson. Wawsogon died in 1869 in Saginaw, Saginaw County. Secondly, Kewaytenoquay married Abram Migesee, or Abram Joshua, the son of

Joshua Migesee. Abram died suddenly at the Ionia House of Corrections on May 6, 1881. At that time, he was the only Anishinabe to have died in that prison. Abram had been incarcerated on a disorderly charge and a default of $200 bail. Abram's father, Joshua, went to the prison and took his son's body home to be buried.

As mentioned previously, James was Kewaytenoquay's third husband. The couple were the parents of two children, a child who died in infancy and a daughter, Wausechewawnoquay (or Mary), born March 31, 1886. After Wausechewawnoquay's birth, the family moved to Elba in Lapeer County so that James could seek work in the wood camps.

On September 30, 1886 or 1887, while living in Elba, Application #624,477 for an invalid pension was submitted for James Ohbowakemo. He cited disease of the lungs (called consumption or tuberculosis), rheumatism, scrofula (tuberculosis of the cervical (or neck) lymph nodes), and injury to the chest as his reasons for the application.

James and his family moved from Elba to stay for a short time on the Canadian Indian Reserve near Sarnia. While there, Kewaytenoquay died and was buried on the reserve in the winter of 1887. James was left to care for his tiny daughter. Shortly after Kewaytenoquay's death, James and little Wausechewawnoquay (Mary) moved back to Isabella County, Michigan.

From the time he came home from the service, James's health had steadily declined. His friends had noticed that he had a persistent cough, which at times produced blood, and that his neck was quite swollen at times. He complained of pain in the left side of his chest and shoulder and exhibited a marked weakness that prevented him from holding a steady job. James treated his ailments with traditional herbs and poultices obtained from local Anishinabek medicine men, one of whom was Thomas Chatfield.

Known as a powerfully strong, healthy man and the best runner in Isabella County before he entered the service, James was hard-pressed to put in a half day's work at manual labor when he returned home. When he was able, he did some hunting and trapping and sold the furs. Sometimes he worked for Henry Pego (who also had moved to Isabella County) at cutting brush and saw logs in the winter. Pego had always considered James a steady, hardworking man and employed him when he was able to work.

When James and his little daughter arrived back in Isabella County, he made the difficult decision to entrust the permanent care and raising of his child to

Bawbaws-noquay. She was the wife of his Company K comrade John Waubanoo, in Weidman of Isabella County.

James married for the fourth time to Lucy Sawgegwonnaybequay/Sawgagwon Petwawetum, the widow of Peter Petwawetum (or Peters). Peters died on December 8, 1889.

The couple's marriage took place on May 15, 1890, in Deerfield Township of Isabella County near Beal City. After their marriage, the pair stayed with Lucy's son, Frank Peters, for one year and raised some corn on Frank's land. The following fall, they moved in with Lucy's son, Isaac Peters, stayed for two years, and farmed on Isaac's property.

In 1893, during their stay with Isaac, James built a little log house on Isaac's land and did some planting when his health would permit. The corn that the couple raised earned a very meager income for them. There were no children of this union.

While living on the Peters's property, James resubmitted his invalid pension claim on November 18, 1890, under the Act of June 27, 1890, and again in November and December 1892. The claim was rejected on August 30, 1895, on the grounds of no disability due to disease of the lungs. He submitted another application on September 29, 1895.

In addition to the earnings from their meager corn crops, James and Lucy were mainly supported by charity from friends and neighbors and with money from the poor funds of the county. Lucy contributed what she could to support the couple by making and selling baskets.

James Ohbowakemo died on December 21, 1895, in Nottawa Township of Isabella County. His demise was from the very causes that he had listed in his original pension claim. He lies at rest in the Anishinabek burial ground in said township.

On January 13, 1896, Application #626,932 for a widow's pension was submitted for Lucy Ohbowakemo. James's claim was finally approved and he received (after his death) Pension Certificate #931,034 issued in March 1897. Lucy finished out James's claim, which paid her forty-two dollars a month, and retroactive to September 30, 1887, up to the date of his death on December 21, 1895. That pension was approved for disease of the lungs (or tuberculosis), scrofula (or tuberculosis of the cervical lymph nodes), rheumatism, and injury to the chest.

Lucy received her Widow's Pension Certificate #443,564 (based on James's diseases listed previously) on May 3, 1896. This certificate paid eight dollars a month and was retroactive to January 13, 1896. She also received an additional two dollars a month for Wawsechewawnoquay's support (as the daughter of the soldier) while she was in Bawbawsnoquay's home. The two dollars a month would cease when Wawsechewawnoquay reached the age of sixteen in 1902.

On July 25, 1896, Jacob Yuncker, a shoemaker from Germany, and the Nottawa Township supervisor and postmaster at Beal City, submitted an application for a Supplemental to the Widow's Pension Certificate #626,932 for a pension for children under sixteen years of age (minor child's claim). This pension application was under the liberal Act of June 27, 1890, and made on behalf of Wawsechewawnoquay's support. Mr. Yuncker had previously been granted guardianship of the estate of Wawsechewawnoquay on February 25, 1896, by the probate court of Isabella County. The guardianship was granted since Wawsechewawnoquay's father and birth mother had died and Lucy Ohbowakemo was in failing health.

The Supplemental to the Widow's Pension Certificate #443,564 was granted to Yuncker on May 3, 1897, by Certificate #443,564 (same number). The certificate then paid two dollars a month (retroactive to January 13, 1896, and ended March 30, 1902) to him as guardian of Wawsechewawnoquay instead of to Lucy Ohbowakemo.

Jacob Yuncker was well acquainted with the James Ohbowakemo family since he saw to their aid from funds available to the poor. He also procured the coffin in which James was buried. Both the coffin and the funeral service were paid for from township funds.

On August 27, 1897, Lucy Ohbowakemo died at her son's residence in Deerfield Township of Isabella County. Her burial site is unknown, although she may have been buried in the Anishinabek burial ground in Nottawa Township.

Jacob Yuncker petitioned the Pension Office on September 1, 1897, to obtain the pension accrued to James Ohbowakemo's widow under the general law of June 1890. Under this law, monthly payments of twelve dollars, which were sent from the date of Lucy's death, would contribute to the support of Yuncker's ward, Wawsechewawnoquay. The petition was granted. Yuncker then submitted Application #662,292, for an original pension for minor children, on September 7, 1897, for further support for his ward. At first, the Pension Certificate #461,296 for Minor Children was granted to Yuncker as guardian in March 1898. The certificate paid twelve dollars a month to Yuncker and was retroactive to December 1895.

On May 3, 1898, the payments under said Pension Certificate #461,296, which paid twelve dollars a month, were stopped. The stoppage was due to the reason that Wawsechewawnoquay was already funded under the general law of June 27, 1890, with Pension Certificate #443,564 and was receiving her increase of twelve dollars a month paid to Yuncker as guardian.

Wawsechewawnoquay (Mary) married at the age of eighteen on September 12, 1904, to Amos Elk and was known as Mary Elk.

On March 18, 1905, Jacob Yuncker died of paralysis at age sixty-seven in Nottawa Township, leaving Wawsechewawnoquay with no legal guardian.

On June 8, 1906, at the legal age of twenty-one and not in need of a guardian, a petition was submitted for Mary that requested that the balance of her Minor's Pension Certificate #461,296 payments of twelve dollars a month be sent to her retroactively from 1899 to 1902.

The general law of 1890 (Pension Certificate #443,564) had expired in 1902 when she attained the age of sixteen, and she had been eligible to then receive her minor's pension retroactively. Her request was granted upon submitting the proper identification of her name and marriage. Evidence indicated that she received the remaining retroactive pension payments.

Otashquabono, Leon, Private

Enlistment: Enlisted as a private on August 27, 1863, at Northport, Leelanau County, by Second Lieutenant Garrett A. Graveraet, First Michigan Sharpshooters, for three years.

Age: Twenty, born January 6, 1842 in Canada.

Occupation: Farmer

Residence: Little Traverse (now Harbor Springs), Emmet County

Physical Description: Five feet ten, black eyes, black hair, and a dark complexion. Examining physician was Dr. George S. Cornell, assistant surgeon, First Michigan Sharpshooters.

Mustered: October 21, 1863, at the confine for Confederate prisoners at Camp Douglas, Chicago, Cook County, Illinois, by Capt. Lowe, First Michigan Sharpshooters. The sharpshooters guarded the prison camp for seven months.

Military Service: Records show that Private Leon Otashquabono was not injured during his service but did suffer from acute rheumatism (painful swelling of the joints—rheumatoid arthritis), swelling of the legs, colds, inflammation of the lungs (pneumonitis or pneumonia), and a cough due to his exposure to the elements while in the trenches before Petersburg, Virginia.

Leon was not admitted to the field hospital, but upon orders from Capt. James S. Deland, he was treated for about four weeks in his company quarters by a regimental physician, Dr. Thomas Eagleson. Dr. Eagleson probably used cupping and blistering for Leon's pneumonia in the thought that the procedure would draw out (absorb) the so-called poison from his lungs into his skin (*Bollet*). Potassium iodide baths (for mild inflammatory effect) and opiates for the rheumatism were administered for pain (*Ibid.*). It would be almost a century before doctors discovered a relationship between an antecedent streptococcal (or strep throat) infection and various rheumatic diseases.

In May 1865, Private Otashquabono was assigned from his company and detailed to the provost guard as a policeman in Washington, DC. He was promoted to the rank of corporal on July 3, 1865.

Discharged: Corporal Leon Otashquabono was mustered out and honorably discharged on July 28, 1865, at Delaney House, Georgetown, Washington, DC. He returned to Detroit on the steamer *Morning Star*. On August 7, he was paid the money owed to him for his service at Jackson, Jackson County.

Upon his discharge, Leon was bedridden with his service-related illnesses for two months. It was difficult for him to hold a job as a laborer because of time lost due to his infirmities. For the rest of his life, Leon's health suffered from the effects of his wartime illnesses. He sought treatment for his ailments from traditional Anishinabek doctors and a Dr. Lewis of Charlevoix.

Biography: Leon Otashquabono was born in Canada, the son of Matihagina and Chingbequa.

His first marriage was to Marianne Giwaise (or Kewesa/Kewesa) on September 6, 1865. She was the daughter of Louis and Lucy Giwaise (or Kewasse, Kewesa). Father Seraphim Zorn, Roman Catholic priest of the mission area of Little Traverse, officiated at the rite of marriage. Witnesses were Daniel and Philomine Nisawakwad. One son was born of this union in 1866.

Marianne died at age twenty-three at Little Traverse on January 30 or 31, 1869. Her demise was caused by inflammation of the lungs (pneumonitis or pneumonia) due to infection caused by one of the pneumococci (*Blakiston*).

After Marianne's death, Leon and his young son went to live with Marianne's parents on their farm in Little Traverse. Leon worked as a farm laborer for his father-in-law and no doubt had loving help from the Kewesa grandparents in caring for the little boy. In the 1870 federal census of Little Traverse, Leon is listed with his son named "Otashquabono," age four, as members of the Kewesa household.

Leon's second marriage was to Mary Ann Kabaashqua Wemickwase on May 7,

1871, in Charlevoix, Charlevoix County. This marriage was also officiated by Father Zorn and witnessed by Basil and Mary Migsawbe.

Mary Ann Wemickwase was previously married (as was reported) for a short time to the widower Rev. Peter Greensky before he died. Greensky was a well-known minister in the Methodist Episcopal Church (see files on Benjamin and Jacob Greensky). The beloved pastor died at 10:00 a.m. on Sunday morning, April 8, 1866. His death was caused by a rapidly fatal form of pulmonary tuberculosis called "florid (bright red) phthisis."

After they were married, Leon and Mary Ann moved to Ironton in Charlevoix County. Sometime after 1875, the Otashquabono family moved from Ironton to Charlevoix in said county and then back again to Ironton in 1879 where they remained.

In the 1880 federal census of Hayes Township in Charlevoix County, the couple were listed with their children: Philomen, age ten; Rosa, age seven; Stephen, age six; Sophia Shigwadja, age five, who was born October 30, 1875; and Mary, age one. Of their children, only Sophia was still living in 1898.

During his postwar years, Leon was a proud member of the Ironton GAR Post #320 in Ironton, Charlevoix County, and Baxter GAR Post #119 also in said county. Leon attended his posts' functions when his health would allow him to do so.

On June 5, 1887, Leon wrote a letter (found in his pension papers) to former Regimental Captain James S. DeLand in response to DeLand. The letter is as follows:

Headquarters
Ironton Post No. 340, G.A.R.
Irronton, Charlevoix Co., Michigan, June 5, 1887

Capt. Jas. S. DeLand

Dear Comrade of Record, your letter of May 31st it found me as well as can be expected. I am very glad I have found you I have been looking for you about two years. There are some of the Boys at Charlevoix and some at Cross Village and some at Suttons Bay. I have not seen them lately there are some at Petoskey and some at Harbor Springs. James AwenKeshig resides at Charlevoix Mich. Francis Tabasash resides at Cross Village Emmet Co., Mich.

Alfred Pishawbay resides at Petoskey Emmet County. John O. Shomin resides at Harbor Springs Emmet Co. Mich. Lewis Shomin resides at Suttons Bay Leelanau Co. Mich. There were some of the Boys at Pent Water or near there I can't tell if they are there or not some up Lake Superior there is some 10 of the Boys around there when I see them I will speak to them or tell them where you are George Ashkebog is dead He died about a year ago at NorthPort Mich Sergt Scott died about seven years ago at Pentwater Mich will I was not sent to the hospital I was treated by the Regt. Doctor I caught cold you sent me to my quarters I was taken with cattarrah and cough ever since I would like to have you do what you can for me My health is very poor.

Please let me know when that reunion is and if I can get the money I will be there hoping to hear from you soon.

I Remain Yours in F.C.K.L.

Leon Otashauabono

On November 9, 1885, Application #553,786 was submitted for Leon Otashquabono for an invalid pension in which he cited his war-related ailments. He received Invalid Pension Certificate #363,488 on June 7, 1887, which paid four dollars a month for disability due to catarrh of head and throat. Catarrh is the inflammation of the mucous membranes of the nose and throat (*Ibid.*). His monthly rate was increased to eight dollars a month from May 14, 1890. Additional applications for increases in payments were rejected on September 6, 1894, September 7, 1900, and February 22, 1902.

On April 24, 1891, Leon applied for a pension under the generous Act of June 27, 1890, citing disease of eyes, headache, pain in his side, cough, and rheumatism. His claim was rejected on November 1, 1892, because he was not entitled to a rating under the Act of June 27, 1890, in excess of the eight dollars a month he already received under the general law. Leon resubmitted his claim on October 21, 1898, and February 28, 1902, with similar results.

Leon Otashquabono died of pneumonia at the age of sixty on April 3, 1902, when he was visiting Harbor Springs. Members of his Charlevoix GAR Post traveled by train to Harbor Springs to bury him with religious rites and military honors in the Catholic section of Lakeview Cemetery called Holy Childhood of Jesus Cemetery. The veterans from J. B. Richardson GAR Post #13 in Harbor Springs met the train and joined the funeral procession and ceremony (*Obit*). Leon's grave site is marked by a military stone and a metal angel memorial.

On May 5, 1902, Application #762,243 for a widow's pension was submitted for Mary Ann Otashquabono. The application was made under the more liberal general law of June 27, 1890. It requested the accrued pension due to Leon and also, to fulfill any unfinished claim. Mary was solely dependent upon her husband for support. He left no insurance but did leave a small house and lot in Eveline Township of Ironton to Mary. The property was located in lot 1 of block 4 of Bird's Addition and valued at seventy-five dollars.

In return for helping her daughter, Sophia, and her family with limited labor, Mary received most of her food and clothing.

Mary's application for a widow's pension was at first rejected on the grounds that the soldier's death from pneumonia was not due to catarrh of head and throat, for which he was pensioned and not shown otherwise to have been chargeable to his military service.

Mary resubmitted her claim, and it was accepted. She was granted a Widow's Pension Certificate #542,020 sometime after 1902. At first she received eight dollars a month, which was later increased to twelve dollars a month. On January 26, 1917 (under the act of September 8, 1916), Mary's monthly payments were increased to twenty dollars, retroactive to September 8, 1916, and remained the same until her death at Ironton sometime during or after 1917. Mary is buried near her husband in said cemetery.

Otto, Marcus, Private

Enlistment: Enlisted on May 18, 1863, at Isabella City (now Mt. Pleasant), Isabella County, by First Lieutenant William J. Driggs, First Michigan Sharpshooters, for three years.

    Age: Nineteen, born in August of 1842 in Gratiot County.

    Occupation: Farmer

    Residence: Isabella County

    Physical Description: Five feet eight, black eyes, black hair, and a dark complexion. Examining physician was Dr. George S. Cornell, assistant surgeon, First Michigan Sharpshooters.

    Mustered: May 26, 1863, at Detroit, Wayne County, by Lieutenant Colonel John R. Smith, First Michigan Sharpshooters

    Military Service: On June 10, 1863, Marcus became ill while training with his regiment and on guard duty at the Detroit Arsenal in Dearborn, Wayne County.

He was sent to the USA Post Hospital near the arsenal, diagnosed with intermittent fever (or malaria). The physicians treated Marcus's illness with doses of quinine from either powdered cinchona tree bark mixed with whiskey or water, or with pills of purified quinine sulfate (*Bollet*). Whiskey worked better because it masked the bitter taste of the quinine. On June 14, he returned to duty with his regiment.

Some military records state that Marcus was wounded on May 11, 1864, during the Battle of the Wilderness. But the Wilderness campaign was fought from May 5 to 6. After May 7, General Meade withdrew his forces from the Wilderness and proceeded to Spotsylvania Court House.

Private Marcus Otto was mentioned in the *Medical and Surgical History of the War of the Rebellion* as having been wounded in the right arm on May 12, 1864, and having undergone a "flap" type of surgery on that day (*Medical and Surgical*).

Captain James DeLand wrote a deposition (found in Otto's pension papers) on March 21, 1865, for Marcus Otto, which stated the following:

> I do hereby certify that Marcus Otto a private in Company K in the First Regiment of Sharp Shooters Michigan Volunteers was present at the Battle of Spotsylvania on May 12, 1864 with his command and was then and there while in the line of his duty as a soldier in action with the enemy was wounded in his right arm from a gun shot.
>
> James S. DeLand
Captain Company K First MSS

The gunshot wound (from a conical missile) that Marcus incurred May 12 shattered the ulna and radius bones of his lower right arm. He was taken immediately to a first aid station where a tourniquet was applied to his arm to staunch the bleeding. His arm was then washed in cold water and hastily bandaged.

From the first aid station, Marcus was then taken by ambulance wagon to his division hospital farther behind the lines where emergency surgery was performed. The doctors anesthetized Marcus with chloroform, amputated the right arm above the elbow, and recovered (or saved) the upper third of the humerus. They concluded the surgery with a flap procedure (*Kuz and Bengtson*). The flap method was used because of the speed in which the surgery could be performed. In this type of operation, flaps were made by placing the amputation knife down to the bone and allowing it to slide over the top of the bone and out the other side of the limb. The same procedure was used on the opposite side of the limb, which would create another flap. Then, with a forceps, arteries and veins were drawn in a distal direction and tied with ligatures of silk or cotton. The large nerves were pulled out as far as possible and cut, which allowed the stumps of the nerves to retract into the soft tissues of the stump. The end of the bone was smoothed with rasps, and then the flaps of muscle and skin would be drawn together over the smoothed end of the bone and sutured with wire or silk. Sometimes the wounds were left open, but mostly they were dressed (*Ibid.*).

After this procedure, the stump would be dressed with simple dressings, which consisted of lint dipped into cold water and held in place with a cloth wrap or adhesive plaster (*Schaadt*). Another method of sealing the stump was to wrap it in bandages coated with a soothing mixture of oils and bees wax called "cerate" and secure the wrappings with adhesive plaster (*Ibid.-Bollet*). The arm was probably supported with a contraption constructed of starch or plaster splints to limit motion. Opium pills were given to the patient to ease his pain. Conclusively, Marcus lost total use of what was left of his right arm.

Private Otto was transferred by ambulance wagon from his division hospital through Fredericksburg to Belle Plain Landing, Virginia, on May 25. He was put onto a hospital steamer and taken to L'Ouverture USA General Hospital in Alexandria, Virginia, where he was admitted on May 26. At L'Ouverture, fresh dressings and sealants were applied to the stump, and additional pain medication was given to him. Marcus could now enjoy a hearty, nourishing diet.

Discharged: Marcus remained at L'Ouverture Hospital until August 18, 1864, when he was mustered out and granted a discharge by reason of complete disability. His wound rendered him unsuitable to reenlist or enter the Veteran Reserve Corps. Otto's certificate was ordered by Major General Augur and granted by Dr. Edwin Bentley, surgeon, US Volunteers, in charge of L'Ouverture USA Hospital. Upon his discharge, Marcus was paid money owed to him for his service, and he returned to Michigan.

As stated in the introduction, by an act of the War Department issued during the Civil War, any soldier discharged from the service by reason of wounds received in battle was to receive a hundred-dollar bounty no matter how short his term of service. Due to his crippling wound, it is assumed that Marcus received this bounty.

After he returned home, Marcus settled on the farm located on his father's government trust land near Weidman in Isabella County.

Biography: Marcus Otto was the son of Wilson (or Wahcum Kenuikegeshik) and Martha Otto. Like his father, Marcus was also known as Kenuikegeshik, which means "the bird that flies at night" (*Otto*). He was the younger brother of Solomon Otto, who enlisted into Company K on the same day as Marcus.

On May 11, 1865, Application #68,140 for an invalid pension was filed for Marcus Otto. It was very difficult for him to hold any steady occupation or to do rigorous farming due to the loss of most of his right arm. After his discharge, the stump of Marcus's right arm had deteriorated to the point that it could not be fitted with a prosthetic extension.

In April 1867, Marcus married Mary Pamosayasquay/Moosaquay (which translates to Mary "Walking Woman") Nottawa, the daughter of Chief Nottawa and his wife, Washeqaway (or Martha), of Isabella County (*Avery*). Mary's siblings included Pemsay, Wakbenagoquay, Tom, Meesowaquay, John, and Mixaway. The Rev. Ernst G. H. Meissler, Evangelical German Lutheran missionary, officiated at the rite of marriage for Marcus and Mary in Union Township of Isabella County.

The couple were the parents of ten children, of which nine are listed as follows: George, born April 1870; twins, Mary and Julia, born 1877, Julia died in 1900; Peter Marcus, born 1878 and died in 1919; John, born in 1879 and died of consumption (or tuberculosis) on April 24 or 28, 1883; William, born in 1882 and died of brain fever (or cerebrospinal meningitis) on July 10, 1884; Esther, born May 22, 1884, and died of cerebrospinal meningitis on April 28, 1902; Joseph Foster, born February 24, 1885, and died in 1975; and Lee, born March 24, 1888, and died in 1921.

Marcus received his Invalid Pension Certificate #47,164 on June 4, 1872, which paid eighteen dollars a month due to the amputation of the lower part of his right arm. His pension was increased to twenty-four dollars a month beginning on June 4, 1874.

In 1879, Marcus applied for an arrears in pay granted by the Act of 1879. By 1889, he was receiving forty-five dollars a month, and his health was rapidly declining. Mary had sole responsibility for his care.

The wound that he incurred in the war had contributed greatly to the cause of his other ailments. He could not dress himself without Mary's aid and was confined to his bed a great deal of the time. He became quite deaf in his left ear, and his left leg was partially paralyzed. One can only imagine the pain that Marcus suffered and the feeling of helplessness of a man with one arm and a bum leg who tried to provide for his family.

Even though his infirmities kept him home most of the time, Marcus was a proud member of the GAR Wabano Post #250 in Mt. Pleasant and attended meetings when he was physically able to do so.

In a letter of August 1, 1900, and addressed to the secretary of the interior, Marcus described a problem that he faced:

Weidman, Michigan

Honorable Secretary of the Interior

I am an Indian and I fought through the War of the Rebellion. I lost one arm and I get from Pension Office $45.00 a month. The White people here at Weidman are about to appoint a guardian for me. I think I am capable of handling the money I receive from Govt. and support a large family with it. Somebody got a petition up and many signed to get a Guardian for me. I don't want no guardian for I have a sound mind. The White people got this petition up simply to make a little something of my income. Can they appoint a guardian for me? I want your opinion. I want you to write me if they can appoint a guardian for me or not.

In August 13, 1900 they will appoint a guardian for me.

Please write.

Mark Otto, Weidman, Mich.

The fact that Mary was doing a good job of handling the finances and taking care of Marcus didn't seem to matter to the folks in Weidman. Unfortunately, when Marcus needed her the most, Mary died on March 4, 1901, at the age of fifty-six.

There was no doctor present at her death, so the cause of death is unknown. Mary's certificate and record of death states that she is buried in the Nottawa Indian Cemetery near Beal City in Isabella County. It's assumed that someone in the family cared for Marcus in his last years, but just who it was is not known for certain.

There is no indication in his pension papers that a guardian was appointed for Marcus. By March 12, 1903, he was receiving fifty-five dollars a month in pension payments.

Marcus Otto died on the night of March 26, 1904, in Nottawa Township when he was going home in his horse-drawn buggy. He was fifty-six years old. His death was the result of the effects of declining health exacerbated by exposure to the elements.

According to the Otto descendants, Marcus lies at rest in an unmarked grave in the family plot in the northwest corner of his Weidman farm. This plot is located on land near Rosebush Road just east of Johnson Road, Nottawa Township, section

18 of Isabella County. But his death certificate lists his burial place as Nottawa Indian Cemetery.

Marcus's wife, Mary, daughter, Esther, and son, William, are also said to be interred in the same family farm plot according to a Marcus Otto descendant. But as mentioned previously, Mary's certificate and record of death states that she is buried in the Nottawa Indian Cemetery near Beal City in Isabella County. Considering that there might have been a change in burial places after the death certificates were signed, the Otto family descendants know where their loved ones are buried.

Otto, Solomon, Private

Enlistment: Enlisted on May 18, 1863, at Isabella City (now Mt. Pleasant), Isabella County, by First Lieutenant William J. Driggs, First Michigan Sharpshooters, for three years.

   Age: Twenty-four, born in 1839 or 1840 near Tittabawassee in Saginaw County.
   Occupation: Farmer
   Residence: Near Isabella City
   Physical Description: Five feet eight, black eyes, black hair, and a dark complexion. Examining physician was Dr. George S. Cornell, assistant surgeon, First Michigan Sharpshooters.
   Mustered: May 26, 1863, at Detroit Arsenal, Dearborn, Wayne County, by Lieutenant Colonel John R. Smith, First Michigan Sharpshooters.
   Military Service: On June 2, 1864, Private Solomon Otto was reported sick and sent by ambulance wagon from his regiment to a depot hospital of the Ninth Army Corps at White House Landing, Virginia, on the Pamunkey River.

Otto was transferred by hospital steamer from White House Landing to Mount Pleasant USA General Hospital in Washington, DC, and admitted on June 11. He was diagnosed with "scrofula" or tuberculosis of the cervical (or neck) lymph nodes (*Blakiston*). The doctors treated Otto's scrofula with the application of a tincture of iodine (used as a paint) to the swollen neck glands (*Evans*). Complete bed rest and a hearty diet were ordered for Solomon.

On June 17, 1864, Otto was transferred from Mount Pleasant Hospital to Haddington USA General Hospital in West Philadelphia, Pennsylvania. An additional diagnosis of rheumatism was made at that time. Otto's rheumatism was treated with opiates for severe joint pain, and quinine or potassium iodide for their mild anti-inflammatory effects (*Bollet*). He was also treated with cool baths and compresses to reduce inflammation.

Private Otto was given a twenty-day furlough from Haddington Hospital to Philadelphia on October 28, 1864. He was reported as deserted in December 1864.

Solomon returned to Haddington Hospital about the middle of December—his previous whereabouts not known, although he may have returned home to be with his family and have traditional treatment for his infirmities.

From Haddington Hospital, Otto was sent back to Michigan and admitted on December 22, 1864, to Harper USA General Hospital in Detroit. Scrofula was listed as the reason for his admittance to Harper. He was treated as mentioned previously and remained at Harper Hospital until May 1865.

Discharged: When he was at Harper Hospital in Detroit, Private Solomon Otto was mustered out, honorably discharged for disability, and paid money owed to him for his service on May 2, 1865. Dr. W. A. Chandler, surgeon of said hospital, signed Otto's release. When he received his discharge, Solomon stated that he wished to have any further correspondence addressed to Mr. John Wahbe in Isabella City.

It was determined by Dr. Chandler that the scrofula illness from which Private Otto suffered was getting worse and had probably existed prior to his enlistment.

Because of this evaluation, Solomon was, of course, deemed unfit for the Veteran Reserve Corps. Also, at this time, the doctors could see that he did not have long to live due to the severity of his illness. So, according to Otto family descendants, hospital personnel put him on a train to go home to Isabella County. He never arrived home. It's thought that Solomon died on his way home, but his body was not found, nor was his grave located.

Biography: Solomon Otto was the son of Wilson (Wahcum Kenewegoshik) and Martha Otto and the older brother to Marcus Otto, who was also in Company K.

Solomon enlisted into Company K on the same day as Marcus.

He was allotted forty acres under the first article of the treaty of August 2, 1855, and second article of the treaty of October 18, 1864, with the Chippewa of Saginaw, Swan Creek, and Black River. It was located in Isabella County, and its description is the northeast quarter of the northeast quarter of section 17, township 15 of range 5 west (*Land Records*).

Due to the disappearance and death of Solomon Otto during the war, a "Marcus Wawbegawmeskum" (or Wawbaygawmeskung), son of the grantee (the grantee was

Solomon Otto), was claimant on Solomon's land allotment certificate granted on May 27, 1871.

Solomon Otto may have been the same soldier named Solomon Kawgayawsung (as the name was spelled in Gruett's 1868 Saginaw Chippewa Index). Some of the Otto descendants believe this entry in the Gruett Index to be true.

Marcus Wawbegawmeskum (named previously) is listed in the Gruett Index as being in the household of Kawgayawsung who is listed as dead (*Gruett*). See file on Solomon Kawgayawsung. There is no pension file for Solomon Otto.

Pakemaboga, John, Private

Enlistment: Enlisted as a private in December 1863 at Camp Douglas, a confine for Confederate prisoners, located in Chicago, Cook County, Illinois. The First Michigan Sharpshooters served as guards at this camp for seven months. Another date of enlistment for Pakemaboga was on October 28, 1863, at Grand Rapids, Kent County, (enlistment officer not recorded) for three years. No bounty was paid.

The enlistment paper for this man is missing from his military service file, hence there is no information as to his age, occupation, residence, or physical description. The following muster date is confusing because it lists John's muster before his enlistment.

Mustered: November 1, 1863, at Grand Rapids by an officer named Collins

Military Service: Private John Pakemaboga was also known as John Penegwah. His military file listed him first as being taken prisoner at the Battle of the Crater before Petersburg, Virginia, on July 30, 1864. A subsequent record listed John as sick of wounds. The last notation of John's fate was recorded as "supposed to have been killed at the Battle of the Crater." With discrepancies as to John's fate, his name was dropped from subsequent military rolls.

Discharged: No discharge given due to death while in the service.

Biography: John Penegwah was born sometime between 1839 and 1845, the son of Joseph and Neganbequa Penegwah. Before his enlistment, he lived in Northport, Leelanau County. He had one stepsister, Eliza, born about 1855 to Joseph and Mary Bashenabe Penegwah.

On March 4, 1881, Application #281,385 for a pension for dependent brothers and sisters was submitted for Eliza Penegwah Keway, who was then living in Little Traverse (now Harbor Springs), Emmet County. In the application, she stated that neither her mother nor her father were living and that she understood that John had died of a fever in May 1864 in a hospital somewhere between Cold Harbor, Virginia, and Washington, DC. There is no pension file for John Pakemaboga/Penegwah.

In the government's appetite for copious amounts of paper, Eliza was subsequently notified that she needed to furnish further evidence of John's service, birth date, and marital status, and the dates of her birth and marriage. Her lawyer, William H. Miller, knew that the information on the application forms was as good as could be attained and that Eliza should receive a pension if the law would allow it.

Eliza Penegwah Keway's application for a pension for dependent brothers and sisters was rejected on April 11, 1888. The government rejected Eliza's claim due to her failure, after a reasonable time and due notification, to furnish further evidence necessary to establish her claim. Therefore, the claim was abandoned. Also, at that time, Eliza was past the age of sixteen and was not eligible for a dependent sister's pension. There is no pension file for John Pakemaboga/Penegwah.

Pemassegay, Daniel, Private

Enlistment: Enlisted as a private on May 18, 1863, at Isabella City (now Mt. Pleasant), Isabella County, by First Lieutenant William J. Driggs, First Michigan Sharpshooters, for three years.
   Age: Twenty-four, born about 1839 in Midland County.
   Occupation: Farmer
   Residence: Isabella City
   Physical Description: Five feet eleven, black eyes, black hair, and a dark complexion. Examining physician was Dr. George S. Cornell, First Michigan Sharpshooters.
   Mustered: May 26, 1863, at Detroit, Wayne County, by Lieutenant Colonel John R. Smith, First Michigan Sharpshooters
   Military Service: Daniel's name on his enlistment paper is spelled Daniel Pamahsegwa. Evidently army life did not appeal to Daniel, and he was listed as deserted on three different dates: June 24, 1863, July 5, 1863, and July 19, 1863, all at Dearborn. His name does not appear on subsequent regimental or company rolls after July 19. It was later discovered that on Daniel's last date of desertion, he went to Canada and took residence there. Philip Gruet's Saginaw Chippewa Index of 1868 lists Daniel as "living in Canada." There is no pension file for Daniel Pemassegay.

Discharged: No discharge given due to desertion to Canada.

Biography: Daniel Pemassegay was the son of Anishinabe Chief Bemassikeh (or Pemassegay) and his first wife, Wawsaychewonnoquay (*Avery*). The names Pemassegay and Bemassikeh are derived from the Anishinabe word *Bimaasige,* meaning "a light shining by" (*Ibid.*).

The chief was known to have had five wives in succession (*Ibid.*). Among the chief's many children, in addition to Daniel, were William, Paul, Lucas, Anna, John, Peter, Jane, Julia, Margaret, Peendugay (or Magdalina), and Mary Ann.

After his band was decimated by smallpox in 1837, Chief Bemassikeh, the headman of the Little Pines Band, purchased 387 acres of land for his people in 1839 and 1842. This acreage was located three miles north of St. Louis in Gratiot County along the Pine River (near the Midland County line) and was called Shingwaksausking or Shimguagonshkom, which means "place of small pine trees" (*Zehnder*).

Desiring education and life skills for his people, the chief was instrumental in inviting Rev. Eduard R. Baierlein, a Lutheran missionary in the Frankenmuth German colony in Saginaw County, to establish a mission and school on the reservation property that he, the chief, had purchased.

Rev. Baierlein accepted the chief's offer. He conferred with Rev. August Craemer, as Craemer was from the same German Colony as Baierlein, and Craemer agreed. The mission and school were opened in 1847 by Rev. Craemer, who was then joined by Rev. Baierlein in May 1848. The Lutheran ministers called this new mission "Bethany," which can mean, among its many translations, "house of poverty," after they had observed the poverty and poor conditions of Bemassikeh's people (*Ibid.*). Bethany was the first mission for the Anishinabek to be established in Gratiot County.

On January 18, 1849, the chief's children, Peter, Paul, Lucas, Maria, and Anna, were baptized in the chief's camp. Among the baptism witnesses were Rev. and Mrs. Baierlein (*Ibid.*).

Old Chief Bemassikeh of the Bethany band of Anishinabek died on May 23, 1850 of 1851, of tuberculosis and was mourned by all who knew him.

Rev. Baierlein was succeeded by Rev. Ernest Gustav Herman Miessler in 1853 when the minister left for India. Rev. Meissler served the Bethany German Lutheran Mission from 1851 to 1859.

With the establishment of the Isabella Reservation, the Anishinabek of Bethany Mission moved to Isabella County. Rev. Meissler followed them and established a new Lutheran mission and school near the reservation. Due to a decrease in church and school attendance, the mission was closed in 1869 *(Ibid.)*.

The original Bethany Mission acreage was returned to the government and the mission farm was sold to Peter Gruet Sr. Only the Bethany Cemetery was kept by the Lutheran synod. The cemetery was rededicated in 1931 and is now a place of quiet beauty with perpetual care.

Among those former Bethany Anishinabek members who were entitled to hold property on the Isabella reservation were Daniel Pemassegay and his siblings Peter Pemassegay and Peendugay, also known as Madaline/Magdalina *(Baierlein)*.

In 1865, Daniel Pemassegay married Mawcawdaymecoquay in Canada. The couple was known to have had at least one daughter, Ogawsequay, born about 1866.

Daniel had thirty-nine and forty-nine hundredths of an acre of allotted land in Isabella County under the first article of the treaty of August 2, 1855, and second article of the treaty of October 18, 1864, with the Chippewa of Saginaw, Swan Creek, and Black River. The acreage is described as the northwest fractional quarter of the northwest fractional quarter of section 1, township 14, range 4 west. His patent certificate was issued on May 27, 1871 *(Land Records)*. There is no pension file for Daniel Pemassegay.

Penaiswanquot, Jacko, Private

Enlistment: Enlisted as a private on June 1, 1863, at Northport, Leelanau County, by First Lieutenant William J. Driggs, First Michigan Sharpshooters, for three years.

Age: Forty, born about 1823 in the Northport area.

Occupation: Farmer

Residence: Northport

Physical Description: Not stated in Jacko's enlistment papers. Examining physician was Dr. George S. Cornell, first assistant surgeon, First Michigan Sharpshooters.

Mustered: June 22, 1863, at Detroit Arsenal, Dearborn, Wayne County, by Lieutenant Colonel John R. Smith, First Michigan Sharpshooters

Military Service: Private Jacko Penaiswanquot (also known as Jacko Pasanoquot) was captured on July 17, 1864, while charging the enemy's works in a battle before Petersburg, Virginia. He was housed in a converted tobacco warehouse with others who were captured from his company and regiment. Shortly after his confinement, he was sent by cattle railcar on a long train ride to Camp Sumter, Andersonville Prison, in Andersonville, Georgia.

Inadequate food and deplorable conditions contributed to his poor health. He became extremely ill with chronic diarrhea and scorbutus (or scurvy), which is a nutritional disorder caused by the lack of vitamin C. During his illness, two Company K comrades, Private Payson Wolfe and Private John B. Shomin, and regimental member Zena D. Ransom of Company C cared for Jacko.

On November 1, 1864, Private Jacko Penaiswanquot was carried to the prison hospital by some of the rebel authorities, where he was laid on a bed of pine straw. His only shelter was a square of canvas pitched like a tent, which he shared with eight to ten men. He died that evening of scorbutus. His body was taken by the comrades who cared for him to a brush arbor dead house, where all usable clothing was removed from the body. Information about Jacko was collected by a record keeper known as Dorance Atwater (also a prisoner), who kept the "Atwater List" of those prisoners who died at Andersonville Prison. Atwater attached a numbered tag to the body for later reference. Then, as quickly as possible, Jacko's remains, along with other bodies, were taken by wagon to the cemetery about a mile from the prison grounds.

At the cemetery, Jacko's body was placed uncovered and shoulder to shoulder with other bodies in a trench about four feet deep. The remains were then covered with dirt (*Encyclopedia*). Many times, a deceased soldier's comrades helped bury him. A small wooden post with a number carved into it was placed at the head of his grave, which identified the soldier and his unit (*Ibid.*).

Private Jacko Penaiswanquot lies at rest in Andersonville National Cemetery under military stone #11705. The headstone states his name as "S. Recalt."

Discharged: No discharge given due to death while a prisoner of war.

Biography: Jacob Penaiswanquot, also known as Jaco Penasewonquot, Jacob Benasewanquot, and Shako Benasewanquot, married Marianne (also spelled Mary Ann) Ogawbayosaqua on August 11, 1844, at Mapleton on Old Mission Peninsula of Grand Traverse County. Father Francis X. Pierz, Roman Catholic missionary of the Little Traverse (now Harbor Springs) area, officiated at the wedding. The marriage was witnessed by Benjamin Pichobe (Pashawba) and David Mongolpin. Louis Agawche (Jacob's brother), Sophia Kawgayawnaqua (Jacob and Louis's mother), and Mary Chibway also attended the wedding.

Jacob and Mary were the parents of eight children: Lewis (or Natahwinodin, which means "first wind"), born about 1846; John (or Kakebonoka, which means "window maker"), born about 1848; Catherine (or Nascan), born about 1850, who would marry Louis Manitowash; Susan (or Shawnosaqua), born about 1852; Simon, born about 1854; William (or Kahbenahe), born about 1856; Andrew, born about 1858; and Mary Ann, born about 1861. The first four children were born on Old Mission Peninsula near Mapleton, Grand Traverse, and the last four siblings were born at Northport, Leelanau County. All the children were baptized in the rite of the Catholic Church.

Another record of baptism for the first four Penaiswanquot children lists Catherine (or Katherine) as born March 10, 1853, Susan as born September 10, 1854, Simon as born February 4, 1857, and William as born August 15, 1858.

Jacob owned property in Bingham, Leelanau County, and farmed there before he and his family moved to Northport.

After Jacob's death in the service in 1864, his oldest sons, John and Lewis, joined Company K (see files on John Jacko and Natahwinodin Jacko). Marianne and the children moved back to Jacob's property in Bingham so that William, Andrew, and Simon could farm their land.

On February 9, 1865, Application #82,393 for a widow's pension was filed under the Act of July 15, 1862, for Marianne Penaiswanquot. Her application was resubmitted (under #363,760) on October 7, 1887. A Treasury Certificate #232,644 was issued to Marianne from the Second Auditor's Office on May 19, 1870, which allowed her to receive Jacob's pay from his death to October 30, 1864. The certificate amounted to about forty dollars.

Marianne tried to support herself by making baskets for the tourist trade. Her children helped as much as they could, with her support, and she did live with her younger sons after they married.

Finally, on January 27, 1890, Marianne received her Widow's Pension Certificate #263,983. It paid eight dollars a month retroactive to October 31, 1864, and was increased to twelve dollars a month retroactive to March 19, 1886. Marianne also received two dollars a month for each child (retroactive from June 25, 1866) until that child attained the age of sixteen. Marianne's payments for child support finally ended when the youngest daughter, Mary Ann, reached the age of sixteen in 1877.

Marianne Penaiswanquot and her family were very close, and she was thought of in the highest regard by all who knew her. She was known to be a kind and honest person. On July 15, 1905, Marianne died near Suttons Bay in Leelanau County, where she resided with her son William.

On October 8, 1925, William Penaiswanquot, who lived in Omena, Leelanau County, wrote to the Pension Commissioner in Washington, DC, and inquired as to any accrued pension that was due to his deceased father, Jacob, or to his mother, Marianne, who died in 1905. The reply (in pension papers) from the Commissioners stated: "there is a pension accrued in this case from June 4, 1905, to the date of death inclusive. Such pension is not an asset of the pensioner's estate. If she left assets sufficient to meet the expense of her last sickness and burial the accrued pension cannot be paid to any one for any purpose."

On April 30, 1925, William again petitioned Washington to request if he could receive any part of Marianne's pension since he cared for her until her death. The reply from the pension bureau was the same as above—his mother's pension was not an asset of her estate.

See file on Natahwinodin Jacko (whose birth name was Louis Penaiswanquot), Marianne's oldest son, for Marianne's application (on December 17, 1896) for a dependent mother's pension. Her application was denied.

Peshekee, Mark, Private

Enlistment: Enlisted as a private on May 19, 1863, at East Saginaw, Saginaw County, by First Lieutenant William J. Driggs, First Michigan Sharpshooters, for three years.

    Age: Thirty, born about 1833 in Saginaw County.

    Occupation: Laborer and hunter

    Residence: Isabella County

    Physical Description: Five feet seven, black eyes, black hair, and dark complexion. Examining physician was Dr. George S. Cornell, assistant surgeon, First Michigan Sharpshooters.

    Mustered: May 26, 1863, at Detroit, Wayne County, by Lieutenant Colonel John R. Smith, First Michigan Sharpshooters

    Military Service: During the Battle of Spotsylvania, Virginia, on May 12, 1864, Private Peshekee sustained a gunshot (missile) wound over his left scapula (or shoulder blade). He was taken immediately to a first aid station, where any bleeding was stopped by compression, his wound was washed, and his shoulder area was hastily wrapped in a bandage sling.

    Mark was taken by ambulance wagon from the first aid station to his division hospital farther behind the lines. At the division hospital, his wound was washed, and if the missile was found to be lodged in Mark's shoulder area, he was anesthetized with chloroform, and it was removed. The open wound area was painted with iodine to impede infection and dusted with morphine powder to ease pain. Lint made from separated threads of cotton or linen fabric, called *charpie,* was placed into the wound (*Schaadt*). The wound site was then bandaged with simple water dressings, which consisted of folded lint dipped into cold water and secured in place by a cloth wrap or adhesive plaster (*Ibid.*). Opium pills were given for pain.

After his medical procedure, Peshekee was kept at the hospital for several days and then transferred by ambulance wagon from the division hospital to a wharf at Belle Plain, Virginia. From the wharf, he was taken by hospital steamer to L'Ouverture USA General Hospital at Alexandria, Virginia, where he was admitted on May 16. He remained at this hospital for additional treatment. On June 1, he was given a twenty-day furlough back home to Michigan.

On June 20, 1864, Private Peshekee, still suffering from the effects of his wound, was sent to USA Post Hospital, Detroit Barracks, in Detroit. He was granted a four-day furlough from the hospital on June 23. He did not return to the barracks hospital until July 8 because he was too ill at home to report. On August 1, Mark rejoined his regiment in Virginia.

Complaining of the effects of his wound and suffering from acute diarrhea, Private Peshekee was admitted to his division hospital on September 9, 1864. The doctors treated Mark's wound as previously mentioned. For his diarrhea, the patient was given narcotics, such as a tincture of opium in an alcoholic solution, which is called laudanum, or opium in the form of pills (*Bollet*). Doses of castor oil and turpentine to cleanse his system and Dover's powder (ipecac and opium) to induce perspiration were also administered to the patient (*Evans*).

Mark was taken from the division hospital by ambulance wagon to the military railroad, put on a mattress in a boxcar, the floor of which was cushioned with straw or hay, and sent to the depot hospital at City Point, Virginia. He was admitted to this hospital on September 13, 1864, and was given similar treatment. No military record mentions that he returned to his company.

Discharged: There is no evidence that a discharge was granted to Private Peshekee, only a notation that he was last paid on April 30, 1864.

The Adjutant General's Office reported that Private Peshekee was reported as "absent sick" and stationed with his regiment near Petersburg, Virginia, for September and October 1864. The AGO further stated that Private Peshekee was listed with those mustered out on July 28, 1865, but there is no evidence of a discharge for this soldier.

It could be assumed that Mark died of the combination of an infection in his wound and from severe diarrhea while at the City Point Depot Hospital. The Phillip Gruett Saginaw Chippewa Index of 1868 mentions, on page 273, that Mark "died in the Army in 1865." The source of this information is presumed to be from his family in Isabella County. Did his death occur in the hospital sometime in 1865 and somehow was not recorded in military records?

Some researchers believe that Mark, who was sick and weak, left the City Point Depot Hospital and traveled a long distance to Madeline Island, Wisconsin. Their opinion is that he died on the island and was buried at La Pointe in the St. Joseph Catholic Mission Cemetery (the Old Indian Cemetery) across from Bayfield of said state. They hold this belief because of their assumption that Mark, because of the similarity of his name (Peshekee is derived from *Bizhiki* and *Pijiki,* which means "buffalo"), was descended from, or related to, the La Pointe, Wisconsin, Ojibwe chief, Bizhiki, who is buried in said cemetery (*Baraga*).

Chief Bizhiki was also known as was Kechewaishke (or Gichiweshkiinh), which means "Great-renewer" (*Wikipedia*). He was born on Madeline Island, was a principal leader of the Lake Superior Chippewa at La Pointe, and died of heart disease on September 7, 1855. The well-revered chief was buried at La Pointe in the St. Joseph Catholic Cemetery (*Ibid.*).

Biography: Mark Peshekee (also known as Mack Peshekee) was a brother to George Wawsawconeyea, Kawgaycumego, and Sawgee. His sisters were Pewawmick and Waybechewawnoquay (*Gruett*).

Mark married Kawgezhegoquay (or Ogawbaygezhegoquay) about 1851. The couple were the parents of at least one daughter, named Quaykechewawnoquay (or Rebecca), and a son named John Mark, who died before the age of one year (*Ibid.*).

Rebecca married Shawwawnawcawmego. Mark's wife died before 1855.

Mark had eighty acres of land in Isabella County, which he was allotted from the first article of the treaty of August 2, 1855, and second article of the treaty of October 18, 1864, with the Chippewa of Saginaw, Swan Creek, and Black River. Its description is the east one half of the northeast one quarter, section 21, township 15, range 4 west. A certificate was granted in 1871 (*Land Records*).

Because the previously mentioned researchers think that there is a familial link between Mark and Chief Bizhiki, which has yet to be proved, they believe that Mark made his way to Madeline Island, died, and was buried in the same cemetery as the Ojibwa chief. But there are many unmarked graves in that cemetery, and some pages of the church's cemetery death register book mysteriously disappeared after the book was borrowed (as told to the author by a Madeline Island resident) sometime between the 1960s and 1980s. So, there is no way to prove that Mark died on Madeline Island and was buried in that cemetery without seeing the actual burial record and plat book, or to know someone who either knows where this book is or can verify another source that lists the burials in that cemetery.

There is also another issue. If Mark Peshekee was of the Christian faith, he may have attended the Methodist Indian Mission Church on the Isabella Reservation. Or he may also have been a follower of traditional Anishinabek beliefs. In either case, Mark would not have been buried in the same cemetery as Chief Bizhiki. The chief was of the Catholic faith, and neither Protestants nor traditional Anishinabek believers would have been buried in a Catholic cemetery on Madeline Island. Until positively proven otherwise, the author believes that Mark's supposed relationship to Chief Buffalo, if there is one, and Mark's burial place, remain unknown. There is no pension file for Mark Peshekee.

Pesherbay, Albert, Private

Enlistment: Enlisted as a private on June 18, 1863, at Little Traverse (now Harbor Springs), Emmet County, by Second Lieutenant Garrett A. Graveraet, First Michigan Sharpshooters, for three years.

    Age: Twenty-five, born about 1838 in Charlevoix, Emmet County (now Charlevoix County).

    Occupation: Farmer

    Residence: Charlevoix

    Physical Description: Five feet eight, black eyes, black hair, and a dark complexion. Examining physician was Dr. Arvin T. Whelan, surgeon, First Michigan Sharpshooters.

    Mustered: July 20, 1863, at Detroit, Wayne County, by Lieutenant Colonel John R. Smith, First Michigan Sharpshooters

    Military Service: In December 1863, when his regiment was guarding Confederate prisoners at Camp Douglas, in Chicago, Cook County, Illinois, Private Pesherbay was detailed as a company cook. He reported sick, illness not stated, at the Camp Douglas Post Hospital on March 16, 1864, and remained in the post hospital when his regiment left Chicago for the front on March 17.

By the middle of April, Albert rejoined his regiment in Annapolis, Maryland.

As he hunkered down in a bombproof shelter before Petersburg, Virginia, on February 20, 1865, Pesherbay stated that he incurred a percussion injury to his head, chest, and lungs due to an artillery shell burst during a rebel bombardment. Although he was not hospitalized at that time, the residual effects would manifest themselves in later years. He shared the bomb proof with Sgt. Francis Tabasasch, who also sustained a percussion injury, Louis Shomin, and Petros Awanaquad. Petros died of his injuries.

In May 1865, Private Pesherbay was detailed from his company to serve as a policeman in the provost guard in Washington, DC.

Discharged: Private Albert Pesherbay was mustered out and honorably discharged at Detroit on August 11, 1865. At his discharge, Albert was paid money owed to him for his service and returned home to Michigan.

Biography: Albert Pesherbay (also known as Peshawbey, Peshaba, and Pashaba) was the son of Black Wolf and Ogemaguan Pashawba.

His first marriage was to Mary Shawnego Wakazoo, the daughter of Chief Peter and Mary Ann Wassa Wakazoo. The couple was married on April 16, 1866, in the township of Charlevoix, Emmet County. John A. Horton, justice of the peace, officiated at the ceremony, which was witnessed by Amanda Horton and Louis Nekisabe.

Mary Ann died of tuberculosis at the age of twenty-five on November 4, 1873. There were no children of this marriage.

Albert's second marriage was of traditional Anishinabek custom and practice (agreement of the couple and their parents) to a woman named Waukegegoquay. She died shortly after the couple's marriage.

The third and last marriage for Albert was to Theresa Trosho (or Trotochaud?). Another pension file record states that Theresa was the daughter of John B. and Martina Trosho. She was also known as Theresa Shotkol. Rev. William Tilden of the Petoskey Methodist Indian Mission Church in Emmet County officiated at the rite of marriage at the church parsonage (minister's home) on September 24, 1878. The ceremony was witnessed by A. P. Moore and C. E. Call.

Before her marriage to Pesherbay, Theresa Trosho was married to Enos Dailey (or Daily), who died at Cross Village, Emmet County, and John Ashquabebay (or

Babamsa), who died at Elk Rapids, Antrim County. It's known that Theresa had three children, Jane, Eliza, and Joseph, during her previous two marriages.

When Theresa married Albert, she brought her children to their marriage. Albert was fond of Theresa's children and listed them as his stepchildren in the 1880 federal census for Emmet County.

Albert and Theresa were the parents of three children: Mary, born about 1875; George, born about 1878; and Lucy, born about 1892.

As with so many veterans of the Civil War, Albert's health declined with age and was aggravated by injuries and exposure incurred during his service.

Application #917,686 for a pension for disability was filed for Albert on August 12, 1890, under the Act of June 27, 1890. Even though there was no documentation of his injuries suffered in the explosion of a shell in his bombproof shelter, except by his own deposition, he was eligible to be pensioned under the Act of June 27, 1890 (a more liberal act), since he had served at least ninety days and was honorably discharged. Albert stated in his application that he believed that the partial muscle weakness of his left side, including his arm and leg, and the deafness in his left ear were the direct result of the shell burst.

Albert's reputation was considered quite good by all who knew him. He was a hard worker at whatever job he could find. Those who made depositions for him stated that the status of his health was in no way due to "vicious habits" (or venereal disease).

An Invalid Pension Certificate #706,289 was granted to Albert on April 5, 1895, for partial inability to earn support by manual labor and for rheumatism, disease of the heart, and deafness of the left ear. The certificate paid twelve dollars at first but was then cut to eight dollars in 1896.

In June 1901, Albert petitioned for an increase of his pension. He related that his health was deteriorating. He had suffered a slight stroke in January, which compounded his muscle weakness and resulted in paralysis. It was hard for him to do manual labor, even to supply wood for his home. He further stated that he could not dress himself or control his limbs due to the paralysis.

Dr. Alexander Worden, chairman of the Emmet County Soldiers' Relief Commission, stated that Albert was indigent and confined to bed with paralysis due to his stroke. Because of these hardships, the doctor related that Albert's family was supplied with food and clothes from the Relief Commission. According to Dr. Worden, Albert was always considered to be a man of good habits and was regarded as an industrious man before his stroke.

Finally, on November 12, 1902, Pesherbay received an increase in pension payments to total twelve dollars a month. He received this amount until his death.

Albert Pesherbay (or Pashawba) died of paralysis due to his stroke on August 29, 1903, in Bear Creek Township, Emmet County. His funeral was conducted out of the Henika Funeral Home.

The old soldier was buried in an unmarked grave in section Z, block 999 of lot 999, of the Potters Field of Greenwood Cemetery in Petoskey. A memorial stone, erected in 2009, now stands in the Greenwood Cemetery and honors the veterans (Albert's name is included) who have no stone markers.

Application #816,581 for a widow's pension was filed for Theresa Pesherbay on November 9, 1904. At his death, Albert left Theresa about ten acres of land, a dozen chickens, a little frame house of three rooms, some furniture, and a little log stable. The total value of said property did not exceed $200. The land was not very arable and was partly swampy.

Theresa hired a man, known as John Camp, who lived across the road from her, to farm what acreage he could in peas, beans, and corn. She did collect about one-third of the farm yield, but that did not amount to over ten dollars a year. To supplement this meager income, Theresa planted and harvested a small garden.

Theresa's health was very poor at the time of her husband's death. She was afflicted with a skin disease that affected her hands so badly that she couldn't work at any type of manual labor for very long. She also suffered from rheumatism. Theresa's daughter, Eliza Daily, did what she could to help her mother.

Even with the little income taken in by the farm, Theresa was still very poor. In addition to county assistance, she accepted help from her neighbors and the local GAR post.

Theresa Pesherbay received an Accrued Pension Certificate #706,289 for money owed to her husband from his last pension payment until his death. The accrued payments started in October 1906.

On October 12, 1906, Theresa was granted a Widow's Pension Certificate #616,707, which paid eight dollars a month retroactive to November 9, 1904. Her pension was admitted under the liberal Act of June 27, 1890, as amended by the Act of May 9, 1900. Under these acts, widows of men who served for ninety days, regardless of the causes of the deaths of their husbands, were eligible for pensions.

Theresa Pesherbay received her pension payments at her home in Bear Creek

Township until her death from stomach cancer on June 5, 1908. Her funeral was held from St. Francis Solanus Catholic Church in Petoskey on June 7, and she was buried in Greenwood Cemetery in said city.

Petozoourquitte, Private

Listed as a member of Company K, First Michigan Sharpshooters, but no enlistment paper has been found. He is thought to be the same man as Petros Awanakwad, who is buried at Poplar Grove National Cemetery in Petersburg, Virginia. See file on Petros Awanakwad.

Porsley, Charles, Private

Enlistment: Enlisted as a private on July 6, 1863, at Little Traverse (now Harbor Springs), Emmet County, by Second Lieutenant Garrett A. Graveraet, First Michigan Sharpshooters, for three years.

    Age: Twenty-five, born about 1838 in Cheboygan, Cheboygan County.

    Occupation: Farmer

    Residence: Burt, Cheboygan County

    Physical Description: Five feet eight, black eyes, black hair, and a dark complexion. Examining physician was Dr. Arvin F. Whelan, surgeon, First Michigan Sharpshooters.

    Mustered: July 20, 1863, at Detroit, Wayne County, by Lieutenant Colonel John R. Smith, First Michigan Sharpshooters

    Military Service: Sometime between September and October 1863, while his regiment was guarding Confederate prisoners at the Camp Douglas confine in Chicago, Cook County, Illinois, Private Porsley lost his waist belt and plate. Much to his chagrin, his wages were docked to cover the negligent loss of military property.

    From April 16 to 21, 1864, Porsley was in the regimental hospital of the First Michigan Sharpshooters in Annapolis, Maryland, with the complaint of diarrhea. The doctors treated Porsley's diarrhea with castor oil (in the morning) to cleanse his system, opium pills for pain (in the evening), Dover's powder (ipecac and opium) to induce perspiration, and turpentine to cleanse his system (*Evans*). These medications were administered with doses of whiskey to mask the bitterness of the medications.

    Boiled water, diluted coffee and tea, barley water, rice water, and broth made of meat extract was the diet that was prescribed for him. As his health and his digestive tolerance improved, the doctors added citrus juices and fresh fruits and vegetables to his diet.

On April 22, 1864, when his regiment had moved out to Washington, DC, Porsley was left behind to be admitted to Division No. 1, USA General Hospital at the United States Naval Academy (Navy Yard) in Annapolis, Maryland, suffering from debility or asthenia – the absence or loss of strength (*Blakiston*). He returned to his regiment in Virginia on May 2nd.

Suffering from emaciation and loss of strength, Private Porsley was admitted to his division hospital in the field on August 10. At the division hospital, Charles was diagnosed with "phthisis pulmonalis," the old term for pulmonary consumption (or tuberculosis) caused by the bacterium *Mycobacterium tuberculosis,* the tubercle bacillus (*Ibid.*). There was no effective treatment for tuberculosis until about the middle of the twentieth century (*Bollet*).

On August 14, Charles was taken by ambulance wagon from the division hospital to the military railroad, put on a mattress in a boxcar, the floor of which was cushioned with straw or hay, and taken to the depot hospital at City Point, Virginia. He was admitted to the hospital at City Point on August 15 and was taken immediately to an isolation ward for patients with tuberculosis.

On August 24, Charles was taken to a dock at City Point, transferred by hospital steamer from the dock at City Point to L'Ouverture USA General Hospital at Alexandria, Virginia, where he arrived the next day. After his arrival, he was again put in an isolation ward. Charles remained at the hospital in Alexandria until he was discharged.

Discharged: While a patient at L'Ouverture Hospital, Private Charles Porsley was mustered out and granted an honorable discharge of disability on December 26, 1864. His discharge was approved by Dr. Edwin Bentley, surgeon, US Volunteers, of said hospital, and the order was given by Major General Auger. It was determined that since Porsley was suffering from tuberculosis of seven months' standing, he was not of any benefit to the service and was not fit to enlist into the Veteran Reserve Corps, so should be discharged. Charles was paid money owed to him for his service at the time of his discharge and returned to Michigan.

Before he left the hospital, Porsley told the authorities that he wished to be addressed at the Burt Post Office with any further communication.

Biography: On August 9, 1865, Application #81,818 for an invalid pension was submitted for the Burt Lake Odawa (Ottawa) Band member Charles Porsley (whose surname was also spelled Porcellay), who was unable to work due to his disease.

In the application, he believed that his illness was due to the rigors of marching, inhaling dust, and exposure to inclement weather while on picket duty and engaged on the skirmish line.

Porsley was notified on April 6, 1870, that his application for an invalid pension was suspended for the lack of evidence of his illness. Even though he had sent in his certificate of disability for discharge paper with all the evidence needed for his reported illness and signed by the doctor in charge of the hospital, rejection of his application was affirmed by the US Pension Office on August 7, 1871. Porsley was notified of the rejection. There is no pension file for Charles Porsley.

Prestawin, Jacob, Private

Enlistment: Enlisted as a private on November 18, 1864, at Traverse City, Leelanau County, by Captain Norman Bailey, First Michigan Sharpshooters and provost marshal for the Fourth District of Michigan, for one year. Credited to the Fourth Congressional District, Bingham Township, Leelanau County.

Age: Twenty-four, born about 1840 in Leelanau County.

Occupation: Farmer

Residence: Bingham, Leelanau County

Physical Description: Five feet nine and a half inches tall, dark eyes, dark hair, and a copper complexion. Examining physician was Dr. Alonzo Mate, First Michigan Sharpshooters.

Mustered: November 18, 1864, at Grand Rapids, Kent County by Captain Norman Bailey, First Michigan Sharpshooters and provost marshal for the Fourth District of Michigan

Military Service: It is the author's belief that Jacob Prestawin and Nahtahwinodin Jacko, who was also known as Louis Penaiswonoquot (or Pasanoquot), may be the same man. See file on Natahwinodin Jacko.

According to a May 9, 1872, report from the Adjutant General's Office, the following notation is found in the pension file for Natahwinodin Jacko. "The man Nai-tah-me-no-ting Jacko is not borne on the rolls of Co. "K", 1st. Michigan S. Shooters, but the name Pestawin Jacko appears on rolls of Co. (whose enlistment and description corresponds with that on the discharge certificate of the first named man) if this is thought to be the man enquire and please renew your application."

The physical descriptions, places of residence, and enlistment information for both men are identical. The differences were: Jacob Prestawin did not receive a discharge paper, but Nahtahwinodin Jacko did; Nahtahwinodin Jacko did not have an enlistment paper (as Prestawin did) but did have a certificate of discharge for disability, which listed the identical information ascribed to Prestawin.

Prestawin was reported sick in May and June 1865. There is no further military record for "Jacob Prestawin (or Pestawin)."

Discharged: No discharge given to a man named Jacko Prestawin (or Pestawin).

Biography: No biographical record found for a man named "Jacko Prestawin (or Pestawin)." Refer to the biographical information for Nahtahwinodin Jacko.

Quoboway, James, Private

Enlistment: Enlisted as a private on May 18, 1863, at Isabella City (now Mt. Pleasant), Isabella County, by First Lieutenant William J. Driggs, First Michigan Sharpshooters, for three years.

Age: Thirty-two, born about 1831 in Eaton County.

Occupation: Farmer

Residence: Isabella City

Physical Description: Five feet five, black eyes, black hair, and a dark complexion. Examining physician was Dr. George S. Cornell, assistant surgeon, First Michigan Sharpshooters.

Mustered: May 26, 1863, at Detroit, Wayne County. No muster officer listed.

Military Service: During the Battle of Spotsylvania on May 12, 1864, Private Quoboway was seriously injured. He sustained a gunshot wound in his left hip in which a missile struck the anterior superior spine of the left ilium (spine of the hip bone), partially destroying the attachment of the *obliquus externus* and the *obliquus internus* muscles of that side and damaging muscles and nerves in the thigh area. The ball also passed through the upper portion of the scrotum and exited through the lower portion of the right buttock, leaving a fistulous opening (a narrow tube or canal formed by incomplete closure). This severe wound would also result in extremely painful sciatica caused by the injury to the sciatic nerve and the wasting of muscles through which the nerve courses (*Blakiston*).

Private Quoboway was taken immediately to a dressing station where his wound was assessed and any bleeding was stopped. He was then moved by ambulance wagon to his division hospital farther behind the lines. At the division hospital, cold water dressings (to reduce inflammation) were applied to his wounds. A cold water dressing consisted of a piece of folded lint that was dipped into cold water, placed on the wound, and secured with a cloth wrap or adhesive plaster (*Schaadt*). James was given opium pills for pain.

After a few days, James was taken by ambulance wagon to the depot hospital in Fredericksburg, Virginia. The depot hospital was located at or near attorney John Marye's house on Marye's heights.

At the hospital, iodine may have been used to paint the areas around the entrance and exit wounds caused by the missile. Cold water dressings were applied to his wounds and changed as often as the overworked staff had time to do so.

On July 28, James was taken by ambulance wagon from the hospital to the wharf at Belle Plain, Virginia, transported to a hospital steamer, and taken to USA General Hospital in York, Pennsylvania. He was admitted to this hospital for further treatment on July 29.

James returned to duty with his regiment on October 27 and rejoined his unit near Petersburg, Virginia. He was able to serve as company cook for a brief time during the month of November 1864 until the effects of his injury grew worse and rendered him unfit for duty.

Discharged: On December 28, 1864, Private James Quoboway was mustered out and given an honorable discharge for disability by Regimental Major Asahel W. Nichols. James's discharge was given on order from Major General Augur.

Due to the severity of his injury, Quoboway was judged unfit for transfer to the Veteran Reserve Corps. He was listed as a good soldier on his discharge paper. James was paid the money due to him for his service upon discharge and returned to Michigan.

As stated in the introduction, by an act of the War Department issued on June 15, 1864, any soldier discharged from the service by reason of wounds received in battle was to receive a hundred-dollar bounty upon discharge, no matter how short his term of service. It is assumed that due to the serious nature of Quoboway's injury, he received this bounty.

Biography: James Quoboway was known to have married in 1867 but related that his wife (name unknown) died in 1869. The couple had no children. In subsequent federal census enumerations, Quoboway listed himself as single.

James had been in constant pain since his injury, and it was extremely difficult for him to walk and almost impossible for him to hold any kind of job. He developed sciatica due to the nerve damage in his thigh, and a constant discharge of pus material oozed from the fistular opening in his right buttock. For many days, he could not get out of bed. Due to extreme pain and muscle weakness, James became quite lame.

Application #89,918 for an invalid pension was filed for the soldier on September 21, 1865. It was filed under the Act of July 14, 1862. He received Invalid Pension Certificate #75,383 on December 19, 1866, which paid four dollars a month commencing (or retroactive) to December 28, 1864.

On June 17, 1878, James submitted a declaration for an increase in his pension comparable to pensions of other soldiers with the same degree of disability. His pension was increased from four dollars a month to six dollars a month from December 30, 1885; from six to eight dollars a month from June 22, 1887, and from eight to twelve dollars a month from May 15, 1889.

Citing total disability, Quoboway submitted another request on December 5, 1896, for an increase in his monthly payments. He received an increase from twelve dollars to fourteen dollars a month to commence on January 7, 1903. James was last paid fourteen dollars a month on December 4, 1905.

James Quoboway died at age seventy-one due to the effects of rheumatism and his battle wounds. His death occurred in Deerfield Township of Isabella County on June 4, 1906. He was buried in an Anishinabek cemetery in said township two days later.

The Pension Agency was notified of his death on February 20, 1907, and his name was dropped from the pension rolls.

Rubberdee, John, Private

Enlistment: Enlisted as a private on September 26, 1864, at Ontonagon, Ontonagon County by A.E.B. Mann, First Michigan Sharpshooters, for three years. Credited to the Sixth Congressional District, Subdistrict 110, Rockland Township, Ontonagon County.

Age: Twenty/twenty-five, born 1839 or 1844 in Michigan.

Occupation: Laborer

Residence: Rockland, Ontonagon County, in Michigan's Upper Peninsula

Physical Description: Five feet eleven, dark eyes, dark hair, and a dark complexion. Examining physician was Dr. George Landon, First Michigan Sharpshooters.

Mustered: October 19, 1864, at Detroit, Wayne County, by Captain Mark Flanagan, Twenty-Fourth Michigan Infantry and provost marshal

Military Service: Private Rubberdee joined his regiment at Peebles Farm, Virginia, on November 4, 1864. No record has been found that showed Rubberdee suffered illness or injury during his time of service.

Discharged: Private John Rubberdee was mustered out and honorably discharged on July 28, 1865, at Delaney House, Georgetown, Washington, DC. He returned to Detroit on the steamer *Morning Star*. On August 7, John was paid money owed to him for his service at Jackson, Jackson County.

Biography: No personal record for John Rubberdee has been located. He probably returned to Ontonagon County, or he may have gone to Wisconsin or Canada. The spelling of John's family surname is incorrect. He was probably of French Canadian/Indian (called Metis) extraction, and his true surname was closer to the French spelling Robidoux, Robideaux, Roberdie, or Raberdoux. His family may have been related to the William Neveaux family of La Pointe, Madeline Island, Ashland County, Wisconsin. The Robidoux name is listed in some of the marriage and baptismal records for that family.

Enlisted Men—Letters S, T, V, and W

Sanequaby, Simon, Corporal

Enlistment: Enlisted as a corporal on June 8, 1863, at Little Traverse (now Harbor Springs), Emmett County, by First Lieutenant William J. Driggs, First Michigan Sharpshooters, for three years.

    Age: Twenty-five, born about 1837 or 1838 in Little Traverse.

    Occupation: Farmer

    Residence: Burt Lake, Cheboygan County

    Physical Description: Five feet eight and a half inches tall, black eyes, black hair, and a dark complexion. Examining physician was Dr. George S. Cornell, first assistant surgeon, First Michigan Sharpshooters.

    Mustered: June 22, 1863, at Detroit, Wayne County, by Lieutenant Colonel John R. Smith, US Army

    Military Service: Corporal Simon Sanequaby was promoted to the rank of sergeant on November 1, 1864. He appeared to have come through his war years without incurring an illness or severe injury, but his health suffered due to the hardships of combat and exposure to inclement weather. After his discharge, Simon was known to be a sickly person.

    Discharged: Sergeant Simon Sanequaby was mustered out and honorably discharged on July 28, 1865, at Delaney House, Washington, DC. He returned to Detroit on the steamer *Morning Star*. On August 7, 1865, Simon was paid money owed to him for his service at Jackson, Jackson County.

    Biography: Simon (also known as Simon Singoby), a member of the Burt Lake band, was raised in Burt Lake Village on Colonial Point in Cheboygan County.

Although he was brought up in the Catholic Church, his first marriage was by traditional Anishinabek custom and practice (agreement of the couple and their parents) to Mary Georgeen Chinquomoqwa. This event took place sometime before Simon joined the army. Simon and Mary were the parents of several children.

About 1870, Mary left Simon and took the couple's children and her mother to an Anishinabek village in Canada where her father had taken residence. She did not return to Michigan. Some years later, Simon learned that Mary and their children had died in Canada. Their deaths were possibly due to consumption (or tuberculosis).

Simon's second marriage was also of the traditional Anishinabek custom and practice to Josette (or Josephina) Giwegoshkam, who was also known as Susan Miskoguon. Susan was the widow of Louis Miskoguon (also known as Kewaquiskum), who was Simon's comrade in Company K. The couple were the parents of a son, James, born in 1873, and a daughter, Margaretta, born in August 1875.

Margaretta was baptized on February 22, 1876, at Holy Childhood of Jesus Catholic Church at Little Traverse (now Harbor Springs), Emmet County. She died four months after her baptism. Since her parents were not married in the eyes of the church, Margaretta was listed as illegitimate on her baptismal certificate.

Sometime after Margaretta's baptism, Simon and Susan agreed that they would go their separate ways and discontinued their relationship. This separation constituted a divorce in accepted Anishinabek custom and practice. Susan remained unmarried.

Simon's third and final marriage was solemnized in the Catholic Church. He married Mary Jane Madwes (or Madwens) Macksunge (or Mocksunge). She was the daughter of Mr. and Mrs. Angelus Madwes, and the widow of Antoine Macksunge, who was also known as Antoine Ahdawish. Father Pius Niermann of Harbor Springs officiated at the marriage of the couple on July 6, 1884, at the Anishinabek Catholic Mission Church in Petoskey, Emmett County. Jacob Eskibwa and Elizabeth Kiwekando were witnesses to the marriage.

Mary was raised in Cross Village, Emmet County, and brought up in the Catholic Church. After their marriage, Simon and Mary lived at Burt Lake and at Bay Shore in Charlevoix County. The couple were known by their friends to be faithful and devoted members of their church. Although they had no children together, Mary brought her son, William Mocksunge, to her marriage with Simon.

Simon's Application #916,812 for a pension for disability was filed for him on October 20, 1890, under the liberal Act of June 27, 1890. He cited injuries to his ankles, knees, legs, and back and disease of the lungs and chest with general debility. He reported that such debilities were of a permanent character and rendered him incapacitated in such a manner that he was unable to earn his living by manual labor.

Although unable to work, Simon did join the GAR George Washington Post #106 at Cross Village in Emmet County and enjoyed the fellowship of the other members.

In November 1891, Simon received his Invalid Pension Certificate #687,755, which paid him twelve dollars a month for disabilities mentioned previously. On March 4, 1895, Simon's monthly pension rate was reduced to eight dollars a month.

On September 18, 1896, and again on November 28, 1898, Simon resubmitted declarations for an increase in pension payments. He cited the additional infirmities of deafness and kidney disease. Simon also stated that he felt that the rate was too low since he was practically unable to perform manual labor to earn wages. These declarations for an increase were rejected, and his pension rate remained at eight dollars a month.

Simon and Mary moved to Charlevoix County from Cheboygan County shortly before the disastrous October 1900 fire that was deliberately set and burned out the Burt Lake settlement at Colonial Point (*Conversations*). The main causes of the tragedy involved the misinterpretation and total disregard for the differences between annuity payments versus taxes by the town's local officials and the state's lack of responsibility in dealing with trust land (*Friday*). This terrible event left the Anishinabek of the settlement homeless and destitute.

On August 20, 1902, Simon again submitted a request for a rate increase, but it was again rejected. During their entire time together, Mary was a devoted wife and tenderly cared for her sickly, emaciated husband. She earned what money she could by her labor of basket making and selling the produce from her garden.

In late 1902, Simon and Mary moved to a little log house on Mitchell Odagemiki's (or Odagomeke's) farm in Hayes Township near Bay Shore (also known as Porcupine Ridge) in Charlevoix County. Mitchell was Mary's brother-in-law whose wife had previously died. The Sanequaby couple rented a small plot of ground for a garden from Mitchell.

Simon Sanequaby died of typhoid fever on June 27, 1903, at his home in Hayes Township. Dr. Lewis of Charlevoix attended him in his last hours. Typhoid fever is an acute infectious disease caused by *Salmonella typhosa* and contracted by ingesting contaminated food or water (*Blakiston*).

Mitchell Odagemiki laid out Simon's body and purchased a coffin from undertaker Charles E. See of Charlevoix. Simon was buried in the Carpenter Cemetery (the Old Indian Cemetery at Bay Shore of Resort Township in Emmet

County) on June 29, 1903. The funeral at the cemetery was attended by family members, close friends, and Company K comrades William Isaac and John Jacko.

Simon had not owned property of any kind, and Mary had a hard time supporting herself in her advanced age. Upon invitation, she divided her time living with widower Mitchell Odagemiki and his grown children in their house and with another brother-in-law, Joseph Kewagoshkum, and his wife. Joseph had married Mary's younger sister, Rosa, and owned a farm adjoining Mitchell's property. These families cared for Mary as best as they could.

On October 26, 1903, Mary Sanequaby's Application #793,645 for a widow's pension was filed for her. She had no one legally bound to support her after her husband's death, and she did need monetary assistance. She submitted her application under the Act of June 27, 1890, as amended by the Act of May 9, 1900.

Mary received her Widow's Pension Certificate #594,494 on June 30, 1905, which paid eight dollars a month. On July 6, 1905, she received the accrued pension of eight dollars a month that was owed to her husband retroactive from the date of his death in 1903. She finally had some money to reimburse her hosts for room and board.

Under the Act of April 19, 1908, Mary's pension payments were increased from eight dollars to twelve dollars per month.

Mary Sanequaby died of severe diarrhea at the age of eighty-five in Hayes Township on August 19, 1913. She was buried near her husband in the Old Indian Cemetery (Carpenter Cemetery).

Sargonquatto, Aaron, Private

Enlistment: Enlisted as a private on February 14, 1865, at Grand Rapids, Kent County, by Captain Norman Bailey, First Michigan Sharpshooters and provost marshal for the Fourth Congressional District, for one year. Credited to the Fourth Congressional District, Leelanau Township, Leelanau County.

Age: Twenty-one, born January 10, 1844, at White Hall, Muskegon County.
Occupation: Laborer
Residence: Leelanau Township, Leelanau County
Physical Description: Five feet seven, black eyes, black hair, and a dark complexion. Examining physician was Dr. Alonzo Mate, First Regiment, Michigan Sharpshooters.

Mustered: February 14, 1865, at Grand Rapids by Captain Norman Bailey, First Michigan Sharpshooters and provost marshal for the Fourth Congressional District.

Military Service: While in the trenches before Petersburg, Virginia, in April 1865, Private Sargonquatto incurred a serious injury that would ultimately leave him blind in his left eye. During the battle, an artillery shell struck the ground near him and exploded. With the explosion, sand and dirt were thrown with such great force into his face and left eye that he was temporarily blinded.

Aaron was taken immediately to a first aid station at the rear of the battle. At the station, both eyes were repeatedly washed out with water, and the inner parts of his eyelids were treated with applications of silver nitrate in water (*Dorwart*).

He returned to his regiment after treatment. But the soreness in his left eye would become progressively worse due to conjunctivitis, or inflammation of the mucous membrane of the eye (*Blakiston*).

In June 1865, Private Sargonquatto was detailed for duty at the Quartermaster Department in Washington, DC.

Discharged: Private Aaron Sargonquatto was mustered out of the army and honorably discharged at Detroit, Michigan, on August 11, 1865. He was paid the money owed to him for his service at his discharge.

Biography: While Antoine Pequongay and his wife, Elizabeth (or Shahwonequa), were in their winter hunting camp near White Hall, Michigan, in January 1842, their son Aaron was born. Even though his family surname was Pequongay, Aaron was known to the Anishinabek as Aaron Sargonquatto, which was also spelled Sahgahnahquato. He would use the name Sargonquatto at his adult baptism, during his military service, and when he signed legal papers, except for his marriage license, when he used the name Aaron Pequongay spelled Puhquonga on the license. The name Sargonquatto is derived from the Anishinabe word (*z)saageaankwad,* which means "clouds are coming" (*Avery*). His siblings included brothers, Shedonequet and Ahbedosegagua, and sisters, Mohdwahgewang and Quisis.

Before he entered the service, Aaron was employed in a sawmill in Manistee, Manistee County. What skills he learned at this mill would aid him in his trade as a carpenter.

On May 8, 1864, Aaron was baptized by Rev. Peter Doughtery, who was the resident missionary to the Presbyterian New Mission Church in Omena of Leelanau County (*Dougherty*). After his baptism, Aaron joined the church and became a lifelong contributing member.

Five years after his discharge from the army, Aaron, age twenty-six, married Susan Allen, age fifteen, the sister of his deceased Company K comrade Sergeant Charles Allen. The couple was married on February 10, 1870, by Rev. Peter Dougherty at Dougherty's home (parsonage) in Omena, Leelanau County. Witnesses to the ceremony were John Kesis, another Company K comrade, and Susan's father, Moses Naskare (or Naishkaze). Refer to Sgt. Charles Allen's file for more on Rev. Peter Dougherty and his Presbyterian mission. After her marriage to Aaron, Susan used the name Susan Pequongay when she was conversing with her English-speaking friends and was also known as Susan Sargonquatto.

Susan was the daughter of Moses (Naskare or Naishkaze) and Annie (or Onjeequa) Allen. She was born in her father's sugar camp west of the village of Omena in the spring of 1852 (*Craker*). Susan and her siblings were also active, baptized members of Dougherty's church. Both Aaron and Susan had attended Rev. Dougherty's mission school (*Ibid.*).

In her later years, Susan described the process of making maple sugar to writer and author Ruth Craker (*Ibid.*). Craker included Susan's description of the process in her book *The First Protestant Mission in the Grand Traverse Region*. Susan's narrative, as told to Mrs. Craker, is as follows:

> "My father often tapped 1,100 trees. When the snow began to melt in the spring and the temperature rose to around 40 degrees, it was time for the people to erect their camps in the sugar bush and tap the trees. The wooden spiles called na-gum-na-quam were driven firmly into a gash in the maple trunk. The sap pails used were 10 quart containers made of birch bark, shaped like a canoe, and called we-gwas-ne-ba-bun. The to-ba-je-gon was a container carved out of a basswood tree and large enough to hold 100 gallons of sap. The sap was stored in these containers when it ran freely and the kettles were overflowing. The maple syrup was boiled in large copper kettles. Inside of the temporary wigwams one might see twelve of these kettles steaming over the open fire. The hole in the roof being the only means for the escape of smoke. They used four foot wood, three lengths long, to burn under the kettles. The Indians made several products from the maple sap. The syrup was called se-wa-ga-ma-da, the delicious wax was known as peg-a-wa-da and the sugar was the siz-a-ah-qua. The sugar was often pulverized and packed in birch bark boxes called

mococks. These mococks had a capacity of from 8-100 pounds. The sugar making time was a family time and a merry time for the Indian people and was anticipated many months before the time. Visitors were always welcome to the Anishinabek sugar camps and were treated to soft sugar and wax on a large maple chip and given little wooden paddles with which to eat it."

Aaron and Susan were the parents of the following children: Lucy, born November 10, 1870; Marion, born July 6, 1872; Julia Ann, born November 15, 1873; Luke, born May 9, 1876; Mary Ann, born November 29, 1878; Harry Jay, born July 2, 1883; John Perry, born September 14, 1884; Louisa Bell, born June 26, 1888; Esther, born September 30, 1890; and Pearl May, born June 25, 1892. One daughter, Lucy, was baptized in June 1871 by Rev. Dougherty at Omena.

Julia would marry Daniel Nokogwon (or Naoquom), the son of Philip and Margaret Naoquom, on April 17, 1894. The couple divorced on November 5, 1909. Julia's second marriage was to Philip King. Lucy married Isaac Andrews on October 23, 1902. Julia Ann and Lucy were the only Pequongay children still living in 1915.

Although his health had begun to fail, Aaron, who was an excellent carpenter, tried to find work to support his family. He often loaded lake vessels along the shore during the summer months and farmed to meet his family's needs.

Aaron joined the GAR Woolsey Post #399 at Northport and was officer of the guard during every year of his membership until his death. He enjoyed reminiscing with his Company K buddies William Newton, Payson Wolf, James Arwonogezice, and John Shomin, as well as other Civil War veterans who were also members of his post.

Aaron's Application #914,740 for an invalid pension was filed for him on September 20, 1890, under the liberal and generous Act of June 27, 1890. He cited blindness in his left eye, eczema that he had acquired in the service, rheumatism, heart trouble, and the inability to do hard manual labor as his reasons for the application.

He resubmitted his application in December 1893 and May 1894. On October 30, 1894, Aaron received his Invalid Pension Certificate #877, 278, which paid six dollars a month retroactive to September 20, 1890.

In January 1895 and again in September 1897 and October 1899, Aaron applied for an increase in his pension payments. He applied because of his increasing inability to do manual labor to support his family. At first, the applications for an increase were denied. Then, in 1903, he was granted a two-dollar increase to bring his total monthly payments to eight dollars.

On May 17, 1907, Aaron submitted an application to be put on the pension rolls under the Act of February 6, 1907. If approved, Aaron would qualify for an increase in monthly payments. In December 1907, Aaron was reissued a pension under the Act of February 6, 1907, and his name was dropped from the rolls of the Act of June 27, 1890. By April 26, 1907, his monthly payments totaled twelve dollars.

Aaron again submitted an application for an increase in his pension on January 16, 1912, in which he cited continued decline in his health. At first, the application was rejected because he could not produce any documents that would verify his advanced age. He explained that the Anishinabek did not keep written records of peoples' ages so he relied upon family and friends to testify on his behalf.

Finally, in December 1912, under the Act of May 11, 1912, Aaron received a reissue of his pension that paid him fifteen dollars a month retroactive to May 28, 1912. Having attained the age of seventy by 1915, Aaron was approved for an increase of three dollars in his monthly pension payments to total eighteen dollars.

On Sunday June 4, 1916, Aaron Sargonquatto died of organic heart disease (caused by something that affected the structure of the heart) at the age of seventy-two at his home in Northport in Leelanau County. He was buried with religious rites and military honors from the Woolsey Post in the Hillcrest Cemetery at Omena. His name is listed as Aaron Pequongay on his death certificate. His military stone lists his name as both Aaron Pequongay and Aaron Sargonquatto.

Susan's Application #1,069,020 for a widow's pension was filed for her on July 10, 1916. In December 1916, Susan applied for the accrued pension owed to her husband before his death.

On April 28, 1917, Susan received Widow's Pension Certificate #824,040, which paid twelve dollars a month retroactive to July 10, 1916. The accrued pension payments, owed to Aaron before his death, were also granted in April 1917 when Susan received her widow's pension. Her payments were increased to forty dollars a month on June 4, 1928, under the Act of May 23, 1928.

Sometime between 1920 and 1930, Susan moved to Traverse City in Grand Traverse County. By 1930, Susan's widowed daughter, Julia King, and grandson, Perry King, were living with Susan.

Susan Pequongay died at her home in Traverse City on Thursday, July 20, 1939, at the age of eighty-seven. Her death was caused by a two-week duration of influenza with the contributory factor of chronic bronchitis. She was buried in the Hillcrest Cemetery in Omena not far from her husband's grave site.

Susan was the last surviving widow of a Company K veteran. She was preceded in death by the only other surviving Company K widow, Mrs. William (Angeline Nebawnegezhik) Newton. Mrs. Newton died in February 1936 at about the age of eighty-six. At the time of her death, Angeline was living in Williamsburg in Grand Traverse County.

Sashkobanquat, Private

Enlistment: Enlisted as a private on May 18, 1863, at Isabella City (now Mt. Pleasant), Isabella County, by First Lieutenant William J. Driggs, First Michigan Sharpshooters, for three years.

Age: Forty-five, born about 1818 in Saginaw County.

Occupation: Farmer

Residence: Pinconning, Bay County

Physical Description: Five feet eight, black eyes, black hair, and a dark complexion. Examining physician was Dr. George L. Cornell, assistant surgeon, First Michigan Sharpshooters.

Mustered: May 26, 1863, at Detroit, Wayne County, by Lieutenant Colonel John R. Smith, US Army

Military Service: In July 1863, Private Sashkobanquot was listed as a company cook when the regiment guarded the Detroit Arsenal at Dearborn.

When his regiment was guarding Confederate prisoners at Camp Douglas in Chicago, Cook County, Illinois, Sashkobanquat was given a pass (or permit) to visit the city of Chicago on the evening of December 27, 1863. As with many soldiers given the freedom of a night out, Sashkobanquat visited a few taverns. On his way back to Camp Douglas, and possibly in an inebriated state, he crossed some railroad tracks and was struck and killed by a train.

What was left of Sashkobanquot's body was most likely buried in Chicago's City Cemetery located six miles north of Camp Douglas. Both Confederate and Union dead from Camp Douglas were buried there. The City Cemetery was a low wet land, and the burial sites deteriorated over time (*Levy*). Instead of names, numbers were inscribed on the headboards and kept on a list.

Some 655 Confederate prisoners and twelve Union guards, who died of smallpox, were buried in the smallpox cemetery across from Camp Douglas. Their graves were marked with headboards inscribed with names (*Ibid.*).

In 1865, the remains from the smallpox cemetery were removed to Oak Woods Cemetery. But in the process of removal, none of the headboards, including those of the twelve Union guards, were removed with the bodies but were thrown aside (*Ibid.*). Today, twelve military stones marked "Unknown U. S. Soldier" can be found in Oak Woods Cemetery.

City Cemetery was closed in January 1867. At its closing, the government purchased two acres in Oak Woods Cemetery for a mass reburial of Confederate prisoners. The reburial area is known as "Confederate Mound," and the interments occurred from April 13 to April 30 of said year. Union soldiers buried in City Cemetery were also reburied at Oak Woods as well as Rosehill Cemetery (*Ibid.*).

Confederate remains were refused reburial at Rosehill due to the expressed animosity of burying Confederate prisoners next to the remains of Union guards in that cemetery (*Ibid.*).

Private Sashkobanquot's grave is as yet to be found. He may be buried at Rosehill Cemetery since it is thought that most of the prison guards were reburied there. But it's possible that one of the unknown Union bodies buried in Oak Woods could be that of the private.

Discharged: No discharge given due to accidental death while on an evening pass in Chicago.

Biography: After Sashkobanquat's death, two women claimed to be his wife. Each woman applied for a widow's pension.

The first woman to make a claim was Etoqua (or Mary) Sashkobanquat, whose Application #54,722 for a widow's pension was filed for her on June 20, 1864. She stated that she was a resident of Buena Vista Township of Saginaw County. Also, she stated that she married Sashkobanquat about 1834 in Sebewaing, Huron County, according to Anishinabek custom and practice (consent of the couple and their parents). The couple were the parents of: Wawwegoshshe, age fifteen; Penasewonquad, age ten; Snakekeghink, age eight; Gawpaykeshinkgoqua, age four; and Wabeskonquad (or Julia), age two. Testifying on her behalf was the much-respected Anishinabe Chief Naugechegumme (also spelled Naugjekomeh) Nauckchegawme and Henry Jackson, who were residents of Saginaw County. Both men stated that Sashkobanquot and Mary Sashkobanquot were always considered husband and wife and that the children were considered their legitimate offspring.

The second woman to make a claim for a widow's pension was Saline Sashkobanquat. Her Application #101,734 for a widow's pension was filed for her on July 5, 1865. Saline stated that she was a resident of East Saginaw, Saginaw County, and that she had married Sashkobanquot on April 4, 1843. She also stated that she and Sashkobanquot were the parents of: Isabell, age twelve; John, age ten; William, age eight; Sarah, age six; Mary, age four; and Henry, age two. Testifying on her behalf was James David, who was a missionary and teacher among the Anishinabek of Saginaw. He stated that Sashkobanquot, Saline, and their children attended his church. The children also attended the church school. James affirmed that Sashkobanquot and Saline were always considered husband and wife and that the children were their legitimate offspring.

Mary Sashkobanquat's claim for a pension was denied on June 14, 1867, because her said husband was killed while on a pass and did not die in the line of duty.

On January 23, 1869, Saline Sashkobanquot was allowed to collect arrears pay for Sashkobanquot's service in the form of Treasury Certificate #194,331. The certificate was retroactive to December 23, 1863. It seems that at that time, the US Treasury Department deemed Saline as the lawful wife from the testimony that the office received.

But on May 1, 1870, upon further study of the testimony given by Mary's friends, Mary (Etoqua) Sashkobanquot was determined to be the true wife of Sashkobanquot and accepted as such by the US government.

Saline Sashkobanquot's claim for a pension was likewise denied on December 9, 1871, for the same reason as Mary's claim—Sashkobanquot was not killed in the line of duty. Saline did not resubmit further claims for a pension.

Being recognized by the government as Sashkobanquot's true wife on September 7, 1887, Mary resubmitted her claim for a pension in September and October 1890 and in July 1891. She cited her condition as being nearly blind, desperately poor, and wholly dependent upon others for support. The US Pension Office sent a final rejection notice to Mary on July 28, 1891. The reason given for the rejection was that even though she was deemed to be Sashkobanquot's true wife, the soldier did not die in the line of duty but while on a pass to the city. Therefore, Mary was not eligible for a widow's pension. Further attempts to file claims for a pension on behalf of Mary (Etoqua) Sashkobanquot were abandoned.

Sawbequom, Adam, Private

Enlistment: Enlisted as a private on July 4, 1863, at Pentwater (some documents also state Elbridge), Oceana County, by Captain Edwin V. Andress, First Michigan Sharpshooters, for three years.

Age: Twenty-eight, born about 1835 in Barry County.

Occupation: Laborer

Residence: Pentwater

Physical Description: Five feet five, black eyes, black hair, and a dark complexion. Examining physician was Dr. Jacob B. McNett, assistant surgeon, First Michigan Sharpshooters.

Mustered: July 11, 1863, at Detroit, Wayne County, by Lieutenant Colonel John R. Smith, US Army

Military Service: On April 2, 1864, Private Adam Sawbequom was admitted from his camp to Division No. 1, USA General Hospital at the United States Naval Academy (Navy Yard) in Annapolis, Maryland, suffering from erysipelas of the face. Erysipelas is a highly infectious disease in which the causative organism is *Streptococcus pyogenes* (*Blakiston*). The resulting infection causes a spreading inflammation of the skin. A fever develops, and the bacteria in the bloodstream (bacteremia) causes severe toxic effects in the patient *(Ibid.)*. The disease can be spread by the unclean hands of medical personnel, dirty instruments and dressings, or by infection in small cuts or wounds.

Upon admission to the hospital, Private Sawbequom had a high fever, a severely swollen face, closed eyes, and painful bowels. The doctors immediately put him into isolation and prescribed a mercury ointment that was prepared from elemental mercury, lard, and suet to be spread on his skin (*Evans*). A tincture of iodine used as a paint was also applied to his skin *(Ibid.)*. To relieve the pain in his bowels and lower his high fever, Adam was given oral medications of potassium iodide and sulfate of magnesium to purge his system *(Ibid.)*. Medicinal whiskey was ordered as a stimulant. By April 4, Adam's condition had improved to the point where the swelling in his face had subsided. His bowels returned to normal, his pulse was regular, his appetite improved, and his pain had disappeared. By April 8, he was able to walk around the hospital yard and required no further treatment.

Adam returned to duty on April 15. He was lucky that his illness was a mild case. His true torment would soon follow and result in his agonizing death.

Private Sawbequom was captured by the rebels on June 17, 1864, while charging the enemy's works in a battle before Petersburg, Virginia. He was first reported as missing in action before knowledge of his capture.

After being held for a few days in a tobacco warehouse on Short Market Street in Petersburg, Adam and other soldiers, including several other Company K comrades, were then loaded onto cattle railcars. The men were then sent on a long journey to a Confederate prison camp. The camp was known as Camp Sumter (also known as Andersonville Prison), in Andersonville, Georgia. It was an open stockade where the prisoners were exposed to the elements and inhumane treatment by their captors.

Due to the lack of proper food, Adam succumbed to scurvy (the lack of vitamin C from fresh fruits and vegetables) and starved to death. His death was recorded on October 26, 1864, and was the same day that he was admitted to the prison hospital.

Sawbequom's body was removed from the prison hospital by his Company K comrades, or by prison guards, and taken to the brush arbor dead house outside of the stockade. Any useful clothing was removed from the body. Information about Adam was collected by a record keeper known as Dorance Atwater (also a prisoner), who kept the "Atwater List" of those prisoners who died at Andersonville Prison. Atwater attached a numbered tag to the body for later identification. Then, as quickly as possible, Adam's remains, as well as other bodies, were taken by wagon to the cemetery a mile from the prison grounds (*Encyclopedia*).

At the cemetery, Sawbequom was placed without a covering into a trench and shoulder to shoulder with other deceased soldiers. His remains were then covered with soil. A small post was placed at the head of his grave with a number carved into it (*Ibid.*). This number matched the number on the body tag and was also noted in the records known about the deceased. Today Adam lies at rest in a grave marked with military stone #11508 that states his name as "Xedan Saw-be-come."

Discharged: No discharge given due to death by disease while a prisoner of war.

Biography: Adam Sawbequom's father died in 1845, leaving Adam as the sole support for his mother, Mary Natamamacy Sawbequom (also known as Mary Naktoma). Adam did not marry.

For ten years before he entered the army, Adam worked at any and all jobs that he could find in order to procure a rented home for his mother and to provide for her needs.

During his service, Adam sent home as much of his pay (when he was paid) as he could. His death left his mother destitute.

On April 24, 1865, Application #90,526 for a mother's pension was filed for

Mary Natamamacy Sawbequom, who, at that time, was a resident of Elbridge, Oceana County. She testified that she had been solely dependent upon her son for support, and since his death, she had no resource by which she could obtain money for rent, interest, or provisions. Since she was not able to work due to her failed health, she was dependent upon charity and friends for support.

Finally, on March 4, 1870, Mary was granted a Widow's Pension Certificate #140,550 under the Act of July 14, 1862, which paid eight dollars a month retroactive to October 27, 1864.

On March 5, 1879, Mary applied for arrears due to her under the act granting arrears of pensions approved January 18, 1879. It's not known if she received these payments. Note that "Adam Sawbequom" and "A. Sockum" are the same man on the Sharpshooter roster for Company K.

Scott, Antoine, Corporal

Enlistment: Enlisted as a corporal on July 4, 1863, at Pentwater (documents also state Elbridge), Oceana County, by Captain Edwin V. Andress, First Michigan Sharpshooters, for three years.

Age: Twenty-two, born about 1841 in the Mackinaw area of Michigan.

Occupation: Laborer

Residence: Pentwater

Physical Description: Five feet five, black eyes, black hair, and a dark complexion. Examining physician was Dr. Jacob B. McNett, assistant surgeon, First Michigan Sharpshooters.

Mustered: July 11, 1863, at Detroit, Wayne County, by Lieutenant Colonel John R. Smith, US Army

Military Service: On April 16, 1864, Corporal Antoine Scott, also known as Antoine LaCroix and Antoine Wayaubemind, was listed as a patient in his regimental hospital in Annapolis, Maryland, suffering from intermittent fever (or malaria). Malaria is an infectious disease caused by one of the genus *Plasmodium* and is transmitted by infected mosquitoes of the genus *Anopheles*. His symptoms included chills, headache, fever, and copious sweat. Treatment consisted of quinine derived from dried, powdered cinchona tree bark that was dissolved in water or whiskey (whiskey masked quinine's bitter taste) or given as pills of purified quinine sulfate (*Bollet*). Quinine was given every few hours during the remission phase, followed by an opium pill if the patient was nauseated or had vomited. Antoine rejoined his regiment when his symptoms were under control.

Corporal Scott distinguished himself in action during the disastrous Battle of the Crater before Petersburg, Virginia, on June 30, 1864. Due to his leadership and example, Corporal Scott was promoted to the rank of sergeant by Regimental Major Asahel W. Nichols on September 1, 1864.

Pursuant to paragraph 7, Special Orders No. 346, Headquarters, Army of the Potomac, dated December 22, 1864, was a request for the names of men who distinguished themselves by conspicuous and daring bravery. Among five men of the Michigan Sharpshooter Regiment mentioned for their bravery was the name of Sergeant Antoine Scott of Company K. He was cited by Regimental Major Asahel W. Nichols for conspicuous gallantry, bravery, and good conduct during the battle to wit: "in refusing to screen himself from the enemy's fire behind the captured works, he stood boldly up and deliberately and calmly fired his piece until the enemy was almost upon him when instead of laying down his arm and surrendering, ran the gauntlet of shot and shell and escaped."

Sergeant Scott was granted a furlough of twenty days on January 11, 1865. He was reported overdue on February 4. Scott returned to his regiment, but the reason for his overdue report was not specified.

Upon the recommendation of Major Asahel W. Nichols, Major General John G. Parke, who commanded the Ninth Army Corps, recommended Sergeant Antoine Scott for the Medal of Honor (the second recommendation) on February 21, 1865, for gallantry, bravery, and good conduct on the field. General Parke echoed Major Nichols's citation to wit: "Sergeant Antoine Scott, Company K, 1st. Michigan S. S. Before Petersburg, 30 July, 1864, instead of screening himself behind the captured works, this soldier stood boldly up and deliberately fired his piece until the enemy was close upon him, when instead of surrendering, he ran the gauntlet of shot and shell and escaped."

The Adjutant General's Office of the US War Department did attach a note to the military record of Antoine Scott in 1887. The note, in the form if a bookmark, was number 1339-A-1887 and verified that General John G. Park did recommend Scott for the Medal of Honor on February 21, 1865. It's not known if Scott knew of his citation and of his recommendation for the Medal of Honor before his death in 1878. Medals of Honor were not awarded posthumously during that time in our country's history.

Five other men of the Michigan Sharpshooter regiment, Sergeant Charles M.

Thatcher of Company B, Corporal Sidney Haight of Company E, Sergeant Charles H. De Puy of Company H, Sergeant Alonzo Woodruff of Company I, and Corporal Benjamin F. Youngs of Company I were also cited and recommended for their conduct under fire (*Bozich*). These men would receive their Medals of Honor by 1896 (*Ibid.*). It's sad that Sergeant Scott, the only Michigan Anishinabe soldier to be recommended twice for this prestigious award, did not receive his country's highest military honor and proudly wear its medal before he died.

On March 15, 1865, Sgt. Scott, feeling ill, and a patient in his regimental hospital, was taken to a military railroad, put on a mattress in a boxcar, the floor of which was cushioned with straw or hay, and sent to the depot hospital at City Point, Virginia. The doctors at City Point confirmed the diagnosis of Scott's regimental physicians. His illness was the venereal disease of primary-stage syphilis.

Syphilis is caused by the microbe *Treponema pallidum*. Symptoms in the primary stage are characterized by small, painless penile ulcers called chancres. These chancres heal over a course of several weeks (*Blackiston*). Among the various treatments for syphilis were the applications of compounds that contained mercury to the primary chancre and penile irrigation administered with a hard rubber syringe. The irrigation procedure may have been done under anesthesia (*Bollet*).

The medications administered to the patient were cathartics (or purgatives), such as calomel (or mercurous chloride) that contained mercury (*Ibid.*), sulfate of magnesium for fever, and castor oil to evacuate the bowels (*Evans*).

On March 23, Scott was taken to a wharf at City Point, and transferred to a hospital steamer which took him to an undisclosed general hospital in Washington, DC.

While Scott was in the hospital in Washington, he was also diagnosed with a second case of venereal disease—gonorrhea. This diagnosis was noted by the doctors on March 26. The disease is caused by the bacterium *Neisseria gonorrhea* and produces a copious, irritating, and thick penile discharge (*Ibid.-Blakiston*). Scott's treatment included penile irrigation treatments (probably under anesthesia as previously mentioned) with solutions of chlorate of potash, chloride of zinc, silver nitrate, and lead or mercury administered with a hard rubber syringe (*Schaadt*). He was also restricted to bed rest and a bland diet. Sometime later, Antoine returned to his regiment. It should be noted that none of the medications used by the doctors to combat venereal disease during the Civil War produced a cure.

Due to an undisclosed infraction, Antoine was reduced in rank from sergeant to private on May 1, 1865. This demotion must have come as a shock to his pride because he improved his demeanor and was promoted to corporal on July 1, 1865.

Discharged: Corporal Antoine Scott was mustered out and honorably discharged on July 28, 1865, at Delaney House, Washington, DC. He returned to Detroit on the steamer *Morning Star.* On August 7, 1865, the soldier was paid money due to him for his service at Jackson, Jackson County.

Biography: Antoine Scott La Croix (the cross) was the son of Petabun (or Petabunaque), also known as Elizabeth, and her second husband, Mitchell La Croix. Petabun was first married to one Niobi Aninewawbe (also known as Nesogod and Niobi Kesheway). Elizabeth and Niobi were the parents of at least one child, a daughter named Margaret Aninewawbe or Margaret Niobi, a half sister to Antoine.

After Mitchell La Croix's death, Petabun married for the third time to Joseph Wayaubemind. Petabun and Joseph were the parents of at least one son, Michael Wayaubemind, who was a half brother to Margaret Niobi and Antoine Scott. Michael was also a member of Company K.

As mentioned previously, Antoine was known by the surnames of LaCroix (his father) and Wayaubemind (his stepfather) in addition to his choice of Scott—the name that he used during his years in the army as well as in his post military years.

Scott was certainly not a well man when he was discharged and returned to Michigan. In addition to his venereal diseases, he was known to have had diarrhea and rheumatism. It's possible that his primary case of syphilis, which could have been in remission at the time of his discharge, may have developed into the secondary phase. The complications of this development would have weakened his health in such a way that he developed pulmonary problems and suffered an early death.

Antoine La Croix Wayaubemind Scott died at the age of thirty-seven on December 10, 1878, in Custer of Mason County. On the state death register for Mason County, Antoine was listed as married, a laborer, and the cause of death was inflammation of the lungs (or pneumonia). It is presumed that he was buried in Mason County. One record in his military papers listed his death as having occurred at Pentwater, although the state death register would be accepted as the most valid record.

Application #415,546 for a mother's pension was filed on February 21, 1890, for Petabun Wayaubemind, then a resident of Bear Creek Township in Emmet County. Her third husband, Joseph Wayaubemind, died in 1883 and left her in need of support.

Margaret Niobe, Antoine's half sister from his mother's first marriage, testified on May 20, 1889, that her mother was dependent upon Antoine for her support before his death. Since her husband Joseph's death, Elizabeth had been dependent upon public assistance and her daughter Margaret's help. Margaret further related that she and her mother were becoming feeble with age and unable to work at any hard labor. Because of their infirmities, Elizabeth and Margaret made birch bark items and ornaments to sell for monetary income.

According to Margaret's deposition, Antoine left neither wife nor children (her mother agreed to this statement) at his death. Since Antoine was listed as married on his death certificate, it has not been ascertained as to his true marital status when he was living.

Not having received any correspondence or answers to further questions posed by the US Pension Office, Elizabeth (or Petabun) Wayaubemind's application for a widow mother's pension was abandoned.

Seymour, Joseph, Private

Enlistment: Enlisted as a private on September 24, 1864, at Ontonagon, Ontonagon County (in the Upper Peninsula of Michigan), by A.E.B. Mann, First Michigan Sharpshooters, for three years. Another record states that Seymore's enlistment was in Greenland of Ontonagon County. Credited to the Sixth Congressional District, Greenland Township, Ontonagon County.

    Age: Twenty, born about 1844 in Ontonagon County.

    Occupation: Laborer

    Residence: Greenland, Ontonagon County

    Physical Description: Five feet eight and a half inches tall, dark eyes, dark hair, and a dark complexion. Examining physician was Dr. George Landon.

    Mustered: October 20, 1864, at Detroit, Wayne County, by Captain Mark Flanagan, Twenty-Fourth Michigan Infantry and provost marshal

    Military Service: Private Seymore joined his regiment at Peebles House, Virginia, on November 4, 1864.

On January 31, 1865, in a battle before Petersburg, Virginia, Seymore sustained a wound to his left leg caused by a piece of shrapnel from an explosion of an artillery shell. He was taken to his aid station where his wound was assessed, washed, and hastily bandaged. From the aid station, Seymore was taken by an ambulance wagon to his division hospital farther behind the lines. The wound was described as a contusion (or bruise) in the popliteal space (a depression or pit) behind his left knee. This hollow area (or fossa) is formed when the knee is flexed or bent.

On February 1, Seymour was taken by ambulance wagon to the military railroad and put on a mattress in a boxcar, the floor of which was cushioned with straw or hay, and sent to the depot hospital at City Point, Virginia.

Treatment at the depot hospital consisted of bathing the area with cold water and applying a cloth of cotton, muslin, linen, or flannel spread with molasses and secured with adhesive bandages (*Powers*). After his treatment, the patient was confined to bed rest.

On February 26, Seymour was transferred to the Convalescent Camp Branch of the depot hospital at City Point. He was detailed as a camp guard on March 9, and on March 20 he was sent back to his regiment.

Discharged: Private Joseph Seymour was mustered out and given an honorable discharge on July 28, 1865 at Delaney House, Washington, DC. He returned to Detroit on the steamer *Morning Star*. On August 7, 1865, Seymour was paid money due to him for his service at Jackson, Jackson County.

Biography: No further information is known about Seymour. He probably returned to his home in Ontonagon County. There is no pension file for Joseph Seymour.

Shabena, Charles, Private

Enlistment: Enlisted as a wagoner with the rank of private on June 11, 1863, at La Croix (renamed Cross Village in 1875), Emmet County, by Second Lieutenant Garrett A. Graveraet, First Michigan Sharpshooters, for three years.

Age: Twenty-three, born about 1840 in La Croix.

Occupation: Farmer and laborer

Residence: La Croix

Physical Description: Five feet eight and a half inches tall, black eyes, black hair, and a dark complexion. Examining physician was Dr. Arvin F. Whelan, surgeon, First Michigan Sharpshooters.

Mustered: July 20, 1863, at Detroit, Wayne County, by Lieutenant Colonel John R. Smith, US Army

Military Service: Private Shabena was a wagoner, or teamster, for Company K. He did not enlist as an infantryman. His job was very important and a vital part in keeping the company supplied for its needs. He was in charge of transporting company property that included forage for the teams, food and cooking utensils, rations for the troops, hospital stores and medicines, weapons, ammunition, clothing, shelter tents, tools, soldiers' knapsacks, officers' baggage, and anything else that the Quartermaster Corps deemed necessary for use by the company. He was expected to keep his wagon in good shape, properly loaded at all times, and to be able to repair it when necessary. In addition to all these tasks, Charles was responsible for the proper care of the mule team that drew the supply wagon (*Wagoner*). It's possible that Charles may have told the recruiting officers that he had experience as a wagoner and that he knew how to care for the mules and rig.

In August 1863, while at the confine for Confederate prisoners known as Camp Douglas, in Chicago, Cook County, Illinois, Shabena served as a company cook. He again served as company cook in October and November 1864 while at the front with his regiment. Like the infantrymen on the picket line or on the march, he was also exposed to inclement weather.

On April 9, 1865, Shabena left with his company from Rainsburgh, Virginia, south of Petersburg, for Cedar Point. The march took two days and one night, during which time the company advanced without intermission.

Many of the men became very ill during the march, including Private Shabena, who caught a severe cold. The men boarded a steamboat at Cedar Point for the trip to Alexandria, Virginia, which took another two days. During this trip, Shabena's cold became worse, and he also suffered from diarrhea.

From Alexandria, the men proceeded to Georgetown where they encamped. It was at this time that Shabena's cold developed into bronchitis and his diarrhea became worse.

Charles was so incapacitated that he was relieved of his duty as a wagoner. His only task was to do light work as a company cook. On the days that he could get out of bed, Charles did not seek medical treatment for his ailments. He didn't trust the regimental doctors. Gradually, Charles's health improved with hot fluids and bed rest and he resumed his duties when he was able to do so.

Discharged: Private Charles Shabena was mustered out and honorably discharged on July 28, 1865, at Delaney House, Washington, DC. He returned to Detroit on the steamer *Morning Star*. On August 7, 1865, Charles was paid money owed to him for his service at Jackson, Jackson County.

Biography: On March 4, 1862, Father Seraphin Zorn, Catholic missionary at La Croix, officiated at the marriage of Charles Shabena (also spelled Shabema), age twenty, and Mary Ann Kijebinessi (also of La Croix), age fifteen. Michael and Mary Kinis of La Croix witnessed the ceremony. Mary Ann was the daughter of

Andrew and Mary Ann (or Kweamokwe) Kijebinessi. Charles and Mary Ann did not have a family.

After Charles returned from the army, he and Mary Ann settled at Little Traverse (renamed Harbor Springs in 1881), Emmett County. Shabena was thought to be a healthy young man when he enlisted, but his war experiences left his health in a broken state. It was thought by some Company K men that Shabena actually had trouble with his lungs at the time of his enlistment, but he was still accepted into the army.

Charles tried to farm and to find whatever jobs he could handle, but his declining health and severe bronchitis resulted in his inability to earn a living. There were many days that he was bedridden. Mary Ann contributed what money she could earn by working as a housemaid.

On September 6, 1866, Application #115,262 for an invalid pension was filed for Charles, who hoped that he would receive a pension.

Because Charles was in danger of dying from suffocation, Father Zorn was summoned several times to his bedside to administer the last rites of the Catholic Church. Finally, on September 13, 1866, Charles Shabena succumbed to pneumonia brought on by the severity of prolonged bouts of bronchitis and possibly other lung ailments. He was buried in Emmet County near Little Traverse.

Before the pension office knew of his death, notification was sent to Charles, which informed him that he would not receive an invalid pension.

After Charles's death, Mary Ann moved back to La Croix to live with her parents. Application #142,530 for a widow's pension was filed for her on February 19, 1867, but she died before her pension application was approved. Her demise was due to the gynecological problem of suppressed periods (the sudden cessation of the menses). She was probably buried near her husband in the Little Traverse area or near her relatives in La Croix.

On February 18, 1869, a Widow's Pension Certificate #125,501 was granted to Mary, which paid eight dollars a month retroactive to July 29, 1865. The certificate was sent before the US Pension Office received notification of Mary's death.

Mary's father, Andrew Kijebinessi (or Kishebinessi), was declared the legal administrator of Mary's estate (and her heir since there were no children) on November 22, 1869. He surrendered Mary's pension certificate and applied for arrears due to a deceased pensioner. Andrew, as Mary's executor of her estate (her pension), received a new pension certificate on March 4, 1870, which granted him Mary's original pension payments of eight dollars a month retroactive from July 29,

1865, until her death on November 30, 1868. Since Mary lived with her parents after her husband's death, the money from Mary's pension could have been used by Mary's father to help pay doctor's expenses and other costs incurred in Mary's care during her illness.

Shaw, Charles, Private

Enlistment: Enlisted as a private on July 4, 1863, at Elbridge (another record states Pentwater), Oceana County, by Captain Edwin V. Andress, First Michigan Sharpshooters, for three years.

Age: Nineteen, born about 1844 in Calhoun County.

Occupation: Farmer

Residence: Pentwater, Oceana County

Physical Description: Five feet nine, black eyes, black hair, and a dark complexion. Examining physician was Dr. Jacob B. McNett, assistant surgeon, First Michigan Sharpshooters.

Mustered: July 11, 1863, at Detroit, Wayne County, by Lieutenant Colonel John R. Smith, US Army

Military Service: Private Charles Shaw deserted from his regiment on July 19, 1863, while stationed as a guard at the Dearborn, Wayne County Arsenal.

On September 9, he returned to his regiment, who was then guarding Confederate prisoners at the Union confine called Camp Douglas in Chicago, Cook County, Illinois. He was restored to duty on the order of Colonel Charles V. De Land. Ten dollars was retained from his pay for the expenses of his arrest, and he was charged with the loss of two .58-caliber Springfield Rifle Muskets.

Due to his arrest and carelessness, Charles had less money to send to his parents in the month of September.

On November 1, 1864, Private Shaw, his deportment improved, redeemed himself from past conduct and was promoted to the rank of corporal.

After his promotion, Shaw was chosen to represent Company K as a member of the regimental color guard (at rank of corporal). In this duty, Charles, who carried a gun, accompanied the color bearer (at rank of sergeant) who carried the regimental flag in battle, and Charles was responsible for protecting the flag and the color bearer, who did not carry a gun (*Color Guard*). This appointment was an honor, and Charles must have understood the significance of it. He was assigned to this position on July 1, 1865. Private Shaw did not incur any injury or illness during his military service.

Discharged: Corporal Charles Shaw was mustered out and honorably discharged on July 28, 1865, at Delaney House, Washington, DC. He returned to Detroit on the steamer *Morning Star*. On August 7, Shaw was paid money due to him for his service at Jackson, Jackson County.

Biography: Charles Shaw, also called Charley Boo Saw Shaw and Charley Shaw, was the son of Shawboosaw and his wife. While in the service, he used only the "Shaw" half of his family name.

In 1860, Charley lived in Weare Township of Oceana County with Charlie Hiskey when the two men worked as laborers.

Charley Shaw married Tebaygomegota (or Nancy) about 1866. Nancy was the daughter of a widow known as Ogawbaishcawmoquay.

By 1870, Shaw was engaged in farming in Elbridge and living with his wife and their son, Kewautaswo, age six months, in Shaw's father's house.

In addition to his work as a farmer, Charles Shaw may have attended meetings of the GAR Joe Hooker Post #26 of Hart in Oceana County, where he enjoyed the fellowship of his soldier buddies.

Charley Shaw died at age fifty-four on or about December 23, 1899. A military stone with Charley Shaw's name on it is located in section C, block 14, lot 3, space 6 in the Hart City Cemetery. The stone is near the military monument of stacked cannon balls erected by the Joe Hooker Post in 1920 to honor the Civil War veterans buried in the city cemetery.

The author was informed by the cemetery sextant that there are no remains buried beneath Shaw's stone and that the stone is considered a military memorial marker for Shaw. The sextant also mentioned that Charley's actual grave site in or near Hart is not listed in the burial records for that area.

There is no pension file for Charley Shaw.

Shawanese, Joseph, Private

Enlistment: Enlisted as a private on June 13, 1863, at East Saginaw, Saginaw County, by First Lieutenant William J. Driggs, First Michigan Sharpshooters, for three years.

Age: Twenty-three, born about 1840 in Shiawassee County.

Occupation: Farmer and hunter

Residence: Chesaning, Saginaw County

Physical Description: Six feet four and a half inches tall, dark eyes, dark hair, and a ruddy complexion. Examining physician was Dr. Arvin F. Whelan, surgeon, First Michigan Sharpshooters.

Mustered: June 16, 1863, at Detroit, Wayne County, by Lieutenant Colonel John R. Smith, US Army

Military Service: According to his medical records, Joseph did not incur any wounds in the war, but he did suffer from physical illnesses. He was admitted to his regimental hospital in the field near Alexandria, Virginia, suffering from intermittent fever (or malaria) on April 6, 1864. The soldier was treated with doses of quinine made from a mixture of powdered cinchona tree bark dissolved in water or whiskey, or in the form of pills of purified quinine sulfate (*Bollet*). Quinine mixed in whiskey instead of water worked better because the whiskey masked the bitter taste of quinine. After a few days, Joseph returned to duty.

On April 26, 1864, Joseph was transferred from his regimental hospital to Mansion House, a branch of Division 1, USA General Hospital at Alexandria, Virginia.

At Mansion House, Joseph was diagnosed with catarrh, which is an old term for congestion of the mucous membranes of the nose and throat (*Blakiston*). It's known that the treatment for catarrh involved the ingestion of warm liquids and some bed rest. About a week later, the soldier returned to his regiment.

On February 25, 1865, Private Shawanese, who was spiting up blood, was sent to Old Hollowell General Hospital (Branch of the 3rd Division General Hospital) in Alexandria and admitted on February 26. His symptom was diagnosed as hemoptysis, the condition in which he spit up blood from his lungs. This occurrence was a sign of consumption or tuberculosis *(Ibid.)*. His treatment included cod-liver oil to evacuate his bowels, whiskey, and a diaphoretic of ipecac and opium called Dover's powder to induce sweating. External applications of flaxseed or bread poultices were applied to his chest to draw out poisons from the lungs (*King*). Additional opium was given to suppress Joseph's cough (*Ibid.*).

Private Shawanese was transferred from Old Hollowell General Hospital to Slough Barracks General Hospital on April 4, 1865, where similar treatment was continued. Medical records stated that he remained at Slough Hospital in Alexandria until his condition deteriorated so much that he was given an honorable discharge of disability from the service.

Discharged: A War Department record states that Joseph Shawanese was discharged on August 18, 1864. But medical records for Private Shawanese definitely state that he was a patient in three different hospitals between April 6, 1864, and May 29, 1865. The final medical record for Joseph states that he was honorably discharged and released from Slough Barracks General Hospital on a surgeon's certificate for disability on May 30, 1865. He was paid money owed to him for his service at his discharge and returned home to Michigan.

Biography: A healthy young man and always ready for the hunt before he entered the service, Joseph returned home in poor physical condition. He sought treatment for his lung disease from one Henry Quewis. Henry was a traditional Anishinabe doctor who treated the Anishinabek of Indian Town (or St. Charles) near East Saginaw, Saginaw County.

Between the years of 1864 and 1868, Joseph married Ellen (Joseph) Turner, the widow of James Turner who died in October 1864. This marriage was of the traditional Anishinabek custom and practice (the consent of the couple and their parents).

Joseph and Ellen were the parents of two children: Samuel, born in January 1868; and Solomon, born in April 1870. Solomon died on December 26, 1871, and Samuel died in July 1880. Both boys were baptized before their early deaths by Rev. A. S. Fair of the Methodist Episcopal Church in St. Charles.

During these years with Ellen and their boys, Joseph tried very hard to support his little family with hunting and trapping, but his lung ailment grew worse with each passing year.

On July 10, 1875, Joseph and Ellen were formally married in a Christian rite officiated by Rev. Fair in St. Charles. The ceremony was witnessed by James Williams and Peter David.

Finally, after years of constant debilitating lung problems, Joseph Shawanese died. Pension records list him as deceased on March 26, 1877. The accepted state death record reported that Joseph died on June 16, 1878, and the final diagnosis was that of consumption (or tuberculosis).

Joseph Shawanese was buried in the Riverside Cemetery of St. Charles. His grave is located in section C, row 3, and is marked with a military stone that reads "Jos. Shawness."

After her husband's death, Ellen made her home in St. Charles with her son, William Turner, from her first marriage.

Ellen Shawanese's Application #243,524 for a widow's pension was filed for her on April 4, 1879. The application claimed that her husband had contracted his lung disease while in the service.

On May 10, 1887, Ellen received her Widow's Pension Certificate #233,307. The pension paid eight dollars a month retroactive from April 4, 1879, and her monthly payments were increased to twelve dollars a month retroactive from March 19, 1886.

Ellen Shawanese died at her son's home on November 11, 1909, of complications due to bowel problems and old age. She was buried near her husband in Riverside Cemetery on November 13 of said year.

On December 13 of said year, William returned his mother's pension certificate and applied to the US Pension Office for the payments accrued up to the pensioner's death. He asked for the accrued money to help pay for expenses incurred for his mother's care, including medicine, groceries, and cemetery charges.

For his efforts, William was issued a check for $11.50 as reimbursement from the US pension agent at Detroit sometime after February 15, 1910.

Shawanosang, Joseph, Private

Enlistment: Enlisted as a private on June 18, 1863, at Little Traverse (renamed Harbor Springs in 1881), Emmet County, by Second Lieutenant Garrett A. Graveraet, First Michigan Sharpshooters, for three years.

Age: Eighteen, born about 1845 or 1846 on Manitoulin Island, Ontario, Canada West. His enlistment paper stated that his birth place was Emmet County.

Occupation: Farmer

Residence: Beaver Island in Manitou County (now Charlevoix County)

Physical Description: Five feet eight and a half inches tall, dark eyes, dark hair, and a ruddy complexion. Examining physician was Dr. Arvin F. Whelan, surgeon, First Michigan Sharpshooters.

Mustered: July 20, 1863, at Detroit, Wayne County, by Lieutenant Colonel John R. Smith, US Army

Military Service: When his regiment was guarding Confederate prisoners at the confine at Camp Douglas in Chicago, Cook County, Illinois, Private Shawanosang was reported to have lost his cartridge box, belt, bayonet, and scabbard. This event occurred sometime between September and October 1863. Consequently, he had a portion of his pay docked for the loss of his equipment. To his chagrin, less pay would mean less money to send home to his parents in Canada.

In October, Joseph was assigned as a cook for his company.

During the Battle of Spotsylvania on May 12, 1864, Private Shawanosang sustained three severe gunshot (missile) wounds to the lower portion of his left leg and foot. These wounds would cripple him for the rest of his life. The first missile passed between the knee and the head of the fibula (the slender bone of the outer part of the lower leg). The second wound was caused by a missile that badly lacerated the lower third of the gastrocnemius (or calf muscle) and the Achilles' tendon. The third wound was caused by a missile that struck the left foot below the external malleolus (a process of bone on the fibula that forms the outside of the ankle bone) and destroyed the bones of the foot in that area. In addition to these wounds, a two-inch piece of pistol ramrod was embedded into the tissue of his foot.

Joseph was taken immediately to his aid station where his wounds were assessed, washed, and hastily bandaged. He was then transported by ambulance wagon to his division hospital farther behind the lines. At this hospital, Joseph's wounds were treated with iodine to impede infection, and then simple water dressings were applied to the damaged areas. Simple water dressings consisted of folded lint dipped into cold water, applied to his wounds, and secured with a cloth wrap or adhesive plaster (*Schaadt*).

On May 17, Private Shawanosang was taken by ambulance wagon to the depot hospital in Fredericksburg, Virginia. The hospital was at or near attorney John Marye's house near Marye's Heights. The doctors in Fredericksburg continued to treat the wounds with iodine and simple water dressings. Joseph was given quinine for fever and an opium pill for pain.

On May 25, Joseph was taken to a wharf at Belle Plain Landing and transferred by hospital steamer to Emory USA General Hospital in Washington, DC. He was admitted to Emory on May 26.

At Emory Hospital, the doctors anesthetized Joseph with ether or chloroform and removed the two-inch piece of pistol ramrod from his foot with a bullet forceps. Iodine and simple cold water dressings were applied to all the wounds and secured as mentioned previously. The dressings were changed several times a day. Frequent changes of cold water dressings helped to control bleeding and wound inflammation (*Ibid.*). The limb was kept immobile, and opium pills for pain were offered to Joseph. Total bed rest was ordered for him.

On May 29, the dreaded postoperative condition of gangrene appeared in Joseph's wounds. The agent of causation is now thought to be that of the bacteria

Staphylococcus pyogenes possibly in conjunction with *Staphylococcus aureus* (*Ibid.*). Gangrene was characterized by the appearance of a small black spot on the healing wound. The discoloration would spread, and the tissue would necrose (or die) and slough (or separate) from living tissue (*Ibid.*). This sloughing appeared in Joseph's wounds on June 1. Because of the contagious nature of gangrene, the doctors isolated Joseph in a separate ward that had been fumigated and disinfected with a bromine solution.

While Joseph was anesthetized with ether or chloroform, the doctors surgically removed the dead tissue from around the wounds. The surgical sites were cauterized with silver nitrate and disinfected with carbolic acid or tincture of iodine (*Bollet*). Yeast poultices were also used to treat the gangrene (*Ibid.*). Simple cold water dressings were again applied to the wounds.

During his stay at Emory General Hospital, Joseph was given a highly nourishing diet. Alcohol, opium, or morphine was continued for pain.

By June 5, the doctors considered his condition as much improved. Joseph was given a furlough from Emory on July 21 and went back to Michigan.

Private Shawanosang returned to Detroit from his furlough on July 27, 1864, and was admitted to St. Mary's USA General Hospital in Detroit on said date. He remained at St. Mary's where iodine and simple water dressings were applied to his wounds. On September 6, he was granted a second furlough to return home for thirty days.

On October 14, Joseph returned from his furlough and was admitted to Harper USA General Hospital in Detroit. He remained at Harper and received additional treatment until his discharge.

Discharged: Private Joseph Shawanosang was mustered out and given a certificate of disability for discharge from Harper USA General Hospital on December 17, 1864. He was one half disabled and considered unfit for the Veteran Reserve Corps. The surgeon in charge of Harper Hospital, Dr. D. O. Farrand, and Lt. Colonel B. H. Hill signed Joseph's discharge paper. Joseph was paid money owed to him for his service at his discharge and related that all further correspondence be addressed to him at his home in Little Traverse in Emmet County.

Biography: Joseph Shawanosang (also spelled Shanernuskin) was born on Manitoulin Island, Ontario, Canada West, about 1845 or 1846, the son of Oscar and Mary Shawanosang. His hospital medical cards listed him as single.

On December 27, 1864, Application #57,490 for an invalid pension was filed for Joseph under the Act of July 14, 1862. He cited his permanent crippled condition and his inability to perform manual labor to any great extent as the reasons for his application for a pension.

Both Captain James S. DeLand and Lieutenant Colonel John R. Smith submitted depositions supporting Joseph's service and his injuries. Joseph resubmitted his application on August 28, 1866.

On October 18, 1866, Joseph received his Invalid Pension Certificate #72,663, which paid $5.33⅓ per month retroactive to December 17, 1864.

Before he went into the service in 1863, Joseph had worked as a farm hand for a Mr. James F. Cable on Beaver Island and was also a fisherman. Mr. Cable thought so much of Joseph and his work ethic that he hired him again after his discharge in 1864. Cable related to Joseph that considering Joseph's severe crippling injuries, he, Cable, only wanted him to complete whatever work he was physically capable of doing.

In the fall of 1867, Cable bought a farm in Attica, Wyoming County, New York. He took his family, including his son, Claude, and Joseph with him when he moved from Beaver Island.

On January 15, 1868, Joseph requested that his pension payments be sent from the Grand Rapids Agency to the Canandaigua Agency of New York. Considering that Attica was five hundred miles from Grand Rapids and only fifty miles from the Canandaigua Agency, it would be much easier for Joseph to collect his monthly payments at the Canandaigua Agency.

On January 18, 1868, Joseph applied for an increase of pension payments from $5.33⅓ to eight dollars while a resident of Attica, New York. By June 27, 1868, his request to have his pension payments sent to the Canandaigua Agency from the Grand Rapids Agency was granted. Joseph's crippled condition and his pain were getting worse. His left leg was now considerably shorter than his right leg due to atrophy.

Joseph resubmitted his application for an increase in pension payments on May 1, 1869. He moved back to Michigan by 1871, as he is reported to have been admitted as a patient to Harper Hospital in Detroit in February 1871. While he was at Harper Hospital, Joseph had additional surgical treatment. He was discharged from the hospital on August 4 of said year.

On March 17, 1873, Joseph applied for a transfer of his pension payments from the Canandaigua Agency back to the Detroit Pension Agency. That request was granted on April 9, 1873. His last payments from the New York agency were made to him on September 4, 1872.

By December 4, 1873, doctors' examinations revealed that Joseph's physical condition had become much worse, as did his pain. He was judged to be two-thirds incapacitated due to his lameness.

A house fire that occurred on February 12, 1879, destroyed Joseph's discharge paper.

By June 19, 1879, Joseph was living in Bay City, Bay County. At that time, he submitted a request to the commissioner of pensions asking for the arrears of pension due to him under the Acts of January 25 and March 4 of 1879.

On July 12, 1879, he submitted an application for a certificate in lieu of discharge to replace the discharge certificate that was destroyed in the house fire. A replacement certificate was sent to him on August 1, 1879. His request for arrears of pension was rejected on August 22, 1879, and his request for an increase of monthly pension payments from $5.33⅓ to eight dollars was not approved.

Joseph Shawanosang died in Bay County sometime after 1879.

Shegoge, John, Private

Enlistment: Enlisted as a private on July 4, 1863, at Elbridge, Oceana County, (another source states Pentwater) by Captain Edwin V. Andress, First Michigan Sharpshooters, for three years.

Age: Twenty-one, born about 1842 in Allegan County.

Occupation: Laborer

Residence: Pentwater, Oceana County

Physical Description: Five feet eight, black eyes, black hair, and a dark complexion. Examining physician was Dr. Jacob B. McNett, assistant surgeon, First Michigan Sharpshooters.

Mustered: July 11, 1863, at Detroit, Wayne County, by Lieutenant Colonel John R. Smith, US Army

Military Service: Private John Shegoge was reported to have lost his .58-caliber Springfield Rifle Musket and all accoutrements between March and April 1864. To compensate the government for the loss of his equipment, John's pay was docked for the cost, which left him less money to send home. This incident occurred either before or after the sharpshooters left for the front, having completed their duty as guards for Confederate prisoners at Camp Douglas, Chicago, Cook County, Illinois.

On June 17, 1864, while charging the enemy's works in front of Petersburg, Virginia, Private Shegoge suffered a gunshot (missile) wound to the right hand. The injury resulted in the destruction of all the metacarpal bones (palm) and the bones of the carpus (wrist). He was taken immediately from the field to an aid station where his wound was assessed and bleeding was stopped by pressure applied to the injured areas. His hand was washed and hastily wrapped in cloth bandages.

John was then transported by ambulance wagon to his division hospital farther behind the lines. At the division hospital, his wounds were treated with iodine to impede infection, and simple water dressings were applied to his hand. These dressings were composed of folded lint dipped into cold water and secured in place by a cloth wrap or adhesive plaster (*Schaadt*).

A few days later, John was taken to a military railroad and put on a mattress in a boxcar, the floor of which was cushioned with straw or hay, for his journey to the depot hospital near City Point, Virginia. He was admitted to that hospital on June 21.

At the depot hospital, applications of iodine and simple dressings were continued as treatment for John's wounds.

Soon the disease of hospital gangrene (caused by the bacteria *Staphylococcus pyogenes* in conjunction with *Staphylococus aureus*) was detected in the wounds, and extensive sloughing (a mass of necrotic or dead tissue that separates from living tissue) occurred (*Ibid.*). To combat the gangrene, Shegoge was isolated from other patients in a separate ward that was fumigated and disinfected with a bromine solution (*Ibid.*). Dead tissue was surgically removed while he was anesthetized with chloroform or ether. The surgical sites were then cauterized with silver nitrate and also disinfected with bromine. Cold water dressings were continued (*Ibid.*).

John was fed a full and unrestricted diet. He was also given quinine for fever, and opium, alcohol, or morphine was administered for pain (*Ibid.*). The surgeons had hoped that they could save a portion of Private Shegoge's hand, but the infection had become too far advanced.

The decision was made by John's doctors to transfer the soldier by hospital steamer from a wharf at City Point to Mount Pleasant General Hospital in Washington, DC. Private Shegoge was admitted to the hospital on June 30.

On July 3, A.A. Surgeon Dr. R. H. King anesthetized Shegoge with ether and amputated his right forearm at the upper third just below the elbow (*Medical*). The surgery was necessary in order to stop the progression of the gangrene. The circular method of amputation was chosen because it produced less secondary hemorrhage (*Kuz and Bengtson*).

In the circular method of surgery, a single-edged amputating knife was used in a circular motion around the limb. The surgeon would divide the skin and subcutaneous tissues down to the level of the muscles. The skin was then retracted like rolling back a shirt sleeve, and the muscles would be divided circularly at the highest level possible. The bone was then cut at this level with a saw. Arteries and large veins were drawn distally with a forceps and tied with silk or cotton ligatures. The large nerves were pulled out as far as possible and cut, which allowed the stumps of the nerves to retract into the soft tissues of the stump of the arm. The end of the bone was smoothed with bone-biting forceps and rasps. At the end of surgery, the skin that was raised from the first layer of muscles was then pulled over the end of the stump, brought together, and loosely sewn with silk or wire sutures (*Ibid.*). The stump was then dressed with bandages smeared with cerate (a preparation of beeswax mixed with oils). Rolls of cotton, linen, flannel, or muslin were used to pad the stump, which would then be supported in splints made of starch or plaster. Whiskey and opium were given to the patient for postoperative pain (*Ibid.*).

On October 25, 1864, Private Shegoge was granted a furlough to go home to Michigan. Still suffering from the effects of his wounds, he was admitted to Harper USA General Hospital in Detroit on February 27, 1865. He remained there until his discharge for disability on June 5, 1865.

Discharged: Private John Shegoge was mustered out and honorably discharged for disability from Harper USA General Hospital on June 5, 1865, by order of Major General Joseph Hooker.

Since Shegoge was considered totally disabled and unfit for the Veteran Reserve Corps, Dr. D. O. Farrand, assistant surgeon in charge of Harper Hospital, signed John's discharge paper. When John was discharged from Harper Hospital, he was paid the money owed to him for his service. At that time, he requested that all further correspondence be addressed to him at Pentwater, Oceana County.

Biography: Application #71,336 for an invalid pension was filed for John Shegoge on June 9, 1865. He cited total disability in his performance of military duty and the inability to perform any labor for meaningful subsistence. At his post in Georgetown, Washington, DC, Capt. James S. DeLand of the First Michigan Sharpshooters signed an Officer's Certificate on July 26, 1865, validating John's service-related wounds.

On March 8, 1866, John was granted an Invalid Pension Certificate #59,537, which paid eight dollars a month retroactive to June 5, 1865.

Again, citing his total disability, Shegoge submitted a request for an increase in his pension payments on September 24, 1866. He request was filed under the Supplementary Pension Act of June 6, 1866.

On December 17, 1866, the pensioner received an increase in his pension payments to total fifteen dollars a month retroactive to June 6, 1866.

John Shegoge's war wounds and the pain associated with those wounds were the causes of the rapid decline of his health. He died on May 26, 1869, at Pentwater and was buried in Oceana County.

Shomin, John B., Private

Enlistment: Enlisted as a private on August 17, 1863, at Little Traverse (renamed Harbor Springs in 1881), Emmet County, by Second Lieutenant Garrett A. Graveraet, First Michigan Sharpshooters, for three years. Credited to La Croix (renamed Cross Village in 1875), Emmet County, Fourth Congressional District.

Age: Twenty, born in April about 1843 or 1845 in St. Joseph, Berrien County.

Occupation: Farmer and carpenter

Residence: La Croix

Physical Description: Five feet eight, hazel eyes, black hair, and a light complexion. Examining physician was Dr. George L. Cornell, assistant surgeon, First Michigan Sharpshooters.

Mustered: October 21, 1863, at Camp Douglas, Chicago, Cook County, Illinois, by Capt. Lowe. Private John B. Shomin was a guard with his regiment at Camp Douglas, which was a confine for Confederate prisoners.

Military Service: On April 1, 1864, Private Shomin was promoted in rank to that of corporal to fill the vacancy of Corporal Peter Burns, who was promoted to sergeant.

On the night of May 6, 1864, during the Battle of the Wilderness in Virginia, Corporal Shomin left the Union breastworks and with his company charged the rebels' fortifications. He soon found himself and the others in full retreat from the enemy and back again behind his regiment's stronghold. When running back to his own breastworks, Shomin ran into a stump. He fell onto the stump and struck the left side of his breast near his heart. The fall bruised his ribs and knocked the wind out of him. He did not seek medical treatment.

During the Battle at Petersburg, Virginia, on June 17, 1864, Corporal Shomin and his company attacked the enemy's defenses. This time he was captured by the rebels and held for a brief time in a converted warehouse on Short Market Street in

Petersburg. He was then sent with other prisoners by cattle railcar to Camp Sumter (also known as Andersonville Prison) in Andersonville, Georgia.

During his imprisonment, Shomin was given extremely poor food and was exposed to inclement weather conditions while confined in an open stockade.

He was subsequently admitted to the prison hospital with scurvy and a bad case of rheumatism. Scurvy is a nutritional disorder caused by the lack of vitamin C in which the patient has spongy gums, a tendency to develop hemorrhages under the skin, and diarrhea and exhibits extreme weakness (*Blakiston*).

Unlike several of his Company K comrades, Shomin lived through his five-month prison ordeal and was exchanged by the rebels at Savannah, Georgia, on November 14, 1864.

Hardly able to walk, except with the aid of crutches, he made his way by steamer to Camp Parole near Annapolis, Maryland. Camp Parole was a camp for paroled prisoners in which both captured Confederates and former Union prisoners who had been paroled by the South were sent for exchange. The camp was also a holding area for Union soldiers who had deserted and whose units were in the area. Doctors on staff provided medical treatment for all the sick and wounded.

To compound his condition of scurvy, he was also found to have the tertian form of the infectious disease of malaria. Malaria in the tertian form is caused by *Plasmodium vivax* in which Shomins's spasms occurred with an elevated fever every forty-five hours. The disease is transmitted by mosquitoes infected with the genus *Anopheles* and is characterized by intermittent or remittent fever and spasms called paroxysms (*Ibid.*). His treatment for malaria at Camp Parole consisted of doses of quinine made from dried, pulverized cinchona tree bark dissolved in water or whiskey. Whiskey worked better as it masked the bitter taste of quinine. Quinine was also dispensed as pills made of purified quinine sulfate (*Bollet*).

To hasten his healing process, Shomin was fed a diet rich in vitamin C, such as various fruits (including lemons and lemon juice) and vegetables, including carrots, turnips, onions, and raw white or sweet potatoes (*Ibid.*). Cooking potatoes destroys the vitamin C content (*Ibid.*). Sauerkraut and a drink that consisted of vinegar, molasses, and water, in addition to cider, were also included in his diet (*Ibid.*).

While he recuperated, Shomin was paid for the months of September and October, which included some of the time that he was imprisoned. He was also granted a furlough to Mackinac Island in the County of Mackinac from December

10, 1864, to January 10, 1865. He returned to Camp Parole after his furlough and rejoined his regiment on May 6, 1865.

Discharged: Corporal John B. Shomin was mustered out and given a certificate of disability for discharge from Washington, DC, on July 3, 1865 (as listed on the muster-out roll taken near Delaney House for July 28, 1865). Shomin's discharge was granted in compliance with paragraph 6 of General Order #77 issued from the Adjutant General's Office on April 28, 1865. He was paid money owed to him for his service at his discharge and returned to his home in Michigan.

John probably become ill again after he rejoined his regiment on May 6, 1865, because he was discharged on July 3 and not on July 28 with the rest of his regiment. General Order #77 was concerned with monetary reimbursement to medical personnel for "the maintenance of sick and wounded soldiers who were placed in private houses or hospitals and other necessary comforts for the sick and convalescing in the various military hospitals" (*Grace*).

Biography: According to information contained in vital records held at La Croix (now Cross Village), John B. Shomin, or John Baptiste Shomin, was born in 1843. The name Shomin is derived from the Anishinabe word *jomin,* which means grape or raisin (*Baraga*). He was the second son of Michael (sometimes called Saki or Michael Saki) and Sophia (Waban) Shomin. John B. was a brother to Louis Shomin, a first cousin to John Shomin (who sometimes signed his name as John O. Shomin) and a fourth cousin to Payson Wolfe, also members of Company K.

John Baptiste's siblings were: Joseph, born about 1841, baptized the same year and died as an infant; Louis (or Ludovicus), born January 11, 1845; Melchior (or Michael), born January 5, 1849; Ignatius, born February 6, 1851, and died October 7, 1894; Maria, born May 13, 1856; Nicolaus, born November 28, 1858, and died as an infant; Joseph, born July 14, 1860, and died on October 17, 1870; and Peter, born February 23. All of Michael and Sophia Shomin's children were baptized at Holy Cross Mission Church at Cross Village (John B's father, Michael, was born in 1823 and baptized in 1831 at said church. He died September 25, 1890. John's mother, Sophie, was also born in 1823.

On May 29, 1868, John B. Shomin married Mary Madelene (or Matilda) Chapman, the daughter of Bela J. and Mary (Charrette) Chapman. The marriage took place at Ste. Anne Catholic Church on Mackinac Island. Rev. Father M. Orth officiated at the rite of marriage with Rev. Father Seraphim Zorn assisting at the ceremony. Elisu Chait and Henrietta Chapman were witnesses.

Mary's siblings were: John, born about 1832; Sarah A., born about 1839; James R., born about 1861; William, born about 1864; and Henry E., born about 1866.

John B. and Mary were the parents of several children. The two children who lived beyond infancy were Nicholas, born in February 1869, and George, born in February 1871.

To support his family, John B. worked as a skilled carpenter and saw his services in demand from his neighbors. He also clerked in John Bates's General Store on Mackinac Island from 1866 to 1879 and did odd jobs when he could find them. As the years passed, his rheumatism and the pains in his chest became worse and interfered with his ability to work at his carpentry trade.

As with his cousin, John Shomin (or John (O.) Shomin), John B. had his problems with his homestead entry. He bought acreage on Application #5293 located in the southeast quarter of section 8 in township 37, north of range 6 west in Emmet County for fourteen dollars on October 22, 1872 (*Land Records*).

There was a dispute at the Bureau of Land Management Land Office about his homestead entry in regards to his not living on the premises. John B. did build a house and barn on the property and cultivated the land. Although he did not live on this acreage, one of his brothers did occupy the property. It's not clear as to the outcome of this dispute or if John B. was able to keep his land.

John B. Shomin's Application #1,110,027 for an invalid pension was filed for him on July 31, 1890. He cited the effects of scurvy, chest pains, and rheumatism as ailments due to his service and imprisonment. During the years after his discharge, John B. sought the services and care of Dr. Moffatt and Dr. S. S. Jessop for his ailments. They both attested to the validity of Shomin's complaints.

Having resubmitted his application on April 25, 1893, John's bid for an invalid pension was rejected on March 14, 1894, with the decision that there was no ratable disability from the ailments cited in the applications. Another rejection was given on November 8, 1894.

John B. again resubmitted his application in April 1897. During those years, his health was in steady decline. Several doctors attested that his deteriorating state of health was due to service-related ailments and stated their desire that Shomin be given a pension.

Finally, Shomin received his Invalid Pension Certificate #978,571 in March 1899. The pension was approved only for rheumatism and was granted under the more liberal General Act of 1890. John received six dollars a month retroactive to May 4, 1897.

In January 1908, Shomin's pension was reissued under the Act of February 6, 1907, which raised his monthly pension payments to twelve dollars retroactive to June 1, 1907.

Shomin's pension was again reissued on February 21, 1913, from the Act of February 6, 1907, which increased his payments to $16.50 a month commencing June 1, 1912, $21.50 commencing April 17, 1915, and twenty-seven dollars commencing April 17, 1920.

After years of declining health, John B. Shomin died on Mackinac Island on September 16, 1913, of chronic endocarditis, or inflammation of the lining of the heart and its valves (*Ibid.-Blakiston*). Shomin's brother-in-law, Andrew J. Chapman, was city clerk of Mackinac Island at the time of John's death and signed his death certificate.

John B's death certificate states that he was buried in Ste. Anne Cemetery on Mackinac Island. So, who is the John B. Shomin whose military stone is in Lakeview Cemetery in Harbor Springs next to John (O.) Shomin? The stone bearing the name "John B. Shomin" in Lakeview Cemetery is probably a memorial stone. A local GAR post most likely went to the island and gave John B. a military burial.

While still a resident of Mackinac Island, Mary Matilda Shomin's Application #1,015,500 was filed for a widow's pension on October 10, 1913. She received her Widow's Pension Certificate #767,503 in November 1913, in which she was paid twelve dollars a month retroactive to October 10, 1913.

On November 21, 1913, Mary Shomin applied for and received the sixty-four dollars of accrued pension owed to her husband up until the time of his death.

After she reached the age of seventy, Mary's monthly payments were increased to twenty dollars per month commencing September 8, 1916, under the Act of September 8, 1916.

As her health declined and she became infirm, Mary went to live with her granddaughter, Miss Agnes Shomin, at 3025 Stanley Avenue in Detroit. Her son, Nicholas Shomin, also provided care for his mother. Under the Act of May 1, 1920, Mary's monthly pension payments were increased to thirty dollars.

On March 6, 1922, Mary became so ill that she required constant assistance and a doctor's care. While still living at her granddaughter's residence, Mary died of bronchial pneumonia on May 7, 1922. Funeral arrangements were under the care of Harvey A. Neely Funeral Director at Stanley and Maybury Avenues in Detroit.

Mary's remains were taken by train from Detroit to St. Ignace on the Michigan

Central Railroad Co. and then by boat to Mackinac Island, where she was interred in Ste. Anne Cemetery near her husband.

The total bill for expenses incurred for Mary's illness and funeral was $226.95. Agnes Shomin applied to the Pension Office for reimbursement for these expenses. The government reimbursed her for sixty-four dollars, which was the accrued pension owed to Mary up to the time of her death. A sum of one hundred dollars was paid toward the bill by the Wayne County Soldiers Burial Fund.

Shomin, John (O), Private

Enlistment: Enlisted as a private on June 11, 1863, at La Croix (renamed Cross Village in 1875), Emmet County, by Second Lieutenant Garrett A. Graveraet, First Michigan Sharpshooters, for three years.

Age: Eighteen, born about 1845 in LaCroix.

Occupation: Farmer

Residence: LaCroix

Physical Description: Five feet eight, black eyes, black hair, and a dark complexion. Examining physician was Dr. Arvin F. Whelan, surgeon, First Michigan Sharpshooters.

Mustered: July 20, 1863, at Detroit, Wayne County, by Lieutenant Colonel John R. Smith, US Army

Military Service: During the Battle of Spotsylvania on May 12, 1864, Private Shomin received a back injury when a tree branch fell on him due to a cannon bombardment from the rebels. There is no record as to medical treatment given to him for this injury, but the injury would bother him for the rest of his life.

While charging the enemy's works in front of Petersburg, Virginia, on June 20, 1864, Private Shomin was shot in the fleshy portion of the upper third of his left forearm. The missile passed from front to back of the arm between the flexor carpi radialis and the palmaris longus muscles, muscles used in flexing the wrist. It also tore through the flexor digitorum profundus and flexor sublimus—the muscles that control the action of the fingers—and exited the arm through the extensor carpi ulnarus, which is another muscle that controls the action of the wrist (*Parker*). As the missile passed through the arm, it lacerated the c. radialis, almost severed the p. longus, and destroyed the median nerve. Fortunately, neither the radius bone nor the ulna bone of Shomin's forearm was fractured.

Shomin was taken immediately to an aid station where his wounds were washed and quickly bandaged. He was given an opium pill for pain.

From the field station, Shomin was taken by ambulance wagon to his division hospital farther behind the lines. At the division hospital, the doctors treated the entrance and exit wounds that were caused by the missile with iodine to impede infection and then applied simple water dressings. The dressings were composed of folded lint dipped into cold water, placed on the wounds, and secured by a cloth wrap or adhesive plaster (*Schaadt*). Private Shomin was taken to a military railroad where he was put on a mattress in a boxcar, the floor of which was cushioned with straw or hay, and sent to the depot hospital at City Point, Virginia.

He was admitted to the depot hospital on June 21 where his wounds were treated as mentioned previously.

On July 1, Shomin was taken from the hospital to a wharf at City Point and transferred by hospital steamer to Washington, DC. He was admitted to the Barracks Branch of Lincoln USA General Hospital on July 2, 1864. Similar treatment for his wounds was continued, and opium pills were given for pain. Shomin returned to duty on October 1, 1864.

On October 29, John was admitted to Augur General Hospital in Alexandria, Virginia, complaining of the partial loss of the use of his left hand. On October 30, Shomin was transferred by hospital steamer from Augur to Barracks Branch of Lincoln General Hospital in Washington, DC.

Shomin remained at Lincoln General Hospital until he was sent to USA General Hospital at Chester, Pennsylvania, where he was admitted on May 13, 1865. He remained at this hospital until his discharge on June 21, 1865.

Discharged: Private John Shomin was mustered out and given a certificate of disability for discharge from USA General Hospital in Chester, Pennsylvania, on June 21, 1865. The discharge was given in compliance with telegram directions from the War Department and the Adjutant General's Office given May 3, 1865. John received the payment due to him for his service at the time of his discharge and returned to Michigan.

Biography: John Shomin sometimes (but rarely) signed his name as John O. Shomin but did so only with business and legal matters. The name Shomin is derived from the Anishinabe word *jomin* and means grape or raisin *(Baraga)*. According to information contained in vital records held at LaCroix (now Cross Village) John (John O.) was the son of Joseph (or Otaiekwatchiwan) and Mary/Maria (or Giokam/Giskwaan) Shomin of La Croix and was known to be fairly well educated. He was a first cousin to brothers and Company K comrades John B. (or Baptiste) and Louis Shomin. John B. and Louis Shomin's father, Michael, sometimes called Saki or Michael Saki, was a brother to John O. Shomin's father, Joseph Shomin.

John's siblings were: Theresa, born April 30, 1841; Catherine, born July 29, 1843; Christina, born March 8, 1848; Aloysia, born October 31, 1850; Lucy, born ca. 1852; Theodorus, born December 7, 1852; Joseph, born ca. 1857; and Christian, born ca. 1859.

During his hospital stays and after his discharge, John's war injuries took their toll on his ability to perform meaningful labor. He experienced a great deal of pain and numbness in his arm and hand. The arm was somewhat diminished in size, and the last two fingers of the left hand were atrophied due to the contraction of the tendons in that area. In extreme weather conditions, it was hard for John to keep his left arm and hand warm. He also suffered from rheumatism, which grew steadily worse.

When he returned from the service, Shomin tried to earn a living at whatever job he could find. He did some plowing and planting on his farm in the summer and cut wood in the winter with his neighbor Horace Angell. For about three winters, he worked hauling railroad ties with neighbor John Wagley, who was a fisherman from Cross Village. He also sailed with Wagley on various lake vessels used in fishing and commerce. But his ability to lift and carry heavy objects and to do strenuous labor was greatly reduced in the passing years due to the pain caused by his war injuries.

The only treatment that John received for his injuries and rheumatism was that of herbal medicines. The medicines were administered by Theresa Quashe, who was considered to be a traditional Anishinabequa doctor.

On many occasions, John acted as an interpreter and a notary public among the Anishinabek for township business and in taking state census. He also served as justice of the peace for Emmet County. On July 28, 1874, John Shomin married thirteen-year-old Hiacintha (or Cynthia) Oguashe (Bonil/Bonit) at La Croix (known as Cross Village since 1875), Emmet County. Rev. Father John B. Weikamp, of Holy Cross Catholic Mission Church, officiated at the ceremony. Witnesses were John Eshkibagowa and Catherine Naganashi. Cynthia's mother was Theresa Quashe (or Oguashe), the Anishnabequa doctor (mentioned previously) of Middle Village (or Good Hart). Cynthia was also known by the following names: Cynthia (or Zita) Makawina (Makawina was her mother's Anishinabequa name), Cynthia Bonil (Bonil was her grandfather's Anishinabe name on her mother's side), and Cynthia Kweshin.

The couple were the parents of seven children, but only four lived beyond infancy. They were: Joseph, born July 13, 1881, at Cross Village and baptized by Rev. Father Weikamp; William Aloysius, born December 2, 1887, and baptized on May 14, 1888, at Harbor Springs by Rev. Father Placidus Krekeler; Paul, born January 14, 1892, and baptized on March 8, 1892, at Harbor Springs by Rev. Father Servatius Altmicks; and Margaret Nina (or Lena), born September 15, 1893, and baptized on October 24, 1893, at Harbor Springs by Rev. Father Norbert Wilhelm. Another son, Aloysius, born June 12, 1883, was listed as baptized by Rev. Father Philip Zorn on June 23, 1883, at Harbor Springs. Aloysius lived only one year.

Application #211,931 for an invalid pension was filed for John on December 24, 1875, when he lived in Cross Village. Former First Lieutenant William J. Driggs, First Michigan Sharpshooters of East Saginaw, Saginaw County, was one of several veteran soldiers connected with his military service who testified on John's behalf.

John received Invalid Pension Certificate #145,119, approved for a gunshot (missile) wound of the left arm, on May 7, 1877. The pension paid two dollars a month retroactive to December 24, 1875.

Shomin resubmitted his application for an increase in payments on November 26, 1877. The application for increase was at first rejected on March 19, 1878. But in 1879, he was granted an arrears of pension of two dollars a month retroactive from June 22, 1865, and ended on December 23, 1875.

Before his marriage, John received a homestead, certificate #4745, of 160 acres on October 23, 1872 (*Letter 1.*). In this case, John signed his name as "John O Shomin." The homestead was a tract of land described as the northeast quarter of section 21, township 37 north of range 6 west in Emmet County. John had cleared three acres of timber, built a board shanty sixteen by fourteen feet, and a long house, sixteen by fourteen feet on his acreage. He considered that his work would more than suffice as "improvement," and he expected to receive a patent for this acreage when all the legalities were straightened out (*Ibid.*).

In 1876, John was very surprised when a man named Ferdinand Mittelstadt applied for the patent for his land. Mittelstadt saw John's homestead acreage advertised (unbeknown to John) in the Traverse City paper (*Ibid.*). On December 27, 1876, there was a hearing on this case in Traverse City. John didn't have any money to travel to Traverse City for the hearing, so he lost his homestead to Mittelstadt.

In a letter to Indian Agent George W. Lee at Ypsilanti, Washtenaw County, on

January 4, 1877, John outlined his continuing problem with Mittelstadt and the loss of his homestead (*Ibid.*).

John wrote again to George Lee on February 8, 1878, and related to Lee that Mittelstadt told him (John) that he could not farm on the homestead in the coming spring because his former homestead was canceled in Washington and belonged to Mittelstadt (*Letter 2*). John pleaded for any help that Lee could give to him. Lee wrote several letters to the government on John Shomin's behalf.

Because of delays, bureaucratic mix-ups, improper registration with the federal government, and the inability to pay taxes on the property, many of these parcels of land chosen by the Anishinabek were lost to land grabbers and squatters.

When the land claims were finely properly recorded, it was discovered that many Anishinabek lost their lands due to preemption laws and errors in the certificates. Under these laws, any non-Anishinabek settlers who moved onto Anishinabek lands and made improvements, such as clearing the land for farming, erecting buildings, and paying delinquent taxes, could have the first claim when that lost acreage was placed upon the open market for sale.

Knowing that the Anishinabek had to travel for miles for staples and were gone for several days at a time, unscrupulous men began to move onto their acreage. These men would erect buildings in the Anishinabek's absence and file for the acreage, claiming that the Anishinabek were not living on the property. When the people returned home, they found that squatters had taken possession of their property. They then found themselves without homes or lands. Thus, like John, many other Anishinabek would lose their land through such unscrupulous and dishonest dealings.

In 1877, John and Hiacintha moved to an area near Harbor Springs in Emmet County. They took residence on a farm, the acreage given to them by John's mother-in-law, Theresa Quashe. The Shomins remained on the farm (next to Quashe's farm) where they raised their family.

Shomin's pension payments for a gunshot (missile) wound of the left arm and rheumatism were increased upon subsequent applications to four dollars a month to commence in 1880, six dollars a month to commence in 1882, and eight dollars a month to commence in 1888.

Whatever problems John had with his homestead acreage in 1872, he eventually did receive ownership of said land with Homestead Certificate #4745 issued to him on October 10, 1888 (*Land Records*).

In the 1880s, John was an active member of the Union veterans' GAR Woolsey

Post #399 at Northport, Leelanau County. For the meeting of September 30, 1889, he was listed as officer of the day.

After an illness (probably severe bronchitis) of seven days, and in declining health, John Shomin died at his home on July 3, 1895, of double pneumonia. He was examined by Dr. Robert Emmett Flood of Harbor Springs shortly before he died. Dr. Flood confirmed that John died of double pneumonia and not tuberculosis.

John Shomin's burial was conducted by his friends Joseph Madwass and Jesse Carmien. The cost of the funeral was at public expense because of the family's poverty. The members of the GAR Harbor Springs J. B. Richardson Post #013 interred John with military rites in section L of lot 49 in Lakeview Cemetery of said city. A military stone marks his grave site.

At his death, John left only a few pieces of furniture and little property of any real value. Cynthia had to make due with making baskets and working as a cook in Petoskey.

On November 4, 1895, Application #622,989 for a widow's pension, enacted under the general act of June 27, 1890, was filed for Hiacinthe (Cynthia) Shomin. By December 26, 1895, Cynthia was granted a Widow's Pension Certificate #438,926, which paid eight dollars a month with an additional two dollars a month for each of the four minor children until each child reached the age of sixteen. These pension payments were retroactive to November 4, 1895.

Cynthia Shomin married for the second time to Bazel Meshkay (Meskekey) of Harbor Springs. Bazel was a farmer who owned forty acres of land. The couple was married at Bay Shore, Emmet County, on September 21, 1896. Rev. Father Bruno Torka of Petoskey officiated at the marriage rites, and witnesses to the ceremony were Simon Green of Horton Bay and Mary Shegonebi of Bay Shore.

Due to her remarriage and having a husband to support her, Cynthia Shomin lost all of her rights to her widow's pension certificate, and the payments to her were terminated on September 21, 1896—the date of her remarriage to Bazel.

On June 14, 1899, a William Clark petitioned the court to be guardian of Cynthia's three minor children under the age of sixteen—William A., Paul, and Margaret. On July 5, 1899, Application #701,466 for a guardian's declaration for pension of minor children was filed for Clark.

The right of guardianship was given to Clark by the probate court of Emmet County on June 19, 1899. The court made it very clear that these children were still in the care of their mother and her second husband and that Cynthia had not abandoned them.

A Pension for Minor Children Certificate #503,423 was granted to William Clark on November 26, 1900, for the support of the three previously mentioned children. The pension provided for payments of eight dollars a month with an additional two dollars per month for each of the children until that child reached the age of sixteen. These payments were sent to Clark and were retroactive to July 5, 1899. Payments would be stopped on September 14, 1909, when Margaret would attain the age of sixteen.

William A. Shomin was known to have attended Mt. Pleasant Government (or Indian) School in Isabella County from 1909 to 1910. At that time, William was twenty-three years old and no longer under Clark's guardianship. He needed money for his schooling and wanted to withdraw the pension money that he understood was in a bank account for him. William felt that he was not in full receipt of the pension payments due to him that had been sent to Clark to be put into his bank account.

William wrote to the US Pension Office and explained his problem. The pension office wrote back to William and stated that the amount of $243.54 (after deduction for lawyer's fees) had indeed been sent to Clark and that William would have to settle the matter with him in probate court to which Clark was accountable.

It is not known whether William actually received the full amount of pension payments due to him that were entrusted to Clark, but the whole matter seemed quite suspicious. Questionable maneuvering on the part of some appointed guardians was not uncommon in their dealings with the Anishinabek—a shameful practice.

Cynthia (Bonil/Bonit) Shomin Meshkay (or Meskekey) died on June 8, 1911, and was buried under the name of Zita Anna Meskekey in Holy Childhood of Jesus Catholic Cemetery in Harbor Springs.

Shomin, Louis, Private

Enlistment: Enlisted as a private on June 11, 1863, at La Croix (named Cross Village in 1875), Emmet County, by Second Lieutenant. Garrett A. Graveraet, First Michigan Sharpshooters, for three years.

    Age: Nineteen, born in 1845 in La Croix.

    Occupation: Farmer

    Residence: La Croix

    Physical Description: Five feet six, black eyes, black hair, and a dark complexion. Examining physician was Dr. Arvin F. Whelan, surgeon, First Michigan Sharpshooters.

Mustered: July 20, 1863, at Detroit, Wayne County, by Lieutenant Colonel John R. Smith, US Army

Military Service: Private Louis Shomin was considered a bright, intelligent, honest man and an all-around good soldier by his commanding officers. He was also fluent in the English language and could communicate very well. The same can be said of Louis's brother, John B., and the men's cousin, John or John (O) Shomin.

Before dawn on April 2, 1865, while charging the rebels' fortifications in front of Petersburg, Virginia, Private Shomin suffered a severe eye injury that would eventually leave him totally blind in one eye. Powder and small fragments from an exploding rebel artillery shell struck Shomin over his right eye and the side of the face, filling said eye with dirt and burning debris. He was taken immediately to an aid station at the rear where one of the doctors washed his eyes with copious amounts of water. At that time, his left eye was not thought to be as severely injured.

From the aid station, Shomin walked or was sent by ambulance wagon to his division hospital farther behind the lines, where he was given additional treatment by Dr. Thomas Eagleson. Dr. Eagleson continued the eye washes and added applications of nitrate of silver in water to the inner portions of both eyelids (*Dorwart*). Opiates were given for pain. Shomin was in and out of this hospital until his discharge but was still able to perform his military duties.

After his injury, Shomin's sight began to deteriorate in his right eye, and he experienced impaired vision in his left eye. For the next five months, there was a constant watery discharge from both of his eyes. It's known that Civil War doctors did treat ophthalmic discharge with gentle washes of borax and alum solutions. Louis would probably have had this additional treatment.

Discharged: Private Louis Shomin was mustered out and honorably discharged on July 28, 1865, at Delaney House, Washington, DC. He returned to Detroit on the steamer *Morning Star*. On August 7, Louis was paid the money due to him for his service at Jackson, Jackson County.

Biography: According to information contained in vital records held at Cross Village (La Croix), Louis Shomin was born January 11, 1845. His family name of Shomin is derived from the Anishinabe word *jomin,* which means grape or raisin (*Baraga*). He was the son of Michael (sometimes called Michael Saki) and Sophie (Waban) Shomin. Michael was born in 1823 and baptized in 1831 at Holy Cross Mission Church. He died September 25, 1890. Sophie was also born in 1823. Louis was a Company K comrade of his brother, John B. Shomin, his cousin John Shomin (who sometimes signed his name John O. Shomin), and his fourth cousin Payson Wolfe. He was also known as Louis Saki.

Louis's siblings were: Joseph, born about 1841 and died as a child; John B. (or John Baptiste), born 1843 or 1845; Melchior (or Michael), born January 5, 1849; Ignatius, born February 6, 1851, and died October 7, 1894; Maria, born May 13, 1856; Nicolas, born November 28, 1858, and died at a young age; a second son named Joseph, born July 14, 1860, and died October 17, 1870; and Peter, born February 23, 1873. Each of the children was baptized at the Holy Cross Mission Church at La Croix in the same year of his or her birth.

When he returned to La Croix after the war, Louis's grandmother treated his injured eye with traditional Anishinabek herbs. But in 1866, he became totally blind in the right eye (complete destruction of the cornea) with only partial vision in the left eye. Also at this time, Louis began to lose the hearing in his right ear due to the concussions of artillery shell bursts during the war years.

Louis married his first wife, Theresa Oquedonequot (or Ogedonaqua, Twagwawgawnay), on August 15, 1867, at Holy Cross Mission Church. Theresa was born December 21, 1845, and was the daughter of John and Margaret (Wakazoo) Poneshing. Father Louis N. Sifferath officiated at the Catholic rite of marriage, and Mary Ahgosa and Lewis Stevens witnessed the ceremony.

The couple were the parents of: Philomene, born ca. 1868; Joseph, born ca. 1869; Jane, born ca. 1870; and Lucy (or Louise), born September 3, 1878. Lucy was the only child to live to adulthood.

Lucy married Samson Blackman on June 22, 1893. He was the son of Paul and Agatha (Pauquaga) Blackman.

Louis was a member of the GAR Woolsey Post #399 of Northport, Leelanau County, and served the post as a junior vice commander. He was also a member of the GAR Washington Post #106 in Cross Village of Emmet County where he served as officer of the guard. Louis was proud to be a member of both posts and enjoyed the companionship of his army buddies.

On February 28, 1880, Application #350,066 for an invalid pension was filed for Louis. In the application, he cited the complete loss of sight in the right eye and partial loss of sight in the left eye due to war-related causes. According to close friends and Company K buddies, Louis suffered terribly with his blindness, especially in cold weather. Many times he could not perform any manual labor or fish to support his family.

On August 19, 1885, Theresa Shomin died of consumption (or tuberculosis) at the couple's residence in Cross Village. Louis was left to care for little Lucy.

Louis's second marriage was to Rosa (Blunt) Ashadagwa, age twenty-five, the widow of Peter Ashadagwa, who died by accidental drowning on June 3, 1885 or 1886. Father Ignatius Mrak officiated at the rite of marriage for the couple on January 10, 1887, at St. Mary's Catholic Church (now known as Kateri Tekakwitha Church) in Peshawbestown (previously known as Eagletown), Leelanau County. Joseph Onenego and Angelina Gishigokwe witnessed the ceremony. Rosa was born in Janesville, Wisconsin, the daughter of Ambrose and Minnie (Landoff) Blunt. She was listed as being white on the marriage certificate. Often Louis used his father's other name of Saki as his surname and did so at his marriage to Rosa. But Father Mrak changed the spelling to "Lake" on the marriage certificate. Therefore, Louis, age forty-one, was married under the name of Louis Lake, not Louis Shomin. The couple and Louis's daughter, Lucy, made their home in Eagletown (Peshawbestown).

Louis received his Invalid Pension Certificate #363,064 in June 1887. The certificate paid six dollars a month retroactive from July 29, 1865, ten dollars a month from April 3, 1884, and twelve dollars a month from April 22, 1885.

Shomin had a homestead of 155 and 39/100 acres in Emmet County. Its description is the north fractional half of the northwest fractional quarter, the southeast quarter of the northwest fractional quarter and the southwest quarter of the northeast quarter of section 4 in township 37 north range 5 west. Homestead certificate #4885 was granted to Louis on October 10, 1888 (*Land Records*).

On April 25, 1890, Louis applied for an increase of pension. This application was rejected. In addition to the health problems he already had, Louis had begun to suffer from lung ailments and developed a persistent cough.

Shomin resubmitted his application for an increase in monthly payments on March 12, 1892, and cited his vision and hearing disabilities as reasons for the increase. He was granted an increase in his payments to sixteen dollars a month in the spring of 1892, which was retroactive to December 4, 1891.

Louis Shomin died between the hours of 4:00 a.m. and 5:00 a.m. on Saturday, April 15, 1893, from consumption (or tuberculosis) and pneumonia at his home in Suttons Bay. He had been treated for his illnesses from 1891 until his death in 1893 by Dr. William M. Payne of same city. At his death, he left no will, but he did leave Rosa and Lucy a small house and lot (lot 2 of block 2) worth $150 in Peshawbestown in the township of Suttons Bay.

Louis Shomin was buried in the cemetery next to Kateri Tekakwitha Church (formally St. Mary's Church) in Peshawbestown and was accorded military honors from his GAR post.

Rosa Shomin's Application #577,576 for a widow's pension was filed for her on May 20, 1893, under the more liberal Act of 1890. Her only livelihood was earned by working as a domestic helper.

On February 4, 1895, Rosa Shomin married Isaac Blackman (son of Mr. and Mrs. John Blackman). The marriage was officiated by Father Bruno Torka of St. Mary's Catholic Church (now Kateri Takakwitha Church, as mentioned previously) in Peshawbestown and witnessed by Leo Frances and Philomena Blackman.

On July 2, 1896, Lars R. Sogge was granted guardianship and manager of the estate of Lucy Shomin by the probate court of Leelanau County. Lar's application #637,596 for a pension for a minor child was filed on July 18, 1896. But since Lucy had attained the age of seventeen by that date, the application was rejected.

Rosa Shomin Blackman received her Widow's Pension Certificate #482,541 on August 21, 1899. The certificate paid eight dollars a month with an extra two dollars a month for Lucy until her sixteenth birthday in 1894. The pension was retroactive to May 20, 1893, with payments for Lucy retroactive to April 16, 1893. But because of her remarriage in 1895 to Isaac Blackman (the US government expected Blackman to support Lucy), payments from that date to 1899 were terminated.

On March 2, 1900, Rosa resubmitted Application #637,596 for a dependent children's pension for her daughter Mary Shomin. She claimed that Mary was a natural daughter of Louis Shomin and was born in the morning of July 8, 1893, three months after her father, Louis's, death. She stated that she did not claim Mary in her former application for a widow's pension because Mary was born after the soldier's death, and Rosa did not think that she was entitled to anything for said child. Little Mary was baptized on September 1, 1893, at St. Mary's Church in Provemont (now Lake Leelanau), Michigan, by Father H. Ruessman, Catholic missionary of said church.

On October 19, 1900, Peter C. Goldschmidt, principal, with C. D. Stanley and W. A. Jackson, were appointed guardians and managers of the estate of Mary Shomin in right of heirship of her deceased father. The appointment was ordered by the probate court of Leelanau County.

On December 13, 1900, Rosa Shomin Blackman received her daughter's Pension for Dependent Children Certificate #504,408. The certificate paid eight dollars a month with an extra two dollars a month until Mary reached sixteen on July 7, 1900. The payments were retroactive to March 8, 1900.

Mary's new guardian, John O. Duncan (who replaced Peter Goldschmitt on March 8, 1907, upon Goldschmitt's resignation), received Mary's pension payments at the increased rate of fourteen dollars a month until July 7, 1909. On that date, Mary attained the age of sixteen.

Mary Shomin married at the age of seventeen to Dominic Chippewa on July 18, 1910, at St. Mary's Catholic Church in Peshawbestown. Dominic was the son of Daniel and Christine (Bebahwe) Chippewa.

After her marriage, Mary wrote a letter to the United States Pension Office in which she stated that she felt that she should be able to draw the full amount of the remainder of her pension payments since she was now married and had previously received payments in small increments for her support. She stated that her guardian told her that when she attained the age of twenty-one, she would no longer need a guardian and could draw upon the remainder of the funds deposited in the bank.

The US Pension Office replied to Mary that total payments of between $1,100 and $1,200 had been paid to her guardian to be deposited in a bank for her support. The letter further stated that under Michigan law, marriage as a minor under the age of twenty-one did not free her from having a guardian. The law also did not require a final settlement by her guardian before she attained age twenty-one. The letter concluded that the matter of a final settlement, and the withdrawal of remaining funds after she reached her age of majority, would have to be concluded between Mary and Mr. Duncan. It's not known if there was a solution to the final monetary settlement.

Smith, Thomas, Private

Enlistment: Enlisted as a private on May 18, 1863, at Isabella City (now Mt. Pleasant), Isabella County, by First Lieutenant William J. Driggs, First Michigan Sharpshooters, for three years.

Age: Twenty-three, born March 14, 1840, in Isabella County.

Occupation: Farmer

Residence: Isabella Township, Isabella County

Physical Description: Five feet ten, black eyes, black hair, and a dark complexion. Examining surgeon is not listed.

Mustered: May 26, 1863, at Detroit, Wayne County, by Lieutenant Colonel John R. Smith, US Army

Military Service: Private Thomas Smith was accepted into Company K even though he had a congenital deformity of his right forearm (he was missing the lower one-third of his arm three inches below his elbow). He convinced the enlistment officer that he could handle the loading and firing of a musket, as he had done so before his enlistment when he hunted game for his family.

On April 21, 1864, Private Smith was admitted to his regimental hospital, suffering from intermittent fever (occurring at intervals) induced by malaria. Malaria is an infectious disease caused by one of the genus *Plasmodium* and transmitted by mosquitoes infected with the genus *Anopheles* (*Blakiston*). The doctors treated Smith's malaria with quinine obtained from dried, pulverized cinchona tree bark that was mixed with water or whiskey. Whiskey worked better since it masked the bitter taste of the quinine. Pills of purified quinine sulfate were also dispensed for malaria (*Bollet*). Thomas returned to duty at the end of April.

On May 3, 1864, Private Smith was taken by ambulance wagon from his company quarters and transferred to the USA General Hospital at Fairfax Seminary near Alexandria, Virginia. He was diagnosed with chronic diarrhea and dysentery (inflammation of the intestinal membrane). Thomas was given extracts made from barley, rice, and meat, which were served with coffee and tea. Medications consisted of tartar emetic and Dover's powder (a combination of ipecac and opium) to induce vomiting and perspiration and to reduce fever. Potassium nitrate was also used to reduce bodily temperature and induce sweating (*Ibid.*). Opium pills were offered for pain. Thomas returned to duty on July 14, 1864.

On August 1, 1864, Private Smith was taken from the field by ambulance wagon and admitted to Washington Hall USA General Hospital in Alexandria, Virginia. At the time of his admission, he was diagnosed with typhoid fever (an acute infectious disease caused by the bacteria *Salmonella typhi* acquired through infected food or drinking water), which resulted in severe diarrhea and dysentery (*Ibid.*). He was isolated from the other patients, and his treatment was much the same as mentioned above for chronic diarrhea. Calomel (or mercurous chloride that contained mercury), quinine for fever, and analgesics to relieve pain were added to his medications (*Ibid.*). Since there were no real effective treatments for typhoid during the Civil War, Smith was fortunate to survive the disease (*Ibid.*). He returned to duty on September 21.

In December 1864, Private Smith was granted a one-day furlough to City Point, Virginia.

When his regiment was in the trenches before Petersburg, Virginia, in February 1865, Private Smith complained of inflamed, sore eyes. He thought that his eyes had become sore due to dust and smoke from artillery and gunfire. It's known that unsanitary camp conditions and the presence of bacteria in soil and dust can cause serious eye inflammation and resultant infection. His condition would become worse in the coming months.

Due to his exemplary conduct, Smith was promoted from the rank of private to that of first sergeant on March 1, 1865. On April 7, First Sergeant Smith was granted another furlough of one day to City Point.

By June, his ophthalmic condition had become much worse Smith was taken by ambulance wagon to a military railroad. At the railroad First Sergeant Smith was put on a mattress in a boxcar, the floor of which was cushioned with straw and hay, and sent to City Point, Virginia, where he was transferred from a wharf to a hospital steamer and sent to a division hospital of the Ninth Army Corps in Washington, DC. He was admitted to this hospital on July 1. The doctors at the corps hospital diagnosed Thomas as having a severe condition of opthalmia or conjunctivitis (inflammation of the mucous membrane covering the anterior portion of the globe of the eye). Treatment consisted of washing the eyes with cold water, and solutions of saline, borax, and chloride of sodium. Every third day, the physicians would evert (turn inside out) Thomas's eyelids and paint those parts with nitrate of silver in water (*Dorwart*).

On July 9, First Sergeant Smith was transferred from the Army Corps hospital to Lincoln USA General Hospital in said city. It was at this hospital that the doctors informed Smith that they diagnosed him as having gonorrheal opthalmia (venereal disease), an acute and severe form of purulent (formation of pus) conjunctivitis. This disease is caused by the bacteria *Neisserea gonorrhoeae* (*Ibid.-Blakiston*). The doctors also told him that there was chronic granulation of his eyelids and that there was really nothing that they could do for him except to irrigate his eyes with warm water and continue the applications of nitrate of silver in water to the insides of his eyelids.

On August 5, First Sergeant Smith was transferred to Armory Square Hospital in Washington, DC. Diagnosis was again that of gonorrheal opthalmia. He was mustered on August 11, 1865, but not paid. Smith was then transferred to Harewood USA General Hospital in the same city, admitted on August 15.

It was at Harewood that Smith was listed and classified with the status of invalid with the loss of sight in his right eye and the severe scarring in his left eye due to destructive inflammation—cause listed as conjunctivitis. He was also described as having a congenital deformity (loss of hand) of his right forearm. The description further stated that even with this congenital condition, First Sergeant Thomas Smith served faithfully for three years in the ranks, carrying his rifle and regularly performing his duties.

On September 6, 1865, a letter was sent by Dr. R. B. Bonlecon, lieutenant colonel and surgeon in charge of Harewood USA General Hospital, to Colonel R. O. Abbott, medical director, Department of Washington. The text of the letter is as follows:

> I have the honor to request the transfer of First Sergeant Thomas Smith, Co. "K", 1st Michigan S. S. Vols to a US Hospital at Philadelphia Pa. He will require treatment for more than sixty days, has destructive inflammation of both eyes, but is able to travel.
>
> Very Respectfully,
> Your obdt. Servant
> Dr. R. B. Bonlecon

A response to Bonlecon was written on September 11, 1865, from the surgeon general's office, authorizing the transfer of First Sergeant Thomas Smith as per instructions in the original letter.

On September 20, Smith was sent by hospital train from Harewood to Mower USA General Hospital at Chestnut Hill near Philadelphia. He was admitted to Mower on September 23, 1865.

From Mower, Smith was sent to Harper USA General Hospital in Detroit and admitted on October 6.

Thomas was finally transferred from Harper to his Post Hospital at the Detroit Barracks and admitted on November 15.

Discharged: After being shuffled from hospital to hospital, First Sergeant Thomas Smith was mustered out of the army and given a certificate of disability for discharge on December 1, 1865, from his Post Hospital at Detroit. He was paid the money owed to him at his discharge and made his way home in a world of darkness.

Another record states that Smith was discharged on August 11, 1865, at Detroit, but that date is in error. Considering that Smith spent considerable time in various hospitals being treated for his opthalmia after the end of the war, as mentioned in his medical file, his date of discharge would naturally be at a later time.

Whether Smith had a severe form of conjunctivitis or gonorrheal opthalmia he was judged to be totally blind upon discharge. The doctors in that era did not have the medical knowledge or the medications to save his eyes and would at times misdiagnose general opthalmia for gonorrheal opthalmia.

Biography: Thomas Smith, who was also known by his Anishinabe name of Shawgwonabay, was the son of William and America Smith of Isabella City. Among his known siblings were Mary Ann, born 1854; Henry J.C., born 1856; Moses, born 1861; and Helen F., born 1863. Thomas was literate and could understand the sometimes complicated rules of land ownership in the United States.

As was mentioned previously, Thomas was born with a congenital deformity of the lack of the lower third of his right arm. He seemed to manage quite well in helping his father with farming chores and in the use of a gun for hunting. His demonstrated ability to use a gun, even with this deformity, allowed his acceptance into the Sharpshooter Regiment when otherwise he should have been rejected for service.

On February 13, 1866, Thomas Smith's Application #102,480 for an invalid pension was filed for him. He cited heart disease, rheumatism, effects of dysentery, and blindness acquired while in the service. Captain James S. DeLand supported that application by signing an officer's certificate for the disability of the soldier.

One examining surgeon's certificate signed on July 18, 1866, stated that he believed that Thomas Smith's blindness was due to "purulent opthalmia" (conjunctivitis with a discharge of pus) and that partial vision might be restored by a surgical operation. On the basis of that surgeon's examination, Smith's application was denied on October 31, 1871, because his prurient opthalmia was not considered to be contracted while in the line of duty. In the judgment of the government, his condition was considered to be due to a sexually transmitted venereal disease and thus the result of "vicious habits."

Thomas had forty acres of land in Isabella County by reason of the first article of the treaty of August 2, 1855, and the second article of the treaty of October 18, 1864, between the United States of America and the bands of Chippewas of Saginaw, Swan Creek, and Black River of Michigan. Its description is the southeast quarter of the northwest quarter of section 9 in township 14 north of range 3 west. His certificate was granted on May 27, 1871 (*Land Records*).

On June 20, 1875, Thomas Smith married Nancy Paymegojing (or Pemegogin) in Isabella Township. The wedding ceremony was officiated by William Chatfield Jr., justice of the peace, in the presence of Thomas Chatfield and Major Francis as witnesses. Nancy, who was born in September 1850, was also known by her Anishinawbequa name of Shebawgozhigoqua. She was the daughter of William and Sarah (or Meckbyhequay) Pabawash. Thomas and Nancy did not have children.

For several years after his service, Thomas visited different doctors. One of these physicians was Dr. B. C. Shaw, who saw Thomas at intervals from August 1888 when Thomas was totally blind in both eyes. It was Dr. Shaw's professional medical opinion that Smith's blindness was not due to a venereal disease caused by "vicious habits" but from severe conjunctivitis.

After many depositions made by his friends and Company K comrades in support of Smith's exemplary character, and those depositions made by other doctors who supported Dr. Shaw's medical opinion, Thomas resubmitted his application for a pension based on disability on August 23, 1890.

The General Act of June 27, 1890, was more liberal to all persons who served ninety days or more for benefit of survivors and their widows and dependents. Thomas stated his inability to earn support by manual labor on account of his blindness. This claim was again rejected by the US Pension Office on December 27, 1892, on the grounds that, in their opinion, his blindness was due to "vicious habits."

Thomas filed another declaration under the same act on June 9, 1894, alleging congenital loss of his right hand and forearm, now as a disabling cause since he had lost his eyesight during his military service. This claim was finally allowed for the loss of the right forearm and hand under the Act of June 27, 1890.

Smith was issued an Invalid Pension Certificate #871,778, which paid twelve dollars a month commencing June 9, 1896, and retroactive from the date of filing his first declaration on August 23, 1890.

In his later adult life, Thomas was hereditary chief (or headman), by succession, of the Saginaw Chippewa tribe in Mt. Pleasant. He and Nancy, who were well thought of and respected, were faithful members of the North Branch Methodist Episcopal Church of Isabella Township where Thomas was trained to be a lay minister.

On March 26, 1900, Thomas was elected chairman of the board of trustees for said church. The other trustees serving with Thomas on the board were Daniel Bennett, Lyman Bennett, Peter Jackson, and James Jackson (*Reuter*).

After years of suffering from his war-related infirmities and of his faithful and devoted service to his church and to his tribe, Thomas died of pneumonia on April

22, 1909, at his home in Union Township. He was buried in the Nippissing Indian Cemetery in Isabella Township. A simple stone marked "Thomas Smith" identifies his grave.

Nancy Smith, who needed support after Thomas's death, applied for monies accrued since his death from his Pension Certificate #871,778. Her application #919,009 for a widow's pension was filed for her on April 30, 1909. Nancy's only support was earned by basket making, a slow and tedious task as age decreased the flexibility of her hands.

The accrued money from Thomas's pension was granted to Nancy, and she received a Widow's Pension Certificate #682,003 on May 22, 1909. Her pension payments amounted to twelve dollars a month. Payments were retroactive to April 30, 1909.

Nancy received this monthly rate until pneumonia claimed her life on May 12, 1910, at her home in Union Township. A large tumor (site unknown) was listed as a contributory factor in her death. She was buried near her husband on May 14 in said cemetery.

South, Peter, Private

Enlistment: Enlisted as a private on June 17, 1863, at Bear River (now Petoskey), Emmet County, by Second Lieutenant Garrett A. Graveraet, First Michigan Sharpshooters, for three years.

    Age: Eighteen, born about 1845 at Bear River.

    Occupation: Farmer

    Residence: Bear River

    Physical Description: Five feet nine, black eyes, black hair, and a dark complexion. Examining surgeon was Dr. Arvin F. Whelan, First Michigan Sharpshooters.

    Mustered: July 20, 1863, at Detroit, Wayne County, by Lieutenant Colonel John R. Smith, US Army

    Military Service: While on guard duty with his regiment at the confine for Confederate prisoners at Camp Douglas in Chicago, Cook County, Illinois, Private South became ill with "intermittent fever" or malaria. Malaria is an infectious disease caused by the genus *Plasmodium* and transmitted by mosquitoes infected with the genus *Anopheles* (*Blakiston*).

Peter was admitted to the USA Post Hospital at the camp on September 25,

1863. His treatment consisted of quinine made from dried, pulverized cinchona tree bark mixed with water or whiskey. Whiskey was better because it masked the bitter taste of the quinine. Quinine was also dispensed as pills made of purified quinine sulfate (*Bollet*). After a few days, South returned to duty with his regiment.

On June 17, 1864, when he was engaged in fighting with his regiment before Petersburg, Virginia, Private South was taken prisoner by the rebels. He was confined for a short time in a tobacco warehouse on Short Market Street in Petersburg and was later sent south on a cattle railcar to Fort Sumter (or Andersonville Prison) in Andersonville, Georgia.

After four months of imprisonment, Pvt. South was admitted to the overcrowded camp hospital, suffering from scorbutus (or scurvy), due to the lack vitamin C found in fresh fruits and vegetables. He exhibited a sallow and emaciated appearance with overall debility and weakness, compounded by chronic diarrhea and starvation.

Private South died in the camp hospital on December 19, 1864, of diarrhea. His body was removed from the prison hospital by his Company K comrades or prison guards and taken to the brush arbor dead house outside of the stockade. In the dead house, any useful clothing was removed. Information about the man's unit, state, and date of death was collected by a record keeper known as Dorance Atwater (also a prisoner), who kept the "Atwater List" of those prisoners who died at Andersonville. Atwater attached a numbered tag to the body. The tag was used for later identification. Then, as quickly as possible, Peter's remains, along with other bodies, were sent by wagon to the cemetery a mile from the prison grounds (*Encyclopedia*).

At the cemetery, South's body was placed without a covering into a trench shoulder to shoulder with other deceased soldiers and buried under prison dirt (*Ibid.*). A small post was placed at the head of his grave with a number carved into it. This number matched the number on the body tag and was also noted in the records known about the deceased. Today, Private South lies at rest under military stone #12,310 in Andersonville National Cemetery.

Peter's mother was solely dependent upon his support since he left neither widow nor child to survive him. After her son's death, she was left destitute.

Discharged: No discharge given. Died while a prisoner of war.

Biography: Peter South, called Paywawnoquot by friends and family, was also known as Peter Kamiskwasigay. He was the only child of Gwamikwasige and Lucy Kamisquahsegay. Lucy was also known as Lucy Shawananokwe.

Peter's father died about 1850 and left Peter as his mother's sole support. Lucy and Peter lived on a piece of land worth about $300. This land was granted to

Lucy and her husband by the Department of Indian Affairs from former treaty negotiations. Peter farmed the land and hunted to support himself and his mother until he left for service in the Union army. Under the rules of the Indian Affairs Department, Lucy had no authority to sell the land and would subsequently have no means by which she could improve it herself after Peter joined the army.

Peter attended the Presbyterian Mission School at Bear River. The school was under the auspices of the Presbyterian Board of Foreign Missions and headed by missionary Rev. Peter Dougherty.

In 1852, Rev. Dougherty sent Rev. Andrew Porter to Bear River to establish an Anishinabek mission and school. The teachers responsible for instructing the students were Mr. and Mrs. Andrew Porter. It was at this school that Peter learned to read and write in English and Anishinabe languages and studied history, mathematics, and geography. The students also learned skills in agriculture and carpentry for the boys and homemaking for the girls.

Peter South's name is listed among the boy students in two attendance reports for the school as recorded by Rev. Andrew Porter in 1860 (*Reports*). Peter had attended eighteen days. He was also mentioned as a student in the same class of the second session that ended September 30, 1860, as was Peter Wells, who attended fifty-two days. Both young men would serve as comrades in Company K (*Ibid.*).

Rev. Porter named Peter "Peter South" for one of Peter's mother's names—Shawananokwe. Her name was derived from the Anishinabe word *jawanong,* which means in the south, to the south, or from the south (*Baraga*). The "kwe" at the end of her name denotes that she was a woman—thus Shawananokwe means a "woman of or from the south."

During his term of service in the army, Peter South, who did not marry, sent home what money he was paid to support his mother in his absence. Lucy did receive a ten-dollar payment just before Peter died.

After Peter's death at Andersonville Prison, of which she was informed by a Company K survivor of the prison, Lucy was a recipient of charity from Emmet County for three months at three dollars a month. The charity money was stopped when she received back pay and bounty from her son's service. Since she had incurred debt in the amount of fifty dollars in trying to make a living, the service money didn't last very long.

Lucy wove baskets of black ash and sweet grass and made containers of birch bark to sell to tourists and interested buyers for a very meager income.

Being destitute and going blind, Lucy's Application #110,435 for a mother's pension was filed for her on September 25, 1865. Her application was approved on March 2, 1869, and she was granted a Mother's Pension Certificate #127,140. The pension paid eight dollars a month retroactive to December 20, 1864. Lucy received these payments until her death at Bear River sometime after 1870.

Stoneman, George, Private

Enlistment: Enlisted as a private on July 4, 1863, at Pentwater, Oceana County, by Captain Edwin V. Andress, First Michigan Sharpshooters, for three years.

Age: Twenty-two, born about 1841 in Montcalm County.

Occupation: Farmer and laborer

Residence: Pentwater

Physical Description: Five feet eight, with black eyes, black hair, and a dark complexion. Examining physician was Dr. Jacob B. McNett, assistant surgeon, First Michigan Sharpshooters.

Mustered: July 11, 1863, at Detroit, Wayne County, by Lieutenant Colonel John R. Smith, US Army

Military Service: On July 19, 1863, Private Stoneman deserted his post at Dearborn, Wayne County, when his regiment was guarding the state arsenal. His whereabouts were unknown. Stoneman did not return to his regiment until September 9 of said year when the regiment was in Chicago, Cook County, Illinois, on guard duty at the confine for Confederate prisoners called Camp Douglas.

George's regiment was ordered to the front to join the Ninth Army Corps on March 12, 1864. The men left Chicago five days later on St. Patrick's Day.

While traveling on the train going from Chicago, by way of Baltimore, to Annapolis, Maryland, Private Stoneman claimed that he incurred an injury to his right eye. He stated that when he put his head out of the window, a cinder from the train's smoke stack struck him in the right eye. The injury caused severe swelling, inflammation of the eye, and partial blindness. He also stated that he sought medical help from the regimental surgeon but did not report the treatment that he was given. This claim of injury would be disputed by a few friends who served with Stoneman when he applied for a pension.

Hospital records state that Stoneman suffered a gunshot (missile) wound to the first and second phalanges (or fingers) of the left hand at the Battle of Spotsylvania (Ni River, Virginia) on May 9 or 10, 1864. He was sent to an aid station where his wound was assessed and washed, and any bleeding was stopped. Cotton bandages were applied to his wounds. He was given some whiskey and an opium pill for pain (*Adams*).

George was then sent by ambulance wagon to his division hospital farther behind the lines. The doctors at the division hospital anesthetized Stoneman with chloroform and performed flap surgery to remove the second (or middle) finger and third (or ring) finger of George's left hand. In this type of surgery, the surgeons excised, or removed, the digits at their metacarpophalangeal joints—the joints that connect the finger bones to the bones (called metacarpals) of the palm of the hand. After surgery, the flaps of muscle and skin, which were cut in the circular method and pulled back before the amputation of the fingers, were brought together and loosely sutured with silk or wire (*Kuz and Bengtson*). Simple water dressings were applied to the stumps of the fingers. These dressings consisted of folded lint dipped into cold water, applied to the wounds, and secured with a cloth wrap or adhesive plaster. George was given an opium pill to ease his postsurgery pain.

On May 12, Stoneman was taken by ambulance wagon through Fredericksburg, Virginia, to Belle Plain landing. He was put on a hospital steamer, transported to Mt. Pleasant USA General Hospital in Washington, DC, and admitted there on May 13. At Mt. Pleasant, the doctors applied a porous mass called "charpie" to Stoneman's finger stumps. Charpie was composed of separated threads of linen or cotton fabric clumped together. This dressing was put on the stumps to absorb drainage and was held in place with bandages of cotton, linen, flannel, or muslin (*Schaadt*). The surgeons closed George's hand over a ball the proper size and held it in place with adhesive plaster (*Ibid.-Kuz and Bengtson*). Opium pills were given to Stoneman to ease his pain, and a nourishing diet was ordered for him.

He was transferred from Mt. Pleasant Hospital on May 27 to Satterlee USA General Hospital in West Philadelphia, Pennsylvania, and admitted on May 28, 1864.

On August 6, he was sent from Satterlee to St. Mary's USA General Hospital in Detroit. Similar treatment was continued as the doctors watched the healing process very closely.

On August 9, 1864, the physicians at St. Mary's determined that the stumps of Pvt. Stoneman's fingers had healed properly and showed no evidence of infection (such as gangrene). He left St. Mary's Hospital on said date and returned to his regiment in Virginia.

Stoneman was admitted to Augur USA General Hospital near Alexandria, Virginia, from his regiment on August 17, 1864. He had complained of chronic rheumatism that was probably brought on by episodes of dysentery and resulted in reactive arthritis. The only treatment available at the time was to administer opiates for severe joint pain and potassium iodide and quinine for their anti-inflammatory effects (*Bollet*). While at Augur Hospital, the doctors determined that Stoneman had lost the sight of his right eye that had occurred from an injury on his initial train trip to the front.

After three months at Augur Hospital, Stoneman was given a furlough on October 26, 1864. He was present and mustered for the months of September and October (before furlough) while in the hospital.

Stoneman was charged with desertion on December 1 and December 31, 1864. He was again charged with the same infraction during the months of January and February 1865. George returned to his regiment on March 14, 1865, and was restored to duty.

On March 21, 1865, all charges of desertion were removed from Stoneman's record by Special Order No. 67 from a board of officers at the headquarters department in Washington, DC. It's possible that some furloughs granted to Stoneman were mistaken for desertion considering time, distance, and communication involved in travel during that era.

From the time he left Augur General Hospital, Stoneman stated that he was not able to perform his military duties because of the injury to his left hand and partial blindness in his right eye. On April 3, 1865, a board of three surgeons from said hospital examined Private Stoneman and pronounced him unfit for military service and unqualified for the Veteran Reserve Corps. They based their decision on the injury to his left hand, inability to perform his military duties, partial blindness, and the diagnosis of the onset of consumption (or tuberculosis) in his left lung. Therefore, Stoneman was eligible for a certificate of disability for discharge.

Discharged: Private George Stoneman was mustered out of the army and given a certificate of disability for discharge from Augur General Hospital, Alexandria, Virginia, on May 8, 1865. He was paid money owed to him for his service at the time of his discharge and returned to Michigan.

Biography: George Stoneman was well thought of and respected. He was headman (or chief) of his band and considered to be a very bright individual who could speak English fluently. When he was home on his furlough, granted October 26, 1864, George married Mary Fox (or Chaquaan/Chaquomoqua also known as Sagooge, Shobboaah, Sawcomemoquay, and Shawpoquawawnogay) on or about November 1, 1864. Although not sweethearts before George left for the army, the couple grew up knowing each other. Their marriage was performed according to Anishinabek custom and practice (consent of the couple and their parents) in the Cobmoosa Government School House near Elbridge, Oceana County. Friends of the couple were also in attendance. Mary said that she was born about 1828 in Grand Haven, Ottawa County. It was reported that she could not speak English.

On March 25, 1867, an invalid pension Application #123,832 was filed for George Stoneman, which stated permanent injuries to his left hand and right eye. He received Invalid Pension Certificate #110,637 on May 25, 1871, which paid two dollars a month retroactive to May 9, 1865. The certificate was only for the missile wound to his left hand.

George Stoneman had 160 acres of land in Oceana County by reason of a cash entry sale of public lands. It's description is the southwest quarter of the northeast quarter, of the southeast quarter of the northwest quarter, the northeast quarter of the southwest quarter and the northwest quarter of the southeast quarter of section 4, in township 16 north, of range 16 west. He was granted Certificate #22088 on March 10, 1874 (*Land Records*).

Several deponents, who were friends and army comrades, testified that before the war they thought that Stoneman had incurred an injury to his right eye (they referred to a white spot on the cornea) or had what we call today a lazy eye or crossed eye. Either condition could have impaired his vision during his service. Due to these discrepancies, the pension office stated that the pension claim was not satisfactorily proven even though the doctors stated that George had incurred the injury to his eye while in the service.

Stoneman submitted a request that he be given an increase of two dollars per month on his pension #110,637 on November 4, 1875. He had hoped that the new request would cover the alleged damage to his eyesight. This petition for monetary increase was rejected on March 20, 1877, for the same reason that it was not covered in the original pension claim. There was no substantial evidence accepted by the Pension Office that the injury to his eye had actually occurred when George was in the service.

Even though Mary and George had no children of their own, a child known as Musneghe, age five, was listed as the couple's daughter in the Oceana County federal census of 1880. If not a natural child of George and Mary's, it's possible that Musneghe was adopted by the couple and given the name Elizabeth (or Eliza). Elizabeth became the future Mrs. Joseph Kelsey. Elizabeth Kelsey is referred to as Mary's daughter and is named as an affiant on a general affidavit for Mary's remarried widow's pension claim.

On the fateful night of July 9, 1887, while his band was harvesting summer berries and camped near Muskegon in Muskegon County, George Stoneman met a tragic death (*Whitehall Forum*). The following newspaper article from the Muskegon County town of Whitehall titled "*Still Another*" gives the details of his death as follows:

The Whitehall Forum
Thursday July 14, 1887

A most distressing accident occurred Saturday night (July 9) near Sweet's Station by which George Stoneman, an Indian well known in this town, was swept into eternity without an instant's warning. The passenger train from Muskegon on that night was delayed by reason of a broken bridge at Muskegon and was something like an hour late. Stoneman was walking on the track from Muskegon and met two of his band who were going to the camp with berries. He expressed himself as wishing to walk alone and his companions permitted him to lag behind. He had evidently been imbibing freely of liquor and must have lain down on the Track and fallen asleep. The two Indians who met him retired in their tents, but soon heard the train rumbling along and bethinking themselves of Stoneman started out to find him. The trainmen were already viewing his mangled remains by the side of the track. A lantern was set by his body and word was brought to town by the train. Coroner Nicholson, Marshal McKinzie, Station Agent Sollau, Reporter Brown and Charley Hinman procured a hand car and repaired to the scene of the accident. The crushed body was placed in a box and brought to town, an inquest being held Sunday morning and the burial taking place in the afternoon. The trainmen say that Stoneman, when he was struck, laid on the rail bed with his head on one of the rails, and the engine and three cars passed over him dragging him about six rods. The coroner's jury rendered a verdict in accordance with the facts, relieving the railway employees of all blame.

Mary was informed of George's death about an hour after the accident. A deposition made by the coroner/undertaker Wayland B. Nicholson stated that

Stoneman was buried in Whitehall's Oakhurst Cemetery in Muskegeon County on the afternoon of Sunday, July 10, 1887 (*Deposition*).

On May 2, 1892, Mary Stoneman married for the second time to David Elliot of Fountain, Mason County. Martin H. Foster, justice of the peace, officiated at the civil ceremony. Witnesses were Daniel S. and Nattie Dyer. Mary lived with Elliott until his death on March 20, 1919.

On June 11, 1896, Mary Elliott received notification that George's application for a two-dollar increase had been reviewed and approved for only the missile wound. She was granted four dollars a month as accrued money owed to George retroactive from September 12, 1883, to his death on July 14, 1887.

After her second husband died in 1919, Mary was eligible to reapply for a widow's pension as the widow of her first husband. Mary Stoneman Elliott's Application #1,175,485 for a remarried widow's pension was filed for her on June 4, 1921. She was too old and feeble to be self-supporting since her second husband, Elliot, had died and she was living in destitute circumstances. Approval was granted for a pension rate of thirty dollars a month under the Act of May 1, 1920. Mary's Widow's Pension Certificate #925,523 was issued on December 13, 1922. Payments were retroactive to June 4, 1921.

Under the Act of July 3, 1926, Mary's pension payments were increased to fifty dollars a month to begin on August 4, 1926. She received these payments until her death on March 12, 1929, at Fountain.

Sutton, Freeman, Private

Enlistment: Enlisted as a private on February 10, 1865, at Grand Rapids, Kent County, by Captain Norman Bailey, First Michigan Sharpshooters and provost marshal for the Fourth Congressional District, for three years. Credited to the Fourth Congressional District, Pere Marquette Township, Mason County.

Age: Thirty-two, born about 1833 in Michigan.

Occupation: Laborer

Residence: Pere Marquette, Mason County

Physical Description: Five feet six, with black eyes, black hair, and a copper complexion. Examining physician was Dr. Alonzo Mate, First Michigan Sharpshooters.

Mustered: February 10, 1865, at Grand Rapids by Captain Norman Bailey

Military Service: While engaged in a skirmish before Petersburg, Virginia, on April 2, 1865, Private Sutton suffered a gunshot wound in his left thigh. The wound was caused by a missile that cut through the sartorius and vastus lateralis (or vastus externus) muscles, just missed the femur (or thigh bone), and lodged in the upper third of his thigh. This wound would cause continuous pain for Sutton and render him permanently disabled.

Sutton was taken to an aid station where his wound was assessed. A tourniquet was applied to his left thigh to stop the bleeding, and the area around the wound was washed (*Bollet*). A temporary cloth bandage was hastily applied to the wound, and the soldier was given an opium pill for pain (*Ibid.*). From the aid station, Private Sutton was sent by ambulance wagon to his division hospital farther behind the lines. After putting iodine on the wound to impede infection, the doctors applied simple water dressings to the wound. Simple dressings were composed of lint dipped into cold water, applied to the wound, and secured with a cloth wrap or adhesive plaster (*Schaadt*).

On April 3, Private Sutton was taken to a military railroad, put on a hospital train, and sent to the depot hospital at City Point, Virginia. The doctors anesthetized Sutton with chloroform and removed the piece of shrapnel. Applications of iodine and simple water dressings were continued. The dressings were changed frequently. Whiskey or an opium pill was offered for pain. A nourishing diet was ordered for the soldier.

On April 5, Sutton was taken to a wharf at City Point, transferred to the hospital ship *State of Maine,* and transported to L'Ouverture USA Hospital in Alexandria, Virginia. He was admitted to L'Ouverture on April 6. His wound was considered to be severe enough to warrant more expert care from the doctors at a large city hospital.

While at L'Ouverture Hospital, treatment of Sutton's wound consisted of: the continued application of simple water dressings; use of carbolic acid, bromine, and tincture of iodine around the wound to impede infection (*Ibid.-Bollet)*; applications of warm poultices made of flaxseed or bread mixed with water used to apply heat to the wound to ward off infection (*Ibid.*); and covering or sealing the wound with "cerate," a waxy substance made of beeswax mixed with oils to keep out insects or other vectors of disease (*Ibid.*). Whiskey or opium pills were given for pain. The scar left by the tract of the missile was large and very painful, and there was a discharge of matter from the wound. While in the hospital, Sutton enjoyed a nourishing, unrestricted diet that the doctors ordered for him to help him to gain strength.

Private Sutton was transferred from L'Ouverture to Slough USA General Hospital in Alexandria, Virginia, and was admitted there on September 16. Simple dressings were continued.

Because of the severity of his wound and the disability that it caused, Private Freeman Sutton was mustered out of service on September 19, 1865, while a patient at Slough Hospital. He was recommended for an honorable discharge of disability by Assistant Surgeon S. D. Twinning of said hospital.

Discharged: Two records state that Sutton was discharged on June 9, 1865, from Slough General Hospital in Alexandria, while two medical records state that he was discharged on September 19, 1865, after he was transferred to Slough General Hospital in Alexandria from L'Ouverture. These two dates lead to a confusion of the facts. Which date is correct? Since Sutton applied for his pension on September 27, 1865, either date of discharge is in line with subsequent events. After Private Sutton was mustered out and received an honorable discharge for disability from Slough, he was paid the money owed to him for his service at his discharge and returned home to Pere Marquette.

Biography: Freeman Sutton was reported to have married one Eliza Kahbayah, also known as Eliza Gunbah, by accepted Anishinabek custom and practice (mutual consent of the couple and their parents) about 1856. The pair separated by mutual agreement shortly before or just after the start of the Civil War. In a marriage of accepted Anishinabek custom and practice, a mutual separation is considered a divorce.

A few days before Sutton enlisted into the Union army, he married a woman known as Pemosawa. Justice of the Peace Sewall Moulton of Mason County officiated at the civil ceremony on February 7, 1865. It is assumed that Pemosawa was also known as Jane or Mary Sutton as found in the census records.

The couple was known to have had the following children: Andrew, born about 1864 and died of measles at age seventeen on July 14, 1881; William, born about 1865; John, born about 1866; Freeman Sutton Jr., born June 10, 1868; Jane, born about 1869; and Johnson (or John), born about 1874 and died of tuberculosis at age seven on July 20, 1881. These children were born to the couple when the family lived in Custer Township in Mason County. It is assumed that none of the other children lived to adulthood because the 1880 census lists Andrew and Johnson as the only children living with the couple, and both of these boys died in 1881. The other children, by their young ages and not being listed in the 1880 census, may have died before the census was taken.

On September 27, 1865, an invalid pension Application #90,655 was filed for Freeman Sutton. The army doctors had declared Sutton to be half-incapacitated, and this was borne out by Sutton's restrictive, noticeable limp and the severe pain that he experienced when walking for any distance. He often complained of the frequent discharge of matter from his wound.

Sutton's second declaration was filed on September 22, 1868. Finally, on June 10, 1882, Sutton was awarded Invalid Pension Certificate #212,234. His pension paid four dollars a month retroactive to June 10, 1865.

On June 24, 1886, Sutton submitted a request for an increase in his monthly payments. The increase was approved September 7, 1886, and he was paid six dollars a month retroactive to August 11, 1886.

Freeman was allotted eighty acres in Mason County under the first article of the treaty concluded July 31, 1855, between commissioners on the part of the United States and the Ottawa and Chippewa Indians of Michigan. The land description is the east half of the southeast quarter of section 8 in township 18, north of range 16 west. Sutton was granted his Certificate #1005 on February 3, 1872 (*Land Records*).

He applied for and received 160 acres in Mason County under the Homestead Act of 1862. The land description is the northeast quarter of section 32 in township 18 north of range 15 west. He was granted his Homestead Certificate #3129 on November 10, 1879 (*Ibid.*).

Sutton's pension was rerated on August 29, 1889, and he was given a third increase of another two dollars, which then allowed him a pension of eight dollars a month, which he received until his death.

On the night of December 13, 1890, Freeman Sutton was struck and killed by a train on the F and P Railway while he was walking along the tracks. According to the accident report, the train engineer notified the section foreman, who in turn informed Jacob Kaplinger, who was justice of the peace in and for Mason County. These men and six jurymen went by handcar to the place of the accident and verified that it was indeed the body of Sutton. The men then removed Sutton's body from the tracks, put him into the handcar, and returned to the handcar house. Sutton's remains were left at this house until the next morning. On the same evening, an inquest into Sutton's death was held by Mr. Kaplinger (*Report*).

Freeman Sutton was buried (place not specified) the next day on Kaplinger's orders. No mention was made as to when Pemosawa was notified of her husband's death.

After her husband's demise, Pemosawa Sutton was left with only sixty dollars' worth of household goods and the money from Freeman's last monthly payment.

On May 12, 1891, a widow's pension Application #515,111 was filed for Pemosawa. She was finally granted Widow's Pension Certificate #388,484 on January 3, 1894, which paid eight dollars a month retroactive to May 12, 1891.

Pemosawa Sutton received her monthly payments until March 4, 1898, when her name was dropped from the pension rolls due to notification of her death in Fountain, Mason County.

Tabasasch, Francis, Corporal

Enlistment: Enlisted as a corporal on June 11, 1863, at La Croix (renamed Cross Village in 1875), Emmet County, by Second Lieutenant Garrett A. Graveraet, First Michigan Sharpshooters, for three years.

Age: Thirty-eight, born December 29, 1827, in LaCroix.

Occupation: Farmer and carpenter

Residence: LaCroix

Physical Description: Five feet eight, with black eyes, black hair, and a dark complexion. Examining physician was Dr. Arvin F. Whelan, surgeon, First Michigan Sharpshooters.

Mustered: July 20, 1863, at Detroit by Lieutenant Colonel John R. Smith, US Army

Military Service: During the months of August and September 1863, when his regiment guarded Confederate prisoners at Camp Douglas in Chicago, Cook County, Illinois, Corporal Tabasasch was given a special assignment for said time period. He was ordered to accompany Second Lieutenant Garrett Graveraet on recruiting service in Michigan. Since both men were popular among their people at home and with their Company K comrades, they were successful in their recruiting efforts.

Being an excellent carpenter, Tabasasch was assigned to the Quartermaster Department at Camp Douglas for construction and repairs to buildings for the months of January and February 1864.

On April 16, 1864, Corporal Tabasasch was admitted to his regimental hospital from his camp outside of Annapolis, Maryland with the complaint of opthalmia. This condition is caused by the inflammation of the conjunctiva of the eye. Treatment for this malady consisted of washing the eyes with a drachm of alum in warm water and applications of nitrate of silver in water to the inner portion of Frank's eyelids *(Dorwart)*. Physicians also administered quinine for fever and ordered iron, cod-liver oil, and a full diet for the corporal *(Ibid.)*.

Having to stand in water up to his knees in the trenches at Petersburg, Virginia, and exposed to a severe rainstorm on June 23, 1864, Tabasasch became sick with diarrhea and mild shakes. He was admitted on June 24 to his division hospital farther behind the lines. His treatment for diarrhea included castor oil given in the morning and opium pills administered at night *(Bollet)*. Calomel, or mercurous chloride that contained mercury, turpentine given orally, and ipecac were also administered along with doses of whiskey *(Ibid.)*.

While combating diarrhea, Tabasasch was also diagnosed with remittent fever (or malaria) at said hospital on June 28. Malaria is an infectious disease caused by one of the genus *Plasmodium* and transmitted by mosquitoes infected with the genus *Anopheles (Blakiston)*. The doctors treated Frank's malaria with doses of quinine made from powdered cinchona tree bark dissolved in water or whiskey. Whiskey worked better because it masked the bitter taste of the quinine. Quinine could also be given as pills made of purified quinine sulfate *(Ibid.-Bollet)*. The patient was also given mercury compounds for bowel complaints and opium pills for pain *(Ibid.)*.

On July 3, Frank was taken by ambulance wagon to the military railroad where he was put on a mattress in a boxcar, the floor of which was cushioned with straw or hay, and sent to City Point, Virginia. At City Point, Frank was taken by ambulance wagon to a wharf, transferred to a hospital steamer and taken to Carver USA General Hospital in Washington, DC. He was admitted to Carver on July 5. Similar treatment was given to the patient.

To add to his misery, Corporal Tabasasch began to experience more severe chills, sweating, pain in his limbs, severe headaches, diarrhea, and intestinal ulcers. His doctors thought that he had typhoid fever. On July 28, Frank was transferred from Carver to USA General Hospital in York, Pennsylvania. He was admitted to USA General on July 29.

At this hospital, Tabasasch was isolated from other patients and given doses of whiskey and quinine. Mercury compounds and opium were also administered to the patient. He also received external therapy called sinapism (or mustard plaster). The plaster was made from ground black mustard seed mixed with flour and water. This mixture was wrapped in a flannel or other cloth and applied to his chest and abdomen. It was thought that the heat caused by the substances in the mustard would draw out "poisons" in the body *(Internet)*.

It's possible that Frank actually had a combination of malaria and typhoid called typho-malaria, which was described as being predominantly malarial or typhoidal in nature. Likely he had one illness or the other, with atypical symptoms, or neither illness, with symptoms due to another cause, or both illnesses at the same time (*Schaadt*). He returned to active duty on October 27, 1864.

On November 26, 1864, Corporal Tabasasch was promoted to first sergeant (or orderly sergeant). Since Tabasasch, who was well liked, was educated at the Holy Cross Catholic Mission School at La Croix and was proficient in both Anishinabe and English languages, he was a very good choice for this promotion. The rank of first sergeant entailed a close working relationship with Captain Andress (who selected him for this rank) in which Tabasasch was responsible for the completion of all daily paperwork for his company and the execution of all orders given by Captain Andress (*Kautz*). At the rank of first sergeant, Tabasasch was paid twenty dollars a month for his service (*Ibid.*).

On March 1, 1865, Sergeant Tabasasch was reduced in rank from first sergeant to fifth sergeant—the most junior grade of this rank. The reason for the demotion was not made clear in his pension papers, but it may have been due to a serious infraction of army regulations or protocol.

Discharged: Fifth Sergeant Francis Tabasasch was mustered out and given an honorable discharge at Delaney House in Tenallytown, DC, on July 28, 1865. He returned to Detroit on the steamer *Morning Star* and was paid money due to him for his service on August 7 at Jackson, Jackson County.

Biography: Francis (or Frank) Tabasasch's original family name was Assinauby or Assinnaby. He changed his surname and that of his children to Tabasasch when he enlisted in the army. After his service and for the rest of his life, Frank's surname would be spelled Tabasasch, as he used this spelling on most of his pension papers. Some of Frank's pension papers are signed "Tabasash." A few of the Tabasasch family records list the family name as "Tabassash." Frank's son, John Baptist, signed his name as "Tabasasch." So the mystery continues—which is the correct spelling? Is it Tabasasch or Tabasash?

Frank was the son of Francis Sr., also called Frank, and Theressa Assinauby (or Assinnaby). Frank Jr. may have had a brother, Joseph, who spelled his surname Tappasash and lived most of his life in Hays Township of Charlevoix County. Joseph died at age ninety-one of old age and heart disease on December 20, 1913 (or 1915).

Francis Jr. married Mary Wobigog (or Wabigog), the daughter of Peter, who was a farmer, and Evangeline (or Angelic) (Panacequa) Wabigog, on February 28,

1851, in La Croix. Rev. Father Ignatius Mrak officiated at the couple's wedding in the Holy Cross Roman Catholic Mission Church.

In the 1860 federal census, Francis Jr. was listed as Francis Assinauby, a mechanic and farmer of La Croix Township. Mary and the couple's children, Madeline, John, and Louisa, were also listed under the surname of Assinauby.

At the time of the 1860 census, Frank's real estate value was $600, and the value of his personal estate was $625.

Also recorded in the 1860 federal census for the same township were Mary Wobigog Assinauby's parents and her siblings who were still at home. The siblings were: Michael, age fifteen; Catherine, age thirteen; Christine, age eleven; Stephen, age nine; and Margaret, age four. Louis and John Baptist Wobegog were listed in the same census and may have been Mary's older brothers.

According to vital records held in Cross Village, Francis Jr. and Mary were the parents of seven children who were duly recorded and baptized during the years of their births by Rev. Father Louis Sifferath. The family included: Magdalena (or Madeline), born May 26, 1855; John Baptist, born August 30, 1857; Rosa, born September 16, 1859 (listed as Louisa in 1860); Louis, born November 29, 1861; Agatha, born February 28, 1864; Joseph, born June 15, 1866; and Anna, born during the early 1870s. Father Sifferath spelled the family name "Tabassash." By 1870, Francis's real estate value was $900.

Rosa, Louis, Agatha, and Joseph would die as young children. Magdeline (or Madeline) died of tuberculosis at the age of sixteen on December 4, 1871. She was known for her exquisite floral appliqué quilt work, and one of her quilts is on display at the Quilt Center of the Michigan State University Museum in East Lansing. Anna, who died between the years of 1894 and 1898, was a student for some years at the Carlisle Indian School in Carlisle, Pennsylvania.

John Baptist Tabasasch was Frank and Mary's only child to attain adulthood. He married Anna Jackson, the daughter of Jacob and Margaret Jackson, on January 15, 1883, at the Holy Cross Mission Church. The young couple had a son, Bazile, born in 1882 before their marriage; a son, Paul, born January 15, 1885 (on his parents' wedding anniversary), and lived only ten days; a daughter, Angeline, born in June 1886, who would eventually marry John Petoskey; and a second daughter, Madaline, born March 4, 1888, and died the day after her birth.

Anna Jackson Tabasasch died on March 6, 1888, of inflammation of the bowel.

Francis Tabasasch's education at the parochial school in Cross Village gave him a firm foundation with which to support his family. He not only learned to be a prosperous farmer, raising various crops and animals, but also acquired woodworking skills by which he became an excellent carpenter and joiner.

In 1860, Francis was elected for a two-year term to the position of Emmet County registrar. He would serve alongside his friend and Company K comrade Henry G. Graveraet, who was elected probate judge the same year.

Application #460,704 for an invalid pension was filed for Francis on September 22, 1882. In the application, he cited chronic diarrhea, fever, ague (a recurrent chill in an attack of malaria), and general debility, which he contracted while in the trenches before Petersburg. His health had deteriorated since his service, and his advanced age contributed to his decline. Also, his hearing had decreased due to the extreme noise of exploding ordinance and gunfire. It was due to these disabilities that Tabasasch blamed his inability to do manual labor, on which he was dependent, for support for himself and his family.

Like many Civil War veterans, Francis joined a Grand Army of the Republic post so that he could enjoy the fellowship of veteran friends who had similar wartime experiences. He served as officer of the guard in the GAR George Washington Post #106 in Cross Village. Among other members of that post were Company K buddies Payson Wolfe, Louis Shomin, Joseph Ashkanok, and Simon Sanaquaby.

Frank would also attend Anishinabek powwow gatherings and war dances in which he would regale the attendees with speeches about his exploits in the Civil War.

After resubmitting his application in 1890 and again in 1891, Francis finally received his Invalid Pension Certificate #731,783 on March 23, 1895. The pension paid two dollars a month retroactive to September 22, 1882. Under the more liberal Act of 1890, Francis received an increase of payments that amounted to twelve dollars a month.

By June 1900, John Baptist Tabasasch was a widower, and he and his daughter, Angeline, were living with Francis and Mary in Cross Village.

Francis was also left a widower when Mary died of a heart attack at the age of sixty-four on August 25, 1900. She is buried in Holy Cross Cemetery of Cross Village. John then assumed complete care of his father in addition to raising his own daughter.

After submitting an application for an increase in payments in 1905, Francis was granted twenty dollars a month on November 9, 1908, under the act of 1907. These payments would continue until his death.

By 1910, Francis was quite ill and infirm. John continued to care for his father during his illness. At the age of eighty-six, Francis died of diarrhea and old age on November 22, 1912, at his home in Cross Village. He is buried in Holy Cross Cemetery near his wife. A military stone marks his burial site.

On October 13, 1913, John Baptist Tabasasch wrote to Washington, DC, to request the last pension payment due to Francis at the time of his death. John needed the payment to reimburse him for the $200 he incurred in the care of his father during his illness and for the cost of Francis's funeral expenses. No record has been located of John having received the last payment.

John Baptist Tabasasch died of dropsy (or edema—the excessive accumulation of fluid in the tissue spaces) at age sixty-two on June 23, 1922, at his home in Cross Village.

Tabyant, Antoine, Private

Enlistment: Enlisted as a private on June 14, 1863, at Little Traverse (now Harbor Springs), Emmet County, by Second Lieutenant Garrett A. Graveraet, First Michigan Sharpshooters, for three years.

Age: Thirty-five/thirty-nine, born about 1834 in Emmet County.

Occupation: Farmer

Residence: Little Traverse

Physical Description: Five feet eight, with black eyes, black hair, and a dark complexion. Examining physician was Dr. Arvin F. Whelan, surgeon, First Michigan Sharpshooters.

Mustered: July 20, 1863, at Detroit by Lieutenant Colonel John R. Smith, US Army

Military Service: When his regiment guarded the confine for Confederate prisoners at Camp Douglas in Chicago, Cook County, Illinois, Private Antoine Tabyant was assigned to extra duty. He served as a company cook for the month of July 1863 and as a waiter to help serve food during the month of December of said year.

During the Battle of Spotsylvania on May 12, 1864, as he charged the enemy's defenses, Tabyant suffered a gunshot wound in the right shoulder. The missile entered his body near the middle of the superior border of the spine of the right scapula (shoulder blade) and broke (fractured) the blade. The path made by the missile passed in front of the spine and cut through several muscles of the upper back and shoulder complex in its trajectory. The result of this wound would affect branches of the seventh cervical and first, second, and third dorsal nerves of the right side of his neck before it exited six inches posterior to the nipple in the left thoracic wall. The injury would leave Tabyant permanently disabled with painful restricted movement of his head and right shoulder. This condition would also result in permanent lameness of his shoulder complex and give him severe pain in the left side of his chest.

After he was wounded, Tabyant was taken to an aid station where any excess bleeding was stopped by the application of direct pressure (*Bollet*). His wound was then assessed, washed, and hastily bandaged. Whiskey or an opium pill was offered for pain.

Tabyant was then taken by ambulance wagon to his division hospital farther behind the lines. At the hospital, the doctors washed and cleaned the entrance and exit wounds made by the missile ball and applied iodine to the wounds to impede infection. Simple water dressings were then put on the wounds. Water dressings consisted of folded lint dipped into cold water, placed on the wounds, and held in place by a cloth wrap or adhesive plaster (*Schaadt*). In addition to the dressings, treatment also consisted of binding Tabyant's arm to his chest with cloth bandages, a trial of various splints, or an abduction pillow that kept his arm out from the chest. The splints also applied traction to the upper arm (*Kuz and Bengtson*). Antoine was given whiskey and an opium pill to ease his pain.

After his treatment at the division hospital, Antoine was taken by ambulance wagon to the depot hospital in Fredericksburg, Virginia, where similar treatment was given to the soldier. The depot hospital was at or near attorney John Marye's house, a short distance from Marye's Heights.

A few days later, Tabyant was sent by ambulance wagon from Fredericksburg to a wharf at Belle Plain Landing. He was put on a hospital ship and conveyed to Harewood General Hospital in Washington, DC.

At Harewood, Antoine was given an opium pill for pain. His wounds were again treated with a tincture of iodine to offset infection and dressed with simple water dressings. Cloth bindings and splints were continued to immobilize his arm and shoulder. Quiet and rest were ordered for the patient, and he was fed a nourishing diet to aid in the healing process.

In addition to his wounds, the doctors at Harewood discovered that Tabyant suffered from trachoma, an infectious disease of the conjunctiva and cornea caused by *Chlamydozoon trachomatis* (*Blakiston*). Trachoma produces an intolerance or sensitivity of light called photophobia, inflamed granulation on the inner surface of the eyelids, pain, and lacrimation (the excessive secretion of tears). The cornea of Antoine's left eye became opaque, and the iris of the right eye was inflamed.

For treatment, Antoine's eyelids were everted to expose the inner portion of the eyelids every third day, and these surfaces were painted with nitrate of silver in water (*Dorwart*). A weak solution of boric acid or a solution of a drachm (or dram) of alum in a pint of tepid water was used several times a day to bath Antoine's eyes (*Ibid.*). Due to the effects of trachoma, Tabayant suffered a total loss of vision in his left eye.

Private Tabyant was given a furlough from Harewood on May 31. He returned to the hospital on June 26. His wounds healed in six months, and he returned to his regiment. After he rejoined his regiment, Antoine saw no further active duty for the duration of the war.

Discharged: Private Antoine Tabyant was mustered out and honorably discharged at Delaney House in Tenallytown, DC, on July 28, 1865. He returned to Detroit on the steamer *Morning Star*. On August 7, 1865, he was paid money due to him for his service at Jackson, Jackson County.

Biography: Antoine Tabyant, also known as Anthony John Tabyant, was the son of Kisabe and his wife. According to church records of Holy Childhood of Jesus Catholic Church in Harbor Springs, Emmet County (found in Antoine's pension papers), the name Tabyant should be spelled as Tabaia or Tobia. The ending "yant" is not of Anishinabe origin, but "aia" is of common use.

Antoine married Mary Ann (or Marian) Skoawabe (or Skawsabe) on August 10, 1846, at Holy Childhood of Jesus Church. Mary Ann was born in 1828 to Debendang and his wife. Rev. Father Francis X. Pierz officiated at the ceremony with Anaasino and Jawanis as witnesses.

The couple were the parents of six children, of which five were listed in the church family register before 1870. The family included: Peter, born in 1855; Susan, born in 1858; Rosalia, whose birthdate is unknown and baptized April 30, 1858; Joseph, born in 1861; and Margaret, born in 1864. Except for Rev. Lawrence Lautishar, who baptized Rosalia, the rest of the listed children were probably baptized by Rev. Father Seraphim Zorn. It may be noted that two other girls were listed in later federal census records as daughters. They were Christine, who may have been born about 1850 and included in the 1880 federal census, and Angeline, born in 1877 and noted in the 1900 federal census. In 1894, only Susan, who was a widow, was still living.

Antoine did his best to support his family by farming and catching fish to sell. But the effect of his wounds resulted in almost total loss of the use of his right arm. The severe pain in his neck quite often effected his ability to do a full day's work.

Even with all of his infirmities, Antoine was known to be an industrious, well-liked, and trustworthy person of his community.

On June 5, 1875, Application #204,769 for an invalid pension was filed for

Antoine Tabaia, which cited his wounds and the blindness of one eye. His application was accepted, and he was granted Invalid Pension Certificate #139,494 on May 13, 1876, for the wounds incurred only in the war. His request to include the total blindness in his left eye as a result of his wounds was rejected. The rate of his pension was two dollars a month retroactive to June 5, 1875.

Due to the decline in his health as he aged, Antoine submitted a request for an increase to his monthly payments on April 9, 1877. He received an increase of five dollars a month to commence on April 27, 1877. Upon Antoine's second request for an increase of monthly payments, he was granted an increase to total six dollars a month to commence on September 10, 1890. Antoine's last request for an increase in monthly pension payments on July 29, 1891, was accepted, and he was given a total monthly payment of twelve dollars retroactive to August 16, 1890.

Antoine Tabaia died at his home in Harbor Springs on May 21, 1894. The cause of death was listed as "whiskey." Even though Antoine did his best to support his family, he suffered a lot of pain because of his wounds. To deaden his pain, he probably imbibed more spirits than he should have. His funeral was held at Holy Childhood of Jesus Church, and he was buried in Lakeview Cemetery in Harbor Springs. He may have been accorded a military burial, including the firing of arms. Today a military stone marks his grave site.

After Antoine's death, Mary Ann was left with no means of support and owned no property. She earned what she could from her daily labor.

On July 6, 1894, Application #598,210 for a widow's pension was filed for Mary Ann Tabaia. She was granted a Widow's Pension Certificate #407,371 and received payments of eight dollars a month to commence on July 6, 1894. Mary Ann also received an accrued pension certificate and voucher payable to her on February 26, 1895. The voucher represented the accrued monies owed to the soldier up to the time of his death. Sometime after 1896, Mary Ann received an increase in her widow's pension. She was given a total of twelve dollars a month and was last paid on September 4, 1911.

Mary Ann (Skoawabe) Tabaia died from the effects of old age in Harbor Springs on September 25, 1911. She was buried in Lakeview Cemetery near her husband.

Tazhedewin, Joseph, Private

Enlistment: Enlisted as a private on July 4, 1863, at Elbridge, Oceana County, by Captain Edwin V. Andress, First Michigan Sharpshooters, for three years.

Age: Nineteen, born about 1844 (or 1845) in Grand Rapids, Kent County.

Occupation: Farmer

Residence: Pentwater, Oceana County

Physical Description: Five feet ten, with black eyes, black hair, and a dark complexion. Examining physician was Dr. Jacob. B. McNett, assistant surgeon, First Michigan Sharpshooters.

Mustered: July 11, 1863, at Detroit, Wayne County, by Lieutenant Colonel John R. Smith, US Army

Military Service: Joseph chose Tazhedewin as the name by which he preferred to be known in the service and by which he would apply for his pension. Tazhedewin may have been his warrior name. His family surname was Poneshing.

While in his regimental camp in Annapolis, Maryland, Joseph became sick with intermittent fever (or malaria). Malaria is an infectious disease caused by one of the genus *Plasmodium* and transmitted by mosquitoes infected with the genus *Anopheles* (*Blakiston*). He was admitted to his regimental hospital on April 6, 1864, and again on April 12. During both stays at the hospital, Joseph was treated with quinine. Quinine was derived from powdered cinchona tree bark mixed with water or whiskey. Whiskey worked better since it masked the bitter taste of quinine (*Bollet*). This medication was also dispensed in the form of pills made of purified quinine sulfate (*Ibid.*).

On May 12, 1864, during the Battle of Spotsylvania, Virginia, Tazhedewin suffered a missile wound that fractured the middle finger of his left hand. Joseph walked with assistance or was taken by ambulance wagon immediately to an aid station where his wound was assessed, and he was given whiskey or an opium pill for pain. Compression was applied to stop the bleeding, and his wound was cleaned with water and hastily wrapped in bandages.

From the aid station, Joseph was taken by ambulance wagon to his division hospital farther behind the lines. At this hospital, iodine was put on the wound to impede infection, and simple water dressings were applied to seal the wound area. Simple water dressings consisted of folded lint dipped into cold water, placed on the wound, and secured in place with a cloth wrap or adhesive plaster (*Schaadt*). A splint was applied to his hand to stabilize the broken finger.

On May 14, due to the sheer numbers of wounded, Joseph was sent by ambulance wagon from his division hospital directly through Fredericksburg, Virginia, to a wharf at Belle Plain Landing. From Belle Plain, he was transported by hospital steamer to L'Ouverture USA General Hospital in Alexandria, Virginia, and admitted on May 16.

On June 1, the surgeons at L'Ouverture Hospital anesthetized Joseph with ether (or chloroform) and amputated the middle finger (second finger or phalange) of the left hand and three-quarters of an inch of the metacarpal bone of the palm at the metacarpophalangeal articulation. The doctors believed that there should be great emphasis on saving the thumb regardless of the severity of injury to the hand.

After surgery, a rasp was used to smooth the end of the metacarpal bone, and flaps of skin and muscle (pulled back from a circular cut during the surgery) were drawn together and sewn with silk or wire sutures (*Kuz and Bengtson*). A waxy substance usually made of beeswax (called cerate) was applied to the wound to seal the raw area and minimize oozing (*Ibid.-Bollet*). The hand was then dressed with simple water bandages and either stabilized with Palmar splints (toward the palm) or was closed over a ball of proper size and held in place with adhesive plaster (*Ibid.-Kuz and Bengtson*). The injury and subsequent surgery would leave Joseph's hand and forearm permanently weakened.

While Joseph was a patient at L'Ouverture, he was given a hearty diet to help him in his physical recovery. The physicians noted that he was suffering from an early stage of pulmonary consumption (or tuberculosis) in both lungs. Tuberculosis is an infectious disease caused by the *Mycobacterium tuberculosis* commonly known as tubercle bacillus (*Ibid.-Blakiston*). The doctors agreed that Joseph was a candidate for an early discharge for disability.

Discharged: Private Joseph Tazhedewin was recommended for an honorable discharge for disability on August 5, 1864, by L'Ouverture Assistant Surgeon Thomas C. Barker. He was mustered out and given a certificate of disability for discharge from L'Ouverture Hospital on August 18, 1864, by Surgeon Edwin Bentley. Joseph was paid money owed to him for his service at the time of his discharge.

From L'Ouverture Hospital, Joseph was sent by hospital steamer to Washington, DC, where he stayed for a month (possibly as a patient in another hospital or medical facility). He then made his way home to Michigan in September.

Biography: Joseph Tazhedewin was known to everyone as Joseph Poneshing Jr. before and after his military service. As stated above, he probably chose the name of Tazhedewin as his warrior name for his military service. He was the son of Joseph and Mary Poneshing Sr.

In the 1860 federal census of Pentwater, Oceana County, Joseph Jr. may have been the person named Poneshing who was one of four young men who worked as laborers in the household of a carpenter named Peter Burdell.

About 1866, Joseph Poneshing Jr. married Mary (or Mawmequa) Negake.

Mary, who was born in March 1850, was the daughter of Jerome and Elizabeth (or Wassayah) Caubmosay/Cobmosay Negake/Onaygake. The ceremony was officiated by Harvey S. Sayles, a farmer and justice of the peace, in Elbridge. Mary's siblings were Rodney, born October 25, 1847, and John, born between 1845 and 1850.

The young Poneshing couple made their home in Elbridge Township and were the parents of eleven children, of whom nine were still living in 1898. The Poneshing children were: Alick (Alex or Lixey), born in February 1868; Margaret, born in 1869; Peter (or Akwnewa), born in March 1872; Lewis, born in February 1876; Mary (or Showayahbenoqua), born in August 1878; Maud, born in March 1885; Agatha, born in February 1888; Joseph (III), born in April 1891; and James, born in September 1892. Two other daughters were listed in the 1880 federal census for Michigan. They were Mawne, born in 1874, and Mawneon, born in 1879. It's not clear whether these girls lived to adulthood.

Joseph provided for his family as best he could. He farmed, worked in a lumber camp and sawmill, and rode logs down the Pentwater River. But as he aged, his ability to use his left hand in handling lumber became a problem. He had great difficulty grasping objects since his hand was weakened by surgery during the war. Sometimes a doctor would have to lance abscesses that would form at the old surgical site. Also, Joseph became thin and emaciated due to the progression of tuberculosis.

On January 14, 1876, Application #212,999 for an invalid pension was filed for Joseph. In the application, he stated that the reason for the need for a pension was the loss of his left middle (or second) finger due to a gunshot (missile) wound that occurred while in battle. He was granted Invalid Pension Certificate #142,516 on November 14, 1876. Payments were two dollars a month retroactive to January 14, 1876.

On December 13, 1890, he submitted a request for additional monthly payments under the General Act of June 27, 1890. This act was more liberal to veterans than any previous law and included all persons who served ninety days or more and who incurred a permanent disability. The law benefited the survivors and their widows and dependents and paid a monthly rate of six to twelve dollars. The rate was proportioned to the degree of disability and stated that the disability need not have originated in the service. Joseph was granted an increase of payments that totaled ten dollars a month retroactive and to commence on June 25, 1890.

On September 29, 1909, Joseph requested another increase in monthly payments. His name was dropped from the rolls under the Act of June 27, 1890, when his certificate was reissued and added to the rolls under the Act of February 6, 1907.

Under this act, Joseph was granted a monthly sum of twelve dollars to commence on September 20, 1909.

Due to increased disability caused by his wound, chronic bronchitis, tuberculosis, and difficulty in trying to support his family, Joseph's monthly payments were increased.

Under the Act of May 11, 1912, as amended by the Act of March 4, 1913, Joseph received sixteen dollars a month to commence on June 22, 1912, twenty dollars a month to commence on July 4, 1914, twenty-four dollars a month to commence on July 4, 1916, thirty-five dollars to commence June 10, 1919, and finally, under the Act of May 1, 1920, Joseph received fifty dollars a month until his death.

Mary (Negake) Poneshing died sometime between the years of 1900 and 1910 at her home in Elbridge and left her husband a widower in ailing health.

By 1910, Joseph was living with his sons James and Joseph (III) and his wife, Elizabeth. Sons Louie, Peter, and Peter's wife and their family were living next door to Joseph. It is assumed that the families shared the care for Joseph in his failing health.

By 1921, Joseph's health declined to the point that the old soldier was confined to bed. He required someone in attendance constantly. His only income was his pension.

On January 3, 1923, Joseph Poneshing Jr. died at the age of seventy-nine at his home in Walkerville (previously known as Stetson), Oceana County. He lies at rest in St. Joseph Catholic Cemetery in Elbridge Township of said county.

Mr. Ray Thompson of Hart, Oceana County, was administrator of Joseph's estate. Thompson appealed to the pension department to forward Joseph's remaining pension money to him (Thompson) since he would need to reimburse the county for the expenses incurred in Joseph's nursing care and burial. It's not certain if the US Pension Agency complied with Thompson's request.

Thomas, Moses, Private

Enlistment: Enlisted as a private on January 27, 1865, at Detroit, Wayne County. His enlistment for a period of three years was witnessed by Captain Mark Flanigan of the Twenty-Fourth Michigan Infantry.

Age: Eighteen, born June/August 27, 1846 (or 1847), on the Kawkawlin Indian Reservation near Bay City, Bay County.

Occupation: Laborer

Residence: White Pigeon, St. Joseph County

Physical Description: Five feet four, with black eyes, black hair, and a dark complexion. Examining physician was Dr. George Landon, surgeon, First Michigan Sharpshooters.

Mustered: January 28, 1865, in Detroit by Captain Mark Flanigan, Twenty-Fourth Michigan Infantry

Military Service: Before he enlisted, Moses was known as Moses Muoguaduey, the same as his father's. The enlistment officer couldn't pronounce Muoguaduey, so he wrote the name "Thomas" as Moses's surname. After his enlistment, he was known as Moses Thomas.

There is no record of Private Thomas having a debilitating illness or suffering a wound during his short term of service. He did complain of rheumatism and was given opiates for pain.

Discharged: Private Moses Thomas was mustered out and honorably discharged at Delaney House in Tenallytown, DC, on July 28, 1865. He returned to Detroit on the steamer *Morning Star.* On August 7, Moses was paid money due to him for his service at Jackson, Jackson County.

Biography: Moses Thomas was the son of Mr. and Mrs. Moses (Muoguaduey) Williams and was the grandson of Tondahgahnee (or Dog), who was a warrior in the War of 1812. Young Moses worked as a laborer before his enlistment.

In 1871, Moses was employed as a mill hand in the Muskegon River lumbering area and was the only Anishinabe in his camp. While working in the woods, Moses suffered a rupture (or inguinal hernia) in his right groin while doing heavy lifting.

Sometime during the 1870s, Moses moved to the Kettle Point Reserve (Indian Reserve 44), County of Lambton, in the Province of Ontario, Canada. His resident address was R.R. #2, Forest, Ontario, Canada. Canadian reservations are called reserves. The Canadian Anishinabek living on the Kettle Point Reserve called themselves Chippewas of Kettle and Stony Point First Nation. Moses's initial reason for the move to Reserve 44 was to work as a missionary and interpreter for the Methodist and Episcopal churches in the area. After his arrival at the reserve, he sought work at the fishery of Mr. James Landon on the shore of Lake Huron.

On October 8, 1883, Moses married Julia Shawnoo. Julia was born April 11, 1861, and was the daughter of Chief Isaac and Elizabeth Shawnoo (or Shawanoo). The marriage took place at the chief's home on the Kettle Point Reserve and was officiated by Rev. John Jacobs. Rev. Jacobs was an Anglican (or Episcopal) clergyman for whom Moses served as a missionary.

Moses and Julia were the parents of at least one known child, Eli, born on the reserve about 1883 (or 1884).

While working at the fishery on one very stormy day in 1887, Moses reinjured his hernia. He incurred his injury as he hauled fishing nets, that were blown down by the storm, into his boat. His physicial condition was serious enough to confine him to bed for several days. His doctor suggested, and Moses complied, that he wear a truss to ease his pain. But Moses complained that wearing the truss caused him additional pain and that he could only wear the support part of the time.

Application #1,133,166 for an invalid pension was filed from Ontario, Canada, for Thomas on August 19, 1892. The application came under the General Act of June 27, 1890, which was more liberal than the previous act. It included all persons who served ninety days or more for benefit of survivors and their widows and dependents. In the application, Moses cited increasing difficulty in earning a living by manual labor due to rheumatism and the pain caused by his hernia.

In the affidavits given by his friends and acquaintances, Moses was praised as an upright, hardworking, and dependable man of good moral habits. He was respected and well liked by all who knew him.

Moses was issued an Invalid Pension Certificate #922,278 on December 28, 1896. The certificate paid eight dollars a month and was retroactive to August 19, 1892.

On April 19, 1904, when Moses and Julia were living in Odanah, Ashland County, Wisconsin, Moses filed a declaration for an increase in his pension allowance. This declaration was under the General Act of 1900, and the provisions were much the same as the General Act of 1890.

He filed a second request for an increase on May 3, 1911, under the General Act of 1907 in which he cited previous terms and stated that he had reached the age of sixty-two. On May 29, 1911, Moses was granted an increase in payments to total twelve dollars per month retroactive to May 3, 1911.

From 1913 to 1922, Moses's yearly payments increased to total seventy-two dollars a month by January 19, 1926. This increase was due to the General Act of 1920, which took into account that the old veterans, by this time, were either helpless, blind, or both, and needed aid and attendance of another person. An increase in payments, which totaled ninety dollars a month, was granted in 1931.

Before the increase in pension payments was granted to Thomas in 1926 and 1931, he sent a letter to the commissioner of pensions in Washington, DC. The letter was sent from Standish, Michigan, on May 17, 1916. It seems that Moses and

Julia were living there for an unspecified time before they returned to Canada. The letter is as follows in its original spelling.

> Standish May 17, 1916
> Commissioner of Pensions, Washington, D.C.
> Could you Please tell me if My Grandfather Tondahgahnee his name has been Kept on Record of the war Department its long time ago I have want to make those Inquires I have under stood My Grandfather was through this a 1812 war your to be old French man living in Bay City your to tell when I was boy My Grandfather was a chief warrior this old man yours to tell me My Grandfather Tondahgahnee (or dog) use to be with this Frenchman Captain Mersack I have seen where the Department have Made Inquires sometime a go but these old war soldiers if the is anything there credited for this old man Tondahgahnee I am his Granson Moses Thomas The reason I am asking the Department I am getting old an for what little I am getting Myself of this pension from this office he don't keep me going everything is so high takes I all I can get to live through I hope the war Department will be so Kind to help me some way if there is anything could be granted to me from this war Department I would be very much Pleased this is all and Please write.
>
> I Am
> Moses Thomas
> Standish Michigan RFD no 3 B.14

The US government responded to Moses's letter and told him that there was no information found in their files about his grandfather Tondahgahnee.

Before 1926, Moses suffered a strangulated hernia (circulation was blocked), and his doctor surgically removed the blockage. By this time, Moses's eyesight was much worse due to cataracts, and his rheumatism was taking its toll. Julia was Moses's sole caretaker and a loyal and attentive wife. But her health was also declining. The couple's son, Eli, did what he could to help his parents, but at the age of fifty-two, he was also in failing health.

Sometime before Moses's death, Julia suffered a paralytic stroke. This type of stroke is caused by a lesion in the brain or spinal cord and results in a sudden loss of muscular power (*Blakiston*). As a result of the stroke, Julia was paralyzed on her left side. She was also plagued with chronic nephritis or the inflammation of the kidneys (*Ibid.*). Eli was left as sole caretaker for both of his parents.

Finally, at the age of eighty-six, the old soldier died on August 25, 1933, at his home on the Canadian Reserve. Thomas's demise was the result of myocardial failure or failure of the heart as a pump with a contributory cause of diarrhea (*Ibid.*). He was attended during his last hours by his physician, Dr. Marshall MacDonald, who was also the physician for the Kettle Point Indian Reserve. On August 28, Moses was buried in the Kettle Point Cemetery. He left a house and lot on the reserve worth about $250 to Julia. At his death, Moses Thomas was the last surviving member of Company K to "walk on" to the spirit world.

Being destitute for monetary support and in need of food and fuel, a widow's pension Application #1,736,502 was filed for Julia Thomas on November 29, 1933. She and many of her loyal friends and neighbors appealed again to the US government in December 1933 and January 1934. The government authorities insisted that Julia wade through more bureaucracy and demanded more and more information that would prove that she was the widow of Moses. During this time, Julia's health declined rapidly. Friends and neighbors helped her, as well as her son and his family, through the winter months as best as they could.

Before her pension application may have been approved, Julia Thomas died at age seventy-three on May 11, 1934. Her death was due to myocardial (or cardiac) failure with the contributory cause of cerebral hemorrhage. Cerebral hemorrhage is due to bleeding from blood vessels in the cerebrum (or chief portion of the brain), either traumatic or due to disease (*Ibid.*). As was with Moses, she was also attended by Dr. Marshall MacDonald in the last hours of life. Burial took place on May 14, and she was laid to rest near her husband in Kettle Point Cemetery.

Eli Thomas petitioned the widows and dependents claims service of the US government for any monetary reimbursement due to his father that would enable him to defray the costs of groceries and burial expenses for both of his parents. An allowance of seventy-five dollars was approved and sent to the undertaker, A. F. Steel and Son, to cover only the cost of burial for Moses. The request for money to pay the grocer was denied.

Since Julia's house and lot were on the reserve, Eli could not sell either one for monies needed. Had she lived to see a possible approval of her pension application, Julia would have received about forty dollars a month until her death.

Valentine, Robert, Private

Enlistment: Enlisted as a private on August 24, 1864, at Jackson, Jackson County, by Captain R. J. Barry, provost marshal for the Michigan Third District.

Private Valentine enlisted for three years as a substitute for Joseph Mills, an enrolled draftee of Lansing, Ingham County. Valentine's enlistment satisfied the requirement for a man from the Third Congressional District, Ingham County, town of Lansing. As the principal or enrolled draftee, Mills would have paid Valentine a sum of about $300 to be his substitute. As a volunteer substitute, Valentine was not eligible for an enlistment bounty since he received a generous sum as a substitute. But he was entitled to receive a hundred-dollar bounty (as were regular enlisted men) if he was discharged due to a serious wound incurred in battle regardless of the length of his term of service.

There were non-Anishinabek men who avoided the service by finding substitutes. Many of these men visited the Michigan reservations and areas with Anishinabek populations. They sought out the men and offered lump sums of money to them if they agreed to serve as substitutes. The Civil War era was a time in which most Anishinabek people were in need of monetary support to provide for their families. The offers of money were hard to refuse.

Age: Twenty-three, born about 1841 in the state of Michigan, possibly in Michigan's Upper Peninsula.

Occupation: Hunter

Residence: Michigan (town not stated), possibly in Michigan's Upper Peninsula

Physical Description: Five feet six and a half inches tall, with black eyes, black hair, and a dark complexion.

Mustered: August 24, 1864, at Jackson (same day as enlistment) by Captain R. J. Barry, provost marshal for the Third District of Michigan

Military Service: There is no medical record of treatment of Private Valentine for an illness or for suffering a wound during his term of service. He was detailed for extra duty at the Quarter Master Department in Washington, DC, in May 1865.

Discharged: One discharge record states that Private Robert Valentine was mustered out and honorably discharged at Detroit on August 10 (or 11), 1865. Another record states that he was discharged at Detroit on August 21 pursuant to Circular 31 of the Adjutant General's Office. At his discharge, Robert was paid money owed to him for his service.

Biography: After he returned to Michigan, Robert Valentine married Mary (or Shawanabenokwe) Condecon (born June 1843) on August 27, 1865. Mary was the daughter of Chief John Waasegiizhig and Mary (or Ikwezens) Blackbird Okandikan Sr. The marriage took place at L'Anse, Baraga County, in Michigan's Upper Peninsula. Rev. George Blaker, an Anishinabe Methodist minister, officiated at the ceremony.

After their marriage, the couple moved to Odanah, Ashland County, Wisconsin, where some of Mary's family lived. It's possible that the couple moved back and forth between Michigan and Wisconsin since Mary had family members who lived in both states.

Mary Condecon was a sister to Henry Condecon, who was also known as Henry Waasegiizhig of Company K. With his marriage to Mary, Valentine gained a brother-in-law and former army buddy.

For reasons unknown, Robert Valentine died on December 22, 1871, at the young age of thirty. It's possible that he may have contracted an illness during his service or during his time at the Quartermaster Department in Washington, DC, and came home ill. Since it's probable that the couple moved residences between Michigan and Wisconsin, Robert's burial place could be in either state. Mary and Robert Valentine did not have children.

In the first part of January 1903, Mary Condecon Valentine stated that she was, at that time, a resident of Odanah, Wisconsin. On January 9, 1903, Application #776,381 for a widow's pension was filed for Mary under the General Act of June 27, 1890. This act was more liberal and stipulated that: the soldier had to have served at least ninety days; was honorably discharged; that the widow had no other means of support; and that the applicant was married to the soldier prior to June 27, 1890, in order to collect survivor benefits. Mary stated in her application that she had not remarried after Robert's death. She requested that all correspondence be sent to her in care of her brother, Henry Condecon, in Odanah.

Upon further investigation of Mary's claim, it was discovered that she had remarried, after her husband's death, to Mr. John (or Jack) Jackson in 1877 and did not inform the government of her second marriage (*Jackson*). John died in 1902.

Mary and John were the parents of five children: John Jr., born 1879 or 1881; Jennie, born 1882 in Rockland, Michigan, in the state's Upper Peninsula (some of Mary's relatives lived in or near Rockland); Dan, born 1884 or 1886; Charlotte, born 1885 or 1887; and Josephine, born 1889 or 1891 (*Ibid.*). Due to not informing the government of her second marriage, Mary's claim to a widow's pension was rejected on April 13, 1903.

Mary (Condecon/Okandikan)Valentine Jackson died at the age of eighty-two on May 8, 1925. She may be buried in the Jackson family plot in Cemetery #2, in Odanah near a road in back of section #2 (*Ibid.*).

Waasegiizhig, Henry, Private

Enlistment: Enlisted as a private on September 24, 1864, in Ontonagon, Ontonagon County, in Michigan's Upper Peninsula by A.E.B. Mann, First Michigan Sharpshooters, for three years.

Age: Seventeen, born April 30, 1847, at Bad River Falls (or Odanah), Ashland County, Wisconsin. Another record states that his birth was in Ontonagon.

Occupation: Laborer

Residence: Pewabic Township of Ontonagon County. Today Pewabic is in Houghton County in Michigan's Upper Peninsula (the U.P.).

Physical Description: Five feet seven, with dark eyes, dark hair, and a dark complexion. Examining physician was Dr. George Landon.

Mustered: October 20, 1864, at Detroit, Wayne County, by Captain and Provost Marshal Mark Flannigan of the Twenty-Fourth Michigan Infantry

Military Service: Private Waasegiizhig joined his regiment at Peebles House, Virginia, on November 4, 1864. There was no medical record found that mentioned any disease or injury incurred by Henry during his military service.

Discharged: On July 28, 1865, Private Henry Waasegiizhig was mustered out and honorably discharged at Delaney House in Tenallytown, DC. He returned to Detroit on the steamer *Morning Star*. On August 7, 1865, Henry received payment owed to him for his service at Jackson, Jackson County, and returned to Michigan's Upper Peninsula. He would remain in the U.P. until he moved to Odanah, Wisconsin, in 1887.

Biography: Henry Waasegiizhig's family surname means "Bright Sky" (*Mayotte*). He was also known as Henry Condecon (or Okandikan) and was descended from a long line of well-respected and revered chiefs. His parents were John Waasegiizhig Okandikan Sr., chief of the Ontonagon band of the Michigan Chippewa (or Ojibwa), and Ikwezens (which means "little girl") Blackbird (*Ibid.*). Ikwezens also used Mary as her first name. She was the daughter of Chief Mukadabenace (or

Makadebinesi) Blackbird, who was headman of the Wisconsin Bad River Band of Chippewa (or Ojibwe).

Chief John Waasegiizhig Okandikan Sr. of the Ontonagon band of Michigan was one of the signers, as second chief, of the September 30, 1854, second treaty of La Pointe, Madeline Island, Wisconsin. In this treaty, the Chippewa (Ojibwe) chiefs ceded all the Lake Superior Ojibwe lands to the United States included in the Arrowhead Region of Northeastern Minnesota in exchange for reservations for the Lake Superior Ojibwe in Wisconsin, Michigan, and Minnesota.

Chief John Sr.'s father (Henry's grandfather), Old Chief Okandikan (Okondokon), whose name meant "buoy" or "to keep the net up," preceded John Waasegiizhig Okandikan Sr. as headman of the Ontonagon band in Michigan.

Old Chief Okandikan (or Buoy) was involved in the colorful history of the Ontonagan Copper Boulder known as the "Manitou" (or spirit). The pure copper rock, which is 4'3" by 3'11" and about eighteen inches thick and weighs about five tons, was sacred to the Upper Peninsula Ojibwa and was used by them as a shrine of worship—a mediator between them and the Great Spirit (*Ontonagon*).

The copper boulder and the abundance of copper in the Upper Peninsula drew people from around the world during the mining rush to Michigan's Copper Country on the west branch of the Ontonagon River (*Ibid.*).

Beginning with Henry Schoolcraft in 1828, many explorers tried to move the enormous rock but had to settle for souvenir pieces of copper that they managed to cut from the boulder.

On an expedition to the Michigan Copper Country in 1841, Mr. Julius Eldred, a wealthy merchant and real estate developer from Detroit, visited the boulder and decided that he had to own it and exhibit it in Detroit (*Ibid.*). He managed to purchase the copper boulder from Chief Okandikan (or Old Chief Buoy) for $150, paid as forty-five dollars in hard cash, with the remaining $105 in merchandise from Eldred's hardware store in Detroit (*Ibid.*).

In 1842, Eldred returned to the Upper Peninsula to move the boulder to Detroit. After much time and effort, he managed to load the boulder onto a barge and float it to Detroit. With all the publicity that was generated by Eldred's copper boulder, the US government took an interest in the matter and considered the rock to be a national treasure. The government officials instructed Eldred to deliver the boulder to Washington, DC, which he did, in November 1843. The boulder made its journey to its DC destination on the cutter *Erie* from Detroit through Buffalo, the Erie Canal, and New York City. In 1847, Eldred and his sons received $5,664.98 for their time and expenses incurred in the purchase and shipment of the copper boulder (*Ibid.*).

The "Ontonagon Copper Boulder" or "copper rock" is now in the possession of the Department of Mineral Sciences, National Museum of Natural History, Smithsonian Institution in Washington, DC *(Ibid.)*.

Old Chief Bouy, as first chief, was one of the signers of the October 4, 1842, first treaty of La Pointe, which involved the ceded lands that are now parts of Wisconsin and Michigan's Upper Peninsula. He was also a signer, as first chief, of the 1854 Treaty of La Pointe, Madeline Island, Wisconsin.

Chief Mukadabenace (or Makadebinesi), as second chief, also made his mark on the 1854 Treaty of La Pointe. The Old Chief's band occupied the land along the lakeshore adjacent to the settlement of Ontonagan in Ontonagan County in Michigan's Upper Peninsula.

Since the Treaties of 1842 and 1854 of La Pointe involved ceded Chippewa (or Ojibwe) lands in exchange for the right to hunt, fish, and gather, and for the establishment of reservations in Michigan, Minnesota, and Wisconsin, the tribes would expect to receive annuity payments of money and goods.

The following story of the Condecon family is an extraction taken from a memoir of Henry's younger brother, John (or Jack) Condecon Jr., entitled *Life History of John Condecon* as told to his daughter Caroline C. Parker (*Life*). The extracted memoir account includes the author's notes (italicized) where appropriate. Please note that the names in the story may differ somewhat in spelling from the family names in the first paragraph under the previously mentioned heading of "Biography."

Life History of John Condecon

Old Chief Okandikan was a member of the traditional Midewiwin or Grand Medicine Society Lodge. Just before his death in 1859, at the age of 82, Okandikan wished to see a priest and be baptized into the Catholic faith. **Author's note:** *The Old Chief was buried in the Methodist Rose Cemetery in Rockland, Rockland County, in Michigan's Upper Peninsula.*

The old chief's mother was also a member of the Midewiwin and several years before her death she was also baptized and became a devout Catholic. She was a member of a society of Catholic women called the Christian Mothers.

Henry Wassegiizhig (or Henry Condecon), was the third child and oldest son in a family of nine children. His siblings were Tom, Annie, Elizabeth, Mary (or Shawanabenokwe), Ellen, John (or Jack) Jr., and Charlotte who was the youngest child. The oldest daughter was accidentally killed while felling trees for firewood.

John Jr. would marry Julia Conner, the daughter of Thomas and Marie Conner on January 5, 1891.

Mary (Shawanabenokwe) was the second oldest child whose first marriage was to Henry's Company K comrade Robert Valentine. **Author's note:** *Robert died in December 1871.* Mary's second marriage was to John "Jack" Jackson in 1877. The Jackson family lived in Odanah, Wisconsin.

The Condecon children held a close relationship with their parents. They appreciated the knowledge that their parents imparted to their brood through loyalty, truthfulness and humor that encompassed the Golden Rule of "treat others as you would want to be treated." Because of these attributes, their mother, Ikwesensish or Ikwezens (Mary) was considered by her family to be a true daughter of a chief.

Although Ikwesensish did not speak English to her family, the children mastered the language. The ability to converse easily in English was of great help to Henry and John Jr. As adults they often met with government officials to discuss tribal business. They felt at ease with the English language in conversations during their employment, when they met with government officials to discuss tribal business and when they conducted their own private business with non speakers.

As with all the Anishinabek, the Condecon family conducted their lives and provided for their sustenance according to seasonal changes provided by Mother Earth for her children. Since the family traveled quite frequently, they lived in wigwams instead of houses.

When going from Ontonagan in Michigan's Upper Peninsula to other points in the peninsula and across the state line into Wisconsin, the family would paddle their twenty-five foot birch bark canoe along the shore of Lake Superior and camp where convenient. Their summer travels availed them of the abundance of whitefish and trout along the shore for their meals and for trade. Chief Wassegiizhig (John Sr.)

Okandikan would always have a net in his canoe. With help from his family there would soon be a boatload of fish to dry at the next camping spot.

During the summer months, the Condecons lived in Ontonagon and in Eagle River in Keweenaw County while they fished and picked blueberries and huckleberries. The delicious fruit was dried and boxed for winter consumption and any extra was sold or traded.

After they prepared their food for the winter, the Condecons journeyed to L'Anse in Baraga County for their annuity payment due from treaties. After they received their payment, the family returned to Ontonagon by way of Houghton, Houghton County and took the opportunity to fish along the Lake Superior shore. The children's mother and the sisters would dry and box the fish and pack the boxes into the canoe.

Henry served during the Civil War in the Michigan Sharpshooter unit. After his discharge from the service, Henry was employed as a laborer and a "land looker," or "cruiser," and an estimator and examiner of lands for a lumber company near Ontonagon. Henry died in 1922 and was given an impressive military burial during a severe snow storm. **Author's note:** *As an experienced woodsman, Henry would estimate prime standing timber for his company with the use of a compass and government maps.*

Author's note: *When he was cutting cordwood for the family fires before Christmas in 1869, Henry sustained a serious wound to his right foot, which would leave him somewhat lame. As he wielded his ax, he accidentally cut across the top of his foot between the toes and the instep. The injury extended from the inner side of the metatarsal phalangeal joint of the big toe across the dorsum (or back) of the foot and terminated at the metatarsal phalangeal joint of the small toe. Henry's father and his brother, Tom, took Henry home, treated him with traditional Anishinabek herbal medicine and poultices, and bound his foot with wrappings. Due to this injury, he did not leave his home for about three months.*

In the fall of 1872, the family returned to Rockland where Henry, and the men of his family, would trap for furs during the late fall and winter months. Mr. James Herring operated a trading post in Rockland and would buy the furs that the Condecon family processed. In trade for the furs, the family would receive what supplies they needed.

Spring brought the "sugar bush" time when the family would make camp and tap the sugar maple trees for the sap. The sap would then be boiled into syrup in copper kettles to make maple sugar. The result weight of the sugar would range from eight to fifteen hundred pounds. Some sugar would be packed for sale to the townspeople – the remainder was for the family's use. **Author's note:** *It was known that sugar cones always delighted the children. They were made by pouring hot maple syrup into birch bark cones that were placed in the snow. After the syrup cooled and solidified into maple sugar, the bark wrappings would be removed, and cones of solid sugar would be given to the eager children.*

During the month of March in 1873, Chief John Sr., Henry, and John Jr. were appointed by the Ontonagan band to be a committee and travel from Ontonagan to L'Anse to collect the annuity payment of money and goods for the entire band. This was indeed a vote of confidence and trust in the Condecon family. The men packed the goods to Ontonagon and then the entire family returned to Rockland.

In the month of April, many types of fish, including pike and sturgeon, came up the Ontonagon River. The Indian families had their own fishing grounds along the Gogebic branch of this river. These fishing areas supplied the Anishinabek with all the fish they needed to eat and sell. Instead of fishing with nets, the families built solid fences across the Gogebic branch of the river and trapped an abundance of fish. They prepared a share of the catch for themselves by drying and packing the fish in boxes. They sold or traded the excess.

In the summer of 1873, the Condecon family went to Bad River Reservation area in Wisconsin. At the reservation the family joined with a large number of Ojibwe who came from Ashland and Odanah *(which means "village")*, Ashland County, Wisconsin on their way to pick blueberries in the prairie county. In addition to blueberries, strawberries, raspberries, and blackberries, both low bush and high bush cranberries were also harvested. What berries were not kept for family consumption were sold for additional income. **Author's note:** *Tribal ties and cultural ways were strengthened when families cooperated in harvesting berries together.*

Author's note: *During that same summer, Henry worked in a quarry that provided stone for the bridge on the Wisconsin Central Railroad at White River.*

In 1875, the Condecon family ceased using wigwams and took up their residence in a house. Chief Waasegiizhig (John Sr.) Okandikan rented a house for his family about one-half mile from Rockland in a village called National Mines in Rockland Township. The family lived there for about ten years.

After the Condecons moved to their rented home, the chief worked at what odd jobs he could get both in town and around the various mines in the area. He planted and tended a garden that supplied vegetables for the farmers who lived around the village as well as for his family's needs. Ikwesensish and her daughters continued their spring task of making maple sugar. Henry would also continue his employment as a land looker in the summer and trap with the men of his family in the winter.

Author's note: *In September 1876, Henry injured his left foot while engaged in trapping, about forty miles from Rockland. In the evening, as he returned to camp with an armful of firewood, he stepped on a sharp piece of snag stubble that penetrated his foot between the large and second toes and broke while in the foot. His brother, John Jr., took him home and treated his wound in the traditional manner with herbs, poultices, and wrappings. It was about six weeks before the remaining piece of stubble worked its way out of Henry's foot.*

After a faithful life of service to both his family and to his Ontonagon band, Chief Waasegiizhig (John Sr.) Okandikan died at the age of eighty in his home on April 25, 1882. The family buried him near his father, Old Chief (Buoy) Okandikan, in the Methodist Rose Cemetery in the town of Rockland, Ontonagon County.

Ikwezens moved from Rockland to Odanah, Wisconsin, in 1884 and resided on the Bad River Reservation, where she remained until her death in 1908.

In 1887, Henry and the rest of his family moved from Michigan to the reservation at Odanah and lived near their mother. Brother Tom, who had lived in Marquette, Marquette County, Michigan for many years, also joined the family and all were enrolled and allotted on the reservation as members of the Wisconsin LaPointe Band of Chippewa Indians.

After arriving in Odanah, Henry joined the GAR George A. Custer Post #140 in Ashland, Ashland County. He was a proud member of his post for one year in which he gained the admiration and respect of his fellow veterans.

As in Michigan, Henry continued employment as a land looker or "cruiser" for a local lumber company and improved his allotment on the reservation after the timber was removed.

It was in Odanah that Henry married first to Louise Mayotte on February 15, 1891. The marriage was officiated by Rev. Father Chrystom Vernyst at St. Mary's Catholic Church in Odanah. Louise brought four children from her previous marriage to her union with Henry. The children included: Mary, born in 1879; Louis, born in 1882; Tom, born in 1887; and John, born in early 1891 and died before the 1894 census.

Henry and Louise were the parents of Julia, born December 17, 1887, and baptized December 24 of same year. Julia died January 25, 1890. A son, Thomas, was born to the couple on January 14, 1891, and baptized on January 19 of that year. Thomas died February 13, 1911, at age twenty.

On October 20, 1890, Application #998,198 for an invalid pension was filed for Henry. He cited injuries to his feet that caused pain in walking as the reason for his need for a pension. His application was made under the generous Act of June 27, 1890, which allowed a pension to any veteran who served for ninety days and was honorably discharged from the service.

Louise died on March 11, 1895, and left Henry with two young stepsons, Tom and Louis, as well as the couple's son, Tom, to support.

In 1895 or 1899 and 1901, Henry and his brother, John Jr., traveled to Washington, DC, as chosen representatives for the Odanah Ojibwe (Chippewa). In Washington they discussed business matters between the tribe and the government. Being fluent in English, as mentioned previously, the brothers did not need an interpreter.

In 1907, Henry received his Invalid Pension Certificate #1,080,261, which paid six dollars a month for injuries he incurred after his service. By 1909, he submitted a request that his payments be increased due to his difficulty in making a living for himself and his children on the amount granted by his pension. Upon the submission of a surgeon's certificate in June 1909, Henry's pension payments were increased to ten dollars a month.

On July 9, 1913, Henry married secondly to widow Mary (Denomie) Pine, whose husband, Mike Pine, died in 1896. Mary was born in Baraga of Baraga County, Michigan, on February 5, 1862. She was the daughter of Samuel Denomie and Agatha Wewasson. Rev. Father Optatus Loeffler officiated at the Condecon (Denomie) Pine wedding at St. Mary's Catholic Church in Odanah. Witnesses to the wedding were Antoine and Jennie Soulier. A daughter, Helena, was born to the couple on December 27, 1918.

In the succeeding years, Henry submitted additional requests for monetary increases as his lameness became worse. He received payment increases from thirteen to nineteen dollars a month (retroactive from 1912) until 1919. Under the Act of May 1, 1920, Henry saw his monthly payments increased to fifty dollars a month by March 4, 1922. This Act of 1920 included any veteran, who, by reason of severe mental or physical disabilities, or nearly helpless, required the personal aid and attendance of another person.

Having gained a great deal of weight during his later years, and suffering in pain for many years with disabilities due to his postwar injuries, Henry Condecon was found dead in bed on Easter Sunday morning of April 16, 1922. Six members of his GAR post journeyed through a late spring snowstorm to Odanah to pay their respects and to give their comrade a proper military burial in the Bad River Cemetery. After Henry's death, only eight veterans remained as members of Post #140 (*Obituary*). Today, Henry lies at rest under a military stone in said cemetery.

Mary moved back to Baraga, Michigan, after Henry died. On October 19, 1922, Application #1,196,762 for a widow's pension was filed for Mary from Michigan. The request was also for accrued monies due to her husband from his last payment on February 4, 1922, to the date of his death on April 16, 1922. For reasons not stated, Mary's application was abandoned, and she did not receive a widow's pension.

Wabano, Thomas, Private

Enlistment: Enlisted as a private on May 18, 1863, at Isabella City (now Mt. Pleasant), Isabella County, by First Lieutenant William J. Driggs, First Michigan Sharpshooters, for three years.

> **Age:** Twenty-four, born about 1839 in Saginaw County.
> **Occupation:** Farmer
> **Residence:** Isabella County

Physical Description: Five feet ten, with black eyes, black hair, and a dark complexion. Examining physician was Dr. George L. Cornell, assistant surgeon, First Michigan Sharpshooters.

Mustered: May 26, 1863, at Detroit, Wayne County, by Lieutenant Colonel John R. Smith, US Army

Military Service: Private Thomas Wabano would serve only five months at Camp Douglas in Chicago, Cook County, Illinois, where his regiment was stationed to guard Confederate prisoners. On November 10, 1863, he reported to his post hospital at the camp, complaining of inflammation and swelling in his groin area and the presence of a painless penile sore (a chancre or ulcer).

Upon examination, it was determined that Private Wabano was showing the primary stage of the "pox," which is an old term for syphilis. Syphilis is a venereal disease caused by the bacterial spirochete *Treponema pallidum* (*Blakiston*). Treatment would have consisted of the application of mercury compounds to the site of the chancre or lesion. Since organic stricture of the urethra can occur with this disease, a metal catheter or dilator may have been used to open a possible stricture (*Bollet*). This procedure was followed by an infusion (or injection) of silver nitrate, chlorate of potash, zinc chloride, or mercury compounds administered by use of a hard rubber syringe (*King*). Anesthesia may have been used during these procedures. Private Wabano returned to duty on December 5.

Toward the end of December, after a period of about six weeks, the doctors determined that Wabano's disease had progressed to the secondary stage where he exhibited cutaneous eruptions (or widespread sores), enlargement of the lymph nodes, systemic toxemia (poisonous products or toxins in the blood), and complained of a sore throat and joint pain (*Ibid.*). After this diagnosis, Wabano was sent home on sick furlough.

Thomas Wabano died on January 7, 1864, (about three days after he arrived home) from the effects of secondary syphilis. His death occurred at the home of his father in Isabella County.

Discharged: No discharge was given due to death in Isabella County while at home on sick furlough.

Biography: Thomas Wabano was the son of John Jones and Nancy (Mesquawawnowquot) Wabano. Before his military service, Thomas married Jane Kakaykoo on March 15, 1861, at Isabella City. Rev. Henry Jackson, an Anishinabe Methodist missionary and interpreter in the area, officiated at the ceremony.

Thomas and Jane were the parents of one daughter, Sarah, born in her parents'

Isabella County home on May 5, 1863. Another record states that Sarah was born in Bay County. She was just three weeks old when her father left for the war.

Application #135,921 for a widow's pension was filed for Jane on October 2, 1866. The application was submitted under the Pension Act of July 14, 1862, which stated that "pensions would be given to those who may be left without provision for their maintenance and support by the death of the soldier." This act made mothers and sisters of deceased servicemen eligible for federal pensions for the first time and increased the rates for some widows and orphans. A later extension of this act would also give benefits to fathers and brothers.

Jane testified that her husband had returned home on a sick furlough from Camp Douglas and that he was quite ill when he arrived. She related that she did not know what illness he had because he had died so shortly after he returned home. No doctor attended him at his death. According to Jane, Thomas entered the army as a very healthy, strong man and became ill while in the service.

Jane's pension application was rejected on March 19, 1868, due to the death of the soldier from syphilis contracted during his service. Thomas's illness was considered by the government to be due to "vicious habits" (or venereal disease) and was therefore not service related.

Even though she did not receive a widow's pension, money owed to Thomas until his death was remitted to Jane.

On April 24, 1884, GAR Wa-bu-no Post #250 was organized at Mt. Pleasant and is known as the only GAR post named for a Native American soldier. Included in its membership were Marcus Otto, George Corbin, and Amos Chamberlain, who were Thomas's comrades in Company K.

A military headstone was placed in honor of Thomas Wabano in the West Side Cemetery (or Riverside Cemetery) in Isabella County. The cemetery sextant informed the author that there are no remains buried under Wabano's stone and that his actual burial site is unknown. The post was disbanded in 1923.

Wabesis, Charles, Sergeant

Enlistment: Enlisted as a sergeant on July 4, 1863, at Elbridge, Oceana County, by Captain Edwin V. Andress, First Michigan Sharpshooters, for three years.

    Age: Twenty-five, born about 1838 in Kent County.

    Residence: Pentwater, Oceana County

Physical Description: Five feet eleven and a half inches tall, with black eyes, black hair, and a dark complexion. Examining physician was Dr. Jacob B. McNett, assistant surgeon, First Michigan Sharpshooters.

Mustered: July 11, 1863, at Detroit, Wayne County, by Lieutenant Colonel John R. Smith, US Army

Military Service: Sergeant Wabesis (also spelled Waubesis) was promoted to the rank of fourth sergeant during the month of August 1863 when he was with his regiment as they guarded Confederate prisoners at Camp Douglas, in Chicago, Cook County, Illinois. Charles also was granted a furlough home during that month.

What Wabesis didn't expect during his service was that he would be arrested and charged with murder. On March 14, 1864, Sergeant Wabesis received permission for a one-day pass to go into the city of Chicago. His pass was signed by Captain Edwin V. Andress and countersigned by Colonel Charles V. DeLand of his regiment.

While in Chicago, Sergeant Wabesis became unintentionally involved in a quarrel with a saloon bartender, John Moynihan, over some postal currency on the counter. Wabesis insisted that the said postal money belonged to him. As the soldier made his way to the door, the bartender insisted that Charles owed him twenty cents before he left the saloon. Words were exchanged, Wabesis pulled out a knife, and the bartender grabbed a cane to try to knock the knife out of Charles's hand. As the two men grappled with each other, Wabesis grabbed Moynihan by the collar and plunged his knife into the bartender's left breast. Wabesis walked out of the saloon as a witness called for a "watch" (a police officer). An officer followed Wabesis and arrested him. The civil authorities were notified, and the soldier was subsequently arrested for the stabbing and charged with manslaughter since Mohynihan died shortly after the confrontation.

The next day, Wabesis pleaded guilty to using a deadly weapon with the intent to do great bodily harm. The full account of this incident was printed in the *Chicago Tribune* (1860–1872) on March 19, 1864, page 4, titled "The Moynihan Murder" (*Murder).

Charles was sent to the Cook County jail for eleven months. During his confinement, his regiment received orders to leave Chicago and proceed to the battlefront. The sharpshooters left Camp Douglas on St. Patrick's Day, March 17, 1864, for Virginia.

Charles's trial was held in February 1865, and it was assumed, correctly, that there was not enough evidence to convict him. So, it was decided that he was to be returned to the county jail to serve a term of six additional months for being involved in the fight, or a "row" as the incident was called.

On July 28, 1865, having been imprisoned for a total of seventeen months (March 16, 1864, to July 28, 1865), Wabesis was released from confinement. His release was on the same day that his unit was discharged from the army. Not knowing what to do, and upon the advice of the sheriff, he returned home to Michigan without notifying the military authorities. This mistake would cause some trouble for him when he applied for a pension.

Discharged: On December 12, 1890, a delayed honorable discharge certificate, furnished by the War Department, was issued to Wabesis, and the charge of desertion was removed from his record (as explained in his biography). This delayed discharge was retroactive to the date of the original discharge of his regiment, as cited previously, and his name was restored to the muster roll of discharged men. He was paid the money owed to him during his confinement and up to the date of April 1865.

Biography: The name Wabesis is derived from the Anishinabe word *wabisi,* which means young swan *(Baraga).* Wabesis is pronounced "Wab-ah-see." Charles was the son of John and Kenoequa Wabesis Sr. His Anishinabe name was Nowcon (or Nawwecaw). Among his siblings were sisters Ashadeanequa, Shanakaqua, and Macadefsequa; and brothers Wabindage (Wahmindego or Wabindago), also known as John Wabesis Jr., Chinguma (or Chingwon), and Post. Wabindage was the youngest son. Charles enlisted into Company K with his youngest brother on the same day.

In the 1860 census, Charles was listed with his first wife, Sarah, and a son, Megoshaage, age three. It's not known what happened to Sarah and Megoshaage.

Charles's second marriage was to Kutoo/Kuttoo/Kittoo Robinson on March 1, 1871 (or February 15, 1871), in the Catholic Church (and Old Government School House) in the township of Elbridge. Father Rivers, a Catholic priest in the township, officiated at the ceremony. Dominic Lewis, Peter Compo, James Cobsequom, and John Perashia were some of the couple's friends who witnessed the wedding.

Kutoo was formerly married to Seth T. Robinson, a non-Anishinabe from New York who was an interpreter for the Anishinabek in the Elbridge area. Kutoo and Seth had a son named Edward (or Edwin) Robinson.

Due to several acts of desertion by Seth, Kutoo obtained a divorce from him on September 7, 1870. The court decreed, at the time of the divorce, that Kutoo would have the care, custody, and education of her son until further order from the court.

Charles, a farmer, and Kutoo were the parents of Jacob Wabesis, born March 15, 1872, and John Wabesis, born July 14 or 15, 1876.

By 1880, Edwin Robinson, age seventeen, was listed in the federal census as living with his father, Seth, and Seth's wife, Hannah.

On December 10, 1880, Charles received his land patent Certificate #4306 for his forty acres in Oceana County under the Homestead Act. The land description is: southeast quarter of the northeast quarter of section 15 in township 15 north of range 16 west of the Michigan Meridian (*Land Records*).

Sometime during his postwar years, Charles joined the GAR Joe Hooker Post #26 located at Hart, Oceana County. He enjoyed the comradeship that it provided to its Union veterans.

Since he needed a pension for support, Charles Wabesis submitted an application on August 11, 1890, to have the charge of desertion removed from his record. In this petition, Wabesis related much the same story of the criminal charges mentioned previously. He said that he could not reproduce the records of the criminal court because those records were destroyed in the Chicago fire of October 9, 1871. Charles also related that being an Indian by birth, he didn't know what to do when he was released from jail. So he did as the sheriff had suggested—he returned home. Charles admitted that he was ignorant of the laws and regulations of war, but in no way did he have any thoughts of deserting his service. Charles's friend and Company K comrade Joseph Tazhedewin (also known as Joseph Poneshing) corroborated Charles's story.

As mentioned previously, Charles was successful in his bid to clear his name. The charge of desertion was expunged from his record, and he was granted an honorable discharge from the army and was given the back pay owed to him.

After notification that his military record had been cleared, Application #1,056,455 for an invalid pension was filed for Charles on September 14, 1891. This pension application was under the generous Act of June 27, 1890, which stipulated that a veteran must have served at least ninety days and received an honorable discharge.

In his pension application, Charles listed rheumatism (generalized aches and pains of his shoulders, neck, and back), and his inability to do any heavy farm labor as the reasons for his need for an invalid pension. One cause of Charles's rheumatism may have been from a childhood bout of acute rheumatic fever initiated by a streptococcal infection. The illness is known to damage the heart.

Due to his death at age sixty in Elbridge, Oceana County, on December 21, 1891, Charles did not receive an invalid pension. His death certificate listed "unknown" as to the cause of his death, but it was known that he suffered from heart trouble.

He was buried in the St. Joseph Catholic Cemetery near his church in Elbridge on December 22 of said year.

Kuttoo Wabesis applied for a widow's pension under the liberal Act of June 27, 1890, citing that she had no other means of support except her daily labor and some assistance from her sons, Jacob and John. She had possession of her husband's forty acres, which he partially improved. The acreage was worth $250, but since it was under a mortgage of $115, it was not worth more than the principal and accumulated interest. Application #547,165 was filed for Kuttoo on April 7, 1892. Those friends who supported her claim for a widow's pension attested to the fact that if she did not receive aid from some source, she would become a ward of the county. Kuttoo did not receive a widow's pension for reasons not clearly explained.

By 1900, Jacob Wabesis, his wife, Mary, and their children, Charley and Lizzie, were living in Elbridge. John Wabesis and his wife, Mary, were also living in Elbridge. Kuttoo is not listed in the household of either family. But in the 1900 federal census of Elbridge, there is a widow named Agatha Wabesis who resided in the household of Samson Robinson. Agatha and Kuttoo may possibly have been the same person. The date of Kuttoo's death is not known. Charles and Kutoo's son, John Wabesis, age forty-two, signed his World War I Draft Registration card as "John Wabsis" on September 12, 1918 (*Draft*). At the time of the draft, John was employed as a laborer at the Hart Cedar Lumber Company in Oceana County.

Wabesis, John, Private

Enlistment: Enlisted as a private on July 4, 1863, at Elbridge, Oceana County, by Captain Edwin V. Andress, First Michigan Sharpshooters, for three years.

Age: Twenty-three, born about 1840 in Kent County.

Occupation: Farmer

Residence: Elbridge Township, Oceana County. Another record states Pentwater, Oceana County.

Physical Description: Five feet nine, with black eyes, black hair, and a dark complexion. Examining physician was Dr. Jacob B. McNett, assistant surgeon, First Michigan Sharpshooters.

Mustered: July 11, 1863, at Detroit, Wayne County, by Lieutenant Colonel John R. Smith, US Army

Military Service: In August 1863, when his regiment was guarding Confederate prisoners at Camp Douglas, in Chicago, Cook County, Illinois, Private Wabesis was given a furlough home. At that time, he was assigned to recruiting duty as well as given home leave. In January 1864, John was detailed as a company cook.

It was first thought that Private Wabesis was taken prisoner by the rebels during the battle before Petersburg (the Battle of the Crater) on July 30, 1864, because he was listed as missing in action after that battle. But after inquiries and depositions, it was discovered that he was killed by shrapnel from the explosion of an artillery shell that landed hear his feet. Artillery shells were filled with gunpowder or iron balls or both. Company K comrades Sgt. Antoine Scott and Pvt. Josiah Light testified that they saw Private John Wabesis dead of the effects of the shell burst. Sgt. Scott testified that: "John Wabesis and I was in a fort (fortification) and the rebels came in on to us and a shell dropped down and bursted and killed several, and I saw John Wabesis lying on the ground and he was lifeless and I supposed that he was dead. I know these facts from personal observation." Scott's testimony was substantiated by some other members of Company K. Whatever the circumstances, Private John Wabesis was neither seen nor heard from again.

Considering the fiasco for the Union at the Battle of the Crater, the Confederates most likely buried John's body in a trench with other unknown Union dead. They probably went about this grizzly task with indifference and disrespect for the boys in blue (*Encyclopedia*).

Discharged: No discharge given due to the eyewitness reports of two company comrades of John Wabesis's death in battle.

Biography: As previously mentioned in his brother Charles's file, the name Wabesis is derived from the Anishinabe word *wabisi,* which means young swan (*Baraga*). Wabesis is pronounced "Wab-ah-see." John was the son of John and Kenoequa Wabesis Sr. and was also known as either Wahnoncegezhik or Wabindage. He was the youngest brother of Sgt. Charles Wabesis, who was also known as Nowcon (or Nawwecaw). John's other siblings were sisters Ashadeanequa, Shanakaqua, and Macadefsequa; and brothers Chinguma (or Chingwon), and Post. John Jr. enlisted on the same day as his older brother Charles.

John Wabesis married Mohtwaynekenoh on March 15, 1856, on the bank of Tamarack Creek near Croton in Newaygo County. The couple were joined in marriage according to accepted Anishinabek custom and practice (agreement between the couple and their parents).

John and Mohtwaynekenoh were the parents of two daughters born in Elbridge.

They were Kahbaynoquay, born October 15, 1857, and Wawbinway, born in 1862. Wawbinway died at the age of five years and three months on September 15, 1867.

After the death of her daughter, Wawbinway, Mohtwaynekenoh married secondly to a man named Chingwon (possibly the brother or a relative to Charles and John Wabesis) in December 1867. This marriage was also conducted according to accepted Anishinabek custom and practice.

Mohtwaynekenoh, in addition to taking care of her surviving daughter, had a son with Chingwon named Edawwawshe, who joined the family in May 1870.

On June 28, 1871, the Second Auditor's Office of the Treasury Department issued a certificate #523,923 in the amount of $225 payable to Mohtwaynekenoh Chingwon as widow of John Wabesis. This payment was for the soldier's service to the time of his death (substantiated by testimony that was accepted by the adjutant general). In addition to that sum, a $175 bounty owed to the deceased was also given to the widow. These monies were allowed under the Acts of July 22, 1861, and July 28, 1866. Under the Act of 1861, a widow whose husband died in the line of duty was eligible for money owed to the soldier up to his death and any bounty money he would have received. Pension money for dependents was approved by 1866.

On March 25, 1872, Mohtwaynekenoh Chingwon, who had remarried (mentioned previously), was appointed as legal guardian for her daughter, Kahbaynoquay. Application #203,469 for a pension for minor children under the age of sixteen was filed for Mohtwaynekenoh Chingwon on April 30, 1872.

A Minor Children's Pension Certificate #167,422 for the amount of eight dollars a month was received by Mohtwaynekenoh Chingwon in February 1875. Even though Kahbaynoquay had attained the age of sixteen on October 15, 1873, the pension payments were retroactive to January 1, 1868, and ended on Kaybaynoquay's sixteenth birthday.

Wakazoo, Joseph, Private

Enlistment: Joseph Wakazoo enlisted first in Company H, Stockton Regiment, Michigan Infantry, which subsequently became Company H, Sixteenth Regiment, Michigan Infantry on November 8, 1861, in Detroit, Wayne County. At his enlistment, Joseph signed up for three years and used the alias T. G. Bay.

On November 27, 1863, Joseph was transferred to Company K, First Michigan Sharpshooters.

Age: Twenty-three, born about 1838 near Kalamazoo, Kalamazoo County.

Occupation: Interpreter and hunter

Residence: Leelanau County

Physical Description: Five feet nine, with dark eyes, black hair, and a dark complexion.

Mustered: Into Company H, Sixteenth Regiment, Michigan Infantry on January 10, 1862, at Hall's Hill, Virginia (located near the District of Columbia), by General David Butterfield.

Military Service: From the time he enlisted in the Sixteenth Infantry, Private Joseph Wakazoo, also known as Joseph P. Wakazoo, had second thoughts about his choice of that unit. There was not another Anishinabe in this regiment, and he felt alone and not completely accepted by his fellow soldiers. He completed his basic training and fought with his unit at the Battle of Fair Oaks on June 1, 1862. After the battle, Joseph wrote a letter to his Congregational minister and close friend, Rev. George Nelson Smith Sr., of Northport, Leelanau County, in which he described the engagement. Rev. Smith had baptized Joseph, admitted him as a member into the Congregational Church in January 1852, and considered him as a son.

During the Battle of Manassas (Second Bull Run) on August 30, 1862, Private Wakazoo deserted the field and headed home to Michigan.

On October 9, 1862, Wakazoo was considered absent without leave, and his name was removed from the rolls of the Sixteenth Michigan Infantry.

During the evening of October 13, Wakazoo had dinner with Rev. Smith at Smith's home. He told his pastor of his desertion three weeks prior to his visit and related his concern and fears of what he had done and of the consequences. He sought Rev. Smith's advice and told him that he wished to join the all-Indian company, Company K of the First Michigan Sharpshooters.

Wakazoo spoke to the Indian Council at the schoolhouse on October 15 and told the assembly of his war experiences.

As he had feared, Rev. Smith heard by letter that Private Wakazoo was arrested for desertion on September 9, 1863, by the military police in Grand Traverse County and was charged thirty-five dollars for the cost of travel to apprehend him. Before he arrived at the detention center at the Detroit Barracks on October 13, Joseph was processed with other deserters and confined to jail in Grand Traverse (*Ibid.-Smith*).

Rev. Smith wrote several letters to the military authorities during Wakazoo's incarceration and explained that the young man wanted to serve his country but desired to be transferred to Company K of the First Regiment Michigan

Sharpshooters. He also related that, since the Sixteenth Michigan Infantry had no other Anishinabek soldiers and Company K was composed of all Anishinabek (except three men from other tribal affiliations), Wakazoo felt that he would be more readily accepted as an equal in that latter company's ranks.

Through the efforts of Rev. Smith, an application requesting a transfer to Company K of the First Michigan Sharpshooters was accepted by the War Department. By order of Lieutenant Colonel B. H. Hill, provost marshal general for the state of Michigan, Wakazoo was transferred to the sharpshooter regiment on November 27, 1863. The charge of desertion was removed from his record at the time of his transfer by First Lieutenant Lemuel A. Nichols of the First Michigan Sharpshooters.

While engaged in the Battle of Spotsylvania on May 12, 1864, Joseph sustained a gunshot (missile) wound to the left hand that injured the fourth metacarpal bone (above the knuckle) of the ring finger. He was taken to the aid station where bleeding was stopped by compression, and the wound was washed and hastily bandaged. He was given an opium pill or whiskey for pain.

From the aid station, Wakazoo either walked or was taken by an ambulance wagon to his division hospital farther behind the lines. At this hospital, iodine was applied to the wound in his hand to impede infection, and a simple water dressing of bandages dipped in cold water was put on his hand and held in place by a cloth bandage or adhesive plaster (*Schaadt*). He was again given whiskey or an opium pill for pain.

On May 15, Joseph was taken by ambulance wagon from his division hospital through Fredericksburg, Virginia, to a wharf at Belle Plain Landing on Potomac Creek. He was transferred from the wharf to a hospital ship and taken to L'Ouverture Hospital in Alexandria, Virginia, where he was admitted on May 16. Similar treatment was continued, and opiates were given for pain. A healthy diet was ordered for the patient.

Joseph was granted a thirty-day furlough on June 14, 1864, from L'Ouverture. While on furlough in Michigan, he was admitted to St. Mary's General Hospital in Detroit on July 9, 1864, for similar treatment and pain management.

Private Wakazoo returned to his regiment on September 16, 1864, still suffering from a great deal of pain and with very limited use of his left hand.

On September 30, Joseph was taken by ambulance wagon to a military railroad. At the railroad, Wakazoo was put on a mattress in a boxcar, the floor of which was cushioned with straw or hay, and sent to City Point, Virginia. He was then taken by ambulance wagon to a wharf at City Point and transported by hospital steamer to Carver USA General Hospital in Washington, DC, for additional treatment. He was admitted to Carver Hospital on October 1.

Still experiencing a great deal of pain in his left hand and not able to perform strenuous military duty, Private Wakazoo was granted a twenty-day furlough from Carver on October 25, 1864, and again returned home to Michigan.

Before he was readmitted to Carver Hospital on November 17, he took the opportunity to vote for Abraham Lincoln in the presidential election of that year.

On February 10, 1865, Joseph Wakazoo was released from Carver Hospital and returned to duty with his regiment.

Due to the serious condition of his wound and in constant pain, Joseph spent most of his military service under continuous treatment and very limited duty. Having attained the expiration of his term of service, Private Wakazoo was discharged from the army and returned to Michigan.

Discharged: Private Joseph Wakazoo was mustered out and given an honorable discharge on February 15, 1865, at Detroit. He was given the pay due to him for his military service at the time of his discharge. Joseph returned to northern Michigan to reside in Northport, Leelanau County, and Petoskey, Emmet County.

Biography: Joseph, also known as Joseph P. Wakazoo, and whose surname was also spelled Wakazo and Wahkazhe, was descended from a long line of admirable and well-respected Ottawa (or Anishinabek) chiefs whose ancestral home was the Red River Valley of Manitoba, Canada. In order to clarify the ancestral lineage of Joseph Wakazoo, the information in the following paragraphs should be carefully noted.

Joseph will be referred to as Joseph P. throughout the rest of this file. He was the son of Chief Peter (or Pendunwan, which means the "sheath" or "scabbard") and Agatha (or Nawzhewayquay) Petoskey Wakazoo (*Old Wing Mission*). Agatha converted to the Catholic faith in 1825, and Joseph P. was baptized after birth by a Catholic missionary.

In addition to Joseph P., the other children of Chief Peter and Agatha Wakazoo were: John Baptist, born about 1829, married an Eliza before 1907, and died April 15, 1910; Mary Shawnego, born July 24, 1836, married David Natiwagonashe Agosa on December 5, 1850, and died November 4, 1873; Moses, born 1840, married Elizabeth Agatha Petoskey on February 14, 1871, and died January 1, 1920; Stephen, born about 1841; and an unnamed infant who died October 27, 1842 (*Ibid.*).

Agatha Petoskey Wakazoo died September 7, 1848. Chief Peter Wakazoo then married for the second and third time, having six children with his third wife,

Mary Ann (or Mesquaba) Okitchigume. Anna, one of the daughters of the chief and Mary Ann and a half sister to Joseph P., married Peter Wells, a Company K comrade of Joseph P. (*Ibid.*).

Joseph P.'s father, Chief Peter (or Pendunwan), was the son of "Old" Chief Joseph Wakazoo and his wife, Choni. Old Chief Joseph was the chief of the Ottawas in Allegan County near Holland, Michigan. Chief Peter's (or Pendunwan) siblings were Kinequa and "Young" Chief Joseph Wakazoo (*Ibid.*). Kinequa took the Christian name of Charlotte upon her baptism into the Roman Catholic Church and was known by both names.

Kinequa Wakazoo married Nyan (or Naon) Miingun (or Maingan), which is the name for wolf. She became the mother of Payson Wolf, thus making Joseph P. and Payson first cousins and Company K comrades (*Ibid.*). Payson Wolf would marry Mary Jane Smith, the daughter of Rev. George Nelson and Arvilla Smith Sr.

Old Chief Joseph, his wife, Choni, and their sons, Chief Peter (Pendunwan) and Young Chief Joseph, converted to Protestantism. Kinequa (Charlotte) would remain a devout Catholic for the rest of her life.

Upon his death about 1835, Old Chief Joseph Wakazoo was succeeded by his son, Young Chief Joseph, as leader of his settlement.

Young Chief Joseph Wakazoo heard the preaching of Congregational Protestant missionary Rev. George Nelson Smith Sr. from Vermont and liked what he heard and saw. The chief decided to recruit Rev. Smith in 1838 to be the settlement's missionary and teacher to his people. When living in Vermont, Rev. Smith had felt a calling to be a missionary among the Anishinabek in Michigan. So, upon Young Chief Joseph's invitation, Smith gladly accepted the offer (*Ibid.*).

"Old Wing" was the name chosen by Young Chief Joseph Wakazoo for the mission and school in memory of his father's brother, Chief Ningwegon (or Negwagon)—"The Wing." This settlement was located along the south branch of the Black River in Allegan County. Rev. Smith would soon come to admire Young Chief Joseph as a brother and counted him as one of his closest friends in mission work (*Ibid.*).

After Young Chief Joseph's untimely death on October 27, 1845, at age forty, Joseph P.'s father, Peter Wakazoo, became Chief. Rev. Smith deeply mourned the young man's death and hoped that the mission and settlement would carry on successfully under his brother Peter's leadership.

In June 1849, Chief Peter Wakazoo helped Rev. Smith move the Ottawas from the Old Wing Mission to Wakazooville (or New Wing Mission) just outside of Northport in Leelanau County on Grand Traverse Bay. This movement was precipitated by the desire to be near other bands, the fear of illness from impure water and poor sanitation, and the continual encroachment of other non-Anishinabek, especially the Dutch, settlers. The Ottawas and the Dutch had their disagreements (*Ibid.*). By 1852, Wakazooville would be annexed to the town of Northport.

As his brother, the Young Chief Joseph, had honored education, Chief Peter also believed strongly in schooling for his children and supported Rev. Smith. Joseph P. and his siblings and half siblings took their early education at the Old Wing Mission School. Later, they continued their classes at New Wing Mission. Both mission schools included lessons in the English language that included spelling, reading, writing, singing, and geography. Some mathematics was also taught as well as vocal music (*Ibid.*).

Even though the mission school was open most months of the year, the Anishinabek children's help was needed by their parents during their seasonal cycle of activities. These activities included processing maple syrup into maple sugar, fishing, farming, berry picking, and hunting. Although these activities cut into the children's class time, the seasonal work not only provided for the Anishinabek's sustenance but also supplied commodities for sale and trade. Rev. Smith's children and other non-Anishinabek children would attend the school on a more regular basis. Only during the cold winter months, when their fathers were hunting and trapping for animal pelts, could the Anishinabek children take advantage of their educational opportunities.

After his mission schooling, Joseph P. (who was known to be a very bright student) spent one year (1845–1846) of advanced schooling in the Wesleyan Seminary at Albion College in Albion, Calhoun County (*Albion*).

After he left Albion, Joseph P. spent two years (1848–1850) at the Twinsburg Institute (also known as Samuel Bissell's School of Ottawas), a school of advanced learning in Twinsburg, Summit County, Ohio (*Smith*). Joseph P.'s brother, Moses, would also attend sessions at Twinsburg. As a student, Joseph P. either boarded out with a family in town or lived in one of the rooms available at the Institute.

Congregational minister Rev. Samuel Bissell established the Twinsburg Institute as a private select school in 1843. The institute emphasized a classical education and included the study of languages, mathematics, elocution, writing, penmanship, music, and art. The school year was divided into three sessions over a forty-two-week period.

In the winter of 1851, Joseph P. was at home in Wakazooville recovering from an illness. As he was recuperating and gaining strength, he found out that he did not have enough money for the next school session at the institute. He decided that when he was well, he would find a job to pay for his school expenses. During his stay at home, Joseph P. was baptized by Rev. Smith and joined the Congregational Church on the first Sabbath in January 1852.

On June 16, 1852, Joseph P., now having sufficiently recovered from his illness, sent a letter to Rev. Bissel discussing his brother, Moses. This letter is the oldest known work written by any of the three scholarly brothers (Joseph, Moses, and Stephen) that still exists and, by today's standards, contains an interesting lack of periods between sentences (*Twinsburg*). The letter states the following:

Grand Traverse June 16, 1852
Rev. S. Bissell

Dear Teacher

I have received your kind letter I write to you to tell you that my brother Moses has been sick this spring & could not go to Twinsburg he is not here & I do not know whether he will be able to go or not I shall not know till I get to Little Traverse on my way where I shall see him as soon as I can get ready I shall go this summer I have not been to school much since I left Twinsburg. I have no special news to write you, we are all usually well I have received a letter from Moses Hamlin he tells me that Augustus has completed his studies and left the school I am very glad that he has got through his course. From your

Sincere Friend
And Pupil Joseph Wakazoo

Before he attended his last session at Twinsburg Institute from April 9, 1860, to March 9, 1861, followed by his graduation, Joseph P. worked as a day laborer on the Presbyterian Mission farm at Omena (called New Mission) on the Leelanau Peninsula. This mission was headed by Presbyterian minister Rev. Peter Dougherty. Money earned from his labors would pay for his last year at Twinsburg. Another student who would attend the same session as Joseph P. was a classmate and friend, Charles Allen, also from the Northport area (*Ibid.-Twinsburg*). Charles would be a future Company K comrade.

After his service in the war, Joseph P. worked as an interpreter in and around the villages of Northport in Leelanau County and Petoskey (or Bear River) in Emmet County.

When he worked as an interpreter, Joseph P. became interested in Christian missionary work among the Anishinabek people. He was influenced by his father, Chief Peter (or Pendunwan), and his uncle, Young Chief Joseph, who had been involved with Rev. Smith and his mission among the Ottawas (or Anishinabe). Joseph P.'s interest in missionary work took him to Lake Winnipeg, Canada, where he ministered among the Canadian Anishinabek for an unspecified period of time.

On May 16, 1879, Application #288,430 for an invalid pension was filed for Joseph P. Wakazoo. In the application, he cited injuries that he incurred in the Battle of Spotsylvania. He mentioned the wound to his left hand and an injury that he claimed caused a severe wound in his right hip. Joseph P. related that the wound in his hip resulted from a piece of shrapnel from the burst of an artillery shell that struck his gun, causing the gun to strike him in the hip. He added that the force of the blow knocked him down, and his comrades carried him to the rear of the action for treatment.

By the end of May 1879 (or by 1880), Joseph P. had relocated to Minnesota and resided on the Leech Lake Indian Reservation in Cass County. Due to his severely crippled left hand, he was not able to do any manual labor as a lumberman or a farmer. While on the reservation, and on other reservations in the surrounding counties, he used his bilingual interpretive skills as a talented teacher.

In 1881, Joseph P. began his life's ministry as a Christian missionary among the Minnesota Ojibwe (or Anishinabek) on the White Earth Indian Reservation and as a lay assistant at Leech Lake Indian Reservation. He also assumed the charge of the Protestant Episcopal Church of St. Antipas for a time. In addition to the Church of St. Antipas, Joseph accepted a charge of the Mission and Church of St. Philip the Deacon at Lake Winnibigoshish. Joseph P. worked under the guidance of Rev. Joseph Alexander Gilfillan, a Protestant Episcopal minister, who had been in charge of all Ojibwe (or Anishinabek) missions in Minnesota since 1873 (*Missions*).

During the early years of his missionary work at Leech Lake, Joseph P. met and married Nesette Fisher. According to church records, Joseph P. Wakazoo and Nesette Fisher (whose father was an Ojibwe or Anishinabe) were married on September 26, 1884, by Rev. Charles (or Charley) T. Wright, a clergyman of the Protestant Episcopal Church. Joseph Butcher and Lizette Taylor were the couple's witnesses. The marriage was performed at Raven's Point on the Winnibigoshish Indian Reservation and was duly recorded in the Parish Register of the Church of the Good Shepherd at Leech Lake.

Nesette's father used the surnames Aiabes, DeJordan, and Fisher interchangeably. Nesette was also known by these three surnames.

Joseph and Nesette were the parents of seven children. The dates of their vitals are as follows: Frank J., born about 1880 and died in 1961; Lizzie, born about 1882 and died in 1900; John, born 1883 and died in 1890; Sophie, born around 1886 and died in 1900; Amus, born about 1889 and died in 1901; Edmond, born November 27, 1893, in Walker, Minnesota, and died in 1962 in Grand Rapids, Michigan; and Sarah, born about 1897 and died in 1905.

Frank would marry Edith Morgan in 1906. Edith was born December 28, 1889, in Minnesota and died in Cass County, Minnesota, on May 6, 1963. Edmond married Ella Fisher (born September 15, 1899, in Suttons Bay, Leelanau County, Michigan) in 1920 in Grand Rapids, Michigan. Ella died October 5, 1975, in Northport of Leelanau County.

Not having heard from the Washington pension office since he left Michigan for Minnesota in 1879 or 1880, Joseph P. resubmitted his claim for disability in 1880, 1881, and 1882. On May 3, 1887, he finally received Invalid Pension Certificate #358,213 for two dollars a month for the injury to his hand. The pension was retroactive to February 16, 1865, the date of his discharge.

His claim of a wound in the right hip was rejected by the Washington Pension Office in 1887. Joseph P. could not provide evidence from comrades in Michigan (those whom he had known well had passed away) for the injury, and there were no hospital records that supported any treatment for this injury. The rejection was made even in the light of testimony to the contrary from several of his neighbors and a physician who swore before a notary public that they observed Wakazoo's scar on his back and that he walked with a limp.

Known for his tireless missionary work among the Ojibwe, Joseph P. was ordained a deacon (presented by Rev. Joseph A. Gilfillan) on January 20, 1887, by Rev. Mahlon Norris Gilbert, bishop coadjutor, of the Minnesota Protestant Episcopal Church (*Deacon*). At the time of his ordination, Joseph P. was in charge of the Indian Mission field at Lake Winnibigoshish. Bishop Gilbert considered Joseph for a doctorate since he admired him as a man of high intelligence who had succeeded in passing a very difficult and creditable examination (*Bishop*).

In 1888, Rev. Wakazoo sent a report to Bishop Gilbert. In his report, he mentioned that he had been at his post for the past year and taught the Indian children in a free day school. He also related that he had carried on the mission work and held services on Sundays and Fridays. It was also noted that twenty children attended the day school and that there were thirty scholars in the summer of 1887. He informed the bishop that the children were learning quite fast and that the bishop would find the number of baptisms and confirmations in Joseph P.'s statistical report.

After the Church of St. Phillip closed, Rev. Wakazoo became assistant pastor at Leech Lake, Cass County. His ministry would require him to move several times in his career.

Under the more generous Act of June 27, 1890, Rev. Joseph P. Wakazoo received a four-dollar increase to his pension, resulting in a payment of six dollars a month. This act covered any military man who had served three months and who was honorably discharged.

In 1898, Rev. Wakazoo and his family were living in Fosston, Polk County, Minnesota. The family was still living in Polk County in 1894 when Joseph petitioned the US Pension Office for a second increase in his monthly payments. He received a second increase that covered the wound of his left hand in addition to rheumatism, disease of the heart, and senile debility due to his age. His monthly payments now totaled twelve dollars. This increase was retroactive to May 11, 1904.

Under the Act of February 6, 1907, Rev. Joseph P. received another increase in his pension payments. He was now paid fifteen dollars a month retroactive to May 9, 1907.

In 1908, the pastor and his family moved to Ebro, Falk Township, of Clearwater County.

Rev. Joseph P. Wakazoo suffered a stroke of paralysis on July 7 or 8, 1910, at his home in Ebro. From the time he was stricken to the date of his death on July 18, the minister was attended by Dr. Turnbull of Fosston. Thus ended Rev. Wakazoo's twenty-year dedication to Christian ministry on the White Earth Reservation.

The revered minister's funeral was held in the little Episcopal Church chapel at Bend of the River on Wednesday, July 20, 1910. Arch Deacon Heman F. Parshall was in charge of the service. He was assisted by the Rev. Charles T. Wright of Cass Lake, Rev. E.C. Ah O Led of Beaulieau, and Rev. Wilkin Smith of Twin Lakes. Friends packed the chapel with many more standing outside. All were anxious to honor the man whom they loved and to offer their sympathy and support to his family. Pastor Joseph P.'s pallbearers were George Wakefield, A. Pederson, Charles Porter, James Madison, Charles Boe, and John Stephens.

After the service, Rev. Wakazoo was buried in the St. Columba Episcopal Mission Cemetery. The cemetery is located at Big Bend, Waubun, Mahnomen County, about six miles out from Ebro (*US Veterans*). His gravestone states:

Joseph Wakazoo
Pvt. US Army
18 July 1910

At his death, the minister left his wife, Nesette, and sons, Frank and Edmond, to feel the deepest loss of his passing.

Application #947,987 for a widow's pension was filed on August 25, 1910, for Nesette Wakazoo, who, at that time, was still a resident of Ebro. She wanted to continue the accrued benefits of her husband's Invalid Pension #358,213 for his service in the sharpshooter regiment. She received approval for the accrued monies of twelve dollars a month (increased from eight dollars a month by the liberal Act of April 19, 1908) on February 8, 1912, retroactive to August 25, 1910.

After the questions concerning discrepancies perceived by the federal government of Nesette's maiden surname(s) and her age at marriage were resolved, she was finally granted a Widow's Pension #736,654 on February 6, 1912. The pension allowed for a payment of twenty-five dollars a month under the Act of April 19, 1908.

Joseph and Nesette's son, Edmond Wakazoo, registered for the World War I draft at the age of twenty-six on May 31, 1917. He was single when he registered and worked as a laborer for the Eureka Lumber Company in Lincoln County, Montana (*Draft*). Edmond served in the United States Eighty-Eighth Army Division, and fortunately, when hostilities ended, he returned to his home in Lengby, Minnesota.

Nesette received her monthly pension payments until her death at the age of fifty-eight on December 10, 1918. She succumbed to bronchial pneumonia complicated by a severe case of influenza. Edmond informed the pension bureau that his mother's death occurred at 3:00 a.m. on said date. Another son, Frank, was listed as the informant on Nesette's death certificate. She was buried near her husband on December 12 of said year.

Watson, James V., Private

Enlistment: Enlisted as a private on July 4, 1863, at Elbridge, Oceana County, by Captain Edwin V. Andress, First Michigan Sharpshooters, for three years.
   Age: Forty-four, born about 1819 in Kalamazoo, Kalamazoo County.
   Occupation: Farmer
   Residence: Pentwater, Oceana County
   Physical Description: Five feet eleven, with dark eyes, dark hair, and a dark

complexion. Examining physician was Dr. Jacob B. McNett, assistant surgeon, First Michigan Sharpshooters.

Mustered: July 11, 1863, at Detroit, Wayne County, by Lieutenant Colonel John R. Smith, US Army

Military Service: Private Watson was given a furlough in August 1863 while stationed as a guard with his regiment at the confine for Confederate prisoners, Camp Douglas, in Chicago, Cook County, Illinois.

He was present for muster during the months of September and October 1863. But during the months of November and December, Watson was reported to be sick in the post hospital and also suffering from partial deafness. The doctors diagnosed his illness as "scrofulous diathesis" with general physical incapacity. Scrofulous diathesis is a disease of hereditary influence. The disease is caused by the tubercle bacillus, which is the agent of tuberculosis of the lymph nodes of the neck called cervical lymph nodes (*Blakiston*). The disease progresses slowly with the development of fistulas and abscesses that ooze pus and heal with difficulty. The doctors were uncertain as to whether he incurred this disease while in the service or from a relative before enlistment.

Private Watson was still very sick and remained in the post hospital when his regiment left Chicago for the front in Virginia on March 17, 1864. Considering the severity of his illness, James was deemed not fit for transfer to the Veteran Reserve Corps in June 1864. The doctors at the post hospital decided to give Private Watson a certificate of disability for discharge from the service. He was paid the money owed to him for his service at the time of his discharge.

Discharged: On June 20, 1864, Private James V. Watson was given a certificate of disability for discharge signed by Dr. J. A. Grove, post surgeon at Camp Douglas. He was paid money owed to him for his service at his discharge and returned home to Pentwater.

Biography: James V. Watson, born in Michigan, emigrated to Canada with his immediate family and then returned to the United States in 1853 with his wife, Mary B., and their son, Amos, born in Canada about 1845. The family was of Potawatomi (Anishinabek) heritage. By the 1860 federal census, they were living in Cheshire of Allegan County in Michigan. In that census, Amos's name is spelled "Ames." James earned the family's living by farming.

In 1863, the Watson family made their home in Pentwater of Oceana County, where James is listed as a farmer.

There is no record of the family in the 1870 or in the 1880 federal census. James probably died from the long-term effects of scrofula sometime after he returned home from his service. It seems that he and his family traveled back and forth between the United States and Walpole Island, Canada, to visit relatives.

Before 1886, Amos Watson married Elizabeth Bazil, who was born about 1844 in Indiana. She was the daughter of John and Elizabeth Bazil.

Amos and Elizabeth (Bazil) Watson were the parents of Nancy J., born about 1886, and Margaret Bazil, born about 1892.

By 1900, the Amos Watson family was living near Athens, Calhoun County, and they were residents on the Potawatomi Nottawaseppei Huron Reservation.

In the 1920 federal census of Athens, a great-granddaughter, Lillie, age eight, was listed as living with Amos and Elizabeth Watson.

It seemed that Amos loved to write about historical events and peoples' personal experiences. He was known to have worked for the *Athens Times* and used the pen name of "Wah-nuh-Wah" (*Article*).

Amos owned a farm of a little over forty acres near East Indiantown northeast of Athens. Because of the decrease in his earning power and the poor harvest of beaver, Amos was forced to sell almost all of his property to earn cash for subsistence.

When Amos's wife died, his granddaughter, Mrs. Mandoka, kept house for him and continued to do so when Amos visited Potawatomi relatives on Walpole Island (*Ibid.*).

Amos died on October 13, 1926. His death was reported in the *Athens Times* on Friday, October 29 of said year (*Ibid.*). There is no pension file for James V. Watson.

Waubenoo, John, Private

Enlistment: Enlisted on May 18, 1863, at Isabella City (now Mt. Pleasant), Isabella County, by First Lieutenant William J. Driggs, First Michigan Sharpshooters, for three years.

Age: Twenty-two, born about 1841 in Saginaw County.

Occupation: Farmer

Residence: Isabella County

Physical Description: Five feet ten, with black eyes, black hair, and a dark complexion. Examining physician was Dr. George L. Cornell, assistant surgeon, First Michigan Sharpshooters.

Mustered: May 26, 1863, at Detroit, Wayne County, by Lieutenant Colonel John R. Smith, US Army

Military Service: About the middle of August 1863, while his regiment was guarding Confederate prisoners at Camp Douglas, Chicago, Cook County, Illinois, Private Waubenoo became ill of an undisclosed cause. After a short time in the post hospital, he was sent home to Michigan on sick furlough. He returned to his regiment about twenty days later.

Sometime between January and February 1864, Private Waubenoo was placed under arrest. No reason was given for his apprehension, but $35.68 was retained from his pay. The monetary reduction in pay for the time of his incarceration resulted in less money to send home to his parents at the next pay period.

For whatever the cause of his misbehavior, Private Waubenoo cleaned up his act, seemed to have impressed his superiors, and received a promotion. He was given an advancement in rank to that of second corporal on November 1, 1864.

On February 25, 1865, Waubenoo was granted a twenty-day furlough for home leave.

During the assault on Petersburg, Virginia, on April 3, 1865, Second Corporal Waubenoo was captured by the Confederates. He was held prisoner for ten days in a tobacco warehouse in Petersburg, and then on April 13, he was released and returned to his regiment. Sometime after his release from capture, Waubenoo received a second promotion to full corporal.

Discharged: Corporal John Waubenoo was mustered out and honorably discharged on July 28, 1865, at Delaney House in Tenallytown, DC. He returned to Detroit on the steamer *Morning Star*. On August 7, 1865, John was paid money due to him for his service at Jackson, Jackson County.

Biography: John Waubenoo, who was also known as Negawnewaywaydung, married Delia (or Obawnebawnoquay) Keezio. Delia's father was Sauginah Kease; her mother's name is unknown. An Anishinabe Methodist missionary officiated at the marriage rites in the year of 1855 (date uncertain) in Union Township of Isabella County. The couple lost their personal marriage certificate in a house fire.

John and Delia made their home in the village of Weidman in Isabella County and were the parents of at least one son, Joseph, born around November 1, 1867. The couple may have had a daughter named Betsy.

Joseph would marry Mary Shawboose, the daughter of John and Mary (Pazhegezick) Shawboose, on July 18, 1892. Daniel Covert, an Anishinabe Methodist Episcopal clergyman, officiated at the couple's wedding, which was witnessed by John and Martha Agahgo.

Application #1,166,185 for an invalid pension was filed for John Waubenoo on April 1, 1895. This application was filed under the liberal Act of June 27, 1890, which allowed a pension to any veteran who served for ninety days and was honorably discharged from the service. John cited severe rheumatism in his arms and legs and resulting heart disease, which he said prevented him from making a living as a farmer.

It's possible that John contracted rheumatic fever either before or during his service. Rheumatic fever is a consequence of an untreated strep throat (or streptococcal bacterial infection) most probably acquired in childhood and can leave the heart valves permanently damaged. This disease can also cause joint swelling and pain (*Blakiston*).

Waubenoo was granted Invalid Pension Certificate #948,468 on November 29, 1897, which was retroactive to April 1, 1895. The pension paid six dollars a month for disability.

On August 24, 1899, the pensioner submitted a declaration for an increase in monthly payments. In his declaration, John related that six dollars was not a sufficient amount to support him with what manual labor he was able to do. The request was filed on August 28, 1899. Other requests were submitted on November 3, 1900, and June 17, 1907.

Finally, on January 7, 1908, Waubenoo's several requests for an increase in monthly payments were accepted under the Act of February 6, 1907, and filed on June 21, 1907. He was granted an increase that amounted to fifteen dollars a month retroactive to June 21, 1907.

Waubenoo suffered for years from painful rheumatism. In his later years, he was plagued with Bright's disease, which is chronic nephritis (or inflammation) of the kidneys (*Ibid.*). This ailment would eventually be the cause of his death.

John Waubenoo died at the age of seventy-five on March 25, 1910, at his home in Nottawa Township. He was buried in Fairview Cemetery of said township and lies at rest under a military stone.

Delia Waubenoo submitted a declaration for a widow's pension on April 8, 1910. But before she would have to navigate the twisting road of government red tape, cardiac insufficiency would claim her life at the age of seventy-seven. She died on April 25, 1910, exactly one month after her husband's death. It's assumed that she was buried near her husband in the same cemetery.

Wayaubemind, Michael, Private

Enlistment: Enlisted on June 17, 1863, at Bear River (now Petoskey), Emmet County, by Second Lieutenant Garret A. Graveraet, First Michigan Sharpshooters, for three years.

Age: Nineteen, born about 1844 at Bear River.

Occupation: Laborer and farmer

Residence: Bear River

Physical Description: Five feet ten, with dark eyes, black hair, and a red (or ruddy) complexion. Examining physician was Dr. Arvin F. Whelan, surgeon, First Michigan Sharpshooters.

Mustered: July 20, 1863, in Detroit, Wayne County, by Lieutenant Colonel John R. Smith, US Army

Military Service: While in camp in Maryland, Pvt. Wayaubemind was assigned to be a company cook during the month of September 1863.

He was admitted to his regimental hospital in his camp outside of Annapolis, Maryland, on April 16, 1864 suffering from the symptoms of intermittent fever (or malaria) in which he suffered alternate periods of chills and fever. Malaria is a disease caused by the parasitic protozoa of the genus *Plasmodium* transmitted by mosquitoes infected with the genus *Anopheles* (*Blakiston*). For treatment, Wayaubemind was given quinine derived from powdered cinchona tree bark mixed in water or whiskey (whiskey masked the bitter taste of the quinine). This medication was also dispensed as pills of purified quinine sulfate (*Bollet*).

On April 22, Michael was admitted to Division No.1, USA General Hospital at the United States Naval Academy (Navy Yard) in Annapolis with the complaint of "debilitas" (debility) or a sense of fatigue, shortness of breath, and general body weakness. Complete bed rest was ordered for him, and he was fed a healthy diet that helped to speed his recovery. Michael returned to duty on May 9.

During the Battle of Cold Harbor on June 3, 1864, Private Wayaubemind was struck in the back by a missile ball which resulted in a contusion (a bruise) in which the skin was not broken. Also, during the same battle, he suffered a severe wound to the second finger of his right hand caused by a piece of iron shrapnel from the explosion of an artillery shell.

The soldier was taken to the aid station to assess his wounds. Bleeding was stopped by compression, and his hand was washed and hastily bandaged.

From the aid station, Michael was taken by ambulance wagon to his division hospital farther behind the lines. The doctors at the hospital used a water dressing of lint dipped into cold water and applied to the wound in his hand. The dressing was held in place by a cloth wrap or adhesive plaster (*Schaadt*). Wet compresses were put on his back to ease the pain of the bruise. He was given whiskey or an opium pill for pain.

On June 6, Private Wayaubemind was transferred by ambulance wagon to White House Landing, Virginia. At the landing, Michael was put on a hospital steamer and sent to Washington, DC.

He was admitted to Mt. Pleasant General Hospital in Washington on June 7, 1864. Cold compresses were again applied to the bruise on his back.

Michael was anesthetized with ether or chloroform, and the second finger of his right hand was amputated at the metacarpophalangeal site—the joints that connect the finger bones to the bones (called metacarpals) of the palm of the hand. The end of the metacarpal bone was smoothed with a rasp. Then the flaps of muscle and skin, which were cut in the circular method and pulled back before the amputation of the finger, were pulled over the metacarpal bone, brought together, and loosely sutured with silk or wire (*Kuz and Bengtson*). Cold water dressings were again applied to the wound left by the removal of the finger. Michael's hand was either stabilized by a Palmar splint (toward the palm) or was placed over a ball of appropriate size and held in place with adhesive plaster. Opiates and whiskey were given to the patient for postoperative pain (*Ibid.*).

During his stay at Mt. Pleasant Hospital, the doctors discovered that Michael had inflammatory disease of the heart valves. This condition may have been caused from the occurrence of acute rheumatic fever sometime in his childhood or contracted after his enlistment with the first complaint of a "sore throat." If he had rheumatic fever in his childhood, the examining surgeon should have detected the inflammation of the heart valves during Michael's enlistment physical. But not all enlistment exams were conducted according to protocol, and an oversight may have been made in Michael's case. Michael's fatigue and weakness had increased due to this physical problem, and the medical personnel could see that his health was deteriorating. Inflammation of the heart valves can result in abnormal heart function and heart failure.

Michael was transferred from Mt. Pleasant Hospital to a hospital steamer and then taken to McClellan USA General Hospital in Philadelphia, Pennsylvania. He was admitted to McClellan on June 13, 1864. He remained in this hospital under total bed rest until he returned to his regiment on July 10.

On July 18, 1864, Private Wayaubemind was admitted to Lincoln USA General Hospital in Washington, DC, from his regiment. Again the diagnosis was inflammatory disease of the heart valves. He remained at this hospital until he was granted a furlough home on August 5.

When he was home recouping from his wounds and trying to cope with his respiratory fatigue, Michael became ill and subsequently overstayed his furlough. When it was noticed that he had not returned to the hospital in the allotted time, Michael was reported by the hospital as a deserter, and a provost marshal (military policeman) was sent to find him and put him under arrest.

He was subsequently released from his arrest and was readmitted to Lincoln USA General Hospital on October 18. Michael left the hospital after a few days and returned to his regiment. His ability to carry out his responsibilities as a soldier became more physically challenging.

Seeing the young soldier's health becoming worse by the day, and hearing him complain of rheumatism (the generalized term for aches and pains), the regimental doctors sent Michael by ambulance wagon to a military railroad. At the railroad, Michael was put on a mattress in a boxcar, the floor of which was cushioned with straw or hay, and taken to the depot hospital at City Point near Petersburg, Virginia, on May 17, 1865. Rheumatism can be another result of acute rheumatic fever, and the pain in the joints can be quite severe. The only treatment for rheumatic pain during the Civil War was to administer opiates and quinine or potassium iodide for their mild anti-inflammatory effect. Baths and compresses were also used for their analgesic effect.

As if Michael didn't have enough infirmities to contend with, he began to experience paralysis of his lower extremities and partial paralysis of his left arm. Michael's medical records do not give a possible explanation for his paralysis.

He was taken by ambulance wagon from the depot hospital to a wharf at City Point, transferred to a hospital steamer and taken to Mt. Pleasant USA General Hospital in Washington, DC, where he was admitted on May 22. When the doctors examined Michael, they agreed that it was time to give him a medical discharge and send him home to stay.

Discharged: Private Michael Wayaubemind was mustered out, given a certificate of disability for discharge, and released from Mt. Pleasant USA General Hospital on June 28, 1865. He returned home to Emmet County. But because of the charge of desertion, he was denied his bounty of seventy-five dollars and wages due to him for his service.

When Captain James S. DeLand received a bill for eight dollars on June 30, 1865, for expenses incurred in Michael's arrest and was informed of the charge of desertion that was leveled against him, he sent a very angry letter to the head provost marshal in Washington, DC. Deland explained that he had not received a notice of Private Wayaubemind having been detained for desertion and that Michael was returned to the regiment with other convalescents and not as a deserter. He further explained that Michael told him that he thought that he had an extension of his furlough but had lost his papers while home. DeLand also related that Michael, as a Native American, did not fully understand US Army rules and regulations. The captain considered Wayaubemind to be a loyal, deserving soldier and knew that Michael never intended, nor considered, to desert his regiment.

On July 14, 1865, by command of Major General C. C. Augur, Headquarters Department of Washington, DC, and on recommendation of company and regimental commanders, the charge of desertion against Private Michael Wayaubemind was removed pursuant to paragraph 3 of Special Order No. 169. The soldier was then allowed to receive the money due to him for his service.

Biography: Michael Wayaubemind was the son of Petabun (or Petabunaque), also known as Elizabeth, and her third husband, Joseph Wayaubemind.

Petabun's first marriage was to Niobi Aninewawbe (also known as Nesogod and Niobi Kesheway). Niobi and Petabun had a daughter named Margaret Aninewawbe or Margaret Niobi.

Petabun married secondly to Mitchell LaCroix. Antoine LaCroix was a son of this marriage. Antoine was also known as Antoine Scott (the name that he used in the service), and Antoine Wayaubemind when his mother married Joseph Wayaubemind. Margaret Niobi, Antoine LaCroix Scott Wayaubemind, and Michael Wayaubemind were half siblings since they shared the same mother. Antoine and Michael would serve as comrades in Company K.

Even though he had returned home a sick man, Michael wanted to marry the girl he loved. It's not known if he knew Teresa before the war or met her on his furlough. Either way, on September 4, 1865, Michael, age twenty-one, and Teresa Missinini, also age twenty-one, and from Burt, Cheboygan County, were united in marriage in Little Traverse (now Harbor Springs), Emmet County. The Roman Catholic rite of marriage was officiated by Father Seraphim Zorn. Charles Bushaw, a Company K comrade of Michael's from Little Traverse, and Mary Pasikwi of Burt were the couple's witnesses.

On June 10, 1868, Michael Wayaubemind and Enos Petoskey, both of Bear

Creek, were witnesses to the marriage of Joseph Misinini of Cheboygan, age twenty, a farmer from Canada, and Theresa Wayaubemint, age nineteen, of Bear Creek, born in Muskegon. The wedding ceremony was conducted by Ignatius Petoskey, justice of the peace. Theresa may have been a Wayaubemind relative of Michael's father, Joseph.

There is no record of a pension application in Michael Wayaubemind's name nor his date of death. But a dependent mother's pension Application #415,546 was filed for Michael's mother, Petabun (or Elizabeth) Wayaubemind, on February 21, 1890, under her son Antoine Scott's service. As noted in Scott's file, Petabun did not receive a pension.

Waygeshegoing, William, Private

Enlistment: Enlisted as a private on May 18, 1863, at Isabella (now Mt. Pleasant), Isabella County, by First Lieutenant William J. Driggs, First Michigan Sharpshooters, for three years.

Age: Twenty-two, born about 1841 in Saginaw County.

Occupation: Farmer

Residence: Isabella Township, Isabella County

Physical Description: Six feet one and a half inches tall, with black eyes, black hair, and a dark complexion. Examining physician was Dr. George L. Cornell, assistant surgeon, First Michigan Sharpshooters.

Mustered: May 26, 1863, at Detroit Arsenal, Dearborn, Wayne County, by Lieutenant Colonel John. R. Smith, US Army

Military Service: Private William Waygeshegoing was cited for desertion on July 19, 1863, while on guard duty for Confederate prisoners at Camp Douglas in Chicago, Cook County, Illinois. William was returned under guard to Camp Douglas where he was restored to duty by Colonel Charles V. DeLand on December 7, 1863.

On April 14, 1864, while at the front with his regiment, Waygeshegoing was diagnosed with opthalmia, which is the inflammation of the mucus membrane that covers the anterior portion of the eyeball. The regimental doctor washed his eyes with cold water, and solutions of saline, borax, and chloride of sodium. About every third day, the doctors would paint the insides of the eyelids with nitrate of silver in water (*Dorwart*).

On June 24, William was listed as sick. He was taken by ambulance wagon to the military railroad where he was put on a mattress in a boxcar, the floor of which was cushioned with straw or hay, and sent to the depot hospital at City Point, Virginia. At the depot hospital, William was diagnosed with chronic diarrhea. He was given the most common treatment at the time for diarrhea, which included oral turpentine, "blue mass" (or mercurous chloride that contained mercury), potassium nitrate, and Dover's powder which was a combination of ipecac (a nauseating expectorant) and opium (*Bollet*).

After his stay at the depot hospital, William was taken to a wharf at City Point on July 4, 1864. At the wharf he was transferred to a hospital steamer and taken to Carver General Hospital in Washington, DC, where he was admitted on July 5. At Carver, William was given much the same treatment for his diarrhea as he had received at the depot hospital.

Pvt. Waygeshegoing was given a forty-five-day furlough from Carver Hospital on October 17, 1864. He went home and sought medical treatment from his traditional medicine practitioners. William was readmitted to Carver Hospital on December 1, 1864, and his treatment at the hospital continued as previously mentioned.

Upon further examination by a medical officer at Carver, it was found that Pvt. Waygeshegoing was suffering from chronic hypertrophy of the heart. In this condition, the heart is enlarged and its valves are deformed. Due to this diagnosis, a decision was made by the medical staff to give the soldier an honorable discharge for disability.

Discharged: Private William Waygeshegoing was mustered out and given a certificate of disability for discharge from the army at Carver Hospital on June 3, 1865. He was paid money owed to him for his service at his discharge and returned to Michigan.

Biography: During his postwar years, William Waygeshegoing (also spelled Waggishegomey) lived mostly in Saginaw County. He was also known by the names of Wahsascum, Long Bill, and Indian Bill. His parents were Waygeshegomey and Waybegewawmoquay.

William was known to have married three times. All the marriages were of traditional Anishinabek custom and practice in which the couple and their parents agreed to the conditions of the marriage. His first marriage was to a woman named Eliza. The couple were the parents of Martha, who would marry Wellington Collins, and a son, Peter. Martha Collins died in 1916. It's not certain what happened to Eliza (*Avery*).

The second marriage for William was to Penasewabenoquay (which means "early bird"). A girl and then a boy, called Joseph, were born of this marriage. It's not known what happened to Penasewabenoquay (*Ibid.*).

William married for the third time to Julia Payshon Chatfield, the daughter of Sampson and Maawasnoqua (or Charlotte) Chatfield. The marriage took place in Isabella County in December 1876. After her marriage, Julia was also known as Pasha Long Bill Skeegocum. This union produced a girl known as Wagezhegome, who died young; a son, John, born August 24, 1879 or 1881, who was also called John Long Bill and who died November 22, 1904; another daughter Jane (or Jennie), born May 15, 1888; and a son Thomas (or Tommy), born September 2, 1891 (*Ibid.*).

Both Jane and Thomas were baptized in Isabella County in the rite of the Methodist Episcopal Church. These two children were known to have attended Mt. Pleasant Indian School in Isabella County. There is a reference to a fourth marriage to a woman named Betsie (or Elizabeth)? in 1886. A daughter, Mary, was supposedly born to the couple on May 10, 1886. But this marriage has not been substantiated.

After his service, William lived mostly in Indiantown (St. Charles) of St. Charles Township in Saginaw County. He worked as a land looker (a person who estimates standing timber) for a lumber company and made ax handles and baskets to support his family. Julia also contributed to the family's income by making baskets.

William's health continued to deteriorate from rheumatism, heart disease, and the effects on his body from chronic diarrhea. His rheumatism may have been precipitated by a bout of rheumatic fever either before or during his military service.

Neighbors and army buddies noticed, mentioned, and testified on affidavits how bad William looked when he came home from the service. They remembered his physical appearance and how he complained about chest pains and rheumatism when they were together in the army.

On February 7, 1887, Application #596,872 for an invalid pension was filed for William. This application cited rheumatism, chronic diarrhea, and disease of the heart. He was granted Invalid Pension Certificate #395,277 on May 12, 1888, retroactive to February 7, 1887, which paid six dollars a month.

In 1889, William petitioned for an increase in payments under certificate #395,277. In 1890, he received an increase of four dollars a month, which gave him a total monthly payment of ten dollars retroactive to 1889.

On the morning of March 27, 1897, William "Long Bill" and his wife, Julia, went to Chesaning in Saginaw County to pick up Bill's pension check. In the afternoon, Julia started on foot for their home in Indiantown, which was about seven miles from Chesaning. Bill stayed in town to visit with his friends and planned to board the evening train to the Fergus stop that night. The following story is extracted from the account of Bill's demise printed in the *Chesaning Argus* of Saturday, April 3, 1897:

> William boarded the train that evening which was a little late and had to pass the south-bound train at Fergus. For some reason he decided to get off at Groveton instead of Fergus. Nothing more was known about him, after he left the train, until a Mr. Mortimer Gallagher would witness a horrible scene. Mr. Gallagher got off the south-bound train at Fergus and started to walk down the tracks to Groveton on his way home. As he walked, he noticed the body of a man lying on the track. Just as he saw the body, a special northbound train came along. Gallagher tried desperately to get to the body to move it away from the tracks but to no avail. The engineer noticed the man on the tracks and tried to stop the train, but it was too late. The engine and four cars passed over the body cutting it into over a hundred pieces.
>
> The remains that could be gathered were taken to St. Charles where an inquest was held. The verdict was that William Waygeshegoing was run over by a Michigan Central train while either already dead or in an unconscious condition. Several men testified that they had spent some time visiting with William and that he was perfectly sober that day and sober on the train in the early evening. *(Argus)*

What really caused William's death? Speculation was that, after getting off the train at Fergus, William changed his mind and tried to catch onto the rear coach as it was leaving the station. He would have been thrown with such force onto the tracks that he would have been rendered unconscious. Another theory was that he suffered a heart attack and died on the track. Anyway, it was a sad demise for William and for his family who depended on him for support. Friends who attended his funeral also mourned his loss.

William's funeral was held in St. Charles, and his remains were buried there. At his death, he was about sixty years of age *(Ibid.)*.

On April 29, 1897, Application #653,176 for a widow's pension was filed for Julia Chatfield Waygeshegoing, citing the need of support for her and her children.

At William's death, Julia and the children were left with two acres of land valued at one hundred dollars and a shanty house.

As William's widow, Julia was granted a Widow's Pension Certificate #454,083 approved on October 16, 1897. The pension paid eight dollars a month with two dollars a month additional for each of her two children, Jane and Thomas. The payments were retroactive to April 24, 1897, and were terminated when each child reached the age of sixteen.

On December 13, 1902, the US Pension Agency received a letter from Julia's sister-in law, Nancy Turner, accusing Julia of living with Nancy's brother, John Williams, and still receiving a pension from her deceased husband's military service.

After receiving the letter from Nancy Turner, the Bureau of Pensions dispatched an examiner to talk to Julia and see if she had violated the federal Act of August 7, 1882, which dealt with (in the opinion of the US government) "open and notorious adulterous cohabitation by a widow who continues to receive her deceased husband's pension."

Upon further questioning of John Williams and Julia about their living arrangement, it was concluded that the couple was cohabiting, and Julia, as a widow, was still receiving her monthly pension payments from her deceased husband's service for herself and her children. Without question, Julia needed the monetary support. At the time of the investigation into the accusation made against Julia, her son John Long Bill, was very ill with tuberculosis and needed constant care. John Williams probably was not able to provide much monetary help but could help Julia with John's physical care.

On November 22, 1904, John Long Bill, who did not marry, died of tuberculosis at the age of twenty-five. He was buried in Riverside Cemetery, which is located in the southwest limits of St. Charles, in section F, row 9. His stone reads "John Wageshcome 1881–1904."

The examiner concluded that Julia was in violation of the August 7, 1882, federal act. Therefore, she was dropped from the roles of pensioners on December 19, 1904. The money that she would have received in the coming months was transferred over to her minor son, Thomas. Because of her violation of the act, she was not eligible to be Thomas's guardian and therefore would not be able to receive the money personally for his needs.

Julia petitioned the probate court of the city of Saginaw, Saginaw County, on November 4, 1905. She asked that Mr. Albert Cantwell be appointed as guardian to handle the money that was transferred from her pension account to the account of her minor child, Thomas Waggishegomey, age fourteen (*Petition*).

On November 23, 1905, Cantwell was appointed to be guardian of Thomas Waggishegomey and was legally bonded in the amount of one hundred dollars to act in the interest of his ward in all matters concerning Thomas's interest of money, goods and chattels, real estate, and all rights and credits that would accrue to Thomas. Cantwell was also ordered to keep a running tab of all transactions and report those activities to the Saginaw County Probate Court.

On March 9, 1906, Mr. Albert Cantwell was informed that his bond was approved and that he had full power as guardian for Thomas (*Probate*). Thomas was now sole heir to his father's real estate of the two acres of farm land worth about one hundred dollars.

William and Julia's daughter, Jennie (or Jane) Waygeshegomey (as she spelled her surname), age twenty-two, married John Fisher, age twenty-four, the son of Jean (or Gene) and Julia Fisher, on March 9, 1907, in Saginaw County. Riley L. Crane, judge of probate, officiated at the marriage. John was a farmer living in St. Charles where the couple met. Witnesses to the marriage were Elizabeth Hesse and Eva Dryden.

Another marriage was recorded for Jennie in which her name is listed as Jennie Wayggishegoney Tinbrook. In this listing, Jennie married Oliver Charles Hoskins, son of Charles Arthur and Ella (Jones) Hoskins, on May 14, 1918, in Lansing of Ingham County. The couple was married by L. Nicola, minister of the Gospel, and the marriage rite was witnessed by C. A. and Ella Hoskins. After their marriage, the couple made their home in Diamondale of Eaton County where Oliver worked as a telephone lineman and Jennie was employed as a seamstress.

In the 1920 census for ward 7 of Lansing, Ingham County, Jennie is a lodger in the home of Glen L. and Grace E. Abbott. Her profession is listed as a seamstress, and she is recorded as married. Since Oliver worked as a telephone repairman, his duties would take him some distance from home for periods of time, which would probably explain his absence on the list of lodgers in the Abbott household.

After he attained adulthood, Thomas Waygeshegoing, or Waygeshegomey (as he spelled his surname), went to Lansing and secured a steady job at the Michigan Screw Company where lug nuts were made. He worked in the plant until he received his World War I Army Draft Registration card at age twenty-four in 1917 (*Draft*).

By 1920, Thomas had attained the rank of sergeant first class in the United States Army. At that time, he was stationed at Camp Gordon United States Military Reservation at Cross Keys, DeKalb, Georgia. He listed himself as a single man (*Georgia*).

In the 1930 federal census, Thomas was living in Lansing where he rented lodging from Mrs. Eva Battin on S. Sycamore Street. He worked as a laborer in the Lansing auto factory.

Thomas Waygeshgoing died in Lansing on January 3, 1943, and was buried in section Q of Mt. Hope Cemetery (*Grave*). His military gravestone was ordered by his sister, Jennie, after his death. Notice the spelling of the family surname. The siblings had a close relationship. His tombstone states:

T. Waggishegomey

Michigan

SGT. 1 CL. 374 Serv. Park Unit

MTC

JANUARY 3, 1943

Jennie died in 1944 and is also buried in section Q of said cemetery in Lansing (*Ibid.*). Her grave is close to that of her brother, Thomas, and her stone reads as follows:

Sister

Jennie Laura Davis

1874 1944

Wells, Peter, Private

Enlistment: Enlisted as a private on June 17, 1863, in Little Traverse (renamed Harbor Springs in 1881), Emmet County, by Second Lieutenant Garrett A. Graveraet, First Michigan Sharpshooters, for three years.

Age: Eighteen, born about 1845 at Bear River, (now Petoskey) Emmet County. Another record states his birth year as 1836.

Occupation: Farmer

Residence: Bear River

Physical Description: Five feet eight, with black eyes, black hair, and a dark complexion. Examining physician was Dr. Arvin F. Whelan, surgeon, First Michigan Sharpshooters.

Mustered: July 20, 1863, in Detroit, Wayne County, by Lieutenant Colonel John R. Smith, US Army

Military Service: According to Peter Wells's military record, it seems that he did not incur any injury, nor was there any mention of illness during his time of service.

Peter was promoted to the rank of corporal on November 1, 1864. He was demoted back to private, with no explanation given, on May 1, 1865.

Discharged: Private Peter Wells was mustered out and honorably discharged at Delaney House, Tenallytown, DC, on July 28, 1865. He returned to Detroit on the steamer *Morning Star.* On August 7, Wells was paid money due to him for his service at Jackson, Jackson County.

Biography: In his formative years, Peter Wells attended Rev. Peter Dougherty's Presbyterian Mission School at Bear River. The teachers responsible for instructing the students were Mr. and Mrs. Andrew Porter. On a list of students for September 1860, Peter, who had attended fifty-two days, was on the same roster as Peter South, who attended eighteen days for that session (*Report*). Both men would be future comrades in arms in Company K of the First Michigan Sharpshooters. The curriculum in this school included the study of reading and writing in both English and Anishinabe languages, geography, history, and mathematics. Also taught were skills in agriculture and carpentry for boys and homemaking for the girls.

On May 29, 1861, Peter Wells (who used the middle initial M) at the stated age of seventeen, married Christimind Wemegwans, age fourteen, of Charlevoix, Emmet County. The couple's marriage was performed by Michael Pitasey, justice of the peace, in the presence of Andrew Porter and W. H. Porter, witnesses. By 1870, Charlevoix was in Charlevoix County.

In 1866, Peter and his wife moved from Bear River to Hayes Township in Charlevoix County, where he earned his living as a woodchopper. That same year, he complained of bleeding from his lungs and was cared for by Dr. James Kaslaw of Bear River. His condition was most likely that of pulmonary tuberculosis.

Sometime between 1866 and 1867, Christimind died. Peter remarried because an 1870 census of Charlevoix (now in Charlevoix County) lists a Peter Wells, a farm laborer, his wife, Elizabeth, and son, Isaac, age two, living in Charlevoix, Charlevoix County.

A third marriage for Peter Wells was recorded in Emmet County on June 28, 1879. On that date, Peter married Anna Wakazoo. The marriage took place at Bear River and was officiated by Hiram Parker, justice of the peace. Simon Petoskey and Thomas Ereveshka witnessed the ceremony.

Anna Wakazoo was born January 9, 1853, at Wakazooville (near Northport in Leelanau County) and was the daughter of Chief Peter (or Pendunwan) and Mary Ann Mesquaba Okitchigume Wakazoo. Mary Ann was Chief Peter's wife of his third marriage (*Old Wing Mission*).

Anna descended from a long line of respected Anishinabe (Ottawa) chiefs. Her siblings were: William, born 1849 and died young; Charlotte, born December 1850; George Nelson, born September 30, 1855; and William (2), born about 1860 or 1861. Anna's half brother, Joseph, was the son of Peter and his first wife, Agatha Petoskey. Joseph was a Company K comrade of Anna's husband, Peter Wells (*Ibid.*).

Anna's father, Chief Peter (or Pendunwan) Wakazoo, was closely associated with the Congregational minister Rev. George Nelson Smith and his mission at Northport in the Grand Traverse area. Rev. Smith baptized Anna and her siblings.

Anna Wakazoo Wells died of pulmonary tuberculosis on July 30, 1883, in Hayes Township of Charlevoix County and is buried in said county.

Application #679,002 for an invalid pension was filed for Peter on November 16, 1888. At the time of his declaration, he was living in Hayes Township of Charlevoix County and had moved there from Bear River (or Petoskey) in 1866 as mentioned previously. Peter testified that he had caught a cold by overexertion and sweating during the assault on Petersburg in 1865 and that this condition had caused his subsequent lung trouble. He also complained of back pain that he thought was the cause of pain in his kidneys.

His medical record, previously mentioned, does not state any lung or kidney problems related to the war. His occupations at the time of his declaration were that of fisherman, farmer, and woodchopper. But he stated that his tuberculosis and kidney pain kept him from working a full day and, at times, resulted in weeks of idleness due to his condition.

On May 2, 1889, a communiqué from the Office of the Board of US Examining Surgeons in Petoskey stated that Peter Wells failed to appear in the specified time to give further testimony of the condition that he claimed for an invalid pension. The order to appear was first issued on December 29, 1888. With Peter's continued failure to appear, the process for a pension was abandoned by the government.

Peter Wells seems to have disappeared from records after November 12, 1888. There is a death record for a Peter Wells who was from Charlevoix that states that this Peter, a farmer born in 1836, died by accidental drowning on December 1, 1888. This death record would agree with Peter's disappearance after November 1888. The record also states that this Peter's parents were Daniel and Sarah Wells. The birth date of 1836 instead of 1845, and the mention of this Peter being married, gives the author pause because there is gap of nine years in the subject's age, and Anna died in 1883. It's possible that this death record is correct for the Peter Wells of this profile, even though the dates of birth disagree, and Peter may have remarried after Anna's death in 1883. Also, it's possible that a mistake could have been made as to Peter's marital status and his birth date in the death record.

It's known that the Peter of discussion had a severe case of pulmonary tuberculosis since he mentioned in his papers that a doctor had treated him for bleeding from the lungs. It's possible that Peter died of his ailment before December 29, 1888, and therefore he was not able to complete the necessary paperwork for his pension.

But the only death record for a Peter Wells in Charlevoix County is the record that mentioned death by drowning. It's the author's opinion that the man who drowned may have been the Peter Wells of Company K.

Wesaw, Thomas, Private

Enlistment: Enlisted as a private on September 26, 1864, in Van Buren Township, Wayne County, by James Hepburn, First Michigan Sharpshooters, for one year.

Age: Twenty-two, born September 24, 1842 (another date lists August 17, 1840), in Calhoun County.

Occupation: Farmer and mechanic

Residence: Van Buren Township

Physical Description: Five feet seven and a half inches tall, with black eyes, black hair, and a dark complexion. Examining physician was Dr. George Landon, Surgeon, First Michigan Sharpshooters.

Mustered: September 24, 1864, in Kalamazoo, Kalamazoo County, by Captain Mark Flanigan, provost marshal

Military Service: When a field gun was loaded with a hollow iron shell filled with gunpowder and set to explode in the air or on the ground, shrapnel, or pieces of the iron shell, would fly in all directions as a result of the explosion. Private Thomas Wesaw sustained a shrapnel wound, also called a gunshot wound, when a piece of shell fragment (from a Confederate artillery shell burst) hit his cheek bone below his left eye and pierced the bone. The injury occurred on March 29, 1865, during the action in which the Union troops retook Fort Steadman in the Siege of Petersburg, Virginia.

The soldier was taken immediately by ambulance wagon to an aid station behind the lines. At the station, any bleeding was stopped by hand pressure and the wound was washed and hastily bandaged.

Thomas was taken by an ambulance wagon to his division hospital farther behind the lines where the doctors swabbed the facial wound with iodine, to impede infection, and applied a simple cold water dressing to his wound. The dressing consisted of folded lint dipped into cold water, placed on the wound, and held secure by a cloth wrap or an adhesive bandage (*Schaadt*). Whiskey was given to Wesaw for shock, and an opium pill was offered for pain.

On April 2, Private Wesaw was taken to the military railroad, put on a mattress in a boxcar, the floor of which was cushioned with straw or hay, and sent to the depot hospital at City Point, Virginia, where he was admitted on April 3.

Since his wound would have been very painful, the doctors probably anesthetized Thomas with chloroform and then proceeded to remove any metal and bone fragments from his face. A tincture of iodine or carbolic acid was applied to the wound to impede infection (*Bollet*). The skin around the wound may have been washed with bromine (or Bibron's antidote) solution and then bandaged with simple cold water dressings (*Evans*). At the time, the physicians believed that cold water dressings of cloth bandages dipped into cold water, placed on the wound, and secured with cloth wraps or adhesive plaster would lessen possible infection and keep inflammation to a minimum. Thomas was offered opium pills for pain.

It was in this depot hospital on April 8 that Private Wesaw met President Abraham Lincoln when Lincoln visited the wounded soldiers. The young warrior admired his president and took a lifelong pride in the fact that he was one of the lucky ones to whom Lincoln offered his strong handshake. Thomas and the other soldiers drew hope from Lincoln's words of condolence, concern, and appreciation for their bravery and for answering their country's call. The vision of that one brief moment with Mr. Lincoln would be etched into Private Wesaw's memory. Just one week later, Thomas would mourn the loss of the life of the nation's leader taken by assassination (*Conversations*).

Thomas's final hospital transfer was to the Convalescent Camp Branch of the depot hospital at City Point on April 9. His injury was very painful and would eventually cause a disease that would leave him blind in the left eye. The injury to the left eye would cause sympathy (the injury to one eye would cause an effect upon the other eye) in the right eye. The scar caused by the wound would fade with advanced age.

Sufficiently recovered to be released from the Convalescent Camp Branch on April 11, 1865, Private Wesaw was immediately assigned to police duty at City Point. He was a member of the police force from April 12 until his discharge.

Discharged: Private Thomas Wesaw was mustered out and honorably discharged from City Point Depot Hospital on June 3, 1865, by reason of the

Military Department Special Order #22. He was paid the money owed to him for his service at his discharge and returned to Michigan.

Biography: Although Thomas's birth surname was Wezoo, he accepted either Wezoo or Wesaw when addressed.

Other members of his family also spelled their surname Wezoo.

He belonged to the Nottawaseppi Huron Band of the Potawatomi tribe of Anishinabek near Athens in Calhoun County. According to one source, the name Wesaw comes from the Pottawatomi word, which means "he, the torchbearer" (*Vogel*). The name may be derived from the word *wassewagan,* which means "torch" (*Baraga*). Although Calhoun County is recorded on his enlistment record as his place of birth, Thomas did testify in his pension papers that he was born in White Pigeon of St. Joseph County.

One of several Wesaw researchers has stated that Thomas was the second son of Louis/Sidone Wezo-Motay, a farmer, and Mary Gaugana or Nuddinnoquay, which means "Lady of the Wind" (*LaLone*). Louis's full siblings were: Isadore Sidone/Moutty, born about 1834; Joseph/Ketosh/ Motay/Wesaw, born about 1844 or 1846; Victory Motay, born about 1848; Peter Motay, born about 1853; and Isaac Motay, born about 1860.

Louis's father, who was a war chief, was the son of Wesaw/Mota and Sinegogua Topenebee. Sinegogua was the daughter of Chief Topenebee and Nogewi.

The following family story is of an incident that occurred in Thomas's childhood. It is recorded in several family sources, including a 1921 recollection by Sarah Isaac, a member of the Athens Anishinabek settlement, and in letters sent to the author by a granddaughter of Thomas Wesaw/Wezoo (*Wells*).

The story is related as follows: Due to the pressure of non-Anishinabek settlers in the area of southern Michigan, the federal government, under the removal acts of 1836 and in the 1840s, sent soldiers to drive out these Potawatomi and send them by force to Kansas. Many of them fled across the straits into the woods of the Upper Peninsula of Michigan, and others escaped into Canada where they settled mainly on Manitoulin and Walpole Islands. The main part of the tribe was escorted from Michigan to what would be their new homeland in Kansas (*Ibid.*).

In the early 1840s, soldiers arrived at Thomas's small encampment of the bands that belonged to Chiefs Mogwago and Pamptopee. Soon panic spread, and the Anishinabek scattered into the woods. In the melee of fear, Thomas's mother, Nuddinoquay, forgot to pick him up and carry him with her. She tried to return to the camp, but the soldiers blocked her passage and led her away. She would die in Kansas. Thomas, just a small child, was left alone by a campfire (*Ibid.*).

After the soldiers and the Anishinabek who were captured had left, the people in hiding came back to the camp. A woman named Magee found Thomas by the campfire and took him to be with her. She cared for Thomas for a short time until Thomas's aunt, his mother's sister, Togah (who escaped and returned from the west as did Mogwago and Pamptopee), assumed the duties of caring for Thomas. Togah raised Thomas until he could care for himself (*Ibid.*).

By 1846, many of the Nottawaseppi Huron Band of Potawatomi had returned to Michigan, and a Methodist Episcopal Church, the Nottawa Indian Mission, was established at the tribal settlement near Athens. Rev. Manasseh Hickey served as missionary to the tribal members. (*Reuter*). Nottawa Indian Mission would become the Athens Indian Methodist Church (*Ibid.*). (End of family story.)

Although Thomas had no formal education, he did teach himself to read the Bible that was translated into the Anishinabe language. He also became a faithful member and class leader of the Athens Indian Methodist Church and a responsible elder of the community. He delighted in singing the Anishinabe hymns in the annual camp meetings and in his church. His rich, melodious voice was enjoyed by all who were in his presence.

After his service in the Civil War, Thomas returned home to settle down, raise a family, and continue his involvement in church activities.

On November 20, 1872, Thomas Wesaw/Wezoo married Rosa Johnson, who was born March 15, 1858. Rosa's mother was from the Mickseninne family. Her father was a non-Anishinabe by the name of John Johnson. S. B. Smith, justice of the peace, officiated at the marriage in Athens with William Cancanby and Louis Smith, both of Athens, as witnesses.

Thomas and Rosa were the parents of eleven children: Eunice, born in 1874 or 1875, who married a Nottaway and died of tuberculosis in 1891; Martha, born in 1880; Agnes, born in 1881 and married Stephen Pamptopee in 1897; Mary, born in 1884 and died in 1884; Lottie, born 1885 and died in 1887; Mina or Ina, born in 1888 and died of fever on March 10, 1895; Nancy, born 1889 and died of scrofula (tuberculosis of the cervical (or neck) lymph nodes) on May 21, 1894; Charly, born in 1890 and died of kidney failure on July 18, 1891; Elizabeth, born October 10, 1892, and married Albert Mackety on January 21, 1912; and Lucile (or Lucy), born in 1899 and married George Whitepigeon (or White Pigeon) in 1919. A son named Dewit, age five, was listed in the 1880 Allegan County census.

After moving to several places while raising their family, the couple finally settled on the Nottawaseppi Huron Band of Potawatomi Reservation in Athens Township of Calhoun County.

Application #523,561 for an invalid pension was filed for Thomas on September 30, 1884. It cited a gunshot wound (shrapnel from an artillery shell burst) of the face and resulting disease of the left eye. The application was approved, and Thomas was granted Invalid Pension Certificate #293,687 on April 18, 1885, which paid four dollars a month retroactive to his application date.

Subsequent appeals for an increase in pension payments resulted in payments of eight dollars a month in 1886 and increased to ten dollars a month in 1889. Monthly payments were again increased under the Act of 1907 to twelve dollars. By 1917, Thomas's monthly payments were increased to $22.50. At the time of his death in 1918, Thomas was receiving thirty-two dollars a month for his injury claims.

In his waning years, as old age took its toll and bouts of pneumonia further weakened him, Thomas related stories of fearful episodes of the Civil War and of his experiences of seeing his friends and comrades die such violent deaths.

Rosa, his beloved wife and companion, died at the age of fifty-nine of complications from diabetes on January 26, 1918. She was buried in the Athens Township Indian Cemetery next to the Athens Methodist Indian Mission Church.

Sometime after Rosa's death, Thomas was reported to have married Lucy Johnson, who may have been Rosa Johnson's sister.

On December 17, 1918, as death was imminent, Thomas rejoiced that he was at peace with his God and with his fellowmen. Knowing that his life was finished on this earth, Thomas was anxious "to walk on" to the great beyond to see his family members who were waiting for him. As he drew his last breaths, he asked his loved ones to sing the "Doxology." His final words were: "Are my feet getting cold yet?" After he had said these words, Thomas folded his hands and went to sleep quietly and at peace. He was laid to rest under a military stone in the Athens Township Indian Cemetery near his wife and his beloved church. Thomas's surname on his gravestone is spelled "Wezoo."

Wesley, John, Private

Enlistment: Enlisted as a private on February 1, 1864, in Kalamazoo, Kalamazoo County, by recruiting officer Captain J. H. Smith, Nineteenth Regiment Michigan Infantry, for three years.

Age: Twenty, born about 1844 in Michigan.

Occupation: Laborer

Residence: Schoolcraft, Kalamazoo County

Physical Description: Five feet five, with black eyes, black hair, and a copper complexion. No examining physician was listed.

Mustered: February 2, 1864, in Kalamazoo, Kalamazoo County, by R. C. Dennison, provost marshal

Military Service: On February 19, 1864, Private Wesley was sent by accident to Camp Nelson outside of Lexington, Kentucky, instead of being sent to Camp Douglas in Chicago, Cook County, Illinois, where his regiment was guarding a confine for Confederate prisoners.

John was moved from place to place until he left Camp Nelson on April 4, 1864, when he was assigned (upon request of Colonel Charles V. DeLand) to DeLand's command in Annapolis, Maryland. He rejoined his sharpshooter regiment in Annapolis sometime during the second week of April.

Private Wesley was reported sick and admitted from the field to Washington Hall USA General Hospital (branch of the Second Division General Hospital) in Alexandria on April 27, 1864. His illness was diagnosed as intermittent fever (or malaria). At this hospital, Wesley was given doses of quinine derived from powdered cinchona tree bark mixed with water or whiskey. Whiskey was better since it masked the bitter taste of quinine *(Bollet)*. Wesley may have also been given pills of purified quinine sulfate.

On May 21, Private Wesley was taken by ambulance wagon from the hospital in Alexandria to a wharf in said city. He was transferred to a hospital steamer, and sent to Satterlee USA General Hospital in West Philadelphia, Pennsylvania. He was admitted to Satterlee on May 22.

In addition to malaria, Wesley was also diagnosed with chronic diarrhea. For treatment of this condition, the doctors always carried a large lump of calomel (or mercurous chloride) with them, which contained mercury and was called "blue mass." Pieces from this blue mass were given to Wesley *(Ibid.)*. Also, oral turpentine was given to the patient, and opiates (or narcotics) in pill form or in an alcoholic solution called "laudanum" were administered for pain *(Ibid.)*. When his digestive system become more tolerant, fluids, including fruit juices, were given to Wesley to help him to regain his strength.

John remained at Satterlee until he was released and rejoined his regiment in the field on October 18, 1864.

On March 1, 1865, Private John Wesley was promoted to the rank of corporal.

Discharged: Corporal John Wesley was mustered out and honorably discharged at Delaney House, Tenallytown, DC, on July 28, 1865. He returned to Detroit on the steamer *Morning Star*. On August 7, he was paid money due to him for his service at Jackson, Jackson County.

Biography: Before he left for the service, John Wesley, the son of John Blackbird, and his wife worked on the river as a lumberjack to earn a living.

After his service, John (who was also known as Nawyahwawsung) lived in Oceana and Mason Counties where he farmed.

In August 1866, John married Mary Pashnanequay (or Mary Sabacoum) Bailey, born in 1849. She was the daughter of Philip and Washsaah Bailey. It can be added that, on her death certificate, Mary's parents were listed as Rully Bailey and Mary Blackjachlattle. The couple's marriage was conducted according to accepted Anishinabek custom and practice (consent of the couple and their parents) at the trading post near Whitehall, Muskegon County.

John and Mary Wesley were the parents of fourteen children, of whom three lived to adulthood: Elizabeth, born about 1871 or 1876 (who married first to James Wilson and secondly to Louie Crampton) and died in 1951; Frank John Wesley, born in April 1884 or 1885 (who married first to Teresa Roundsky and secondly to Alice Nancy Russett) and died in 1978; and Emma Wesley, born in December 1894. Emma married first to a Rawson, secondly to David Marshall, and thirdly to a man named Shawano. She died in 1964.

During his postwar years, John's diarrhea became worse. Anishinabequa doctor Mary Sangoagi (whose father was an Anishinabe doctor) treated John's condition with medicinal herbs. Through the years, and especially in his later years, this disease would task his strength so much that he was not able to do a full day's work of farming.

John owned ninety-one and one-tenth acres of public domain through the Homestead Act of 1862. His Homestead Certificate #5220 was granted to him on August 1, 1883. The acreage was located in Eden Township of Mason County, and its location was described as the southeast quarter of the northwest quarter and the lot numbered 3, of section 20 in township 17 north of range 16 west (*Land Records*).

On August 21, 1889, Application #723,953 for an invalid pension was filed for John Wesley. The application cited chronic diarrhea contracted while in the service. In addition to the claim of diarrhea, he also mentioned ankylosis (the stiffness or fixation of a joint) of the left wrist and injury to the left hand due to the bursting of his gun while hunting previous to 1889. At the time of his application, John and his family were living in Fountain of Mason Country.

Even though the hunting accident had no bearing on his service, John was granted Invalid Pension Certificate #735,445 on March 2, 1892, for the injury to his hand and received twelve dollars a month retroactive to July 17, 1890. Due to the passage of the generous Act of June 27, 1890, all veterans with honorable discharges were granted a pension on the conditions that: they served at least ninety days regardless of any injury or illness incurred either before or after their service; proof of the soldier's death; the widow was without other means of support than her daily labor; the widow was married to soldier prior to June 27, 1890; that all pensions under this act commence from the date of receipt of application in the US Pension Bureau.

A family friend suggested to John and Mary that they should legalize their marriage according to the white man's law. So, on May 2, 1892, the couple was married at Fountain by Martin H. Foster, justice of the peace. Witnesses to the ceremony were Daniel L. and Nettie Dyer.

Having been weakened by malaria and chronic diarrhea and in poor health, John Wesley contracted what was called quick consumption (or tuberculosis) and died on September 26, 1908. The term used today for such a demise is galloping tuberculosis, which is a rapidly fatal form of pulmonary tuberculosis (*Blakiston*). There was no medical attendant at his death since he expired so quickly.

John Nawyahwawsung Wesley was buried in an unmarked grave in Grant Township Cemetery near Free Soil in Mason County. This cemetery is also known as Maple Grove Cemetery and Free Soil Cemetery (*findagrave*).

Mary submitted a request for the accrued monies left over from John's last pension payment on September 17, 1909, in the amount of $12.80. Her petition was approved, but friends reported that she received only $6.40, or half of what was due to her.

Application #908,553 for a widow's pension was filed for Mary on November 25, 1908. The application was rejected on the grounds that there was no evidence of tuberculosis in John's service record or at his discharge.

Mary resubmitted claim #908,553 on October 27, 1910, under the Act of April 19, 1908. The claim was filed in November 17, 1910. This act was more liberal for widows of Civil War veterans and increased the pension rate from eight dollars to twelve dollars a month. The act required that the widow was married prior to June 27, 1890, which eliminated the requirements as to dependence. It also superseded the Act of 1890 in the majority of widows' claims.

On March 20, 1912, a government agent named Mr. F. G. Sims visited Mary in her cabin and described her as a hard worker and well liked by the non-Anishinabek folks. But her cabin was not maintained and was so open that any occupants would suffer from the cold. The agent also related that Mary needed a guardian since she was helpless in caring for what she had and that any money that she earned should go toward food and clothing.

Finally, in April 1912, Mary was granted a Widow's Pension Certificate #739,536. This certificate paid twelve dollars a month retroactive from November 17, 1910, which was the date of filing the claim under the Act of April 19, 1908.

On May 13, 1912, Thomas S. Stevens of Free Soil, Mason County, was found to be a suitable guardian for Mary in the judgment of the court. He posted a $400 bond and was appointed by the probate court of Mason County to handle Mary's affairs since she was adjudged to be incompetent.

By April 13, 1916, John E. Bennett had replaced Thomas S. Stevens as Mary's new guardian. There was no explanation in the court documents as to why Bennett replaced Stephens. The probate court of Mason County found Bennett to be a suitable replacement for Stevens, and he posted a $400 bond.

Pension payments for Mary were increased until she received thirty dollars a month until her death. According to the Mason County Probate Court, Bennett managed Mary's estate in good faith and notified the court of her death.

Mary Wesley died of acute dilation (or stretching) of the heart in the evening of July 4, 1925. Dilation (stretching) of the heart is an increase in one or more of the cavities of the heart arising from the weakening of the heart muscle (*Ibid.-Blakiston*). This condition is associated with the failure of circulation resulting in congestion of the lungs and other organs.

Mary's funeral service was held at the Church of Jesus Christ of Latter-Day Saints (Mormon) in Free Soil. She was buried near her husband and other members of her tribal affiliation in Grant Township Cemetery.

Whiteface, Charles, Private

Enlistment: Enlisted as a private on July 4, 1863, in Elbridge, Oceana County, by Captain Edwin V. Andress, First Michigan Sharpshooters, for three years.

    Age: Twenty-two, born about 1841 in Ionia County.

    Occupation: Laborer

    Residence: Pentwater, Oceana County

Physical Description: Five feet eight and a half inches tall, with black eyes, black hair, and a dark complexion. Examining physician was Dr. Jacob B. McNett, assistant surgeon, First Michigan Sharpshooters.

Mustered: July 11, 1863, in Detroit, Wayne County, by Lieutenant Colonel John R. Smith, US Army

Military Service: Private Whiteface was stricken with an illness on December 3, 1863, while serving with his regiment as a guard at the confine for Confederate prisoners at Camp Douglas in Chicago, Cook County, Illinois.

He was admitted immediately to his USA Post Hospital at the camp where the doctors diagnosed his ailment as pneumonia. He probably developed pneumonia from a cold or bronchitis brought on by severe weather when he was on guard duty. Treatment for his ailment consisted of the painful procedure of cupping and blistering his chest, which was thought to cause the blood to accumulate in the skin where the treatment was applied and draw out the poison from his lungs. The process was thought to be an anti-inflammatory measure (*Bollet*). The doctors treated his pain and suppressed his cough with opium pills (*Ibid.*).

Private Whiteface returned to guard duty on December 9.

On December 22, 1863, the soldier was reported to be absent without leave. He returned to Camp Douglas two days later. No reason was given for his absence.

The day before Christmas in 1863, Charles gave twenty dollars to his Company K comrade Amos Ashkebugnekay (Amos Green) to give to Charles's father while Green was on a furlough home. Both Amos and George Stoneman, also a Company K soldier, vouched for Charles's concern for his father and that he did what he could to support his father's needs.

Private Whiteface was readmitted to the Post Hospital on February 14, 1864, suffering from consumption (or tuberculosis) and complications of pneumonia. He died that same day. His body was prepared for burial by the camp burial detail and put into a wooden box identified with his name. Charles was buried first in the Camp Douglas Cemetery. Later, his body was disinterred and reburied in the Civil War soldiers' section of Rosehill Cemetery in Chicago. His tombstone mistakenly reads "C V WHITBRAIN PVT 1 MICH SHARPSHOOTERS."

Discharged: No discharge given due to death by disease while in the Post Hospital.

Biography: Charles (Charley) Whiteface (or "Washed face") was also known as Nowquoum and Wahboose. Wahboose is derived from the Anishinabe word "wabos," which means "rabbit" (*Baraga*). He was the son of John (or Wobbundayquayse) and Bungkeeshee (or Punggeshe) Whiteface. His parents were married by accepted traditional Anishinabek custom and practice (consent of the couple and their parents). Charles had at least one sister, named Kahbahshemoqua. His mother died about 1854 or 1858 at or near Saranac, Ionia County. After Bungkeeshee's death, John and his children moved to Oceana County.

By 1860, John was becoming more feeble and was no longer able to hunt and fish to supply food for his family. He was now dependent upon Charles for life's necessities.

About 1862, Charles Whiteface began to live, according to Anishinabek custom and practice, with Susan Kewaquahum. She was also known as Sookatt Kewaquahum Whiteface. The couple lived as husband and wife and had only one child, a daughter, born early in 1863.

Not long after their daughter was born, Charles and Susan separated due to Susan's ill treatment of Charles (according to pension records). When the couple agreed to go their separate ways, which was considered a divorce in an Anishinabek marriage of custom and practice, Charles decided to enlist in the army.

On January 21, 1866, Rev. Isaac K. Greensky officiated at the wedding of Susan Whiteface and Louis Ogejewahnon according to the rite of the Methodist Episcopal Church in Pentwater of Oceana County. Witnesses to the ceremony were Joseph Elliot (an Anishinabe interpreter) and Joseph Taunchey. The couple were the parents of two children, a daughter who died at a young age, and a son. Louis died sometime after the children were born.

In March 1870, the daughter of Susan and Charles Whiteface died. In 1872 or 1873, Susan filled out an application form for a widow's pension, claiming that she was the legitimate widow of Charles.

By 1874, Susan was married to William McCoo, alias Kookooshshob, by Anishinabek custom and practice.

On December 4, 1874, Application #218,729 for a father's pension was filed for John Wobbundayquayse Whiteface, who did not remarry since Bungkeeshee's death. At the time of the application process, John was living at Ludington, Mason County. He was late in having his claim filed because he could not speak English, nor could he find anyone to translate for him. Also, he didn't understand all the paperwork that was involved in the submission of an application.

John had forty acres of wild timber land that he received from the government as an allotment. After Charles died, he had to sell the land for $125 in order to have enough money to buy food and clothes. When that source was depleted, he lived on county charity. By the time his representative filled out John's application for a father's pension in 1874, John was advanced in age and quite feeble.

John asserted that Susan's claim was false since she had had two husbands who supported her after Charles's death and there was no living child of Susan and Charles as a legitimate dependent under the age of sixteen.

On January 25, 1875, John was notified that he would receive a Treasury Certificate #617,138 in payment of a hundred-dollar bounty due to Charles for his service before his death.

The first application that was submitted for John in December 1874 was denied because of the murky situation of who was the legitimate recipient of a pension—the father, John, or the former wife, Susan. At the time of the rejection, the US Office of Indian Affairs was of the opinion that Charles left a wife and child who would be entitled prior to the father's claim. But the office made it clear that any evidence filed that showed that no wife or child was left would be considered. An interpreter, John Smith, who had been helping John Whiteface, became ill shortly after filing the application and was delayed in investigating the evidence and proofs needed to expedite the father's claim.

A second request for a father's pension for John Whiteface was submitted on July 12, 1879. Many letters were sent to the US Pension Office, including a letter from interpreter John Smith, that attested to John's honesty and truthfulness. It seems that the US government may have agreed that John Whiteface was the worthy recipient but requested more proofs for the father's case.

The last notation in Whiteface's file was that the decision for his pension was "pending." As far as is known, John Wobbundaquaysse Whiteface did not receive a dependent father's pension, and his date of death has not been located. What is known is that John was given assistance by county charity and by his friends until he died.

On June 13, 1915, William Genereau of Fountain in Mason County wrote a letter to the Committee on Agriculture asking if Charles's sister, Kahbahshemoquay, would be entitled to a pension or other relief on account of Charles's service. By the time the letter was written, Kahbahshemoquay was over the age of sixteen and was not eligible for a minor's pension.

Williams, James, Private

Enlistment: Enlisted as a private on May 29, 1863, in Dearborn, Wayne County, by Lieutenant Joseph O. Bellair, First Michigan Sharpshooters, for three years.

Age: Eighteen, born about 1845 on Walpole Island, Lambton County, Ontario, Canada.

Occupation: Farmer

Residence: Lapeer, Lapeer County

Physical Description: Five feet six and a half inches tall, with dark eyes, dark hair, and a red complexion. Examining physician was Dr. Arvin F. Whelan, surgeon, First Michigan Sharpshooters.

Mustered: June 16, 1863, in Detroit, Wayne County, by Lieutenant Colonel John R. Smith, US Army

Military Service: Private James Williams deserted from his regiment on July 5, 1863, while the sharpshooters were on guard duty for the weapons and munitions at the Dearborn Arsenal in Wayne County.

James was apprehended sometime in April 1864. By then his regiment had relocated and was encamped near Annapolis, Maryland. It's not known if Private Williams deserted because he didn't like the army, was sick, or that he just wanted to go home to see his family. After he was arrested, James was sent to the Paroled Prisoners Camp (or Camp Parole) three miles outside of Annapolis, as mentioned in a later memorandum attached to his military record. At Camp Parole James had a physical examination and was given medical treatment, nourishing food, and a new suit of clothes.

Private Williams remained at Camp Parole until December 10, 1864, when he was given a furlough for thirty days. He reported to the Detroit Barracks from his furlough on January 14, 1865. Three days later on January 17, Williams was sent back to the Paroled Prisoners Camp in Maryland. It's very possible that the soldier was suffering from a lingering illness.

Camp Parole was a barracks for prisoners that included both captured Confederates and former Union prisoners who had been paroled by the South and sent for exchange. The camp was also a bivouac for soldiers who had deserted from their units that were stationed in the area. The doctors on staff provided medical treatment for all the sick and wounded.

After Private James Williams returned to Camp Parole in January 1865, any trace of him is lost. There is no record of his death at Camp Parole. James may have deserted again and returned to his former residence in Lapeer, gone back to his birthplace in Canada, or died en route from Camp Parole to his destination.

Discharged: There is no record of a discharge for James Williams.

Biography: It's possible that James and Samuel Williams may have been brothers or relatives since both of them were born in Canada, had the same residences, and enlisted and deserted on the same day.

There is no pension file for James Williams.

Williams, Joseph, Private

Enlistment: Enlisted as a private on June 5, 1863, in Isabella City (now Mt. Pleasant), Isabella County, by recruiting officer First Lieutenant William J. Driggs, First Michigan Sharpshooters, for three years.

Age: Twenty-seven, born about 1836 in Saginaw County.

Occupation: Farmer

Residence: Isabella Township, Isabella County

Physical Description: Five feet seven, with dark eyes, black hair, and a reddish complexion. Examining physician was Dr. George S. Cornell, first assistant surgeon, First Michigan Sharpshooters.

Mustered: June 16, 1863, by Lieutenant Colonel John R. Smith, US Army in Detroit, Wayne County

Military Service: Between the months of September and October 1863, Private Joseph Williams lost the bayonet to his .58-caliber Springfield Rifle Musket. He was charged for a replacement, which probably impressed upon him the importance of keeping track of his battle gear.

Around 10:00 p.m. on June 17, 1864, Williams was captured along with seventy-seven other men of his regiment during the battle at Petersburg, Virginia. The men were taken prisoner by the Rebels of Ransom's Brigade of the Thirty-Fifth North Carolina Infantry (*Howe*).

Williams and fourteen other Anishinabek of Company K were marched into the town of Petersburg with the rest of the captured men of the regiment and housed in an old tobacco warehouse. All fifteen of the Anishinabek prisoners were divested of their rifles that they were carrying at the time of their capture (*Ibid.*). These rifles were treasured by the prisoners since most of the men decorated the stocks of their guns with carvings of animals, birds, and flowers. The rebels soon made use of these rifles against their Union foes and would not relinquish the weapons until Robert E. Lee surrendered the Confederate army at Appomattox Court House, Virginia (*Ibid.*).

After a short stay in the confine of the warehouse, the prisoners were loaded upon cattle railcars and taken to Camp Sumter, also known as Andersonville Prison, in Andersonville, Georgia. At the prison, Joseph and the rest of his comrades were exposed to inclement weather, scarce food, poor medical care, and mistreatment by the prison guards. Joseph's health suffered due to the ordeal of his imprisonment.

After five months at Andersonville, Private Williams was sent to another prison camp, Camp Lawton in Millen, Georgia, on November 11, 1864. The Union forces were all but upon the rebels by then. Joseph as one of seven Anishinabek prisoners who would survive the prison camp, was paroled at Savannah, Georgia, on November 26, 1864, and then transported to Camp Parole, Annapolis, Maryland. At Camp Parole, he had a physical examination and was given medical treatment, nourishing food, and a new suit of clothes.

Camp Parole was a camp for paroled prisoners in which both captured Confederates and former Union prisoners who had been paroled by the South were sent for exchange. The camp was also a holding area for soldiers who had deserted from their units stationed in the area. Doctors on staff provided medical treatment for all the sick and wounded.

On December 10, Joseph was given a furlough home for thirty days. He returned to Camp Parole on January 21, 1865, and was then sent to Camp Chase, Ohio, on February 16.

Camp Chase was a military staging and training camp established in Columbus, Ohio, in 1861. The camp contained a section for use as a prison camp and a section designated as a Confederate cemetery where more than 2,200 Confederates are buried.

Joseph was again granted a thirty-day furlough home from Camp Chase on February 24.

After his return from his second furlough in March, Joseph was ordered to report to his commanding officer at the Detroit Barracks to await his muster-out. The furloughs home attest to Joseph's poor health from his imprisonment and the need for rest and recuperation.

Discharged: Private Joseph Williams was mustered out and honorably discharged at Detroit on June 20, 1865. He received the pay due to him at that time and returned home.

Biography: Joseph Williams was also known as Joseph Nesogot. He was the son of William (a Shikbahouk or an Anishinabe doctor) and Sawkawsowayquay (or Anne) Nesogot. Joseph used his father's first name as a surname when he enlisted in the army. His siblings were John and Samuel.

According to the Gruett Saginaw Chippewa Index. Joseph married

Ogawbaygezhegoquay (or Sarah) around 1860. The couple were the parents of a son, named John, who was born about 1863.

Before 1871, Sarah took her son, left Joseph, and moved to Canada.

Joseph married secondly to Eliza Showshowomobins in Isabella County on March 6, 1871. The marriage was officiated by Rev. John Irons, Anishinabe Methodist Episcopal minister, and witnessed by Jacob Jackson and Peter Atawish. The couple were the parents of a daughter, Jane, who was born deaf.

Joseph Williams (or Joseph Nesogot), a man of very poor health due to his confinement in a prison camp, died sometime after 1872. He was buried in the Taymouth Indian Cemetery in Saginaw County near his brother Samuel. Joseph's military stone reads Joseph Shoyat, a corruption of the name Nesogot.

There is no pension file for Joseph Williams-Nesogot.

Williams, Moses, Private

Enlistment: Enlisted as a private on July 4, 1863, at Marquette, Marquette County, by Thomas Smith, assistant recruiting officer, First Michigan Sharpshooters, for three years.

Age: Thirty, born about 1833 in Marquette.

Occupation: Farmer and hunter

Residence: Marquette, Marquette County

Physical Description: Five feet eight, with black eyes, black hair, and a dark complexion. Examining physician was Dr. Arvin F. Whelan, surgeon, First Michigan Sharpshooters.

Mustered: July 20, 1863, in Detroit, Wayne County, by Lieutenant Colonel John R. Smith, US Army. Moses's Final Statement of his service lists July 11, 1863, as his mustering date.

Military Service: Private Moses Williams was reported present for duty from his enlistment until the action before Petersburg, Virginia, on July 30, 1864, called the Battle of the Crater. On that date, Williams was listed as having been taken prisoner. By December 31 of said year, Moses's fate, from the testimony of two Company K comrades, was updated to "killed in action" in the Crater.

The Battle of the Crater was a fiasco for the Union troops. It's most likely that the Confederates buried Moses Williams's body with indifference and disrespect in a trench near the battlefield *(Encyclopedia)*. His place of rest would not be in the soil of his ancestors and forever be unknown to his loved ones.

Discharged: No discharge given. Killed in battle.

Biography: There is no pension file for Moses Williams.

Williams, Samuel, Private

Enlistment: Enlisted as a private on May 29, 1863, at Dearborn, Wayne County, by Lieutenant Joseph O. Bellair, First Michigan Sharpshooters, for three years.

Age: Twenty, born about 1843 on Walpole Island, Lambton County, Ontario, Canada.

Occupation: Farmer and hunter

Residence: Lapeer, Lapeer County

Physical Description: Five feet five, with dark eyes, dark hair, and a red complexion. Examining physician was Dr. George S. Cornell, first assistant surgeon, First Michigan Sharpshooters.

Mustered: June 16, 1863, in Detroit, Wayne County, by Lieutenant Colonel John R. Smith, US Army

Military Service: Private Samuel Williams deserted from his regiment on July 5, 1863, while the sharpshooters were on guard duty for the weapons and munitions at the Dearborn Arsenal in Wayne County. It's not known if Private Williams deserted because he didn't like the army, was sick, or he just wanted to go home to see his family.

Discharged: There is no record of a discharge for Samuel Williams.

Biography: Nothing more is known about this soldier. It's possible that Samuel Williams and James Williams may have been brothers or relatives since both of them were born in Canada, had the same residences, and enlisted and deserted on the same day.

There is no pension file for Samuel Williams.

Wolf, Payson, Private

Enlistment: Enlisted as a private on August 3, 1863, at Northport, Leelanau County, by Sergeant Charles Allen, First Michigan Sharpshooters, for three years.

Age: Thirty, born about 1831 or 1833 in Middle Village, also called Good Hart,

Emmett County. Wolfe family lore states Payson's birthplace as the Canadian island of Manitoulin, which is located in the northeastern part of Lake Huron.

Occupation: Farmer

Residence: Northport

Physical Description: Five feet seven, with dark eyes, dark hair, and a dark complexion. Examining physician was Dr. George S. Cornell, first assistant surgeon, First Michigan Sharpshooters.

Mustered: August 8, 1863, at Dearborn Arsenal in Detroit, Wayne County, by Lieutenant Colonel John R. Smith, US Army

Military Service: Private Payson Wolf left for Dearborn with his enlistment officer and friend, Sgt. Charles Allen, on August 1, 1863. Allen had been granted a twenty-day furlough on July 12 for the purpose of recruiting men from the Northport area. The two friends boarded the wooden steamer *Tonawonda* at Union Dock in Northport at 1:00 p.m. Both men, along with other recruits, were accompanied to the dock by their respective families who, with sadness and aching hearts, saw them off and wished them well *(Smith)*.

Filled with patriotic pride and considering themselves worthy warriors for their people, Allen and Wolf could not imagine what lay ahead for them and what horror and bloodshed each would experience. One soldier would return to his family, who would rejoice at his homecoming but be saddened at how much he had changed. The other soldier would be mourned by his loved ones due to his tragic death.

When he was with his regiment as they guarded Confederate prisoners at Camp Douglas, Chicago, Cook County, Illinois, Payson wrote several letters to his wife, Mary Jane. One of these letters *(courtesy of Clarence [Bud] and Avis Wolfe)* is transcribed as it was written in its original form.

Camp Douglas, Chicago, Ill. January 16, 1864

My dear wife,

I just received two letters from you within the last four days. Was very glad indeed to hear from you so much when I understand your letters to say that you are enjoying your self well. I like to hear you say or write you are doing the best you can, I wish you happiness all the while. My dear wife if I had wished otherwise I would not have left you for the good of you and our children. I have undertaken such a work as this now and not that I should be permitted in good reputation before men. When I know you to be lonely or getting sick of me I also get uneasy for you. You know not dear wife how much I love you, I say the truth I love you. Should I see anything I could possibly do for you in this world, I would do it. And now although I would have been very glad to stay with you at home to see me every day, and know that my mother loves me very much for I am her only son living my brothers all died long ago. And that she has to feel very bad about me if I did leave for soldering where I may have to endure hardships. And although I knew that I should have to put a piece of wood under my head for a pillow and have to sleep on a bare floor or ground. All this did not stop me. I determined to go for the good of you my dear wife. If you think over this, you will see.

And you well know, that none persuaded me to enlist it was my own will that brought me here. And I often, very often spend my time in thinking about you, in my heart you are always near as in, keep steady in your mind and always try to be in good nature, and happy you'll be. Above all pray to the Lord for blessing if his will is that we should meet again that will be done. These are my constant thoughts. If I should meet you again I shall not be as I have been before.

About the money I sent you I want to be particular. I do not know whether you received the $30.00 I sent you, by the captain of the Alleghany, but the $35.00 by my mother I know that you received it. I sent you all that I have been paid.

I always rather have you take and use my wages and fortunes. As I have said before, for your good I am here.

But for this time I shall keep a little of my pay, for I need a few things for the winter such as gloves and c. We are going to be paid off in two or three days. The pay is for two months as up to the last of December. The rest of the money I will send you. You will want to take care of your money well. Because if we should go south soon, it may be a long time before we'll get paid again. One soldier who has been in the field told me that he was not paid for nine months in one time. Pay-days are not regular down there. You will know here that I haven't been on guard for two months almost, for I have been rather unwell. Now I am stronger and gaining every day, except the ear-ache sometimes.

Osah-o gwah-you and Kewagoshkom are getting well. About the papers, I send them to you once in a while that you may read them with pleasure. I don't know as you get them all and as all my things for you get through.

I give you my best respects and love to Father and Mother, and Annie. Also my own mother for me and children, kiss them for me.

I am one who loves you and your beloved husband and a soldier.

Payson Wolf

Payson's comment in his loving letter to Mary that "if he and Mary should meet again (hoping that he would survive the war) he would not be as he was before" was a prophetic statement that would ultimately result in profound sadness for his family.

During his duty as a guard with his regiment at the confine for Confederate prisoners at Camp Douglas in Illinois, Payson did complain of an earache (or otalgia). The doctors treated the problem by putting drops of a sweet oil, such as olive oil or castor oil, into the auditory canal. A heated brick wrapped in a towel or warm compresses were applied to the outside of the ear to draw out any infection (*Internet*). Payson also experienced bouts of general malaise, as attested to in the above letter to his wife. Except for homesickness, Payson's physical health was generally good.

Mary Jane and Payson's mother, Kinequa (or Charlotte), visited him several times while he was at Camp Douglas. When possible, some of the children accompanied their mother and grandmother. Included in the items that Payson received on those visits, or by mail, were new moccasins, shirts, socks, wool gloves for the winter, canned fruit (in glass jars), cakes, and pails of whitefish (*Ibid.-Smith*).

When the regiment moved to the front and settled in camp at Annapolis, Maryland, Payson became ill with intermittent fever (or malaria). He was admitted to Division No. 1 USA General Hospital at the United States Naval Academy (Navy Yard) in Annapolis on April 22, 1864. As a patient at the hospital, he was given quinine for the malaria in the form of powdered cinchona tree bark dissolved in water or whiskey. Whiskey worked better as it masked the bitter taste of the quinine. Payson received this medication three times a day. Quinine was also dispensed as pills made of purified quinine sulfate (*Bollet*). A nourishing diet was also ordered for Payson. Considered well enough to be discharged from the hospital, the soldier returned to duty with his regiment on May 2, 1864.

Private Wolf was taken prisoner during the action before Petersburg, Virginia, on June 17, 1864. After a few days of confinement in a tobacco warehouse, he and other prisoners were sent by cattle railcars to a stockade prison camp called Camp Sumter (Andersonville Prison) in Andersonville, Georgia. The trip was especially uncomfortable and noxious because of the filthy conditions of the train's cattle cars used to transport the prisoners.

The men arrived at the stockade on June 28. They wanted to stay together as a group, so they settled in the northwest part of the prison grounds where they had their own little area of "real estate" (*Ripple*). On the day of their arrival, it was extremely hot, and an evening thundershower created almost unbearable humidity. Their ordeal of untold suffering due to neglect, mistreatment, disease, inclement weather, and starvation had begun. It was known that assaults and robbery by other prisoners were common in the stockade, but the Anishinabek men were known to defend themselves well (*Ibid.*).

During his imprisonment, Payson suffered from diarrhea and scurvy (lack of vitamin C) due to the absence of fresh fruits and vegetables. Scurvy caused his gums to bleed and become spongy. He also lost some teeth. His legs and feet swelled so much that even walking was extremely painful. The muscles of his left arm and hand become very weakened and atrophied from the lack of proper nutrition brought on by scurvy. Due to the atrophy of his left hand, a part of his forefinger dropped off. He soon lost the use of that hand. Payson experienced constant pain, and his weight plummeted until he was only a skeleton of himself.

Private Wolf was finally released from Andersonville prison and sent to Savannah, Georgia, where he was paroled on November 26, 1864. From Savannah, he was then sent on the steam ship *Constitution* to Camp Parole in Alexandria, Virginia. When he boarded the ship, Wolfe received his first suit of clean clothes. Upon arrival at Camp Parole, Payson was given a physical, enjoyed his first bath in clean water, received a second new suit of clothes, and partook of nourishing food.

Camp Parole was a camp for paroled prisoners in which both captured Confederates and former Union prisoners who had been paroled by the South were sent for exchange. The camp was also a holding area for soldiers who had deserted and whose units were stationed in the area. Doctors on staff provided medical treatment for the sick and wounded.

On December 1, Mary received a letter from Payson from Camp Parole telling her that he had survived his ordeal and expected to get his first furlough home. On December 10, Payson arrived home at 2:00 p.m. for a thirty-day furlough. He was welcomed at the dock by his happy and much-relieved family.

During the thirty days of his first furlough home, Payson revealed to his family and friends the horror that befell him and his comrades while they were prisoners at Andersonville. The prisoners were robbed of anything useful. He related that starvation would lead the men to do unthinkable things to obtain anything to eat. Weak from starvation (sometimes not having anything to eat from two to four days) and being nauseous, it was very difficult for the men to keep any rations, such as beans, in their stomachs. As soon as they swallowed the beans, they would vomit the contents, and others would rush up to eat the vomit. Payson said that most of the time the boiled rice that they received contained maggots. It was either eat the rice and the protein that the maggots supplied or starve (*Ibid.-Smith*).

Payson reported back to Camp Parole in January 1, 1865, after his first furlough. He became ill from his infirmities while in camp and remained there until he was able to travel for his second thirty-day furlough home. He arrived back at Northport at about 5:00 p.m. on March 27, 1865. After his second furlough had expired, Payson reported to Camp Chase, Ohio, on April 28 to remain there until his formal discharge.

Camp Chase was a military training camp for Union troops, which included a section for use as a prison camp for Confederate prisoners. The Confederate cemetery contains 2,260 graves.

Discharged: Private Payson Wolf was mustered out and honorably discharged from Camp Chase, Ohio, on June 13, 1865. He was paid money owed to him for his service at his discharge and returned to Detroit. A short time later, he boarded the steamboat *Wenona* for the trip home to Northport. When he arrived at the Northport dock at 3:00 p.m. on June 25, he was escorted home by his grateful family and friends.

The ravages of war, seeing his buddies die, and the terrible experiences of the Andersonville imprisonment would leave Payson with not only physical but also psychological scars. Today we call these battle scars post-traumatic stress disorder. In the mid-nineteenth century, there was no professional help for PTSD. These issues, and the ramifications of other problems that would occur, ultimately resulted in the dissolution of his marriage with the only girl he truly loved.

Biography: Payson Wolf was the son of Nayan (or Naon) and Kinequay, also known as Charlotte, (Wakazoo) Miingun (or Maingan) which means "wolf."

Kinequay Wakazoo was from a noble family of Anishinabek chiefs of the Ottawa tribe originally from Lake Winnipeg, Canada, who were intermediaries between fur gatherers and buyers for the large northern fur-trading companies. Her family was also recognized as having great medicine healers (or Medewid). Kinequay was born in the Manitoba, Canada, Red River Country about 1801 when her parents, "Old" Chief Joseph Wakazoo and Choni, were camped in that area (*Kinnequa*). See file on Joseph Wakazoo.

According to the Anishinabek journeys during the seasonal changes, the tribal family bands moved their camps back and forth from Manitoba into Michigan Territory by way of a stop on Manitoulin Island. Michigan was warmer in the winter, and Manitoba was cooler in the summer. As the families made their annual trek, they hunted, trapped, fished, grew crops, and made maple sugar for their economy. Furs could be sold at the Astor Company at Fort Mackinac. Black Lake (or Lake Macatawa in Ottawa County) was one of their favorite winter camps.

An intelligent, headstrong, and remarkable lady, Kinequay was trained as a medicine woman (or Midekwe) with great healing powers. Her knowledge of roots and herbs was legendary among her people, and she was known to travel very long distances to procure these natural medicines for her treatments (*Ibid.*).

Her first husband and their six children were reported to have died in a small-pox epidemic. Try as she did, all of her healing powers were no match for such a disease (*Ibid.*). Kinequa, her parents, and her two siblings, Joseph and Peter (or Pendunwan), were spared.

After their deaths, Kinequay, now in early middle age and chaffing at the incessant urging of her male relatives to remarry, married a young Ottawa chief, Nayan (or Naon) Miingun (or Maingan) half her age. The men in the family wanted the Wakazoo line of chiefs to continue and hoped that the couple would produce an heir, a son or daughter, who would inherit Kinequa's powers of healing (*Ibid.*).

Naon and Kinequa were married in a Catholic ceremony in the fall of 1830. Kinequay was a devout Catholic who took the Christian name of Charlotte upon her conversion. The Wakazoo and Miingun families were also practitioners of the faith, having been converted by French priests of the Order of the Society of Jesus—the Jesuits (*Ibid.*).

Kinequa gave birth to a son in 1831 or 1833 whom she named Payson. There is a discrepancy as to just where Payson was born—Manitoulin Island (during his parents' seasonal travel cycle) or Middle Village (between Cross Village and L'Arbre Croche) as he stated on his enlistment paper. Two other sons, Mitchell and Louis, would eventually join the family, but they would die young (*Ibid.*).

When they finally settled down in L'Arbre Croche (which means the Crooked Tree), the Miinguns and Wakazoos (except Kinequay) became disaffected with the

Catholic faith and separated from the church's teachings. Kinequay remained a Catholic (*Ibid.*).

In 1833, word spread from other Anishinabek, who traveled up and down the western coast of Michigan, that there was a Congregational preacher, Mr. George Nelson Smith, who had arrived in the Michigan Territory. Mr. Smith preached the Gospel based on the Protestant faith. He had established churches at Plainwell and Otsego in Allegan County and at Richland (or Gull Prairie) in Kalamazoo County (*Ibid.*).

Smith and his wife, Arvilla Almira (Powers) Smith, had emigrated from Vermont to the Michigan Territory in 1833. George had felt a call to preach to the settlers in the territory and a special call to teach and minister to the Anishinabek. He trained to be a minister with the Michigan Presbyterians in 1834. On April 2, 1837, Smith was formally ordained as the Rev. George Nelson Smith. He would have the honor to be the first Congregational minister to be ordained in the newly minted state of Michigan.

In the fall of 1837, "Young" Chief Joseph Wakazoo (son of "Old" Chief Joseph) traveled to hear Rev. Smith speak at a church in Allegan County. He liked what he saw and what he heard from the minister and formed a close friendship with Smith. That special relationship would last until the chief's untimely death at age forty in 1845.

In 1838, Chief Joseph asked Rev. Smith to be teacher and minister to his thirty Ottawa families. Smith and his family were soon joined by Joseph's band. The settlement was named Old Wing Mission for Old Chief Joseph's brother Chief Negwegon (or "The Wing"). This mission was located in the northwest part of Allegan County just within the present Allegan County line and was complete with a school and church. Smith's school offered courses in mathematics, English, geography, reading, writing, and singing. In addition to academic studies, classes in carpentry and farming for the boys and sewing and cooking for the girls were taught to give the students domestic skills with which they could make a living.

After intense study of the Ottawa language for about eight years, Rev. Smith became fluent to the point that he did not need an interpreter for his sermons. His efforts delighted the Anishinabek. The Smith children would also become fluent in the Ottawa language.

In addition to his preaching and teaching duties, Rev. Smith was a judge and adviser-general combined when he settled disputes among the members of the colony. He also doctored the sick, delivered babies, and performed noninvasive surgery.

When Young Chief Joseph Wakazoo died in 1845, Smith was devastated by the loss of his right-hand man and stalwart supporter. Joseph's brother, Peter (or Pendunwan which means "scabbard" or "sheath"), succeeded Joseph as chief and, in respect for his brother, fully supported Rev. Smith in his ministry and academic teaching. Chief Peter's son, Joseph Wakazoo (refer to his file), was a first cousin to Payson Wolf and would serve as a comrade with Payson in Company K.

With continued unfortunate incidents dealing with cultural differences between the growing number of immigrants from the Netherlands who had also settled near Allegan and the Anishinabek families, Rev. Smith had to make an important decision. The minister moved his family and Chief Peter Wakazoo's family bands to a portion of land near what is now Northport in Leelanau County. The group relocated in 1848, and the new settlement was named "Wakazooville" for Chief Peter. Wakazooville was annexed to Northport in 1852.

Rev. and Mrs. Smith again established a school for the Anishinabek children with the Smith children also in attendance. The same academic and life skills courses were offered as were taught in Allegan.

The Smiths would become frustrated (as they were in Allegan) in trying to educate the Anishinabek children. The children's parents would need their help in the cycle of seasonal occupations to obtain food for consumption, sale, and trade. The students would miss many days of school.

First, there was maple sugar making in the early spring. This was a very important time since the sugar was shipped in barrels to markets in Chicago. Next was the spring planting of corn, beans, and squash, followed by spring fishing. As their gardens grew, the Anishinabek would go to berry-picking camps to harvest fruit to be sold fresh and dried. The gardens would be harvested in the summer, followed by more fishing. Cranberries were picked in the fall and dried for personal use and sale. Passenger pigeons, taken in the fall hunt, would be exported out of state to upscale restaurants.

So, even though Smith's school was open throughout the year, the only time the Anishinabek children could attend for any length of time was during the cold months of winter when their fathers would hunt fur-bearing animals for their valuable pelts.

Rev. Smith would complain that some of the Anishinabek children did not learn to speak English very well due to the various interruptions during their school year. Some students would excel in their studies, and Smith would send them to Wesleyan Seminary in Albion, Calhoun County, and Twinsburg Institute in Twinsburg, Ohio, for further education. Sending these children out for additional education was done only with their parents' permission.

As more non-Anishinabek came to Wakazooville, Chief Peter established a settlement out from the town and named it Onumeneseville, where his Anishinabek people would not feel so pressured from other cultures moving into the area.

In 1851, Rev. Smith organized the Northport Congregational Church for both Anishinabek and non-Anishinabek congregations. He held three services every Sunday.

Rev. and Mrs. Smith were the parents of ten children: George Nelson Smith Jr., born June 20, 1832; an unnamed son, born in 1834 and died shortly after birth; Mary Jane, born Nov. 14, 1835, in Gull Prairie; Arvilla Aurelia, born March 30, 1838, at Gun Plain; Esther Eliza, born Aug. 10, 1840, at Old Wing Mission and died Mar. 18, 1844; an unnamed daughter, born May 5, 1843, and died shortly after birth at Old Wing Mission; Esther Eliza (2), born April, 12, 1844, and died shortly after birth at Old Wing Mission; an unnamed son, born May 15, 1845, and died shortly after birth at Old Wing Mission; Esther Ann (or Anna) Eliza, born September 1, 1846, at Old Wing; and an unnamed son, born in 1849, who died shortly after his birth at Old Wing.

The Smith children knew no other playmates but the Anishinabek. They had been taught by their father that these people of the forests were as good as white people and that God loved them too. So, when the Smith's oldest daughter, Mary Jane, and Payson fell in love and wanted to marry, the situation not only rocked the congregation but also the community. If Rev. Smith refused to consent to the marriage, he knew that his life's work of teaching tolerance and acceptance would be for naught. Payson was an upright young man who did not drink, accepted Christianity, and joined Smith's Northport church in 1850. He was also Mary Jane's classmate at the Old Wing Mission School (*Old Wing Mission*).

Both Smith and Arvilla were torn over creating a division in their congregations. But they finally acquiesced to the marriage and realized that the young folks would not be dissuaded. Arvilla had a very hard time accepting the situation and had a premonition that their marriage would be a troubled one.

The extraction of an entry about the marriage of Payson Wolf and Mary Jane Smith from Rev. Smith's *Memoranda and Diaries of July 31, 1851 (Courtesy of Clarence (Bud) and Avis Wolfe)* is as follows: Rev. Smith solemnized the marriage of Payson Wolf, aged nearly nineteen years, and his oldest daughter, Mary Jane Smith, aged nearly sixteen years, at 3:00 p.m. on July 31. Rev. Smith noted that all the people of the settlement were present except the chief and family. He further stated that entertainment was enjoyed by all and that the occasion was pleasant.

Kinequay (or Charlotte) was not in attendance at the ceremony. She did not approve of her son's marriage to a white girl. Charlotte respected Rev. and Mrs. Smith and had the highest regard for the work that they did among her people. But she disliked white people as a group and held them in contempt (*Ibid.-Old Wing Mission*). She believed, as did her brothers, that the white traders were liars and cheats and gave the Indians liquor in order to steal their trade goods. She knew that Mary Jane, as a daughter of the respected Smith family, was an upright person in the community. It took some time, but Kinequay reluctantly accepted the fact that her son had married a white girl.

After their marriage, Payson built a comfortable home for his young bride and worked as a carpenter, hunter, and farmer to support her and their children (*Ibid.*).

Payson had forty acres by reason of a cash entry sale and received his certificate #486 for the acreage on December 1, 1858. Its description is the southeast quarter of the southwest quarter of section 3 in township 31 north of range 11 west in Leelanau County (*Land Records*).

He had eighty acres by reason of the amended fifth clause of the first article of the treaty concluded July 31, 1855, between the commissioners on the part of the United States and the Ottawa and Chippewa Indians of Michigan. He was awarded his certificate #1163 on June 26, 1872. Its description is the west half of the northwest quarter of section 10 in township 31 north of range 11 west in Leelanau County (*Ibid.*).

Payson and Mary Jane were the parents of thirteen children; George Payson, born May 23, 1852, baptized on June 1, and died May 18, 1860, in Northport; Arvilla Aurelia "Tissie," born December 11, 1853, and died December 23, 1945; William Powers, born November 27, 1855, and drowned in the sinking of the schooner *Kimball* in Lake Michigan on May 8, 1891; Esther Eliza "Ettie," born July 16, 1857, and died January 5, 1936; Charles Freemont, born March 5, 1859, and died April 25, 1925; George Payson (2), born December 22, 1860, and died May 17, 1883; Edwin Andress (named after a favorite military officer of Payson's Company K), born February 3, 1863, and died September 18, 1920; Jessie Annie, born October 9, 1865, and died in 1955; Allen Burnside "Birney," born March 16, 1867, and died in 1943; Mary Jane, born February 1, 1869, and died Mary 22, 1949; Mabel Helen, born February 22, 1871, and died July 15, 1949; Clara Belle, born February 1873 and died May 28, 1958; and Stella Minnie, born December 17, 1874, and died January 17, 1935. The Wolf children and their descendants would add an "e" to their surname in adulthood (*Wolfe*).

As Payson and Mary Jane's children began to arrive, Kinequay became a doting and loving grandmother. She accepted her bicultural grandchildren and had a respectful relationship with her daughter-in-law.

When she traveled around the area, Kinequay would take her pet rooster and a little red travel trunk known as "Kinequay's trunk" with her (*Ibid.*). She never learned the English language and only spoke to her grandchildren in the Ottawa dialect. Mary Jane and Payson would translate the conversations.

After his discharge from the army, Payson returned to Northport a very different man from the one who had left for the war. The horrors of battle and Andersonville Prison took their toll on him as he relived these experiences in his nightmares. Payson's personality and demeanor began to change in a dark and troubling way (*Ibid.*).

He couldn't really talk to Mary Jane about his horrible experiences. She wasn't there with him, she couldn't share his anguish, and she was unable to offer a catharsis for his physical and mental pain. Adjusting to civilian life was troublesome for Payson, especially since he had no use of his left arm and hand for anything that required hard manual labor. Mary Jane would suffer her own sadness with Payson's trials.

During his postwar years, Payson was in conflict as to who he really was. He loved his wife and children, had adapted to white ways, and had many white friends. Even though he walked in two worlds, he still tried to adhere to the values of his Anishinabe heritage. He felt unaccepted by both cultures (*Ibid.*).

Payson joined the Northport GAR Woolsey Post #399 in Leelanau County and the Washington GAR Post #106 at Cross Village in Emmett County. In these fraternal gatherings, he could vent his frustrations and commiserate with fellow veterans who had similar war experiences and understood his torment.

He did his best to provide for his rapidly growing family with part-time wage work for his father-in-law. This behavior reflected his obligations as an Ottawa man to his wife's parents (*Ibid.*). His other economic pursuits involved hunting passenger pigeons and packing them in wooden barrels for sale in Chicago, selling fish and maple sugar, and trading horses between Chicago and northern Michigan.

An invalid pension Application #109,071 was filed for Payson on May 30, 1866.

He received Invalid Pension Certificate #78,903 for disability on March 16, 1867, with the monthly payment of six dollars retroactive to June 13, 1865. Eventually, Payson would receive an increase of fourteen dollars a month until his death.

With more mouths to feed and his inability to properly provide for his family, tensions continued to rise, and the Wolf marriage began to deteriorate. During his dark moods, it was hard for Mary Jane and the children to live with him. The Smiths helped by taking some of the children into their home and providing for them. Rev. Smith had many talks with his son-in-law to try to understand Payson's trouble and to offer some help, if Payson wanted it.

As the situation between Payson and Mary continued to worsen, Rev. Smith, with a heavy heart, made a very difficult decision. He asked Payson to leave Northport. Payson agreed and moved to Cross Village (Old L'Arbre Croche), Emmet County, in 1876 to be near his mother, Kinequa, who had moved there.

Soon after Payson left town, Rev. Smith accompanied Mary Jane to the Leelanau County Court House so that she, with a heavy heart, could file for divorce. Her divorce from Payson was finalized and granted on October 21, 1879.

Payson Wolf died of heart failure (failure of the heart as a pump) at Cross Village on December 7, 1900, and was buried in the Old Catholic Cemetery (Holly Cross Cemetery) near his mother. A military stone marks his resting place.

Mary Jane Smith Wolf died on October 5, 1905. She was buried near her parents in the Northport City Cemetery.

With the best of two worlds blended into a bicultural family, the adult Wolfe children distinguished themselves in their own right. The second George Payson became a railroad engineer, but he and his brother, William Powers, died young and unmarried in freak accidents; Burnside (or Birnie) taught school and supported himself as a sign painter; Edwin Andress, a violinist, and his brother, Charles Fremont, a printer, lived in Chicago where Edwin also supported himself as a sign painter.

Among the Wolfe sisters, Jennie graduated from the University of Michigan with a nursing degree; Arvilla Aurelia (or "Tissie") (Wolfe) Emerson was a professional pianist; Clara Belle (Wolfe) Joyce Perry became a newspaperwoman like her sisters, Esther Eliza ("Ettie") (Wolfe) Wilson, Jessie Annie (Wolfe) Hilton, and Stella Minnie (Wolfe) Champney Grieshaber; Mabel Helen (Wolfe) Bennett did not have a profession outside of her home.

Thus, the Wolf/Wolfe clan distinguished itself as the "First Family of Northport."

Discharge Papers

To all whom it may Concern.

Know ye, That _William Isaacs_ a _Privt_ of Captain _James S. DeLand_ Company, (K) _First_ Regiment of _Michigan Sharpshooters_ **VOLUNTEERS,** who was enrolled on the _Eleventh_ day of _May_ one thousand eight hundred and _Sixty three_ to serve _three_ years or during the war, is hereby **Discharged** from the service of the United States this _Twenty Eighth_ day of _July_, 1865, at _Delany House D.C._ by reason of _S.C.o No 178 AG.O Wars Dept. Washington July 24 1.6_ (_No objection to his being re-enlisted is known to exist._)

Said _William Isaacs_ was born in _Isabella co_ in the State of _Michigan_, is _Twenty_ years of age, _Five_ feet _Nine_ inches high, _Dark_ complexion, _black_ eyes, _black_ hair, and by occupation, when enrolled, a _Farmer_

Given at _Delany House_ this _August Eighth_ day of _July_ 1865

☞ *This sentence will be erased should there be anything in the conduct or physical condition of the soldier rendering him unfit for the Army.

[A. G. O., No. 99.]

Sylvester Keyser
Capt & Brevt Lt Col A D Co
Commanding the Reg't.
1st Div 9 A.C.

James S. DeLand
Capt Co K 1st M.S.S
Comdg Co.

Regular discharge paper of Private William Isaacs, Company K, First Michigan Sharpshooters. Copy of the original paper that is held in the Clarke Historical Library, Central Michigan University, Mt. Pleasant, Isabella County.

ARMY OF THE UNITED STATES.

CERTIFICATE

OF DISABILITY   FOR DISCHARGE

Private Jacob Collins, of Captain _____
_____ Company, (_K_) of the _1st Mich S.S._ Regiment of the United States
Volunteers was enlisted by _W. J. Driggs_ _____ of
the _____ Regiment of _June_ at _East Saginaw Mich_
on the _Tenth_ day of _June_, 186_3_ to serve _Three_ years; he was born
in _____ in the State of _____, is _____
years of age, _____ feet _____ inches high, _____ complexion, _____ eyes,
_____ hair, and by occupation when enlisted a _____ During the last two
months said soldier has been unfit for duty _____ days.* _____

From Partial Description List for A.G.O.

STATION: _Campbell Hospital D.C._
DATE: _March 29th 1865._   _Ed B Rossiter_
                                            Lieut Vet Res Corps
                                            ──Commanding Company.──

I CERTIFY, that I have carefully examined the said _Jacob Collins_
of Captain _____ "_K_" Company, and find him incapable of performing the duties of a
soldier because of † _Partial loss of use of left arm_
from G.S.W. received in battle. He
is unfit for the V.R.C.
Disability total

                                            A Shuecten
                                            _____ Surgeon. U S

◆──◆◆◆◆──◆

DISCHARGED, this _Thirteenth_ day of _April_, 186_5_, at _Campbell_
U.S. Gen Hospital Washington D.C.
                                            A Shuecten
                                            Surgeon U.S. in charg
                                            ──Commanding the Reg't.──

The _Soldier_ desires to be _addressed_ at
      Town _Saginaw_ County _Saginaw_ State _Michigan_

* See Note 1 on the back of this.   † See Note 2 on the back of this
[A. G. O. No. 100 & 101—First.]   [DUPLICATES.]

Certificate of disability for discharge for Private Jacob Collins, Company K,
First Michigan Sharpshooters. National Archives, Washington, DC.

475

Photographs

CERTIFICATE IN LIEU OF LOST OR DESTROYED
DISCHARGE CERTIFICATE

CIVIL WAR
JAN 22 1920

To all Whom it May Concern:

Know ye, That *Thomas Kechittigo* a *Sergeant* of *Company K,* *First* Regiment of *Michigan Sharpshooters* VOLUNTEERS, who was *enrolled* on the *third* day of *May*, one thousand *eight* hundred and *sixty-three*, to serve *three years* was **Discharged** from the service of the United States on the *Twenty-eighth* day of *July*, one thousand *eight* hundred and *sixty-five*, by reason of *Muster out of company.*

This Certificate is given under the provisions of the Act of Congress approved July 1, 1902, "to authorize the Secretary of War to furnish certificates in lieu of lost or destroyed discharges," to honorably discharged officers or enlisted men or their widows, upon evidence that the original discharge certificate has been lost or destroyed, and upon the condition imposed by said Act that this certificate "shall not be accepted as a voucher for the payment of any claim against the United States for pay, bounty, or other allowances, or as evidence in any other case."

Given at the War Department, Washington, D. C., this *first* day of *February*, one thousand nine hundred and *thirteen*

By authority of the Secretary of War:

LAW DIVISION
JAN 10 192_

(A. G. O. 150)

W H Ladd
Adjutant General.

004309

Certificate in lieu of lost or destroyed discharge certificate of Sergeant Thomas Kechittigo, Company K, First Michigan Sharpshooters. National Archives, Washington, DC.

Capt. Edwin V. Andress, Company K, First Michigan Sharpshooters (courtesy
of the Burton Historical Collection, Detroit Public Library)

First Lieutenant William J. Driggs, Company K, First Michigan Sharpshooters
(courtesy of the Burton Historical Collection, Detroit Public Library)

Second Lieutenant Garret A. Graveraet, Company K, First Michigan Sharpshooters (courtesy of the Bentley Historical Library, University of Michigan, Ann Arbor)

Henry G. Graveraet, Company K, First Michigan Sharpshooters (courtesy of the Bentley Historical Library, University of Michigan, Ann Arbor)

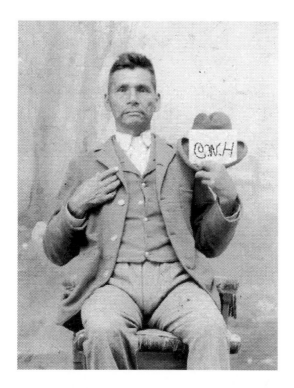

Cornelius W. Hall, Company K, First Michigan Sharpshooters
(courtesy of the Carol Ardis family collection)

Florence (Nibnesey Hill) Hall, wife of Cornelius W. Hall (courtesy of the Carol Ardis family collection)

Cornelius W. Hall, Company K, First Michigan Sharpshooters and grandchildren. Circa 1903.
(Courtesy of the Wexford County Historical Society Museum.)

Thomas Kechittigo, Company K, First Michigan Sharpshooters and his wife, Mary
(Campau Elke) Kechittigo. Circa 1915. (National Archives, Washington, DC.)

Leon Otashquabono, Company K, First Michigan Sharpshooters (courtesy of the Burton Historical Collection, Detroit Public Library)

Marcus Otto, Company K, First Michigan Sharpshooters (courtesy of the Simon Otto collection)

Aaron Pequongay (Aaron Sargonquatto), Company K, First Michigan Sharpshooters, his wife, Susan (Allen) Pequongay, and daughter and grandson. Circa 1915. (Courtesy of the Collections of the Grand Rapids Public Museum.)

Joseph Poneshing (Joseph Tazhedewin), Company K, First Michigan Sharpshooters and his family. Circa 1914. (Courtesy of the Grand Rapids History and Special Collections, Archives, Grand Rapids Public Library, Grand Rapids, Michigan.)

HENRY CONDECON

Henry Wassagezhic (Henry Condecon), Company K, First Michigan Sharpshooters.
Picture from the booklet *Proceedings of the La Pointe band of Chippewa Indians
in General Council and Assembled at Odanah, Wisconsin, 1907.*

Thomas Wezoo, Company K, First Michigan Sharpshooters, his wife, Rosa (Johnson)
Wezoo, and daughter, Elizabeth (courtesy of the Alberta Wells family collection)

Payson Wolf, Company K, First Michigan Sharpshooters
(courtesy of the Avis D. Wolfe family collection)

Mary Jane (Smith) Wolf, wife of Payson Wolf (courtesy
of the Avis D. Wolfe family collection)

Selected Names for Handwriting Analysis

The analysis of a man's signature can tell a lot about his personality. For the task of interpreting a sample of handwriting from seventeen men of Company K, the author chose Mrs. Geraldine Moore Schram, who is an internationally renowned master certified graphoanalyst. Her handwriting analysis is amazing.

Among Mrs. Schram's many certifications, memberships, honors, and awards are the following: diploma, master in graphoanalysis from the International Graphoanalysis Society; registered professional document examiner, World Association of Document Examiners; court-qualified state of Michigan—Circuit Court; certified facility officer—Defense Industrial Security Program for Defense Investigative Service, Washington, DC—administered by Department of the Army—Newport News, Virginia, for Department of Defense Programs, secret clearance and COMSEC manager; professional memberships in the American Society of Industrial Security, National Security Institute, Michigan Chapter of Graphoanalysis, of which she was president 1987–89, 1979–1981, and the World Association of Document Examiners; international seminar lecture presentations, including "Anger—Second Most Powerful Force" International Professionals—Teachers—Postgraduates and "Terrorist-Terrorism-Business," which addresses the similarities of gangs and terrorists.

Mrs. Schram was also recognized as Michigan Graphoanalyst of the Year, 1978, and International Graphoanalyst of the Year, 1994.

Her many publications include: *Suicide Profile*, 1985; *Insights Seminar Book of Signatures*, 1984; *Personalities at Risk*, 1994; and *Disabled Personalities*, 2013.

Signature Analysis of Seventeen Men Selected from Company K

1. **Charles Allen:** 1863—Although very intelligent with a strong ability to focus on one thing at a time, everything had an emotional impact on Charles. He

was very honest and would not give in to pressure when he started, but by 1863, this had changed. He felt like he was being taken advantage of, and it created an anger that could influence his ability to hear other sides of a situation. His experiences influenced his opinion, and that was not going to change. By the later part of 1863, he was feeling more insignificant. His sense of caution became a self-blame for something that happened. It was a form of self-punishment and completely nonproductive for him and did not mean he was actually responsible. It was only what he believed.

2. **Joseph Ashkanok:** 1894—Joseph was honest and responsible in his obligations. Although he had difficulty with persons who acted with authority, whether it was real or not, it was a source of stress for him and many times promoted feelings of anger. He loved to learn and became restless if learning was not available. He was a problem solver and could identify a situation well before others became aware of it. He was not realistic with something that directly affected him. Thus he tended to change to fit what he felt and wanted. He had a minor tremor, which may have been stress. By 1898, Joseph had very strong emotions here with a strong need for personal recognition. He started out proud and now feels insignificant. Although his mental process is still very strong, he feels less hopeful. He wanted to be liked but would fight to survive.

3. **Louis Gibson:** 1864—Strong mental fluidity with the ability to mentally move from one avenue of thought to another without any hesitation or loss of original information. There was much worry and anxiety here. Worry is founded in real situations, anxiety is in what doesn't exist and did not actually happen. Anxiety is a misplaced imagination and a waste of energy. He did not give up regardless of how negative a situation appeared to be. Strong emotions contributed to his drive to accomplish despite circumstances. Very intelligent but preferred to have as much information as possible before making a decision, which made him appear slow to respond when under pressure. It added to his need for recognition and many times the misunderstanding of others.

4. **Garret Graveraet:** 1864—Garret had a strong dislike for someone he was working with at the time and as a result tried not to think about the circumstances involved. A lack of trust in others allowed him to be independent in his decisions. He had a strong temper, which he kept under control most of the time, yet a

release of this could be astounding. He did not feel accepted for who he was even in his own family. He was very intelligent with a natural writing talent and creativity, which made him feel out of step with many others. Garret had a strong ability to argue a point that was a form of release for him. He never felt that his mother (or dominant female in his developing years) cared for him and that the dominant male did not defend him when he needed to be defended. Garret was a very strong individual despite these feelings.

5. **Henry Graveraet Jr.:** 1863—There was evidence of frustration. He preferred things to be orderly and attractive, and a totally messy environment was a real harassment to him. He had the ability to know things without reading about them or being told. This was a form of ESP, which is rare. Along with the ESP was a creative ability in music and math or numbers. This combination made him feel isolated. He believed that he was being asked to do more than he was receiving back in appreciation, and still felt that he did not have the right to refuse or to say no to others. He could then become stubborn, which worked against his reasoning and intelligence and caused him to be afraid to share his ideas and perceptions.

6. **Jacob Greensky:** 1864—Very honest and put more value on personal information and communication than on what would be considered business, effort or military. His value rested only on his opinion and decision. There was anxiety here that increased for him because he refused to listen to other people's ideas. He had difficulty being with persons different from himself. This was because he had difficulty with his identity and felt that his family was more important than he was. As a result, he would mentally resist authority figures, especially if they embarrassed him. This sample of his signature indicated that he had some help or guidance.

7. **Cornelius Hall:** 1864—As with Jacob Greensky, Cornelius felt that his father and family were more important than he was. Even though he was intelligent, he felt everything was a competition, and on a personal basis, he would use communication to try to get something for himself. He would not give in easily and was uncomfortable working with his hands. 1892—Anxiety strong here, still being very honest and not using communication in a negative manner. Good memory in

keeping details but needed someone he could rely on. There is evidence that he was less stressed working with his hands now.

8. **James H. Hamlin:** 1864—Was direct and honest in his personal communication. He was also self-conscious about his mental process and his ability to investigate mentally and be correct. He dealt with only what was evident, and added to this was an excellent ability with details, which he never forgot. James felt strongly that his father (family) did not contribute to his development and that he was solely responsible. He did not hold onto emotional feelings very long; these were quickly replaced by current happenings, and the past feelings forgotten. He had a strong artistic ability and line value.

9. **John Jacko:** 1891—Only signature number three was dated. He had the ability to know if someone was being untruthful. He was very honest, and as "John" the individual, he liked responsibility. Signature number two indicated some neurological tremor that was not evident in the other two signatures. His identity needs were very strong, and by 1891 he felt even more insignificant and more emotionally stressed. Yet, through all of it, he remained straightforward and honest in all communication and responsibility.

10. **Josiah Light:** 1863–1869—Very fluid thinking. He had the ability to see opportunity and to take the first step toward it. What held him back was his belief that he truly was alone and alienated from his immediate family. In signature number two, he had lost his self-confidence and identity as Josiah. As a result, temper had developed to handle this deprivation. His deep emotions and attention to details did not allow him to forget the incidents that contributed to this downfall. As a result, he was in constant turmoil inside and would only trust one person at a time.

11. **Leon Otashquabono:** 1894—In signature one, his emotional response was strong and stayed with him for a significant amount of time. He had a strong temper that he kept under control, but if he thought someone was taking advantage of him, he would vent verbally and could be physical as well. Although he was very honest, he had his own opinion on everything. He also had ESP, and the difference here is that he relied on it. In signature two, his temper was more out of control, and he developed aggressive behavior but with less emotional drive. Leon was still very honest in his communication. His personal self-image had

weakened and became less strong. Writing was shakier with tremor, indicating some level of physical deterioration.

12. **Albert Pesherbay:** 1890—Albert felt that his paternal family was more important than he was and that he was insignificant. This opinion affected everything that he did. He was very creative and had a natural talent with music. Albert had difficulty with messy surroundings, which caused him anxiety. He preferred orderliness, which, to him, made everything less confusing. He was very honest and yet would not share the creative ideas that he had because of his lack of self-belief. To deal with this attitude, he had chosen to use a controlled temper. He did not like to be totally alone and yet felt socially isolated. As with a few of the other men, he had an ESP that he was afraid to use, which caused him more stress.

13. **Aaron Sargonquatto:** 1865–1900—Note: In all these signatures, none were spelled exactly the same; therefore all were examined in a forensic structure to determine authenticity. Usually, unless under extreme stress, individuals do not misspell their names. As a result, signatures two, three, and four were considered authentic. Aaron had the ability to concentrate and to focus on one issue at a time. Although intelligent, he preferred short-term projects and responsibility, which had an impact on his interest level. Emotionally he did not carry things from the past with him for long and yet was being held in a past event and waited for approval from the person involved. He needed to acquire things in order to feel worthwhile. Aaron was very honest in his communication and yet could be aggressive if the situation called for this behavior. He occasionally would overvalue himself, thought that he was better than others, and at the same time, felt that he was being used and not given recognition. There were major emotional changes in his final signature and most likely some physical changes.

14. **Antoine Scott:** 1863–1866–1873—Of the four signatures, one was retraced, two were not considered authentic, and one had evidence of minor guided hand and was authentic. Antoine was self-critical, and yet he could be very positive about what he emotionally believed. Therefore, he preferred to be more in control of events. Although he was positive in some ways, he was not a hopeful person. Antoine existed in the moment to make all of his decisions, and if his past became involved, his determination increased. If it meant that he had to be involved in a future event or push decisions, he became hesitant and not strong on follow-through. He did not share information but kept much to himself. He would not give up any critical information.

15. **Henry Waasegiizhig:** 1894—Henry had finger dexterity and creativity but not full hand dexterity. He loved to learn and to question everything, which, in that era, probably caused him some problems. He was very open about everything and preferred being around people. Henry was not prejudiced, although he did have some very specific opinions. He liked change and preferred not to be stuck in the same learning situation for long periods. In signature number two, he was even more modest and was feeling socially alone. Henry did not give in easily and yet would not give himself credit for his strengths.

16. **Joseph Wakazoo:** *Minister*—1907—He argued his point and added additional reasoning with what he considered facts. He was capable of analyzing but tended to hold it in control. Joseph liked physical movement and needed to be around people. He did not do well if alone too long. Isolation was a stress for him. Although he liked people in general, he had difficulty with anyone who appeared to be a know-it-all. He had the ability to see and identify opportunity and then take the first step to work toward its success. There were minor neurological tremors indicated also. He preferred to be identified as responsible and accepted additional responsibility without being asked.

17. **Payson Wolf:** 1862–1864–1866–Note: One 1862 and one 1864 signature were not his. He preferred to be responsible for what was around him. There was something that happened to him that he had difficulty facing directly, and so he, only in his mind, changed the event so that he could handle this issue more comfortably. He needed and wanted recognition for being strong and not giving in to extreme pressure. Although he liked being with people, he was emotionally and mentally stuck in a past event that caused him to feel ignored and to not really experience present time. This happened to him between the ages of five and eight. The need for approval and closure of this event was with him all the time and influenced his decision even in the military. Payson had a unique ability to understand others' needs and ideas.

Summary: Although writing samples were minimal, it was very interesting to note the many similarities in these men. They were honest, responsible, and intelligent, and for the most part, very creative. Holding information to themselves was also a common thread. Their isolation and loneliness were evident in all them. There was no deceit toward their superiors or their families. Yet communication and understanding had to be difficult and stressful for all them. In addition to all their experiences, not being able to understand their creative abilities, along with a lack of personal recognition and ability to use their creativity, must have been emotionally and mentally difficult for all them.

Geraldine Schram
Certified Master Graphoanalyst
Registered Forensic Document Examiner

Bibliography

Primary Resources Researched for All Files

Civil War Compiled Military Service Records, carded Military Medical Records and Military Pension Files located at the National Archives in Washington, DC.

The Descriptive Roll of Company K, First Regiment, Michigan Sharpshooters in the Archives of the State of Michigan, Lansing, Ingham County.

Births, marriages, and deaths (Vital Records) reported by both church and state records in the Library of the State of Michigan, Lansing, Ingham County.

County Probate and Vital Records held at the Family History Library of the Church of Jesus Christ of Latter-Day Saints, Midland, Midland County.

Grand Army of the Republic (GAR) veteran organization (or Posts) in the various counties. Microfilm located in the Archives of the State of Michigan in Lansing, Ingham County.

Gruett, Philip. 1868 Saginaw Chippewa Index (family associations and genealogy) held at the Clarke Historical Library located on the ground floor of Parke Library on the campus of Central Michigan University in Mt. Pleasant, Isabella County.

Land Records. Internet records listed in the files found in BLM-GLO (Bureau of Land Management, General Land Office, US Department of the Interior).

Genealogy, Family Trees and Family History Records online—at Ancestry.com.

Research in newspapers, magazines, and books at the Hoyt Public Library in Saginaw, Saginaw County; and the State of Michigan Library, Lansing, Ingham County.

Secondary Sources Researched for the Following Files

Andress, Edwin V. Captain

Bollett, Dr. Alfred Jay. *Civil War Medicine Challenges and Triumphs*, 314. Tucson, Arizona: Galen Press, 2002.

Evans, Dr. Bruce A. *A Primer of Civil War Medicine—Non Surgical Medical Practice during the Civil War Years*, 49, 65. Knoxville, Tennessee: Bohemian Publishers, 1998.

Hartwick and Tuller. *1890 Oceana County Pioneers and Business Men of to Day*.

Hooppell Family Genealogy on Ancestry.com. Internet search.

Schaadt, Dr. Mark J. *Civil War Medicine—An Illustrated History*, 67–68. Quincy, Illinois: Cedarwood Publishing, 1998.

Graveraet, Garrett A., Second Lieutenant

Bailly. *Descendants of Joseph Bailly*—Roots Web.com—Internet Search.

Bollet, Dr. Alfred Jay. *Civil War Medicine Challenges and Triumphs*. Galen Press, Tucson, Arizona, 2003, p. 93.

Cemetery. Conversations with the office staff of the Historic Congressional Cemetery, Washington, DC.

Detroit *Advertiser and Tribune*—post Graveraet death (June 30, 1864) announcement. Clarke Historical Library, Central Michigan University, Mt. Pleasant. Courtesy of the Clarke Historical Library.

Graveraet. *Graveraet Family Genealogy* at Ancestry.com. Internet search.

Herek From Buckbee. Raymond J. Herek. *These Men Have Seen Hard Service*, Wayne State University Press, Detroit, Michigan, 1998, p. 150. From the Memoirs of Julian Edward Buckbee Private collection of John Buckbee.

Kuz, Dr. Julian and Dr. Bradley P. Bengtson. *Orthopaedic Injuries of the Civil War*, Kennesaw Mountain Press, Inc., Kennesaw, Georgia, 1996, pp. 28, 37.

Lefevere 1. http://archives.nd/edu/calendar/c184509.htm

1845 Sep. 3

(Graveraet, Sophie) (?): Point St/ Ignace, Michigan)

to (Bishop Peter Paul Lefevere.: Detroit, Michigan)

She gives a report of the Catholic school at Point St. Ignace with a list of the boys and girls and their ages. They improve in their studies. Some, especially the older boys, do not attend regularly because obliged to attend to fishing and other labors.

III-2-h-A.D. unsigned - 1 p. - 4to. - (20) University of Notre Dame Archives: Online Calendar – University of Notre Dame, South Bend Indiana.

Lefevere 2. http://archives.nd.edu/calendar/c184709.htm
1847 Sep 20
Graveraet, Sophie: Mackinac, (Michigan)
to Bishop (Peter Paul) Lefev(e)re,: (Detroit, Michigan)

Mrs. Graveraet's husband wishes to move from Point St. Ignace with their family but has not yet fully decided to do so. He can get into no business there and her salary, which both think too small, is all they have to depend on. She would like to remain and asks that her wages be increased to twelve dollars a month. If Lefevere sees fit to do so, she will agree to remain.

III-2-h – A.L.S. - 1p. - 8vo. - (1) University of Notre Dame Archives: Online Calendar-University of Notre Dame, South Bend, Indiana.

Lefevere 3. http://archives.nd.edu/calendar/c184805.htm
1848 May 12
Graveraet, Sophie: Mackinac, (Michigan)
to Bishop P(eter) P(aul) Lefevere: (Detroit, Michigan)

Mrs. Graveraet acknowledges the receipt of Lefevere's letter of May 3 enclosing a certificate of deposit for $36. She will continue to keep the school in the best possible order and make the report as he requests. The school is doing very well. In a postscript she adds that a blank receipt is enclosed (no enclosures).

III-2-h – A.L.S. - 1p. - 8vo. - (1). University of Notre Dame Archives: Online Calendar –University of Notre Dame, South Bend, Indiana.

Medical. Chapter IX, "Wounds And Injuries of the Upper Extremities," Section IV, "Injuries of the Shaft of the Humerus" in *Medical and Surgical History of the War of the Rebellion 1861–1865, Part II, Volume II,* 51; and "Amputations of the Arm—Fatal Cases," in *Volume X of Medical and Surgical History of the War of the Rebellion, 1861–1865,* 801.

Smith, Emerson R. papers. *Our Country and the Civil War May 18, 1961.* Courtesy of the Bentley Library, University of Michigan, Ann Arbor.

Agahgo, Charles, Private

Baraga, Frederick. *A Dictionary of the Ojibway Language*, Minnesota Historical Press, St. Paul, New Material, 1992, p. 179.

Bollet, Dr. Alfred Jay. *Civil War Medicine Challenges and Triumphs.* Galen Press, Tucson, Arizona, 2003, pp. 201–202;

Ibid., pp. 233, 235.

Encyclopedia of Death and Dying, Civil War, US, p. 5. Internet search.

Evans, Dr. Bruce A. *A Primer of Civil War Medicine-Non Surgical Medical Practice during the Civil War Years.* Bohemian Publishers, Knoxville, Tennessee, 1998, p. 100.

Medical. *Medical And Surgical History Of The War Of The Rebellion, 1861-1865, Volume VI - Erysipelas, Case 29*, p. 671.

Rutkow, Dr. Ira M. *Bleeding Blue and Gray—Civil War Surgery and The Evolution of American Medicine.* Random House, New York, 2005, p. 26.

Allen, Charles, Sergeant

Catalogue. *Catalogue of the Instructors and Students of Twinsburg Institute for the Academic Year Commencing April 9, 1860 and ending March 9, 1861. Twinsburg Historical Society, 8996 Darrow Road, Twinsburg, Ohio.* S. and J. Featherstone Publishers, Cleveland, Ohio, 1861. The Catalogue roster lists Charles Allen from Grand Traverse, Michigan for that school year. Courtesy of the Twinsburg Historical Society.

Clifton, James A., Cornell, George L., and McClurken, James. *People of the Three Fires The Ottawa, Potawatomi and Ojibway of Michigan*, Grand Rapids Inter-Tribal Council, 1986, p. 31.

Craker, Ruth. *The First Protestant Mission In the Grand Traverse Region.* Rivercrest House, Mt. Pleasant, Michigan, 1979, pp. 50, 66, 69.

Dougherty, Rev. Peter. *Minutes of the Old Mission and New Mission (Grove Hill) Church 1843–1871.* Indian Mission Church (Grand Traverse Bay, Mich.) Session minutes and statement of organization, 1843–1871, including: session minutes by Rev, Peter Dougherty, 1843–1871; with statement of organization (1 vol.). From sources held at the Presbyterian Historical Society, Philadelphia, Pennsylvania. Call Number: UPPERVAULT V M146 G7644.

Guide. Conversations with an interpreter and guide at Fredericksburg National Battlefield Park, Fredericksburg, Virginia.

Ibid.

Captain. Sixth US Cavalry, Brig. – Gen. US Volunteers. *Customs of Service For Non-Commissioned Officers and Soldiers Practiced In The Army Of The United States.* Philadelphia, J. B. Lippincott and Co., 1864, pp. 419 to 436, "The First Sergeant."

Ibid.

Noodin, Dr. Margaret Ann, Associate Professor of English and American Indian Studies, University of Wisconsin, Milwaukee. Conversations with Dr. Noodin.

Reed, Dr. William Howard. *Hospital Life in the Army of the Potomac, Chapter II.* Boston, Massachusetts, 1866.

Ibid.

Ibid.

Ibid.

Romig, Walter. *Michigan Place Names.* Detroit: Wayne State University Press, 1986.

Roy, Dr. Caroline Helen Peltier, Instructor of Ojibwe language, Saginaw Chippewa Indian Tribe, Mt. Pleasant, Isabella County, Michigan. Conversations with Dr. Roy.

Schaadt, Dr. Mark J. *Civil War Medicine—An Illustrated History.* Cedarwood Publishing, Quincy, Illinois, 1998, pp. 59–60.

Tanner, Dr. Helen Hornbeck. *Mapping the Grand Traverse Indian Country—The Contributions of Peter Dougherty.* Leelanau Press, Glen Arbor, Michigan, 2009, p. 3. Conversations with Dr. Tanner.

Amderling, Peter, Private

Blakiston's Illustrated Pocket Medical Dictionary. McGraw-Hill Book Company, Inc., 1952, p. 393.

Bollet, Dr. Alfred Jay. *Civil War Medicine Challenges and Triumphs.* Galen Press, Ltd. Tucson, Arizona, 2002, p. 235.

Pfanz, Donald C. *The Depot Field Hospital At City Point, Virginia,* 1988.

Andrew, John, Private

Evans, Dr. Bruce A. *A Primer of Civil War Medicine—non Surgical Medical Practice during the Civil War Years.* Bohemian Publishers, Knoxville, Tennessee, 1998, p. 65.

Reuter, Dorothy. *Methodist Indian Ministries in Michigan 1830-1990*. Eerdmans Printing Company, Grand Rapids, Michigan, 1993, p. 294. Conversations with Mrs. Dorothy Reuter.

Rutkow, Dr. Ira M. *Bleeding Blue and Gray—Civil War Surgery and the Evolution of American Medicine*. Random House, New York, 2005, p. 238.

Schaadt, Dr. Mark J. *Civil War Medicine—An Illustrated History*. Cedarwood Publishing, Quincy, Illinois, 1998, pp. 67–68.

Aptargeshick, Oliver, Private

Blakiston's Illustrated Pocket Medical Dictionary. McGraw-Hill Book Company, Inc., 1952, p. 168.

Bollet, Dr. Alfred Jay. *Civil War Medicine Challenges and Triumphs*. Galen Press, Tucson, Arizona, 2003, pp. 235–236.

Ibid., p. 308.

Ibid.

Ibid.

Encyclopedia of Death and Dying, Civil War, US, p 5. Internet search.

Evans, Dr. Bruce A. *A Primer of Civil War Medicine—Non Surgical Medical Practice during the Civil War Years*. Bohemian Publishers, Knoxville, Tennessee, 1998, p 92.

Arwonogezice, James, Private

Baraga, Frederick. *A Dictionary of the Ojibway Language*. Minnesota Historical Press, St. Paul, New Material, 1992, pp. 132, 402.

Reuter, Dorothy. *Methodist Indian Ministries In Michigan 1830–1990*. Eerdmands Printing Company, Grand Rapids, Michigan, 1993, p. 158. Conversations with Mrs. Dorothy Reuter.

Ibid., p. 152.

Ashkanak, Joseph, Private

Blakiston's Illustrated Pocket Medical Dictionary. McGraw-Hill Book Company, Inc., 1952, p. 76.

Evans, Dr. Bruce A. *A Primer of Civil War Medicine—Non Surgical Medical Practice during the Civil War Years*. Bohemian Publishers, Knoxville, Tennessee, 1998, p. 65.

Holy Cross. *Holy Cross Catholic Church Family Records (1869–1895)*. Archives of Holy Cross Catholic Church at Cross Village, Emmet County. Conversations with Father Albert Langheim OFM.

Langheim, Father Albert OFM. *The Catholic Mission At Cross Village The First 200 Years—Anamiewatigoing (or Prayer Place Near the Cross)*. Conversations with Father Langheim.

Schaadt, Dr. Mark J. *Civil War Medicine—An Illustrated History*. Cedarwood Publishing, Quincy, Illinois, 1998, pp. 67–68

Ashkebug, George, Private

Baraga, Frederick. *A Dictionary Of The Ojibway Language*. Minnesota Historical Press, St. Paul, New Material, 1992, p. 49.

Blakiston's Illustrated Pocket Medical Dictionary. McGraw-Hill Book Company, Inc., 1952, p. 326.

Schaadt, Dr. Mark J. *Civil War Medicine—An Illustrated History*. Cedarwood Publishing, Quincy, Illinois, 1998, pp. 67–68.

Ashkebugnekay, Amos, Private

Potter, Jerry O. *The Sultana Tragedy America's Greatest Maritime Disaster*. Pelican Publishing Company, Gretna, Louisiana, 1992, p. 83.

Ibid., p. 84.

Land Records.

Ashman, Daniel, Corporal

Dorwart, Dr. Bonnie Brice. *Death Is In The Breeze: Disease during The American Civil War*. Bonnie Brice Dorwart, M.D., and the National Museum of Civil War Medicine, Frederick, Maryland, 2009, p. 51.

Encyclopedia of Death and Dying, Civil War, US, p. 5. Internet search.

Ibid.

Fancher, Honorable Isaac A. *Past and Present of Isabella County, 1911*, p. 79.

Something About Everything Military—The Life of a Drummer, pp. 1–4. Internet Search.

Ibid.

Ibid.

Awanaquad, Petros, Private

Bollet, Dr. Alfred Jay. *Civil War Medicine Challenges and Triumphs.* Galen Press, Tucson, Arizona, 2003, pp. 236–237.

Ibid., p. 233.

Encyclopedia of Death and Dying, Civil War, US, p. 5. Internet search.

Ibid.

Evans, Dr. Bruce A. *A Primer of Civil War Medicine—Non Surgical Medical Practice during the Civil War Years.* Bohemian Publishers, Knoxville, Tennessee, 1998, p. 108.

Schaadt, Dr. Mark J. *Civil War Medicine—An Illustrated History.* Cedarwood Publishing, Quincy, Illinois, 1998, pp. 52, 53.

Ibid., p. 69.

Benasis, John, Private

Baraga, Frederick. *A Dictionary of the Ojibway Language.* Minnesota Historical Press, St. Paul, New Material, 1992, p. 86.

Lafernier—Conversations with and information from Susan Lafernier.

Reuter, Dorothy. *Methodist Indian Ministries in Michigan 1830–1990.* Eerdmans Printing Company, Grand Rapids, Michigan, 1993, p. 351. Conversations with Mrs. Dorothy Reuter.

Bennett, Louis, Private

Beaubien Family. Internet Search for Beaubien or Beaubin on RootsWeb at Nishnawbe-L Archives and the Morrow Family Tree on myfamily.com in Ancestry.com. Internet search.

Ibid.

Blakiston's Illustrated Pocket Medical Dictionary. McGraw-Hill Book Company, Inc., 1952, p. 555.

Records of the Office of the Judge Advocate General (Army). Record Group 153, 1692–1981 (bulk 1800–1967), National Archives, Washington, DC.

Burns, Peter, Private

Bollet, Dr. Alfred Jay. *Civil War Medicine Challenges and Triumphs* Galen Press, Ltd. Tucson, Arizona, 2002, p. 233.

Ibid.

Evans, Dr. Bruce A. *A Primer of Civil War Medicine-Non Surgical Medical Practice during the Civil War Years.* Bohemian Publishers, Knoxville, Tennessee, 1998, p. 104.

Bushaw, Augustus, Private

Bollet, Dr. Alfred Jay. *Civil War Medicine Challenges and Triumphs.* Galen Press, Ltd., Tucson, Arizona 2002, p. 233.

Ibid.

Ibid., p. 238.

Ibid., p. 308.

Evans, Dr. Bruce A. *A Primer of Civil War Medicine-Non Surgical Medical Practice during the Civil War Years.* Bohemian Publishers, Knoxville, Tennessee, 1998, p. 104.

Ibid., p. 109.

Cabecoung, William, Private

Baraga, Frederick. *A Dictionary Of the Ojibway Language.* Minnesota Historical Press, St. Paul, New Material, 1992, pp. 179, 180.

Bollet, Dr. Alfred Jay. *Civil War Medicine Challenges and Triumphs.* Galen Press, Ltd. Tucson, Arizona, 2002, p. 232.

Evans, Dr. Bruce A. *A Primer of Civil War Medicine-Non Surgical Medical Practice during the Civil War Years.* Bohemian Publishers, Knoxville, Tennessee, 1998, p. 107.

Schaadt, Dr. Mark J. *Civil War Medicine—An Illustrated History.* Cedarwood Publishing, Quincy, Illinois, 1998, pp. 90, 91.

Carter, Charles, Private

American Indians in Maryland. Internet search.

Encyclopedia of Death and Dying, Civil War, US, p. 4. Internet search.

Nanticoke/Southern Delaware: Native Languages of the Americas—History of the Nanticoke (Southern Delaware) tribe—Internet search.

Chamberalin, Amos, Private

Avery, Chad. Conversations with Chad Avery, Anishinabe genealogist and historian.

Bollet, Dr. Alfred Jay. *Civil War Medicine Challenges and Triumphs.* Galen Press, Tucson Arizona, 2003, pp. 233 and 236.

Ibid., p. 238

Ibid., p. 236.

Gruett, Philip. *The 1868 Saginaw Chippewa Index.* (see Primary Resources Researched) p. 35.

Kautz, August V. *The 1865 Customs of Service for Non-commissioned Officers and Soldiers.* Stackpole Books, Mechanicsburg, Pennsylvania, p. 95, section #288.

Land Records.

Chatfield, Charles, Private

Bollet, Dr. Alfred Jay. *Civil War Medicine Challenges and Triumphs.* Galen Press, Tucson, Arizona, 2003, p. 232.

Ibid., pp. 233, 235.

Ibid., 233, 236

Dorwart, Dr. Bonnie Brice. *Death Is In The Breeze: Disease during the American Civil War.* Bonnie Brice Dorwart, M.D. and the National Museum of Civil War Medicine, Frederick, Maryland, 2009, p. 51.

Evans, Dr. Bruce A. *A Primer of Civil War Medicine—Non Surgical Medical Practice during the War Years.* Bohemian Publishers, Knoxville, Tennessee, 1998, p. 65.

Gruett, Philip. *The 1868 Saginaw Chippewa Index* (see Primary Resources Researched) p. 303.

Ibid., p. 51.

Ibid.

Land Records.

Ibid.

Schaadt, Dr. Mark J. *Civil War Medicine—An Illustrated History.* Cedarwood Publishing, Quincy, Illinois, 1998, p. 68.

Chatfield, Samuel C., Private

Avery, Chad. Conversations with Mr. Chad Avery, Anishinabe genealogist and historian.

Encyclopedia of Death and Dying, Civil War, US, p. 4. Internet search.

Gruet, Philip. *The 1868 Saginaw Chippewa Index* (see Primary Resources Researched), p. 38.

Ibid., p. 211.

Land Records.

Reuter, Dorothy. *Methodist Indian Ministries in Michigan 1830–1990*. Eerdman's Printing Company, Grand Rapids, Michigan, 1993, p. 108. Conversations with Mrs. Dorothy Reuter.

Church, Albert, Private

Schaadt, Dr. Mark J. *Civil War Medicine-An Illustrated History*. Cedarwood Publishing, Quincy, Illinois, 1998, p. 95.

Collins, Jacob, Private

Bollet, Dr. Alfred Jay. *Civil War Medicine Challenges and Triumphs*. Galen Press, Tucson, Arizona, 2003, pp. 101, 102.

Ibid., p. 101.

Kuz, Dr. Julian and Dr. Bradley P. Bengtson. *Orthopaedic Injuries of the Civil War*. Kennesaw Mountain Press, Inc., Kennesaw, Georgia, 1996, p. 28.

Schaadt, Dr. Mark J. *Civil War Medicine—An Illustrated History*. Cedarwood Publishing, Quincy, Illinois, 1998, pp. 67, 68.

Collins, John, Private

Avery, Chad. Conversations with Mr. Chad Avery, Anishinabe genealogist and historian.

Ibid.

Bollet, Dr. Alfred Jay. *Civil War Medicine Challenges and Triumphs*. Galen Press, Tucson, Arizona, 2003, pp. 235 and 240.

Evans, Dr. Bruce A. *A Primer of Civil War Medicine-Non Surgical Medical Practice during the Civil War Years*. Bohemian Publishers, Knoxville, Tennessee, 1998, p. 107.

Gruett, Philip. *The 1868 Saginaw Chippewa Index* (see Primary Resources researched), p. 302.

Ibid.-Bollet. pp. 236–237.

Internet search—*"Brief History of Mustard Plasters,"* p. 2.

Land Records.

Ibid.

Ibid.

Schaadt, Dr. Mark J. *Civil War Medicine—An Illustrated History*. Cedarwood Publishing, Quincy, Illinois, 1998, pp. 88, 90.

Collins, William, Corporal

Gruett, Philip. *The 1868 Saginaw Chippewa Index* (see Primary Resources Researched), p. 182.

Ibid., p. 33.

Land Records.

Newspaper (1.) *Bay City Tribune of* Bay City, Bay County, February 9, 1899.

Newspaper (2.) *Bay City Times* of Bay City, Bay County, February 9, 1899.

Ibid.

Corbin, George, Corporal

Avery, Chad. Conversations with Mr. Chad Avery, Anishinabe genealogist and historian.

Bollet, Dr. Alfred Jay. *Civil War Medicine Challenges and Triumphs.* Galen Press, Tucson, Arizona, 2003, p. 308.

Evans, Dr. Bruce A. A *Primer of Civil War Medicine—Non Surgical Medical Practice during the Civil War Years.* Bohemian Publishers, Knoxville, Tennessee, 1998, p. 103.

Ibid.-Evans, pp. 50, 71, 91, 106.

Ibid.-Evans, p. 94.

Ibid.-Evans.

Gruett, Philip. *The 1868 Saginaw Chippewa Index* (see Primary Resources Researched), p. 40.

Land Records.

Ibid.

Schaadt, Dr. Mark J. *Civil War Medicine—An Illustrated History.* Cedarwood Publishing Company, Quincy, Illinois, 1998, pp. 67, 68.

Crane, Amos, Private

Emory, Mrs. Gretchen. Conversations with and information from Mrs. Emory about Madash and Noquet history.

Lafernier, Susan. Conversations with and information from Susan Lafernier about the heirship estate of Amos Crane: The source of the heirship papers is: Department of the Interior, Office of Indian Affairs—*The heirship estate of Amos Crane, Mackinac Agency, L'Anse and Vieux Desert Reservation: Law-Heirship, 20545–15. C E T.*

Land Records.

Reuter, Dorothy. *Methodist Indian Ministries in Michigan 1830–1990*. Eerdmans Printing Company, Grand Rapids, Michigan, 1993, pp. 351, 352. Conversations with Mrs. Dorothy Reuter.

Dabasequam, Jonah, Private

Craker, Ruth. *The First Protestant Mission In the Grand Traverse Region*. Rivercrest House, Mt. Pleasant, Michigan, 1979, p. 50.

Encyclopedia of Death and Dying, Civil War, US, p. 4. Internet search.

Ibid.

Guide. Conversations with an interpreter and guide at Fredericksburg National Battlefield Park, Fredericksburg, Virginia.

David, John, Private

Avery, Chad. Conversations with Mr. Chad Avery, genealogist and Anishinabe historian.

Blakiston's Illustrated Pocket Medical Dictionary. McGraw-Hill Book Company, Inc., 1952., p. 765.

Encyclopedia of Death and Dying, Civil War, US, p. 5. Internet search.

Evans, Dr. Bruce A. *A Primer of Civil War Medicine—non Surgical Medical Practice during the Civil War Years*. Bohemian Publishers, Knoxville, Tennessee, 1998, p. 32.

Ibid., 33.

Ibid., 92.

Schaadt, Dr. Mark J. *Civil War Medicine—An Illustrated History*. Cedarwood Publishing, Quincy, Illinois, 1998, p. 88.

Ibid., p. 90.

Ibid., p. 95.

Ibid.

Dutton, Luther, Private

Avery, Chad. Conversations with Mr. Chad Avery, Anishinabe genealogist and historian.

Ibid.

Gruett, Philip. *The 1868 Saginaw Chippewa Index* (see Primary Resources Researched), p. 44.

Land Records.

Reuter, Dorothy. *Methodist Indian Ministries in Michigan 1830–1990*. Eerdmans Printing Company, Grand Rapids, Michigan, 1993, p. 125. Conversations with Mrs. Dorothy Reuter.

Schaadt, Dr. Mark J. *Civil War Medicine—An Illustrated History*. Cedarwood Publishing, Quincy, Illinois, 1998, p. 68.

Etarwegeshig, John, Private

Encyclopedia of Death and Dying, Civil War, US, p. 4. Internet search.

Ibid.

Guide. Conversations with an interpreter and guide at the Fredericksburg National Battlefield Park, Fredericksburg, Virginia.

Lee. Letter of George Lee, Indian agent, Office of Mackinaw Indian Agency (in Ypsilanti, Michigan) to the commissioner of Indian Affairs, Washington, DC. Letter dated June 22, 1877, and held in the collections of the Clarke Historical Library, Central Michigan University, Mt. Pleasant, Isabella County. Courtesy of the Clarke Historical Library.

Genereau Jr., Louis, Sergeant

Blakiston's Illustrated Pocket Medical Dictionary. McGraw-Hill Book Company, Inc., 1852, p. 250.

Bollet, Dr. Alfred Jay. Civil *War Medicine Challenges and Triumphs*. Galen Press, Tucson, Arizona, 2003, p. 213.

Evans, Dr. Bruce A. *A Primer of Civil War Medicine—non Surgical Medical Practice during the Civil War Years*. Bohemian Publishers, Knoxville, Tennessee, 1998. p. 33.

Genereau Family on Genealogy Wise—Internet search—posted by James P. LaLone, March 29, 2011.

Ibid.

Jackson, Michigan Prison Records, Michigan Department of State, State of Michigan Archives—Louis Genereau, May 25, 1840 to August 15, 1841.

Kuz, Dr. Julian and Dr. Bradley P. Bengtson. *Orthopaedic Injuries of the Civil War*, Kennesaw Mountain Press, Inc., Kennesaw, Georgia, 1996, p. 52.

Michigan Pioneer and Historical Collections—Made By the Pioneer Society of the State of Michigan, Wynkoop, Hollenbeck Crawford Company State Printers, 1908, Lewis Gen-ro, Vol. 10, p. 161.

Ibid.

Ibid.

Oral History. *The Tree That Never Dies, Oral History of the Michigan Indians*, edited by Pamela J. Dobson, Grand Rapids Public Library, Grand Rapids, Michigan, 1978, p. 129.

Schaadt, Dr. Mark J. *Civil War Medicine—An Illustrated History*. Cedarwood Publishing, Quincy, Illinois, 1998, pp. 67–68.

George, David, Private

Encyclopedia of Death and Dying, Civil War, US, p. 5. Internet search.

Gruett, Philip. *The 1868 Saginaw Chippewa Index* (see Primary Resources Researched), p. 172.

Land Records.

Medical and Surgical History of the War of the Rebellion—Part I, Volume II Chapter I.—Wounds And Injuries of the Head. Section III—Gunshot Contusions of the Cranial Bones, p. 120.

Schaadt, Dr. Mark J. *Civil War Medicine—An Illustrated History*. Cedarwood Publishing, Quincy, Illinois, 1998, pp. 67–68.

Gibson, Joseph L.

Craker, Ruth. *The First Protestant Mission In the Grand Traverse Region*. Rivercrest House, Mt. Pleasant, Michigan, 1979. p. 50.

Ibid., p. 66.

Ibid., p. 75.

Ibid., p. 71

Ibid., p. 70

Ibid., p. 71

Ibid.

Ibid., p. 77

Ibid., p. 74

Encyclopedia of Death and Dying, Civil War, U S, p. 5. Internet search.

Ibid.

Report. *Report of the Presbyterian Indian Mission School at Bear River, Emmet County as taught by Rev. Andrew Porter.* An enumeration of both boys and girls who were students at Porter's mission school for the first quarter of the year 1860 commencing January 3 and ending March 31. Source held at the Clarke

Historical Library, Central Michigan University, Mt. Pleasant, Isabella County. Courtesy of the Clarke historical Library.

Traverse. *The Traverse region, historical and descriptive, with illustrations of scenery and portraits and biographical sketches of some of its prominent men and pioneers.* Ann Arbor, Washtenaw County, Michigan: University of Michigan Library, 2005. p. 130.

Going, Samuel, Private

Encyclopedia of Death and Dying, Civil War, US, pp. 4–5. Internet search.

History 1. *History of Allegan and Barry Counties, Michigan With Illustrations and Biographical Sketches Of Their Prominent Men And Pioneers.* D. W. Ensign and Company, Philadelphia, Pennsylvania, 1880, pp. 42, 354, 472, 474.

History 2. *History of Barry County, Michigan by Hon. W. W. Potter. With Biographical Sketches Of Prominent Men By Ford Hicks And Edward Butler.* W. W. Hart's Steam Book and Commercial Printing House, 1883, p. 13.

Graveraet Jr., Henry G., First Sergeant

Bailly, Joseph—Wikipedia, the free encyclopedia—Internet search.

Blakiston's Illustrated Pocket Medical Dictionary. McGraw-Hill Book Company, Inc., 1952, p. 753.

Bollet, Dr. Alfred Jay. *Civil War Medicine Challenges and Triumphs.* GalenPress, Tucson, Arizona, 2003, pp. 233, 235, 236.

Ibid., p. 240.

Encyclopedia of Death and Dying, Civil War, US Internet Search, p. 5.

Herek, Raymond J. *These men Have Seen Hard Service.* Wayne State University Press, Detroit, Michigan, 1998, pp. 148,150. From the Memoirs of Julian Edward Buckbee in the Private Collection of John Buckbee.

Native Americans in Michigan 1.—*Graveraet Family Page*—Internet search.

Native Americans in Michigan 2.—*Graveraet Family Page*—Internet search.

Ibid.

New York Colonial Muster Rolls 1664–1775—Report of the State Historian of the State of New York, Volume II. Genealogical Publishing Co., Inc.

Schaadt, Dr. Mark J. *Civil War Medicine—An Illustrated History.* Cedarwood Publishing, Quincy, Illinois, 1998, pp. 96–97.

Schoolcraft, Henry R. Papers 1806–1875. From Library of Congress 68 reels. MICRO. Source - Clarke Historical Library, Central Michigan University, Mt. Pleasant, Isabella County. Courtesy of the Clarke Historical Library.

Greensky, Benjamin C., Private

Encyclopedia of Death and Dying, Civil War, US, p. 4. Internet Search.
Ibid.
Frassanito, William A. *Grant and Lee The Virginia Campaigns 1864–1865*. Charles Schribner's Sons, New York, p. 48.

Greensky, Jacob, Private

Avery, Chad. Conversations with Mr. Chad Avery, Anishinabe genealogist and historian.
Blakiston's Illustrated Pocket Medical Dictionary. McGraw-Hill Book Company, Inc., 1952, p. 760.
Ibid., p. 169.
Conversation (1.) with a Greensky descendant about Peter Greensky. The descendant is an Anishinabe speaker and language instructor.
Ibid.
Conversation (2.) with a Greensky descendant about Peter Greensky. The descendant is an Anishinabe speaker and language instructor.
Ibid.
Land Records.
Reuter, Dorothy. *Methodist Indian Ministries in Michigan 1830–1990*. Eerdmans Printing Company, Grand Rapids, Michigan, 1993, p. 148. Conversations with Mrs. Dorothy Reuter.
Ibid.
Ibid., p. 152
Schaadt, Dr. Mark J. *Civil War Medicine—An Illustrated History*. Cedarwood Publishing, Quincy, Illinois, 1998, p. 68.
Ibid., pp. 98–99
Ibid., p. 88
Ibid.
Ibid., p. 91.
Walker, Louise Jean. *Beneath the Singing Pines,* Hillsdale Educational Publishers, Inc., Hillsdale, Michigan, pp. 25, 33.

Gruet Jr., Peter, Private

Moll, Harold W. Michigan historian and genealogist. Conversations with Mr. Moll and letters from Mr. Moll about the Gruet family history.

Ibid.

Hall, Cornelius, Private

Blakiston's Illustrated Pocket Medical Dictionary. McGraw-Hill Book Company, Inc., 1952, p. 97.

Ibid., p. 739.

Ibid., p. 110.

Evans, Dr. Bruce A. *A Primer of Civil War Medicine—Non Surgical Medical Practice during the Civil War Years.* Bohemian Publishers, Knoxville, Tennessee, 1998, p. 33.

Ibid., p. 75.

Ibid., p. 50.

Land Records.

Schaadt, Dr. Mark J. *Civil War Medicine—An Illustrated History.* Cedarwood Publishing, Quincy, Illinois, 1998, p. 68.

Hamlin, James H., Private

Encyclopedia of Death and Dying, Civil War, US p. 5. Internet search.

Ibid.

RootsWeb: Nishnawbe-L Re: Hamlin and Jendron/Gaudron/Jandreau. Internet search.

Hannin, Joseph, Private

Bollet, Dr. Alfred Jay. *Civil War Medicine Challenges and Triumphs.* Galen Press, Tucson, Arizona, 2003, pp. 296, 297.

Ibid., pp. 285, 286.

Dorwart, Dr. Bonnie Brice. *Death Is In The Breese: Disease during The American Civil War.* Bonnie

Brice Dorwart, M.D. and the National Museum of Civil War Medicine, Frederick, Maryland, 2009, pp. 132, 51.

Oneida. *First Allies-Oneida Indian Nation* at Oneida Indian Nation.com. Internet search.

Richards, Cara E. *The Oneida People.* Indian Tribal Series, Phoenix, Arizona, 1974, p. 1.

Hubert, Charles, Private

Blakiston's Illustrated Pocket Medical Dictionary. McGraw-Hill Book Company, Inc., 1952, p. 501.

Census. *1836 Census of Ottawa and Chippewa Mixed Breed.* Internet Search.

Denney, Robert E. *The Distaff Civil War.* Tafford Publishing, 2006, p. 227.

Internet. Wikipedia search—*Brief History of Mustard Plasters,* p. 2.

Schaadt, Dr. Mark J. *Civil War Medicine—An Illustrated History.* Cedarwood Publishing, Quincy, Illinois, 1998, p. 68.

Isaacs, William, Private

Altic, Stephen. *Epidemic Kerato-Conjunctivitis in the 71st. Ohio Volunteer Infantry,* 1996, pp. 1–4. Internet search.

Dorwart Dr. Bonnie Brice. *Death Is In The Breeze: Disease during The American Civil War.* Bonnie Brice Dorwart, M.D. and the National Museum of Civil War Medicine, Frederick, Maryland, 2009, pp. 132.

Ibid., p. 51.

Evans, Dr. Bruce A. *A Primer of Civil War Medicine—Non Surgical Medical Practice during the Civil War Years.* Bohemian Publishers, Knoxville, Tennessee, 1998, pp. 33, 34.

Ibid. p. 107.

Gruett, Philip. *The 1868 Saginaw Chippewa Index* (see Primary Resources Researched), p. 47.

Internet Wikipedia search - *Brief History of Mustard Plasters,* p. 2.

Land Records.

Schaadt, Dr. Mark J. *Civil War Medicine—An Illustrated History.* Cedarwood Publishing, Quincy, Illinois, 1998, pp. 67, 68.

West, Mrs. Blanche Chatfield. Letter of September 15, 1958 housed in the Clarke Historical Library, Central Michigan University, Mt. Pleasant, Isabella County. Courtesy of the Clarke Historical Library.

Ibid.-West.

Jacko, John, Private

Blakiston's Illustrated Pocket Medical Dictionary. McGraw-Hill Book Company, Inc., 1952, p. 267.

Ibid., 415.

Bollet, Dr. Alfred Jay. *Civil War Medicine Challenges and Triumphs*. Galen Press, Tucson, Arizona, 2003, p. 236.

Ibid.-Bollet., pp. 285, 286.

Evans, Dr. Bruce A. *A Primer of Civil War Medicine—Non Surgical Medical Practice during the Civil War Years*. Bohemian Publishers, Knoxville, Tennessee, 1998, p. 77.

Internet Wikipedia search—*Brief History of Mustard Plasters* p. 2.

Jacko, Natahwinodin, Private

Blakiston's Illustrated Pocket Medical Dictionary. McGraw-Hill Book Company, Inc., 1952, p. 765.

Bollet, Dr. Alfred Jay. *Civil War Medicine Challenges and Triumphs*. Galen Press, Tucson, Arizona, 2003, p. 274.

Ibid.-Bollet., pp. 235, 236.

Ibid.-Bollet., p. 232.

Ibid.-Bollet., p. 238.

Evans, Dr. Bruce A. *A Primer of Civil War Medicine—Non Surgical Medical Practice during the Civil War Years*. Bohemian Publishers, Knoxville, Tennessee, 1998, pp. 32, 33.

Ibid.-Evans., p. 77.

Jackson, Edward Andrew, Private

Blakiston's Illustrated Pocket Medical Dictionary. McGraw-Hill Book Company, Inc., 1952, p. 765.

Bollet, Dr. Alfred Jay. *Civil War Medicine Challenges and Triumphs*. Galen Press, Tucson, Arizona, 2003, pp. 273.

Ibid., pp. 235, 236.

Ibid., pp. 232, 238

Evans, Dr. Bruce A. *A Primer of Civil War Medicine—Non Surgical Medical Practice during the Civil War Years*. Bohemian Publishers, Knoxville, Tennessee, 1998, pp. 32, 33.

Foresters. *Independent Order of Foresters*, Internet search.

Jackson. *Our Jackson Kin*, Internet search.

Temperance. *Royal Templars of Temperance*, Internet search.

Jeandron, Michael, Private

Claims, Michael Jaudron, Sr. Mackinac County Original Land Claims. Book No. 6. Claims within the County of Michilimackinac, Year 1828. Claims in Michigan, pp. 224 and 225. Internet search.

Ibid.

Encyclopedia of Death and Dying, Civil War, US p. 5. Internet.

Ibid.

Land Records

Johns, William, Private

Blakiston's Illustrated Pocket Dictionary. McGraw-Hill Book Company, Inc., 1952, p. 767.

Bollet, Dr. Alfred Jay. *Civil War Medicine Challenges and Triumphs.* Galen Press, Tucson, Arizona, 2003, p. 92.

Evans, Dr. Bruce A. *A Primer of Civil War Medicine—Non Surgical Medical Practice during the Civil War Years.* Bohemian Publishers, Knoxville, Tennessee, 1998, pp. 49, 65.

Kabaosa, Louis, Private

Evans, Dr. Bruce A. *A Primer of Civil War Medicine—Non Surgical Medical Practice during the Civil War Years.* Bohemian Publishers, Knoxville, Tennessee, 1998, p. 65.

Internet Wikipedia search—*Brief History of Mustard Plasters,* p. 2.

Kabayasega, George, Private

Altic, Stephen. *Epidemic Kerato-Conjunctivitis in the 71st. Ohio Volunteer Infantry,* 1996, pp. 1–4. Internet search.

Blakiston's Illustrated Pocket Medical Dictionary. McGraw-Hill Book Company, Inc., 1952, p. 240.

Dorwart, Dr. Bonnie Brice. *Disease is in the Breeze: Disease during the American Civil War.* Bonnie Brice Dorwart, MD, and the National Museum of Civil War Medicine, Frederick, Maryland, 2009, pp. 51–52.

Evans, Dr. Bruce A. *A Primer of Civil War Medicine—Non Surgical Medical Practice during the Civil War Years.* Bohemian Publishers, Knoxville, Tennessee, 1998, pp. 77, 108.

Kadah, Joseph, Private

Bollet, Dr. Alfred Jay. *Civil War Medicine Challenges and Triumphs*. Galen Press, Tucson, Arizona, 2003, p. 308.

Encyclopedia of Death and Dying, Civil War, US, p. 5. Internet search.

Evans, Dr. Bruce A. *A Primer of Civil War Medicine—Non Surgical Medical Practice during the Civil War Years*. Bohemian Publishers, Knoxville, Tennessee, 1998, p. 103.

Ibid., pp. 91,48 and 71.

Ibid., p. 92.

Kakakee, Joseph, Private

Baraga, Frederick. *A Dictionary of the Ojibway Language*. Minnesota Historical Press, St. Paul, New Material, p. 183.

Ibid., p. 248.

Grey County Historical Society, Ontario, Canada. Conversations with Susan Schank Communication Chair for the Society. Informational material received from researcher Susan Schank.

Ibid.

Ibid.

Ibid.

Ibid.

Ibid.

Ibid.

Ibid.

Ibid.

Land Records.

Nahnebahwequa. Internet, Wikipedia search.

Ibid.

Ibid.

Kaquatch, Samuel, Private

Dorwart, Dr. Bonnie Brice. *Death Is In The Breeze: Disease during The American Civil War*. Bonnie Brice Dorwart, M.D. and the National Museum of Civil War Medicine, Frederick Maryland, 2009, p. 94.

Encyclopedia of Death and Dying, Civil War, US p. 5. Internet search.

Evans, Dr. Bruce A. *A Primer of Civil War Medicine—Non Surgical Medical Practice during the Civil War Years.* Bohemian Publishers, Knoxville, Tennessee, 1998, p. 65.

H.R. 8498. Congressional serial set, Issue 3048, 52nd. Congress, 1st. Session, House of Representatives, Report No. 1880. March 3, 1893.

Internet Wikipedia search—*Brief History of Mustard Plasters,* p. 2.

Schaadt, Dr. Mark J. *Civil War Medicine—An Illustrated History.* Cedarwood Publishing, Quincy, Illinois, 1998, p. 68.

Will. *The Last Will and Testament of Michael Kaquatch,* Little Traverse (Harbor Springs) Emmet County. Emmet County Probate Court, January 1, 1875.

Kawgayawsung, Solomon, Private

Gruett, Philip. *The 1868 Saginaw Chippewa Index* (see Primary Resources researched), p. 365.

Ibid.

Kechittigo, Thomas, Sergeant

Avery, Chad. Conversations with Mr. Chad Avery, Anishinabe genealogist and historian.

Bollet, Dr. Alfred Jay. *Civil War Medicine Challenges and Triumphs.* Galen Press, Tucson, Arizona, 2003, p. 212.

Campbell, George W., "Old Choctaw," *The National Tribune,* September 11, 1913.

Gruett, Philip. *The 1868 Saginaw Chippewa Index* (see Primary Resources researched), p. 110.

Land Records 1.

Land Records 2.

Schaadt, Dr. Mark J. *Civil War Medicine—An Illustrated History.* Cedarwood Publishing, Quincy, Illinois, 1998, p. 68.

The Avalanche of Grayling, Crawford County, October 25, 1894.

Ibid., November 1, 1894.

White, Wyman S. *The Civil War Diary of Wyman S. White, First Sergeant of Company F, 2nd. United States Sharpshooter Regiment, 1861–1865.* Baltimore Butternut and Blue, pp. 249–250.

Ibid., p. 250.

Kejikowe, Simon, Private

Conversations and Correspondence with Mr. Curtis Chambers, Tribal Chairman of the Burt Lake Band of Ottawa and Chippewa Indians, and with Mrs. Loretta Parkey, Tribal Enrollment Officer and Historian of the Burt Lake Band of Ottawa and Chippewa Indians at Brutus, Cheboygan County.

Friday, Matthew J. *Michigan Historical Review, Spring 2007* pp. 87–97.

Guide. Conversations with an interpreter and guide at the Fredericksburg National Battlefield Park, Fredericksburg, Virginia.

Ibid.

Reed, Dr. William Howard. *Hospital Life in the Army of the Potomac, Chapter II.* Boston, Massachusetts, 1886.

Ibid.

Ibid.

Schaadt, Dr. Mark J. *Civil War Medicine—An Illustrated History.* Cedarwood Publishing, Quincy, Illinois, 1998, p. 68

Traverse Magazine, November 2006, pp. 43–47.

Kenewahaneby, John, Private

Conversation with an interpreter and guide at the Fredericksburg National Battlefield Park, Fredericksburg, Virginia.

Reed, Dr. William Howard. *Hospital Life in the Army of the Potomac, Chapter II.* Boston, Massachusetts, 1886.

Internet search—*Brief History of Mustard Plasters,* p. 2.

Kesas, John, Private

Baraga, Frederick. *A Dictionary of the Ojibway Language.* Minnesota Historical Press, St. Paul, New Material, 1992, p. 137.

Kewacondo, Benjamin, Private

Blakiston's Illustrated Pocket Medical Dictionary. McGraw-Hill Book Company, Inc., 1952, p. 767.

Bollet, Dr. Alfred Jay. *Civil War Medicine Challenges and Triumphs.* Galen Press, Tucson, Arizona, 2003, p. 92.

Evans, Dr. Bruce A. *A Primer of Civil War Medicine—Non Surgical Medical Practice during the Civil War Years.* Bohemian Publishers, Knoxville, Tennessee, 1998, pp. 49 and 65.

Record. Ancestry.com - *American Civil War Soldiers*. – Benjamin Kewaconda.

Register. *US Army Register of Enlistments 1798–1914*, p. 124.

Schaadt, Dr. Mark J. *Civil War Medicine—An Illustrated History*. Cedarwood Publishing, Quincy, Illinois, 1998, p. 68.

Kitchibatise, Amable, Private

Baraga, Frederick. *A Dictionary of the Ojibway Language*, Minnesota Historical Press, St. Paul, New Material, 1992, p. 193.

Bozich, Stanley J. *Michigan's Own—The Medal of Honor—Civil War to Vietnam War*. Polar Bear Publishing Company, Frankenmuth, Michigan, 1987, p. 67.

Danville. Danville National Cemetery—National Cemetery Administration, Danville, Virginia. Internet search.

Encyclopedia of Death and Dying, Civil War US, p. 5. Internet search.

McFall Jr. Conversations with Mr. F. Lawrence McFall, Jr. and information from his book, *Danville in the Civil War*, The Virginia Regimental History Series. H.E. Howard, Inc., Lynchburg, Virginia, 2001.

Ibid.

Ibid.

Ibid.

Ibid.

Lamourandere, Thaddeus, Private

Encyclopedia of Death and Dying, Civil War US, p. 4. Internet search.

Ibid.

Guide. Conversations with an interpreter and guide at the Fredericksburg National Battlefield Park, Fredericksburg, Virginia.

Lidger, Daniel, Private

Oneida. *First Allies-Oneida Indian Nation* at Oneida Indian Nation.com. Internet search.

Richards, Cara. *The Oneida People*. The Indian Tribal Series, 1974, p. 1.

Light, Josiah, Private

Internet search—Earache Remedies—*Blind Pig and the Acorn*.

Obituary for Josiah Light in the *Ludington Record*, Mason County under Eden News, October 23, 1884 (between October 16 and October 30, 1884).

Riverton Indian Church Registry—Methodist Church—Riverton, Mason County, Indians Eden Township Baptisms. Microfilm held at the Church of Jesus Christ of Latter-Day Saints (LDS) Family History Library, Midland, Midland County.

Marks, Louis, Private

Blakiston's Illustrated Pocket Medical Dictionary. McGraw-Hill Book Company, Inc., 1952, p. 420.

Bollet, Dr. Alfred J. *Civil War Medicine Challenges and Triumphs.* Galen Press, Ltd. Tucson, Arizona, 2002, p. 347.

Ibid., p. 350.

Diary. Entry of June 17, 1864 in the *Charles Campbell Diary* held in the Earl Gregg Swem Library, Manuscript Division of the College of William and Mary in Williamsburg, Virginia.

Land Records.

Marquette, Frank (Francis), Private

Barry. *History of Barry County by the Honorable W.W. Potter (1869–1940) Illustrated With Biographical Sketches of Prominent Men by Ford Hicks and Edward Butler.* Engraved and Printed by The Reed-Tandler Company, Grand Rapids, Michigan, 1912, p. 10.

Blakiston's Illustrated Pocket Medical Dictionary. McGraw-Hill Book Company, Inc., 1952, p. 369.

Evans, Dr. Bruce A. *A Primer of Civil War Medicine—Non Surgical Medical Practice during the Civil War Years.* Bohemian Publishers, Knoxville, Tennessee, 1998, p. 68.

Mashkaw, James, Private

Baraga, Frederick. *A Dictionary of the Ojibway Language.* Minnesota Historical Press, St. Paul, New Material, 1992, p. 221.

Encyclopedia of Death and Dying, Civil War, US p. 4. Internet search.

Ibid.

Letter. From a letter received at the Michigan Mackinac Agency (located at that time in Ypsilanti, Washtenaw County) addressed to the commissioner of Indian Affairs and written on April 14, 1876, by interpreter John Smith. The information cited in James Mashkaw's profile is located on page 4 of said letter. This letter is included with other correspondence sent to the Mackinac Agency from the years

1874–1876. It is found in Mackinac Agency M 234, Roll no. 411 held at the Clarke Historical Library on the campus of Central Michigan University in Mt. Pleasant, Isabella County.

Mashkaw, John, Private

Baraga, Frederick. *A Dictionary of the Ojibway Language.* Minnesota Historical Press, St. Paul, New Material, 1992, p. 221.

Encyclopedia of Death and Dying, Civil War, US p. 4. Internet search.
Ibid.

Letter. From a letter received at the Michigan Mackinac Agency (located at that time in Ypsilanti, Washtenaw County) addressed to the commissioner of Indian Affairs and written on April 14, 1876, by interpreter John Smith. The information cited in John Mashkaw's profile is located on page 4 of said letter. This letter is included with other correspondence sent to the Mackinac Agency from the years 1874–1876. It is found in Mackinac Agency M 234, Roll no. 411 held at the Clarke Historical Library on the campus of Central Michigan University in Mt. Pleasant, Isabella County.

Miller, Thomas, Private

Blakiston's Illustrated Pocket Medical Dictionary. McGraw-Hill Book Company, Inc., 1952, p. 135.

Bollet, Dr. Alfred Jay. *Civil War Medicine Challenges and Triumphs.* Galen press, Tucson, Arizona, 2003, p. 252.

Craker, Ruth. *The First Protestant Mission In the Grand Traverse Region.* Rivercrest House, Mt. Pleasant, Michigan, 1979, pp. 71, 73.

Evans, Dr. Bruce A. *A Primer of Civil War Medicine—Non Surgical Medical Practice during the Civil War Years.* Bohemian Publishers, Knoxville, Tennessee, 1998, p. 108.

Internet Wikipedia search—"Brief History of Mustard Plasters," p. 2.

Misisaius, Edward, Private

Blakiston's Illustrated Pocket Medical Dictionary. McGraw-Hill Book Company, Inc., 1952, p, 656.

Bollet, Dr. Alfred Jay. *Civil War Medicine Challenges and Triumphs.* Galen Press, ltd. Tucson, Arizona, 2002, p. 234.

Encyclopedia of Death and Dying, Civil War, US, p. 5. Internet search.

Guide. Conversations with an interpreter and guide at the Fredericksburg National Battlefield Park, Fredericksburg, Virginia.

Ibid.

Reed, Dr. William Howard. *Hospital Life in the Army of the Potomac, Chapter II.* Boston, Massachusetts, 1886.

Schaadt, Dr. Mark J. Civil War Medicine—An Illustrated History. Cedarwood Publishing, Quincy, Illinois, 1998, p. 68.

Miskoguon, Louis, Private

Evans, Dr. Bruce A. A Primer of Civil War Medicine—non Surgical Medical Practice during the Civil War Years. Bohemian Publishers, Knoxville, Tennessee, 1998, p. 104.

Potter, Jerry O. *The Sultana Tragedy America's Greatest Maritime Disaster.* Pelican Publishing Company, Gretna, Louisiana, 1992, p. 83

Ibid., p. 84.

Mixinasaw, Thomas, Private

Encyclopedia of Death and Dying, Civil War, US, p. 5.

Ibid.

Smith, Rev. George Nelson. Smith Memoranda and Diaries-Notes from February 23, 1868. Courtesy of Clarence and Avis Wolfe.

Ibid. Smith's Memoranda and Diaries-Notes from March 11–13, 1868. Courtesy of Clarence and Avis Wolfe.

Mixonauby, Thomas, Private

Bollet, Dr. Alfred Jay. *Civil War Medicine Challenges and Triumphs.* Galen Press, Ltd., Tucson, Arizona, 2002, pp. 201, 202.

Internet Wikipedia search—"Brief History of Mustard Plasters," p. 2.

Evans, Dr. Bruce A. *A Primer of Civil War Medicine—non Surgical Medical Practice during the Civil War Years.* Bohemian Publishers, Knoxville, Tennessee, 1998, pp. 106, 107.

Land Records.

Reuter, Dorothy. *Methodist Indian Ministries in Michigan 1830–1990.* Erdmans Printing Company, Grand Rapids, Michigan, 1993, p. 164. Conversations with Mrs. Dorothy Reuter.

Schaadt, Dr. Mark J. *Civil War Medicine—An Illustrated History*. Cedarwood Publishing, Quincy, Illinois, 1998, p. 71.

Mogwahgo, George, Private

Kuz, Dr. Julian and Dr. Bradley P. Bengtson. *Orthopaedic Injuries of the Civil War*. Kennesaw Mountain Press, Inc., Kennesaw, Georgia, 1996, pp. 36, 37.

Schaadt, Dr. Mark J. *Civil War Medicine—An Illustrated History*. Cedarwood Publishing, Quincy, Illinois, 1998, pp. 68, 69.

Mwakewenah, Daniel, Private

Baraga, Frederick. *A Dictionary of the Ojibway Language*. Minnesota Historical Press, St. Paul, p. 209.

Craker, Ruth. *The First Protestant Mission In The Grand Traverse Region*. Rivercrest House, Mt. Pleasant, Michigan, 1979, pp. 70, 71.

Ibid.-Craker, p 77.

Dougherty, Rev. Peter. *Minutes of the Old Mission and New Mission (Grove Hill) Church 1843–1871*. Original microfilm held at the Presbyterian Historical Society, 425 Lombard Street, Philadelphia, Pennsylvania 19147-1516. Call Number: UPPERVAULT V M146 G7644, Indian Mission Church (Grand Traverse Bay, Michigan), Session Minutes and statement of organization, 1843–1871 including: session minutes by Rev, Peter Dougherty, 1843–1871; with statement of organization (1 vol.).

Ibid.

Ibid.

Kuz, Dr. Julian and Dr. Bradley P. Bengtson. *Orthopaedic Injuries of the Civil War*. Kennesaw Mountain Press, Inc., Kennesaw, Georgia 1996, pp. 36, 37.

Newspaper. *Saginaw Weekly Enterprise, June 30, 1864, p. 2—"A Michigan Indian Sharpshooter."*

Ibid.

Ibid.-Newspaper a.

Ibid.-Newspaper b.

Probate. January 22, 1868 Emmet County Probate Court Guardianship Records for Ann Rood/Rodd as guardian for John and George Mwakewenah. Copies of the original papers found in Daniel Mwakewenah's pension file.

Romig, Walter. *Michigan Place Names*. Detroit: Wayne State University Press, 1986, p. 415.

Schaadt, Dr. Mark J. *Civil War Medicine—An Illustrated History.* Cedarwood Publishing, Quincy, Illinois, 1998, p. 68.

Traverse Region. *The Traverse Region of Michigan Historical and Descriptive* p. 129. Internet search.

Narquaquot, Joseph, Private

Bollet, Dr. Alfred J. *Civil War Medicine Challenges and Triumphs.* Galen Press, Tucson, Arizona, 2003, p. 235.

Internet Wikipedia search—*"Brief History of Mustard Plasters,"* p. 2.

Levy, George. *To Die in Chicago—Confederate Prisoners at Camp Douglas, 1862–1865.* Evanston Publishing, Inc., Evanston, Illinois, 1994, p. 295. Conversations with Mr. George Levy.

Ibid., pp. 294–300.

Ibid.

Ibid.

Nauquam, Thompson, Private

Reuter, Dorothy. *Methodist Indian Ministries in Michigan 1830–1990.* Eerdmans Printing Company, Grand Rapids, Michigan, 1993, p. 156. Conversations with Mrs. Dorothy Reuter.

Nelson, Thomas, Corporal

Avalanche. Grayling, Crawford County *Avalanche* Newspaper *1879–1940s,* November 1, 1894.

Ibid December 28, 1911.

Avery, Chad. Conversations with Mr. Chad Avery, Anishinabe genealogist and historian.

Blakiston's Illustrated Pocket Medical Dictionary. McGraw-Hill Book Company, Inc., 1952, pp. 51, 553.

Ibid.–Blakiston, p. 546.

Bollet, Dr. Alfred Jay. *Civil War Medicine Challenges and Triumphs.* Galen Press, Tucson, Arizona, 2002, pp. 236, 237.

Land Records.

Newspaper. Saginaw, Saginaw County *Weekly Enterprise* July 28, 1864, p. 3.

Reuter, Dorothy. *Methodist Indian Ministries in Michigan 1830–1990.* Eerdmans Printing Company, Grand Rapids, Michigan, 1993, p. 278. Conversations with Mrs. Dorothy Reuter.

Schaadt, Dr. Mark J. *Civil War Medicine—An Illustrated History.* Cedarwood Publishing, Quincy, Illinois, 1998, pp. 68, 69.

Neveaux, William, Corporal

Bayfield. *Bayfield County Press Part VI: Moving On, Remembering the War—Veterans Meet on Madeline Island, 1913.*

Blakiston's Illustrated Pocket Medical Dictionary. McGraw-Hill Book Company, Inc., 1952, p. 46.

Cadotte. Mrs. Mary Cadotte. Conversations with Mrs. Cadotte and a visit to St. Joseph Catholic Mission Cemetery on Madeline Island, Ashland County, Wisconsin.

Land Records.

On The Rock. The History of Madeline Island Told Through Its Families. Madeline Island Historical Preservation Assn., Inc., La Point, Wisconsin, New Past Press, Inc., Friendship, Wisconsin.

Research. Information given to the author from a genealogy researcher in Wisconsin.

Ibid.

Ibid.

Ibid.

Schaadt, Dr. Mark J. *Civil War Medicine—An Illustrated History.* Cedarwood Publishing Company, Quincy, Illinois, 1998, pp. 67,68.

Sivertson, Howard. *The Illustrated Voyager,* Lake Superior Port Cities Inc. Duluth, Minnesota, 1999, p. 11.

Newton, William, Private

Blakiston's Illustrated Pocket Medical Dictionary. McGraw-Hill Book Company, Inc., 1952, p. 691.

Ibid., p. 558.

Reuter, Dorothy. *Methodist Indian Ministries in Michigan 1830–1990.* Eerdmans Printing Company, Grand Rapids, Michigan, 1993, p. 250. Conversations with Mrs. Dorothy Reuter.

Ohbowakemo, James R., Private

Blakiston's Illustrated Pocket Medical Dictionary. McGraw-Hill Book Company, Inc., 1952, p. 558.

Bollet, Dr. Alfred Jay. *Civil War Medicine Challenges and Triumphs.* Galen Press, Ltd. Tucson, Arizona, 2002, p. 252.

Ibid., p. 240.

Ibid., p. 236.

Ibid., p. 233.

Otashquabono, Leon, Private

Blakiston's Illustrated Pocket Medical Dictionary. McGraw-Hill Book Company, Inc., 1952, p. 558.

Ibid., p. 135.

Bollet, Dr. Alfred Jay. *Civil War Medicine Challenges and Triumphs.* Galen Press, Ltd. Tucson, Arizona, 2002, p. 252.

Ibid., p. 308.

Obit. Indian burial in *Independent Democrat, Harbor Springs News* Column on April 11, 1902.

Otto, Marcus, Private

Avery, Chad. Conversations with Mr. Chad Avery, Anishinabe genealogist and historian.

Bollet Alfred J. *Civil War Medicine Challenges and Triumphs.* Galen Press, Tucson, Arizona, 2003, pp. 236, 237.

Ibid.-Bollet, p. 233.

Kuz, Dr. Julian and Dr. Bradley P. Bengtson. *Orthopaedic Injuries of the Civil War,* Kennesaw Mountain Press, Inc., Kennesaw, Georgia, 1996, p. 37.

Ibid.

Medical and Surgical History of the War of the Rebellion, Volume X, Section IV—Intermediary Amputations In The Arm, p. 757.

Otto, Simon. *Grandmother Moon Speaks.* Thunder Bay Press, Lansing, Michigan, p. 52.

Schaadt, Dr. Mark J. *Civil War Medicine—An Illustrated History.* Cedarwood Publishing, Quincy, Illinois, 1998, pp. 68, 69.

Otto, Solomon, Private

Blakiston's Illustrated Pocket Medical Dictionary. McGraw-Hill Book Company, Inc., 1952, p. 651.

Bollet, Dr. Alfred J. *Civil War Medicine Challenges and Triumphs.* Galen Press, Tucson, Arizona, 2003, p. 308.

Evans, Dr. Bruce A. *A Primer of Civil War Medicine—Non Surgical Medical Practice during the Civil War Years.* Bohemian Publishers, Knoxville, Tennessee, 1998, p. 65.

Gruett, Philip. *The 1868 Saginaw Chippewa Index* (see Primary Resources researched), p. 365.

Land Records.

Pemassagay, Daniel, Private

Avery, Chad. Conversations with Mr. Chad Avery, Anishinabe genealogist and historian.

Ibid.

Ibid.

Baierlein, E. R. *In the Wilderness With the Red Indians, German Missionary to the Michigan Indians, 1847–1853.* Wayne State University Press, 1893, p. 139.

Land Records.

Zehnder, Herman F. *Teach My People The Truth—The Story of Frankenmuth, Michigan.* 1970, p. 83.

Ibid., p. 78.

Ibid., p. 215.

Ibid., pp. 80–82.

Penaiswanquot, Jacko, Private

Encyclopedia of Death and Dying, Civil War, US, p. 5. Internet search.

Ibid., p. 5.

Peshekee, Mark, Private

Baraga, Frederick. *A Dictionary of the Ojibway Language.* Minnesota Historical Press, St. Paul, New Material, 1992, p. 354.

Bollet, Dr. Alfred Jay. *Civil War Medicine Challenges and Triumphs.* Galen Press, Tucson, Arizona, 2003, p. 285.

Evans, Dr. Bruce A. *A Primer of Civil War Medicine—Non Surgical Medical Practice during the Civil War Years.* Bohemian Publishers, Knoxville, Tennessee, 1998, p. 70.

Gruett, Phillip. *The 1868 Saginaw Chippewa Index* (see Primary Sources researched), p. 351.

Ibid.

Land Records.

Schaadt, Dr. Mark J. *Civil War Medicine—An Illustrated History.* Cedarwood Publishing, Quincy, Illinois, 1998, p. 68.

Ibid.

Wikipedia—the free encyclopedia—Internet search for *"Kechewaishke"* (or Great Renewer) on p. 1.

Ibid., p. 11.

Porsley, Charles, Private

Blakiston's Illustrated Pocket Medical Dictionary. McGraw-Hill Book Company, Inc., 1952, p. 189.

Ibid., p. 760.

Bollet, Dr. Alfred Jay. *Civil War Medicine Challenges and Triumphs.* Galen Press, Tucson, Arizona, 2003, p. 287.

Evans, Dr. Bruce A. *A Primer of Civil War Medicine—Non Surgical Medical Practice during the Civil War Years.* Bohemian Publishers, Knoxville, Tennessee, 1998, pp. 91, 92, 94.

Quoboway, James, Private

Blakiston's Illustrated Pocket Medical Dictionary. McGraw-Hill Book Company, Inc., 1952, p. 648.

Schaadt, Dr. Mark J. *Civil War Medicine—An Illustrated History.* Cedarwood Publishing, Quincy, Illinois, 1998, p. 68.

Sanequaby, Simon, Corporal

Blakiston's Illustrated Pocket Medical Dictionary. McGraw-Hill Book Company, Inc., 1952., p. 765.

Conversations. Conversations with Mr. Curtis Chambers, tribal chairman of the Burt Lake Band of Ottawa and Chippewa Indians, and Mrs. Loretta Parkey, tribal enrollment officer and historian for the Burt Lake Band of Ottawa and Chippewa Indians, at Brutus, Cheboygan County.

Friday. Article by Matthew J. Friday in the *Michigan Historical Review, Spring 2007,* pp. 87–97.

Sargonquotto, Aaron, Private

Avery, Chad. Conversations with Mr. Chad Avery, Anishinabe genealogist and historian.

Blakiston's Illustrated Pocket Medical Dictionary. McGraw-Hill Book Company, Inc., 1952, p. 169.

Craker, Ruth. *The First Protestant Mission In the Grand Traverse Region.* Rivercrest House, Mt. Pleasant, Michigan, 1979, p. 86.

Ibid., pp. 82, 83.

Ibid., pp. 85, 86.

Dorwart, Dr. Bonnie Brice. *Death Is In The Breeze: Disease during The American Civil War.* Bonnie Brice Dorwart, M.D., and the National Museum of Civil War Medicine, 2009, pp. 50, 51.

Dougherty, Rev. Peter. *Minutes of the Old Mission and New Mission (Grove Hill) Church 1843–1871,* p. 14. Indian Mission Church (Grand Traverse Bay, Mich.). Session minutes and statement of organization, 1843–1871, including: session minutes by Rev. Peter Dougherty, 1843–1871; with statement of organization (1 vol.). From sources held at the Presbyterian Historical Society, Philadelphia, Pennsylvania. Call Number: UPPERVAULT V M146 G7644.

Sashkobanquot, Private

Levy, George. *To Die In Chicago—Confederate Prisoners At Camp Douglas 1862– 1865.* Evanston Publishing, Inc., Evanston, Illinois, 1994, p. 288. Conversation with Mr. George Levy.

Ibid., p. 294.

Ibid.

Ibid., p. 297.

Ibid., p. 295.

Sawbequom, Adam, Private

Blakiston's Illustrated Pocket Medical Dictionary. McGraw-Hill Book Company, Inc., 1952, p. 250.

Ibid.

Encyclopedia of Death and Dying, Civil War, US, p. 5. Internet search.

Ibid.

Evans, Dr. Bruce A. *A Primer of Civil War Medicine—Non Surgical Medical Practice during the Civil War Years.* Bohemian Publishers, Knoxville, Tennessee, 1998, p. 64.

Ibid., p. 65.

Ibid., p. 68.

Scott, Antoine, Corporal

Blackiston's Illustrated Pocket Medical Dictionary. McGraw-Hill Book Company, Inc., 1952, p. 715.

Ibid.-Blakiston., p. 304.

Bollet, Dr. Alfred Jay. *Civil War Medicine Challenges and Triumphs.* Galen Press, Tucson, Arizona, 2003, pp. 316, 317.

Ibid., p. 235.

Bozich, Stanley. *Michigan's Own—The Medal of Honor—Civil War to Vietnam War.* Polar Bear Publishing Company, Frankenmuth, Michigan, 1987, pp. 67, 68.

Ibid.

Evans, Dr. Bruce A. *A Primer of Civil War Medicine—Non Surgical Medical Practice during the Civil War Years.* Bohemian Publishers, Knoxville, Tennessee, 1998, pp. 68, 70.

Schaadt, Dr. Mark J. *Civil War Medicine—An Illustrated History.* Cedarwood Publishing, Quincy, Illinois, 1998, p. 96.

Seymour, Joseph, Private

Powers, Shon. *A Look at the United States Greatest Conflict From the Point of View of a Civil War Buff.* Author House, Bloomington, Indiana, 2011, p. 383.

Shabena, Charles, Private

Wagoner. *Wagoner in the Civil War—*Photos and Stories—FamilySearch.org., Internet search.

Shaw, Charles, Private

Color Guard. *Description of the duties of the Third Maine Color Guard Company K. Reenactment Group.* Internet search.

Shawanese, Joseph, Private

Blakiston's Illustrated Pocket Medical Dictionary. McGraw-Hill Book Company, Inc., 1952, p. 135.

Ibid., p. 322.

Bollet, Dr. Alfred Jay. *Civil War Medicine Challenges and Triumphs.* Galen Press, Tucson, Arizona, 2003, p. 236.

King, Janet, RN, BSN, CGRN.—*Vermont in the Civil War—Civil War Medicine.* Internet search, p. 6.

Ibid.

Shawanosang, Joseph, Private

Bollet, Dr. Alfred J. *Civil War Medicine Challenges and Triumphs.* Galen Press, Tucson, Arizona, 2003, p. 212.

Ibid., p. 213.

Schaadt, Dr. Mark J. *Civil War Medicine—An Illustrated History.* Cedarwood Publishing, Quincy, Illinois, 1998, pp. 67, 68.

Ibid., p. 68.

Ibid., p. 72.

Ibid.

Shegoge, John, Private

Kuz, Dr. Julian and Dr. Bradley P. Bengtson. *Orthopaedic Injuries of the Civil War.* Kennesaw Mountain Press, Inc., Kennesaw, Georgia, 1996. p. 37.

Ibid.

Ibid.

Schaadt, Dr. Mark Jay. *Civil War Medicine—An Illustrated History.* Cedarwood Publishing, Quincy, Illinois, 1998, p. 68.

Ibid., p. 72.

Ibid., pp. 71, 72.

Ibid., p. 72

Ibid.

The Medical and Surgical History of the War of the Rebellion, (1861–1865), Volume X., Intermediary Amputations In the Forearm, p. 983.

Shomin, John B., Private

Baraga. Frederick. *A Dictionary of the Ojibway Language*, Minnesota Historical Press, St. Paul, New Material, 1992, p. 175.

Blakiston's Illustrated Pocket Medical Dictionary. McGraw-Hill Book Company, Inc., 1952, p. 651.

Ibid., p. 415.

Ibid.-Blakiston., p. 230.

Bollet, Dr. Alfred Jay. *Civil War Medicine Challenges and Triumphs*. Galen Press, Tucson, Arizona, 2003, p. 236.

Ibid., p. 343.

Ibid., p. 344.

Ibid., p. 359.

Grace, William. US Army Medical Department, *The Army Surgeon's Manual, General Orders No. 77*, Norman Publishing Company, San Francisco, California, 1992, p. 51.

Land Records.

Shomin, John (O.), Private

Baraga, Frederick. *A Dictionary of the Ojibway Language*. Minnesota Historical Press, St. Paul, New Material, 1992, p. 175.

Parker, Steve. *The Human Body Book*. DK Publishers, New York, 2007, pp. 56,57.

Letter (1.) Letter of John O. Shomin to Indian Agent, George W. Lee on January 4, 1877. Letters received at the Office of Mackinaw Indian Agency, Ypsilanti, Michigan. Letter held at the Clarke Historical Library, Central Michigan University, Mt. Pleasant, Isabella County. Courtesy of the Clarke Historical Library. See Primary Resources Researched.

Ibid.

Ibid.

Ibid.

Land Records.

Letter (2.) Letter of John O. Shomin to Indian Agent George W. Lee on February 8, 1878. Letters received at the Office of Mackinaw Indian Agency, Ypsilanti, Michigan. Letter held at the Clarke Historical Library, Central Michigan University, Mt. Pleasant, Isabella County. Courtesy of the Clarke Historical Library. See Primary Resources Researched.

Schaadt, Dr. Mark J. *Civil War Medicine—An Illustrated History.* Cedarwood Publishing, Quincy, Illinois, 1998, p. 68.

Shomin, Louis, Private

Baraga, Frederick. *A Dictionary of the Ojibway Language.* Minnesota Historical Press, St. Paul, New Material, 1992, p. 175.

Dorwart, Dr. Bonnie Brice. *Death Is In The Breeze: Disease during The American Civil War.* Bonnie Brice Dorwart, M.D. and the National Museum of Civil War Medicine, Frederick, Maryland, 2009, p. 51.

Land Records.

Smith, Thomas, Private

Blakiston's Illustrated Pocket Medical Dictionary. McGraw-Hill Book Company, Inc. 1952, pp. 415, 492.

Ibid.-Blakiston., p. 304.

Bollet, Dr. Alfred Jay. *Civil War Medicine Challenges and Triumphs.* Galen Press, Tucson, Arizona, 2003, p. 236.

Ibid., p. 233.

Ibid., pp. 272–273.

Ibid., p. 274.

Ibid.

Dorwart, Dr. Bonnie Brice. *Death Is In The Breeze: Disease during The American Civil War.* Bonnie Brice Dorwart, M.D. and the National Museum of Civil War Medicine, Frederick, Maryland, 2009, p. 51.

Land Records.

Reuter, Dorothy. *Methodist Indian Ministries in Michigan 1830–1990.* Eerdmans Printing Company, Grand Rapids, Michigan, 1993, p. 144. Conversation with Mrs. Dorothy Reuter.

South, Peter, Private

Baraga, Frederick. *A Dictionary of the Ojibway Language.* Minnesota Historical Press, St. Paul, New Material, 1992, p. 167.

Blakiston's Illustrated Pocket Medical Dictionary. McGraw-Hill Book Company, Inc., 1952, p. 415.

Bollet, Dr. Alfred Jay. *Civil War Medicine Challenges and Triumphs.* Galen Press, Tucson, Arizona, 2002, p. 236.

Encyclopedia of Death and Dying, Civil War, US, p. 5. Internet search.

Ibid.

Reports. (1.) Report of the Presbyterian Indian Mission School at Bear River, Emmet County, as taught by Andrew Porter, teacher to the Chippewa and Ottawa Indians. An enumeration of both boys and girls who were students at the school for the first quarter session beginning January 3 and ending March 31, 1860. Report held at the Clarke Historical Library, Central Michigan University, Mt. Pleasant, Isabella County. Courtesy of the Clarke Historical Library.

(2) Report of the Presbyterian Indian Mission School at Bear River, Emmet County, as taught by Andrew Porter, teacher to the Chippewa and Ottawa Indians. An enumeration of both boys and girls who were students at the school's second session ending September 30, 1860. Report held at the Clarke Historical Library, Central Michigan University, Mt. Pleasant, Isabella County. Courtesy of the Clarke Historical Library. See Primary Resources Researched.

Stoneman, George, Private

Adams, George Worthington. *Doctors In Blue The Medical History of the Union Army in the Civil War.* Morning Side Press, Dayton, Ohio, 1985, p. 116.

Bollet, Dr. Alfred Jay. *Civil War Medicine Challenges and Triumphs.* Galen Press, Tucson, Arizona, 2003, p. 308.

Deposition. Deposition of Wayland B. Nicholson, undertaker, found in Stoneman's pension papers as follows: "Whitehall, Michigan July 22, 1887 This is to certify that George Stoneman was buried in the Whitehall Cemetery July 10, 1887, and that I Wayland B. Nicholson undertaker officiated at his funeral as such and that I saw him buried. Wayland B. Nicholson, Undertaker."

Kuz, Dr. Julian and Dr. Bradley P. Bengtson. *Orthopaedic Injuries of the Civil War.* Kennesaw Mountain Press, Inc., Kennesaw, Georgia, 1996, pp. 36, 37.

Ibid.-Kuz and Bengtson., p. 36.

Land Records.

Schaadt, Dr. Mark J. *Civil War Medicine—An Illustrated History.* Cedarwood Publishing, Quincy, Illinois, 1998, pp. 68, 69.

Whitehall Forum. Article in Muskegon County's *Whitehall Forum* Newspaper titled *Still Another*, Thursday, July 14, 1887, page not numbered. Courtesy of the White Lake Community Library, White Hall, Michigan.

Sutton, Freeman, Private

Bollet, Dr. Alfred Jay. *Civil War Medicine Challenges and Triumphs*. Galen Press, Tucson, Arizona, 2003, p. 101.

Ibid.

Ibid.-Bollet., p. 212.

Ibid., p. 213.

Ibid., p. 233.

Land Records.

Ibid.

Report of Jacob Kaplinger found in Sutton's pension papers as follows: "County of Mason, State of Michigan, Please certify that on the night of Dec, 13, 1890 I held an inquest on the remains of an Indian killed on rail way track of the F and P Railway who was supposed to be Freeman Sutton and who was Buried by my order. Jacob Kaplinger, Justice of the Peace in and for Mason County, Mich."

Schaadt, Dr. Mark J. *Civil War Medicine—An Illustrated History*. Cedarwood Publishing, Quincy, Illinois, 1998, p. 68.

Tabasash, Francis, Corporal

Blakiston's Illustrated Pocket Medical Dictionary. McGraw-Hill Book Company, Inc., 1952, p. 415.

Bollet, Dr. Alfred Jay. *Civil War Medicine Challenges and Triumphs*. Galen Press, Tucson, Arizona, 2003, p. 236.

Ibid., 237.

Ibid.-Bollet, pp. 235, 233, 236.

Ibid., p. 235.

Dorwart, Dr. Bonnie Brice. *Death Is In The Breeze: Disease during the American Civil War*. Bonnie Brice Dorwart, M.D., and the National Museum of Civil War Medicine, Frederick, Maryland, 2009, p. 132.

Ibid., p. 51.

Internet Wikipedia search—*Brief History of Mustard Plasters*, p. 2. Volunteers.

Kautz, August V. *Customs of Service For Non-Commissioned Officers and Soldiers Practiced In The Army Of The United States*. Philadelphia, J. B. Lippincott and Co., 1864 "First Sergeant."

Ibid.

Schaadt, Dr. Mark J. *Civil War Medicine—An Illustrated History.* Cedarwood Publishing, Quincy,
Illinois, 1998, p. 84.

Tabyant, Antoine, Private

Blakiston's Illustrated Pocket Medical Dictionary. McGraw-Hill Book Company, Inc., 1952, p. 749.

Bollett, Dr. Alfred Jay. *Civil War Medicine Challenges and Triumphs.* Galen Press, Tucson, Arizona, 2003 p. 101.

Dorwart, Dr. Bonnie Brice. *Death Is In The Breeze: Disease during the American Civil War.* Bonnie Brice Dorwart, M.D. and the National Museum of Civil War Medicine, Frederick, Maryland, 2009, pp. 50, 51, 52.

Ibid., p. 132.

Kuz, Dr. Julian and Dr. Bradley P. Bengtson. *Orthopaedic Injuries of the Civil War.* Kennesaw Mountain Press, Inc., Kennesaw, Georgia, 1996, p. 25.

Schaadt, Dr. Mark J. *Civil War Medicine—An Illustrated History.* Cedarwood Publishing, Quincy, Illinois, 1998, pp. 68, 69.

Tazhedewin, Joseph, Private

Blakiston's Illustrated Pocket Medical Dictionary. McGraw-Hill Book Company, Inc., 1952, p. 415.

Ibid.-Blakiston., p. 760.

Bollet, Dr. Alfred Jay. *Civil War Medicine Challenges and Triumphs.* Galen Press, Tucson, Arizona, 2003, pp. 236, 237.

Ibid.

Ibid.-Bollet., p. 233.

Kuz, Dr. Julian and Dr. Bradley P. Bengtson. *Orthopaedic Injuries of the Civil War.* Kennesaw Mountain Press, Inc., Kennesaw, Georgia, 1996, p. 37.

Ibid.-Kuz and Bengtson, p. 36.

Schaadt, Dr. Mark J. *Civil War Medicine—An Illustrated History.* Cedarwood Publishing, Quincy, Illinois, 1998, pp. 68, 69.

Thomas, Moses, Private

Blakiston's Illustrated Pocket Medical Dictionary. McGraw-Hill Book Company, Inc., 1952, p. 698.

Ibid., p. 466.

Ibid., p. 129.

Ibid., p. 322

Valentine, Robert, Private

Jackson, John (Jack). From the Leonard Paquette family home **page:** information about John Jackson, Mary Condecon Jackson, and the Jackson family from Genealogy.com family tree maker online. Internet search.

Ibid.

Ibid.

Waasegiizhig, Henry, Private

Life. *Life History of John Condecon* as told to his daughter, Caroline Condecon Parker (Mrs. George), at Odanah, Wisconsin, in 1935. *Creator: United States. Works Progress Administration: Chippewa Indian Historical Project Records, 1936–1942.* A printed text (that the author copied at the Ojibwe Bad River Reservation library near Odanah, Wisconsin) can be found in Envelope 12, Part 1, IV.A18, pp. 70–77 in a binder held in the library. This WPA project was a collection of records of Chippewa Indian folklore sponsored by the Great Lakes Indian Agency and directed by Sister M. Macaria Murphy FSPA (Franciscan Sisters of Perpetual Adoration) of St. Mary's Indian School, Odanah, Wisconsin. The Condecon story can also be found on two reels of microfilm (35) mm housed at the Area Research Center, History Center and Archives, Northern Great Lakes Visitor Center; owned by the Wisconsin Historical Society, Library—Archives Division. The call number is Northland Micro5; Micro 532. At the time she recorded her father's history, Caroline was John's oldest living child and the niece of John's brother Henry Waasegiizhig.

Mayotte. Credit to Mr. Patrick Mayotte, also known as Gizhibaa'aanakwad, of the Bad River, Wisconsin, Band of Ojibwe (Anishinabe). Conversations with Mr. Mayotte and information sent to the author from Mr. Mayotte.

Ibid.

Obituary. *Wa-Sa-Se-zik Passes Away, Henry Condecon, of Odanah, Whose Indian Name Was Wa-sa-se-zik, Was Found Dead in Bed Easter Morning.* Ashland, Wisconsin *Daily Press,* Monday, April 17, 1922.

Ontonagon. Ontonagon County—part of the MIGenWeb of The USGENWEB PROJECT—Internet search. *A Brief History of Ontonagon,* pp. 1–3.

Ibid., pp. 1, 2.

Ibid., p. 2.

Ibid.

Ibid., p. 3.

Ibid., pp. 2, 3.

Wabano, Thomas, Private

Blakiston's Illustrated Pocket Medical Dictionary. McGraw-Hill Book Company, Inc., 1952, p. 715.

Bollet, Dr. Alfred Jay. *Civil War Medicine Challenges and Triumphs.* Galen Press, Tucson, Arizona, 2003, pp. 314, 316, 317.

King, Janet, RN, BSN, CGRN. *Vermont In The Civil War—Civil War Medicine—Venereal Disease,* p. 11. Internet search, VermontCivilWar.Org Database.

Ibid.

Wabesis, Charles, Private

Baraga, Frederick. *A Dictionary of the Ojibway Language.* Minnesota Historical Press, St. Paul, New Material, 1992, p. 393.

Draft. *United States World War I Draft Registration Cards, 1917–1918.* Internet search on Ancestry.com.

Land Records.

Murder. *The Moynihan Murder.* Chicago *Tribune (1860–1872),* article of March 19, 1864, p. 4. ProQuest Historical Newspapers; Chicago Tribune (1849–1988) p. 0–4.

Wabesis, John, Private

Baraga, Frederick. A *Dictionary of the Ojibway Language.* Minnesota Historical Press, St. Paul, New Material, 1992, p. 393.

Encyclopedia of Death and Dying, Civil War, US, p. 4. Internet search.

Wakazoo, Joseph, Private

Albion. 1845–1846 Catalogue of the Wesleyan Seminary at Albion College listing the Indian students in attendance. Material found in the archives of the United Methodist Church in Albion College, Albion, Calhoun County, Michigan.

Bishop. Mahlon Norris Gilbert: Bishop Coadjutor of Minnesota 1886–1900, By Francis Leseure Palmer, Milwaukee, Wisconsin: The Young Churchman, 1912, Chapter X. The Work of a Bishop p. 3. Churchman, 1912, Chapter X, The Work of a Bishop.

Deacon. Mahlon Norris Gilbert: Bishop Coadjutor of Minnesota 1886–1900, By Francis Leseure Palmer, Milwaukee, Wisconsin: The Young Churchman, 1912, Chapter XI. The Indian Missions p. 2.

Draft. *US World War I Draft Registration Cards, 1917–1918* at Ancestry.com.

Missions. Domestic Missions: *The Indian Deacons at White Earth* by Rev. Joseph A. Gilfillan, from the Archives of the Minnesota. Historical Society, published in 1881.

Old Wing Mission. *Old Wing Mission Cultural Interchange as Chronicled by George and Arvilla Smith in their Work with Chief Wakazoo's Ottawa Band on the West Michigan Frontier.* Edited by Robert Swierenga and William Van Appledorn. William B. Eerdmans Publishing Company, Grand Rapids, Michigan, 2008, pp. 623–626.

Ibid., p. 625.

Ibid.

Ibid., p. 624.

Ibid.

Ibid., p. 480.

Ibid., p. 38.

Ibid., pp. 42–44.

Ibid., pp. 554–555

Schaadt, Dr. Mark J. *Civil War Medicine—An Illustrated History.* Cedarwood Publishing, Quincy, Illinois, 1998, p. 68.

Smith. George N. Smith's Memoranda and Diaries 1839–1849, entry of December 27, 1848. In Old *Wing Mission* edited by Robert Swierenga and William Van Appledorn. William B. Eerdmans Publishing Company, Grand Rapids, Michigan, 2008, p. 343. Courtesy of Clarence and Avis Wolfe.

Ibid.-Smith. George N. Smith's Memoranda and Diaries entry of September 10, 1863. Courtesy of Clarence and Avis Wolfe.

Twinsburg. Letter of Joseph Wakazoo to Samuel Bissell, Twinsburgh Institute, Summit County, Ohio, dated June 16, 1852, in MS 116 of Samuel Bissell Papers, container 1, folder 2. Kept at Research Center Reference Division, Western Reserve Historical Society (WRHS) Library Research Center, 10825 East Boulevard, Cleveland, Ohio. Courtesy of WRHS.

Ibid.-Twinsburg. *Catalogue of the Instructors and Students of Twinsburgh Institute for the Academic Year Commencing April 9, 1860, and Ending March 9, 1861.* Twinsburg Historical Society, 8996 Darrow Road, Twinsburg, Ohio. S. and J.

Featherstone Publishers, 1861. The Catalogue roster lists Joseph Wakazoo from Grand Traverse, Michigan, for that school year. Courtesy of the Twinsburg Historical Society.

US Veterans Gravesites, ca. 1775–2006, from Ancestry.com.

Watson, James V., Private

Article. Death Claims Indian Scribe—Athens Times Newspaper, Friday, October 29, 1926, Athens, Calhoun County.

Ibid.

Ibid.

Blakiston's Illustrated Pocket Medical Dictionary. McGraw-Hill Book Company, Inc., 1952, p. 651.

Waubenoo, John, Private

Blakiston's Illustrated Pocket Medical Dictionary. McGraw-Hill Book Company, Inc., 1952, p. 628.

Ibid., p. 110.

Wayaubemind, Michael, Private

Blakiston's Illustrated Pocket Medical Dictionary. McGraw-Hill Book Company, Inc., 1952, p. 415.

Bollet, Dr. Alfred Jay. *Civil War Medicine Challenges and Triumphs.* Galen Press, Tucson, Arizona, 2003, pp. 236, 237.

Kuz, Dr. Julian and Dr. Bradley P. Bengtson. *Orthopaedic Injuries of the Civil War.* Kennesaw Mountain Press, Inc., Kennesaw Georgia, 1996, pp. 37.

Ibid., p. 36.

Schaadt, Dr. Mark J. *Civil War Medicine—An Illustrated History.* Cedarwood Publishing, Quincy, Illinois, 1998, pp. 68, 69.

Waygeshegoing, William, Private

Argus. The Chesaning *Argus,* Chesaning, Saginaw County, Saturday, April 3, 1897, no page numbers listed.

Ibid.

Avery. Conversations with Chad Avery, Anishinabe historian and genealogist.

Ibid.

Ibid.

Bollet, Dr. Alfred Jay. *Civil War Medicine Challenges and Triumphs.* Galen Press, Tucson, Arizona, 2003, pp. 233, 235–236.

Dorwart, Dr. Bonnie Brice. *Disease is in the Breeze: Disease during the American Civil War.* Bonnie Brice Dorwart, MD, and the National Museum of Civil War Medicine, Frederick, Maryland, 2009, p. 51. *1917–19*

Draft. US World War I Draft Registration Cards 1917–1918 for Thomas Waggeshigomey on *Ancestry.com.*

Georgia. Sergeant First Class Thomas Waygeshegomey found on the Fourteenth Census of the United States: 1920—Population, January 14, 1920, Camp Gordon United States Military Reservation at Cross Keys, DeKalb, Georgia, on Ancestry. com.

Grave. Internet search for online cemetery records and memorials at findagrave. com. Internet search.

Ibid.

Petition. Petition to the Probate Court of Saginaw County, State of Michigan for the Appointment of a Guardian for Tommy Waggishegomey, November 4, 1905.

Probate. State of Michigan, The Probate Court for the County of Saginaw, In the Matter of the Estate of Thomas Waggishegomey, Minor, March 9, 1906.

Wells, Peter, Private

Old Wing Mission. *Old Wing Mission Cultural Interchange as Chronicled by George and Arvilla Smith in their Work with Chief Wakazoo's Ottawa Band on the West Michigan Frontier.* Edited by Robert Swierenga and William Van Appledorn. William B. Eerdmans Publishing Company, Grand Rapids, Michigan, 2008, pp. 623–626.

Ibid., p. 625.

Report of the Presbyterian Indian Mission School at Bear River Emmet County as taught by Andrew Porter, teacher to the Chippewa and Ottawa Indians. An enumeration of both boys and girls who were students at the school's second session ending September 30, 1860. Source for this report is held at the Clarke Historical Library, Central Michigan University, Mt. Pleasant, Isabella County. Courtesy of the Clarke Historical Library. See Primary Resources Researched.

Wesaw, Thomas, Private

Baraga, Frederick. *A Dictionary of the Ojibway Language.* Minnesota Historical Press, St. Paul, New Material, 1992, p. 266.

Bollet, Dr. Alfred Jay. *Civil War Medicine Challenges and Triumphs*. Galen Press, Tucson, Arizona, 2003, p. 212.

Conversations. Conversations with Mrs. Alberta June Mackety Wells, granddaughter of Thomas Wezoo, and letters sent to the author by Mrs. Wells.

Evans, Dr. Bruce A. A *Primer of Civil War Medicine—Non Surgical Medical Practice during the Civil War Years*. Bohemian Publishers, Knoxville, Tennessee, 1998, p. 49.

LaLone. Submitted by James P. LaLone to RootsWeb:Nishnawbe-L (Nishnawbe) Topenebee at Nishnawbe-L Archives. Internet search.

Reuter, Dorothy. *Methodist Indian Ministries in Michigan 1830–1990*. Eerdmans Printing Company, Grand Rapids, Michigan, 1993, pp. 160–166. Conversations with Mrs. Reuter.

Ibid., pp. 166–175.

Schaadt, Dr. Mark J. *Civil War Medicine—An Illustrated History*. Cedarwood Publishing, Quincy, Illinois, 1998, pp. 68–69.

Vogel, Virgil J. *Indian Names in Michigan*. University of Michigan Press, Ann Arbor, 1986, p. 60.

Wells. Story written (about 1921?) by Sarah Isaac and letters sent to the author by Alberta June Mackety Wells, granddaughter of Thomas Wesaw/Wezoo.

Ibid.

Ibid.

Ibid.

Wesley, John, Private

Blakiston's Illustrated Pocket Medical Dictionary. McGraw-Hill Book Company Inc., 1952, p. 169.

Ibid.-*Blakiston*., p. 210.

Bollet, Dr. Alfred Jay. *Civil War Medicine Challenges and Triumphs*. Galen Press, Ltd., Tucson, Arizona, 2002, p. 236.

Ibid., p. 235.

Ibid., pp. 236–238.

Find A Grave Memorial (at findagrave.com)—Internet search.

Land Records.

Whiteface, Charles, Private

Baraga, Frederick. *A Dictionary of the Ojibway Language.* Minnesota Historical Press, St. Paul, New Material, 1992, p. 394.

Bollet, Dr. Alfred Jay. *Civil War Medicine Challenges and Triumphs.* Galen Press, Ltd. Tucson, Arizona, 2002, p. 252.

Ibid., p. 240.

Williams, Joseph, Private (also known as Joseph Nesogot)

Howe, Thomas J. *The Petersburg Campaign, Wasted Valor, June 15–18, 1864,* The Virginia Civil War Battles and Leaders Series. E. H. Howard, Inc. Lynchburg, Virginia, 1988, p. 78.

Ibid., Footnote #46, p. 172.

Ibid.

Williams, Moses, Private

Encyclopedia of Death and Dying, Civil War. US p. 4. Internet Search.

Wolf, Payson, Private

Bollet, Dr. Alfred J. *Civil War Medicine Challenges and Triumphs.* Galen Press, Tucson, Arizona, 2003, pp. 236–237.

Internet search—Earache Remedies—in *Blind Pig and the Acorn.*

Kinnequa. Charlotte Waukazoo, aka Kinnequa, aka Kinnequay. From Historical Collections: Collections and Researches made by the *Michigan Pioneer and Historical Society, Vol XXX,* 1905, Lansing, *LIFE AND WORK OF THE LATE REV. GEORGE N. SMITH, A PIONEER MISSIONARY,* BY MRS. ETTA SMITH WILSON, granddaughter of Kinnequa.

Ibid.

Ibid.

Ibid.

Ibid.

Ibid.

Ibid.

Ibid.

Land Records.

Ibid.

Old Wing Mission. *Old Wing Mission Cultural Interchange as Chronicled by George and Arvilla Smith in their Work with Chief Wakazoo's Ottawa Band on the West Michigan Frontier.* Edited by Robert P. Swierenga and William Van Appledorn. William P. Eerdsman Publishing Company, Grand Rapids, Michigan, 2008, pp. 489–490.

Ibid.-Old Wing Mission, p. 489.

Ibid., p. 490.

Ripple, Ezra Hoyt. *Dancing Along the Deadline—The Andersonville Memoir of a Prisoner of the Confederacy.* Presidio Press, Novato, California, 1996, p. 25.

Ibid., p. 26.

Smith. Rev. George Nelson Smith. Memoranda and Diaries entry of August 1, 1863. Courtesy of Clarence and Avis Wolfe.

Ibid.-Smith. Entry of November 25, 1863.

Ibid.-Smith. Entry of December 30, 1864.

Wolfe. Conversations with Clarence and Avis Wolfe and information and photos sent to the author from the couple.

Ibid.

Ibid.

Ibid.

Ibid.

Index

bold denotes Company K members, enlisted men and officers; *italics* denotes photo

A

adhesive plaster 21, 22, 40, 47, 57, 67, 90, 97, 115, 123, 128, 142, 149, 159, 160, 163, 179, 192, 199, 206, 214, 241, 251, 256, 272, 291, 303, 313, 342, 346, 354, 374, 379, 388, 391, 392, 419, 433, 446

Agahgo, Charles (enlisted man) 33, 496

alcohol 10, 31, 39, 45, 50, 55, 80, 81, 96, 113, 139, 169, 172, 346. *See also* laudanum; *See also* whiskey

Allegan County xiv, 134, 212, 213, 244, 248, 253, 254, 255, 269, 345, 421, 428, 448, 468

Allen, Charles (enlisted man) 36, 496

ambulance corps 9, 100

Amderling (Anotagon), Peter (enlisted man) 43, 44, 73, 497

"America's First Allies," Oneida as known as, 13

amputation 26, 67, 251, 256, 269, 290, 292, 346, 374, 433

Andersonville Prison 37, 60, 61, 64, 65, 68, 130, 153, 166, 176, 218, 228, 229, 242, 249, 263, 264, 276, 277, 300, 328, 349, 371, 441, 458, 459, 465, 494, 503, 506, 521, 524, 529, 532, 534, 538, 539. *See* Camp Sumter (Georgia)

Andress, Edwin Von Shultz (V.) (officer) 20

Andrew, John (enlisted man) 46, 497

anesthetics 9. *See also* chloroform; *See also* ether

Anishinabe/Anishinabek
    attempts by to enlist in Union army 189, 380
    defined x, 95
    in First Michigan Sharpshooters 5
    occupations and life ways 6
    personalizing of gun stocks by 5
    reasons for enlistment by 5, 6

Anishinabe Methodist Episcopal Church 48, 53

antiseptics 9. *See also* bromine; *See also* iodine

Aptargeshick, Oliver (enlisted man) 49, 498

Arwonogezice, James (enlisted man) 51, 498

Ashkanok, Joseph (enlisted man) 54

Ashkebug, George (enlisted man) 57, 58, 499

Ashkebugnekay, Amos (enlisted man) 60, 499

Ashman, Daniel (enlisted man) 63, 499

Athens Indian Methodist Church 448

Athens Methodist Indian Mission Church 449

Awanakwad, Petros (Peter) (enlisted man) 66

B

Baierlein, Eduard (E. R.) (reverend) 298

Baraga County 74, 107, 108, 109, 110, 140, 400, 405, 409

Baraga, Frederic (Catholic bishop) 45

Barry County xiv, 122, 133, 134, 231, 232, 234, 253, 327, 508, 518

Battice, John (enlisted man) 70

Battle at Petersburg (Virginia) xi, xii, xiv, xv, xvi, 5, 13, 15, 21, 26, 27, 33, 35, 37, 40, 44, 46, 47, 50, 52, 55, 57, 60, 64, 66, 67, 73, 75, 79, 80, 83, 85, 87, 90, 91, 92, 95, 97, 98, 103, 107, 111, 115, 119, 122, 123, 124, 128, 130, 133, 136, 140, 142, 149, 153, 156, 159, 161, 165, 166, 169, 171, 175, 178, 179, 186, 187, 192, 199, 200, 206, 208, 214, 216, 217, 218, 219, 221, 222, 227, 228, 231, 232, 234, 237, 240, 241, 242, 246, 249, 251, 252, 255, 256, 263, 266, 267, 268, 276, 280, 285, 291, 294, 296, 297, 299, 302, 303, 306, 309, 310, 313, 315, 320, 328, 330, 331, 333, 334, 335, 339, 342, 345, 346, 348, 353, 354, 360, 365, 366, 371, 373, 374, 375, 379, 380, 383, 388, 391, 401, 412, 418, 419, 428, 430, 433, 434, 437, 445, 446,

458, 460, 464, 465, 485, 497, 505, 506, 509, 516, 517, 518, 520, 541

Battle of Spotsylvania (Virginia) xi, xii, xiv, xv, xvi, 5, 13, 15, 21, 26, 27, 33, 35, 37, 40, 44, 46, 47, 50, 52, 54, 55, 57, 60, 64, 66, 67, 73, 75, 79, 80, 83, 85, 87, 90, 91, 92, 95, 97, 98, 103, 107, 111, 115, 119, 122, 123, 124, 128, 130, 133, 134, 136, 140, 142, 149, 153, 156, 159, 161, 165, 166, 169, 171, 175, 178, 179, 186, 187, 192, 199, 200, 201, 206, 208, 214, 216, 217, 218, 219, 221, 222, 227, 228, 231, 232, 234, 237, 240, 241, 242, 246, 249, 251, 252, 254, 255, 256, 263, 266, 267, 268, 280, 285, 290, 291, 294, 296, 297, 299, 302, 303, 306, 309, 310, 312, 313, 315, 320, 328, 330, 331, 333, 334, 335, 339, 342, 345, 346, 348, 353, 354, 360, 365, 366, 371, 373, 374, 375, 379, 380, 383, 387, 388, 391, 401, 412, 418, 419, 424, 428, 430, 433, 434, 437, 445, 446, 458, 460, 464, 465, 485, 497, 505, 506, 509, 516, 517, 518, 520, 541

Battle of the Crater (Petersburg, Virginia) xii, xv, 14, 44, 46, 50, 52, 60, 64, 67, 75, 85, 90, 92, 97, 107, 115, 130, 149, 153, 156, 159, 165, 175, 178, 179, 187, 192, 200, 208, 216, 219, 227, 242, 246, 249, 263, 285, 296, 299, 303, 306, 309, 313, 320, 328, 330, 333, 345, 348, 353, 360, 366, 371, 379, 383, 416, 430, 434, 445, 458, 460, 464

Battle of the Ni River (Virginia) xi, xii, xiv, xv, xvi, 5, 13, 15, 21, 26, 27, 33, 35, 37, 40, 44, 46, 47, 50, 52, 55, 57, 60, 64, 66, 67, 73, 75, 79, 80, 83, 85, 87, 90, 91, 92, 95, 97, 98, 103, 107, 111, 115, 119, 122, 123, 128, 130, 133, 136, 140, 142, 149, 153, 156, 159, 161, 165, 166, 169, 171, 175, 178, 179, 186, 187, 192, 199, 200, 206, 208, 214, 216, 217, 218, 219, 221, 222, 227, 228, 231, 232, 234, 237, 240, 241, 242, 246, 249, 251, 252, 255, 256, 263, 266, 267, 268, 280, 285, 291, 294, 296, 297, 299, 302, 303, 306, 309, 310, 313, 315, 320, 328, 330, 331, 333, 334, 335, 339, 342, 345, 346, 348, 353, 354, 360, 365, 366, 371, 373, 374, 375, 379, 380, 383, 388, 391, 401, 412, 418, 419, 428, 430, 433, 434, 437, 445, 446, 458, 460, 464, 465, 485, 497, 505, 506, 509, 516, 517, 518, 520, 541

Battle of the Wilderness (Virginia) xi, xii, xiv, xv, xvi, 5, 13, 15, 21, 23, 26, 27, 29, 33, 35, 37, 40, 44, 46, 47, 50, 52, 55, 57, 60, 64, 66, 67, 73, 75, 79,

80, 83, 85, 87, 90, 91, 92, 95, 97, 98, 103, 107, 111, 115, 119, 122, 123, 128, 130, 133, 136, 140, 142, 149, 153, 156, 159, 161, 165, 166, 169, 171, 175, 178, 179, 186, 187, 192, 199, 200, 206, 208, 214, 216, 217, 218, 219, 221, 222, 227, 228, 231, 232, 234, 237, 240, 241, 242, 246, 249, 251, 252, 254, 255, 256, 263, 266, 267, 268, 280, 285, 290, 291, 294, 296, 297, 299, 302, 303, 306, 309, 310, 313, 315, 320, 328, 330, 331, 333, 334, 335, 339, 342, 345, 346, 348, 353, 354, 360, 365, 366, 371, 373, 374, 375, 379, 380, 383, 388, 391, 401, 412, 418, 419, 428, 430, 433, 434, 437, 445, 446, 458, 460, 464, 465, 485, 497, 505, 506, 509, 516, 517, 518, 520, 541

Bay County xvi, 101, 102, 104, 177, 179, 202, 324, 345, 394, 411, 504

Bay Shore 53, 147, 317, 318, 358

Beaver Island 341, 344

Bemassikeh (Pemassegay) (chief) xiv, 88, 147, 298

Bemassikeh (Pemassegay), Wawsaychewonnoquay 298

Benasis, John (a.k.a. John Bird) (enlisted man) 73, 500

Bethany German Lutheran Indian Mission 298

bilingualism 4, 37, 46, 137, 424

Bissell, Samuel (reverend) 141

Black Lake (Lake Macatawa) 467

blistering 83, 99, 169, 172, 237, 247, 280, 286, 454

blood poisoning 29, 34, 48, 208, 241, 248
    pyemia 34, 248
    septicemia 29, 48, 208, 241, 256

blue mass 34, 44, 90, 103, 136, 157, 172, 261, 437, 450

blue pills 99, 103

Bodawatomi (Potawatomi) 2, 158, 179, 180, 212, 224, 232, 233, 235, 252, 428, 429, 447, 448, 449, 496

Bradley Indian Mission xiv, 213

bromine, as antiseptic 9, 22, 34, 115, 142, 163, 179, 215, 248, 343, 346, 379, 446

bronchitis 14, 66, 83, 165, 182, 183, 218, 237, 324, 335, 336, 358, 394, 454

The Bureau of Pensions: Its History, Activities and Organization (Weber) 11

Burnside, Ambrose E. 9

Burns, Peter (enlisted man) 78, 500

Bushaw, Augustus (enlisted man) 80, 501

C

Cabecoung (Caybaicoung), William (enlisted man) 53, 82, 83, 84, 96, 101, 501

Calhoun County 15, 155, 212, 252, 253, 254, 337, 422, 429, 445, 447, 449, 469, 536, 538

Campbell, Charles W. (reverend) 141

Camp Chandler (Kalamazoo) 3, 125, 152, 181, 211, 212, 225, 242, 246, 251, 254, 280, 418, 427, 445, 449, 450, 468

Camp Chase (Ohio) 12, 15, 37, 42, 61, 136, 138, 243, 244, 245, 276, 422, 459, 466, 469, 496, 511, 513, 532, 537

Camp Douglas (Illinois) ix, xi, xiv, 8, 9, 11, 22, 25, 33, 37, 38, 39, 51, 60, 66, 75, 78, 86, 90, 92, 95, 99, 101, 102, 113, 115, 118, 119, 122, 127, 130, 133, 140, 159, 162, 185, 191, 216, 221, 227, 233, 235, 240, 242, 254, 255, 261, 262, 265, 266, 276, 285, 296, 305, 306, 309, 324, 325, 335, 337, 341, 345, 348, 370, 373, 382, 387, 410, 411, 412, 416, 428, 430, 436, 450, 454, 462, 464, 494, 497, 498, 499, 500, 501, 502, 503, 504, 505, 506, 507, 508, 509, 510, 511, 515, 516, 517, 520, 521, 522, 523, 524, 526, 527, 528, 529, 531, 532, 533, 534, 537, 538, 540

Camp Lawton (Georgia) 37, 60, 61, 64, 65, 68, 130, 153, 166, 176, 218, 228, 229, 242, 249, 263, 264, 276, 277, 300, 328, 349, 371, 441, 458, 459, 465, 494, 503, 506, 521, 524, 529, 532, 534, 538, 539

Camp Parole (Maryland) 9, 11, 21, 25, 26, 33, 49, 51, 64, 78, 80, 85, 90, 113, 115, 122, 159, 181, 229, 237, 276, 306, 309, 310, 327, 329, 349, 350, 373, 382, 391, 432, 450, 457, 459, 464, 465, 466, 499, 501, 502, 510, 511, 513, 514, 531, 533, 534, 539

Camp Sumter (Georgia) 37, 60, 61, 64, 65, 68, 130, 153, 166, 176, 218, 228, 229, 242, 249, 263, 264, 276, 277, 300, 328, 349, 371, 441, 458, 459, 465, 494, 503, 506, 521, 524, 529, 532, 534, 538, 539

capsicum 149

carbolic acid (phenol) 343, 379, 446

Carter, Charles (enlisted man) 85, 501

Cass County 177, 424, 425, 426

castor oil 34, 50, 79, 87, 90, 99, 103, 113, 122, 136, 149, 157, 162, 169, 172, 186, 231, 248, 281, 303, 309, 331, 383, 464

Cathartics 162. *See* castor oil

Catholic Mission School (Point St. Ignace) 30, 153, 154, 384, 494, 495

cerate 27, 291, 347, 379, 392

Chamberlain, Amos (a.k.a. Pahnosewawnequat) (enlisted man) 86

Charles Mears (steamer) 20, 21, 27, 33, 37, 44, 45, 47, 55, 57, 58, 61, 66, 71, 73, 76, 79, 80, 81, 83, 87, 88, 91, 95, 96, 98, 100, 103, 104, 107, 123, 124, 128, 142, 157, 160, 163, 166, 169, 175, 178, 180, 181, 182, 183, 186, 192, 200, 212, 214, 215, 224, 225, 229, 237, 243, 244, 252, 256, 268, 272, 277, 281, 286, 291, 294, 303, 310, 313, 315, 316, 331, 332, 334, 335, 338, 342, 346, 349, 354, 360, 366, 374, 383, 384, 389, 391, 392, 395, 401, 420, 430, 433, 434, 437, 443, 450, 451, 462

Charlevoix County 13, 52, 53, 58, 140, 141, 143, 145, 147, 164, 166, 167, 168, 239, 242, 244, 245, 259, 260, 265, 287, 305, 317, 318, 341, 384, 443, 444, 445

Chatfield, Charles (enlisted man) 89, 502

Chatfield, Samuel C. (enlisted man) 92, 502

Cheboygan County xiii, 66, 135, 163, 164, 196, 206, 219, 245, 309, 316, 318, 435, 516, 527

Chippewa County 72, 108, 141, 143, 159, 160, 272

Chippewa (Ojibwa, Ojibwe) vii, xiii, 2, 48, 72, 74, 76, 83, 84, 91, 92, 100, 105, 108, 109, 116, 117, 129, 132, 141, 143, 145, 147, 156, 159, 160, 177, 197, 201, 230, 232, 233, 235, 248, 268, 269, 270, 272, 274, 295, 296, 297, 299, 304, 364, 369, 381, 401, 402, 403, 408, 459, 471, 483, 493, 497, 502, 503, 504, 505, 507, 511, 515, 516, 525, 526, 527, 532, 535, 539

chloroform 9, 26, 40, 67, 123, 136, 179, 251, 256, 290, 303, 342, 343, 346, 374, 379, 392, 433, 446. *See also* anesthetics

chronic endocarditis 352

Church, Albert (a.k.a. James Moses) (enlisted man) 94, 503

circular amputation 346

cloth wrap (cloth bandages) 21, 90, 97, 103, 115, 123, 128, 142, 149, 159, 160, 163, 192, 199, 206, 214, 240, 267, 272, 291, 303, 313, 342, 346, 354, 374, 379, 388, 391, 433, 446

Collins, Jacob (enlisted man) 97, 503

Collins, John (enlisted man) 98, 503

Collins, William (enlisted man) 100, 504

Company K (First Michigan Sharpshooters) ix, xi, 1, 11, 20, 23, 25, 96, 218, 221, 418, 419, 443

as all-Indian Company 1

as attached to Ninth Corps 9

deaths in battle, from wounds, or from disease of 154

deployment of 51

membership of 52, 322, 411

officers of 2, 7, 176

religious backgrounds of 7

source of biographical profiles of 11

sources of names used for biographical profiles 11

Confederate army, surrender of 5, 458

conjunctivitis (opthalmia) 64, 157, 162, 163, 320, 366, 367, 368, 369, 382, 436, 511, 513

Connecticut (steamer) 21, 27, 33, 37, 44, 45, 47, 55, 57, 58, 61, 66, 71, 73, 76, 79, 80, 81, 83, 87, 88, 91, 95, 96, 98, 100, 103, 104, 107, 115, 123, 124, 128, 142, 157, 160, 163, 166, 169, 175, 178, 180, 181, 182, 183, 186, 192, 200, 212, 214, 215, 224, 225, 229, 237, 243, 244, 252, 256, 268, 272, 277, 281, 286, 291, 294, 303, 310, 313, 315, 316, 331, 332, 334, 335, 338, 342, 346, 349, 354, 360, 366, 374, 383, 384, 389, 391, 392, 395, 401, 420, 430, 433, 434, 437, 443, 450, 451, 462

Constitution (steamer) 21, 27, 33, 37, 42, 44, 45, 47, 55, 57, 58, 61, 66, 71, 73, 76, 79, 80, 81, 83, 87, 88, 91, 95, 96, 98, 100, 103, 104, 107, 123, 124, 128, 131, 142, 157, 160, 163, 166, 169, 175, 178, 180, 181, 182, 183, 186, 192, 200, 212, 214, 215, 224, 225, 229, 237, 243, 244, 252, 256, 268, 272, 277, 281, 286, 291, 294, 303, 310, 313, 315, 316, 331, 332, 334, 335, 338, 342, 346, 349, 354, 360, 366, 374, 383, 384, 389, 391, 392, 395, 401, 420, 430, 433, 434, 437, 443, 450, 451, 462, 465

consumption (tuberculosis) 12, 22, 45, 59, 77, 82, 90, 93, 95, 96, 104, 107, 108, 109, 110, 116, 117, 120, 125, 126, 144, 145, 146, 151, 167, 170, 181, 182, 204, 212, 213, 226, 237, 238, 265, 268, 269, 270, 281, 282, 283, 287, 292, 294, 298, 306, 310, 317, 339, 340, 358, 362, 375, 380, 385, 392, 393, 394, 405, 406, 428, 440, 443, 444, 445, 448, 452, 454, 469

contusion 90, 128, 333, 432

Cooper, Richard 28, 29, 130, 136, 255

Copway, George 2

Corbin, George (a.k.a. Puhquas and Wabmaygo) (enlisted man) 102, 504

Crane, Amos (enlisted man) 106, 504

cupping 83, 99, 162, 169, 172, 237, 247, 280, 286, 454

D

Dabasequam, Jonah (a.k.a. Kemwanashkam) (enlisted man) 111, 505

Danville Prison (Danville, Virginia) 13, 217, 218, 219, 517

David, John (a.k.a. Taybawsegay or Tabaseka) (enlisted man) 112, 505

dead house 65, 131, 153, 176, 218, 249, 300, 328, 371

debridement 22, 214

Delaware Tribe (Lenni Lenape) 85

depot hospital 21, 33, 37, 40, 41, 44, 47, 55, 66, 79, 83, 87, 91, 92, 95, 98, 115, 128, 142, 149, 159, 160, 166, 169, 180, 186, 199, 200, 206, 207, 214, 241, 246, 247, 256, 267, 294, 303, 304, 310, 313, 331, 334, 342, 346, 354, 379, 388, 434, 437, 446

　Alexandria, Virginia 169

　City Point, Virginia 15, 27, 44, 47, 66, 79, 80, 83, 87, 91, 92, 95, 98, 103, 115, 166, 186, 246, 303, 310, 331, 334, 346, 354, 366, 379, 383, 419, 437, 446, 497

　Fredericksburg, Virginia 21, 33, 37, 40, 55, 95, 111, 128, 136, 199, 206, 214, 222, 241, 252, 256, 267, 313, 342, 374, 388, 391, 419, 497, 505, 506, 516, 517, 520

　White House Landing, Virginia 294, 433

De Puy, Charles H. 218, 219, 331

Descriptive Roll of Company K, First Regiment Michigan Sharpshooters, Volunteers 12

Detroit Advertiser and Tribune 7, 29, 494

diarrhea 44, 45, 48, 49, 50, 61, 66, 78, 79, 80, 81, 82, 83, 87, 89, 90, 91, 96, 99, 103, 104, 105, 149, 156, 157, 165, 166, 169, 170, 172, 176, 186, 228, 231, 237, 243, 244, 277, 281, 300, 303, 304, 309, 319, 332, 335, 349, 365, 371, 383, 386, 398, 437, 438, 450, 451, 452, 465

Disabled Personalities (Schram) xv, 485, 491

discharge papers 474

diseases. See specific diseases 95, 218, 283, 286, 332. *See* anesthetics

Doughtery, Peter (reverend) 141

Dover's powder 34, 50, 66, 67, 79, 80, 81, 87, 90, 96, 99, 103, 113, 142, 166, 169, 183, 186, 237, 243, 247, 281, 303, 309, 339, 365, 437

Driggs, William J. (officer) 2, 20, 22, 23, 24, 29, 44, 47, 51, 55, 152, 172, 175, 204, 212, 257, 296, 312, 322, 347, 358, 361, 365, 368, 386, 395, 412, 437, 449, 458, 459, 460, 462, 471, 485, 516, 527

drug addiction 10

drum feasts 4

Dutton, Luther (a.k.a. Luke Dutton, Isidor Abendunk, and Chittimon) (enlisted man) 114, 505

Duverney, William 5

E

earache 159, 225, 464, 517, 541

embalming 10, 194, 262

emetics 169, 172. *See* castor oil

Emmet County xiv, 14, 25, 32, 51, 54, 66, 68, 69, 74, 80, 82, 111, 120, 126, 127, 129, 135, 136, 139, 140, 141, 143, 145, 156, 166, 167, 177, 191, 195, 196, 206, 216, 219, 220, 221, 227, 230, 240, 242, 244, 245, 255, 258, 259, 260, 265, 285, 287, 296, 305, 306, 307, 308, 309, 317, 318, 332, 334, 336, 341, 343, 348, 351, 353, 355, 356, 357, 358, 359, 361, 362, 370, 372, 382, 386, 387, 389, 420, 423, 432, 434, 435, 442, 443, 473, 499, 507, 515, 521, 532, 539

enlistment 3, 4, 5, 6, 7, 12, 17, 18, 19, 20, 23, 25, 33, 36, 43, 46, 49, 51, 54, 57, 60, 63, 64, 66, 70, 72, 73, 74, 78, 80, 82, 85, 86, 89, 92, 94, 96, 97, 98, 100, 102, 106, 107, 111, 112, 114, 118, 120, 121, 122, 127, 129, 133, 134, 135, 136, 140, 141, 147, 148, 153, 156, 159, 160, 161, 162, 165, 168, 169, 171, 174, 175, 177, 179, 181, 182, 185, 187, 191, 195, 197, 198, 206, 208, 211, 213, 214, 215, 216, 221, 223, 225, 227, 231, 232, 234, 236, 240, 242, 246, 249, 251, 255, 261, 263, 264, 265, 266, 271, 275, 280, 285, 289, 294, 295, 296, 297, 299, 302, 305, 309, 311, 312, 314, 316, 319, 324, 327, 329, 333, 334, 336, 337, 338, 341, 345, 348, 353, 359, 364, 365, 370, 373, 378, 382, 387, 390, 394, 395, 399, 401, 409, 411, 415, 417, 427, 428, 429, 432, 433, 436, 442, 445, 447, 449, 453, 456, 458, 460, 461, 462, 467

inducements for enlistments 3

oath taken at 17

paper of Cornelius Ward Hall 150

paper of Robert Valentine 19

Enrollment Act of March 3

erysipelas 34, 122, 248, 327, 496

Etarwegeshig, John (a.k.a. John Wamegwon) (enlisted man) 118, 506

ether 9, 21, 136, 214, 342, 343, 346, 392, 433.

as anesthetics

F

families, effect of wartime experiences on

.58-caliber Springfield Rifle Muskets 5, 95, 99, 113, 276, 337, 345, 458

First Michigan Sharpshooters ix, x, xi, 1, 2, 4, 5, 9, 11, 15, 18, 19, 20, 23, 25, 28, 31, 33, 36, 43, 46, 49, 51, 54, 57, 60, 63, 66, 73, 74, 75, 76, 78, 80, 82, 83, 85, 86, 89, 92, 94, 96, 97, 98, 99, 100, 102, 103, 111, 112, 114, 118, 122, 127, 129, 130, 133, 135, 140, 141, 142, 147, 148, 149, 153, 156, 158, 159, 160, 161, 162, 165, 168, 169, 171, 174, 175, 177, 179, 181, 185, 187, 191, 197, 198, 206, 208, 213, 214, 216, 218, 221, 224, 225, 227, 231, 232, 234, 236, 237, 240, 242, 246, 249, 251, 253, 255, 261, 263, 265, 266, 271, 274, 275, 276, 280, 285, 289, 294, 296, 297, 299, 302, 305, 309, 311, 312, 314, 316, 319, 320, 324, 327, 329, 333, 334, 337, 338, 339, 341, 345, 347, 348, 353, 356, 359, 360, 364, 370, 373, 378, 382, 387, 390, 391, 395, 401, 409, 410, 411, 412, 415, 417, 418, 419, 427, 428, 429, 432, 436, 442, 443, 445, 453, 454, 456, 457, 458, 460, 461, 462, 474, 475, 476, 477, 478, 479, 480, 481, 482, 483, 484

Company K (First Michigan Sharpshooters) vii, ix, x, xi, xii, xiii, xv, xvi, 1, 2, 4, 5, 6, 7, 11, 12, 13, 15, 18, 19, 20, 23, 25, 26, 37, 40, 41, 42, 44, 45, 48, 60, 61, 65, 67, 68, 69, 73, 74, 82, 84, 85, 88, 91, 96, 100, 101, 102, 105, 106, 124, 125, 130, 131, 136, 146, 147, 148, 153, 154, 156, 158, 161, 163, 166, 167, 168, 170, 171, 176, 177, 178, 179, 180, 189, 194, 195, 198, 199, 200, 203, 209, 210, 218, 221, 224, 227, 230, 238, 243, 244, 245, 246, 253, 255, 263, 269, 270, 278, 280, 283, 290, 292, 295, 300, 301, 309, 317, 319, 321, 322, 324, 328, 329, 330, 332, 334, 336, 337, 349, 350, 355, 361, 365, 369, 371, 372, 382, 386, 398, 400, 404, 411, 413, 414, 416, 417, 418, 419, 421, 423, 435, 443, 444, 445, 454, 458, 460, 469, 471, 474, 475, 476, 477, 478, 479, 480, 481, 482, 483, 484, 485, 493, 528

mustering of into United States service 5

flap amputation 26

Fredericksburg National Battlefield Cemetery (Fredericksburg, Virginia) 21, 33, 37, 40, 55,

547

95, 111, 128, 136, 199, 206, 214, 222, 241, 252, 256, 267, 313, 342, 374, 388, 391, 419, 497, 505, 506, 516, 517, 520

Fredericksburg, Virginia 21, 33, 37, 40, 55, 95, 111, 128, 136, 199, 206, 214, 222, 241, 252, 256, 267, 313, 342, 374, 388, 391, 419, 497, 505, 506, 516, 517, 520

G

general court-martial 75, 161

Genereau, Louis, Jr. (enlisted man) 12, 20, 21, 122, 123, 124, 125, 126, 127, 456, 506

Genereau, Louis, Sr. 20, 21, 125

George, David (a.k.a. David Nayyawtoe or Naygatoe) (enlisted man) 127, 507

George Leary (steamer) 21, 27, 33, 37, 44, 45, 47, 55, 57, 58, 61, 66, 71, 73, 76, 79, 80, 81, 83, 87, 88, 91, 95, 96, 98, 100, 103, 104, 107, 123, 124, 128, 142, 157, 160, 163, 166, 169, 175, 178, 180, 181, 182, 183, 186, 192, 200, 212, 214, 215, 224, 225, 229, 237, 243, 244, 252, 256, 268, 272, 277, 281, 286, 291, 294, 303, 310, 313, 315, 316, 331, 332, 334, 335, 338, 342, 346, 349, 354, 360, 366, 374, 383, 384, 389, 391, 392, 395, 401, 420, 430, 433, 434, 437, 443, 450, 451, 462

Gibson, Joseph L. (a.k.a. Joseph Nabawnayasang and Louis J. Gibson) (enlisted man) 129, 507

Going, Samuel (a.k.a. Sam Tondoqua) (enlisted man) 133, 508

gonorrhea 331

Grand Army of the Republic (GAR) xiv, 11, 24, 25, 52, 53, 56, 59, 62, 63, 82, 84, 88, 106, 152, 163, 167, 168, 203, 204, 205, 274, 278, 287, 288, 292, 308, 318, 322, 338, 352, 357, 358, 361, 363, 386, 408, 409, 411, 414, 472, 493

Grand Medicine Society Lodge (Midewiwin) 268, 403

Grand Traverse Mission Church (Old Mission) and school 41

Graveraet, Garret A. (a.k.a. Garrett A. Graveraet) (officer) 28, 29, 51, 54, 57, 80, 111, 129, 136, 139, 140, 159, 191, 195, 206, 216, 240, 242, 249, 257, 265, 285, 305, 309, 334, 341, 348, 353, 359, 370, 382, 387, 442

Graveraet, Henry Garret, Jr. (a.k.a. as Henry Garrett Graveraet, Jr.) (enlisted man) 137

Graveraet, Sophia 28, 29, 195

Greensky, Benjamin C. (enlisted man) 140, 509

Greensky Hill Indian Mission 53

Greensky, Jacob (enlisted man) 141, 509

Greensky, Peter (reverend) 141, 144

Greensky, Susan 141, 143, 144

Grove Hill New Mission Church 42, 132, 258

Gruet (Grewett), Peter, Jr. (enlisted man) xiv, 147, 148, 270, 271, 297, 299, 502, 510

H

Hagerstown, Maryland 85

Hall, Brickerd (Ann) (Mahwazoo) 150

Hall, Cornelius Ward (a.k.a. Negawnesay or Kawgaygawbowe) (enlisted man) 150

Hall, Florence (Nibnesey Hill) 479

Hall, Kawgaygawbowe (Frederick) (chief) 150

Hamlin, James (or Jacobert/Jackoba) Hatch (enlisted man) 153, 510

handwriting analysis, selected names for 485

Hannin, Joseph (enlisted man) 156, 510

Harwich, Kent County (Ontario, Canada) 20, 49, 157, 158, 161, 171, 172, 188, 341, 343, 395, 396, 456, 461, 514

Herek, Raymond J. 9, 494, 508

Hickey, Manasseh (reverend) 141

Holmes, Thomas 10, 28, 256

Holy Childhood of Jesus Catholic Cemetery 359

Holy Childhood of Jesus Catholic Church and school 195, 229, 245, 317, 389

Honor Indian Mission 53

Houghton County 45, 108, 401, 405

Hubert, Charles (enlisted man) 159, 511

Hyde Park, Dutchess County (New York) 13, 23, 75, 87, 91, 138, 156, 157, 171, 172, 186, 223, 224, 344, 402, 413, 496, 498, 508, 509, 530

I

illnesses 9, 48, 82, 170, 224, 286, 339, 362, 384

Indian agents
   DeWitt C. Leach 29, 106
   George W. Lee 356, 530
   Henry R. Schoolcraft 135, 137
   Richard Cooper 28, 29, 130, 136, 255

Indian missions 269, 537
   Athens Methodist Indian Mission Church 449
   Bethany German Lutheran Indian Mission 298
   Bradley Indian Mission xiv, 213
   Greensky Hill Indian Mission 53
   Honor Indian Mission 53
   Isabella Indian Mission 71, 88, 105

Methodist Riverton Indian Mission 226
Nottawa Indian Mission and Cemetery 448
Oceana Indian Mission 125
Oneida Indian Mission 157
Petoskey Methodist Indian Mission Church 306
Pine River Methodist Indian Mission 143, 144
Salem Indian Mission 269
Taymouth Indian Mission 269
Indiantown 102, 190, 429, 438
indolent ulcer 214
Insights Seminar Book of Signatures (Schram) xv,
485, 491
iodine 9, 27, 34, 47, 55, 90, 179, 181, 192, 199,
200, 206, 241, 266, 294, 303, 313, 327,
342, 343, 346, 354, 379, 388, 391, 419, 446.
as antiseptics
Irons, John (reverend) 141
Isaacs, John (enlisted man) 160
Isaacs, William (enlisted man) 161, 511
Isabella County xv, 7, 46, 48, 63, 71, 78, 82, 86, 88,
89, 91, 92, 93, 97, 98, 100, 101, 102, 105, 106,
109, 112, 116, 117, 118, 127, 129, 161, 164, 167,
168, 184, 197, 201, 202, 205, 206, 263, 266,
269, 280, 281, 282, 283, 284, 289, 291, 292,
293, 294, 295, 297, 298, 299, 302, 304, 312,
314, 324, 359, 364, 368, 409, 410, 411, 429,
430, 436, 438, 458, 460, 474, 493, 497, 499,
506, 508, 509, 511, 519, 530, 532, 539
Isabella Indian Mission 71, 88, 105

J

Jacko, John (enlisted man) 165, 511
**Jacko, Natahwinodin (a.k.a. Louis/Lewis
Penaiswanquot)** (enlisted man) 168, 512
Jackson, Edward Andrew (enlisted man) 171, 512
Jackson, William (enlisted man) 174
Jeandron (Jondreau), Michael (enlisted man) 154,
175, 176, 177, 513
Jesuits (Order of the Society of Jesus) 467
John, David (enlisted man) 177
John, William (enlisted man) 179

K

Kabaosa, Louis (enlisted man) 181, 513
Kabayacega, George (a.k.a. George Sockatup)
(enlisted man) 182
Kadah, Joseph (enlisted man) 185, 514
Kahgayahsung, Solomon (a.k.a. Solomon Foster)
(enlisted man) 197

Kakakee, Joseph (enlisted man) 187, 514
Kalamazoo County 125, 152, 211, 212, 225, 242,
246, 251, 254, 280, 418, 427, 445, 449,
450, 468
Kaquatch, Samuel (enlisted man) 191, 514
Kawkawlin Indian Reservation 394
Kechittigo, Mary Ann (Campau/Campeau Elke) 480
Kechittigo, Thomas (Tom) (a.k.a. Neodegezhik)
(enlisted man) 198, 515
Kedgnal, John 5, 123
Kejikowe, Simon (enlisted man) 206, 516
**Kenewahaneby, John (a.k.a. John
Kenewahnaneppi/Keniwahnaneppi)** (enlisted
man) 208, 516
Kent County 33, 35, 53, 60, 78, 118, 141, 148, 165,
168, 171, 172, 173, 185, 187, 208, 231, 232,
233, 235, 246, 254, 261, 275, 281, 296, 311,
319, 378, 391, 411, 415
Kesas, John (enlisted man) 211, 516
Kettle Point Reserve (Indian Reserve #) (Lambton,
Ontario, Canada) 395
Kewacondo, Benjamin (enlisted man) 213, 516
Kitchibatise, Amable (enlisted man) 216, 517

L

Lake Macatawa (Black Lake) 467
Lamourandere, Thaddeus (Taddy) (enlisted man)
221, 517
Lapeer County 46, 48, 84, 86, 89, 91, 92, 93, 100,
202, 263, 282, 457, 461
La Pointe, Madeline Island, Ashland County
(Wisconsin) 15, 43, 45, 46, 72, 76, 77, 108,
123, 271, 272, 273, 274, 304, 315, 362, 396,
400, 401, 402, 403, 404, 406, 407, 408, 483,
497, 523, 535, 536, 537
laudanum 45, 50, 80, 81, 87, 166, 169, 172, 303, 450.
See also specific medical treatments
lay preacher/minister 52, 74, 146
Leach, Dewitt C. 29, 106
Lee, George W. 356, 530
Leelanau County xiv, 15, 36, 42, 52, 57, 69, 132, 141,
153, 165, 167, 168, 170, 171, 206, 208, 209,
216, 236, 238, 239, 240, 244, 249, 250, 258,
277, 278, 285, 296, 299, 301, 302, 311, 319,
320, 321, 323, 358, 361, 362, 363, 418, 420,
422, 423, 425, 443, 461, 469, 471, 472, 473
Lee, Robert E. 5, 458
Lenni Lenape (Delaware Tribe) 85
Letterman, Jonathan 9, 238

Lidger, Daniel (a.k.a. David Lidyer) (enlisted man) 223, 517

Light, Josiah (enlisted man) 225, 517

M

Mackinac County 25, 30, 74, 76, 77, 135, 139, 153, 154, 155, 159, 175, 177, 202, 213, 214, 513

Mackinac Island 25, 29, 30, 74, 76, 77, 135, 136, 137, 138, 139, 148, 153, 154, 175, 202, 213, 214, 349, 350, 351, 352, 353

malaria 10, 87, 90, 99, 165, 266, 290, 329, 339, 349, 365, 370, 383, 384, 386, 391, 432, 450, 452, 464

Marks, Louis (enlisted man) 227, 518

marksmanship, as requirement for enlistment 7

Marksmanship Required for Enlistment 7

Marquette County xiv, 108, 138, 147, 407, 460

Marquette, Frank (Francis) (enlisted man) 231, 518

Marye, John 21, 33, 40, 55, 95, 128, 133, 200, 206, 214, 241, 256, 267, 313, 342, 388

Marye's Heights 21, 33, 40, 55, 95, 128, 133, 200, 206, 214, 241, 256, 267, 313, 342, 388

Mashkaw, James (Jim) (a.k.a. Kahkuhgewa) (enlisted man) 232, 518

Mashkaw, John (enlisted man) 234, 519

Mashkaw (Maishkaw), John, Sr. (chief) 14, 232, 233, 234, 235, 236, 518, 519

Mashkaw, Wahonoquay 233, 235, 236

Mason County 62, 63, 72, 123, 135, 150, 151, 152, 178, 187, 189, 190, 191, 225, 226, 246, 248, 249, 262, 277, 332, 378, 380, 381, 382, 451, 452, 453, 455, 456, 517, 518, 533

Medal of Honor 14, 15, 219, 330, 517, 528

The Medical and Surgical History of the War of the Rebellion 28, 34, 128, 290, 529

medical treatment 21, 47, 87, 229, 243, 335, 348, 349, 353, 437, 457, 459, 465

Meissler, Ernst G. H. (reverend) 141

Methodist Church School (Bay Mills) 108, 143

Methodist Riverton Indian Mission 226

Midewiwin (Grand Medicine Society Lodge) 268, 403

Miingun (Maingan) (Wolf) family 421, 466, 467

Miingun (Maingan) (Wolf), Kinequa (Kinnequa) (Charlotte) 421, 466, 467

Miingun (Maingan) (Wolf), Naon (Nayan) (chief) 421, 466, 467

Miller, Thomas (a.k.a. Thomas Kahgee) (enlisted man) 236, 519

Misisaius, Edward (enlisted man) 240, 519

Miskoguon, Louis (a.k.a. Kewaquiskum and Awkebemosay) (enlisted man) 242, 520

Mixonauby (Micksenawbay), Thomas (enlisted man) 246, 247, 248, 249, 520

Mixunasaw, William (enlisted man) 249

Mogwahgo (Moguago), John (chief) 251, 252, 253, 254, 521

Mogwahgo (Moguago), Roxana 252

Mogwahgo (Moogargoe), George W. (enlisted man) 251, 252, 253, 254, 521

monetary compensation
    as inducement for enlistment 6
    upon discharge 268, 313, 368

Morning Star (steamer) vii, 21, 27, 33, 37, 44, 45, 47, 55, 57, 58, 61, 66, 71, 73, 76, 79, 80, 81, 83, 87, 88, 91, 95, 96, 98, 100, 103, 104, 107, 123, 124, 128, 142, 157, 160, 163, 166, 169, 175, 178, 180, 181, 182, 183, 186, 192, 200, 212, 214, 215, 224, 225, 229, 237, 243, 244, 252, 256, 268, 272, 277, 281, 286, 291, 294, 303, 310, 313, 315, 316, 331, 332, 334, 335, 338, 342, 346, 349, 354, 360, 366, 374, 383, 384, 389, 391, 392, 395, 401, 420, 430, 433, 434, 437, 443, 450, 451, 462

morphine 9, 97, 123, 142, 252, 256, 267, 303, 343, 346

Mt. Pleasant Indian School (Isabella County) xv, 7, 46, 48, 63, 71, 78, 82, 86, 88, 89, 91, 92, 93, 97, 98, 100, 101, 102, 105, 106, 109, 112, 116, 117, 118, 127, 129, 161, 164, 167, 168, 184, 197, 201, 202, 205, 206, 263, 266, 269, 280, 281, 282, 283, 284, 289, 291, 292, 293, 294, 295, 297, 298, 299, 302, 304, 312, 314, 324, 359, 364, 368, 409, 410, 411, 429, 430, 436, 438, 458, 460, 474, 493, 497, 499, 506, 508, 509, 511, 519, 530, 532, 539

mustard plaster (sinapism) 99, 103, 162, 165, 182, 261, 383

Mwakewenah, Catherine (Ningasigekwe) 258

Mwakewenah, Daniel (chief) (enlisted man) 255, 521

myocardial failure 398

N

Nanticoke 85, 86, 501

Narquaquot, Joseph (enlisted man) 261, 522

Narwegeshequabey, Jackson (a.k.a. Nowkeshe) (enlisted man) 263

National Archives xi, xiii, 11, 18, 19, 475, 476, 480, 493, 500

Naugechegumme (Naugjekomeh) (chief) 7, 201, 325

Nauquam, Thompson (enlisted man) 265, 522

Nelson, David (a.k.a. Chief David Nelson Shopnagon/ Shoppenagans and Shawbwawnegonse "Little Needles") vii, 14

Nelson, Mary (Awnemequoung or Amnemequon) 203

Nelson, Thomas (enlisted man) 266, 522

nephritis 25, 152, 398, 431

Neveaux (Neveau), William (enlisted man) 271, 272, 273, 274, 275, 315, 523

Newton, William (a.k.a. Wawachen, Wabwahchin, and Itwogezhick) (enlisted man) 275, 523

Ninth Corps, Company K as attached to 9, 40, 44, 67, 128, 199, 207, 241

Noquet Tribe 108

Northport Congregational Church 470

Northport, Leelanau County 36, 52, 57, 141, 165, 167, 170, 216, 236, 240, 244, 249, 250, 278, 285, 296, 299, 301, 358, 361, 418, 420, 461

Nottawa Indian Mission and Cemetery 293, 294

O

Oceana County xi, xiv, 20, 33, 35, 51, 60, 72, 118, 121, 122, 125, 133, 141, 148, 150, 181, 182, 185, 221, 222, 225, 232, 233, 234, 235, 246, 255, 261, 275, 327, 329, 337, 338, 345, 347, 348, 373, 376, 390, 391, 392, 394, 411, 414, 415, 427, 428, 453, 455, 494

Oceana Indian Mission 125

Odaawaa (Odawa, Ottawa) 2

Ogitchedaw (warriors) x, 2, 4, 6, 8, 12, 37, 51, 157, 224, 228, 462

Ohbowakemo, James (a.k.a. James R. Oshburn) (enlisted man) 280, 524

Ojibwa (Ojibwe, Chippewa) 2, 83, 116, 143, 160, 188, 220, 305, 401, 402

Okandikan (Okondokon), John Waasegiizhig, Sr. 400, 401, 402

Okandikan (Okondokon), Old Chief (a.k.a. Old Chief Bouy) 400, 401, 402, 403, 405, 407

Old Mission 36, 41, 42, 51, 112, 131, 132, 168, 170, 236, 238, 257, 258, 260, 300, 301, 496, 521, 527

Old Wing Mission 420, 421, 422, 443, 468, 470, 471, 537, 539, 542

Omena, Leelanau County 206, 236, 238, 302, 321

Oneida County (New York) 13, 23, 75, 87, 91, 138, 156, 157, 171, 172, 186, 223, 224, 344, 402, 413, 496, 498, 508, 509, 530

Oneida Indian Mission 157

Oneida Indian Nation 157, 224, 510, 517

Ontonagon County xiii, 43, 45, 314, 315, 333, 334, 401, 407, 535

Onumunese, Leelanau Township, Leelanau County 250

opiates 10, 50, 80, 99, 104, 107, 157, 162, 165, 181, 186, 192, 215, 225, 261, 281, 286, 295, 360, 375, 395, 419, 433, 434, 450

opium 9, 21, 26, 27, 34, 40, 45, 47, 50, 54, 55, 57, 66, 67, 79, 80, 81, 83, 87, 90, 96, 97, 98, 99, 103, 113, 115, 122, 123, 136, 142, 149, 159, 166, 169, 172, 182, 183, 186, 192, 199, 200, 206, 209, 214, 231, 237, 240, 241, 243, 247, 252, 255, 256, 267, 281, 291, 303, 309, 313, 330, 339, 342, 343, 346, 347, 354, 365, 374, 379, 383, 388, 391, 419, 433, 437, 446, 454

opthalmia (conjunctivitis) 64, 157, 162, 163, 320, 366, 367, 368, 369, 382, 436, 511, 513

oral turpentine 50, 90, 437, 450

Order of the Society of Jesus (Jesuits) 467

orthopedic surgeries 9

otalgia 464

Otashquabono, Leon (enlisted man) 285, 524

otitis media 159, 225

Ottawa County 123, 187, 189, 262, 376, 467

Ottawa (Odaawaa, Odawa) xiii, 2, 12, 14, 15, 21, 72, 123, 132, 134, 138, 145, 150, 156, 160, 177, 187, 189, 207, 212, 220, 222, 228, 230, 232, 233, 235, 248, 259, 262, 277, 310, 376, 381, 420, 444, 466, 467, 468, 471, 472, 496, 511, 516, 526, 527, 532, 537, 539, 542

Otto, Marcus (enlisted man) 289, 524

Otto, Solomon (enlisted man) 294, 525

P

pain relief 9, 142, 165, 281. *See also* opium; *See also* morphine

Pakemaboga, John (enlisted man) 296

Paybawme (chief) vii, xiii, xiv, 7, 8, 14, 20, 88, 116, 117, 137, 138, 143, 147, 150, 160, 184, 188, 193, 201, 203, 207, 233, 235, 252, 259, 268, 269, 277, 292, 298, 304, 305, 306, 325, 369, 375, 395, 397, 398, 400, 401, 402, 403, 404, 406, 407, 420, 421, 422, 424, 443, 444, 447, 467, 468, 469, 470, 537, 539, 542

Pemassegay, Daniel (enlisted man) 297
Penaiswanquot, Jacko (a.k.a. Jaco Penasewonquot,
    Jacob Benasewanquot, and Shako
    Benasewanquot) (enlisted man) 299, 525
pensions 10, 11, 106, 171, 196, 211, 308, 314, 329,
    345, 396, 397, 411, 440, 452
People of the Three Fires 2, 496
Pequongay, Susan (Allen) xii, 12, 15, 36, 37, 38, 39,
    40, 41, 42, 43, 48, 134, 169, 209, 210, 238,
    280, 321, 423, 461, 462, 471, 482, 485, 496
Personalities at Risk (Schram) xv, 485, 491
Peshekee, Mark (a.k.a. Mack Peshekee) (enlisted
    man) 302, 525
Pesherbay, Albert (enlisted man) 305
Petoskey Methodist Indian Mission Church 306
Petozoourquitte (enlisted man), . See also
    Awanakwad, Petros (Peter) 68, 69, 309
phthisis pulmonalis (pulmonary tuberculosis), . See
    also pulmonary tuberculosis 95, 310
Pierz, Francois (reverend father) 195, 209
Pine River Methodist Indian Mission 143, 144
plastic surgery 10
pneumonia 53, 83, 89, 90, 99, 101, 103, 110, 151,
    162, 167, 168, 173, 191, 192, 208, 237, 247,
    261, 262, 280, 285, 286, 288, 289, 332, 336,
    352, 358, 362, 369, 370, 427, 449, 454
podophyllin 149
Popular Grove National Cemetery (Petersburg,
    Virginia) xii, xv, 44, 46, 50, 52, 60, 64, 67, 68,
    75, 85, 90, 92, 97, 107, 115, 130, 149, 153, 156,
    159, 165, 175, 178, 179, 187, 192, 200, 208,
    216, 219, 227, 242, 246, 249, 263, 285, 296,
    299, 303, 306, 309, 313, 320, 328, 330, 333,
    345, 348, 353, 360, 366, 371, 379, 383, 430,
    434, 445, 458, 460, 464
Porsley, Charles (enlisted man) 309, 526
post-traumatic stress disorder 9, 10, 37, 466
potassium iodide 50, 80, 104, 186, 241, 286, 295,
    327, 375, 434
Potawatomi (Bodawatomi) 2, 158, 179, 180, 212,
    224, 232, 233, 235, 252, 428, 429, 447, 448,
    449, 496
pox 410. See also smallpox
Prestawin (Pestawin), Jacob (enlisted man). See
    also Jacko, Natahwinodin (a.k.a. Louis/Lewis
    Penaiswanquot) 169, 311, 312
prosthetics 9
pulmonary tuberculosis . See also phthisis pulmonalis
    (pulmonary tuberculosis) 22, 95, 107, 144,
    268, 270, 287, 443, 444, 445, 452

purgatives 99, 162, 169, 331. See also castor oil
pyemia (blood poisoning) 29, 34, 48, 208, 241, 248

Q

quinine 10, 34, 35, 50, 64, 66, 80, 87, 90, 99, 103,
    104, 113, 157, 165, 169, 172, 182, 186, 231,
    237, 248, 266, 290, 295, 329, 339, 342,
    346, 349, 365, 371, 375, 383, 391, 432, 434,
    450, 464
Quoboway, James (enlisted man) 312, 526

R

Reed, William Howard 207, 241
religious backgrounds 7
rheumatism 34, 50, 53, 61, 62, 81, 84, 104, 105, 149,
    156, 158, 186, 187, 190, 191, 204, 211, 213,
    223, 228, 273, 274, 275, 277, 282, 283, 285,
    286, 288, 294, 307, 308, 314, 322, 332, 349,
    351, 355, 357, 368, 375, 395, 396, 397, 414,
    426, 431, 434, 438
Rubberdee, John (enlisted man) 314

S

Saginaw County 14, 20, 23, 48, 72, 78, 84, 86,
    94, 96, 97, 99, 102, 112, 114, 116, 117, 127,
    147, 162, 167, 174, 182, 183, 184, 198, 202,
    257, 264, 266, 269, 270, 281, 294, 298, 302,
    324, 325, 326, 338, 339, 340, 356, 409, 429,
    436, 437, 438, 440, 441, 458, 460, 493, 522,
    538, 539
Salem Indian Mission 269
Sanequaby, Simon (a.k.a. Simon Singoby) (enlisted
    man) 316, 526
Santee Sioux uprising () 3
Sargonquatto, Aaron (a.k.a. Aaron Pequongay)
    (enlisted man) 319
Sashkobanquat (enlisted man) 324, 325, 326
Sawbequom, Adam (enlisted man) 327, 527
Schoolcraft, Henry R. 135, 137, 509
Schram, Geraldine Moore xv, 485
scorbutus (scurvy) 61, 62, 64, 65, 80, 81, 130, 153,
    228, 229, 243, 249, 277, 300, 328, 349, 351,
    371, 465
Scott, Antoine (a.k.a. Antoine LaCroix and Antoine
    Wayaubemind) (enlisted man) 329, 528
scrofula (tuberculosis) 12, 22, 45, 59, 77, 82, 90, 93,
    95, 96, 104, 107, 108, 109, 110, 116, 117, 120,
    125, 126, 144, 145, 146, 151, 167, 170, 181,
    182, 204, 212, 213, 226, 237, 238, 265, 268,

269, 270, 281, 282, 283, 287, 292, 294, 295, 298, 306, 310, 317, 339, 340, 358, 362, 375, 380, 385, 392, 393, 394, 428, 429, 440, 443, 444, 445, 448, 452, 454

septicemia (blood poisoning) 29, 34, 48, 208, 241, 248, 256

Seymour, Joseph (enlisted man) 333, 528

Shabena, Charles (enlisted man) 334, 528

Shawanese, Joseph (enlisted man) 338, 529

Shawanosang (Shanernuskin), Joseph (enlisted man) 341, 342, 343, 345, 529

Shaw, Charles (enlisted man) 337, 528

Shegoge, John (enlisted man) 345, 529

Shomin, John B. (enlisted man) 348, 530

Shomin, John (O.) (enlisted man) 348, 353, 530

Shomin, Louis (enlisted man) 359, 531

Siege of Petersburg (Virginia) xi, xii, xiv, xv, xvi, 5, 13, 15, 21, 26, 27, 33, 35, 37, 40, 44, 46, 47, 50, 52, 55, 57, 60, 64, 66, 67, 73, 75, 79, 80, 83, 85, 87, 90, 91, 92, 95, 97, 98, 103, 107, 111, 115, 119, 122, 123, 128, 130, 133, 136, 140, 142, 149, 153, 156, 159, 161, 165, 166, 169, 171, 175, 178, 179, 186, 187, 192, 199, 200, 206, 208, 214, 216, 217, 218, 219, 221, 222, 227, 228, 231, 232, 234, 237, 240, 241, 242, 246, 249, 251, 252, 255, 256, 263, 266, 267, 268, 280, 285, 291, 294, 296, 297, 299, 302, 303, 306, 309, 310, 313, 315, 320, 328, 330, 331, 333, 334, 335, 339, 342, 345, 346, 348, 353, 354, 360, 365, 366, 371, 373, 374, 375, 379, 380, 383, 388, 391, 401, 412, 418, 419, 428, 430, 433, 434, 437, 445, 446, 458, 460, 464, 465, 485, 497, 505, 506, 509, 516, 517, 518, 520, 541

signature analysis 485. *See* handwriting analysis

simple cold water dressings 21, 54, 55, 199, 200, 214, 271, 342, 343, 446

sinapism (mustard plaster) 99, 103, 162, 165, 182, 261, 383

smallpox 202, 218, 262, 298, 324, 325

Smith, Arvilla Almira (Powers) 334, 467, 468, 471, 473, 528

Smith, George Nelson, Sr. (reverend) 141

Smith, Nancy Paymegojing (Pemegogin) 368

Smith, Thomas (a.k.a. Shawgwonabay) (enlisted man) 364, 531

South, Peter (a.k.a. Paywawnoquot) (enlisted man) 370, 531

State of Maine (steamer) 21, 27, 33, 37, 44, 45, 47, 55, 57, 58, 61, 66, 71, 73, 76, 79, 80, 81, 83, 87, 88, 91, 95, 96, 98, 100, 103, 104, 107, 123, 124, 128, 142, 157, 160, 163, 166, 169, 175, 178, 180, 181, 182, 183, 186, 192, 200, 212, 214, 215, 224, 225, 229, 237, 243, 244, 252, 256, 268, 272, 277, 281, 286, 291, 294, 303, 310, 313, 315, 316, 331, 332, 334, 335, 338, 342, 346, 349, 354, 360, 366, 374, 379, 383, 384, 389, 391, 392, 395, 401, 420, 430, 433, 434, 437, 443, 450, 451, 462

State of Michigan Archives and Library 11

steamers

   Charles Mears 20

   Connecticut 115

   Constitution 42, 131, 465

   George Leary 27

   Morning Star vii, 45, 58, 71, 73, 76, 83, 88, 96, 100, 104, 107, 124, 157, 163, 166, 175, 178, 180, 182, 183, 200, 212, 215, 224, 225, 229, 244, 272, 277, 281, 286, 315, 316, 332, 334, 335, 338, 360, 384, 389, 395, 401, 430, 443, 451. *See Morning Star* (steamer)

   State of Maine 180, 379

   Sultana 61, 218, 243, 499, 520

   Tonawanda 37

   Wenona 466

Stephenson, B. F. 11

St. Joseph County 156, 158, 179, 181, 223, 224, 251, 252, 394, 447

Stoneman, George (enlisted man) 373, 532

Suicide Profile (Schram) xv, 485, 491

Sultana (steamer) 21, 27, 33, 37, 44, 45, 47, 55, 57, 58, 61, 66, 71, 73, 76, 79, 80, 81, 83, 87, 88, 91, 95, 96, 98, 100, 103, 104, 107, 123, 124, 128, 142, 157, 160, 163, 166, 169, 175, 178, 180, 181, 182, 183, 186, 192, 200, 212, 214, 215, 218, 224, 225, 229, 237, 243, 244, 252, 256, 268, 272, 277, 281, 286, 291, 294, 303, 310, 313, 315, 316, 331, 332, 334, 335, 338, 342, 346, 349, 354, 360, 366, 374, 383, 384, 389, 391, 392, 395, 401, 420, 430, 433, 434, 437, 443, 450, 451, 462, 499, 520

surgery. *See also* amputation; *See also* anesthetics; *See also* antiseptics

   orthopedic surgeries 9

   plastic surgery 10

Sutton, Freeman (enlisted man) 378, 533

syphilis 21, 136, 263, 331, 332, 410, 411

T

Tabasasch, Francis (Frank) (enlisted man) 382
Tabyant, Antoine (a.k.a. Anthony John Tabyant) (enlisted man) 387, 534
Taymouth Indian Mission 269
Tazhedewin, Joseph (a.k.a. Joseph Poneshing Jr.) (enlisted man) 390, 534
These Men Have Seen Hard Service (Herek) 9, 26, 136, 494, 508
Thomas, Moses (enlisted man) 394, 534
Tonawanda (steamer) 21, 27, 33, 37, 44, 45, 47, 55, 57, 58, 61, 66, 71, 73, 76, 79, 80, 81, 83, 87, 88, 91, 95, 96, 98, 100, 103, 104, 107, 123, 124, 128, 142, 157, 160, 163, 166, 169, 175, 178, 180, 181, 182, 183, 186, 192, 200, 212, 214, 215, 224, 225, 229, 237, 243, 244, 252, 256, 268, 272, 277, 281, 286, 291, 294, 303, 310, 313, 315, 316, 331, 332, 334, 335, 338, 342, 346, 349, 354, 360, 366, 374, 383, 384, 389, 391, 392, 395, 401, 420, 430, 433, 434, 437, 443, 450, 451, 462
tourniquet 26, 54, 67, 97, 266, 290, 379
trachoma 388, 389
triage method 9
tuberculosis 12, 22, 45, 59, 77, 82, 90, 93, 95, 96, 104, 107, 108, 109, 110, 116, 117, 120, 125, 126, 144, 145, 146, 151, 167, 170, 181, 182, 204, 212, 213, 226, 237, 238, 265, 268, 269, 270, 281, 282, 283, 287, 292, 294, 298, 306, 310, 317, 339, 340, 358, 362, 375, 380, 385, 392, 393, 394, 428, 440, 443, 444, 445, 448, 452, 454. *See also* consumption (tuberculosis); *See also* pulmonary tuberculosis; *See also* scrofula (tuberculosis)
turpentine wraps 83
Twinsburg Institute (Twinsburg, Ohio) 12, 15, 37, 42, 422, 423, 469, 496, 537
typhoid fever 96, 113, 169, 170, 172, 173, 318, 365, 383

U

Union army 2, 64, 65, 85, 189, 234, 372, 380, 532
    inducements for enlistments 3
upon discharge 268, 313, 368

V

Valentine, Robert (enlisted man) 399, 535

W

Waasegiizhig, Henry (a.k.a. Henry Condecon or Okandikan) (enlisted man) 401, 535
Waasegiizhig Okandikan Sr., Ikwezens (Mary) (Blackbird) 401, 402
Waasegiizhig Okandikan Sr., John (chief) vii, xiii, xiv, 7, 8, 14, 20, 88, 116, 117, 137, 138, 143, 147, 150, 160, 184, 188, 193, 201, 203, 207, 233, 235, 252, 259, 268, 269, 277, 292, 298, 304, 305, 306, 325, 369, 375, 395, 397, 398, 400, 401, 402, 403, 404, 406, 407, 420, 421, 422, 424, 443, 444, 447, 467, 468, 469, 470, 537, 539, 542
Wabano, Thomas (enlisted man) 409, 536
Wabesis, Charles (enlisted man) 411, 536
Wabesis, John (enlisted man) 415, 536
Wakazoo, Agatha (Nawzhewayquay) (Petoskey) 420
Wakazoo, Joseph (a.k.a. Joseph P. Wakazoo) (enlisted man) 417, 536
Wakazoo, Peter (Pendunwan) (chief) 420, 421, 424, 443, 444, 467, 469
Walpole Island, Lambton County (Ontario, Canada) 20, 49, 157, 158, 161, 171, 172, 188, 341, 343, 395, 396, 456, 461, 514
warriors (Ogitchedaw) x, 2, 4, 6, 8, 12, 37, 51, 157, 224, 228, 462
Watson, James V. (enlisted man) 427, 538
Waubenoo, John (a.k.a. Negawnewaywaydung) (enlisted man) 429, 538
Wayaubemind, Michael (enlisted man) 432, 538
Waygeshegoing (Waggishegomey), William (enlisted man) 436, 437, 439, 441, 538
Wayne County 3, 20, 22, 23, 25, 30, 33, 36, 43, 46, 47, 49, 52, 54, 57, 60, 63, 66, 73, 75, 78, 80, 83, 86, 89, 92, 94, 97, 99, 101, 102, 111, 113, 114, 115, 118, 122, 127, 133, 135, 147, 153, 156, 159, 161, 162, 171, 175, 177, 178, 179, 181, 186, 191, 197, 198, 214, 221, 223, 224, 225, 227, 232, 234, 237, 249, 261, 263, 265, 266, 271, 276, 289, 294, 297, 299, 302, 305, 309, 312, 315, 316, 324, 327, 329, 333, 334, 337, 339, 341, 345, 353, 360, 365, 370, 373, 391, 394, 401, 410, 412, 415, 417, 428, 429, 432, 436, 442, 445, 454, 456, 457, 458, 460, 461, 462
weapons. See .-caliber Springfield Rifle Muskets 334, 457, 458, 461
Weber, Gustavus A. 11
Wells, Peter (enlisted man) 442, 539

Wenona (steamer) 21, 27, 33, 37, 44, 45, 47, 55, 57, 58, 61, 66, 71, 73, 76, 79, 80, 81, 83, 87, 88, 91, 95, 96, 98, 100, 103, 104, 107, 123, 124, 128, 142, 157, 160, 163, 166, 169, 175, 178, 180, 181, 182, 183, 186, 192, 200, 212, 214, 215, 224, 225, 229, 237, 243, 244, 252, 256, 268, 272, 277, 281, 286, 291, 294, 303, 310, 313, 315, 316, 331, 332, 334, 335, 338, 342, 346, 349, 354, 360, 366, 374, 383, 384, 389, 391, 392, 395, 401, 420, 430, 433, 434, 437, 443, 450, 451, 462, 466

Wesaw (Wezoo), Thomas (enlisted man) 445, 446, 447, 448, 539, 540

Wesleyan Seminary 422, 469, 536

Wesley, John (enlisted man) 449, 540

Wezoo, Elizabeth 483

Wezoo, Rosa (Johnson) xiii, 53, 93, 212, 293, 380, 448, 449, 483

whiskey 21, 26, 27, 40, 54, 55, 57, 66, 67, 87, 90, 97, 98, 99, 103, 115, 123, 142, 165, 185, 186, 190, 199, 200, 206, 214, 227, 240, 241, 255, 266, 267, 290, 309, 327, 329, 339, 347, 349, 365, 371, 374, 379, 383, 388, 390, 391, 419, 432, 433, 446, 450, 464

Whiteface, Charles (Charley) (enlisted man) 453, 541

White, Wyman S. 199, 515

Williams, James (enlisted man) 456

Williams, Joseph (a.k.a. Joseph Nesogot) (enlisted man) 458, 541

Williams, Moses (enlisted man) 460, 541

Williams, Samuel (enlisted man) 461

Wolf, Mary Jane (Smith) xii, xvi, 15, 26, 33, 36, 46, 49, 54, 57, 60, 63, 74, 75, 78, 80, 83, 86, 89, 92, 94, 97, 99, 101, 102, 111, 113, 114, 118, 122, 124, 127, 133, 135, 147, 161, 162, 184, 190, 191, 197, 198, 206, 221, 225, 227, 232, 234, 237, 244, 249, 250, 251, 261, 263, 265, 266, 269, 271, 276, 280, 289, 294, 297, 299, 302, 305, 309, 316, 324, 327, 329, 334, 337, 339, 341, 344, 345, 353, 360, 364, 365, 366, 367, 368, 369, 370, 373, 382, 387, 391, 410, 412, 415, 418, 419, 421, 422, 423, 424, 426, 428, 429, 432, 436, 442, 444, 448, 449, 454, 456, 457, 458, 460, 461, 462, 464, 466, 468, 469, 470, 471, 473, 484, 496, 518, 519, 520, 531, 537, 539, 541, 542

Wolf, Payson (enlisted man) 461, 541

Y

yeast poultices 122, 343

Z

Zorn, Seraphim (reverend father) 68, 286, 350, 389, 435

TRUE DIRECTIONS

An affiliate of Tarcher Perigee

OUR MISSION

Tarcher Perigee's mission has always been to publish books that contain great ideas. Why? Because:

GREAT LIVES BEGIN WITH GREAT IDEAS

At Tarcher Perigee, we recognize that many talented authors, speakers, educators, and thought-leaders share this mission and deserve to be published – many more than Tarcher Perigee can reasonably publish ourselves. True Directions is ideal for authors and books that increase awareness, raise consciousness, and inspire others to live their ideals and passions.

Like Tarcher Perigee, True Directions books are designed to do three things: inspire, inform, and motivate.

Thus, True Directions is an ideal way for these important voices to bring their messages of hope, healing, and help to the world.

Every book published by True Directions– whether it is non-fiction, memoir, novel, poetry or children's book – continues Tarcher Perigee's mission to publish works that bring positive change in the world. We invite you to join our mission.

For more information, see the True Directions website:

www.iUniverse.com/TrueDirections/SignUp

Be a part of Tarcher Perigee's community to bring positive change in this world!
See exclusive author videos, discover new and exciting books, learn about upcoming events, connect with author blogs and websites, and more!
www.tarcherbooks.com

TRUE DIRECTIONS
AN AFFILIATE OF TARCHER PERIGEE

Printed in the United States
By Bookmasters